GYN (CELLO1)
Waterstones
Feb 02

10284993

WALES AND CINEMA

THE FIRST HUNDRED YEARS

DAVID BERRY

Published in co-operation with the Wales Film Council and the British Film Institute

UNIVERSITY OF WALES PRESS 1994

This publication has been made possible through the support of the Wales Film Council.

The publishers wish to acknowledge the initial funder, Ffilm Cymru, and the financial assistance of TAC – Teledwyr Annibynnol Cymru (Welsh Independent Producers).

This paperback edition has been published with the financial support of the Arts Council of Wales.

The images on the front cover are (clockwise from top right): Mike and Robert Gwilym in **On the Black Hill** (dir. Andrew Grieve, 1987); Florence Turner in **A Welsh Singer** (dir. Henry Edwards, 1915); director Endaf Emlyn on the set of **Gadael Lenin (Leaving Lenin**, 1992); Les Adlam in **Today We Live** (dir. Ralph Bond, 1937); Ifan ab Owen Edwards, director of the first Welsh-language sound film – **Y Chwarelwr** (**The Quarryman**, 1935).

First published, 1994
Paperback edition, 1996

Designed by
Neil James Angove

Printed in Great Britain
at The Bath Press

British Library Cataloguing-in-Publication Data
A catalogue record for this book is available from the British Library.

ISBN 0-7083-1370-1

For Marion (1913 – 1985) and Jack (1914 – 1989)

You have to begin to lose your memory, if only in bits and pieces, to realise memory is what makes our lives. Life without memory is no life at all. Our memory is our coherence, our reason, our feeling, even our action. Without it we are nothing.

(Luis Buñuel in his autobiography *My Last Breath*, 1982)

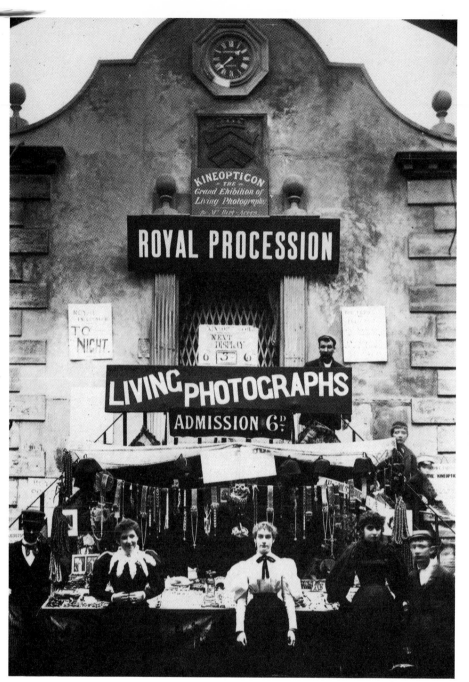

This is the only known photographic record of Birt Acres's Kineopticon display of early movies at Cardiff's Fine Art and Industrial Exhibition in 1896. 'Royal procession' refers to a royal visit that year, shot by the film-maker and later screened for the future King Edward VII in the first 'royal command performance'.

CONTENTS

vii

The 1994 hardback edition of this book coincided with the centenary of the first film shown in Wales, on the Edison Kinetoscope 'peepshow' machine – showing images to be seen by only one viewer at a time. This edition, with the symmetry beloved of publishers, surfaces near the end of a crowded year of celebrations marking 100 years of *projected* cinema in the UK and in Wales. On 5 May 1996 – exactly 100 years after Birt Acres became the first to show films to a Welsh audience – the Wales Film and Television Archive, Aberystwyth, screened the world première of Maurice Elvey's 1918 British silent **The Life Story of David Lloyd George**. The film had been rediscovered after seventy-six years of oblivion. This book's *raison d'être* is to help the reader rediscover and reassess the *entire* legacy of films made about Wales and its people. The reprint allows corrections to the first, hardback, edition. Financial constraints prevent the indexing of references in this preface, in which I have taken the opportunity to update the main text (if not the appendices and filmographies) in a year which could yet prove a watershed for Welsh film.

The backdrop

The backdrop to Welsh screen production has changed little since 1994. Talent still emerges despite the low budgets and impecunious state of Welsh-based screen funding bodies. Money from British Screen and, perhaps more crucially, the Arts Council of Wales Lottery Unit, offers encouragement that Welsh film may be about to build significantly on the promise so evident two years ago. Former S4C programme controller Euryn Ogwen Williams has expressed the belief that more Welsh-based directors will be able to break free from the strait-jacket of dependency on television, with its slot-filling imperatives and tendency to opt for safe commissions.

British Screen has now backed two Welsh films for cinema release – Endaf Emlyn's S4C/BBC Wales feature **Y Mapiwr** (**The Making of Maps**) (1995) and Marc Evans's English-language drama **House of America** (in production in late 1996 and based on a stage play by south-Walian Edward Thomas). Lottery money amounting to £250,000 apiece has been awarded to the Evans film and to **Darklands**, an 'industrial thriller' cum pagan horror story set in urban south-west Wales and directed by Newport's Julian Richards, a National Film School graduate. The lottery grants sent these two films' individual total budgets beyond £1m (still a modest sum, even by UK standards).

Since 1994 it has become increasingly apparent that neither Screen Wales (the ostensible marketing agency for Welsh film) nor the Wales Film Council (responsible for bursaries, production, film education and culture and funding the Wales Film and TV Archive) has enough money to make much of an impact on the indigenous movie scene. The WFC's latest year's budget, little more than £400,000, speaks for itself and includes a mere £61,000 for production.

If the UK and American distributors' innate suspicion of (or bias against) Welsh-language film is to be overcome, more aggressive marketing from Wales is needed. The baffling case of **Hedd Wyn**, still to find a British distributor despite its Oscar nomination and Royal Television Society Best Drama award, does not bode well. A public film body with more clout, representing all aspects of films in Wales including their marketing, now has its appeal and in late 1996 a merger was agreed between the WFC and Screen Wales in a move towards creating the infrastructure the industry patently needs.

The recent films

Y Mapiwr was an eloquent rites-of-passage film in which events, played out against the backdrop of the 1962 Cuban Missile Crisis, seemed tantalizingly out-of-kilter. What seemed initially to be a suspense thriller with a teenage boy (Gavin Ashcroft) seeking to solve the mystery disappearance of a dancing student at his mother's school, metamorphosed into a study of sinister, symbiotic family relations, adultery and murderous collusion. The eerie, largely unpeopled landscape carried a primal charge of its own, thanks partly to Nina Kellgren's often offbeat photography.

The BBC Screen Two drama **Streetlife**, made for around £330,000 by Karl Francis (BBC Wales drama head from January 1996), might have enjoyed a successful and early cinema release in the UK if the BBC hierarchy in London had been prescient enough to gauge its impact on audiences and organizers at the Edinburgh Film Festival in 1995. In **Streetlife** Francis resisted his usual tendency to extrapolate and encourage his audiences to draw (sometimes questionable) political generalizations from the particular. The film proved an intensely claustrophobic exploration of a jilted single mother's slide into depression and tragedy on a south Wales valleys' housing estate rife with drugs and prostitution. The director coaxed a consummate performance from actress Helen McCrory as the unfortunate Jo. The work was undermined by a slightly implausible finale, but there was no denying its visceral charge.

The Englishman Who Went Up a Hill But Came Down a Mountain (1995), written and directed by Chris Monger, was released on the back of its star Hugh Grant's instant celebrity after **Four Weddings and a Funeral**. The Englishman enjoyed a modest hit, the humour smacking of such Ealing comedies as **Whisky Galore** and **The Maggie** with Welsh rustics gulling two English mapmakers (Hugh Grant and Ian McNeice, superb as a toping Blimp).

Anthony Hopkins made his directing début with **August** (1996), based on a stage play by Newport's Julian Mitchell which transplanted Chekhov's *Uncle Vanya* to Victorian north Wales. A few *frissons* were had from this cultural displacement, but the film was a tame, timorous affair.

The drama-doc continues to be the natural *métier* of Colin Thomas whose finest recent work is **The Reel Truth** (1995), an amusing and spirited S4C/Channel Four series exploring, in both English and Welsh, the fakery in many 'classic' documentary movies, particularly of the silent era. It remains to be seen whether Cardiff's Teliesyn can remain a force in the drama-doc genre following the death in 1995 of the co-operative's scripting mentor, inspirational historian Gwyn Alf Williams.

In animation, Wales consolidated its reputation in 1996 with Cardiff hosting the International Animation Festival for the third time. The pick of the new 'local' films shown was Cardiff-based independent Gerald Conn's sand-on-glass short **Eastern Promise** (1995), a sly tourist's-eye view of India.

Rediscovered wealth

The Life Story of David Lloyd George is a fairly complete rough cut rather than a final cut – as you might expect from the circumstances of its virtual seizure (see chapter 4). This significant biopic, trailing an intriguing history of suppression, ran two and a half hours (at 18 frames per second) and, at over 10,000 ft. was at least 4,000 ft. longer than indicated in Denis Gifford's *British Film Catalogue* (and *Wales and Cinema's* Film Milestones section). Much more pertinently, the movie proved a remarkable social document of seductive political propaganda and hagiography, with Elvey, in innumerable vivid setpieces, demonstrating a precocious feel for documentary-style immediacy.

The version shown in Cardiff in 1996 was assembled, with due fidelity to the director's assumed intentions, by the Wales Film and Television Archive technician John Reed – taking advice from political and screen historians. The film, restored by the National Film Archive, has been coloured in a London lab, adhering as closely as possible to 1918 tinting and toning instructions found on the negative. The movie tells us much about British film at the time – the occasional sluggish editing is typical, with UK directors apparently oblivious to the influence elsewhere of D. W. Griffith's cross-cutting techniques. In the suffragette riot scenes outside London's Queen's Hall, Elvey *does* employ skilful montage, handling potentially dangerous crowd scenes with panache. The most impressive sequence embraces Lloyd George's visits as Minister of Munitions to aircraft and armaments factories during the First World War. These moments have a strangely moving 'documentary' veracity, aided by Norman Page's dignified performance as the 'Welsh wizard'. Modern audiences are as likely to dwell on the startling setpiece special effects, notably Elvey's effective use of superimposition when denizens of a workhouse 'float' through its walls, symbolizing the liberating effects of Lloyd George's introduction of old-age pensions.

Shot out of Twickenham studios, the film was a considerable achievement – especially as Elvey was on the set of his (much inferior) biopic, **Nelson** as late as July 1918. He was even forced into a six-week re-shoot of Nelson following a lab fire, and started filming the Lloyd George feature in the last week of August at the earliest.

Understandably enough, the **Life Story**'s rediscovery deflected attention from other significant 'finds'. The WFTVA identified Welsh-based director William Haggar's 1904 Urban film **The Bathers' Revenge**, which had been in the National Film Archive in London since 1936 under the descriptive title (in lieu of any words on the print) of **Bathers Pull Couple Into Water**. No more than 75 ft. long, the film is a park-bench comedy of exemplary construction.

In 1995 the Netherlands Film Museum screened a coloured print from their archives of the 1898 British Biograph phantom train ride to Conway Castle – shown at London's Palace Theatre, Shaftesbury Avenue, in March that year. This evocative film, with superb panoramic shots, is not yet available in a British archive. The hand-tinted colouring would seem to have been carried out later (but probably well before 1910) as contemporary reports of successful 1898 screenings do not refer to colour.

Much research clearly remains to be done on all aspects of films in Wales (in the field of exhibition, and audience response, for example). I hope this book will encourage far more specific research, to help prove that Welsh film history is much richer than most UK historians have hitherto either acknowledged or suspected.

David Berry
September 1996

ACKNOWLEDGMENTS This book is the work of an enthusiastic film critic and writer rather than a professional historian. Several cinema and film histories have been of great assistance – the work of John Barnes, Denis Gifford, Rachael Low, in particular, and of that zealous journalist Terry Ramsaye (much maligned by purists) whose colourful, and intoxicating description of early cinema, *A Million and One Nights* (1926) fuelled my desire to know more about the formative years. Jenny Steele's research – on archival sources and film holdings – for the Welsh Arts Council in 1977 was a valued starting point.

I am grateful to all film directors, actors and actresses who have given up valuable time to be interviewed or to answer my queries. I would also like to thank sincerely all those who helped with this project over thirteen years, including staff at the National Library of Wales, Aberystwyth; the British Library, London and Newspaper Library, Colindale; Central Library, Cardiff; Aberdare Library; Clwyd Record Office; Gwynedd County Council; the British Film Institute's Information Department and Library in London; and *World's Fair* newspaper, Oldham. I am also grateful to the Wales Film Council; Gareth Morris (manager of library services, BBC Wales) Luke McKernan (BFI Cataloguing Department); to Stephen Lyons, Philip Lloyd, Mervyn Heard and Richard Brown for granting access to their original research and material; to Iola Baines, Gwenan Owen and John Reed of the Wales Film and TV Archive, Aberystwyth; to Ed Buscombe (BFI); to Charles Silver at the Museum of Modern Art, New York, for extracts from the D. W. Griffith Papers; Martyn Howells, former Wales Arts Council film officer; Claire Pollak; Madeline Matz at the Library of Congress, Washington; staff at Eastman House, Rochester, NY; also Geoffrey Hill, Peter Morgan, Martin Roberts and members of the Haggar family: Roy Haggar sen., Roy Haggar jun., Grace Greenland, John Haggar, the late Jo Haggar – and the late Madge Rastall (who would have so liked to see this book). A number of film-makers and actors helped me greatly but have since passed on, leaving enduring legacies: John Ormond, Jack Howells, Donald Alexander, Ralph Bond, Clifford Evans. Thanks are also due to Bill Barrett, Geoff Dart, Terry Dimmick, Terry Downey, John East, Alan and Sue Edmunds, John Hessey, Bert Hogenkamp, Bruce Kennedy, Mansel Jones, Janet McBain (of the Scottish Film Archive) Luned and David Meredith, John O'Beirne, Mary Simmonds, Lyn Williams, Deryk Williams (of S4C) and Euryn Ogwen Williams (formerly S4C), the press office at the Welsh Fourth Channel and Roger Worsley.

I am indebted to Elaine Burrows, Jackie Morris, Bryony Dixon, Clive Truman and Julie Rigg in the National Film Archive's viewing services department, London, for putting up with me during years of visits and screenings; to Linda Pariser, film programmer at Cardiff's Chapter Arts Centre, for her encouragement and help and to other Chapter staff, particularly Glen Manby, Graham Jones, Rachel Calder, Siân Ifan and Rob Kennedy for their unfailing courtesy in screening much material for me. Nia Roberts, formerly of BAFTA Cymru, and Julie Paschalis assisted considerably with translations; Steve Freer and Steve Groves advised on aspects of the text; Peter Stead read and commented usefully on the manuscript; Richard Staniforth gave impetus to the early stages of this project; Liz Powell, editor at the University of Wales Press, helped correct errors and omissions.

John Hefin of the Wales Film Council deserves particular thanks for his practical support and faith. He did perhaps more than anyone to make this book possible. Janine Cooper's friendliness and hard work over more than two years in typing the manuscript through its various revisions – and dealing with my hieroglyphics – was a constant encouragement.

BFI	British Film Institute
CCVW	Cardiff (Chapter) Community Video Workshop
CEE	*Cardiff Evening Express*
CFW	Chapter Film Workshop (later Filmworks, Wales)
dir.	director
dist.	distributor
IWM	Imperial War Museum
MFB	*Monthly Film Bulletin*
MOMA	Museum of Modern Art, New York
NFT	National Film Theatre
NFA	National Film Archive
p.c.	production company
RR and A	*Rhyl Record and Advertiser*
SWDP	*South Wales Daily Post*
SWE	*South Wales Echo*
SWEP	*South Wales Evening Post*
SWML	South Wales Miners' Library
WAC	Welsh Arts Council
WM	*Western Mail*
WFA	Wales Film and TV Archive

Film was never made to feel very welcome in Wales. As a two or three year old infant, stinking slightly of gin and the sweat of the fairground, it ran slap up against Evan Roberts and the [religious] Revival of 1904–5 and was severely mauled. It survives – but remains retarded to this day.

(Film-maker Wil Aaron in *The Arts in Wales 1950–1975*, Welsh Arts Council, 1979)

In many countries film is recognized as an important form of cultural expression capable of reaching a great many people. It is time that those people who can influence cultural policies in Wales recognized that fact and began to establish the framework that would allow such a film culture to develop.

(Film director and media lecturer Michele Ryan in Tony Curtis (ed.), *Wales: The Imagined Nation*, 1986)

In 1977 a Welsh feature film surfaced which intrigued and even excited some of those present at its rare public screenings. **Above Us the Earth** centred on the ailing Ogilvie Colliery in the Rhymney Valley and an old miner succumbing to emphysema – a victim of 'pit dust'. The plight of the colliery was real – it had closed down after losses of £580,000 in eight months in 1975 – but the decline of the pitman, the human drama touched off by the social dilemma, was a screenplay fiction.

The director Karl Francis, from nearby Bedwas in Gwent, had invented the narrative thread running through the real events in his film, and yoked aspects of communal and private grief and trauma in a vibrant dramatized documentary which clearly held no brief for either the National Coal Board or the leaders of the National Union of Mineworkers. **Above Us the Earth** displayed a scepticism similar to Jill Craigie's 1949 fictional feature **Blue Scar** – also set in Wales – which focused on a mining community's problems from a working-class perspective but also challenged the socialists' euphoria about the successful battle for nationalization of the pits and hinted at the schism in the miners' ranks in the battle for a five-day week. Francis's own ambivalence towards the coal industry which the miners had sustained, and been sustained by, was obvious and gave his film a bracing tension. The unusual blend of documentary and reconstruction and the use of weathered familiar faces from Valleys villages, was affecting, but the sentiment expressed on screen was offhand, almost brusque, and the humour which leavened the script was sardonic and clenched. The film, with its all-amateur cast, was far removed from a Hollywood confection. It seemed then that no outsider could have made this feature in the same way, so refreshingly free of clichés and stereotypes. Even the slight awkwardness of several non-pros (including the director's mother Gwen) in partly improvised situations bespoke an integrity which went beyond the dramatic effectiveness of individual scenes. Windsor Rees, as the broken miner, constantly snatching lungfuls of air, could scarcely have provided a performance of such truth if he had not suffered the same chronic breathing problems himself.

The director, who shot part of the film at his mother's home, spent months at the colliery – almost from the time news first broke of the impending closure – and much preparation was spent 'shooting' without film in the camera to build up the miners' confidence and ensure that people could experience 'the feel of filming and regard the camera as naturally as they would a pit prop'.[1]

The enthusiasm I felt watching the film – a compelling record of a community in the throes of radical change – stemmed not merely from the intuition that it marked the arrival of a talented director, an impression confirmed by the bulk of Francis's later work. It sprang from realizing that this kind of feature by an independent was possible in Wales and that in the right hands there could be an indigenous Welsh cinema which made pertinent points about urban life and ordinary Valleys people, drew on film-makers' experiences and recognized the potential for drama in actual events as the south Wales coalfield came under threat. That kind of observational realism based on real experience had been the forte of directors working in other areas (Ken Loach in Yorkshire, Bill Douglas in Scotland, for example). There was also, of course, a rich lode of Welsh history, rural and urban, to be mined on screen.

Above Us the Earth offered scenes of south Wales very different from the anodyne view of working-class life filtered through the lenses of Hollywood or the major British studios in the forties and fifties – and certainly in the bulk of mining films of that period. It was a shock to realize that mining was *central* to a Welsh film conceived for the cinema (not TV) for the first time since Craigie's **Blue Scar**. It was also the first time a Welsh director had defied convention to use an amateur in a significant lead role (outside strict documentary) since director Paul Dickson asked D. R. Griffiths, school caretaker and brother of former Welsh minister Jim Griffiths, to play himself in the poignant 1951 Festival of Britain film, **David**. The last film focusing with similar passion on the plight of unemployed miners in Wales, **Today We Live** – set in Pentre, Rhondda – was made back in 1936–7. Yet in the intervening years, when dozens of films (especially on TV) were set in the principality, scarcely a handful of cinema features had dealt in any depth with social life and problems in the south Wales valleys. It was also sobering to reflect that almost all the popular or influential films of the thirties and forties which conditioned the way people outside Wales saw the nation were made by outsiders. Many were fascinating works which merit serious discussion in any history of the Welsh cinema – but they were compromised, either by box-office demands or by the nature of their sponsorship and financing. It's difficult to bite the hand that feeds you.

The Citadel (1938), an often compelling indictment of insanitary living conditions in the Valleys and corruption and insidious apathy in a *laissez-faire* medical profession, was at least based on the first-hand observations of the novelist and sometime Tredegar and Treherbert doctor, A. J. Cronin. But it was one of three features made by MGM in Britain just before the Second World War as an expedient to maintain a toehold in British markets and satisfy British 'quota' requirements.[2] And the presence of its co-star Rosalind Russell for box-office ballast crucially affected the plotting.

The Proud Valley (1940), regarded by many as the archetypal Welsh mining film (or confection) was made largely at Ealing Studios, with pit exteriors shot in Staffordshire collieries after south Wales mineowners refused the crew permission to film there. It was directed by an Old Etonian, Pen Tennyson (great-grandson of the poet) whose experience of Wales had been gained mainly as a house-guest of the coalowning Davies family of Llandinam.[3]

The first, 1945, version of the Emlyn Williams stage play **The Corn is Green**, with Bette Davis as Williams's schoolmistress/mentor, was shot entirely in America with virtually an all-Stateside cast. The 1979 version by that doyen of Hollywood directors George Cukor was a shameless vehicle for Katharine Hepburn, who even helped Cukor with the casting.[4]

How Green Was My Valley (1941), the film most often pilloried by Welshmen, is best seen not as a misguided attempt to evoke Richard Llewellyn's already highly coloured vision of the south Wales Valleys but as a work central to the romantic *oeuvre* of director John Ford, an American of Irish descent – with the casting bordering on the farcical. Sara Allgood as the mother was hotfoot from Dublin's Abbey Theatre; Maureen O'Hara, and the inimitable Barry Fitzgerald and his brother Arthur Shields were all from Ireland. Small wonder south Wales film historian Peter Stead has dubbed the setting 'an Irish Shangri-la'. The father was played by Scotsman Donald Crisp; the Canadian Walter Pidgeon was oddly effective as Mr Gruffydd, that clerical monument to sanity and self-sacrifice. Rhys Williams (playing Dai Bando and long in exile in America) was the only Welshman in a key role – apart from those ubiquitous choir members . . .[5]

That evocative, handsomely mounted curio **The Last Days of Dolwyn** (1949), the

DAVID LLOYD GEORGE
AND D.W. GRIFFITH

D. W. Griffith, the greatest director of his day, meets one of the greatest politicians, David Lloyd George. The photo was almost certainly taken when Griffith shot part of the war propaganda film *Hearts of the World* (1918) in Britain – at the UK government's behest.

one screenwork both scripted and directed by Emlyn Williams, was patently by an exile – its fatalistic romanticism shot through with the writer's own ambivalent feelings towards Wales and its alleged parochialism.

During these years there was no Welsh film industry. Lack of finance dictated *that* – and the parlous state of the British cinema and its prevailing values. UK screen war dramas and documentaries gained the national cinema kudos and in 1947 British films were even more popular than American features at the UK box office – but much domestic cinema was mired in hidebound studio films, often from geriatric stage plots. The stilted drawing-room comedies, the fanciful melodramas of the mid- and late thirties were no match for the brash, fast moving, confident and cinematic Hollywood films which flooded the UK markets in the interwar years. The British cinema was only briefly revitalized in the late thirties during the empire-building of Alexander Korda at London Films and during the war when significant new talents such as Carol Reed, David Lean and Launder and Gilliat emerged. The upper-middle-class values which generally made British cinema so airless and introspective had been perpetuated by film bosses like Oswald Stoll, who grew up in Cardiff and played a significant part in the history of film in Wales as proprietor of the Empires at Cardiff, Newport, Swansea and the capital's Philharmonic Hall, in particular. Stoll was xenophobic, flying the flag for all things British – yet he failed to recognize the possibilities on his own doorstep.[6] As head of the biggest movie studio in Britain in the 1920s, he neither responded to the intrinsic drama of social events in Wales nor was able to see how Welsh writing talent or locations could be used – and he failed to capitalize on that brief flowering of films set in Wales, and featuring some of the most popular silent screen stars of Britain and Hollywood, between 1913 and 1922. However, even if he *had* reacted to the industrial and social maelstrom of the twenties and thirties, British film censorship would have prevented accurate representation of the social forces at work (trade-unionism, for example, was effectively banned from the screen). Before the Second World War the prevailing middle-class mores of the British cinema *were* challenged – by men like Ralph Bond, who bitterly resented the stereotyping of the working class as comic butlers and parlour maids and who made the Welsh section of **Today We Live** not merely to show people the plight of the unemployed (and force some action) but to present the dignity of proletarian labour and give the working class a voice on the screen. Even Bond was an outsider, a London-based Communist, and his film, centred on jobless miners building their own leisure centre, was sponsored by the government-backed Council for Social Service. This prevented anything more than token criticism of the unemployment situation (or for that matter of 'do-gooding' building schemes to keep people occupied in lieu of full-time jobs). Humphrey Jennings who made **Silent Village** (1943) and part of **Spare Time** (1939) in Wales was a Cambridge University graduate who first studied the working classes as a founder of the Mass Observation Movement which conducted vox pops in Bolton, Lancashire ('Worktown') in the 1930s to see how the proletarians lived.[7]

Blue Scar was unquestionably a brave film and featured implicit criticism of the NCB hierarchy, post-nationalization, but it's reasonable to suppose the message was at least partly diluted because half the cash backing came from the Coal Board. Certainly, the film's love story deflected attention from the politics.

All these factors militated against the Welsh seeing themselves, or their actual lives, reflected on screen. Yet ever since cinema's birth, the Welsh have had film-makers whose work has been largely ignored by British screen historians. Before the First World War the work of pioneer showman William Haggar on melodramas, chase films and thrillers was as highly regarded by Gaumont as any of his contemporaries – and as popular with the public. The maverick entrepreneur Arthur Cheetham was scarcely less significant, shooting films before the turn of the century. Between the wars there were lone creative voices working within Wales – notably C. H. Dand, whose 1933 north Wales quarry film **Men Against Death** was one of the first works in the British cinema to make the dangers of the working man's life virtually the *raison d'être* of a film, albeit within a flimsy narrative. And Ifan ab Owen Edwards broke new ground in 1935 when his **Y Chwarelwr** (The Quarryman) became the first Welsh-language sound film.

The film industry between the 1930s and 1950s was heavily biased towards the metropolis. Studio bosses were seemingly unwilling to shoot outside London, as talented British director Michael Powell found in 1935 when he was ordered back from north Wales while making the melodrama **The Phantom Light** because the set was deemed too far away for the production company to monitor the production. But in the forties and fifties, through its writers and above all its performers, Wales still made a significant contribution to film as the movies enjoyed a post-war boom in the principality. The number of cinemas, which climbed over 250 in the 1920s, reached 315 by 1946 and many cinema-goers attended two or three times a week. Its actors (particularly Stanley Baker, Rachel Roberts and Richard Burton) played crucial roles, helping the British cinema to slough off its middle-class past.

Sir Ifan ab Owen Edwards – director of the first Welsh-language sound film.

Acting opportunities for the Welsh on the big screen were reduced as the advent of television hit the cinema box office and by December 1952 more than 38,200 viewers in Wales had TV licences. BBC Wales's 'live' television dramas flourished after the opening of the Wenvoe transmitter that year, and the provision of a studio in a converted chapel in Broadway, Cardiff, by 1956 helped equip many stage performers for the screen – though the only outlet for many were B films or 'programmers' of often inferior quality. Yet that television tradition, begun largely by adapting the European literary classics or works from established novelists and stage playwrights such as Richard Llewellyn, Emlyn Williams and Dylan Thomas, was important in harnessing new talent – Alun Owen and Elaine Morgan, for instance – and the influence of dramas produced by such as Dafydd Gruffydd, David Thomas, Emyr Humphreys and George Owen remains today. Television in the sixties and seventies also made viewers aware of the great Welsh-language contribution made by the country's premier stage dramatist Saunders Lewis and provided outlets for other considerable writing talents such as Rhydderch Jones and Ewart Alexander.

In the past eighteen years – since **Above Us the Earth** – the situation has changed for film in Wales, even though British cinema production has dwindled dramatically. Fine independent directors have made – mostly for TV – salient, even trenchant, features focusing on the way we live now. Works have spanned aspects of Welsh life previously ignored on the screen, and output has included impressive genre features of the kind which must be the life-blood of any indigenous film culture. There has been a burgeoning interest in Welsh film – and a mini-production boom which could hardly have been foreseen when **Above Us the Earth** was premièred at London's Other Cinema. Karl Francis has continued to dissect the mining communities and the political and social forces for change in Wales in a string of combative works, notably **Ms Rhymney Valley** (1985) and **The Angry Earth** (1989). A clutch of other directors and writers are now prepared to focus on the problems and preoccupations of contemporary Wales.

Film-makers such as Stephen Bayly, Chris Monger and Stephen Weeks have made an impact in the commercial cinema. Spectacular strides have been made in animation with directors such as Joanna Quinn, Dave Edwards, Phil Mulloy, Clive Walley, Candy Guard and Alison Leaf in the vanguard. Quinn's Annecy Festival winner **Girls' Night Out** (1987), a robust, exhilarating work, drew humour from ordinary life – an area strangely ignored in too much animation work – and Valleys vernacular, experimenting bravely with both form and content. New talent has emerged in both drama (Marc Evans, Paul Turner) and documentary (Colin Thomas). Yet it took the advent of S4C (the Welsh Fourth Channel – Sianel Pedwar Cymru) and Channel Four in 1982 to tap the potential and energy in Wales, to provide a lifeline to young independent directors and confirm that the nation can forge an identity through its own films rather than accept images grafted on by outsiders. The time is ripe for an assessment of all their past work – and the present burgeoning of talent.

Wales is in the throes of its most invigorating creative film period since William Haggar delighted crowds with his shows in the British cinema's first decade. Independent production flourishes – especially in Cardiff, Caernarfon and Bangor. There is now a substantial body of work set in and about Wales or simply offering images of Welshness through characters and casting 'representative' actors. Yet there are still large areas of film-making in which directors and writers have failed to fulfil potential. (There is still a marked lack of genre films, for example.)

The Irish have unearthed probably the strongest batch of feature film-makers in the Celtic countries, including Pat O'Connor, Neil Jordan, Jim Sheridan, John Davies, Pat Murphy and Thaddeus O'Sullivan. Welsh films have yet to make an impact in British cinemas as the Irish have done with superb post-1980 works such as **Acceptable Levels, Maeve, Cal, Angel, The Crying Game, My Left Foot, Ballroom Of Romance** and **The Dawning**, or the Scots with Bill Douglas's famous trilogy, the early works of Bill Forsyth and features such as **Venus Peter** and **Soft Top, Hard Shoulder**. But there is enough talent in Wales and much fine recent work to build on. The formation of the Wales Film Council in 1993 promised a higher level of future funding, and marketing support from the recently structured Screen Wales augurs well for future prospects, even if a much higher level of government subsidy or industrial sponsorship is needed.

How many British directors have created anything like the consistent body of work boasted by Karl Francis? How many UK directors have produced comedies, rooted in real life, of the quality of **Joni Jones** and **Coming Up Roses**? Few documentary series in recent years have had the political thrust and bite, the depth of analysis and the entertainment value and exuberance, of **Cracking Up, The Dragon Has Two Tongues** and **Writing On the Line** – all the work of one Cardiff independent company, Teliesyn. Not too many film workshops in Britain have managed work as invigorating as Chapter's **Contortions, Voice Over** or **Walter Ego**, and we need not be defensive about a Welsh mini-'industry' which can produce work in the past decade or so of the standard (or variety) of, say, **Un Nos Ola Leuad (One Full Moon), Hedd Wyn, Boy Soldier, Ballroom, Aderyn Papur (And Pigs Might Fly), Gwenallt, Gadael Lenin (Leaving Lenin), Contortions** and **Elenya**.

An analysis of all this past work and the cinema's role in Wales spanning the past century is long overdue. It certainly seems odd that the cinema – often described as the greatest twentieth-century art form (and certainly the biggest mass entertainment) – has been so ignored within Wales's cultural discussions and the Welsh literary tradition. No previous book on the cinema in Wales or the Welsh contribution to film has ever been published. Go into many Welsh libraries and you would suspect the cinema never existed. When I first arrived to work for the *South Wales Echo* I was dismayed to find that the newspaper's library contained virtually no information on John Grierson, the acknowledged father of the British documentary movement – even though he edited his **This Wonderful World** TV programmes in the *Echo*'s own building in Cardiff. As the north Wales producer-director Wil Aaron has suggested, film has never been given its rightful role within Welsh culture. A rich legacy of screen work has been virtually ignored. Almost all the fascinating silent films about Wales between 1896 and 1922 have been lost, and much post-war TV output here has been junked.

This book attempts to assess the legacy and the losses and to embrace the different strands and creative film trends in the cinema and TV today: the production, distribution and exhibition – and the level of public funding, which has always been abysmal in Wales. (It is a major indictment of the Welsh Arts Council – and the British Film Institute that the peppercorn £11,700 budget for Chris Monger's 1980 **Voice Over** remained in early 1990 the highest single production grant handed out by the WAC.) The following chapters trace the output of Welsh cinema from the days when films were just a five- or ten-minute 'turn' on music-hall bills or a fairground diversion. Other sections of the book look at the creative contributions of Welsh performers to the British screen and international cinema. Some will be familiar – Richard Burton, Ray Milland, the Rachels (Roberts and Thomas), Anthony Hopkins and, in particular, Stanley Baker, who played a crucial role in changing the emphasis in British cinema (and the way it was perceived), and in the career of the director Joseph Losey. Certain actors have been unfairly reduced to cursory mentions or footnotes in official UK histories (Mervyn Johns, Edmund Gwenn, for example). Other important performers are still comparatively unknown outside Wales – such as Sue Roderick, Iola Gregory and Dafydd Hywel. Many have worked primarily in the Welsh language – where there is still more scope *within* Wales than in English, an anomaly discussed in these pages.

The creative contribution of silent stars is not ignored. Ivor Novello, once 'discovered' by D. W. Griffith and much more than a matinée idol, was surely destined for many more major roles (perhaps in Hollywood) if his career had not been curtailed by a punishing round of theatre commitments caused by his own excessive creativity . . . Gareth Hughes, who played lead roles in more than twenty Hollywood films, remains almost completely unknown or forgotten outside his native Llanelli.

This book also explores the work of documentary directors such as John Ormond, Jack Howells and Richard Watkins, and the Welsh-language pioneers – Ifan ab Owen Edwards and John Roberts Williams. Any history must embrace the important social conscience/mining films but also the traditions of Welsh comedy and the satirical stereotyping of the Welsh and their humour in work like **A Run For Your Money**, **Only Two Can Play**, **Grand Slam** and familiar British comedies by the Boulting Brothers and Launder and Gilliat. There is also much to fascinate in the cinema's role and impact in Wales and its growth from the early fairground days of bioscopes (travelling cinemas) ablaze with myriad lights, and colourful and raffish organ frontages, through the boom in cinema buildings from 1910 to 1914 to the spread of film as a mass entertainment in the twenties and thirties, and its struggles from the 1950s on.

More general questions are asked here. What is a Welsh film? Is it one produced in

Shooting *Gadael Lenin* (*Leaving Lenin*): Endaf Emlyn (and Lenin) in St Petersburg. Audiences voted the film their favourite UK feature at the 1993 London Film Fesstival.

Wales or one which, though originating outside, catches the spirit, the aspirations of the nation's people? Do people receive a valid and accurate image of Wales from the cinema or TV screen – and does it matter? Has continued preoccupation with myth, the Celtic or medieval past and Arthurian legend seen in many Welsh Office promotional films, Welsh Film Board shorts and much S4C work, retarded or debilitated film in Wales? How much is the general conception of Wales outside the country based on images of a sentimentalized or sanitized past? All are issues broached in discussions of individual films. There was hardly a mining picture in the forties and fifties without a choir scene or a moment when colliers expressed their camaraderie in song. At times the screen choir has been the *entrée* to a closed community (as Paul Robeson's itinerant ship's stoker found in **Proud Valley**). At others the choir's constitution and the status of locals within it has triggered most of the intrinsic drama or comedy – witness **Valley of Song** (1953) and a Cardiff Film Society version of Eynon Evans's play **Jubilee Concert** (1983). Is or was the choir an accurate indicator of social hierarchy (a question that might be raised by any exposure to work about Wales)? At what point does stereotyped imagery cease to have emotional validity? When do the almost obligatory shots of pit-head machinery (which so offended Graham Greene as cliché back in 1940) or of keening, shawled women waiting at a disaster scene for their men, cease to carry their own charge?[8] When does such film 'shorthand' or visual metaphor become outmoded or damaging in suggesting how a nation might be perceived? Does the colonization of Wales by film-makers from the US and England who choose to set work in the principality result in a glossing over of realities, a failure to grasp essential detail? For years Welsh people have been forced to see themselves on screen as often uninformed visiting film crews have seen them. All too frequently the view offered has told us more about the film-maker than about Wales.

The past – and the future

What better time than the early 1990s to try to put all this past work in perspective? S4C has completed its first chequered decade; a Wales Film Council, with wide-ranging responsibilities, has succeeded Ffilm Cymru, itself set up in 1989 by BBC and S4C to make features; a Wales Film Archive is struggling belatedly into life and

Welsh confidence: buoyant self-promotion for Stephen Bayly's *Coming Up Roses*, with Iola Gregory and Dafydd Hywel.

even metropolitan critics are becoming aware of the phenomenon of Welsh-language film, especially since two S4C features, **Boy Soldier** and **Coming Up Roses** (both in Welsh with English subtitles) made history in 1987 showing at commercial West End cinemas and gaining limited release on the Cannon circuit.[9] In 1985 the National Film Theatre acknowledged the Welsh contribution with a season of films about, or set, in Wales. In 1991 Wales BAFTA (BAFTA Cymru) staged its own awards ceremony for the first time. It is only now that film is beginning to be viewed within Wales as a serious art form, or an entertainment at least worth serious discussion – a sharp irony at a time when huge tracts are now barren of cinemas and the country boasts 50–60 venues compared to a peak of 300-plus during the immediate post-war years.

This history – itself subjective and the work of an 'outsider' (in Wales since 1974) – aims to show that Wales has had far more to offer the cinema than Richard Burton, Anthony Hopkins and **How Green Was My Valley** (the triumvirate many might select if asked for their 'idea' of 'Welsh film'). The book makes no claims to be definitive. As Wales's well known historian Gwyn Alf Williams has acknowledged, all accounts of history are selective and personal (even partisan!).[10] I have tried to consider the films and performances in the context of British film history and its industry, and of the period, and to explore some avenues worth further research and investigation. The work accommodates, at one end of the spectrum, the film- and video-makers whose work has tried to catch the temper and tenor of the times. At the other are those whose work is rooted in the 'heroic' tradition and regularly harks back to a Celtic past enshrined in myth and folk tale, notably Stephen Weeks and Paul Turner (in his earlier films). The first works of Teliesyn, south Wales's first non-workshop film co-operative, and much S4C output of Wil Aaron's Caernarfon-based

Ffilmiau'r Nant and Cardiff's Scan Films (Geoff Thomas, Frances Gallaher) have tended to dwell on Wales's past – though Teliesyn have increasingly drawn analogies with the present. This study also suggests what the future may hold for Welsh film and the cinema at a time when TV is being radically re-shaped, more money is being poured into Wales-based features and co-productions and big screen 'dwindling box office' trends have at last been reversed. There is no reason, if the right infrastructure is established, why future films in Wales should not be made for the cinema, as I attempt to show in chapter 24.

But indigenous Welsh film can only develop by building on the lessons, and profiting from the failures, of previous work and seizing on the clues offered up by that still largely 'hidden bequest' of films embraced in this book. That fertile legacy from the past century makes a flourishing Film and TV Archive and increased awareness of a Welsh screen culture a necessity.

SECTION 1   SILENT FILM DAYS

CHAPTER 1
CHAPTER 2
CHAPTER 3
CHAPTER 4
CHAPTER 5

Scene in a barber's shop: An accurate photograph quickened into life of a scene that has actually occurred . . . even the smoke on the customer's cigar . . . is blown across the scene and slowly disperses in the air – a most remarkable example of Kinetoscopic reproduction . . . What would the theatrical public give for such reproduction of, say, Garrick? Yet the next century may, possibly, be able to have an accurate reproduction of Irving's voice and gesture.

(Advertisement for Edison's Kinetoscope presentations at Stoll's Panopticon, Cardiff, *Western Mail*, 17 December 1894)

Cardiff was a privileged and prospering town in 1896. The Ocean and Powell Duffryn companies and entrepreneurs like David Davies and the Cory Brothers were riding high on a coal export boom, which was to make Cardiff and Barry the busiest ports anywhere just prior to the First World War. The pits were yet to feel the tremors from the industrial disputes which in 1898 would lead to a six-month stoppage and the formation of the South Wales Miners' Federation. Life revolved around the docks and the town had a thriving transport system based on the waterways and the tramways built up by the enterprising patriarch Solomon Andrews and his family (later to play no small role in developing south Wales cinemas). In 1896 the Cardiff port was the second busiest in the world, behind New York, if judged by annual shipping tonnage. The air of well-being among Cardiff businessmen reached its apogee as they prepared to set their stall out for the world – with one of the largest industrial exhibitions ever held in Britain planned for Cathays Park. Choral and orchestral recitals were favoured as entertainment by the upper and upper-middle classes, while the middle and labouring classes preferred the stage melodramas of companies run by Wilson Barrett and Ben Greet and the more robust fare offered by Oswald Stoll at his Empire Music Hall in Queen Street and Philharmonic Hall, St Mary Street, where he also provided a bewildering range of novelty acts and curios in one particular room, the Panopticon. D'Arcs Waxworks, also in St Mary Street, catered for the appetite for novelties in the great decade of discovery concluding Victoria's reign – providing effigies of such luminaries as W. G. Grace, the Boer War heroes Lords Roberts and Kitchener, and even notorious murderers (including Charles Peace, later immortalized on film in Wales by William Haggar).

One novelty act in the Panopticon, from 17 December 1894, presaged the arrival of arguably the greatest twentieth-century art form. In the same month as Polish pianist Paderewski was entertaining audiences at Cardiff's Park Hall, and music-hall star Vesta Victoria appeared at the city's Empire, two penny-in-the-slot Kinetoscope cabinets, developed in Thomas Edison's 'Black Maria' studio in Orange, New Jersey, were introduced into the curio hall. These offered spectators a peep-hole view of short films made by Edison's employee William Kennedy Dickson – including haircutting in a barber's shop, one round of a prizefight, skirt dancing and the strongman Eugene Sandow 'performing physical jerks' and lifting weights. A large *Western Mail* display advert touted 'Edison's new and wonderful invention' and gave a detailed description of the first film ever seen in Wales, set in a barber's shop in which a 'coloured gentleman' – 'a porter, boot black and general utility' – shares a joke in the newspaper with a customer while the barber shaves another client who betrays the results of his 'immoderate haste' by 'sundry grimaces and winces . . .' The writer of a *Manchester Guardian* review cited in the advert stressed that this was not an imaginary event from 'the pen or brush of some artist' but an accurate photograph 'quickened into life' of a scene that had actually occurred. Even the blink of an eyelash – 'so marvellously distinct and true to nature' – was recorded and 'the smoke of the cigar which the man smokes is blown across the face of the scene and slowly disperses in the air . . . Most remarkable evidence of the fidelity of kinetoscopic reproduction.'

Dickson had been experimenting with shorts since 1889 and the films, no more than 40–50ft. long, were shown on 35mm., but at 43–46 frames a second (compared to silent films' 16 frames a second), which would have caused some jerkiness of movement.[1] *The Manchester Guardian* article (of 14 October) said the cabinet, 4ft. high, 2 ft. wide, would remind other people of earlier 'scientific toys' exploring the principle of continuous motion – such as 'the zoetrope, the zoogyroscope . . . and

The *Western Mail* advert for the first screenings of the Edison Kinetoscope at Cardiff's Philharmonic Hall, St Mary Street, December 1894. This attraction competed for attention with Magneta, the Floating Lady, and tight-rope artists, the Lloyd Brothers.

STOLL'S PANOPTICON, PHILHARMONIC-HALL & BUILDINGS,
ST. MARY-STREET.

OPEN ALL DAY.—ADMISSION SIXPENCE.

Attractions in the Theatorium:—
THE LLOYD BROTHERS ON THE TIGHT-ROPE,
And Other Specialists.
IN OTHER SECTIONS OF THE EXHIBITION,
Amongst manifold items of interest, the features are
MAGNETA, THE FLOATING LADY,
Whose Evolutions in Mid-air, entirely unsupported, are an incomprehensible and unsolvable mystery; and
EDISON'S LATEST INVENTION,
THE GREATEST SURPRISE OF THIS GENERATION,
THE EDISON KINETOSCOPE.
SEE IT THIS WEEK, FOR WHEREAS THE FEE FOR SO DOING IS INCLUDED IN THE
ORDINARY ADMISSION CHARGE OF 6d. PAID ON ENTRANCE,
NEXT WEEK A SEPARATE EXTRA CHARGE MUST BE MADE.
THE EDISON KINETOSCOPE IN OPERATION!
SCENE IN A BARBER'S SHOP.

The beholder, who is looking down through the window of the Kinetoscope Cabinet, sees the interior of a barber's shop.

A man is reclining upon a barber's chair, about to be shaved. The barber goes to his case, secures his cup, makes a lather, and with this proceeds to lather the man's face. Meanwhile a coloured gentleman, who is probably acting in the capacity of porter, boot-black, and "general utility," is moving about the room. He picks up a paper and sits down to read it. Another customer comes in, pulls off hat and coat, takes a cigar from his vest pocket, lights it, picks up a paper, and sits down to smoke, read, and await his turn. The coloured gentleman aforesaid finds something very funny in the newspaper he is reading, and thereupon he crosses the room and points out the amusing article to the waiting customer. They both laugh, and show every sign of amusement.

Meanwhile the barber has been shaving his man, and both the "shaver" and the "shavee" have been going through many motions, the one plainly evincing his desire to hurry through the work of shaving and be ready for the "next"; the other as plainly showing the results of this immoderate haste on the part of his "executioner" by sundry grimaces and winces when the razor takes off sections of his cuticle. On the wall is seen the appropriate sign, "With or Without Chloroform," which is readily understood after witnessing the torture of the man in the barber's chair. Now, it should be understood that this is not an imaginary scene, emanating from the pencil or brush of some artist, but an ACCURATE PHOTOGRAPH QUICKENED INTO LIFE OF A SCENE THAT HAS ACTUALLY OCCURRED.

Every movement, from the walking of the man across the floor to the sweep of the razor, and even the very blink of an eyelash (so marvellously distinct and true to nature is the re-production) is recorded, and is witnessed by the beholder through the window of the kinetoscope. Even the smoke of the cigar which the man is smoking is blown across the face of the scene, and slowly disperses in the air—a most remarkable evidence of the fidelity of kinetoscopic re-productions.

ON OCTOBER 14th LAST THE "MANCHESTER GUARDIAN"
Said in a Leading Article on
THE EDISON KINETOSCOPE,
"Mr. Edison, who has accomplished many marvels, is not content to rest upon his laurels, but is developing new and startling inventions. One of these, the 'kinetoscope,' is intended to re-produce motion as the phonograph re-produces sound, though not in the same manner. The basis of the kinetoscope is photography. If, for example, Mr. Edison desires to show us a moving picture of a man taking off his coat, the data of the actual scene are first recorded by the camera at the rate of forty-three successive photographs in each second. When these separate pictures of the changes of attitude that occur to a man when disembarrassing himself of his outer covering are set in motion at the same speed as that at which they were taken they unite to form one complete picture, and the photographic figure is seen to take off its coat with an absolute fidelity to nature. This will, no doubt, remind some readers of the zoetrope, the zoogyroscope, and other scientific toys with even more aggravating designations. But practical applications will, doubtless, be found for Mr. Edison's latest invention. We are told that 'the apparatus in which this re-production takes place is a cabinet about 4ft. high, 2ft. wide, and 1ft. 9in. deep. It contains the celluloid film band, the apparatus for re-constructing the disjointed views, and a small electric motor for driving the apparatus. The chief detail of the mechanism is a flat metal ring having a slot in it, which makes about 2,000 revolutions per minute. The film passes rapidly over the ring, beneath which is a light. The spectator looks through a lens on to the film, and every action recorded on it passes under his view.' The marvels now told of the kinetoscope are in the green wood; what may we expect in the dry? Mr. Edison now shows on a small scale all the features of an original stage production,' but by and bye he proposes to make a partnership between the phonograph and the kinetoscope, and by enlarging the figures and throwing them on a screen produce or re-produce a drama. What would the theatrical public give for such a re-production, say, of 'Garrick'? Yet the next century may, possibly, be able to have an accurate repetition of Irving's voice and gestures. How will the new machine affect the action and delivery of the orator who knows that every movement of voice and limb is being recorded for the admiration or the amusement of posterity? The possibilities of the kinetoscope are great and multifarious."

other toys with even more aggravating designations'. But the writer thought 'practical applications will doubtless be found for Mr Edison's latest invention, containing a celluloid film band, and a small electric motor.' The writer showed prescience in observing that the films recorded 'on a small scale the features of an original stage production' – it was to be a year before the first rudimentary *projected* fiction films were made – but Edison clearly had a vision of the future. The advert claimed that he hoped to link his new phonograph with the kinetoscope and 'by throwing them on the screen produce or reproduce a drama'.

The first local report of the invention, in the *Western Mail* on 18 December, noted that the instrument 'passes before the eye about 1,200 photographs in 25 seconds' and adds, 'when looking through the disc one can hardly imagine that he [*sic*] is not looking directly on the scene portrayed, through the wrong end of a field glass.' Despite the size of the newspaper advert on 17 December, by Christmas week Edison's presentation of 'photographs of actual life and every figure in motion' received only sixth billing at the Panopticon, below a wax tableau of the Death of Nelson; a live act – the Lucases' 'dem darkees from Old Kentucky'; a levitation specialist – Magenta 'the floating lady'; a comedy turn, and the Punch and Judy act of Prof. Richard Codman (father of the north Wales cinema pioneer John Codman).[2] Not until the films were projected did they create any kind of impact – and the first Cardiff screenings caused scarcely a ripple. The south Wales press certainly ignored the historic first screenings of projected cinema, as we know it, by the Lumière brothers in Paris in December 1895. The following year the chief entertainment remained the music-hall at Stoll's Empire – re-opened, after a facelift, with room for 2,300.[3] Within months the hall hosted visits from such vaudevillians as Harry Tate, Harry Champion and one Charles Chaplin – 'dramatic and light comedy vocalist' – father of the screen comedian.[4]

The event of the year was the great Fine Art, Industrial and Maritime Exhibition in Cathays Park which pulled in 898,000 visitors over six months. The local press, with customary hyperbole, claimed the exhibition made every single event in Wales in the past 'dwindle into insignificance'.[5] But not even the most prescient audience could have foreseen the eventual impact of the unheralded exhibition diversion which was to usher out the music-hall within a few years.

Birt Acres in Cardiff

The screenings of films by a scientist and inventor named Birt Acres – each less than a minute long – gained relatively meagre column inches from reporters clamouring for information on the latest products of the heavyweight commercial companies displayed at the event, the exploits – and fatal misadventures – of youthful balloonists and such esoteric ephemera as Wat Tyler's boots.[6] It seems ironic that all other events which set the public's adrenalin flowing in anticipation before the great Cardiff showpiece opened in May should now seem dwarfed by the significance of the Acres movie shorts in Wales. It was a happy accident that brought him to Cardiff to present almost certainly the first public screening of his films outside London – and made it possible for him to shoot a royal visit. *That* film proved the coup of the first official 'Royal Command' screen performance in London in July after Acres was summoned to Marlborough House to show his work – and the favourable judgements of the then Prince and Princess of Wales gave the new 'moving pictures' the respectability and kudos they needed.[7] Until then most people aware of film regarded it as an inferior entertainment, a transient novelty, the preserve of boffins and photographers vying with each other – in the wake of the Dickson/Edison peep-show Kinetoscope and Kinetograph – to exhibit and sell ever more sophisticated camera and projection equipment.

Acres, flushed with his command-performance success, helped consolidate the new invention's popularity by staging a public première of his royal film in a programme at the Metropolitan Music Hall in London's Edgware Road in August. At the finale, the audience cheered the film and the operator of his machine, the Kineopticon. The command performance would perhaps have been important enough as a watershed for film, but helping Acres with the lighting at Marlborough House was the redoubtable Cecil Hepworth, the son of a magic-lanternist. That screening sold Hepworth instantly on the invention, and he was to make the film **Rescued By Rover** (1905), an often-revived UK film from cinema's first decade, and head the most influential of Britain's early production studios at Walton-on-Thames. Hepworth, in turn, played a crucial role when leading American and British box-office stars (including Chrissie White, Ivy Close and Florence Turner) featured in silent films set in Wales around the time of the First World War. He distributed British films by the American ex-Vaudevillian Florence Turner, and in 1915 she starred in tandem with director Henry Edwards in the **Welsh Singer**, one of three films made from best-selling novels by west-Wales-born Allen Raine.[8]

Birt Acres was just one of the major screen pioneers to visit south Wales only months after the Lumières' historic show in Paris on 28 December 1895. The same month that Acres first demonstrated his invention to audiences at the exhibition in Cardiff, the Cinématographe – the machine developed by the Lumières – screened some of the brothers' films to audiences

Birt Acres, who filmed at the great Industrial Exhibition in Cardiff in 1896.

in the town, and in October the 'daddy of the British cinema' Robert William Paul – Acres's former employer, exhibited his machine and, more importantly, shot two short films of traffic, in Queen Street, Cardiff – almost certainly the first Welsh street scenes.

The scientists and photographers who first brought 'cinema' to the bustling music-halls and the lecture halls of south Wales may have harboured illusions that their inventions would ultimately remain the preserve of the laboratory and classroom. They saw themselves as educators rather than entertainers, but they were soon disabused by the robust showmen of an earthier, more pragmatic stamp and by an urban working class which soon recognized the merits of a new entertainment which could take them even further away from their hard lives than the stage acts and melodramas which previously provided the prime form of proletarian 'escapist' entertainment. More austere members of the middle classes in Wales took more convincing, as their consciences warred with the dogma of chapel and Nonconformist puritanism. Many saw the cinema as both disreputable, with its music-hall links, and palpably inferior – with its 'dumb shows' and early narrative limitations no substitute for the 'legitimate' stage.

It may seem remarkable that less than seven months after the first public cinema screenings by the Lumière brothers in Paris, Cardiff had not only staged a show of the Lumières' films on their own machine, the Cinématographe, but also hosted visits from two men, Acres and Paul, who not only shot film in Wales in 1896 but are now recognized as Britain's first two film-makers. It doesn't seem as surprising, perhaps, that people in urban south Wales weaned on music-hall and vaudeville 'turns' and sleight-of-hand stage effects should take to the new medium, and its capacity – within a year or two – for magical 'trick' films and visual coups which could not be reproduced by even the most sophisticated of stage entertainers. From the time improved technology allowed primitive fiction film, the movies took tentative hold. In Wales, in particular, the ability to present actual sporting events (even days later) – or re-stage them for the camera – also appealed to the music-hall's predominantly male audiences. And it seems inevitable that so many of the most popular 'actuality' or 'topical' films (forerunners of newsreels or documentaries) should feature the fight game. Films were not long enough, initially, to encompass anything other than the sketchiest storyline. It was imperative that early subjects should provide action and movement. What better than boxing – never more popular in Wales than in late Victorian days and the years up to and during the First World War? Welshmen had fought a succession of World and British title battles, and pugilism rather than education was seen by some families as an escape route from Valleys poverty. But the vogue for boxing films was relatively shortlived as fiction films became longer (allowing scope for weightier or more ingenious storylines) – though fiction movies with boxers as heroes persisted through the 1920s.

In 1896 the average length of a film was around 40ft. – running less than a minute – and shows of a dozen or even twenty shorts were soon commonplace. By 1914 the longest British films were eight-reelers of around 7,500ft. and film-makers could now do much more than the simple one-idea 'park bench' or chase films and could draw for inspiration on the literary classics, or 'penny dreadfuls' and comic strips. D. W. Griffith and Edwin S. Porter in America and the great French, Italian and German directors, had introduced many of the narrative screen devices which were to make the cinema a unique art form. Chaplin had arrived on the scene and tiros in Hollywood were gearing up to flood world screens.

In retrospect it seems scarcely surprising that in 1896, when films were just fragments or reproductions of a single event or basic comic situation, the new medium should have been seen as no more significant as entertainment than Röntgen's newly discovered X-ray plates, for example – which drew large crowds into Welsh music-halls and other public venues in 1896. Yet by 1914 it was *inevitable* that cinema would usurp those music-halls as the new mass entertainment.[9]

The early screenings

> This wonderful instrument is one of the great inventions of the age . . . It may be described as an adaptation of the Kinetoscope and the Magic Lantern, enabling the audience to witness upon a screen on which the light is thrown the movements of a crowd or of individual persons . . . The performance was a remarkable success and all present declared themselves astonished with the series of pictures thrown upon the screen.

> (*South Wales Echo* account, 6 May 1896, of the first Kineopticon performance at the Cardiff Fine Art, Industrial and Maritime Exhibition)

Birt Acres, (1854–1918), born in Virginia, USA, but living and working in Barnet, Herts., stole a march over all the other pioneers when he screened the first films ever to be projected in Wales – on 10 April 1896, for the Cardiff Photographic Society.[10] Acres showed various films to the Cardiff photographers: of men playing cards; a review of the troops by the German Emperor at the Kiel Canal; shots of the 1895 Derby – 'the preliminary canter, the exciting finish and the surging of the crowd after the race'; and of a southwester off Dover, capturing the 'roll of waves and the dashing spray'. Acres was apologetic about the quality, complaining about the density of the gelatine film and the dull limelight (rather than electricity) he used to screen it but the audience cheered him 'again and again' and insisted he show the Derby short once more. The success of the Dover film may seem inexplicable today but as each breaker rolled in 'rounds of applause' were accorded by the delighted spectators.[11] The studies of waves taken from the pier 'made one feel inclined to stand back for fear of getting wet', wrote one journalist.[12]

Film historian John Barnes has stressed that shots of flying seaspray and waves surging over rocks were more popular than the more obvious, live-action subjects which had been filmed for the Kinetoscope screenings at 40–46 frames a second but were being projected at 20 on Acres's Kineopticon by 1896 (compared with the normal silent speed).[13] The speed discrepancies must have made the characters' actions seem jerky or absurd. Interestingly, the same rolling waves effect had triggered high excitement in 1854 when John Dilwyn Llewellyn (relative by marriage of the cameraman and inventor Henry Fox Talbot) exhibited in London's Bond Street four photographs called *Motion* and one shot of the steamboat *Juno* at Tenby which 'fixed instantaneously the floating smoke and steam'. Queen Victoria was so enamoured by some of these works – the first photographs to show waves breaking – that she had carried them home and Llewellyn had to send home for replacements.[14] Nearly forty years later, Acres also submitted a series of shots of waves to the Photographic Society in London – work described as 'his masterpiece'.[15]

That first visit by Acres to fellow photographers in Cardiff was scarcely reported, but critics soon succumbed to his displays at the Cathays Park exhibition. On 5 May, to an 'invited audience', he screened his Derby, Emperor and Dover films, plus **Beertime in a Carpenter's Shop**, images of the 'lightning' cartoonist Tom Merry at work and a primitive story, **Arrest of a Pickpocket**. The *South Wales Echo* reporter was euphoric about the screenings by Mr Birdacre (*sic*), finding the Derby shots 'very exciting and interesting' and thought 'the sea dashed at intervals over the seawall in the most realistic style.' 'This wonderful instrument is one of the great inventions of the age,' gushed the *Echo*, understandably. All present declared themselves astonished with 'the series of pictures thrown upon the screen', and the display, on a machine described by the journalist as an adaptation of the Kinetoscope and the magic lantern, was deemed 'a remarkable success'.[16] The *Western Mail* on 6 May reported 'The photographs are secured on a continuous film . . . one picture gives place to the other before any single one can impress itself on the retina of the eye.' The same paper reported (4 May) that Acres Cardiff open displays, presumably from 5 or 6 May on, were the first public exhibition of this 'unique discovery' (the Kineopticon) – and this may have been the case.

A royal peep-show

By June, Acres had added further films to his display – each on average some 40ft. long – including the Niagara Falls and Tower Bridge, both 'in motion'. But his prize attraction was the moving picture he took on 27 June, at the Cardiff exhibition, of the then Prince of Wales (later Edward VII), Queen Alexandra and the Princesses Victoria and Maud.[17] The work, destined to cause furore in the press, was obtained by 'cutting a little hole through the canvas of the main entrance so that we could get an uninterrupted view of the ceremony', wrote Cardiff's Samuel Allen, who introduced Acres to the audience at official exhibition presentations.[18] The *Amateur Photographer* magazine reported that Acres had received permission (but not apparently from royalty) to tear a hole in the exhibition walls, and 'pointed his peculiar camera full at the Royal Party'.[19] Unfortunately, the camera caught the Prince scratching his head and Acres was roundly rebuked for his breach of protocol by the London-based *Globe* newspaper which dubbed him a 'photographic fiend'. Acres refuted allegations of any impropriety. The movement, he said, was 'probably to brush away an intrusive fly'.[20]

The film, long vanished, was 80ft. long (twice his norm) and contained shots of Cardiff's Mayor, Lord Windsor and Lady Windsor, the royals arriving by carriage with their escort of yeomanry, Mr Robert Forrest, the exhibition chairman – and a *Western Mail* representative 'notebook in hand'. The party was seen being rushed into the exhibition and there were glimpses of a few Cardiff bobbies' helmets.[21] When Acres asked permission to show his scoop publicly he was summoned to London where the royals 'expressed their great delight with it' and the prince was 'intensely amused' by the work, screened on 21 July 1896 (the eve of Princess Maud's wedding) with the help of Hepworth's electrical arc lamp.[22] The

Era newspaper reported that the royal party film was loudly applauded – and repeated by request – and the prince gave Mr Aires (*sic*) permission to photograph the wedding the following day.[23] Acres had hedged his bets, arriving with twenty-one films to screen, including his first fictional work **Arrest of a Pickpocket** and shots of a train travelling through Highgate Tunnel – but also his footage of the 1896 Derby won by the prince's own horse, Persimmon.[24]

That August, at Cardiff Photographic Society's invitation, Acres also filmed a military tournament in Cathays Park when his Kinetic camera 'similar to a diminutive barrel organ' filmed in front of the main grandstand and shot a sword duel, a boxing match, a maypole dance, a mounted quadrille and mule battery and – an obvious crowd-pleasing sketch – 'Cleaving the Turk's Head'.[25]

The inventor viewed the success of his camerawork with mixed feelings and when his Kineopticon wooed crowds at London's Metropolitan Music Hall it was, significantly, exhibited by an agent, Lewis Sealy, rather than the inventor. But both Acres and Sealy basked in the glory of the Marlborough House coup (the Kineopticon was even

---

Queen's Hall, at 7.30 and 9 o'clock.

✳✳✳

The Kineopticon,

INVENTED AND PATENTED BY

BIRT ACRES, ESQ., F.R.Met.S., F.R.P.S.

Introduced by MR. T. C. HAYWARD.

✳

A Selection will be shown from the following List of Subjects:—

1. SEA WAVES AT DOVER.
   The waves roll up in a most realistic manner, breaking against the Admiralty Pier, each wave as it breaks throwing up a great cloud of spray.
2. GOLFING EXTRAORDINARY—5 GENTLEMEN.
   This is a Golf Scene, in which one gentleman in attempting to strike the ball misses and falls headlong, much to the amusement of the bystanders.
3. TOM MERRY, "LIGHTNING CARTOONIST," SKETCHING GLADSTONE.
4. TOM MERRY, "LIGHTNING CARTOONIST," SKETCHING SALISBURY.
   In these two pictures Mr. Tom Merry, the Lightning Cartoonist, is seen busy at work upon portraits of Mr. Gladstone and Lord Salisbury.
5. BOXING MATCH OR GLOVE CONTEST.
   Having an interval introduced, during which the combatants sit down for a brief rest, and are vigorously fanned by two attendants, concluding in the last round with one of the boxers being floored.
6. HIGHGATE TUNNEL.
   A goods train issues from the tunnel and passes through Highgate Station; a gentleman, waiting for his train, strolls up and down the platform and watches the passing trucks.
7. HENLEY REGATTA.
   This year's picture, showing the whole surface of the river crowded with boats, &c.

The Birt Acres Kineopticon show at London's Queen's Hall in 1896 features his film of the Prince and Princess of Wales's visit to Cardiff, with Princesses Victoria and Maud.

8. THE ARREST OF A PICKPOCKET,
In which the man is pursued by a constable, runs right across the picture, they struggle together and the policeman's helmet is knocked off, then the pickpocket, by slipping out of his jacket, manages to escape, but runs full tilt into the arms of a sailor, with whose assistance he is finally secured, handcuffed, and marched off to justice.

9. BROADWAY—NEW YORK.
A busy scene at Broadway, with carriages, trams, carts, and pedestrians moving about.

10. PRINCE AND PRINCESS OF WALES AT CARDIFF, JUNE 27TH.
A view of the Prince and Princess of Wales, the Princesses Victoria and Maud, and their suite, on the occasion of their visit to the Cardiff Exhibition, in which portrait pictures of the Royal group are faithfully reproduced.

The above subjects are the identical pictures exhibited before H.R.H. The Prince of Wales and the Royal Wedding Guests, at Marlborough House, on Tuesday, July 21st, 1896. At the close of the Entertainment, H.R.H. complimented Mr. Acres on the successful exhibit, and honoured him by a special permission to photograph the Royal Wedding on the following day.

Promenade Concert

In the QUEEN'S HALL, at 8 o'clock.

THAMES IRON WORKS' MILITARY BAND

(By kind permission of A. F. HILLS, Esq.),

Conductor: MR. JOHN H. WILLIAMS, Bandmaster Thames Iron Works' Military Band, and 2nd Kent Volunteer Artillery.

Vocalists: MISS ANNIE SWALLOW, MR. ARTHUR WESTON,
MR. FRED DANIELS, Coster Comedian.

1. MARCH—"Argandab"	*T. Thompson.*
2. SONG—"The Carnival"	*Molloy.*
MR. ARTHUR WESTON.	
3. OVERTURE—"La Ruche D'or"	*E. Brepsant.*

temporarily re-christened the Royal Cinematoscope).[26] Yet, despite Acres's efforts – and the publicity he gained from a fairly sycophantic photographic trade press – the Lumières remained front runners in silent cinema in 1896, trawling for markets throughout the world.

Mr Trewey's sleight of hand

On 11 May, barely a week after Acres's exhibition screening, Lumière's Cinématographe – 'this startling novelty' – was the main attraction at Cardiff's Empire, unveiled by the brothers' London-based manager Felicien Trewey, the virtuoso magician and shadowographer.[27] The machine, a camera-projector which took 35mm. film and screened films at 35 frames a second (an improvement on the Kinetoscope), had made its bow at the Regent Street Polytechnic and was to show 'shorts' at the London Empire, Leicester Square, for more than a year. Trewey also screened in Cardiff a Derby film of 1895 – probably shot by Acres – which allowed onlookers to show the 'excitement depicted on every face', at the finish. They stole the thunder from Acres's Kineopticon, which was still advertised – if infrequently – at the Cardiff exhibition among the 'sideshows and novelties': it received such scant attention that the Cardiff Photographic Society complained, 'our animated photographs are left out in the cold'.[28] Cardiff Empire's proprietor, Oswald Stoll, featured the Lumière show as a principal attraction when films normally appeared way down the music-hall bills, but he knew a good thing and from 22 June film shows were regular features at Stoll's Panopticon. In July, the Lumière agent was back, with more shows, when the machine was booked for £125 a week.[29] Another breakthrough came when Stoll announced that from now on the Lumière Cinématographe would appear in the middle of the programme at *each* music-hall performance. It is remarkable that the year cinema came to Britain, Stoll had film shows running at two separate Cardiff entertainment centres (the Empire and Panopticon) – surely a unique occurrence outside London. His Panopticon also claimed the first south Wales screening of the **Famous Butterfly Girl** – Loie Fuller, a dancer and rudimentary stripteaser – in a film considerably more *risqué* than anything else in official circulation.[30]

The Cinématographe made its début at the Empire in Swansea on 13 July and in

Newport on 20 July and Trewey paid several visits to south Wales that year. His film selection included a London street scene, the Lumières' famous arrival of a train (always a big attraction as locos moved towards and loomed over front row audiences), **A Flirtation** and **The Coronation of the New Czar**. At Swansea Empire, when there was some criticism of film quality, the wily Trewey was ingenious enough to hit on the idea of running through pictures of a fire brigade call in reverse – showing the men and women running backwards – which naturally delighted unsophisticated patrons. That bill also included, intriguingly, shots of the pleasureboat, the *Brighton*, entering Swansea. Fifteen Lumière Company films appeared in one Swansea bill, including more film of Princess Maud's wedding, **Blacksmiths at Work** (also known as **The Forge**) and **Pranks on a Gardener** – the Lumières' famous **L'Arroseur Arrosé – Teasing the Gardener**, one of their best-known surviving films and one of the earliest works with a fictional storyline. It features an incorrigible youngster who steps on a water hose, then off it, sending a jetstream of water into the gardener's face, before receiving a good beating.[31]

A film patriarch: R. W. Paul

In October 1896, Cardiff finally played host to R. W. Paul himself.[32] Apart from his Queen Street shorts, the inventor or his agent screened twelve films on his Theatrograph or Animatographe, including shots of the 1896 Derby, Princess Maud's wedding (again!), his 80ft. fictional work **The Soldier's Fortune**, his **Papermakers**,

Robert William Paul, who took moving pictures in Queen Street, Cardiff, in 1896.

Arrival of the Pony Express and shots of the renowned music-hall entertainer – 'Chirgwin, The White Eyed Kaffir'.[33] Already in Paul's shrewd blend of actuality (or current event) film, stage act records and fiction, there were signs that he was alive to the medium's entertainment value. But his publicity was couched in the usual defensive self-improvement terms of the day, stressing that the projector 'processed features not merely for the music-hall habitué but for the scientist'.[34]

Acres and Paul were an interesting pair. There was lively competition between many of the pioneers for business *and* kudos; rows surrounding rival cinema invention claims by the great Thomas Alva Edison and his talented employee Dickson, and the various fracas about US film patents, were mirrored in squabbles between Paul and Acres conducted in photographic journals after the two men split up in 1895. The rift was lifelong.

Paul (1869–1943), an electrical engineer and scientific instrument maker in London's Hatton Garden, had been asked to make copies of Edison's Kinetoscope or peep-show machines by two Greek businessmen planning to install them in entertainment venues throughout Europe. Edison had patented his company's camera, the Kineto-graph, and the films shot at his Black Maria studios at Orange, New Jersey, but failed to take similar safeguards with his viewing machines. Paul threw scruple to the wind and reproduced the peep-show machines after an overture to Edison about a possible partnership had been ignored. But Paul's first actual camera was shaky. Acres helped out with a clamping device to stabilize the motion, but it was not until 1936 that Paul conceded he had worked out his ideas 'due to Acres'.[35] Acres, in 1896, claimed the Boat Race and Derby films of 1895 were shot on the Kinetic Camera he had patented by May that year, but Paul claimed both films were his and were shot by Acres on a camera he developed with the American as his employee.[36] By October 1896, Acres – who also claimed to have shown films privately in August 1895 (before the Lumières) – finally shed any vestige of false modesty, describing himself – with little justification – as the 'original inventor of animated photography' and the first to present a successful exhibition of moving pictures.[37]

Paul continued to visit south Wales. In November 1896 at the Swansea Empire his Theatrograph was billed below the legendary actress Lillie Langtry, and the same month in a Paul bill at the Newport Empire a street-fight scene and the arrest of offenders by police and a bathing scene 'caused much laughter'.[38] By then, the Merthyr Theatre Royal and Opera House had also booked the Theatrograph.[39] Paul was soon to outstrip Acres as a force in the embryo British cinema – creating the first film studios at Muswell Hill (New Southgate) making many fiction films and 'trick' shorts inspired by the *trompes-l'oeil* of the French magician and theatre owner, Georges Méliès.

The Lumières eclipsed

Trewey returned to the Cardiff and Newport Empires and Stoll's Panopticon in 1897, when the *Cardiff Evening Express* noted that the Cinématographe's popularity 'had not waned in the slightest' and large crowds attended the Newport screenings. The machine was back in June and September when Trewey was just one exhibitor to show in Wales film of Queen Victoria's jubilee procession.[40] Any self-respecting film pioneer managed to find a place somewhere along the route – as film-makers were to do for the monarch's funeral procession footage four years later – and the result was a glut of these actuality shorts.[41] Yet, despite the endless pursuit of fresh material, film-makers could not always satisfy audiences or their own often exacting standards. There is ample evidence that, at this stage, many shows and projection standards were poor – with material shown at the 'wrong' speed.

The Lumières at first seemed beyond criticism. Their films were said to be 'the most perfect ever exhibited', while Stoll's Newport Empire billed the Cinématographe as 'unequalled'.[42] But the days of their supremacy were numbered as more sophisticated equipment arrested public interest. Competition increased as exhibitors billed their shows under increasingly exotic titles to pull in crowds. A spectacular blow was struck to the Cinématographe's pre-eminence by the arrival of 70mm. film, shown in Wales on the American Biograph by British agents of the US Mutoscope and Biograph company and shot with a camera partly developed by Edison's former employee Dickson – though the invention was credited to Herman Casler, a leading light in developing 'What The Butler Saw' machines. Oswald Stoll, who had regularly praised the superiority of the Lumière machine, was swift to switch horses. The Biograph, already a hit with London crowds, was billed as 'the latest wonder', and an advert for the Cardiff and Swansea Empires claimed the show was 'a marvellous improvement on the Cinématographe . . . Everything is shown lifesize.'[43]

In July, the press reported Biograph films had 'perfect stillness' and 'none of the dazzling effects associated with similar machines',[44] and an August report of a performance including the jubilee procession and the Henley regatta described the films as 'perhaps the best displayed by any animatographe'.[45] There was standing room only at the Biograph's first appearance in Swansea when the 'pictures were shown with a steadiness that was very acceptable after the jerkiness of other picture shows and as they were much larger in area the result was all that could be desired'.[46] Work shown included **Stable on Fire**, **Niagara Lower Rapids**, **Caught in the Act** (more rudimentary fiction – 'a merchant is discovered by his wife kissing a typewriter girl'), **A Hard Wash** or **The Piccaninny's Bath**, **The Horseless Fire Engine** and **A Pillow Fight**.

The public were perhaps soon sated with the diet of actuality film (often formal processions, the abridged news film of its day) and the brief fiction works. But the predominantly male audiences who flocked to Welsh music-halls were soon to discover films which effectively reproduced on screen their other leisure interests. As longer films were made, melodrama based on stage works became popular (as Haggar's films demonstrated). Right from these first Acres and Lumière Derby screenings, the public had also responded warmly to sports events on screen and local events were soon featured. Action from a Wales soccer international at Swansea was seen in 1901, and the annual Cardiff Horse Show, soon to be almost a yearly screen attraction, made its début on film in 1902. In north Wales, the Pwllheli Horse Show was shown the same year by Fred E. Young, the amateur magician and estates manager for Solomon Andrews, Cardiff's tramway king.[47] But no other early sports event on screen matched for popular appeal the great scoop of 1897.

Fight films – and Peerless Jim

Cardiff's Philharmonic Hall in St Mary Street – home of Stoll's Panopticon – trumpeted the screening of the World Heavyweight title fight between American, Gentleman Jim Corbett (later, briefly, a film fiction star in his own right), and the Cornishman Bob Fitzimmons (who had staged exhibition bouts in the 1896 Cardiff Fine Art and Industrial event). The Hall advertised '165,000 photographs – two miles of film on the Veriscope' – a projector developed by one Enoch J. Rector who clinched the deal to shoot the bout at Carson City, Nevada.[48] The film, when seen in America, had grabbed the imagination and established the screen as 'definitely low brow, an entertainment for the great unwashed commonality', screen historian Terry Ramsaye claimed.[49] It certainly became a talking point in Wales even if its standards left much to be desired and Mr W. Rotherham, travelling with the Veriscope in an American entourage including an electrician, a chief operator and a lecturer, told the press 'little could be done to control the vibration' and 'blamed the weather for the variation in quality'.[50] These lecturers were common in silent film days, often providing a general description of scenes and frequently inserting their own dialogue and witticisms.

Prizefights were soon recognized as failsafe attractions in Wales in their own right, and sometimes re-staged for the screen with film-makers demanding that knock-outs take place precisely at the ideal spot in the ring for the cameras. It must also be remembered that staged but illegal prizefights were still in the 1890s a feature of Valleys life. Boxing, in both fairgrounds and halls, was a huge spectator attraction when Wales boasted a clutch of World or British champions including flyweight Jimmy Wilde – 'The Ghost With a Hammer in His Hand' (later a feature film actor before entering cinema management) – Freddie Welsh and Peerless Jim Driscoll. It was hardly surprising that as two- and three-reelers developed, fighters like Wilde, James J. Corbett, Bombardier Billy Wells and Jess Willard played leads in fictional screen dramas. In June 1907, the audience at Cardiff's Andrews Hall cheered as Driscoll unwrapped a Sunday punch on screen to floor former bantamweight World Champion Joe Bowker in London days before – and Peerless Jim was present at each Cardiff performance.[51]

But just as popular was film of the 1899 Bob Fitzimmons v. James J. Jeffries fight on Coney Island, screened at Swansea's Albert Hall in 1900 by Chas. W. Poole's United Amusements. Poole claimed to have spent £250 to obtain the only print in Britain of the fight, screened on the Cinematoscope of Lubin, who founded the powerful US theatre chain. Lubin had earlier pirated the 1897 Corbett–Fitzimmons fight employing two freight handlers to restage the fight while a prompter read a blow by blow account from a local newspaper.[52] Poole's adverts for his show captured the xenophobic, imperialistic mood of the day – 'It is being able to protect himself with his fist that makes the Britisher so much feared by foreigners.'[53]

Boxing films, fact and fiction, remained popular in the 1896–1918 period but the jingoism and patriotism – evident in the Poole show – had also found release in the flood of Boer War films and shorts about the exploits of Kitchener and Roberts in the next few years (many of them shamelessly recreating incidents for the screen and dressing them up as the real event). Poole had introduced his cinema as an addition to the family's specialist Myriorama entertainment featuring paintings of panoramic views and drawings of disasters and other events on a wooden backdrop which moved along on rollers. Poole's, ingenious stage entertainers since 1837, regularly supplied their shows with a battery of sound effects including gunpowder explosions for the battle scenes.[54] The family regularly changed the names of their various shows and the magic lanterns and projectors they used from 1901 onwards. The titles embraced the Pooleograph, the Myriograph and, most spectacularly – when acting as agents for the Edison company – the Edison–Poole Eventographe.[55] Edison, of course, was anxious to make up for lost time, and his first projecting machine, the Projectoscope (or Projectorscope), screened films at Cardiff's Theatre Royal in December 1897 – 'the latest triumph of science showing lifesize living pictures of local and general interest.'[56] The early showmen and exhibitors searched restlessly for screen novelties to keep the public happy, but an increase in Welsh film material by 1898 must have created more interest in the burgeoning medium in south Wales.

The funeral processions for Gladstone – in Westminster and from his north Wales country retreat at Hawarden – were screened to huge crowds. Other attractions of 1898 included travelling shots of Conwy Castle shown on the American Biograph at the Cardiff Empire.[57] But, above all, people loved to see themselves on screen and exhibitors were willing to oblige. Enterprising showmen increasingly took street shots of as many residents as possible, and included them in their programmes as bait for their main attractions. Cardiff's Corpus Christi procession was shown on London-based Phil and Bernard's Cinématographe in 1898 and the march became an annual screen attraction; and in 1901 Cardiff Fire Brigade emulated other firemen in Britain in going through their paces before a camera.[58]

A creative breakthrough

With film a fragile infant and still frequently a lowly attraction on music-hall bills in the new century's first decade, it is hardly surprising that many could not see its long-term prospects. Yet it is not entirely fanciful to suggest that before 1900 some Welsh showmen must have felt the first stirrings of an embryo art form.

The first inkling probably came to Wales in 1898 at the Albert Hall, Swansea, show, by the magician David Devant, for Maskelyne and Cooke, proprietors of London's famous Egyptian music-hall. He presented films by the great magician and 'trick' director Georges Méliès which had a rapturous reception from the local press, and were hailed as 'by far the finest films seen in Swansea'. They included **The Haunted Castle** – 'a weird and ghostly spectacle' which gave spectators 'a creepy, thrilling sensation'; and **Faust's Laboratory** – 'the most lengthy and unquestionably the most wonderful picture taken'.[59] Méliès, a Paris theatre-owner, used stop-motion and splicing to create fantasy and shock effects (disembodied heads and torsos were a speciality) and his showman's panache, his theatrical flourishes and timing and editing skills, made his simple narrative films a huge attraction.

The press reporter noted that Devant's machine was 'obviously a much improved one for that unpleasant whirring noise has been done away with, whilst the pictures are made more dramatic by the accompanying sounds from the back of the stage, including the sound of a discharged gun'. A few years later Joseph Danter, the south Wales travelling cinema pioneer, always had a shotgun on hand to add authenticity to his silent melodramas and comic 'screamers'; and his sister-in-law Louise came back regularly from the local store with a pram-load of crockery 'seconds' which she smashed with a mallet behind screen during slapstick scenes.[60]

The Méliès pantomime and fairytale films soon became a regular Christmas entertainment at Cardiff's Philharmonic Hall (**Little Red Riding Hood** in 1901 and 1903; **Blue Beard** in 1902, when the Frenchman's best-known film today, **A Trip to the Moon**, was also seen). The screen pantomime also became a tradition with the Pathé Frères Company. Cardiff saw its **Aladdin and His Wonderful Lamp** (in 1906), **Ali Baba and the 40 Thieves** (in 1907 and at New Year 1910) and **Puss in Boots** (1909). The Méliès films were to become a tremendous liberating force and inspiration for other directors, including Paul, Hepworth and Haggar, who all made 'trick' shorts in cinema's first decade.

Early sound and other experiments

Another novelty – sound – had arrived earlier. An early sound-on-disc system, Edison's Kinetophone, was certainly seen by a small Cardiff audience in 1896 but more serious attempts were made five years later when Cardiff Empire advertised 'the most wonderful adaptation of the age' with celebrities 'not only seen but heard by means of the Phono Bio-Tableaux'.[61] And by 1901 Bromhead of Gaumont was talking of synchronizing pictures with sound.[62] In 1906, the year after Cardiff finally achieved city status, St Louis Animated Pictures announced 'talking pictures' at the Park Hall with the aid of the Gaumont Chronophone – 'Pictures That Sing: Pictures That Live! The Human Voice Reproduced as in Life!'[63] But these sound-on-disc systems were badly flawed and the process of switching to 'talkies' was too expensive. William Haggar sen. also used Gaumont Chronophone which roughly synchronized sound and image by electrical connections between motors, but film-goers were only able to hear in the first few rows.[64] At the Park Hall Cinema in 1907, Scots entertainer Harry Lauder could be heard and seen on the Chronomegaphone as film showman Ralph Pringle exploited a brief vogue for short 'singing and dancing' pictures. Other pieces shown starred George Robey and the British film and music-hall comedian Will Evans.[65]

The lust for new screen sensations left the *South Wales Daily Post* reporter cold. He claimed, slightly presumptuously, that the 'biograph . . . had exhausted its material in the world of fact' and had turned to mere illusions; he cited, disparagingly, a film with a man cracking an egg to find his decapitated head inside.[66] Others were more than prepared to experiment with the use of film outside the usual context. As early as 1899 animated photographs were shown during a stage melodrama at the Merthyr Theatre Royal and Opera House; and Alexandra, Howe & Cushing's, a menagerie and circus entertainment, provided films on the Cinématographe in south Wales with their eighty animals, curiosities and freaks as live entertainment. An exhibitor named Le Clair showed films at Pontypridd as a diversion to his act with a dog troupe – and in 1898 at Wrexham the cinematographe was shown in the pantomime *Aladdin*.[67]

It is small wonder that film struggled to retain its appeal in the face of rival attractions. There were visits to Cardiff from Beerbohm Tree and Sir Henry Irving and the stage melodramas which were soon to provide silent cinema with so much source material. In July 1908 alone, Harry Lauder, Harry Tate and the inimitable W. C. Fields – 'eccentric juggler' – all appeared in south Wales halls.[68] It was a vintage decade for other Cardiff visitors such as the Fred Karno troupe who developed the talents of Arthur Jefferson (Stan Laurel) and Charlie Chaplin; and Western showman Buffalo Bill with his Rough Riders paid the first of several visits to Wales in 1899 and was captured on film by the indefatigable north Wales businessman and entrepreneur Arthur Cheetham in 1903. For a few years cinema suffered in comparison with these live attractions, but Stoll retained faith and gave the medium impetus in 1906 when he embarked on a long-running series of shows relying mainly on film to attract an audience.[69] By then he had become the first in Wales to screen Edwin S. Porter's Western, **The Great Train Robbery** (1903), with its enterprising close-ups, and the prestige British film, **Rescued by Rover**. He was also to introduce Welsh audiences in 1909 to the first films of D. W. Griffith.

Grinding down the Mrs Grundys

As film gained popularity it inevitably suffered a backlash from Nonconformist clerics and puritans who had previously vented their spleen on the music-hall. South Wales showman Henry Studt, a member of a 'travelling cinema' (bioscope) family, had incurred clerical wrath earlier with his theatre activities, merely for taking workhouse inmates and pauper children to pantomimes. A Revd John Davies stormed out of a Swansea Board of Guardians meeting after a vote of thanks to the showmen, and claimed they were 'injuring the morality of children', and didn't support 'our churches and chapels'.

In August 1897, it was Oswald Stoll's turn to be upbraided, facing the brimstone of Alderman Rawlings in Swansea. Rawlings claimed modern entertainment 'stimulated evil passions', and he attacked the 'frivolity, unhealthy excitement and downright vulgarity' of the music-hall 'which made it impossible for anyone to frequent it in the spirit of Christ'.[70] Stoll pointed out that nearly a million people in Britain attended theatre and music-halls each night.[71] But whatever their public postures, the showmen were acutely sensitive to the press and public feelings – especially after an 1899 police crack-down on alleged *risqué* material in penny-in-the-slot machines, which were removed from Rhyl sands, a Swansea venue and a Merthyr shop. When Stoll re-opened the Swansea Empire after conversions in 1900, he appealed for support from those 'who do not believe that any amusement is wrong in principle', and a slogan at his halls claimed: 'To amuse and entertain is good, to do both and instruct is better.'[72] He made his bid for lasting respectability on Good Friday 1907, when the Pan-opticon staged **The Life and Passion of Christ**, 'a most significant coloured film of more than 40 scenes or views obtained at enormous cost'.[73] This was probably the celebrated but very static surviving film – effectively a series of tableaux – by the screen's first woman director, Alice Guy Blaché, made for Gaumont the previous year. The film was so that popular it was screened at least twice more by Stoll within twelve months.

The entrepreneur, who had been known to threaten his audience with a fire exting-uisher dousing, was something of a puritan himself. His attitude can be gleaned from the *Stoll Editorial News*, the house journal of his film company operating at Crickle-wood from around 1921. It described him as a pioneer of British films, 'who cleansed the music-hall stage', bringing to it 'great' – and by implication 'respectable' – players from the theatre such as Irving, Beerbohm Tree and Ellen Terry.[74] The quotes provide a fairly damning indication of the prevailing ethos of Stoll's film company and go some way to explain why its work seemed so lacking in vitality and reality.

As film's popularity grew, the showmen, scientists and exhibitors tried to stifle dis-senting voices by playing Sacred Concerts on Sunday and regular benefits for charity or disaster funds, while other film-makers followed the magic-lanternists in shooting heavily moralistic, pious works – notably about the evils of drink. Despite the critics' strictures, 'cinema' was gaining a measure of respectability in the years up to the

1914–18 war, with the French and Italian dramas gaining favour and American comedy shorts increasingly popular. It was rapidly leaving behind the originators.

End of the beginning

Paul was no longer making films by 1910 and the Lumière brothers had long vacated the field by then – their father Antoine's now infamous advice to Méliès lingered after them: 'The invention isn't for sale,' he advised. 'But if it were it would ruin you. It can be exploited for a while as a scientific curiosity – beyond that it has no commercial future.'

Acres continued making shorts until 1900, then returned to his laboratory and dark rooms. He resented that animated photography had been made the 'instrument of the showman', and was associated 'in its infancy so intimately with the music-hall'.[75] 'He dreaded his Kineopticon becoming accepted by the unappreciative public as a show instead of a really remarkable scientific spectacle,' wrote one trade journal.[76] It is significant that when the Kineopticon was advertised as the 'simplest, cheapest and best projection machine on the market', the wholesale agents for the apparatus were the British Toy and Novelty Company of Ludgate Hill, London.[77] It took the boom in permanent cinema buildings, a world war and the first flood of work from Hollywood, to lift film above the status of just another toy, ephemeral attraction or variety act.

Look out for the entertainments . . . at the Town Hall by A. Cheetham with local living pictures taken at Rhyl during this season and exhibited a few days afterwards. Also entertainments by the loudspeaking, talking machine, the gramophone . . . Pictures of the Rhyl May Day procession taken by himself and of the steam roller at work in Queen Street came in for a particularly warm expression of approval and much laughter was evoked by the procession being shown . . . moving backwards.

(*Rhyl Record and Advertiser*, 4 June 1898)

Within two years of the moving pictures' birth in Britain, two film-makers and showmen in Wales had embarked on careers bridging the gap between the first 'animated photograph' novelty shows in halls to the days of permanent cinemas. Both Arthur Cheetham, a sometime 'quack', incorrigible self-publicist and flamboyant entrepreneur in north and mid Wales, and William Haggar, a former itinerant theatre actor in south and west Wales, brought films to communities which would otherwise have been starved of the new invention. In the teeth of the Welsh Nonconformist revival, they screened their work in many areas under the thumb of chapel elders, where all forms of modern entertainment were anathema. A third Welsh-based pioneer, John Codman – operating in the same areas as Cheetham – experimented with his own fiction films (mainly comedies and dramas) in the cinema's first 10–15 years. Codman also took his camera around Wales to provide early travelogues and basic comedies and dramas, and if he remains a peripheral film figure, his family – sister Leah Marlborough and brother-in-law John M. East – were at the hub of British studio film-making in its first challenging period. If Acres and Paul saw film as an extension of their photographic or scientific experiments, the Welsh-based trio came from the other dominant strand of cinema trailblazers. They were neophytes with the nous to see the invention's obvious potential to woo crowds, complement their stage acts or change the direction of their careers.

Arthur Cheetham, at a family wedding, 1913.

Cheetham (1864–1936), burly and charismatic, staged concerts in Rhyl (his first Welsh base) plus song and dramatic recitals, often appearing in them himself; Codman ran minstrel shows in Llandudno; and Haggar led his travelling theatre troupe – mainly members of his large family – by traction engine and 'living wagon' (caravan) around Wales, before plunging into cinema, with his bioscope (travelling shows). Haggar, with his 30-odd films – distributed mainly by Gaumont and Charles Urban – embraced an impressive variety of genres (from chase films to melodramas, 'actuality' shorts to 'trick' films and iconoclastic comedies). His creative range and durability as a theatre showman, entrepreneur and cinema proprietor confirm his stature as the key creative figure within Wales in early cinema days. But Cheetham, for all his hyperbole and self-promotion, retains a secure place in any history – as the first film-maker within the country and the first to shoot events specifically to screen them in his own shows.

Exhumed: a pioneer's 'lost' films

Between 1972 and 1982, two separate collections of films in dusty cans – the long-forgotten remnants of a career – were discovered and 'exhumed'.[1] The works were on potentially explosive nitrate (non-safety) stock, but most proved not merely salvageable, but servicable and viewable. They provided remarkable confirmation of

CHAPTER 2

North and
Mid Wales:
Mountebanks,
Minstrels and
Welsh Picture
Showmen

TOWN HALL, RHYL,

Two Nights Only—
MONDAY and TUESDAY, July 31st & August 1st,
Grand Exhibition of Mr Cheetham's

SILVOGRAPH ANIMATED PICTURES.

Two Fine New Pictures :
" E. H. WILLIAMS' MERRIE MEN."
A DOUBLE DANCE by Jimmy Charters and Fred Egan.

And the Screaming Sketch, " THE SCHOOL,"
And a fine selection of other copyright Pictures, the sole property of Mr Cheetham.

Illustrated Songs by **Madame Rose Garton.**

Reserved Seats, numbered 2s. Reserved Seats, unnumbered 1s 6d. Front Seats, 1s. Back Seats (limited) 6d.
Plan may be seen, Reserved Seats Booked and Tickets obtained at Mr Cheetham's, 30 Queen Street.

A local newspaper advert for Arthur Cheetham's Silvograph show at Rhyl in 1899.

the early film days of Arthur Cheetham, who arrived in Rhyl in 1889.[2] Cheetham, born in Derby and later a printer's apprentice in Manchester, was obviously familiar by 1897 with early film – despite the paucity of north Wales screenings – and his first subjects, mail boat and train arrivals, simple records of stage acts, street scenes, soccer matches and processions, all reflect the influence of early film-makers such as the Lumières and Acres. He was not an innovator and rarely ventured outside these prescribed areas. Yet his films nestle comfortably in the mainstream of early British shorts, providing insights into the popular subject matter and technical shortcomings of the day. Cheetham also left behind literature of his first shows which reflects how film was perceived, showmen's relationship with audiences and his own defensive desire, amidst all the tub-thumping, to stress the respectable nature of his entertainment.

Cheetham made around thirty films between 1897 and 1903 and at least twelve of his documented works survive, providing an arresting record of early film practices, form and preoccupations in the days when the cinema still struggled for wide public acceptance. Cheetham remains in obscurity – his name is unknown even to most British film historians, but it is ironic, perhaps, that so much of his work is extant while only two of Haggar's documented films survive. There is no evidence that Cheetham made any more than simple actuality films, turning the camera on events before him (or restaging them), and most contain no more than two or three static camera set-ups. In his film of the Duke and Duchess of York's visit to Conwy (1899), for example – 'four times the length of ordinary pictures' – he shot the royal carriage from sideways on, then the front, then from the rear, or reverse angle.

From the outset, Cheetham adopted aggressive advertising campaigns and *outré* public postures which must have upset dog-in-the-manger local worthies. He soon attracted the suspicion of councillors who thought him something of a huckster after they were alerted to his displays of phrenology (character reading from forehead bumps) on Rhyl Sands near his Queen Street home, where by the late 1890s he was offering 'electric medical treatment' in his 'Electro-Curative Institute'.[3] As a phrenologist, he charged between 2s. 6d. and two guineas a time and prepared charts of his findings from his own dictation into the Edison–Bell Phonograph; by 1900 he was listed in a Rhyl guide merely as 'a character-reading specialist, medical electrician and hygienist'. Yet by January 1897 he had introduced animated photographs into his Town Hall entertainments and a year later shot his own films. He also introduced electricity into Rhyl at his printing works in Queen Street.[4]

Children Playing on Rhyl Sands – a Cheetham film of 1899.

Silver screen days

Moving pictures were first brought to Rhyl by Moore and Burgess, the London-based minstrels who appeared at the town's Winter Gardens in August 1896 showing a tooth-pulling scene in a dentist's operating room and footage 'from a Parisian Boulevard'.[5] Five months later – in January 1897 – the *Rhyl Journal* touted Mr A. Cheetham's 'New and marvellous entertainment of living pictures or animated photographs by the Cinematograph'. Pictures shown were **Bicycling in the Park**, **Stable on Fire** 'showing the rescue of horses', a garden scene and the perennially popular 'waves against a breakwater during a storm'.[6] All of these, of course, were works by other pioneers.

Cheetham, and his wife Rose, sang on stage during the traditional Easter Sunday sacred concerts and also to accompany images on screen. They also provided regular gramophone entertainment – no doubt to promote Cheetham's gramophone shop in Queen Street.[7] Extrovert exhibitors were often entertainers in their own right. William Coutts, for instance, the great west-Wales cinema proprietor, apparently recited Shakespeare on stage.[8] Leon Vint, later a film producer and owner of a cinema chain stretching beyond south Wales, was formerly a local ventriloquist and mesmerist whose act was a popular theatre attraction in the first year of cinema in Britain.[9]

With a predilection for fads and gadgets, Cheetham emphasized novelty elements at his early screenings, making great play of his 'silver' screen, 'which brings the pictures out almost as well as electric light', and he swiftly dubbed his screen the Silvograph.[10] He made his first short in January 1898, announcing to audiences that he had 'perfected his machine for taking animation photographs'. The *Rhyl Record and Advertiser* hailed his film of children playing on a beach as 'a good success' at the Town Hall that month and noted that the 'children were at once recognised by the audience'.[11] The director had caught the moving picture bug and in the next eighteen months – and particularly between January and March 1898 – moved through north and mid Wales shooting a bewildering variety of shorts. These included film of

CHAPTER 2

North and
Mid Wales:
Mountebanks,
Minstrels and
Welsh Picture
Showmen

The mailboat *Munster* at Holyhead – from Arthur Cheetham's film.

Wrexham High Street, a Rhyl May Day procession, slate being loaded onto waiting ships at Porthmadog, the mailboat *Munster* arriving at Holyhead from Dublin, a horse fair at Llangollen, ladies boating at Aberystwyth Bay, the Irish Mail 'flying' through Rhyl station, a rough sea in Rhyl from the west promenade, and shots of a steamroller in the town's Queen Street. The mailboat film is the lone survivor of this group.[12] Cheetham was also soon aping Trewey in pursuing cheap laughs by reversing film to show the Rhyl May procession moving backwards.[13]

In March 1898 and May 1899 the film-maker also screened his work at the Grand Pavilion, Rhyl – and the 1899 show included the arrival of a train at Llanrwst.[14] He was now well enough established in the community to enjoy a special 'benefit' performance and that year shot the surviving film of the royals' visit to Conwy – with the Duke and Duchess of York, the future King George V and Queen Mary, disembarking from a carriage and entering the castle. He was shrewd enough to include 'human interest' elements – a colourful flat-capped local and a dog, for example.[15] On 31 July and 1 August 1899, Cheetham advertised new films including shots of E. H. Williams and his popular local concert party of minstrels appearing on the beach at Rhyl. The act, 'the rage of the town', included a frenetic dance, 'vigorous fancy footwork' by Jimmy Charters and Fred Egan, accompanied by a double bass and harpist – and 'a screaming sketch, The School'. Cheetham also showed 'a fine selection of other copyright pictures'.[16] The E. H. Williams extant film – shot from in front of the stage – shows the leader introducing the performance. Lettering on the changing-room door at the rear of the stage announces the £120 rental for a pitch and that the Merrie Men and seventeen star artists will give Town Hall performances in wet weather. Boys in caps and boaters can be seen peeking disarmingly around the sides of the stage at the entertainment. In the school sketch, a headmaster gives a boy a hearty caning with a cricket bat.

Perhaps the most endearing, and interesting, surviving Rhyl film from that period – probably by Cheetham – shows scenes outside the Christchurch and Clwyd Street schools, Rhyl, with boys scurrying to and from the building, leapfrogging over each

Cheetham's *E. H. Williams and His Merrie Men* (1899).

other and palpably enjoying the camera's presence. These smack of carefully staged scenes, with horses passing within feet of the lens and a chimney sweep lounging, decoratively, centre-frame.[17] It is possible that these school scenes are actually separate films and certainly the total length of the scenes – 550 ft. (9 mins.) is greater than any of the film-maker's other shorts. There is no documentary proof that they were by the pioneer, though there is strong anecdotal evidence and they had been carefully stored with the other Cheetham work. If the Christchurch and Clwyd street scenes *are* his, they suggest that he composed carefully within the frame and concerned himself in the most basic way with *mise-en-scène.*

Cheetham continued to travel extensively to screen films. In one March week in 1900, his shows were at Llanidloes, Dolgellau and Bala and he regularly made more films to add to his repertoire.[18] In 1903, for example, he shot the Rhyl Gorsedd and a Rhyl cycling club outing. Buffalo Bill Cody's renowned Wild West show went bankrupt in the First World War but his Congress of Rough Riders paid several visits to Wales and in 1903 their procession of 800 with 500 horses travelled in 'four special trains'. Most fascinating of all Cheetham's Rhyl footage is the film of Cody taken in that year when the pulp dime magazine hero and rodeo showman was sworn into the town's Royal Antediluvian Order of Buffaloes. Cody can be seen moving through the crowd in a ten-gallon hat and being driven away later in a landau. The work was screened on 30 May with shots of the May Day procession and carnival queens and the local press praised its 'great animation and clearness'.[19]

There is no hard evidence that Cheetham ever ventured into fiction but one adventurous short followed a skirmish with the local council.[20] Entrenched attitudes to the new medium died hard and the film-maker's robust advertising methods led to rifts with the Rhyl local authorities. When council workmen arrived to remove a sign at the Central Hall for some alleged infringement, the unabashed showman turned the camera on them and showed the results to his patrons a few days later.[21] Those

Western showman Buffalo Bill (right) visits Rhyl in 1903 and is captured for posterity by the indefatigable Arthur Cheetham.

CHAPTER 2

North and
Mid Wales:
Mountebanks,
Minstrels and
Welsh Picture
Showmen

who hoped this huckster with his hard-sell methods would soon leave were disappointed. But by 1906 – when he accompanied some films with Dame Nellie Melba recordings – he faced competition from a travelling picture-showman Sydney Carter, who had shown films in Liverpool, Leeds and Birmingham and arrived at Rhyl's Victoria Hall in July with his New Century Pictures containing an 'irreducible minimum of flicker'. Another Rhyl venue, the Palace, also screened films that year – on Poole's Myriograph.[22]

On Whit Monday 1906, Cheetham opened probably the first permanent cinema in north Wales when he hired Rhyl's Central Hall 'all year round' stressing the auditorium had been 'redecorated and made into a perfect drawing room'.[23] The advert was another sop to that middle class which Cheetham, along with early pioneers, was so anxious to cultivate. He opened a short-lived cinema in Colwyn Bay, in 1908. Unfazed, he mounted screenings elsewhere in the town. An article in a souvenir brochure c. 1910–13 for his second Colwyn Bay cinema – a converted chapel in Conway Road – claimed he first exhibited in the town in 1897 – and assured any customers imputing base motives that he 'did not attach himself to the business because there was money in it'.[24] 'He is in truth one of the PIONEERS who had had to educate the people to the usefulness of the Cinematagraph [sic], both as an Educational factor and a sound, healthy recreative amusement,' the brochure asserted; ' . . . only the well-informed people could appreciate the marvellousness as well as the possibility of the new invention.' Flattery clearly had its uses. The old hygienist, doubtless with one eye on economy, reasserted himself: 'Carpets are entirely dispensed with,' he announced grandly. 'Thus one of the most potent causes of germ-spreading is entirely removed. For the same reason drapery on the walls is entirely avoided.' Special regard had been paid to hygiene – as 'Colwyn Bay is first and foremost a Health Resort.'

Cheetham's claims for the films he screened were typically grandiose: 'The steadiest pictures in the world – amusing, entertaining, educational and refined.' 'Refined' was the key word of the period among exhibitors in their untiring efforts to break down residual hostility. Objective aesthetic standards had yet to apply to films in those early days, so it is small wonder that when film operators advertised their wares they also relied on superlatives, or hailed their films as the longest or their screens as the biggest, or harped on some other extraordinary presentation feature. Cheetham, who had earlier hyped his silver screen, later miraculously found special virtues in shots of the production of Palethorpe's sausages at Dudley Port: 'This film is about half a mile long and the longest film ever made' – and he claimed his own 1898 Blackburn Rovers v. West Brom soccer short was, at 250ft., the longest of its type made at that time. It was certainly among the first football films ever shot and the magazine *Photography* claimed he achieved 'good sharpness and remarkable likenesses'. In late 1898 he was also making another camera capable of taking 'animated photographs of 1,000 feet at one time'.[25]

The Silvograph at Central
Hall, Market Street, Rhyl.

Pushing back the boundaries

The Rhyl jack-of-all-trades had also expanded into mid-Wales, opening the Electric
Picture Palace and Theatre, Aberystwyth, 'the first daily all year round entertainment
in the town', in the New Market Hall at Market Street. Films had been shown in
Aberystwyth as early as 1898 on the Velograph, 'the latest Photo-Electric Marvel', at
the Royal Pier Pavilion, and by Fred E. Young at the same venue in 1899. Young also
staged a show at the Pareezer Hall – later the Rink Picture Theatre – in 1899 on
'Edison's latest and most perfect machine, 30 magnificent pictures'.[26] Young, a
resourceful showman, was recreation and fêtes manager at Pwllheli by 1900, and the
next year showed movies as a diversion from the usual concert-party entertainment at
the Assembly Rooms, including **The Rivals**, **The Piccaninny's Bath**, and **Washing
Day**, plus footage of the local horse show, tennis and croquet. He also introduced
shorts at the Hall, Cricieth, in 1901. By 1910 he was forgotten, but Cheetham, who
opened a permanent cinema at Cheetham Hill, Manchester, was installed
permanently in the Palladium, Market Street, Aberystwyth, and ran year-round shows
there for some years.[27] His family later produced films in the town between 1923 and
1928, including surviving footage of the Town Schools gymnastics display – a subject
dear to his heart – offering, as an intertitle says: 'health and proportional
development of the growing child'. The Cheethams (probably his sons) also shot an
Aberystwyth Town Harriers five-mile run when large crowds lined the route.[28] When
Cheetham retired, sons Gus and Bernie helped run the Rhyl cinema ventures – later
taken over by the Shannon Brothers, who, around 1919/20, also made 'actuality'
shorts of local events, no doubt inspired by the flair and resource of a fiercely
independent director who had confounded his early detractors.[29]

CHAPTER 2

North and
Mid Wales:
Mountebanks,
Minstrels and
Welsh Picture
Showmen

TELEGRAMS: "J. CODMAN, LLANDUDNO."　　　　**NATIONAL TELEPHONE 42.**

J. CODMAN'S
ENTERPRISES
New Empire American
and ROYAL WELSH
Electric Animated Pictures
THE FINEST IN THE WORLD. AND　　　(REG.)
VARIETY AMUSEMENT AMALGAMATION.

SUPPORTED BY THE
New Empire Orchestra.
WITH FULL EFFECTS FOR PICTURES.

Letterhead from John
Codman's 'New Empire
American and Royal Welsh
Electric Animated
Pictures' enterprises – sent
from Aberystwyth in
1909.

John Codman's lost legacy

John Codman's New Empire and Animated Picture Company presents New
Pictures, brimful of humour and pathetic interest! Extraordinary dissolving and dio-
ramic effects! Full Orchestral Band! High Class Company of Eminent Artists!
Absolutely rock steady! Projected by the latest fire-proof machinery!

(Codman advertisement, c.1909–10, cited in John M. East, 'Neath the Mask, George
Allen and Unwin, 1967)

Son of the Llandudno Punch and Judy man, 'Professor' Richard Codman
(1831–1909), John Codman (1876–1935) made a significant contribution to early
film in north Wales. Codman had a 'living picture' machine by December 1900
(possibly a magic lantern showing slides), and screened films all through Wales in pre-
war days. At one stage, while based at the Pier Show, Llandudno, he reputedly
mounted shows at six different halls in a day.[30] He was an authentic travelling film
man, hauling his projector and screen equipment and a 600-seat caravan theatre with
a traction engine generating enough power to operate the projector. Codman and his
brother Herbert enticed audiences to shows by touring towns with megaphones,
shooting films through the day and offering locals 'immortality on film – a chance to
see themselves'. Often the camera was not even loaded after the first few minutes.[31]

A string of lost films made between 1905 and 1909 have been attributed to Codman,
notably a (probably re-staged) **Passion Play at Oberammergau**, a **Tour of North
Wales**, and four fictional shorts: **Mr Hughes and His Christmas Turkey**, **Luck of a
Diver**, **Mr Troublesome** and a Welsh drama, **The Miner's Daughter**. Codman's
claims as a film-maker now rest almost solely on the testimony of his relative, the
author John East, but his credentials as a showman are in no doubt.[32] At the peak of
his film activity he offered 'New Empire American and Royal Welsh Electric
Animated Pictures' (plus a variety show or 'amusement amalgamation'), supported by
the New Empire Orchestra with 'full effects for pictures'. He claimed to run nine
separate entertainment shows around Britain, and sent out 'experienced operators and
photographers only' with each show – 'local animated pictures taken in each town'.[33]

Codman certainly had the right family connections. His sister, Leah Marlborough
(1868–1953), a silent-film actress often billed merely as an 'exotic adventuress' in the
days before screen credits, appeared in early R. W. Paul shorts at his Muswell Hill
studios. She also featured in other British films by Cricks and Sharp at Mitcham,
Cricks and Martin at Croydon, London's Clarendon pictures (whose products
saturated Stoll's Cardiff cinema bills in the immediate pre-war years) and the noted
pioneer James Williamson at Hove.[34] The actress has recalled how she filmed

'reaction' close-ups with her head thrust through a flap in a stage flat. Her head would appear on screen (in the days of irising and heavy masking), followed by a cutaway to an incident. Like many stage actresses, she regarded film as a necessary evil and never acquired the enthusiasm for the screen shown by her husband, John M. East, a film producer and screen actor, primarily for Neptune films at Borehamwood.[35]

Whatever his creative credentials, Codman was a bustling, irrepressible early showman. Films were originally sold by the foot – never rented or hired – which accounts for exhibitors listing the film footage on posters and handbills. But by 1908, when rentals were finally introduced, the enterprising Codman was in the vanguard of these deals advertising his passion play for exchange.[36] In his prime, he leased halls in twelve towns in Wales and the borders, travelling as far south as Nantymoel and Ogmore Vale in Glamorgan.[37] In 1909 his New Empire Animated Pictures were at the Athenaeum Hall, Llanelli, and in 1910 when he took over the Victoria Hall, Newtown, he renamed the film entertainments Codman's Picturedrome and engaged his brother-in-law, John Miller, to provide harp accompaniment to his silent movies.[38] His halls all became known as Picturedromes and – to capitalize on the success of US films – he advertised shows under the 'New Empire American Animated Picture Co.' banner (with slight variations). But the increased costs of the film business and the arrival of more sophisticated purpose-built cinemas spelled the end of his screen career and drove him into bankruptcy by 1915.[39]

John Codman
(1876–1935).

The other leading entrepreneur in the area was J. R. Saronie (James Roberts) (1872–1967). He introduced films to Prestatyn, screened his 'world renowned Electric Pictures' weekly at the Town Hall from 1910, and also exhibited at Colwyn Bay in 1909. By 1920, he was operating films permanently at two or three venues, including the army camp at Kinmel Park, near Rhyl.[40] By 1910 cinema, thanks largely to Cheetham, Codman and Saronie, was firmly established as a spectacle in north Wales. West Wales, where many chapel-goers were cowed by the bloodcurdling anti-entertainment rhetoric of Revivalist preachers like Evan Roberts, was a little slower to embrace the movies.[41] Certainly Harry and Fred Poole with their Myriograph were at the Assembly Rooms, Carmarthen, in 1899, and Cecil Hepworth screened some of his own films in Cardigan in 1901, but films made only tentative inroads into the area, most notably among sideshow attractions in fairs such as Portfield (at Haverfordwest), Newcastle Emlyn and Pembroke, where the travelling bioscope families screened shorts.[42] At Llanelli, William Haggar set down cinema roots in 1910 at the former Royalty Theatre, creating a permanent cinema where the family's theatre act had first entertained crowds in 1892. By then, Haggar was at the apogee of his fortunes. He had shot all his films, built the foundations of a family cinema chain and done as much as anyone to ensure that cinema had a firm foothold in many rural towns and villages even before the genius of Chaplin, Sennett and Griffith changed the nature of the medium – and the public's perception of it – for good.

None of our competitors had such a wonderful organ, nor a better programme . . . We attracted the crowds because we had a change of programme every night, with films that father had taken himself. This was a big advantage over our rivals. All travelling cinemas [at least] had one centre entrance . . . the engine to generate electricity being at one end and an old-fashioned barrel organ the other. The new Marenghi organ front [meant] we had two entrances, which was a big advantage on a busy day when we would be open at 10.30 a.m. and keep going until 11 p.m.'

(Lillian Haggar, unpublished manuscript, 1969)

In a remarkable moment in an early British film, a killer and adulterer disguised as a clergyman fills the screen and thumbs his nose at police pursuers who have been lulled into accepting his false identity. His action and wall-to-wall grin invite the audience's complicity even though the screen character was based on a murderer executed just twenty-six years previously. The audacity, assurance – and iconoclasm – of this scene from **The Life of Charles Peace** (1905)[1] tell us much about both the relationship Wales-based director William Haggar assumed with his audience and his knowledge of popular working-class taste. No other images in cinema before the First World War sum up more eloquently the division between the cinema's scientific pioneers who saw the film as an 'invention' and a medium for technical experiments, and directors who sought to appeal to unsophisticated audiences weaned on music-hall acts, penny-dreadful crime novels, comics, or the touring stage melodramas of the day.

Arthur William Haggar (1851–1925) made thirty-four documented films –

William Haggar sen. and his wife Sarah.

around sixty in all, according to his family – and his stock was remarkably high with Gaumont, who distributed most of his work in Britain and principally in mainland Europe. One 1905 film, **The Salmon Poachers** (or **A Midnight Mêlée**), sold 480 copies – more than any other British film, including Hepworth's still-celebrated **Rescued by Rover** (1905).[2] Haggar's status was remarkable for a man who travelled outside Wales infrequently – and whose films were rarely seen in city-centre cinemas, even in the principality. The director, a cheerful, bluff man, was the first in Wales to employ the close-up for impact (in the Peace film) and to develop relatively elaborate scenarios on film and, though he usually shot with a static camera, he used the screen frame with perception and was clearly versed in the conventions of early British cinema. He also varied angles intelligently to create a sense of immediacy and bustle as characters exited in chase scenes as close as possible to the camera to both right and left.[3] They might then re-enter, in the foreground, in a reverse angle. This was a standard device of leading British film-makers of the period.

More importantly, Haggar also operated with his own stock company (mainly his family, who had wide experience in his stage melodramas), well before the idea had been developed by D. W. Griffith at Biograph or Mack Sennett at Keystone.[4] Haggar's films embraced some of the subjects and themes shot by his only significant British rivals outside London and Sussex – Yorkshire's Bamforth and Mottershaw – but Haggar was the only pioneer of his time *as close* to rural working-class film- and theatre-goers. Mottershaw, in Sheffield, with his regular film shows at the city's

Cutlers Hall, and Bamforth in Leeds were also closer to provincial working-class audiences than their southern counterparts and tended to be preoccupied with the themes of working-class crime, comic melodrama and domestic peccadilloes that preoccupied Haggar. But the Welsh-based showman was the only film-maker, of any standing, weaned in the hurly-burly of the fairground or the theatre, where he performed his stage potboilers before introducing his early films to audiences. Many fairgoers had never seen moving pictures before they attended shows by Haggar and other travelling cinema pioneers in Wales. It is important also to recognize that Haggar films embraced most genres – it would be possible by studying the catalogue entries for his 'lost' work to reconstruct, or extrapolate, a history of British cinema of the period.

No study of the film-maker can be attempted unless we understand his roots. By 1901, Haggar, born in Dedham, Essex, had been a showman for thirty years – first with a small band, then as a puppeteer – before setting up his own drama company, the Castle Theatre, which functioned from the 1880s in Wales.[5] Haggar was a travelling showman who hauled his fit-up theatre and props originally by horseback, then by traction engine, and later opened bioscope shows, often screening the family's own films. In the showgrounds he competed with other film pioneers who also made their own shorts to increase the choice available to customers. All were battling for the same proletarian audience. In 1891, with the birth of a daughter, Lillian (Lily May), the Haggars had eight surviving children who were to form the regular casts of the films, and give William an advantage over other Wales bioscope owners whose forays into film-making were limited to 'topicals'.

Haggar obtained a projector from the London opticians, J. Wrench and Son, and his first film show – according to Lillian – was at Aberavon in 1898 when he screened **Turn Out of the London Fire Brigade** (almost certainly the Lumière 1897 film), and a **Train Emerging from a Tunnel** – probably Acres's **Highgate Tunnel** (1896) or **Phantom Train Ride through Chislehurst Tunnel**, made by the London-based Chard and Co. in 1897. Later he regularly presented 16–20 shows of shorts each day, but his own fortunes fluctuated with the troughs and peaks of the south Wales coal industry.[6] The family motto became 'follow the coal' after his bioscope activities were almost wiped out in the great six-month stoppage of 1898 as pitmen tightened their belts.[7] For nearly twenty years before 'cinema' was a glint in Edison's eye, Haggar's nomadic company were dab hands at Grand Guignol and the lustier melodramas – travelling from mid and west Wales to the south Wales valleys, regularly wintering in Aberdare and constantly renewing their repertoire of material, from the classics to burlesque. In the hustle and scurry of the fairground he often acted as barker enticing customers personally into his shows. As an actor regularly staging potboiler dramas and farces he had a greater appreciation of the taste of ordinary men and the wish of that 'great unwashed commonality' to see films which occasionally discomforted or derided the authority figures of their day. These spectators might, if not at a fairground, be watching a vigorous illegal prizefight. Haggar certainly was not the only director pre-1910 confident enough to create screen characters who upset law and order before (generally) succumbing to the prevailing morality and inevitable come-uppance at the film's finale. But it is significant that much of his output reveals an irreverence for convention. More than a decade before Chaplin's tramp antics and violent reprisals against Eric Campbell's bullying cop in **Easy Street** (1917), for example, Haggar was presenting underdogs up-ending normal values and, in the case of the Peace film, placing them in a more radical context than Chaplin (at least before

A business card/letterhead for W. Haggar and Son's Royal Electric Bioscope – one of the family's travelling picture shows.

The Immigrant (1917). Apart from the Peace film – described by one writer as the birth of 're-creative reportage' in Britain – Haggar created on screen a comedy series with the character Mirthful Mary, a corpulent, toping slattern much given to tangling with 'beaks' and 'bluebottles'.[8] And in at least four of his other films, police are the butt of humour. In **The Meddling Policeman** (1904), an officer is 'strung with sausages and pelted with eggs'. In **Bathing Not Allowed** (1905), a 'bobby' and a farmer are dipped into the briny by mischievous boys. In **The Rival Painters** (1905), a PC is demeaned as he rages impotently, unable to stop a paint-slapping battle between two artists, and in **The Salmon Poachers** (same year), miscreants dump two pursuing officers into the river before escaping with their catch. They are later arrested and placed in a boat to be taken to the lock-up but escape again and once more pitch their captors into the water, beating them off with their oars.[9] These comedies indulged the lowbrow tastes of audiences who enjoyed seeing the authorities lampooned – and they undoubtedly provided vicarious relief to many who had spent the week cowed in harsh working conditions. Many of Haggar's 'heroes' were reprobates and soaks who kicked over the traces, notably the drunk Irishman in the 1904 **Flynn's Birthday Celebrations**, who throws his wife through the window.[10]

This was bellicose slapstick with the kind of vitality which Britain's film industry leaders, such as Oswald Stoll, sapped when they sought to woo wider audiences in the early 1920s with a diet of stiff drawing-room dramas and humour and classbound exotic romances.

The surviving films

It is a chastening thought that Haggar's reputation rests heavily on testament from former Gaumont-British chief executive Col. A. C. Bromhead – and the survival of the film-maker's own potted, picaresque **Life of Charles Peace**.[11] Only one other Haggar film, the 220ft. **A Desperate Poaching Affray** (1903), is viewable in its entirety, and its true importance, as we shall see, has only been acknowledged following recent US academic research.

The Peace film was shot in Pembroke with Haggar's son Walter in heavy stage make-up as the whey-faced killer, presented here as the type of pocket villain around whom legends cluster. The screen killer is unprepossessing, diminutive and frail-looking.

Walter Haggar in the con-
troversial hanging scene
from *The Life of Charles
Peace* (1905).

Walter, wearing outsize clothes, cuts an almost pathetic figure in a calculated bid to arouse the sympathies of an audience who would be familiar with the violin-playing Peace's deeds and the stories of his execution at Armley Jail, near Leeds, in 1879. Haggar's version, twenty-six scenes with eleven titles, was released just before a rival production from Frank Mottershaw's Sheffield Photo company but still seems concise and clear compared with Mottershaw's laboured and convoluted scenario which survives catalogued in twelve scenes.[12] The film opens with Peace's attempts to woo Mrs Dyson, a friend's neighbour, and moves swiftly through the villain's slaying of her cuckold husband to his discovery by the law hiding under bedclothes with a family posse (including William Haggar's first wife Sarah) in attendance. Peace's rooftop escape – on a blatant stage set – is choreographed by Haggar with humour and brio as the criminal leaves police in his wake. Tension is dissipated neatly in the ensuing scene when stop-motion photography allows Peace to don his cleric's garb before sanctimoniously handing out leaflets to the cops who scatter them as they continue the chase. Then, in the most daring moment of this 13-minute film, Peace moves centre-screen foreground for the one authentic close-up, tweaks his nose joyously into camera at receding police, before fastfooting it in the opposite direction. The scene seems even more courageous weighed against the earlier shot of Peace preening himself after shooting Dyson. The criminal's capture by PC Robinson after a fist fight is a splendidly rumbustuous affair and the train journey – third class – in which Peace dives out of a carriage to elude police taking him for trial is amusing and effective, despite the crude props. It is a fine example of the film-maker's ability to wed the techniques of his actuality films – including his early 'phantom rides' (with a travelling camera aboard the vehicles) – to his fictional melodramatic material. The patent use of a dummy only slightly mutes the impact of the villain's ingenuity in leaving one officer clutching an empty boot as Peace escapes through a carriage window and hobbles along the track (towards the camera) – adding a little elementary suspense before he is overhauled by police. The sequence provides excellent examples of Haggar's cutting *within* the scene. The audience is shaken up once more as the anti-hero attacks Mrs Dyson when she picks him out at an identity parade. The noose is soon fastened around Peace, the hood clamped on his head, last rites are

49

spoken, then the trap door springs and the rope swings as the criminal disappears from the bottom of the screen. Even Haggar balked at showing his protagonist dangling. The scene may still have been strong meat for an audience used to relatively staid and anodyne screen fare (outside the trick films of Méliès, Hepworth or G. A. Smith). At Swansea Quarter Sessions in 1908, penny 'orribles and bioscope pictures were said to have influenced two youths to embark on a life of crime; their favourite reading was **The Life of Charles Peace**. They stole a revolver and a dagger to arm themselves 'like the hero of the pictures' – (according to the cinema trade magazine *Bioscope*). But incidents much more frightening had no doubt garnished the melodramas provided by Haggar and his company and their stage contemporaries on journeys through Wales.

Haggar knocked Frank Mottershaw's nose out of joint by rushing his Peace film out before the Sheffield company released its version – and Mottershaw made great play of *his* supposed superior taste when he excised the execution scene from his own film 'as we believe it is too ghastly and repulsive'. Mottershaw's catalogue entry also stresses that shots of Peace's Banner Cross murder and the sensational leap from the train were taken on the actual spot and even that the engine driver he used was 'the very same man who escorted Peace on his journey'.[13] The Mottershaw film also featured blue-tinted night scenes, and there are significant variations in the films. It is Mrs Dyson in the Sheffield version who throws a note into Peace's garden forbidding his unwelcome intrusion into the family. In Haggar's drama Peace places a note for Mrs Dyson on a bush and steps out from cover as she reads it. Mottershaw also shows Peace captured following a safe-break and a struggle after hiding the spoils in a field. Haggar's version begins differently with a break-in (featuring his daughter Lillian as Walter's supposedly male accomplice).[14] The Sheffield version's scenario contains an abrupt cut from Peace's capture after a burglary in the Manchester area in scene five to the moments when he approaches a house at night carrying a violin case in which he usually totes a rope ladder for scaling the wall. This is the scene which opens Haggar's version.[15]

Mottershaw's film no longer exists but on the evidence of the catalogue synopsis it lacks the simple narrative development of Haggar's version. The Haggar film also has a pleasing gusto; in the pursuit of Peace and the chases along the railway line and over waste ground full of building rubble Haggar achieves pace and fluidity – by using the frame so intelligently. Interiors are admittedly risible with crude drawings of inset windows, hastily scratched out on stage flats, a recalcitrant door which makes a chimney shake and a literal paper moon. But the film's vitality and Haggar's use of cinematic elements in **A Desperate Poaching Affray** (US title, **The Poachers**) (1903), give the lie to comments by former National Film Archive head Ernest Lindgren that Haggar was merely a primitive, still bound to theatrical tradition and the idea that characters must move from side to side against a stage backdrop. The legacy of Haggar's background is obvious but his use of depth and foreground action in the Peace finale is a saving grace and effectively complements the clumsier proscenium-arch scenes. And in **Desperate Poaching Affray**, he threw off the stage mantle completely, essaying his first panning shot. In this work, featuring son William jun. as the chief villain, the poachers fire on their police pursuers two or three times, are chased down an incline and over a gate, and then cut off – after lively river skirmishes – by police and helpers who outflank them. The extant National Film Archive print is in fine condition, enabling us to admire how Haggar uses natural lighting contrasts to good effect on outdoor shots – but it is his use of the frame which impresses most.

Frame enlargement from Haggar's *A Desperate Poaching Affray* (1903), with William Haggar jun., at right.

The pursuers are nowhere to be seen, then burst onto the screen from the front. William leads the way as the villains dash out of shot to the left, then emerge, after a cut, in the foreground of the screen, left, in a shot which suggests that the chase has continued longer than actual 'film time'. Haggar continues to employ different angles in demonstrating more than a rudimentary command of early film grammar and conventions. In the final shot, the dishevelled criminals are grabbed and marched off, again in the foreground. Apart from William jun.'s slightly overgenerous gestures when he floors an adversary with a haymaking right hand, there is not the slightest hint of theatricality and staging.

A Desperate Poaching Affray (The Poachers) was screened *c.*1903 in the United States by travelling cinema pioneer Lyman H. Howe from Pennsylvania who, in his early days, generally presented respectable movies for Methodist groups. The Haggar film was 'filled with sensationalistic violence completely uncharacteristic of Howe's usual bill of fare', wrote his biographer, the US historian Charles Musser. 'Perhaps because it was one of the cinema's first chase films it proved an irresistible choice.'[16] More significantly, Musser has elsewhere cited American catalogues and trade journals, from the nickelodeon era, as evidence that Haggar's film and Mottershaw's British short **A Daring Daylight Burglary** initiated the entire US 'film chase craze' which began in 1903. It may well be, from this evidence, that Haggar influenced other film-makers – on both sides of the Atlantic – almost as much as he was inspired by other directors of his day. Musser underlines his claims by stressing that Walter (*sic*) Haggar's **Desperate Poaching Affray** was one of at least three UK films copied and sold by Edison, Biograph and Sigmund Lubin's company between June and October 1903.

Unfortunately, only one other William Haggar film survives even in an incomplete form – a mere 37ft. fragment of the 420ft. **Message from the Sea**. This was a fairly elaborate shipwreck drama but won praise as a 'splendid idea capitally worked and notable for genuine pathos'.[17] The existing footage merely shows a sailor, Harry Mainstay (played by William Haggar jun.) taking leave of his family. The film was tinted in blue, according to Gaumont catalogues.

Many Haggar movies, from contemporary accounts, were considerable achievements given their production conditions. He never had a studio and many shorts were shot by the river – film after film involves a dunking – and shooting was sometimes wrapped up in an hour and a half. Small wonder that some of his lost films are scarcely distinguishable from each other in bare plot synopsis. In **Wanted – a Wife**, the 'sets' were all on the back of a flatbed lorry.[18] There is no doubt that Haggar was held in great esteem by Gaumont, who even presented him, gratis, with a film camera and mechanical tripod with a revolving head, released his films in most of Britain and Europe and supplied him with film stock. Haggar naïvely handed over the negatives in return for retaining the rights in south Wales – and must have lost heavily when **Salmon Poachers** sold those 480 prints at £6. 17*s*. apiece for Gaumont. The company praised the 274ft. film's 'magnificent quality throughout' and touted it as 'the most realistic moonlight effect picture we have ever issued', and thirty years later Gaumont chief A. C. Bromhead spoke in glowing terms of the film.[19]

Yet despite his pre-eminence in Wales before 1914, Haggar has, until relatively recently, occupied a tenuous place in official British film histories. If his Peace film had not survived it is doubtful whether any serious critic would have valued his contribution to the cinema in the days when R. W. Paul, Cecil Hepworth and Brighton pioneers James Williamson and G. A. (George Albert) Smith were building the industry. For forty years – and as recently as 1990 – film historians have persisted in laying false trails by claiming that Walter, not William, made the films even though Walter, for all his creative talents, was not a director.[20] Until the late 1940s it was commonly believed that Frank Mottershaw made the surviving version of Charles Peace. It was not until Haggar's daughter Lillian recognized the work at a screening that it was properly identified – even though Mottershaw's film (the longest in Britain at that time) contained 100 ft. more and it seems difficult to confuse them from respective catalogue entries.[21] Railway and screen historian John Huntley has also pointed out that the handles of the railway carriages in the Haggar film betray their GWR origin.

The vanished works

Haggar's contribution to film essentially began when he changed his early Wrench machine for a projector from Maguire and Baucus and became a friend of that firm's London manager Charles Urban, whose own Kinemacolor productions later introduced the revolutionary two-colour process to cinema in Wales.[22] Haggar, who had dabbled in still photography for years, was finally spurred to make his own films when Harry Scard, senior manager of Wadbrook's travelling show, had the Wales–England 1901 soccer match filmed and screened exclusively in his show.[23] Not to be outdone, Haggar acquired his own portable generating machine (costing around £600), to replace limelight power.[24] Haggar was never slow to adopt new practices. He experimented with primitive 'talkies' – the Cinephone (sound on disc) – and even attempted a colour film of 'a lady disrobing', with red used for one petticoat, blue for the next, but the attempt was abandoned because the dyes were of varying density and created a laughable effect.

William Haggar jun., right foreground, in the opening, surviving moments of *A Message from the Sea*. A frame enlargement from the 37 ft. extant fragment of this 'lost' movie.

Lillian and Walter Haggar suggest (in unpublished documents) that their father's first film was of a train arriving at Burry Port station in 1902, but certain evidence suggests the distinct possibility of an earlier film.[25] The *Showman* reported on 9 August 1901 that Haggar at Swansea Fête and Gala had proved 'another big draw with views taken from his bioscope'. These could conceivably, of course, have been lantern slides but **The Dumb Man of Manchester** – in Haggar's shows at the Villiers Ground, Briton Ferry, and at Blaina in 1901 – could also have been an earlier Haggar screen version of his melodrama of the stage title listed in the 1908 Gaumont catalogue.[26]

No one could reasonably have expected the Wales-based showman to be innovative at the outset, and he aped the films of others. He plumped early on for train or tram films which allowed movement and presented attractive Welsh locations – his early **Phantom Ride Through Swansea** (*c.*1902) – shot from the front of a tram – would have been of this familiar type. When Haggar had the temerity to present pseudo-documentary war footage he may have picked up a wrinkle or two from the many shameless Boer War reconstructions purporting to be genuine 'topicals' containing actual footage of combat, or from Urban who in 1902 screened supposed bona fide footage of Edward VII's coronation and interior shots purporting to be of the Westminster Abbey ceremony. These shots were culled from a filmed reconstruction of the event by Georges Méliès.[27] Haggar landed up with egg on his face when he shot, in south Wales, supposedly genuine battle scenes in the snow featuring heavily made-up actors and the ruse was discovered. He also recreated Boer War material, more legitimately dramatized the invasion of the French at Fishguard in 1797 and also reputedly made a film at Mumbles Head where his daughters had 'to pull red petticoats over their heads to appear like soldiers because people wanted action by this time, not just rough seas'.[28]

The film-maker, according to his family, also shot a mass funeral at Mumbles for six men drowned on the breakwater at Aberavon docks and gave copies to Moss Empires and Harry Scard.[29] Haggar also shot processions through Aberdare – as eyewitnesses have testified – and a Welsh National Pageant (*c*.1909) in Cardiff; but it was the documented fictional films which place him in the forefront of the pioneers.[30]

One trick short, **D.T.'s – the Effects of Drink** (1905), obviously owed a debt to Méliès's sleight of hand and possibly an 1899 film, of the same title, now credited to Philipp Wolff.[31] In Haggar's a man returns from his club, sees visions and reforms. When he throws off his coat in the bedroom it assumes a dog's form and walks off. Vases metamorphose into owls, a bed is transformed into a monster taking him around the room on its back and finally vanishes in a cloud of steam which spouts him into the air. It seems obvious that this genuflection to the pious conventions of the day was much more intent on providing screen humour.

More typical of the film-maker's broader outlook and eye for audience approval was his Mirthful Mary series of very short squibs: **A Case for the Black List**, **Mirthful Mary in the Dock** and **Mary is Dry**, all distributed by Gaumont between 1903 and 1905.[32] In the **Black List** film Mary, the bane of barmen's lives, is already the worse for liquor when refused entry to a country inn. A policeman is called in and strikes her with a truncheon. Mary grabs the stick – and 'repays the blow with interest', according to a title.[33] It takes three policemen to subdue her. Finally a handcart is produced; she is placed on it, struggling, and wheeled off out of frame. 'This is a really A1 comic,' said Gaumont, who regularly singled out Haggar films for superlatives. **Mirthful Mary in the Dock** was distributed in the US (as **Mary in the Dock**) by Biograph acting as agents for Gaumont.

Characters' foreground entrances and exits from the frame were characteristic of Haggar – and perhaps understandable given the reaction of audiences to Lumière material with trains rushing towards the front stalls. This elementary choreography could look hopelessly stage-managed (a terrified policeman's flight with his hands held up in horror during the Charles Peace film is an example) but employing cinema depth gave the film great verve and worked successfully in lieu of the close-ups which some early film-makers favoured more regularly. **A Case for the Black List** proved popular, allowing Gaumont – in their catalogue preamble to **Mirthful Mary in the Dock** – to claim that 'hundreds of thousands have watched this case from the commencement.' This second film (a 'roof raiser') involved more obvious nose-thumbing, with hints of police brutality. Mary in court bears 'visible traces of her recent arrest', says the catalogue, and 'the courthouse has been cleared of the public.' Mary refuses to be sworn in and castigates the magistrate as 'an ould thief'. A PC catches the full force of an elbow from the Amazon and 'is left mourning a mouthful of loose teeth'. The clerk of the court, seeking order, is then seized by Mary and a 'whirlwind of disorder' sweeps through the building. 'Coppers fall like skittles, books and papers fly in all directions.' Then Mary hurls everything at the magistrate who is struck in the eye with an inkpot before the harridan is hustled to the cells. This is material which might have come from the comic pages of Ally Sloper, and Haggar was clearly more interested in raising guffaws than in portentous moralizing and knew his audiences loved to see authority take a pratfall. In **Mary is Dry**, the 'mirthful one' – always played by one of Haggar's discoveries, a fat lady known only as Mog – enters a pub, and gulps down a customer's beer. When the barflies protest, she drenches them with a soda syphon, smashes glasses, jumps on the counter and wrecks the place. There is, significantly, no mention in the potted plot of a come-uppance.[34]

Haggar also produced irreverent tramp films, notably **Weary Willie and Tired Tim Turn Barbers** (1903), one of several – by different directors – featuring the slothful comic-strip heroes.[35] But the richest sources for Haggar's film-making were his own popular stage entertainments. At the zenith of his theatre company's fortunes a fresh play was performed almost every night for three- or four-month stretches – so there was no shortage of possible screen material. Regular items in his stage repertoire down the years included *East Lynne*, *Maria Marten* (or *The Red Barn Mystery*), *The Maid of Cefn Ydfa* (all filmed by the showman), *Sweeney Todd*, plus the gamut of Shakespeare – and the company had a cavalier attitude to copyright, merely changing titles of popular plays in performance. That old warhorse *The Sign of the Cross* became *The Shadow of the Cross*, for example, in Haggar theatre shows.[36] The film-maker's son Will jun. and his wife Jenny Linden performed similar stage material, with their company based in Pontardulais, after William sen. decided to concentrate on his film-making.[37] They took their familiar stage roles in William sen.'s 1908 **Dumb Man of Manchester** in which a lawyer loses a locket and a witness is needed to save a deaf mute from the gallows. Haggar sen.'s daughter Violet played the lead in **The Red Barn Mystery** (1908), one of the director's longest works at 685ft. Only two are longer, **Sign of the Cross** (1904) at 700ft., starring Will jun. and Jenny Linden, and the Charles Peace film, 770ft.

'The Maid'

Perhaps the Haggars' favourite subject was **The Maid of Cefn Ydfa**, the Welsh tragedy based on a legendary romance between a thatcher and musician, Wil Hopcyn and heiress Ann Thomas, first performed on stage around 1870.[38] At least two or three screen versions were made by the family. William sen. shot the drama in 1908 and the sole surviving film – by Will jun. and his Pontardulais-based stage company – appeared in 1913–14. This last work features, in the comic relief role of Lewis Bach (dubbed Dai Lossin in the film), Will Fyffe of 'I belong to Glasga' fame, a member of the Haggar company and odd-job man before branching out on his own. Twenty years later he became a star of the British cinema.[39]

The Maid film was rediscovered in 1984 by a member of the Haggar family who found it in a stairwell of a house near Swansea and offered the nitrate copy in three cans (and rapidly disintegrating) to the British Film Institute whose restored copy ran twenty-six minutes and bears the subtitle **The Love Story of Ann Thomas**.[40]

Will Haggar jun. (b. *c*.1871, d. 1935) and Jenny (d. 1954) feature as the starcrossed lovers, and Will's breastbeating and elaborate blown kisses seem crass on screen now. The film, one of the longest British features of its day, at around 3,000ft., has little considered use of camera angles and does not appear to bear Haggar sen.'s signature. The frequent static long and medium shots seem unnecessarily stilted and the work has little animation.[41] Will's declamatory style owes more to the stage company's traditional mummery than the screen. Jenny's performance as the mettlesome Ann, rejecting a forced marriage, is adequate if a little stiff. But the sets contain elaborate artwork to suggest stained-glass windows and inlaid designs on walls and there is some ingenuity in re-working the legend. The traditional version is faithfully followed in early scenes of burgeoning romance after Ann, a 'charity worker' (according to the film's titles), encounters Wil thatching a cottage. But when Ann rejects the suit of Anthony Maddocks, son of landed gentry, Haggar takes liberties with the legend in which Wil disappears on hearing that Ann has finally succumbed to pressure from the

Maddockses and her mercenary mother and has married. In the film, two thieves are first paid to drown Wil after the thatcher has struck Maddocks for insulting Ann during an outing to Bridgend fair. The scheme goes awry – Morgan (a seer) rescues Wil, who has been pushed into water (which scarcely seems knee-high!). The loving pair are re-united but a clever scripting device ensures that Ann assumes wrongly that Wil has accepted a bribe and deserted her and Wil, equally deceived, is persuaded to travel abroad believing he can win her hand by proving himself. In a close-up which would obviously have appealed to audiences bred on melodrama, Ann, reduced to a prisoner in her own house, uses a hairpin to scratch on a leaf in her own blood a plea to Wil to save her. Hopcyn arrives too late – cue for much ineffectual flamboyant agonizing at the church door – and the film's restored version ends abruptly with Ann sliding into madness, shackled to a perpetually drunken husband, and grieving at the graveside for the loss of her dead child. She replaces her wedding ring with Wil's in a gesture of defiance. In the legend, Ann Maddocks of Llangynwyd, Glamorgan, died of a broken heart soon after her marriage to Maddocks, a lawyer. A sub-plot involving Ann's father's will is left unresolved and it is a pity no record of any other screen version of **The Maid** or a script of the family stage-play exists.

Fyffe enjoys two setpieces – when he makes off with a rival's lady friend after escaping a beating early on and in a crude scene when he is wheeled home in a barrow by Gwennie (Kate Haggar), tied up with ribbons and pledges never to be drunk again.

William Haggar jun. and his wife Jenny, in *The Maid of Cefn Ydfa* (1914).

Exhibition and distribution

Discussion of Haggar's films should not be divorced from the world in which he
operated. The years 1903 to 1908 marked the apex of Haggar's creative career, but his
impact on cinema goes much beyond that – as an influential bioscope entrepreneur
and later cinema owner. His creative peak coincided with his most hectic years
running a travelling cinema, when Wales was in the vanguard of fairground film
entertainment with a clutch of families making and/or showing their own works.

The Haggar family often set up their bioscope (travelling cinema) with 'living
wagons' – caravans – (and later organs) providing the stage frontage, where
entertainers known as 'paraders' lured the crowds into the film shows. The Haggars
took space from families like the Studts and Danters who owned roundabouts and
rented the ground for seasonal shows. But they also sometimes ran their own show in
a field, a practice known as 'private business'. The blackest days for the Haggars came
early with the south Wales coalfield at a standstill during 1898, when the family had
to sell off two living wagons. The showman reverted to stage pantomime, staking cash
on an ambitious *Cinderella* which saved the family from destitution.[42] Sunday Sacred
Concerts also helped pay the rents and Haggar, even with his enthusiasm for making
pictures, was never blind to expediency. In 1899 he laid up his bioscope for the
winter months, returning to the stage in partnership with son James as W. and J.
Haggar's Dramatic Company.

Haggar's 'Royal Bioscope' was at Neath Fair with an 89-key Gavioli organ in 1898
alongside other film shows. By 1907 as many as six shows fought for business there
and it was small wonder that competitive instincts were finely honed in those days
when Haggar brought his shows from west Wales to the heart of the south Wales
valleys.[43] By 1908 he was established at Aberdare where, at Christmas, he confounded
sceptics by filling the Market Hall with a 'gigantic' variety company, and the
adjoining yard with his bioscope show.[44] The original Haggar show frontages, with
the living wagons, were plain enough and a Savage light engine provided power. But

Haggar's Kosy Cinema,
Aberdare, *c.* 1915.

William sen. was probably the first in Wales to gamble on using an organ to front his stage when he bought a 44ft. Marenghi with a repertoire of Harry Lauder songs, Sousa marches and operatic selections. In May 1905, he startled and delighted audiences by introducing at Llanelli his 'electric bioscope' – dubbed in deference to the thunderous Marenghi organ. Around 1907 he introduced a more sophisticated Coliseum Bioscope show with a frontage of gold work, an ornate stage roofing design and a 110-key Gavioli.[45] It is barely possible now to imagine the impact these travelling shows, with their gaudy colours, flashing lights and shimmering edifices, must have made when showmen arrived in towns and villages with their traction engines on wet and mournful midweek days. The entertainment must have seemed awesome to remote west Wales outposts often bereft of any other comparable form of entertainment for months on end. The annual or seasonal fairs were rallying points for the travelling 'cinemas' or 'bioscopes' whose status was often marked by the elaborate fairground music and frontage, and quality of their 'paraders', ranging from acrobats and dancers to clowns and 'midgets'.

Contemporary accounts make clear that Haggar's bioscope show frontage was perhaps the most photogenic and impressive in Wales until Sidney White, the Cardiff and west Wales showman, 'amusement caterer', and later cinema entrepreneur, took delivery in 1909 of a 112-key Gavioli Orchestraphone – 'the largest and grandest organ ever produced in Europe and a ton heavier than any other organ'.[46] The merits of film programmes seem often to have been of secondary concern to audiences but evidence abounds of the showground appeal of Haggar's entertainments throughout the century's first decade. It seems, superficially, strange that little record exists of Haggar's films playing in the city and major town music-halls. **Desperate Poaching Affray** was screened at the Cardiff and Newport Empires in 1903.[47] In the *same week* of September 1906, Stoll's Panopticon showed **A Message from the Sea** and **The Maid of Cefn Ydfa** (possibly the first *c.*1902/3 screen version of the legend – attributed to Will Haggar jun.'s company by Walter), and in 1907 the same venue screened **The Salmon Poachers** (or **Midnight Mêlée**).[48] Certain other films shown may have been by Haggar but the general absence of his films from urban halls may be directly attributable to Haggar's decision to go it alone in Wales, rather than allow Gaumont to handle his films in the principality.[49] In 1907, the Haggars were certainly still flourishing in the fairgrounds, with two film enterprises operating concurrently. Their no. 1 show was at Aberdare, their no. 2 venture at Maesteg.[50] But after wife Sarah's death in 1909, William sen.'s travelling ceased and the family settled into various cinemas between 1910 and the twenties. It was natural that they should set down roots where their shows were most popular, such as Llanelli, Pembroke – and, most notably, Aberdare (where Haggar ran the permanent Kosy cinema from 1915 after years in the temporary Shanty cinema in the nearby Market Yard). Haggar continued to exert a huge influence, installing his children as managers in his cinemas – Will jun., Henry, James and Lillian all remained in the business which absorbed their youthful and adult lives.[51] The full legacy of the Haggar family may not yet be known. It will be interesting to see if the Wales Film and TV Archive can unearth more of their films so we can better assess the creative contribution of the two Williams in particular.

The fairground bioscopes – and families

Scant justice has been done in film histories to other Welsh-based fairground bioscope families whose colourful shows were a magnet for Valleys crowds starved of entertainment. Their contributions to film were admittedly ephemeral – it was just one more diversion and vied for pride of place in a showman's entertainment with his lions, menagerie or roundabouts and other sideshows.

The Dooners, a West Country family, were travelling showmen before 1850, but the patriarch during their halcyon showground days was James Dooner sen. (1840–1910) who, with his son Richard 'Dickie' Dooner, reputedly staged tableaux vivants and living pictures or slides as early as the mid-1890s. Dickie Dooner (born at Eastwood, Notts., died 1951) operated a film machine made by Charles Urban and reputedly

shot a passion play and a version of a notorious local murder at Cwmafon. The
Dooners were originally best known for their lions and wild beasts act, but moved
into cinema permanently after gaining experience with travelling picture-shows billed
– at various times – as the Royal Empire Show, the Bioscope of Passing Events, the
Grand Bioscope and the Electrograph of Animated Pictures.[52] As the bioscopes'
popularity increased, the Dooners faced strong competition – at Neath Fair in 1901,
for instance, they battled for audiences with Wadbrook's 20th Century Electrograph,
Crecraft's Lion and Picture Combination and Testo's Marionettes and Living
Pictures.[53] The younger Dooner continued itinerant shows into the early 1930s, long
after other peripatetic cinema pioneers had settled for bricks and mortar. But the
family began to show films in workers' institutes and halls through the mining valleys
and in 1935 Dooner built the 'super' Plaza cinema in Maesteg – one of his haunts in
travelling days – and ran a chain of cinemas to rival Haggar's.[54]

The Studts, with roots in Germany and Austria, were a fairground family in Britain
back in the 1830s or 1840s.[55] The bioscope of 'Long' or 'Honest' John Studt, the
charismatic 6ft. 4in. showman, and John and brother Jacob's film shows were a
regular attraction for years at the Hayes in Cardiff. The Studt family later took over a
permanent cinema at Pontyclun, Mid Glamorgan.[56] The Scards, originally from
France, gained a foothold in the bioscope business as associates of the Wadbrooks.
Henry James Scard (b. 1859) married Mary Polly Wadbrook in 1886, and his son
Harry Scard jun. and Henry Wadbrook, another film pioneer, ran the travelling
cinema and the original permanent cinema at Market Square, Milford Haven,
demolished by fire in 1920, and replaced the same year. The showbusiness families
were closely linked and marriage consolidated family businesses. When Dickie
Dooner married Helen Wadbrook of Wadbrook's Cinematograph Show, the church
was crowded with the 'élite of the travelling world'.

Edward Danter, of the famous Danter showground family, also ran early film-shows

Crecraft's Bioscope
showfront 1912, with
paraders and the legendary
Mrs Elizabeth Crecraft
(centre, and inset with her
two sons).

and reputedly shot local footage himself, notably of Whitsun processions in old Tredegar. The bioscope's organ frontage was originally provided by John Danter sen., the originator of the family's fairground performances.[57] A more permanent Danter cinema, the Coliseum, was operating c.1914 at Tirphil in the Rhymney Valley run by Joseph Danter, one of five brothers.[58]

Wadbrook's bioscope show operated by 1898, and by 1901 that family was apparently making its own films.[59] At Gorseinon Fair that year, they screened the Ireland v. Wales soccer match and 'other local pictures' plus a passion play – 'This show is advertised as the pride of Wales and is certainly so with the grand carved front (recently new) and magnificent Orchestraphone . . .' At that year's Neath show, the Wadbrook's bioscope '20th Century Electrograph' was 'the attraction of the fairground', featuring film of Queen Victoria's funeral, Joan of Arc, and Lord Roberts's triumphant return to London after his campaign against the Boers.[60] In 1902, Wadbrooks at Neath offered a Wales–Scotland soccer match and at Morriston near Swansea – when the family screened Méliès's **Blue Beard** – 'admiration was seen on all faces at such a magnificent looking exhibition'.[61]

The Crecrafts were among the first fairground families based in Wales to tap into cinema's potential. They originally ran a waxworks exhibition, then a menagerie, but screened films as one attraction from around 1900. The family boasted in Mrs Elizabeth Crecraft, a near-legendary matriarch (b. 1818 in Chelsea, d. 1916), who ran the family's entertainments on the fairground as late as 1910 when she was ninety-two and billed as 'the oldest show proprietor in the world'.[62] She dominated her two sons Charlie and Joe and cut an intimidating figure on stage in her distinctive black garb. The Crecraft picture-shows appeared regularly at Glynneath and it was no surprise when they finally moved into a permanent cinema there in 1912.[63]

Other notable fairground exhibitors included the Manders' waxworks and cinematograph show, Pat Collins of the family now associated with Barry Fair, and Sidney White and his Electric Coliseum.[64] John or 'Jack' Scarrott, the celebrated boxing showman, ran an animated picture booth at Tonypandy as early as 1901, no doubt learning where his future lay after fierce competition with the Haggars. Even circus entertainments such as Chipperfields', Sangers and Bostock and Wombwells' often would not risk appearing in Wales without films or slides as a diversion.[65]

Taking the flak

As interest in the film business snowballed, it was scarcely surprising that cinema shows attracted outbursts from puritans, and the tendency of itinerant proprietors to herald their shows with lavish displays of paraders – particularly leggy female dancers – sparked outbursts. In 1908, Jacob Studt defended his show against letter writers to the *Hereford Times* who criticized the 'half naked' girls outside one or two shows in that area, and Tom Poole of Poole and Poole denied any moral impropriety imputed to his wife who wore a 'three quarter dress' for a Studt show in Wales.[66] Haggar advertised shows which were 'instructive, elevating and entertaining' – despite his taste for robust snook-cocking fare – and cultivated the favour of local worthies by his charity donations, and Sunday Sacred Concerts, with his family often singing accompaniments to religious lantern slides.[67] He was sufficiently brimstone-proof by 1911–12 to complement his sacred concerts with Sunday programmes of meatier screen entertainment in Aberdare – and he was shortly to win election to the Merthyr

Board of Guardians and Aberdare Urban Council, and join the establishment he had earlier satirized.[68] But he was not immune to the calumny of less diffident clergy such as the fundamentalist W. Cynog Williams who claimed in the *Aberdare Leader* of 9 March 1912 that the streets of one Aberdare area 'teemed with moral consumptives'. He complained that a delegation to Aberdare District Council which pressed for no cinema shows on Sunday had been treated with contempt. 'Because Mr Haggar gave an occasional benefit concert some people in Aberdare closed their eyes on certain things. A benefit concert was the sop to many a conscience,' he claimed.

A letter from 'Old Pal (Aberdare)' defended Haggar from the 'Rev Charitable Cynon Williams': 'It does not require anyone to champion Mr Haggar. It is well known that he has been the means of collecting, and has given, hundreds of pounds to various causes in the last 10–15 years.' Another writer, 'Trecynonyte', was even less sympathetic to Cynog Williams: 'These periodical outbursts of vituperation are nauseating.' One writer enquired, sarcastically, whether Cynog would allow himself to

William Haggar's generosity is celebrated in the cinema trade paper *The Bioscope* in 1910.

be screened accompanied by 'his great sermon on the gramophone in order to smash Haggar and Poole'.[69] A few months later, Williams appeared to have won one battle as Sunday shows were banned by Aberdare Council. By 1913 local councillor T. Walter Williams was pressing for a watch committee there and inveighing against films – placarded around town – 'which had a demoralising tendency'. In the prevailing atmosphere, it is little wonder that the Empire, Aberdare, insisted that all films were of 'a clean character'.[70]

But there was no stopping cinema's development – even though the First World War ended the travelling picture-show days for many families. The pioneering generation was fast disappearing. James Dooner died in 1910, John Studt (b. 1849) in 1912, and Mrs Crecraft in 1918. As the 1914–18 war approached, it became increasingly difficult for wandering showmen to satisfy the insatiable demand for new fiction, and old habits died hard. A. C. Bromhead of Gaumont noted that 'long after the principles of exhibition and distribution [film rental] had been established, showmen continued to buy films.' And though it was still common practice to offer fairly brief shows of short films, some proprietors sought to keep patrons happy for longer. The *World's Fair* newspaper (14 June 1913) noted with pleasure that some travelling shows were matching permanent cinemas in showing big programmes and they cited the achievements of Edwards and Page at the Picture Palace, Ystradgynlais, in showing three three-reelers, four two-reelers and a one-reeler in one four-hour programme. 'Surely this constitutes a record?' they asked.

Dwindling fortunes

By 1913, the travelling shows were in irreversible decline. Portfield Fair at Haverfordwest – thriving with five bioscopes in 1909 – hosted its last bioscope shows only four years later.[71] The Cinematograph Act of 1909, laying down rigorous safety standards, spelled the end of the road for many showmen and led directly to the rash of permanent cinemas created before the First World War. Walter Haggar, years later, complained that, as the first purpose-built cinemas sprang up (and took films on rental), it became harder to go to a fair with a programme of films that the audience had not seen. 'We all rushed around trying to find somewhere that hadn't got a local cinema. When we did, our visits, which would normally last only two or three days, were extended to six or seven weeks with business . . . perhaps 20 per cent of what it used to be.'[72] The arrival of permanent cinemas virtually coincided with the first spate of fiction films with Welsh settings. They were not, ironically, from Wales but from British studios in London and the South East – and from America. By 1918, British screens were saturated with American product and the once-glamorous 'travelling pictures' were mainly a memory. The audiences had outgrown the fairgrounds and portable shows. As Ada Roberts, Walter Haggar's wife, lamented: 'People wouldn't come into the fields into the mud to see our shows any more.'[73]

It is questionable whether any town in the kingdom can vie with Swansea in the doubtful honour of the number of urchins who parade its streets in the alleged garb and with the alleged mannerisms of Chaplin. It is in the way of becoming a public nuisance.

(Bioscope, 28 October 1915. Chaplin and Mabel Normand impersonation competitions were held that year all over Wales.)

In fifteen years, from 1912 to 1927, with silent cinema in its pomp, no fewer than twenty-six fictional films, including at least fourteen features, were set or part-set (not merely shot) in Wales, as major British studios and Hollywood-based crews – liberated by film's technical advances – began to venture to outside locations. It is ironic that only four of these movies from this first fertile period of features about Wales appear to have survived – including two films made by a Cardiff company. The loss of the others is an indictment of the casual way the UK industry developed. Films for some decades were given little intrinsic or aesthetic value and no attention was paid in the principality itself to storage or the need for an archive. Film had no worth beyond the ephemeral and first-run box-office receipts. The London-based film industry had shown little interest in shooting in Wales in the century's first decade – though Hepworth, Warwick, Urban and Heron (a subsidiary of Universal) all made early travelogues. Yet between 1912 and the advent of talkies there was almost a surfeit of material produced featuring some of the finest stars of the British and American silent cinema. The sudden fascination developed not, as the more naïve might suppose, because Wales from 1910 to 1912 was at the peak of its industrial prosperity, a maelstrom of social dissent and a fascinating area of political struggle. These were, after all, the years of the Tonypandy riots, the Llanelli rail-strike shootings and stop-outs, and increased tension in the battle for wages and better coalfield conditions. The arrival of film crews did not, as far as we can tell, reflect in any way an upsurge of interest in urban south Wales, riding high with coal production and exports reaching such record levels that Barry in 1911 had the highest coal exports of any port in the world – shipping 11 million tons in the boom after the new dock opened there in 1889.

Filming forays into Wales sprang, rather, from a recognition of the country's photogenic locations, in the years when US companies were gearing themselves up to consolidate their British markets. UK film-makers, aware for the first time of keen competition from across the Atlantic and feeling the financial pinch, began to move further out of London to capture authentic (and comparatively cheap) backdrops. The growth in film-making in Wales also coincided, of course, with the rise of the cinema palaces – the arrival of permanent buildings, many replacing the old music-halls.

A west Wales phenomenon

The fine characteristics of the children of Wales are shown at their best in this tale of a Welsh youth and maid who, born in the poorest circumstances, attain to fame as sculptor and a great prima donna.

(*South Wales Echo* advertisement for **A Welsh Singer**, 14 March 1916)

The most significant of these early films was **A Welsh Singer**, made in 1915 from a novel by a best-selling west Wales novelist, Allen Raine – Anne Adaliza Evans from Newcastle Emlyn, Cardiganshire. In 1905, Hutchinson claimed, astonishingly, that her books that year outsold any other living novelist on their lists. In five years (from 1915 to 1920) no fewer than three of her novels – all set in her native county – were adapted for the screen.[1]

Raine's work has long been out of print, but her slightly florid prose, taste for rural romance and plots exploiting extraordinary coincidences made her much in demand

Opposite:
Florence Turner in A Welsh Singer.

by film-makers of the period. There were other appealing facets of Raine's work. She took a caustic view of native superstition and parochialism – but her ability to work within the classbound conventions of the day yet identify with lowly-born characters, and the feeling she conveyed of belief in her protagonists (even within the most lurid plots) all helped explain her popularity. Her style by the standard of the day and the genre (romantic melodrama) was admirably concise; her story-lines cogent if improbable; and her books, though steeped in tragedy, invariably had an affirmative finale. She was ripe for screen adaptation. **A Welsh Singer** marked the first screen appearance of the British actress Edith Evans – but it starred Florence Turner, the famous Vitagraph Girl who became the first to sign a screen contract when she joined J. Stuart Blackton's celebrated American company, Vitagraph, in 1906.[2] Turner, a former Vaudevillian whose *métier* was mimicry and comedy, played a huge variety of character roles in Hollywood, and in a brief British sojourn from 1913 to 1916 she demonstrated her versatility and eclecticism. Her parts in Britain ranged from Mifanwy the shepherdess in **A Welsh Singer** (playing opposite the film's director, Henry Edwards), the Shepherd Lassie of Argyle and Bathsheba in **Far from the Madding Crowd**, to a Lancashire millgirl in **For Her People**.[3] Silence was golden for Turner, who did not have to worry about perfecting accents.

Florence Turner, the former Vitagraph Girl, star of *A Welsh Singer* (1915).

In **Florence Turner Impersonates Film Favourites** (alternative title **Film Favourites**) (1914), she appeared as Sarah Bernhardt, Keystone's Mabel Normand, 'Wild West Billy' (obviously film's first cowboy star Bronco Billy Anderson) and a Biograph star (probably a skit on a D. W. Griffith tearjerker). Turner, only 4ft. 10in. tall, was reputedly one of the US cinema's main money-earners in the years before Chaplin and Mary Pickford set their own terms. When Turner uprooted herself from America with her regular director, Larry Trimble, the *New York Dramatic Mirror* claimed no actress had a larger following and the *Motion Picture World* stressed that she had increased the 'sale of Vitagraph pictures over all other makes'. Her stature is best illustrated by comments from fellow silent star Norma Talmadge who recalled an early visit to the Vitagraph lot – 'I would rather have touched the hem of her skirt than shaken hands with St Peter.'[4] Turner finally formed her own company in the US but the vertical combinations of major companies producing, distributing and exhibiting their own films froze her out of the early circuits to some extent and may have prompted her sudden exit to Britain. She was received into Hepworth's studio at Walton-on-Thames which became a base; Hepworth later described the arrival of Turner, Trimble and the rotund American comedian John Bunny as 'one of the more portentous events of my long life'. It's not surprising perhaps that Turner, casting around for British material, should alight on Raine's novel – which had notched up sales of 316,000 by 1908 when the writer's total sales had topped 1.7 million. They were soon to top two million. Trimble co-wrote the screenplay with Edwards, already a matinée idol in his own right, and the film proved so popular it was re-released in 1918. In 1922, Butchers, the distributors, disclosed that 1,740 prints had been released and the number of bookings had 'never been approached by us on any subject'.[5]

Raine's biographer Sally Jones – who writes very little about the films – describes the novel as 'a study of snobbery', and it does seem fairly preposterous today. It has the staple ingredients of romantic folk tales: mistaken and concealed identities, a scheming rejected lover, a blaze threatening the heroine's life, and a blighted love miraculously revived. Mifanwy is the daughter of a poor farmer and his wife who adopt a supposed orphan, Ieuan, later to become a talented sculptor. Ieuan is employed as a youth by his own father but only belatedly discovers his boss's true identity. Later, as his career prospers in London, he becomes fond of the farmer's niece, Laissabeth (Una Venning). Mifanwy graduates as a singer from Pomfreys Circus to become 'La Belle Rose', a renowned London diva. Ieuan (Henry Edwards), who attends her first public appearances, fails to recognize her but her voice stirs memories of the mountain girl he knew and he invites her to see a model he has made of Mifanwy. Ieuan, soon besotted by La Belle Rose, incurs Laissabeth's jealousy – and she locks the embryo lovers in a room when fire breaks out in the theatre. Both lose consciousness – and are rescued, a formula plot device in Welsh films of the period (in **Torn Sails**, **Aylwin** and shorts by Sidney Northcote, for example). Mifanwy is at pains to remind Ieuan of his promise to return to the Welsh girl and, in a bizarre twist, she hotfoots it back to Wales, dons old clothes and is reunited with Ieuan who remains unaware of her identity – only revealed after he has proposed.

Reviews suggested Trimble and Edwards treated the story with great fidelity except that the novel's Mifanwy was herself adopted by the farming couple, Shân and Ianto. The class consciousness and racist values implicit in the novel run deep. It is interesting that Laissabeth, of the privileged class, suffers no retribution while Mifanwy is only acceptable as Ieuan's bride when her new urban life-style has given her a milky complexion and she has ceased to resemble the 'brown'-skinned shepherdess of youth. **A Welsh Singer** was also the first feature set in Wales to stress the value of education – particularly in English – as an escape route, though Ieuan and Mifanwy and folk in their own area converse in Welsh.

Reviews for the film were ecstatic. The *Bioscope* praised its 'beautifully arranged and reproduced camera studies intensifying the emotional force of situations',[6] and the *Cinema Magazine* highlighted Edwards's conscientious artistic care and taste as a producer while *Kine Weekly* described Turner's performance as 'one of her greatest triumphs'.[7] Even if we accept that reviewing standards were wayward and no British film critic of any enduring credibility had yet emerged, the opinions expressed in trade magazines were by no means always bland or sycophantic and are a much better yardstick than local press reviews of the period. Only two or three still photographs of the film survive, but these are atmospheric enough to ensure regret that no copy of the full feature appears to exist. Turner's visit to the Cardiff Empire in 1914, when she 'fairly brought down the house' with character 'studies' did box-office prospects no harm.[8] Her career faltered in the 1920s despite leading roles for Metro, and in Britain early in the decade. At one stage she was marooned penniless in Britain and her journey home was financed by the film star Marion Davies, a regular visitor to south Wales as mistress of newspaper mogul William Randolph Hearst, who had bought St Donat's Castle as a second San Simeon (his California home) and staged lavish parties there. In 1937 Turner, then on her uppers, was hired by Louis B. Mayer as a film extra.

Henry Edwards's fortunes continued to wax as players began to attract the adoration of fans, whose appetite for any morsel on their favourites was served by the plethora

of magazines. In 1918 *Pictures and Picturegoer* chose Edwards as the first of a series of Famous Men portraits 'partly because we receive more letters about him than . . . any other British male artist'. Hepworth Picture Plays' publicity of the time claimed: 'Chrissie White, Alma Taylor and Henry Edwards are the greatest picture players in Britain'.[9] Husband-and-wife team Edwards and White were to play the leading roles in another 'Welsh' film, **Aylwin** (1920).

Torn Sails, from the novel by Welsh author Allen Raine.

In the same year, another Raine novel was adapted for the screen, and shot in and around Newcastle Emlyn – the five-reeler **By Berwen Banks**, directed by Sidney Morgan for the Progress company and released by Butchers. Little is known about it save that it featured 'an Anglican vicar's son who secretly weds a dissenter's daughter and recovers from amnesia in time to save her from shame'.[10] The third Raine novel filmed was **Torn Sails** (also 1920), directed by A. V. Bramble for the Ideal company, starring Milton Rosmer and Mary Odette. The novel is much more persuasive than *A Welsh Singer* with a greater maturity of style and plausibility in plotting and characterization – with odd notable exceptions. The *Western Mail* reviewer, interestingly, found the novel a 'decided advance upon any of its predecessors – a clear and faultless reflection free of all affectation of the inner life of rural Wales'.[11] The story is built around Hugh Morgan, owner of a sailmaking business, who marries an employee Gwladys Price; she remains smitten with love for Hugh's right-hand man, Ivor, but will not betray her husband. In one scene Ivor saves Gwladys from drowning and the shooting proved costly. A boat used for filming was dashed against the rocks and overturned, and several cast members had to be pulled to safety.

Sally Jones considers *Torn Sails* 'by no means' one of Raine's best novels but she was fascinated with one character, Gwenny, a thwarted mother who becomes mentally

Poster for *Aylwin*, a romantic melodrama set in Wales, from the novel by Theodore Watts-Dunton. (The spelling of 'Aylwyn' on this poster varies from Allen Raine's novel – and from the film, according to historians Rachael Low and Denis Gifford.)

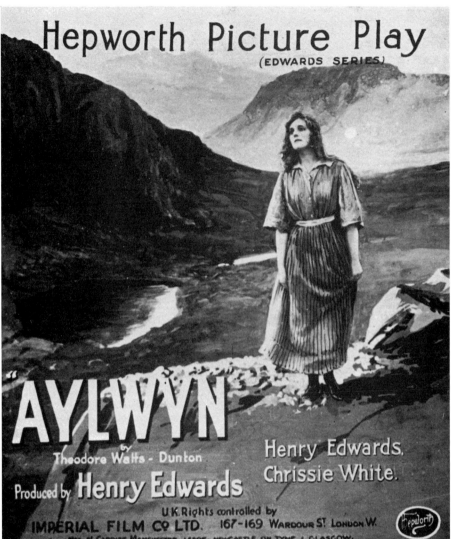

unhinged by grief and starts the blaze which kills Hugh (who on his death-bed 'bequeaths' Gwladys to Ivor). Jones compares the treatment of Gwenny, who unwittingly chokes a child by feeding it a blend of roasted mouse and brown sugar (as a potential cure), to Caradoc Evans's sardonic treatment of Nanny and the Rats and the force of superstition in his cautionary short story 'Be This Her Memorial'.[12] It would be fascinating to know if the choking scene was retained in the film.

The *Bioscope* complained that the 'Welsh atmosphere scarcely extended beyond the settings', the 'small-part types' should have been more carefully selected, and Mary Odette's performance as Gwladys 'lacked depth and subtlety'.[13] The reviewer thought the romance between Ivor (Rosmer) and Gwladys should have been the main theme of the story and not treated as of 'quite secondary importance'. It seems probable that the film placed greater stress on the bonds between Hugh and his employee, Ivor.

Allen Raine's acquaintance, Florence Hope of Newcastle Emlyn, forecast a fresh interest in the writer's books 'through the advertisement of the cinema, for however much we despise the pictures they have come to stay and, to my mind, the more stories like *Torn Sails* are put on screen the better it is for everybody.'[14] Her observations are only too revealing of the attitude still held in the 1920s by a certain

One of Britain's leading silent stars, Chrissie White, in *Aylwin*.

social stratum. Raine has now suffered almost total critical eclipse in Wales, even though Emlyn Williams has acknowledged her influence, but at her peak she equalled in popularity such potboiler authors as Marie Corelli and Hall Caine whose work inspired so many films of the period.[15] Raine herself was conscious of criticism that her work was bland or idealistic – 'I am quite aware there are some dark stains on the morals of Wales. These I purposely leave unportrayed for I do not consider it necessary to wade through the mud lying underneath the stream when there are so many flowers growing on its bank waiting to be culled.'[16] British film-makers were similarly loath in the 1920s to explain the undercurrents of social life.

Aylwin (1920), shot around Snowdonia from a convoluted and, at times, opaque novel by Theodore Watts-Dunton, was a five-reel tragedy focused on a well-heeled man's affection for a girl in defiance of his mother's wishes. The girl, Winifred, goes mad after her drunken father, Tom Wynne, dies in a landslide leaving evidence of his theft of the Aylwin family jewels from the author Philip Aylwin's grave. The story hinges on even more extraordinary coincidences than **A Welsh Singer**. Hero Hal Aylwin, Philip's son, thinks he has lost his love who disappears to London but recognizes her portrait when he visits his friend Wilderspin (Gerald Ames). Surgery is needed to restore Winifred's sanity after the giddy excesses of the plot.

Watts-Dunton, an editor of George Borrow's books, was heavily influenced by the writer, but his own novel is an unappetizing farrago of mysticism, quasi-spiritualism and verbosity and it is almost unreadable. The almost interminable digressions by the mournful self-centred Hal on the strange atavistic theories of his father, and some even more bizarre reflections on alleged gypsy folklore, constantly blur the narrative and dissipate tension. The book should surely only have been adapted (as a silent) by concentrating on just one or two plot threads.

The *Bioscope* reviewer praised the exceptionally beautiful Welsh scenery and (more

Ivy Close – the mother of British director Ronald Neame – starred in the short tragedy *Mifanwy* in 1913.

bewilderingly) the quality of the original novel – 'cleverly interpreted' by director Henry Edwards.[17] But the writer pointed out that the violated tomb episode, Hal's love quest and Winifred's cure were 'three distinct subjects . . . Edwards should have concentrated on one element – the love pursuit.' The film was 'pure melodrama of a not very convincing type' and the reviewer criticized its 'loose construction' and remarked that Wynne's death in the landslide was 'neither very convincing nor very thrilling'. Chrissie White escaped the critic's strictures but was damned with faint praise. As the 'demented' Winifred she revealed a 'surprising capacity for temperamental acting'. She was an artist of 'real versatility and power although one still likes her best as the perfect embodiment of the quiet, even natured, warm hearted *English girl*' (my italics).[18]

Weepies and folklore

Another leading silent-film star to turn to Wales was Ivy Close, mother of the durable British director Ronald Neame and wife of her regular screen director Elwin Neame. Close played the title role in her own company's short work, the 13-minute (675ft.) **Mifanwy** (1913), a romance tragedy set in Wales in which the central character rejects the local rector's advances and later dreams of her lover who has died at sea and now beckons her into his arms midst the waves. Mesmerized, she follows him into the water and is found dead on shore the next morning. It was directed by Neame and released by Hepworth, but information remains scarce and the film is not even included in most filmographies of the actress who ran her own studios at Esher, Surrey, with her husband, and later worked for the Kalem company in America.[19]

Yet another Mifanwy or Myfanwy was the heroine of the **The Pedlar of Penmaenmawr**, one of four films of 15–20 minutes set in Wales and shot by Sidney Northcote between 1912 and 1913 and written by the prolific Harold Brett for the British and Colonial Kinematograph Co. Dorothy Foster played the lead, Myfanwy Griffiths, who is saved from a cliff mishap by a hawker. Foster also starred in the other three shorts: **The Belle of Betws-y-Coed** (US title: **The Belle of North Wales**), **The Smuggler's Daughter of Anglesea** [*sic*], and **The Witch of the Welsh Mountains**. All three feature rescues and date from the era of the cliffhanger serials of Pearl White and others. In **The Belle of Betws-y-Coed**, a girl returns to her sweetheart after he 'thrashes tramps who've carried out a vicious attack'.[20] But the most intriguing of the Northcote quartet seems to be **Witch of the Welsh Mountains**, centred on a wounded widow who recovers in time to save the 'wrong girl' from being burned at the stake.[21]

Other Welsh films of the day placed heavy emphasis on religion, Celtic mysticism and ritual pastorale, forlorn romance and identity puzzles. Typical was Martin Thornton's feature **Gwyneth of the Welsh Hills** (1921), starring Madge Stuart and Eille Norwood, famous through the 1920s as a stodgy, remarkably uncharismatic screen Sherlock Holmes for Oswald Stoll's company. The film was adapted from a novel written four years previously by Edith Nepean from Llandudno, a journalist and inveterate traveller who, like Allen Raine, did her most significant writing after moving to London and also drew ideas from gypsy folklore.[22]

Tragedy and redemption were popular ingredients of this kind of material, when plots were lubricated by contrivances such as apparent loss of memory, or myopia. The longest Welsh film of the period was the Alliance Company's **Love and the Whirlwind** (1924, 6,858ft.) (dirs. Harold Shaw and Duncan MacRae) about 'a Lord's son who poses as a fisherman when a poacher frames him for shooting his mother'.[23] The notable British star Clive Brook featured, opposite Marjorie Hulme. Less angst permeated **The Croxley Master** (1921), obvious box-office fare culled from the Arthur Conan Doyle story and directed by prolific British film-maker, Percy Nash. The hero is a doctor's assistant who boxes a local champion 'to buy the practice and win the doctor's daughter'.[24]

Other Welsh features contained usual melodramatic staples. **The Little Welsh Girl** (1920) centred on an expelled priest accused of murdering a servant girl and was directed by actor Fred Paul, who made many films from 1914 on, originally for the Ideal company.[25] **Love in the Welsh Hills** was a Regent Company crime thriller (dir. Bernard Dudley, 1921) featuring a ruined farmer who frames a petty officer for theft but later confesses robbery and murder after falling over a cliff. The naval officer Robert Lloyd (James Knight) has been suspected of the murder after earlier knocking out the victim, accusing him – falsely – of adultery with his wife Nan (Marjorie Villis). In fact the dead man had seduced her sister Gwen (Constance Worth). The *Bioscope* reviewer was impressed by the film's scenic charm – its 'outstanding feature' – but thought the 'strong human melodrama' was marred by a 'clumsy scenario and bad continuity'. The popular device of amnesia was used in **Land of My Fathers** (dir. Fred Rains, 1921): 'a woman weds a man with no past memory and drowns herself when he's cured by meeting an ex-fiancée . . .'[26]

The social and class values of these works were typical of a British cinema atrophied in a generally mythical past or a distinctly upper-middle-class present; they seemed increasingly sterile as the 1920s wore on. (Sound, with its early limitations on movement, made the films seem even more stilted than before.) It would be possible to conclude from the films that industrial Wales did not exist at all and that rural Wales was composed entirely of mentally fragile shepherdesses, gypsies and potential suicides pursued by worried, usually rather rich and apparently myopic young men who needed rather more than earthly powers to effect the obligatory last-ditch rescue. The real world, as most Welsh people understood it, rarely appeared in this material. Mining features fairly centrally in just one film, the Edison company's first sally into the principality, **The Foreman's Treachery** (1914) – and it hinged around copper rather than coal. It was made by Liverpool-born Charles Brabin, sometime husband of the screen vamp Theda Bara, and was shot among 'some of the most beautiful scenery in North Wales, including Llangollen, Snowdon, Swallow Falls and Beddgelert village'.[27]

After a rich vein of ore is discovered on pit property by the foreman Griffiths, he steals a miner's horde to buy the land which is up for sale with its copper reserves officially almost exhausted. Disturbed by the theft victim, Griffiths hurls him down a well and frames for the crime a worker, David Llewellyn, boyfriend of Anna Lloyd, the miner's daughter. The *deus ex machina* proves to be the girl's slightly simple brother, a witness to the struggle at the well (that fatal coincidence again). The foreman, of course, can only atone by death and he is duly destroyed by blasting operations while fleeing across the mountains. The film, heavily promoted, was one of a string of Edison films made in Britain between 1912 and 1914 by a small UK-based company unit. The stars were almost invariably Marc MacDermott and Miriam Nesbitt (Llewellyn and Anna Lloyd in **The Foreman's Treachery**). *Bioscope* thought the film compared favourably 'even with the best production of its studio . . . A good strong drama of an old-fashioned type remarkable for the beauty of its settings with magnificent views of Llangollen and district.'[28]

The only work which apparently attempted to treat Welsh historical legend was George Ridgwell's **The Last King of Wales** (1921), with Charles Aston as Llywelyn, and American actress Malvina Longfellow as Queen Eleanor. Longfellow, who played Lady Hamilton in the 1919 British production of **Nelson**, had previously appeared in the five-reel **Betta the Gypsy**, also set in Wales, inspired by an operetta and made in 1918 with Marga La Rubia in the title role.

Censored: the Prime Minister

One of the most fascinating Welsh projects of the era was a biography of David Lloyd George (1918), completed but never released and long thought to be lost or destroyed.

Scenes were shot around Caernarfon at the National Eisteddfod and at the statesman's Cricieth home, and were directed by Maurice Elvey, the film-maker with the most prodigious output in UK cinema history. Harry Rowson, founder of the film's producers, Ideal, thought the film 'exceeded every expectation' and that Elvey had 'excelled himself', handling a formidable cast including well-known West End actor Norman Page as the chameleon politician, Alma Reville (later Hitchcock's wife) as Megan Lloyd George, Douglas Munro as Disraeli and the cadaverous Ernest Thesiger as Joseph Chamberlain.[29] 'The picture had everything . . . a boy-makes-good story and plenty of humour', Rowson said later. American companies in Wardour Street clamoured for distribution rights, Carl Laemmle of the Imp company wanted first option in handling a US release. Why then did it never see the light of day?

Research in recent years, based on Harry Rowson's surviving memoirs and papers, has unearthed a remarkable story.[30] There is strong evidence that the film was effectively suppressed after Lloyd George or his advisers developed cold feet following an article in the patriotic, tub-thumping magazine *John Bull*, edited by the now-notorious Horatio Bottomley. It alleged that senior Ideal company executives were of German origin and insinuated that they were not fit to handle such a biography. Rowson stated that government Chief Whip, Capt. Guest, told Ideal that Lloyd George did not want the film released, but Guest claimed the decision had nothing to do with the article – even though the government had previously approved the project. It seems likely that Lloyd George or the Home Office feared that Bottomley could whip up enough ill will to cause political damage. *John Bull* boasted a circulation of 1.7 million, was highly influential and the magazine's profits of £113,000 in 1918 trebled those of its publishers, Odhams. The publishers were acutely embarrassed by Bottomley's broadside, especially as their trade paper *Kine Weekly* had lauded the movie in large display advertisements for eight successive weeks.

Originally Ideal had planned to make a feature on the causes of war. The company approached Winston Churchill to write the film in tandem with Ideal's regular scenario writer Elliot Stannard, but Churchill bowed out when he joined Lloyd George's Cabinet. Rowson then decided to make a film on Lloyd George: 'the most important man in the world'. Simon Rowson, Harry's brother, took over the project, and historian Sir Sidney Low went to north Wales for a month to research the script –

and completed it in seven weeks. The scenario spanned Lloyd George's early home and school life, his first court cases as a lawyer and, more importantly, his political opposition to the Boer War (including his flight disguised as a policeman from Birmingham Town Hall after one unpopular speech) and his clash with Joseph Chamberlain on Chamberlain's tariff proposals. The film went on to show Lloyd George's transformation when the 1914–18 conflict began and his final recognition as the 'man who won the war'. Norman Page visited the Commons every day, studying the politician's mannerisms, and delivered a fine performance, according to Harry Rowson.

Lloyd George meets Hitler: a 'rediscovered' film of the MP's much-criticized visit to Germany in 1936. The première of this film led to Viscount Tenby, a descendant of Lloyd George, submitting the long-lost 1918 feature on the statesman to the Wales Film and TV Archive.

As interest rose in the build-up to the film's release, Ideal resisted demands from exhibitors to help boost their profits by shooting the material as a serial rather than a feature. In October 1918 the blow fell. Bottomley claimed Ideal was a German-constituted company and pointed out that the Rowsons had changed their name from Rosenbaum. Bottomley had called for a vendetta against all 'Huns', naturalized or not, Street points out. Ideal took libel and slander actions against *John Bull*; *Cinema* magazine sprang to Ideal's defence, referring to 'most unpleasant inferences' to be drawn from the offending article and stressing the company's 'very high reputation' and 'many notable and excellent productions'. *Cinema* also published a list of those involved with Ideal who were with one exception (a man with four sons in the British Army) all born in Britain – even though the Rowsons (like many others in wartime) had changed their name. Despite such 'exoneration', Ideal faced pressure from friends and the industry to shelve the movie 'to prevent this, at all costs, from becoming a Jewish question – the only way we could look at it'. Harry Rowson thought the film's release could trigger an 'embarrassing world scandal'.

Ideal succumbed and the government paid £20,000 in compensation – the cost of the movie's production. A representative of government solicitors arrived at Rowson's office one day, peeled off the money in £1,000 notes and the negative and positive of the film left with him in a taxi. Rowson claimed the company lost £100,000 on potential UK business alone, and it was clearly scant consolation to him when *John Bull* withdrew all imputations and paid full costs. The film disappeared for seventy-six years. Then in May 1994 negatives of the complete feature were deposited among sixteen cans of Lloyd George material (mainly nitrate stock) at the Wales Film and TV Archive, Aberystwyth. The negatives, supplied by Viscount Tenby (a grandson of the statesman) were in cans officially sealed in 1920 – as an accompanying legal document confirmed. The total material submitted also included long-lost footage of a First World War 'Kine Views' movie from the Hepworth company containing interviews with various luminaries (including politicians such as Bonar Law) about the conflict, and a number of Topical Budget programmes from the early 1920s alluding to Lloyd George. The discovery of this material alone, particularly the only UK feature ever made on a contemporary home statesman, more than confirmed the worth of the new archive and set one wondering how much material might have been unearthed had the Welsh Arts Council, or the TV companies, had the prescience to establish it two decades earlier.

Ideal resurrected the Lloyd George project in the Second World War but the statesman died before he could reply to company overtures and the planned film was aborted.[31] The only version of Lloyd George's life to emerge during his palmy years was a seemingly innocuous 750 ft. animation movie, **The Romance of Lloyd George** (1917), 'founded on sittings given to the artist' by the Prime Minister. Made by Kine Comedy cartoons and drawn by Ernest Mills, it featured Lloyd George's escape from Birmingham Town Hall – plus recognition of his insurance and pension achievements.[32]

A lone survivor

The only extant pre-war feature-length film of special Welsh interest, apart from Will Haggar jun.'s **Maid of Cefn Ydfa**, is, curiously enough, **Ivanhoe** (1913), made for Carl Laemmle's pioneering Imp company, a forerunner of Universal – with Chepstow Castle and the surrounding countryside doubling for the locations of Sir Walter Scott's novel.[33] The director was the Irish-born Herbert Brenon, an autocrat whose taste for extravagant sets led to regular conflicts with backers and producers. Brenon, in Britain to make a spy thriller, saw a stage production of *Ivanhoe*, and the film-maker, who shot one- and two-reelers at the phenomenal rate of one a week around 1912, persuaded Laemmle to bankroll the project and even extend it from three to four reels. The company was sufficiently worried about its length to inform patrons that there was 'no padding', but the final budget of £3,500 was large for its day – hardly surprising as Brenon, true to form, shot 20,000 ft. to obtain the 3,500 ft. in the actual print.[34]

Welsh involvement was far from token. Walter Thomas, a local amateur actor, had a showy cameo as Robin Hood, hogging one scene when he beats Friar Tuck in a quarterstaff joust. Five hundred locals were used as extras at 5*s*. a day. As this was more than the local shipyard (or menial jobs elsewhere) offered they stopped work when the sun shone and scurried to the castle – 'Everywhere in the town could be seen Chepstowians in armour, chain mail and Lincoln green.'[35]

Fine prints of this film are still accessible and Brenon makes superb use of his locations. The work, a severely truncated version of the classic, is impeccably lit. The *Bioscope* singled out the 'beautiful camera studies . . . never introduced for their own sake alone', and the writer thought **Ivanhoe** proved that 'for beauty of scenery and setting England [*sic*] stands before any country in the world.'[36] Scenes when Rebecca (Leah Baird), daughter of the wealthy Jewish merchant Isaac of York (played by Brenon himself), is pictured in solitary confinement have grace and emotional eloquence thanks to subtle use of shade and chiaroscuro lighting – a contrast to some of the film's battle scenes clumsily framed in dreary mid-shot with a static camera.

Motion Picture World reviewer W. Stephen Bush praised the 'splendid acting' of the leads and 'magnificent settings' but more problematic today is the leaden performance as hero of King Baggot who strikes stilted postures and looks unhappy throughout.[37] His lack of range seems strange for an actor deemed talented enough to play all ten roles in Imp's two-reeler **Shadows** (1914) and to receive star billing in the company's trade advertisements long before the practice was generally accepted. **Ivanhoe**'s most

A poster for *Ivanhoe*, shot by America's Imp company in and around Chepstow Castle.

dramatic moments – the horsemen's storming of the castle seen in high angle from Rebecca's vantage point, and the hero's intervention when he defeats Font de Boef at the climactic joust to save Rebecca from incineration as a witch – are handled with the panache of the better silent serials. Brenon switches angles with dexterity but he was obviously hampered by the four-reel format. Lady Rowena, the nominal heroine (Evelyn Hope), disappears from the screen for longish spells and seems almost a subsidiary character exerting only a nebulous hold on the audience. The film generally has a languid beauty, with Brenon displaying a flair for composition, but it lacks verve and a certain imagination.[38] The captions, interestingly, are succinct and always relevant from a director who decreed that they should be 'short, virile and colloquial'.[39] These lessons unfortunately were not absorbed by the British film industry of the 1920s.

The Chepstow film is perhaps best seen today as a dry run for Brenon's later desert castle siege scenes in **Beau Geste** (1926) starring Ronald Colman, when a bigger budget helped the director to achieve much more genuine animation and fluidity. **Ivanhoe** proved a considerable success and more than 100 prints were distributed immediately in London. The film also helped convince Laemmle that even a five-reel feature might be not only practical but desirable especially when in July 1913 Zenith, the British company, rush-released an equally successful six-reel Ivanhoe version, **Rebecca the Jewess**. The success of the Imp feature also prompted **Pimple's Ivanhoe**, a short 1913 satire featuring the popular British screen comedian 'Pimple' (Fred Evans), a comedy re-issued in 1915 – and the 1915 British feature **Jane Shore** (dirs. Bert Haldane, Martin Thornton), also partly shot at Chepstow Castle.[40]

An aberration: Mascot Star

At least one Welsh company functioned in the early 1920s, after a fashion, and the paltry efforts of Cardiff's Mascot Star which made two films in 1919 and 1920, survive. It operated as a screen acting college and production outfit under the 'principal', Ernest Edmunds, between 1918 and 1922. They offered to train performers, claiming at one stage to have engaged an American producer, but found themselves in competition with London and Provincial Studios a few doors away, who canvassed for students for film acting classes: 'Big salaries to be earned: 15s. a day upwards.'[41] Mascot Star countered with: 'Mary Pickford earns £4,000 a week, Charlie [Chaplin] earns £250,000 a year. What do you earn? We want British talent for our new picture.'

An early company advert also boasted – inaccurately – that the college had already produced 'the first and only comedy in Wales'.[42] The claim referred to **Coals and Courtship** (1919), which featured Ernest Edmunds in a small role as a marriage registrar. The company trumpeted the appeal of 'the famous Welsh laughtermakers Fred Harris and Miss C. A. Edmunds', and Harris was certainly billed as 'the king of Welsh comedians' at Cardiff's Hippodrome in 1918. Yet the film contains much artless burlesque and buffoonery, fatuous characterization and stereotyping – and it is interesting chiefly for what it reveals of the film-maker's attitudes and notions of audience sympathies. Even accepting the company's status as virtual amateurs, they seemed to have little idea of film. Both Harris, grimacing wildly, and Miss Edmunds, with an exaggerated fey courtesy, constantly acknowledge the cinema-goer as they might a theatre audience. The film is a series of loosely linked events, acts or 'attractions' (almost like a vaudeville review) rather than a coherent narrative film. The action is supposedly set in 'Pwllgain Colliery, Pontypridd' (fictitious) and the facetious tone can be gauged from the opening title: 'We can now introduce you to a "striking" example of a Welsh miner.' Then: 'Dai, hard at work, look you.' There are shots of the pitman Dai Lossin – possibly based on the popular *Western Mail* character of the day – as he tries vainly to persuade a pit pony, hauling a coal truck, to move. Then we see Margaret Ann (Edmunds), dumpy and graceless, sitting on a coal heap. One or two infantile rhymes precede the entry of 'Lord Lank, Squire of Cwmscotton'. 'PC Pint', observing trouble from a nearby rooftop, topples to the ground, hits out at the supposed aristocrat – for some unfathomable reason – and a brawl ensues. Dai is embroiled in the mêlée – 'a thrilling representation of a conflict between police and miners – indeed to goodness'. Dai is bundled into a police vehicle but a title tells us an armistice has been agreed. They all adjourn to the pub and in a later scene Dai and his girl are seen swigging liquor on a bench. Miss Edmunds is seen blatantly giving instructions to the film's cameraman – or taking them – before resuming a drunken pose, and in a later scene at 'Cwmscotton Fair' she also seems to be painfully aware of the camera. The scene includes revellers shying at cardboard effigies of the Kaiser and German Crown Prince. Another fracas is the prelude to Dai and Margaret Ann's wedding (with the marriage on a flimsy stage set) followed by a toe-curling sentimental ending. The last of the film's twenty-six titles refers to 'the play' and the cast line up outside the register office facing the camera for the final fade-out. The term 'photoplay' was still common screen parlance then – a reflection of most directors' and companies' stagebound approach.

In March 1920 the company touted a proposed film (apparently never made) starring 'Mr Sid Coleman of Cardiff'. The next month Mascot Star was making **Down on the Farm**, a two-reel comedy 'supervised' by Ernest Edmunds, including fifty local performers and shot around Cardiff.[43] This second travesty was screened as a support at the Cardiff Cinema, Queen Street, in June, and its initial one- or two-night run was extended to a week, supposedly by popular demand.[44] The short featured one Leon Lyne as Lucky, 'a knight of the road', who is dazed in a crash aboard a child's trolley and dreams of farm adventures with an attractive girl – 'Rita Vallee, a buxom vamp' (Esta Latner) – and frolicsome campers. Romantic entanglements and reprisals ensue, but the film is characterized by relentlessly crude editing and slapstick.

Mascot Star claimed 'lady artistes were especially engaged to teach your children film acting by American methods' and 'parts were guaranteed', but the company soon disappeared.[45] The demise was no loss to the cinema which had then been established for some years as the popular mass entertainment in Wales. This success was assured by the appeal of the serials, the one- and two-reel comedies (particularly Chaplin's) and technical innovations (most publicized – and obvious – in the films of D. W. Griffith, whose new productions were all accompanied by huge adverts in the local press listing the entire 'star cast'). 'The Tramp' during the 1914-18 war ousted in public affection the early European comics such as Tontolini, Foolshead and even the great Max Linder.

Film's popularity had gained spectacularly in the decade from 1910 to 1920 as the cinema boom began in earnest, but astonishingly little had been seen of contemporary urban Wales or its people on screen.

Documentaries and topicals

The only existing stereoscopic-life motion pictures in the annual colours of nature. The latest and most perfect phase of cinematography . . . Melodies of colour . . .

(Cardiff's Olympia cinema advertising Charles Urban's revolutionary two-colour Kinemacolor in the *South Wales Echo*, 14 August 1911)

It took years before the first documentaries were made of key events in Welsh history – apart from royal processions and visits and significant funerals – though cinema managers were not impervious to the impact of tragedies on their audiences, and Welsh proprietors at film-shows took collections for bereaved dependants of mining victims from 1896 – the year of the Tylorstown disaster.

Some of the earliest locally screened topicals were of Boer War derring-do.[46] The first outside companies drawn to Wales were intent on recording the scenery – witness the films of the River Conwy and the town by the American Biograph Company in 1898, the Warwick Company (1900), and Cecil Hepworth (1909), and primitive north Wales – and Conwy – travelogues by the Heron company.[47] In 1902, Warwick also filmed a Wales–Scotland rugby match and an Eisteddfod at Caerphilly.[48] All Charles Urban's early visits to Wales after leaving Warwick in 1903 were prompted by the appeal of the locations. In 1909 he offered footage of the Dinorwic Slate Quarry – then the largest in the world – and followed with at least three more shorts: **Excursion into Wales** (a 'fine travel subject' of old castles, halls and moats in Chester, Conwy, Menai Straits and Llandudno), **Glimpses of the Wye Valley** and **The River Banks of Wales**.[49] But the footage which caught the imagination was undoubtedly the 1911 colour film Urban took of the royal investiture at Caernarfon. Gaumont shot the event with titles in both Welsh and English (probably the first Welsh–English bilingual film ever made), but their monochrome effort was eclipsed by Urban's company who captured the ceremony in Kinemacolor, the exciting mechanical two-colour (red and green) process perfected by the inventor, G. A. Smith. The arrival of non-hand-tinted colour on screen was timely, reviving palates jaded by the hitherto relatively limited film diet.[50]

A black-and-white version survives revealing a talent for composition – with Urban essaying a series of cuts to telescope time, during a mounted procession accompanying the royal carriage. In the following castle ceremony, Urban tilts the camera and ventures modest pans. As the prince descends from the rostrum there is a cutaway and an impressive shot, through an archway, of the prince and a high-angle view of the royal party. Horses pass very close to camera and the film ends as the royal carriage is caught, centre frame. The film, employing neat lighting contrasts, has a visual sophistication unusual in topicals of the time. Another surviving version – almost certainly Gaumont's as it bears company logos – is also quite sophisticated, taken with multiple cameras from favourable vantage points. A print of this film – lacking the polish and symmetry of the Urban short – was recently acquired by the Wales Film and TV Archive.

There were certainly some film-makers in Wales prepared to capture contemporary events, even if there seems in retrospect a disappointing dearth of indigenous film to chronicle one of the most turbulent periods in Wales's industrial history.[51] James Haggar, William's son, screened pictures (almost certainly the surviving Pathé film) of the 1911 Llanelli rail strike and the aftermath of the riot at the GWR railway goods yard, when two men were shot dead by soldiers. Extant Pathé footage contains shots of the military, police and firemen clearing the wreckage around damaged carriages, and a Market Street scene of people boarding up windows.[52] The next month Haggar filmed a labour protest demonstration and 'secured a fine picture . . . This was dispatched to London by the 8.38 p.m. train on Sunday . . . and was actually developed, printed, fixed and dried and sent back to Llanelli and shown at the second performance on Monday night to the delight of the huge audience.'[53]

In December, 1911, Haggar boasted that he had secured footage of the shipwreck at Burry Port of a Cardiff-bound schooner.[54] When 439 men perished in the worst Welsh pit disaster – at Senghenydd in 1913 – it was the newly opened Llanelli Cinema in Stepney Street that screened the film in the town and held a relief performance for the bereaved families, with Brynmawr miners collecting donations.[55] Other pitmen were less than happy to see shots of the tragedy on screen so soon. The *World's Fair* (25 Oct. 1913) reported that Western Valley miners, meeting at

Abertillery that month, had called on patrons to boycott the film and passed a resolution protesting about its 'depressing influence on spectators'. The reactions reflect the conditioning of ordinary men totally unused to seeing 'real life' or industrial conditions or problems depicted on screen. But the Senghenydd film was shown widely in Wales that year – often at benefit shows for miners and dependants.

Other footage survives from the period. C. B. Stanton, then a fiery left-wing miners' agent and later Merthyr MP before a political change of heart, can be seen addressing strikers outside the Aberaman gasworks in a Pathé film, *c.*1910, and there is also, in the National Film Archive, Pathé film of union leader Havelock Wilson speaking to dockers from a balcony in Cardiff during the docks strike of 1910–11.[56] It includes shots of police, some with bayonets, arriving at the docks at 5 a.m. (according to a title) and mounted officers passing through ranks of pedestrians.

No 'event' or 'interest' film could match in popularity the footage of the 1910 clash between two of Wales's greatest boxers, Freddie Welsh, from Pontypridd, and Peerless Jim Driscoll, shown all around Wales in 1911. Gaumont and Pathé offered numerous other topicals shot in south Wales as the First World War approached – the longest was probably Pathé's 1913 444ft. film of slate quarrying and blasting at Blaenau Ffestiniog.[57] Both companies were quick to cash in on the cinema boom. Gaumont's offices in Wharton Street, Cardiff, opened in March 1912 and in July 1913 the *Gaumont Weekly* magazine, carrying news of the hire service run by 'the largest film renting concern in the world' noted the 'phenomenally rapid growth of the cinematograph business in South Wales and the West of England'.[58] Gaumont, Pathé and Warwick all battled for supremacy with their early newsreels and screen magazine programmes and Gaumont's Cardiff offices boasted two cameras and its 'own operators' offering special local films on demand – 'everything from funerals to music-hall sketches'. The *Gaumont Weekly* highlighted a topical of the royal visit to south Wales in 1913.[59] Walterdaw also had offices in Cardiff in 1913 and 'an excellent little camera for filming topicals'.[60]

Cinemas: the early boom

The documentaries, 'topicals' or screen magazine programmes flourished as fillers as the whole film business expanded with increasing investment in permanent cinemas following licensing legislation. The move towards full-time cinemas had been anticipated by Oswald Stoll when he made film the top attraction at his halls, and by 1910 there were 162 halls and other venues showing film in Wales, even if many held infrequent screenings.[61] By 1919 there were 183 with fourteen serving Cardiff's 182,000 population, but by 1920 the venues had soared to 252.[62] From 1909 to 1914, dozens of permanent purpose-built cinemas opened and many other halls began to show film as virtually the sole entertainment.

The 648-seat Electric in Queen Street, Cardiff, built in 1909 and revamped a year later, can lay claim to be the Welsh capital's first permanent cinema, run by London and Provincial Electric Theatres of Charing Cross Road. It boasted: 'Dainty teas served by dainty maids.' In 1910, eight different sites served Cardiff's 164,000 population, including the Cory Hall, then regularly used for film shows, the 2,000-seat New Theatre, the Park Hall cinema (2,500 capacity), the 2,000-seat Empire (reconstructed 1916), and the Panopticon/Philharmonic Hall (1,800).[63] Remarkably, Swansea, with a population of 70,000, boasted the same number of venues – a tribute to the entrepreneurial energy of the indefatigable William Coutts, who ran twelve theatre and picture palaces in the area by 1912, and even advertised his own bioscope school for the training of projectionists.[64] The crucial years for Cardiff cinema development were 1911 to 1914, when new film premises opened included the Olympia (formerly the Andrews Hall in Queen Street, later the ABC and the Cannon, now MGM), the Penylan in Roath (later the Globe), the Splott Cinema, the Picture Playhouse (also known as the Cardiff Cinema Theatre) in Queen Street, Solomon Andrews's baby, the Central, and the oldest surviving building still used as a cinema – the 792-seat Imperial (launched in 1911, but housing the Odeon from 1936).[65]

The scramble for custom meant that managers could not wait to embrace novelties. Singing pictures (notably Vivaphone's sound-on-disc method and Clarendon's 'sound pictures') continued to be popular as late as 1914, when the Gaiety in City Road, Cardiff, held exclusive rights in the city to Edison's 'marvel' – yet another new vaunted sound system, the Kinetophone, 'the eighth wonder of the world'. But Edison's optimism soon evaporated.

Much more excitement was generated by the introduction of Kinemacolor. Georges Méliès had produced glorious hand-tinted film earlier, but south Wales showmen were soon queuing up to display the wonders of a more sophisticated technological colour system. The Prince of Wales expressed admiration for the process at a special London screening in 1911, and later that year the Olympia in Cardiff touted the new attraction. 'Everybody is talking about Kinemacolor, the best that can be produced in natural photographic colours', the cinema declared. The Cardiff Cinema was soon on the bandwagon, and in Swansea, the Empire snapped up exclusive rights. The snag was – the process only worked in good sunlight. It was still all the rage for a year or two with Urban achieving worldwide recognition for his extraordinary two-and-a-half hour programme of film from the Delhi Durbar processions and festivities.[66] Later, more film studios used artificial lighting; and a vapour lamp strong in showing black-and-white film but weak on red and greens proved unsuitable for Kinemacolor, and the process was dropped for features, though Urban continued to use it for newsreel, travel and educational film. He sent out road shows of the Delhi Durbar – including one to Wales – always showing a colour version after first screening the monochrome film. In fifteen months, this one film grossed more than £150,000, even if interest in the black-and-white version was soon exhausted. In 1913, Urban clinched a deal to supply colour film to Stoll's Coliseum in London and other theatres on the Stoll circuit, but the process soon fell into disuse when proprietors found it was twice as expensive as black and white, ran at twice the normal speed and caused heavy wear and tear on projectors. There was also some 'fringing' or 'ghosting' around images.[67]

Kinemacolor wound up operations in 1916, but as late as 1915–16 a separate company, Kinemacolor Ltd., offered a 1,385ft. film, **A Holiday in North Wales – from Llandudno to Caernarfon**.

The battle for audiences

The more progressive cinemas were already booking orchestras as the battle for huge potential audiences hotted up. The fifty-strong Canton Male Voice Choir accompanied film at the Olympia in Cardiff. The Park Hall, revamped as a permanent cinema in 1915, boasted the largest cinema orchestra in the city and a grand organ. One manager, at Ystrad Mynach, even made a virtue of featuring 'a purely local orchestra entirely of colliers'.[68] Cardiff Cinema, announcing the screening of the £50,000 Italian epic **Cabiria**, claimed, curiously, 'the largest British orchestra in Wales', a comment perhaps prompted by the success of Herr Rauscher's Austro-Hungarian Orchestra at the Cardiff Picture Playhouse. Cinema openings continued even in the war years and, in 1916, the Pavilion opened on the site of the former Philharmonic Hall in St Mary Street.

The pioneer permanent-cinema proprietors were flourishing by the First World War but they suffered headaches earlier in meeting the tough regulations of the 1909 Cinematograph Licensing Act (operating from 1 Jan. 1910).[69] Coutts told Swansea Town Council that the Act meant considerable expense for alterations. The bioscope box or cabinet had to be placed outside the auditorium and substantially constructed of fire-resisting materials. Coutts said placing it away from the auditorium, except at the Palace, was impossible. Mr P. C. Rowe, manager of the Swansea Empire, insisted, optimistically, that the Act was only intended to apply to 'little shop exhibitions which were a danger to the public'. In most cases local authorities compromised, allowing cinema licences if proprietors banished projection boxes and equipment to the back of the auditorium – though some cinemas still hit trouble. The Cardiff Hippodrome promised to provide a 'non-inflammable' operating box near the exit after a fire in the auditorium in 1914.

Coutts obviously solved his problems and continued to run his halls with panache, screening Pathé colour films successfully in 1911; and he even experimented with Cinephone Sound in 1910. Undeterred by its failure he apparently attempted to introduce a primitive form of 3D projection in the Picture House, Swansea, in 1914, again unsuccessfully. Coutts was not the only cavalier publicist. When David Richards of the Café Monica, Swansea, opened a bioscope hall in 1909, he boasted pictures 'interspersed with grand opera selections and suitable illustrated solos'.[70] Swansea's peak development years were 1912–14. They saw the arrival, as permanent cinemas, of the Rialto (formerly the Theatre Royal) in Wind Street, the Carlton (Oxford Street), the Electric (Union Street), the Castle, Elysium and the Shaftesbury Hall.[71]

Perhaps the most intriguing south Wales gimmick of all in these years was the opening for a spell in 1911 of a Newport base of Hale's Tours – an enterprising business set up in America to cater at once for the public's fascination with travel and the new medium. In these shows, audiences sat in railway carriages on rockers, while travelogue films were shown, providing them with the illusion of movement.[72]

Lively showman Leon Vint, the Jackson Withers group and Will Stone were already building up cinema chains in south Wales between 1910 and 1920. Vint, who ran the Picture Theatre at Llanelli by 1911 and opened the Electric Palaces at Neath (1910) and Llanelli (1912), was even ingenious enough to cater for his cosmopolitan audience of seafarers at Barry Dock in 1913/14 by advertising films on a board outside in seven different languages.[73] Vint, like John Codman, was just one pioneer to overreach himself and decline within a few years into bankruptcy, even though he had taken the precaution of buying up the film rights of potboiler novels. The Romilly at Barry, not to be outdone by this grandstanding old sweat, introduced family boxes by 1913 as the south Wales docks enjoyed unprecedented wealth, and the manager added to programmes by making topical slides of local events. Fortune again turned full circle as the cinema was gutted in a blaze in 1920.[74] Jackson Withers were licensees of the Theatre Royals at Cardiff and Merthyr, the Grand at Aberaman and proprietors of the New Theatre, Bargoed, and Will Stone's 20th Century Picture Company ran venues at Tonypandy, Dowlais and Ton Pentre.[75] Another circuit, Pitts Electric Theatres, ran ten halls in south Wales during the decade blighted by the First World War, as more and more permanent cinemas opened up in the Valleys. When the Kings Hall, Pentre, opened in 1913, the July *Bioscope* reported there were 'now seven cinemas in the Rhondda'.

Licensing authorities had to be vigilant to clamp down on 'cowboy' builders who sniffed easy pickings. At Swansea police court, a builder Willie White, was fined for breaking by-laws in erecting a Pontardulais cinema without planning permission. The prosecution said the building was 'jerry and slipshod and would prove a death trap to the audience'. The rural council had rejected White's original proposals and a revised plan, and an independent surveyor said it was 'one of the worst buildings' he had seen.[76]

But opposition to permanent cinemas was breaking down rapidly. Workmen's halls and institutes rejected the reservations about cinema from their more old-fashioned members and film performances were soon regarded as an invaluable boost to coffers. The Blaengarw Workmen's Hall club staged film shows from 1900. Regular cinema ran at Blaenafon and at Aberaman Workmen's Hall by 1910. Aberaman – known as Poole's Picture Palace at one time – was described in 1915 as the 'largest and most comfortable hall in the Aberdare valley', with 1,500 seats.[77] In 1913, miners of Nine Mile Point Colliery, Cwmfelinfach, devoted the whole top floor at their new institute to a 'cinematograph theatre' hoping it would raise more than half of the institute's total cost of £11,000 – and workers also owned and managed a 'successful' cinema venture at Ogmore Vale.[78] Miners from Mardy and Eastern collieries ran the workmen's hall at Pentre and, by the early years of the century, the 1,900-seat hall at Ferndale, Rhondda, boasted 'a new operating box of solid concrete to take two machines'.[79]

The rash of picture houses coincided with a boom in roller-skating rinks which generally proved shortlived. In some cases, cinemas replaced the rinks – in Aberystwyth, Rhyl and Wrexham, for instance. Many more halls switched from live variety to picture palaces, with success often depending on the fierce energy and flair of individuals. At Buckley in north Wales, for instance, Thomas Cropper, a printer and businessman in the Cheetham mould, not content with funding the town's choir and orchestra, built the Palace cinema in 1915.[80] Another driving force was the former film-maker Will Onda (real name Hugh Rain) who, in 1910, ran the New Hall cinema in Caernarfon and a string of Lancashire halls from his Preston base.

In west Wales, Sidney 'Daddy' White, the flamboyant showground doyen, sold his Palace cinema at Haverfordwest during the 1914–18 war, but returned with due ballyhoo in 1920 to run the permanent picture house in Ammanford.[81] Opposition to cinema in west Wales was melting more slowly, but predictably the area's Non-conformists fought a vigorous last stand, creating a *cause célèbre* in 1914 with the Pavilion, Cardigan, built just two years previously, at the eye of the storm. A sectarian and morality dispute opened a serious rift in the community, with the rumpus centred on a screening of **From the Manger to the Cross** (1912), the only six-reeler ever made by America's Kalem company, a Biblical epic shot in the Holy Land and featuring British actor Robert Hamilton-Bland as Christ.[82] It was directed by Irish-born Sidney Olcott and scripted by the actress Gene Gauntier, who played the Virgin

Mary. At that time, many clerics were against the Almighty's portrayal by any actor, and the company was obviously going where angels feared to tread in embarking on such a subject on this scale. To head off squalls, they staged a special screening for 1,000 clergy in London. Kalem's president, Frank Marion, pledged the film would not offend any doctrine or creed, and he must have been euphoric at the clerics' positive response and a notice from the *Sunday Express* reviewer who 'left the Albert Hall yesterday longing for an exhibition in all the Cathedrals, Churches and Chapels in the land'.

This scribe's apocalyptic vision had no doubt faded by 1914 after the film had been banned by various authorities, including Liverpool – and his views cut no ice in Cardigan. The minister of the Bethesda Welsh Baptist chapel there was a shareholder of the cinema and was discomforted when Pavilion manager Don Williams suggested that a special choir might be formed to accompany the film. Worse followed. Civic leaders who had paid pious lip service to the film earlier found that during its run all performances on three nights played to capacity crowds of 500 while attendances at the official local choir meetings dwindled. The cinema's own choir did well – even though some members dropped out 'bowing to pressure brought to bear on them by their friends who objected to the picture'.[83]

Splenetic church elders charged blasphemy that Muslim bit-part actors had played Christians and objected to payments to those taking part. Their anger was fuelled further by the appearance in the audience at one performance of thirty members of a nearby Catholic monastery only recently exiled from Brittany in an anti-clerical purge. The Pavilion's manager boxed clever. A popular local author was enlisted to take the heat off by reviewing the film, and duly obliged with a panegyric. But hostilities increased and Don Williams, also a local schoolmaster, left his cinema-manager's post around 1916 after claims that his film duties were incompatible with classroom responsibilities.

A rump of chapel hardliners found it impossible to stop the inexorable march of the new medium, as more wily pragmatic clerics forecast. By 1922, a residue of chapels were even competing with established cinemas for films, and south Wales exhibitors voiced concern about the increasing number of chapel cinemas in the area and pressed licensing authorities to 'impose the same conditions on chapel people as bona fide proprietors'.[84] The cinema's appeal as relatively cheap entertainment was perfectly understandable – especially in the post-war mood of the 1920s with the public relaxing after the toll of war. Prices in Cardiff by 1919 ranged from only 3*d.* in the cheapest seats at the Hippodrome, Westgate Street, and the Clifton Picture Palace, to 2*s.* 4*d.* for the best spots at the Cardiff Castle cinema and the 950-seat Canton Coliseum.[85] Lowest commercial cinema prices in Wales that year were 1½*d.* at the Windsor Kinema, Penarth, owned by Willmore Bros., and 2½*d.* at the Pavilion, Cardigan. Occasional screenings at the Parish Hall, Chirk, cost 2*d.* Venues run by workers naturally tended to be cheaper. Llanbradach colliers charged only 1½*d.* for the cheapest of 800 seats at their hall, and Abergwynfi pitmen's performance cost 3*d.* By 1920, Penrhiwceiber pitmen in Glamorgan were quoting the lowest prices in Wales – 2½*d.* including matinées.

It was small wonder that businessmen profiting from the coal and docks determined to gain a slice of the new industry's profits. When British Famous Films Cinema Pictures, producers and renters, were set up with £300,000 capital by 1920, directors included Walter Thomas Gould (chairman of Gould steamships), Albert Joseph

Solomon, another steamship director of Roath Park, and Cardiff shipowner John Evans Lewis. The prospectus claimed the time was ripe for establishing a wide-ranging British film production company, 'the ideal business combination controlling every branch from production of the films to distribution to the cinema theatres'. The new company would acquire the renting contracts and rights of six feature films already produced by an existing Famous Pictures Ltd. at the Woodlands studio, Whetstone, London (including the Welsh-set **Betta the Gypsy**).[86] Euphoria was brief. The bottom fell out of the shipping market and some owners were soon on their uppers as British industry stagnated. Gould himself went bankrupt. The British film industry was no more stable, with traumatic days ahead in the 1920s.

But British showmen and cinema proprietors, bolstered by the surfeit of Hollywood product, were largely inured to the vagaries of world market changes. At the start of the decade, warnings had been sounded about building bans preventing showmen and entrepreneurs meeting all the post-war demand. Yet by mid-decade, many cinema managers were still reaping handsome profits, despite the industrial slump, as the public appetite for Hollywood films seemed insatiable. But a chorus of anguish was swelling within the film trade, with some criticism of men like Oswald Stoll who had failed to stave off the fierce competition from the US by raising screen standards. In Wales, as elsewhere, cinemas were soon monopolized by the much more vigorous Hollywood features which caught the tempo of their times. That stranglehold was soon consolidated with the arrival of the 'talkies'.

Balcon's chief British glory was Ivor Novello – the young actor-dramatist-composer who looked beautiful enough to delight both sexes and appeared in nine Gainsborough films between 1925 and 1930.

(Geoff Brown, *Michael Balcon, The Pursuit of British Cinema*, 1984)

Only two Welshmen could safely be described as bona fide stars of the silent era – and one of those is scarcely known in his native country and forgotten even by more assiduous cineastes and critics in Britain where few of his films are available for viewing. Other redoubtable Welsh performers from the silent days, such as Edmund Gwenn and Lyn Harding, had long careers on screen, but before talkies they were mainly leads in indifferent British fodder or reliable character or support actors, and their best work was reserved for the sound era.

Ivor Novello (David Ivor Davies) (1893–1951) and the now obscure, Llanelli-born, Gareth Hughes (1894–1965) regularly, and in careers spanning over a decade, enjoyed regular leads or principle-support roles before 1928. In that year, when sound features first appeared in Britain, Novello was voted the outstanding film star (English or American) by readers of *Picturegoer*, perhaps the most influential of all fan magazines. He featured high in film-goers' polls in the twenties – despite universal apathy to the pallid British product in competition with the much more energetic, virile films from America – and made twenty-two films between 1920 and 1934, surviving a false start in Hollywood and an even more abortive second visit. Novello has been poorly served by biographers who have concentrated almost exclusively on his stage achievements. W. McQueen-Pope, in the course of his hagiography, insisted, with the arrogance born of ignorance, that we should forget the silent films altogether – as 'a thing of the past'.[1] Yet Novello was not merely a box-office success – no one seeing **I Lived With You** (or **The Rat**, for that matter) today would doubt his ability to command the screen, or the skill of his timing and the appeal of his urbane wit as both performer and writer. He was to prove the saviour of Michael Balcon's career in its faltering early days, and his screen potential seemed on the brink of fulfilment in the sound era when theatre commitments and his own prodigious stage creativity forced him to abort his film career just as the talkies promised to be his natural *métier*. It was an achievement to attract a following to British films in the 1920s, and Novello's successes should be considered against the fragile state of the 'home' industry at that time.

British film in the doldrums

Many British companies made films which depended solely on plot or even just words – they seemed to be scarcely aware of the developments in editing, composition and cinematic storytelling in the US and Europe (by the Russians and Germans, for instance,) and practised by such European exiles as Murnau, Stiller and Eisenstein in Hollywood.

Critics claimed that Oswald Stoll, the south Wales music-hall showman, had much to answer for as British film standards hit rock bottom. By 1927, many British cinema managers simply did not want to book UK features, and the home industry was in a sorry financial state as production dried up. Stoll made a fortune from music-halls, variety and his links with Moss Empires before moving to the London area where he opened his first film studio, Regent House, in Surbiton in 1918. Two years later, after the launch of his film production company, he was confident enough to switch to the former Nieuport Aviation Company premises which became Britain's biggest studio – with a main £20,000 shooting stage – at Cricklewood, north London.[2] But his rapidly declining screen fortunes thereafter were mirrored by the slump of many smaller companies unable to cope with Hollywood competition.

The UK industry slumped spectacularly between 1920 and 1927, from 145 films a year to forty-five and actually plunged to thirty-seven in 1926. The government-appointed Moyne Committee estimated that in 1927 only 5 per cent of films shown on British screens were from this country, with 85 to 90 per cent of product American. That year, to protect the home industry from foreign competition, the committee fixed a minimum percentage of British films which exhibitors and distributors could handle.[3] Stoll himself plotted a disastrous course from the beginning – he scarcely acknowledged the influence of Hollywood talent or the aesthetic appeal of the great European films. Instead he revealed a deep xenophobia. He tried to stem the tide of Hollywood success by blustering appeals to audience patriotism using the slogan, 'British films for British theatres' and this became the parrot cry of the house magazine, *Stoll Editorial News*. He accused British exhibitors of being obsessed with American movies and neglecting indigenous films, suggested they did not know what the public wanted and claimed, revealingly, that audiences never desired to see pictures of other nationalities 'at the expense of pictures of their own, wherein they can see British life and ideas in a British atmosphere and revel in the feeling there is no place like home'. A *Bioscope* editorial tartly reminded Stoll that UK films had 'in many instances' killed themselves 'with their low quality'.[4] Another slogan, 'Stoll films are dull films', became the most pervasive of its day and as the film historian Rachael Low has noted, acidly, the studio – as the biggest single UK producer – must have contributed largely to the poor reputation of British films.[5]

Stoll relied far too heavily on the appeal of existing novelists, irrespective of whether their work would adapt comfortably for the screen. He initially announced his Eminent British Authors plans and an ambitious programme based on novels or plays by 'proven' populist writers such as A. E. W. Mason, Jeffrey Farnol, Rafael Sabatini, Marie Corelli and Ethel M. Dell.[6] Managing director Jeffrey Bernerd said British films could take advantage of 'the best . . . stories in the world' and the programme would show what 'the great English [*sic*] people responds to – fine wholesome stories set in the perfect beauties of the English scenery or in appropriate settings in every part of Europe.'[7]

In hindsight, an early warning note in 1920 from the *Morning Post* drama critic seems prescient: 'Sir Oswald Stoll is the biggest brain in the show industry but his genius is financial rather than artistic and his experience of the drama desultory and somewhat discomfiting [*sic*].'[8] In 1921, the *Kine Year Book* warned there was 'still far too great a tendency to buy titles and authors' names without reference to the suitability of the material and to save money by hack scenarios and cheap methods of production'. Stoll failed to take heed: in 1921, he announced a second series of Eminent Authors. His productions included more adaptations from Dell and Mason, plus Edgar Wallace's **The Four Just Men** and also feature films to pull in the public familiar with a Stoll Sherlock Holmes series starring Eille Norwood.[9] Too many of these were unsuitable for the screen. Audiences failed to respond, Stoll could never crack the American market, and the small British market could not support an industry on the scale he envisaged. A prime example of the Stoll house style is **A Daughter of Love** (dir. Walter West, 1925), a stultifying, hilarious museum piece reeking of class and snobbery while implicitly condemning it. Just as bad is the 1921 **Hound of the Baskervilles**, which lacks all suspense or narrative drive with the director, Maurice Elvey, relying on titles and dialogue rather than images. Seeing it now you wonder how Stoll managed to make three separate series of fifteen two-reelers centred on Holmes, plus one other feature, **The Sign of Four** (1923). Stoll was not alone.

Hepworth also relied heavily on work by middlebrow authors, with disastrous results. It was precisely this kind of atrophied lack-lustre fare – and the prevailing values of the UK cinema – that London-based communist director Ralph Bond was rebelling against when he criticized the drawing-room comedies and dramas and the condescending portraits of working-class characters. He sought to make **Today We Live**, shot partly in south Wales, to redress the balance.

Novello and Carole Dempster in *The White Rose*.

Keeping home fires burning: Ivor Novello

Even in this arid climate, when British audiences turned their back on the UK cinema, Novello's pulling power was undeniable. His appeal as a theatre writer and suave, dominating presence in so many stage hits had much to do with this, but some of his films, though uneven in quality, do have much more vitality, humour and tension than the average feature of the day.In an era when so many British studios were obsessed with merely translating novels, or West End stage hits, Novello was fortunate to work for fine directors – the stylist Louis Mercanton, Hitchcock's mentor the grossly neglected Graham Cutts, and Hitch himself. Yet he never, for example, worked in features by Victor Saville, whose free-wheeling musicals and visual flair allowed Jessie Matthews to eclipse every musical performer in British film.[10] Saville's touch, choreography and editing skills and ability to liberate the camera would surely have allowed Novello's talent for musical comedy full expression. It must be remembered that in Novello's **I Lived With You** – a work of quicksilver wit and a devastating critique of class hypocrisy – Novello was working under a journeyman director, Maurice Elvey.[11] The Welsh actor was incarcerated in too many studio-bound productions which centred on class divisions already broken down, to some extent, by the First World War. Three or four of his still-viewable features remain to show us just how good Novello could be. Interestingly, he rarely appeared as a Britisher in films – his aquiline good looks, the famous 'profile', lent themselves to playing Latins or other Europeans, or ambiguous characters who were often the catalyst for change. He was best as the outsider, often fairly villainous or wanton, disrupting the status quo and unconstrained by society's conventional attitudes and morality. At times he seemed the antithesis of the 'matinée idol'. Occasionally, as in **I Lived With You**, he eroded class barriers and became the agent exorcizing social pretensions. Novello's ability and energy in mercurial roles gave a tension to some films which might have seemed vapid without him, and the trenchant humour of his best scripts supplied a resonance which few contemporaries in Britain could achieve.

With better vehicles, and a prolonged stay in Hollywood, he might conceivably have been a heart-throb to rival Valentino in the 1920s and become an assured droll or light humorist in both musical and screwball comedies at their apogee in the 1930s. Novello claimed to love seeing films but loathed making them. He was worried that he was unable to improve on his performance once the film was in the can, and by the lack of response from the camera:[12] ' . . . even if the director seems pleased he's only one man. Just compare that with a night at Drury Lane with 2,500 people showing their interest by their laughter, their silence and their deeply appreciated applause.'[13]

Gareth Hughes also frequently expressed disaffection with his films. He only admired one, **Sentimental Tommy**, and that was from a lauded stage work by J. M. Barrie. But he was certainly capable of pathos and of engaging earnestness, even intensity, on screen. Both Welshmen were not always the best judges of their own work and the films they have left behind are now ripe for re-evaluation.

Novello's success

Ivor Novello's opening career gambits, at least in Hollywood, were scarcely impressive. But his début in an American film could hardly have been made for a more celebrated director. David Wark Griffith chose him for **The White Rose**, reputedly for his resemblance to the US star Richard Barthelmess. History was to repeat itself, curiously, with Griffith when he made one of his stranger decisions by choosing another Welshman, Emlyn Williams, to play the famous fated-Chinaman role – created by Barthelmess on screen – in a remake of **Broken Blossoms** (1936).[14] Novello's performance opposite American actresses Mae Marsh and Carole Dempster in the part of a fallen, priggish minister Joseph Beaugarde in Griffith's **The White Rose** (1923) was scarcely electrifying, according to film historian and critic Iris Barry. 'Though spiritual looking, his torment is not believable,' she wrote, then added, crushingly, 'and as a hero he is a milksop.'[15] The *New York Times* reviewer was slightly kinder. 'Novello', the writer noted, was a 'handsome young man' whose clergyman wore a 'perpetual expression of gloom. Only the flicker of a smile once passes over his face. He is filled with grief for the world just before he becomes a minister and his expression of melancholia increases when he is ordained.'[16] Miss Barry's judgement seems singularly harsh, in retrospect. Surviving prints, at the Museum of Modern Art, New York, and Eastman House, Rochester, reveal that Novello played the role with some sensitivity but was hampered by the melodramatic story-line and – in the spectators' eyes – the breaks of continuity inevitable with some 200 intertitles. His theatrical gestures, far removed from his usual much more naturalistic style, were clearly demanded by Griffith in a work of moralistic fervour to bring the theme of guilt and atonement into sharper relief.

The plot is contrived and melodramatic. Beaugarde, of an aristocratic family, has been devoted since childhood to Marie Carrington (Dempster), another blueblood, but on a walking holiday after finishing his seminary training he seduces and impregnates orphan girl Bessie Williams, known as Teazie, a waitress at a riverside inn. Beaugarde takes up his calling and confesses his guilt to Marie. Teazie, thrown out of her lodgings with her baby, unable to find work, traipses around at night before arriving at the Carringtons' home where she collapses gravely ill. Beaugarde is summoned as the local cleric to provide comfort, recognizes her and confesses his love. In a romantic coda, we discover the girl is now recovering slowly with Beaugarde

Novello renouncing his vows as the errant cleric of D. W. Griffith's *The White Rose*.

in doting attendance (having renounced the church following an impassioned confession from the pulpit of his – generalized – 'sins'). Marie meanwhile will, we surmise, marry former butcher's boy John White 'from poor white trash' (according to a Griffith title) who has long been besotted 'from a distance' but has now become wealthy and is presumably no longer beyond the social pale.

The Dickensian travails of Teazie, the purplish intertitles and the plot contrivances are standard devices of the period and typical not merely of Griffith who presents his character with some warmth and understanding. But the director's hand can be seen more obviously in the recurrent use of heavy romantic symbolism surrounding the white rose which Beaugarde picks for Teazie as they linger beside the river's edge prior to the seduction; in the irises used for key close-ups; and in the racism which betrays Griffith's Southern conservatism and which manifests itself chiefly in the treatment of Apollo, Beaugarde's black servant, as a figure of fun.

Novello scarcely conveys the impression that his clergyman is 'as innocent of the roaring world as a child', as one title insists, but he is good in the wooing scenes and handles the character's piety and hypocrisy (and Griffith's didactic style) with reasonable assurance. The characters – as is usual with the director – must pay heavily for their sins, Beaugarde in quitting the church and Teazie for being corrupted by flighty hotel staff and allowing her generosity of spirit to lead to unwise flirtations.

The audience at the New York première occasionally applauded the beauty of the scenes, shot mainly in the bayous of Louisiana with much effective use of slow pans.

The wage sheet at the D. W. Griffith studio at Mamaroneck for the week ending 12 June 1923. It shows that Ivor Novello received $500 a week, Mae Marsh his co-star $400, and Griffith's legendary regular cameraman G. W. 'Billy' Bitzer $50.

NAME	OCCUPATION	RATE	TOTAL TIME DAYS REGULAR	TOTAL TIME HOURS OVERTIME	ACCT. NO.	CHECK NO.	AMOUNT	TOTAL AMOUNT	PROD.
A L Grey	Gen Mgr	150.			Exp104	28153	150.00		
A L Grey	" "	350.			"	28154	350.00	c	
Geo W Bitzer	Camera	50.			U5	28155	45.00	c	
Geo W Bitzer	"	50.			"	28156	5.00	c	
Robert B Austin	Cashier	65.			MOS	28157	65.00	c	
F Weil	Steno	35.			"	28158	55.00	c	
Helen Draper	Operator	22.			"	28159	22.00	c	
Jack Sherman	Off. Boy	18.			"	28160	18.00	c	
E. Maitland	Steno.	30.			"	28161	30.00	c	
O'Kane Conwell	Designer	100.			U5	28162	100.00	c	
Neil Hamilton	Actor	125.			"	28163	125.00	c	
John Powers	Publicity	150.			Exp104	28164	150.00	c	
A Pesce	Musician	250.			" "	28165	250.00		
Mae Marsh	Actress	400.			U5	28166	400.00		
Jos. Burke	Actor	200/			"	28167	200.00		
Ivor Novello	"	500.			"	28168	500.00	c	
F Rollins	Wardrobe	30.			"	28169	30.00	c	
John Matheson	Stills	18.			"	28170	18.00	c	
Marie Foy	Actress	175.			"	28171	175.00	c	
Jane Thomas	"	300.			"	28172	300.00	c	
Marie Foy	"	175.	1(12/30)		"	28173	25.00	c	
Jane Thomas	"	300.	1(12.30)		"	28174	42.86	c	
Chas. Kirk	Art Dir				.	28176	25.00	*	
B. Turner	Elec	100.			WS	28177	100.00	c	

* Increase in Salary

The *New York Daily News* was more impressed with Novello as a fine actor, and Paul Gallico also lauded his talents.[17] Novello apparently received a contract guaranteeing him $500 a week for his first Griffith film, with options on further films with the director – and steady salary increases rising to $1,000 a week. But, by the end of 1923, relationships had broken down and Novello was threatening to sue for $11,200, claiming an option had been taken for two films after **The White Rose** – films paying $700 a week, each movie offering a minimum of eight weeks' salary. Novello claimed that Griffith had broken his contract. The Welshman thought the first extra movie would be an American Revolutionary biopic, 'Nathan Hale', but this project was dropped, and the studios thought Novello unsuitable for a lead role in the next film Griffith completed – **America** made in 1924. Griffith sought to 'farm out' the actor to other studios but Novello was opposed to this and wished to work in America only for Griffith. He turned down an offer to star in Elmer Clifton's **The Warrens of Virginia**, and a settlement was apparently reached in Novello's favour after Griffith's studio at Mamaroneck went bankrupt in 1925.[18]

By the time of his first US visit Novello – born in Cowbridge Road, Cardiff, to the singing teacher and choir leader Madame Clara Novello Davies – had built up a rapport with audiences through his earlier features **Gypsy Passion** (the US title of his début film, Louis Mercanton's **Call of the Blood**), and **The Bohemian Girl** (1922). Novello had left Wales for London in his teens but his embryonic talent for composing dialogue and lyrics and projecting himself on stage was nurtured in his Cardiff days when he won a National Eisteddfod prize as a boy tenor.[19] At sixteen, he had starred with Thelma Kaye (the future Mrs Ronald Colman) in a Cardiff Amateur Dramatic Society musical, and after some fame as a composer with 'Keep the Home Fires Burning' (1915), he wrote a trio of stage successes. By his twenties he was a national celebrity. But Mercanton, best known as the director of Sarah Bernhardt in the silent screen version of **Queen Elizabeth** in 1911, took a gamble when choosing Novello – yet to play a major stage role – reputedly on the basis of a photograph.[20] **Call of the Blood** (**L'Appel du Sang**, 1920) released by Stoll, remains one of the actor's best films – a courageous work of impressive assurance.[21] It has a toughness one does not associate with Stoll – or readily with the image of Novello. The latter is notably unsympathetic as Maurice Delaney, a novelist, whose 'generous heart' leads him to betray his wife (Phyllis Neilson-Terry) and form a deadly liaison with a fisherman's daughter. Mercanton clearly shielded the inexperienced Novello as much as Hitchcock was to do in **The Lodger**, but the actor was notably ill at ease in opening sequences when his natural poise seemed to desert him. It may be the lack of composure which forced Mercanton into improvising – he repeatedly employs silhouettes in the most expressive setpieces including, for example, the character's moonlit boat ride with his new love, a cavemouth kiss and a clandestine hotel meeting during a memorable fairground scene and firework display. It is noticeable that Mercanton is much less reticent in allowing Neilson-Terry her share of anguished close-ups.[22] The chiaroscuro lighting, the fine cutting and framing and intelligent use of the rocky Sicilian landscape distinguished the film, even though the denouement with the mercenary Salvatore ambushing Delaney, then casting his lifeless body onto the rocks, is strangely muffled. But Novello was established even here as an actor who could appear predatory and dangerous – and he was to remain at his most effective when his characters were ambiguous or insouciant or when suggesting a feckless nature and an inability or unwillingness to be easily assimilated into society.

Yet Novello's early screen period was not particularly distinguished.[23] **The Bohemian Girl** (dir. Harley Knoles) was well shot and was moderately successful with audiences but it appears now as ludicrous hokum with the actor as a Polish refugee, merely a rather amorous foil to Gladys Cooper's aristocratic Bohemian girl. The audience associated Novello only with escapism and were probably oblivious to the film's murky values – racist and nationalist. They warmed to the female stars and were disarmed by C. Aubrey Smith's relaxed, authoritative playing as Novello's itinerant mentor, and Constance Collier's termagant gypsy queen, much larger than life. After more stage successes and a screen hit in Harley Knoles's **Carnival** (1921), Novello was paid £350 a week by 1923, the year he took the (matinée idol) role of Bonnie Prince Charlie, for Gaumont (dir. C. C. Calvert). It was populist hogwash with James Harding dismissing it as 'untainted by any relationship with history'. Douglas Fairbanks jun. later played the role with the same conspicuous lack of success. Novello enjoyed a wider range in the stagey and tediously protracted **The Man Without Desire** (1923), a curious blend of melodrama, sci-fi, medical sophistry and romantic adventure which foreshadowed the eighties and nineties screen vogue for time travel. However, the film was directed limply by Adrian Brunel, who was later 'slated' to make **The Rat** but replaced by Cutts. Novello played Count Vittorio, an impetuous eighteenth-century Lothario whose body is preserved by a scientist after he feigns suicide when his married lover kills herself. Revived 200 years later, the count mistakes a young girl for his erstwhile paramour and, on discovering the truth, finds all life savourless – becoming literally 'a man without desire'. Caroline (C. A.) Lejeune described the work as a 'testimonial to native production and worth all the British film weeks put together' – a strange assessment of a dull feature shot partly in Italian and German studios. She was not alone in praising the film; the *Kinematograph Weekly* writer thought Novello's acting a revelation and *The Times* said Novello had 'done nothing better for the films'.[24]

The Rat and *The Lodger*

> It's only my profile they like, yet every butcher boy in Naples has one twice as good.

> (Novello, after viewing rushes of his box-office hit, **The Rat**, cited in Michael Balcon, *A Lifetime of Films*, 1969)

Novello's fertile period with Balcon and Gainsborough consolidated his screen career. Balcon described him later as 'by far the most important star' of the studio's Islington days and he developed the kind of protective affection for his protégé that he later bestowed on **Proud Valley** director, Pen Tennyson.[25]

Novello's link with Balcon began with **The Rat** (1925), a hugely entertaining camp trifle from a stage hit written by Novello and Constance Collier under the combined pseudonym David L'Estrange.[26] The film is notable, apart from Novello's mercurial performance, for director Graham Cutts's tracking and dolly shots (certainly among the first in a British feature) plus pans and even zooms; and also for the extraordinary baroque décor of the main Parisian setting, the White Coffin Club, the haunt of Novello's capricious character, a dance club 'Apache' (gigolo).[27] The kitsch settings suggest the modishness of those around him and the direction gives the film a distinction the script, co-written by Cutts, scarcely merits overall. Novello plays a brittle egoist who loves women's attentions but has a flippant attitude to romance – 'love is a game without rules,' he tells an acquaintance in a sequel. But, despite his philandering, he loves his wife, Odile, and fatally wounds a gangster who tries to molest her. Then he agonizes and tries to prevent her accepting blame for the murder. Yet after affecting disdain for the aristocrat Zellie de Charmet (Isabelle Jeans) in amusing scenes which satirize romantic conventions, he falls under her spell, especially when she provides him with a false alibi. Novello's switches of mood at the whim of a wildly uneven script are hard to swallow but there is no gainsaying the energy, magnetism and confidence of the actor by this stage in his career, and the film – which cost £18,000 and made £80,000 – has disarming humour and vitality. This film alone gave Gainsborough the financial ballast it needed and spawned two financially successful sequels, **Triumph of the Rat** (1926) with Novello again partnering Jeans as Zellie (by then his mistress), and **Return of the Rat** (1929), plus a 1937 sound remake of the original with Anton Walbrook in the Novello role, and Ruth Chatterton. **The Rat** films undoubtedly consolidated Balcon's career during a shaky period.

Novello's other films for Gainsborough were by no means as rewarding, and Balcon describes the company's first AGM as a far from happy event. His opinions provide more insight into the faults of the British cinema. 'Simply to examine the films in progress at the time of the formation of the new public company is sadly illuminating in retrospect,' Balcon wrote. They were **Downhill**, **The Vortex** (both 1927), and **The Constant Nymph** (1928). 'It seems all too obvious we were not over-exercising our intellectual power in our choice of subjects. All three were stage plays, two were skilfully constructed for the theatre – and almost all relied exclusively on verbal images rather than visual action,' said Balcon. 'Both **The Vortex** and **The Constant Nymph** were demonstrably unsuitable for adaptation to a medium without the power of speech.'[28]

The Vortex is an overheated cautionary tale about aristocratic decadence centred on a mother's damaging flirtations and her excesses, including drug taking. Coward's humour emphasized the destructive potential in the age disparity between a mother, Florence Lancaster, and her young lover, while hinting that economic differences were just as harmful in creating dependencies militating against loving relationships. The mother's vanities are regularly punctured by Novello as the son, who is seen not merely as a wet blanket but a hypocrite. He is

Novello in the title role of *The Rat*.

interested in his mother dropping her new young lover mainly because he sees the interloper as a possible rival in his own pursuit of a female house guest. It was an unrewarding role in a film hopelessly bogged down in long, if frequently witty, titles seeking to reproduce the flavour of Coward's amusing sallies and badinage and Novello seemed merely petulant in the role played by Coward on stage. We savour the lines but wince at the attempts to bring them to life. Problems also stemmed from the film company's decision to bowdlerize the text, as the director, Adrian Brunel, stressed.[29]

Hitchcock's **Downhill** was worse – a dismal, dated picaresque tale of a young man's plummeting fortunes after he assumes guilt (a little too altruistically) for a friend accused of seducing a waitress. Even Hitch could hardly distract the audience from the crass dialogue and it is more than possible that the director, more intent on refining his technical skills, took a perverse delight in the more stupefying inanities. When Roddy Berwick (Novello) is expelled from school by the head for his immoral behaviour, he can only stutter: 'Does that mean, sir, I shall not be able to play for the old boys?' Balcon still savoured the line years later and it became a catchphrase at the Islington studio. Novello is required to look first hangdog then faintly dissolute and dishevelled as he tumbles from grace with his banishment first from the family, then his own marital home. The director makes good use of the studio to evoke low-life locales as Roddy is 'flung to the rats of Marseilles', and later introduces a panoply of dissolves, tracks and hand-held shots of the prodigal's return to Britain in delirium. Novello, little more than a pawn in this bravura technical display, could do nothing with the thankless role.

Ivor Novello in
Hitchcock's *The Lodger*.

The teaming with Hitchcock bore more fruit in **The Lodger** (1926), hailed by the *Bioscope* as 'perhaps the finest British production ever made'. The director, perhaps influenced by **Downhill**'s failure, was forced to cast Novello at Balcon's insistence and had to dilute the ending in deference to the star's growing popularity.[30] For by then Novello had few box-office peers in the British cinema. In 1926 he topped a British screen popularity poll run by the national *Daily News*, and in 1928, he was voted most popular British or American star by readers of *Picturegoer*. Yet Hitchcock's film needed some re-editing after disappointing previews, before gaining favour with audiences.

Novello was certainly more comfortable and suitably enigmatic as **The Lodger**, despite his tendency to overplay his hand in more melodramatic scenes. The lighting effects and subtle use of shadow often masked the actor or lent ambivalence to his actions. The most celebrated setpiece – the moment when this mysterious tenant can be seen through a glass ceiling as he paces the room above – is the kind of flourish Hitchcock could not resist. The Novello character's aloofness, even arrogance, helps keep the audience in thrall to Hitchcock's many variations and embellishments on the Edna May Lowndes script. Near the climax, Novello, pursued by the mob, is pinned against railings in the screen foreground, arms outstretched in the crucifixion position – an image which probably lingered in the audience's minds longer than any in the actor's later Balcon films, **The Gallant Hussar** (dir. Geza von Bolvary, 1928), made in Germany, and his last silent film, **A South Sea Bubble** (dir. T. Hays Hunter and released 1928).[31] The actor's first sound film, **Symphony in Two Flats** (dir. V. Gareth Gundrey, 1930), another transplant of a stage hit, made no impression on either critics or public, though he did win a Metro contract soon afterwards and *Bioscope*, closely monitoring the speaking voices of the silent stars, gave Novello a vote of confidence for his 'ready and natural charm', and for revealing 'a delightful sense of humour in lighter moments'.[32]

The Welshman's return to Hollywood proved chastening. Asked to adapt his theatre play, *The Truth Game*, which ran six months in London, he beavered away for six months and 'eight treatments later' all that remained in the company's first draft treatment were the characters' names and even they were changed on the first day of production.[33] *The Truth Game* was finally directed by Jack Conway and released in 1932 as **But the Flesh is Weak**, starring Robert Montgomery, despite Novello angling for the main role. It seems inconceivable that MGM, in these heady days under Irving Thalberg, could not recognize Novello's worth as a performer, even given their crowded star roster. Novello made only one film (**Once a Lady**, 1931) during the second Hollywood sojourn – on loan to Paramount – and spent much of his time on routine writing assignments, with the playwright Frederick Lonsdale on **Lovers Courageous** (starring Montgomery) – and also working on **Mata Hari** and even on **Tarzan the Ape Man** (with its much-mocked and much-misquoted Tarzan/Jane exchange, though the film's female star Maureen O'Sullivan thought Novello's dialogue 'witty and charming').[34]

A fine madness

Filmed in 1933, [**I Lived With You**] is one of the British cinema's undiscovered treasures . . . It was directed competently and unobtrusively by Maurice Elvey but is wholly the creation of Ivor Novello, who wrote the stage play, stars in the film and gathered round him several members of the original cast to recreate their roles on celluloid.

(Jeffrey Richards, *The Age of the Dream Palace*, 1984, p.311)

The Hollywood stay was frustrating but hardly fruitless. During idle periods in and out of the Los Angeles studio Novello wrote his best stage play, according to James Agate. Transferred to the screen by Twickenham Films, **I Lived With You** proved a bracing antidote to many contemporary flavourless British confections.[35] Novello's impoverished Russian prince, Felix, discovered on a bench in the Hampton Court maze by a working-class girl, Gladys (Ursula Jeans), proceeds to expose the cant and dissensions within her family. The film is a hilarious parody of bourgeois aspirations, consumer values and crippling class consciousness. The delusions of the two daughters and their mother are graphically reflected, together with the infidelities of a comic-strip caricature of a hangdog sedentary husband in a house of women. This male worm turns, thanks to the encouragement of Novello's waggish interloper and pursues, with embarrassing results, a flighty young gold-digger.

Jeffrey Richards, alone of British film critics, has given due praise and weight to this film, comparing it with Pasolini's **Theorem** (1968) in which Terence Stamp plays the outsider who wrecks a family's complacency and parades their double standards. Elvey's film could, more profitably, be compared with that superb Renoir feature **Boudu Saved from Drowning** (1932), where Michel Simon, as the slothful tramp befriended by a bourgeois couple, proceeds to question the morality of his hosts' actions and motives despite his own boorish behaviour and base ingratitude.[36]

Novello made a sound version of **The Lodger** (1932), this time directed for Balcon at Gaumont-British by Maurice Elvey, and appeared in another relatively unsympathetic role in Anatole Litvak's **Sleeping Car** (1933) with Madeleine Carroll. The actor again appeared as the outsider upsetting the status quo, a sinuous train attendant flirting with a gallimaufry of women passengers on a journey from London to Budapest. The film, with sumptuous settings and fine camerawork (by Günther Kampf and Glen MacWilliams) influenced by German Expressionism, offered Novello great scope for the same kind of effortless, if superficial, charm and sense of mischief he brought to **I Lived With You**.

Unfortunately, Novello was too prolific to pursue two careers simultaneously, and increasingly stage commitments were forcing him to reject tailor-made screen roles. In the 1930s, Twickenham producer Julius Hagen made strenuous efforts to persuade

Opposite:

Exotic Novello . . . in Anatole Litvak's *Sleeping Car.*

him to make a film every three years and even offered a role in **Spy of Napoleon** (1936) which, ironically, went to Richard Barthelmess.[37] The Welshman made only one more film, Basil Dean's **Autumn Crocus** (released 1934), from Dodie Smith's stage play, set (like **The Constant Nymph**) in the Tyrol. Novello's flirtatious hotel keeper gives Fay Compton's middle-aged schoolmistress transient happiness on vacation. The film, with second unit direction by Carol Reed, now looks painfully twee. Compton's little-girl voice is an irritation, especially set against the hectoring jingoism of her xenophobic female companion, Edith (Muriel Aked). The slim material lacked the febrile good humour of Novello's own screenplays. Novello himself is too mannered and ingratiating, poor backdrops strain credibility and, despite odd moments of poignancy and genuine feeling, the film languishes.

Novello provided only the music when the screen version of his huge 1934 Drury Lane stage hit, **Glamorous Night** (1937), was made at Elstree by Brian Desmond Hurst with Barry McKay, Mary Ellis and south Wales tenor and former miner Trefor Jones as Miss Ellis's singing partner, in a Ruritanian-style romance. Dennis Price starred in the Technicolor version of his **The Dancing Years** (dir. Harold French, 1949) and Herbert Wilcox directed **King's Rhapsody**, which flopped, with Errol Flynn and Anna Neagle in the leads, in 1955. These three films, for all their patent shortcomings, at least allowed audiences to savour much of Novello's most creative music. The Welshman *was* due to appear in **The Rat** sound remake in 1937 but could not cram it into his schedule.[38] Twice Novello had three productions running on the London stage simultaneously; in 1933, when he was forced to abandon the screen; and 1949 when he had five productions touring Britain – *Perchance to Dream, The Dancing Years, We Proudly Present, King's Rhapsody* and *Careless Rapture*.[39] It seems a pity that Novello did not stay around to thrive in the increasingly sophisticated films of the thirties, as Hitchcock, Victor Saville and Carol Reed all found their feet to give the British cinema credibility. But at least he did leave behind a clutch of works of undeniable interest and Balcon was able to build on his box-office pull to achieve later impressive successes for MGM British, such as **The Citadel**, and his cherishable canon of Ealing films, including **Proud Valley** and **A Run For Your Money**.

A 'juvenile lead'

Gareth Hughes was not in Novello's class. Yet he succeeded where Novello failed – in establishing himself in California. At his peak, he earned $2,000 a week; he made forty films between 1919 and 1932, was regularly employed in Hollywood in its buoyant first decade, and worked for such major companies as MGM, Fox, Famous Players Lasky and First National – frequently in tandem with major female stars of the era. But his career was in decline when he suddenly washed his hands of cinema altogether and returned to the theatre. Finally, in a bizarre career twist worthy of any risible Hollywood 'melo', he became a priest working among the Indians. The reasons for Hughes's obscurity are not hard to fathom – quite apart from the inaccessibility today of most of his work.

He was rarely in lavish productions – and in his bigger-budget films, **The Enemies of Women** (1923, directed by Alan Crosland, later to make **The Jazz Singer**) and in Goldwyn's **The Christian** (dir. Maurice Tourneur, 1923), he was well down the cast. Often he supported 'second string' stars in small production units within the major companies. And he scarcely ever worked for directors who have since been championed by critics devoted to the *auteur* theory, though he did appear in features by much respected 'second or third pantheon directors' such as W. S. (Woody) Van Dyke, Maurice Tourneur, Herbert Brenon, John M. Stahl, William Beaudine and Rowland V. Lee.[40]

More crucially, Hughes was only 5ft. 5ins. tall and 8½ stone at the peak of his career. His youthful and frail appearance meant he was consigned to male *ingénu* or shallow glamour-boy roles.[41] He lacked the authority to move on to more challenging adult parts; and it is significant that for a *Photoplay* questionnaire in 1924 he described his type of role as 'juvenile lead'. By that time, he had already been in Hollywood five or six years. Hughes was also in many films culled from insubstantial, ephemeral literary work – many were spun out, often to their detriment, from short stories in the *Saturday Evening Post* as the insatiable studios devoured contemporary material. The authors were not all nonentities, and a Scott Fitzgerald story – 'Head and Shoulders' – inspired **A Chorus Girl's Romance** (dir. William C. Dowlan, 1920) which earned Hughes a long-term Metro contract.[42]

Significantly, Novello and Hughes, who both bowed out of film early, had one thing in common. To them, perhaps, the cinema had still not come of age when they left it, and they both much preferred stage to film work.

A forgotten talent

Gareth Hughes's disenchantment with the screen might be understandable when one considers that he often appeared in low-budget, under-publicized independent work; he only ever worked with one major director whose films are still revived – Raoul Walsh – and that was in the film-maker's first feature. Yet he often garnered good reviews in slight vehicles, and starred for some of the leading directors of the twenties. Walsh's **Every Mother's Son** (1919) was the first of several films featuring the actor as a soldier caught up in the First World War. Hughes played, for him, a typical role – a doting mother's boy with pacifist leanings who joins up only after witnessing suffering at first hand in helping to care for wounded survivors from a ship sunk by a German U-boat near his home. He was often the vacillating or diffident small-town youth driven by circumstances into heroism, as in the comedy **A Chorus Girl's Romance**, when his wimpish bookworm turns, after receiving a thrashing, and becomes first an athlete, then a trapeze artist. In **Enemies of Women**, a meandering and almost interminable 11-reel melodrama adapted from a Blanco-Ibanez novel, he played a sybaritic musician and member of Lionel Barrymore's aristocratic and misogynistic circle, who gambles heavily and remains on the fringe of orgiastic revels but is finally overcome with remorse. Mindful of his group's unsavoury reputation, he joins up in the First World War where he is blinded. When the Hughes character first turns up on leave in his soldier's outfit he is greeted by sneers and guffaws from Barrymore's unrepentant hedonist: 'Now I'm convinced that in every man there is a soldier.'

This was not the stuff of which real macho heroes were made and Hughes, though expressive and energetic enough on screen when required, never quite shed an aura of boyish subservience. In George D. Baker's **Don't Write Letters** (1922), for example, he played Bobby Jenks, who lies outrageously in his letters – again from the First World War trenches. The missives exaggerate Jenks's muscular development and he is so embarrassed after his proxy marriage proposal is accepted that on his return he masquerades as the letter-writer's brother.[43]

Hughes's rather ascetic appearance meant he was often cast as the artist, synonymous almost with 'weakling' in the new Hollywood. He was a dramatist in Philip Rosen's **The Lure of Youth** (1921), for instance, an orchestra leader in Wilfred Noy's **The Midnight Girl** (1925), and a designer of ladies' gowns in **Life's Darn Funny** (dir. Dallas M. Fitzgerald, 1921).[44] Yet he often won the girl, and the transparent integrity of many of his fictional characters obviously enabled him to pass muster with studios and audiences. Hughes's films epitomize the ludicrous plotting, lurid melodramas and laughable and crass moralizing of so much screen entertainment hell-bent on winning a mass audience yet desperate to strike the right moral poses. Hughes spent his early career on stage, most often in unambitious touring productions, until he went to America and, in his first significant screen role, played the brother of the star, Clara Kimball Young, in Albert Parker's 1919 feature **Eyes of Youth**.[45] He was mainly confined to doling out advice to Young, who agonizes over whether to 'marry a wealthy man, become an opera singer or settle for marrying the man she loves'. Young's character, Gina Ashley, is allowed by a mystic to gaze into a crystal ball enabling her to see her future life and make the correct choice, and in one of these projected 'lives' the protective brother (Hughes) is so distraught that he shoots the opera entrepreneur who has made Gina his mistress and dishonoured the family. Among Gina's supposed manipulators in this big-budget production was 'Rudolpho Valentino', who attracted critics' attention and (although on screen less than five minutes in two scenes) was billed as the film's star when it was re-released after the ageing Kimball Young's supposed screen charms faded.

Publicity photo for Hollywood silent-movie star, Llanelli-born Gareth Hughes.

Hughes, flitting between Metro and Famous Players Lasky in his early days, must have been buoyed by the effusions of the respected American actress, Mrs Maddern Fiske, who told the acerbic wit and critic, Alexander Woolcott – the model for **The Man Who Came To Dinner** – that she could believe acting was 'an immortal art when watching the glow of a performance by Gareth Hughes'.[46] The actor was, for a short time, a leading light for The Welsh Players theatre group, which also included Edmund Gwenn, and as early as 1915 mooted the possibility of appearing in a group of films 'of Welsh customs' for a New York company. These projects never materialized but Hughes made nine films in his eighteen months in Hollywood from 1918, including **Isle of Conquest** (dir. Edward José) for the Norma Talmadge Production company.[47] And he appeared for producer Adolph Zukor in Famous Players Lasky's 1919 version of **Mrs Wiggs of the Cabbage Patch** as the lone adult male among the brood of Mrs Wiggs, a cheerful matriarch in a 'poor settlement'.[48] Hughes, starring opposite well-known silent heroine Marguerite Clark, tended to be overshadowed by other characters. The film, directed by Hugh Ford, was weighed down by more than 110 intertitles.

Another romantic lead performance for Famous Players – as Tommy Sandys in **Sentimental Tommy** (dir. John S. Robertson, 1921) – proved Hughes's biggest career breakthrough after a loan-out from Metro, and it earned his best reviews.[49] The performance was convincing enough to persuade Robertson that Hughes would be a perfect screen Peter Pan, but the director – originally 'slated' for the film – was

Gareth Hughes in his
favourite role as J. M.
Barrie's Sentimental
Tommy.

F 229-51

replaced on the Barrie classic by Herbert Brenon.[49] In **Sentimental Tommy**, Hughes
played a romancer with a literary bent who befriends the twelve-year-old Grizel,
daughter of a 'painted lady' in the village of Thrums. Later returning to the area, he
proposes impetuously. Grizel (May McAvoy), is not impressed by his conviction and
turns him down but pines and becomes progressively unhinged as Tommy pursues a
middle-aged aristocrat (Virginia Valli). Inevitably the former friends are reconciled for
the fade-out.

Hughes sometimes landed the girl even if his characters had a dubious or notorious
past, as in **The Hunch** (dir. George D. Baker, 1921), and **Men of the Night** (dir.
Albert Rogell, 1926).[50] In Rogell's film, for example, Hughes played a reformed safe-
robber. But, as in certain Novello films, matches were often made on the basis of class
rather than dramatic logic, as in **Ginger** (dir. Burton George, 1919), where the
working-class newsboy (a childhood friend of the heroine) is killed off conveniently
in the last reel to allow Ginger (Violet Palmer) to marry a judge's son, Bobby
Trowbridge (Hughes). In the 1919 film, **The Red Viper**, which featured a young

'Jack' (John) Gilbert below Hughes in the cast list, the Welshman was more interestingly cast as a newsboy himself, David Belkov of 'foreign descent' in 'New York's crucible, The East Side'.[51] He joins an anarchist group after witnessing the eviction of a poor family and, as usual, redemption is only possible after suffering, in this case a near-fatal shot from the anarchist leader. The same atonement idea is the climax of a 1928 Hughes film, **Comrades** (dir. Cliff Wheeler), when he plays a coward who takes the glory for his brother's valorous deeds and can only redeem himself with the ultimate sacrifice – shielding his kin from a bullet.

In **And the Children Pay** (1918), Hughes was cast as a genuine villain in a film with a plot faintly similar to that of Griffith's **The White Rose**.[52] The synopsis suggests a scenario of hilarious improbabilities. Hughes plays a college boy, Billy, who makes his girlfriend drunk and pregnant, then refuses to marry her. The child is born blind and crippled, but that's only the beginning . . . The father, recognized by his former girlfriend (now a prostitute) while visiting a brothel, is ordered to pay child support – but the baby dies in court. Billy is denounced from the pulpit only to be taken ill himself and expire in his mother's arms. The film is interesting, now, as an anti-VD movie. A title announcing that the child was born 'with a crippled body' and a final shot of Billy in an advanced state of physical decay 'suggest this was originally a disease propaganda story', noted the *Bioscope* reviewer (13 May 1920). It appeared to be a 'drastically censored Venereal disease film. The propaganda has for the most part been eliminated, leaving only a framework of rather lurid and pointless melodrama,' added the writer, who found the film morbid and 'somewhat unpleasant', and complained that frequent Biblical quotations impeded 'whatever dramatic interest it possesses'.

Actually, the film had a fascinating genesis and Hughes was directly responsible for certain changes. The actor was engaged to appear in the film as early as late 1915 but the Veritas Photo Company hit financial problems and the movie was never completed. In 1918 the production was bought by a Chicago firm who wanted to distribute it under the title **Girls Don't Tell** and 'starring Gareth Hughes'. The Welshman, in an apparent fit of puritanism, instructed lawyers to prepare an injunction, in a bid to change the film title or remove his name from the billing. So the film became **And The Children Pay**.

The plot was only slightly more implausible than the extraordinary script of **Woman Under Oath** (1919), which revealed much about male-dominated Hollywood thinking in the days when Dorothy Arzner was the only female director. In John M. Stahl's film, Hughes played a shipping clerk accused of murder after he is discovered with a gun, standing over the corpse. The film opens with a subtitle asking if women are temperamentally suited to be jurors and then loads the dice when the central character, Grace Norton (Florence Reed), the first female juror in New York, finally admits she is the killer in the case she is judging. At least Miss Norton has the decency to protest Hughes's innocence, deadlocking the vote during an all-night session with eleven to one in favour of finding him guilty.[53]

Hughes's most interesting role in these early days seems to have been the incorrigible fantasist and liar he played in Metro's **The Garments of Truth** (dir. George D. Baker, 1921). Here he invents an elaborate story of saving the mayor's niece, after a dam burst supposedly threatens his village. Medical treatment reverses his 'illness' and he insists on telling the truth, however unpalatable. The grocery firm which employs him is less than amused when he acquaints customers with the staleness of the products; then he wrecks a real estate scheme which could have brought the town prosperity.

Hughes's later links with Famous Players brought him into more exalted company in two Pola Negri vehicles directed by **Ivanhoe** director, Herbert Brenon – **The Spanish Dancer** (1923), and **Shadows of Paris** (1924). In the later film, as a prisoner (Lazarillo), he enjoys a bravura scene when his ingenuity helps rescue from execution one of the film's stars, Antonio Moreno. Both films also featured Adolph Menjou, and Wallace Beery was an unlikely King Philip IV in **The Spanish Dancer**.[54] These were Hughes's only excursions into the more glamorous productions, but he was prolific throughout the decade. He played a bewildering range of roles: from a bohemian 'advocate of free love' in Greenwich Village in Fox's **Woman, Woman!** (dir. Kenean Buel, 1920), to a captured German soldier, Lieut. Fritz von Lang (an obvious in-joke, reference to director Fritz Lang) in **Top Sergeant Mulligan** (dir. James P. Hogan, 1928), and a boy hobo opposite cowboy star William Desmond in a 'Western romance', **The Sunset Trail** (dir. Ernst Laemmle, 1924). In George D. Baker's **Little Eva Ascends** (1922), Hughes even spent much of the film dressed as a little girl – playing an actor performing as the character, Little Eva, in a version of *Uncle Tom's Cabin* staged by his screen mother's repertory company.

Generally, Hughes seemed more at ease as homely helpmate and lover or flawed innocent than as wordly man-about-town. In Frank Mattison's 1927 silent **Better Days** he is initially playing a self-confident journalist and wide boy but winds up as an almost anonymous second fiddle to Dorothy Devore's spunky heroine as the pair tangle with racetrack swindlers. Only one Hughes role pointed towards the direction and preoccupations of the more vibrant, energetic, socially conscious cinema of the 1930s. In George Fitzmaurice's **Kick In** (1923), he played a pocket hood who plans one last big heist to give his baby a good start in life and is shot by a policeman for his pains. May McAvoy, Hughes's sweetheart in **Sentimental Tommy**, was his lover again.[55]

Hughes's monk, Brother Paul, in Goldwyn's **The Christian** (directed by Maurice Tourneur from the Hall Caine potboiler) hinted unwittingly at the direction of his later life.[56] It also placed him in a singularly strong cast, headed by Richard Dix, Mae Busch and Phyllis Haver. Most of his appearances from then on were for smaller companies. He even shared top billing with a dog, Champion, in **Silent Sentinel** (dir. Alvin J. Neitz), a silent made as late as 1929, and he scarcely ventured into talkies – despite advertising in casting directories in the early sound years.[57]

By 1930 the soggy sentimentality of the kind of films in which Hughes thrived in his early Hollywood days had been largely left behind. It was still a surprise when the Welshman, who became a naturalized American by the mid-twenties, retired from the screen. More eyebrows were raised in the late thirties when he became a missionary on the Nevada reservation for the Paiute Indians. In later life he shamelessly acted out the gospels in the pulpit. There had been hints earlier of a spiritual and religious interest. In a letter in a personal Hughes file in New York, the actor refers to his love of collecting old bibles, and back in 1922 he was making curious pronouncements hinting at this future.[58] 'I love jewels that suggest resplendent altar cloths and stained glass windows. One day I shall fit up one of my rooms as a cloister,' he told an interviewer.[59] But to another journalist, after his Hollywood 'defection', he was perhaps even more revealing: 'I am a ham, I do my soul more good than I do the Indians, maybe. I am a ham, for Christ's sake.'[60]

It has still to be established just how much the arrival of sound influenced Hughes's decision to retire from the screen, but he had no great affection for film and there seems no reason to suspect he was just another 'casualty' of the talkies. The story of his career and later life was deemed interesting enough for RKO in the 1950s to moot a biopic, which remained on the drawing board.[61]

Before Hughes and Novello made their mark, the Welsh had made little impact in studio features. Abortive attempts were made in the twenties to promote another Welsh star. The opera singer Gwilym Evans featured in the Napoleonic melodrama **A Royal Divorce** (1923), a version of the old stage warhorse popular with Cardiff audiences for at least the previous two decades. Evans was cast – opposite Ruth Chatterton – for no better reason, apparently, than his supposed likeness to the emperor. His performance cut no ice with the film's writer, Walter Summers.[62] 'He was dreadful. The French laughed at him. They thought he was a terrific joke as Napoleon,' said Summers. 'He was a singer really. He wasn't a good actor but he did play in opera – that was his only acting experience as far as I know.'[63] The film, an 'epic' of some 11,000 ft., was made by British producer G. B. Samuelson and director Alexander Butler, and with a reasonably distinguished cast including Gerald Ames, Gertrude McCoy and Lillian Hall-Davis.[64] Made only two years before Abel Gance's seminal **Napoleon**, it flopped at the box office and attracted only derision from critics. It was not surprising that Evans, who appeared in the operetta *Castles in the Air* in 1911 on that historic London Scala bill which first showcased Kinemacolor, was never heard of in the cinema world again.

Ring favourites – and Queenie

A more colourful candidate for film stardom was the deceptively frail-looking Rhondda boxer Jimmy Wilde, the world flyweight champion. Wilde was undoubtedly a charismatic figure who earned pay and 'nobbins' in his youth in the same fairgrounds which nurtured the Welsh cinema pioneers. Superlatives and nicknames clustered around Wilde and his lethal punching – the Tylorstown Terror, the Mighty Atom and the Ghost with a Hammer in his Hand. A. E. Coleby, the British director and producer whose three-hour, 17-reel **The Prodigal Son** (1923) was dismissed as soporific and gave Stoll's company a bad name, decided to capitalize on the enthusiasm shown for fighters in documentaries or 'actuality' films. In 1917 after featuring the famous Bombardier Billy Wells in the fictional **Kent the Fighting Man**, Coleby presented Wilde in another feature, the **Pitboy's Romance**, for his Tiger company. Wilde and Tommy Noble played boxing and whippet-racing rivals. Wilde as the collier, Jimmy Davies, beat the screen villain's protégé (Noble) in the ring and foiled a planned betting coup. The narrative provided Jimmy with a childhood sweetheart Mifanwy Griffiths, and sometimes, in defending her, the hero was forced to 'lay out opponents'. Coleby left little to chance, featuring no fewer than five *rounds* from the crucial fight, and allowing Wilde to feature in final close-up dressed, patriotically, in khaki to keep the wartime audiences happy. The film does not appear to have done that well. It was actually sold off by auction to distributors, The Film Bureau, for £2,800, after bidding started at £1,000, and was 'not as brisk as expected'. Little evidence exists of screenings, though it played the Picture House, Leeds, after a trade show in the city. The *Bioscope*'s reviewer, at least, thought Wilde's 'boyish naturalness' suited the role and that 'he could not have done better if he had years of training for the film'.[65] But despite all the contemporary fight fervour Wilde never

Cardiff's Queenie Thomas starring opposite Basil Rathbone in the silent British version of *School for Scandal.*

starred in another fictional work. He later entered the film business, first as a renter in Cardiff then as a cinema proprietor. Wilde only appeared in one other fiction feature, in a cameo in **Excuse My Glove** (1936) starring the boxer Len Harvey, directed by Redd Davis for independent producer Joe Rock and released by Associated British. The Welsh heavyweight Tommy Farr also featured in a small role – the year before his unforgettable world title fight against Joe Louis – and fighters Billy Wells and Gunner Moir also played cameos. James J. Corbett and Jess Willard both featured in popular transatlantic serials shown in Wales; Georges Carpentier and Jack Dempsey also appeared in fictional movies. Other British sports stars also capitalized on their fame in the silent era with fictional screen roles, notably jockey Steve Donoghue in a 1926 series, and the same year the legendary Wales soccer winger Billy Meredith played himself (the lead role) in **The Ball of Fortune** (dir. Hugh Croise), a movie also featuring Mabel Poulton, and about a footballer who marries a magistrate's daughter.[66]

Efforts were also made to promote Queenie Thomas (b. 1898 or 1900) – billed locally as 'Cardiff's own film star' and educated in the city – as a significant new British talent.[67] She made at least twenty films plus two series of shorts between 1915 and 1928, often in leading roles. Working mainly for producer Bertram Phillips, she was described as his 'pupil and protégé'. She worked initially with the Clapham-based Holmfirth Company which swallowed up the more famous screen outfit Bamforth's in 1915 and, later, principally for Phillips's own BP Films. Her career, interrupted for two to three years by marriage, was spent in modestly budgeted films which failed to stir critics or the box office and, by the sound era, she was virtually forgotten. Thomas's material varied from the melodramatic – again with the almost inevitable emphasis on gypsy lore – notably **A Little Child Shall Lead Them** (1919) and **Meg o' the Woods** (1918), to material illustrating popular songs or more traditional material.[68] Predictably, some of the films had a strong moral strain. **Rock of Ages** (1919), for example, described as 'the first of her own photoplays', was billed as 'a fascinating and pictorial story from the old family hymn' when advertised at Cardiff's Castle cinema in the first week of 1920. Thomas played an Irish girl, Biddy Kinsella, who 'converts an atheist by posing for a church mural'.[69] The film's publicists, clearly imbued with some of Stoll's jingoism, touted the work as 'an all-British masterpiece which can compete with any American productions'.[70]

Thomas occasionally worked for bigger companies such as Butchers (who normally distributed the Phillips films) or G. B. Samuelson, but rarely featured in films as apparently ambitious as Phillips's own 1923 version of **A School for Scandal** (6,350ft.), when she played Lady Teazle, with Basil Rathbone as Joseph Surface, in a production showcased in a special British Film Week.[71]

Across the divide

Other Welsh performers destined to become leads or important support players straddled the sound and silent eras.

Edmund Gwenn (1875–1959) enjoyed a forty-year screen career, even though he only embarked on films in his early forties after launching his stage career in the year the cinema first began in Britain. Gwenn was born in Glamorgan, according to most film histories, but recent research suggests he may even have been born in Wandsworth, of Welsh parents. He entered cinema in 1916 with **The Real Thing at Last**, but his most memorable silent role was in the 1920 version of Galsworthy's **The Skin Game** (dir. B. Doxat-Pratt), as a bluff *nouveau riche* industrialist upsetting the equilibrium of a complacent landowning family. Gwenn succeeded in amusing, however outrageous his behaviour, and his character won over the audience to some extent with his energy and capacity for delivering uncomfortable home truths. Gwenn, who generally specialized in more benign and avuncular roles, repeated the characterization in Hitchcock's 1931 sound version.[72]

Another actor with strong Welsh connections to play starring roles spanning sound and silent eras was John Longden (1900–71). Described in some contemporary publicity and filmographies as 'a former South Wales miner', he made his mark as the policeman boyfriend of Hitchcock's heroine, Anny Ondra, in the first British sound film **Blackmail** (1929). He also played in Hitch's **Juno and the Paycock** (1929) and **Young and Innocent** (1937). Longden, born in the West Indies, was a staple of British films in the thirties, often as a dogged lawman, an officer or suitor. He also directed at Elstree **Come Into My Parlour** (1932). His risibly slow metronomic delivery as a ship's officer in a frequently seen sequence from the German director E. A. Dupont's early (1929), Elstree-made, sound film, **Atlantic**, showed just how difficult some experienced performers found it to time lines and deliver them smoothly where they could be picked up by concealed microphones.

E. E. (Edward) Clive (b. Monmouth 1879, d. 1940) switched to films from the stage in his fifties. He specialized in butler roles, or as the quintessential staid or stolid Britisher. Clive came late to Hollywood but his career embraced, remarkably enough, more than seventy films in the last seven or eight years of his life and he appeared, often in cameos, in some of the more memorable features of the period 1933–1940, including **The Bride of Frankenstein, Captain Blood, Camille, Hound of the Baskervilles** and the Hitchcock thriller **Foreign Correspondent**.

Lyn Harding (b. Newport 1867, d. 1952), much better known in Wales as a stage actor, made his screen début in Stoll's **The Barton Mystery** (1920), and earned good reviews playing a 'humbug and charlatan' who solves the murder of a rogue. He attracted more attention as Henry VIII, opposite Marion Davies's unlikely Mary Tudor, in the comedy **When Knighthood Was In Flower** (1921) and later starred with her in **Yolanda** for MGM in 1924.[73] Gwenn, Harding and Clive were to deliver their most subtle and persuasive performances in the thirties and forties when a clutch of fellow countrymen, most notably Ray Milland, in Hollywood, and Emlyn Williams, Mervyn Johns, Naunton Wayne and Roger Livesey, mainly in Britain, also featured regularly in rewarding and significant roles.

Despite the increasing impact of Welsh stars it would be some years after the first talkies before any fiction films emerged which dealt seriously with working-class life in Wales, or focused on the country in any meaningful way and took account of the previous few tumultuous decades.

By 1925 the depressed state of the British industry was causing general concern . . . it was felt that from the point of view of British culture and ideals it was unwise to allow the United States to dominate the cinemas of this country . . . cinematograph audiences then were made up of the most impressionable sections of the community, and it was felt to be of the utmost importance for our prestige, for our trade, and, it was even asserted, for our morals that they should see at least some proportion of British films.

(Board of Trade evidence to Moyne Committee on the film industry, 1936)

The post-war cinema boom of the twenties and thirties coincided, paradoxically, with a slump in Britain's fortunes. The euphoria which had seized the south Wales coal-owners just before the onset of war – reflected in Powell Duffryn's forecast of a four and a half million tons annual output for the next 100 years – was soon dispelled as markets were lost, particularly as Russia and South America found alternative sources of supply. The south Wales coalfield, which had achieved record tonnage in 1913, was in sharp, inexorable decline after 1924. Production halved between 1923 and 1943; 241 pits open in the early twenties shut down by 1926; the Cardiff and Barry ports which, pre-1914, had led the world, declined sadly while production companies were struggling and trying to cut their losses by the late twenties. But the public, however impecunious, found in the cinemas respite from unpalatable realities outside. The cinemas, in response pegged prices and found a ready audience for the cheap seats, and programmes changed two or three times a week. Welsh audiences were as enthusiastic as any, soaking up thrillers, Westerns and romantic melos featuring stars such as Mary Pickford, her husband Douglas Fairbanks sen., and Lillian Gish, prior to sound. They responded increasingly to spectacle in the films of D. W. Griffith and De Mille and to the comics, Chaplin, Keaton and Harold Lloyd who by the early twenties, had outgrown their origins in one- and two-reelers, and were starring in features. The talkies added a new dimension; the gangster genre, with its pithy, hardboiled dialogue, came into its own as the antithesis of the saccharine weepies and romances of the Pickford era. In the wake of Al Jolson's unprecedented talkie success, musicals became part of the staple diet, creating a new breed of screen entertainer, often capitalizing on Broadway successes as the jazz age with its ubiquitous flappers gathered momentum. The 1920s, ushered in on a wave of optimism in cinemas in Wales, more than justified most of the high hopes of showmen and entrepreneurs.

It was the most glamorous yet mercurial decade in screen history. Both film and the new picture palaces came of age and the crowds flocked to the grand new venues, often with baroque façades, art deco interiors, fountains and even the kind of sweeping staircases which you somehow associate with the opulent *fin de siècle* cinema and mellifluous camera movements of the great stylist, Max Ophuls. Customers were beguiled by the sumptuous decor, serenaded by café orchestras, wooed by spruce flunkeys and blitzed with a surfeit of mirrors and kitsch. The foyers often resembled the cluttered sets of those early talkies in which resourceful sound men hid microphones in every second aspidistra. The cinema became for many in Wales a second home, a refuge from the industrial and social strife outside. Even as the General Strike and other disputes took their toll of some cinemas – forcing staff cuts and even cinema closures – overall attendances remained buoyant. Forecast demands for 2,000 extra British cinemas proved over-optimistic in the financial climate but around 1,000 UK cinemas were built between 1924 and 1932, and many venues were given a facelift to boost their capacity.

But there was another side to the twenties. The paucity of ideas and talent in the British cinema was exposed more than ever by the arrival of racy American drama, the witty idiomatic repartee of gangsters and their molls – and, in the early sound years, by the first American musicals. UK studios were obsessed with merely culling films from novels, often retaining self-consciously literary dialogue. As Welsh artist Augustus John (a member of the London-based Film Society) complained: 'The filmwriters, never out of their shirtsleeves, are day and night engaged in boiling down more and more novels, reducing them to the pap-like consistency considered acceptable to the edented jaws and tired stomachs of the crowd.'[1]

Many Welsh exhibitors who had drooled over long queues early in the 1920s and sighed with relief when the worst excesses of the Entertainment Tax were curbed, found themselves struggling to survive when sound came along and expensive talkie equipment had to be installed to enable them to compete. Miners' institute cinemas, seeing commercial cinemas around them gambling on sound, had to opt for talkies to maintain their revenue. Cinemas and institutes which tried to cut costs and install cheap equipment often had to strip it out again and find alternatives, while business slumped during the time they were not wired for sound. Some cinemas closed never to re-open, and for many these watershed years became a nightmare. Cinemas such as the Cardiff Imperial, unable to change quickly, tried to make a virtue of their apparent shortcomings, presenting themselves as specialist houses and homes of silent film where the 'pure art' of cinema could still be seen. This was not quite the naïve gambit it seemed as many audiences were frankly disillusioned with early sound films on inferior equipment, directed by refugees from Broadway who had no idea of framing, composition, cinematic movement or fluent editing skills. Previously fleet stage actors suddenly seemed to have concrete boots and to boom out their lines while trying to locate the nearest sound mike concealed in a convenient pot-plant on set. Sound also put paid to the cinema orchestra, some around 30-strong, a fixture at town-centre and many Valleys cinemas from the First World War period. Thousands of musicians lost their livelihoods. Yet, by the early thirties most cinemas, after weathering the transition, were buoyant again and had embarked on a spree which was to last – for some – until the early 1950s. There were 321 cinemas in Wales in 1934 – a figure never equalled – and from the thirties the sound quality was certainly good enough to do justice to newly developing film genres, the musicals and 'screwball' comedies.

Bolt-holes and cheap seats

Ominous rumblings could be heard amidst the prevailing optimism as the twenties began. Strong fears were expressed that the demand for housing after the war, particularly after Lloyd George's famous 'homes fit for heroes to live in' speech, would blight hopes of a major building expansion in cinemas. The Entertainment Tax, introduced to fill government coffers during the Great War, was increasingly burdensome to cinemas for a few years, especially to small exhibitors often hiring public halls two and three times a week.[2] In 1920, a 2*d.* tax was charged on all 4*d.* to 7*d.* seats, 1*d.* on 2½–4*d.* seats, and up to 2*s.* on those between 10*s.* 6*d.* and 15*s.*[3] Housing *did* take priority in Wales in the 1920s and there was a pronounced building upsurge between 1925 and 1928, before a sharp decline in the 1930s, but box-office figures in Wales continued to rise as audiences sought escapist entertainment.[4]

Not all post-war material shown was simple escapism. In 1919 Cardiff actress Joan Vivian Rees was at the centre of one of the worst censorship rows in the British cinema up to that time. She starred in the G. B. Samuelson company's **Damaged Goods** as Edith Wray, an orphaned country girl who is raped by her employer, M. Rouvenal (James Lindsay), in a big-city fashion house and turns to prostitution after placing her illegitimate child in a convent. She fails to find work after being banished by her employers and she passes on venereal disease to a client, George Dupont (Campbell Gullan), who in turn infects his lover who then has an illegitimate baby. The film was a British remake of an American feature of 1915, and Rees had played the same role in a stage version in 1917. Yet the censors refused to pass Alexander

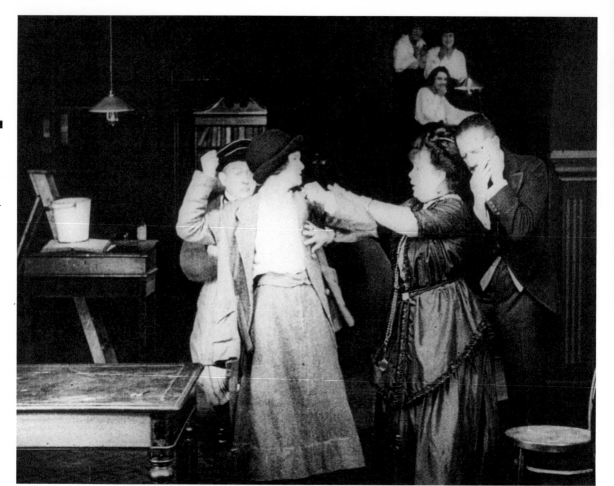

Butler's 1919 UK feature, even though it was supposedly less graphic than the American version and had a screen doctor relaying the dangers through captions and highly melodramatic intertitles, expressly forbidding George from marrying until completely cured: 'There is not only your wife. There are her children, your children whom you may contaminate too. It is the future of the race I am defending.' George takes the advice of a quack instead, marries, his baby sickens, his wife leaves him and he is forced to seek the GP's help to salvage his life.

Cardiff's Joan Rees (left), as the VD victim dismissed from her job, strikes back in the 1919 British film *Damaged Goods.*

The censors had no power to influence local authorities, but the Cinema Exhibitors' Association tried to persuade councils not to show it. The film, 'an all-British production', apparently received only isolated public screenings but it certainly had an agent in Wales. The rise in VD after 1914 and the government's worries over its effect on the war effort probably led Samuelsons to delay the movie after advice from the BBFC in 1917 that it could hardly be accepted in its stage form. The same kind of worries over morals were expressed, somewhat more eccentrically, by Merthyr councillor and temperance man W. Lewis, who pressed unsuccessfully for cinema closures at 9 p.m. 'in view of the fevers and moral conditions of our young men'. He opined that cinemas were more dangerous than 'public houses'.[5]

Another VD film, **The Dangers of Ignorance**, an educational, non-fiction work, was screened in Cardiff in 1928 at the Imperial and Queen's cinemas in Queen Street and, at both venues, men and women were segregated, men attending at 4.30 and 8.30 p.m., women at 2.30 and 6.30 p.m. This Wardour film – billed as 'a powerful sermon dealing with the social evil which is undermining the physical and mental health of the nation' – was approved by the Central Council for Health Education. Its run was extended when it played to large crowds at the Imperial in March.[6]

Whatever their fare, the cinemas were forced to gear prices to the pockets of working-class audiences hit by declining income, especially in south Wales where miners' wages slumped and there were long periods of unemployment. Attendances naturally reflected the vagaries of the coalfield, but generally the upward trend in audiences and in cinema building increased as crowds demanded escapism. Occasionally there were problems within the film industry itself, such as the 1920 projectionists' strike. In 1924 there was some general relief with a remission on the Entertainment Tax – wiped out altogether for seats up to 6*d.* in price and cut for those up to 1*s.* 3*d.*[7] Reductions carried the rider that all the cuts must be passed on to customers.[8] There was optimism in the south Wales cinema trade that year, with attendances in most areas holding up. A spot in the cheap seats enabled even the humblest viewer to 'live out' their fantasies as Hollywood came into its own. By 1928, it was still possible for adults to see films for as little as 5*d.* in many Cardiff cinemas, with top prices 2*s.* at venues like the Capitol, Queen's and Park Hall. Many cinemas in mining and rural areas of Wales still had 3*d.* seats. Generous allowances were obviously made for the grim situation in south Wales, as prices contrasted sharply with London, where charges as early as 1920 ranged from 21*s.* to 10*s.* 6*d.* at the plusher venues.

Glitter – and gloom

> Never before has anything come along which is so adapted to the needs of the common people . . . as the cinema industry. Few there are, even in the poorest colliery districts, in the slums of the cities, who cannot afford the 5*d.* to see the greatest artists of the world. Nothing else can bring Matheson Lang, Henry Ainley, Charlie Chaplin, Pola Negri and Ivor Novello into the tiny villages of the country.

(Geo. Roberts, Porth exhibitor, cited in *Bioscope*, 3 June 1924)

The silent cinema reached its creative zenith from the early twenties on, with directors and studios compensating for lack of dialogue with emphasis on spectacular sets, flamboyant editing, bravura camera flourishes, and subtle lighting effects and movement. Hollywood gained much from the experience of stylish European *émigrés* such as Murnau, Lubitsch and von Sternberg. The Welsh also responded to the epics of D. W. Griffith. According to one authoritative account, 750 people were somehow crammed into a performance of his **Way Down East** at Buckley's Picture Palace, north Wales (official capacity 350), and they were regaled with an ice-breaking machine used to simulate the sounds of Lilian Gish's river ordeal.[9]

Orchestras were one outward symbol of an individual cinema's status, but the picture palaces also vied with each other in opulence, many aping the interiors of Hollywood films. Some developed laughable pretensions; the Plaza in North Road, Cardiff, for example, built in 1928, was even billed as 'La Plaza' during its first year, when Cardiff boasted twenty cinemas serving a 200,000 population. Managements competed with each other on advertising, and on 'stunts' to pull in customers. When a movie called **The False Alarm** played in Cardiff in 1924 the Pavilion cinema management arranged for a fire alarm to be smashed in a busy main street, and the fire brigade to turn out.

Cardiff's Capitol cinema, opened in 1921 by Tilneys' Kinemas Ltd., claimed to be the 'greatest theatre in the principality' and was certainly the largest – with 3,158 seats, impressively wide staircases and a suspended balcony. Attractions there included Lionel Falkman's orchestra or combo (variously billed as 'Augmented Orchestra', 'Syncopated Five' and 'Jazzmanians'), a café, terrace and soda fountain.[10] The local press was suitably smitten, describing it as 'magnificent'. Its splendours 'couldn't be exaggerated', purred one critic. Three years in the building, the Capitol opened on Christmas Eve with Tilneys declaring they wanted to make a special feature of British films. They began with the popular UK comedy, **Nothing Else Matters**, featuring (in film débuts) Mabel Poulton, the Cockney co-star of Novello films, and Betty Balfour, the British favourite who was present at several south Wales cinema openings in the thirties, and directed by veteran George Pearson.[11] It was accompanied by an edition of Pathé's light-hearted magazine, **Eve's Film Review**. But the Capitol's chauvinism soon gave way to expediency with the cinema booking the latest US blockbusters.

Certain British film personalities remained in demand for prestige cinema events. Ivy Duke and Guy Newall attended the Cardiff Press Ball in 1920 (but significantly, part of the evening was devoted to impersonations of the Hollywood stars Mary Pickford, Mae Marsh, Norma Talmadge and Nazimova). Alma Taylor, John Stuart and Maurice Elvey were all invited to attend a cinema Carnival at Cardiff's City Hall in January 1928, and the following month Chrissie White, appearing with Henry Edwards at the New Theatre, was a guest at a city gala ball. British stars Betty Balfour and Mary Odette contributed brief syndicated articles to the local press.[12] But the bulk of box-office hits in the twenties were American, and there always seemed to be a surfeit of good films around. The Cardiff Plaza opened as it meant to go on with **Camille**, starring Norma Talmadge and Gilbert Roland. Another city cinema, the redbrick Regent 'Super Cinema' in Ely, one of a chain owned by the Splott (Cardiff) Company – 'the largest entertainers of the Cardiff public' – featured, on its first bill, Novello in the British film **The Constant Nymph**, with Howard Hawks's US feature **A Girl in Every Port** (starring the screen Lulu, Louise Brooks) as the support. Three days later the cinema screened Murnau's classic, **Sunrise**, with Janet Gaynor and George O'Brien, accompanied by Archie Roberts's 'high class orchestra'.[13]

As the decade wore on, there was a growing sense of well-being and buoyancy in film exhibition. Even after the General Strike took heavy toll in some towns and villages, net UK business was satisfactory and building developments were 'unparalleled in the history of the trade'. In London and the provinces there was a scramble for new sites and 'the latest kinemas had never been approached in luxury or capacity.' Existing theatres had been 'enlarged to super dimensions', the *Kinematograph Yearbook* claimed, and 'seating capacity must have increased by hundreds of thousands.'[14] In 1928, an accountant estimated Cardiff cinema attendances at between four and five million a year.[15] Even the ailing British film industry, after the slump in the early 1920s, began later in the decade to benefit from the government-imposed quota for a 5 per cent (minimum) showing of British-made films, though *Kine Weekly* editor S. G. Rayment was premature in 1928 in stating that indigenous production had enjoyed 'a welcome revival'. Certain groups like the South Wales Cinema Co. made great play of programming their British films conspicuously, to meet quota requirements. When they screened a Fay Compton feature at Swansea's Carlton cinema in 1928 they expressed the view that 'the British people will be surprised to see how far British films have progressed in photography, production and direction.' Yet, with a few exceptions, British cinema production remained *creatively* moribund until the mid-thirties.[16]

Cardiff's Capital Cinema does justice to D. W. Griffith in 1922.

Some south Wales cinema owners could not share the general prosperity buoyancy. Their business was hit as local collieries closed down and major industries declined. The docks area in Barry, in particular, was affected as coal exports and docks trade suffered. Alfred Rees of the Picture Palace, Cadoxton, went bankrupt, claiming business had declined and citing his 'lack of capital and heavy working expenses'.[17] The same fate befell Maurice Meskin of the Park Cinema, Aberdare, in 1928, when he blamed 'excessive overheads and trade depression following the 1926 General Strike'. David Thomas Williams of the Picture Palace, Cwmaman, Aberdare, also went through the hoop, attributing his failure to 'the trade depression caused by stoppage of the local collieries and forced discontinuance of business at the Kinema'.[18]

More dramatic was the demise of the flamboyant Leon Vint, that consummate showman, then of Long Acre, London, who faced bankruptcy proceedings and had public liabilities of £15,000 by 1927.[19] Vint had leased his first hall at Kettering in 1906, then acquired a string of other venues, including the Barry Docks cinema, operating them as Leon Vint Organizations. In 1911 he formed Leon Vint Theatres, taking over as going concerns seven venues in England and Wales, including cinemas at Neath, Llanelli and Aberavon. He blamed his collapse on a slump in the theatre and cinema business, depreciation of his shares in the two companies, living beyond his income, high interest on money borrowed, betting losses and 'heavy expenses in entertaining and travelling to obtain business'. Another noted Valleys man was Rowland Williams, a former actor and opera singer who had teamed up with William Coutts to form a Cardiff Film Exchange and Club, a focal point for exhibitors and distributors, in 1920. He filed for bankruptcy after suffering losses from leasing cinemas including the Rialto at Whitchurch, Cardiff, the Palace (Pengam) and

Victory (Abertridwr). The two or three years around the miners' lock-out of 1926 were undoubtedly bleak for many – one Welsh showman estimated that a quarter of Wales's 260 cinemas in 1928 were closed down – but most rallied with the talkies.

The talkie revolution

SECTION 2

Talkies
and the
Picture
Palace Boom

The trouble for others lay ahead – *with* sound. Cinemas such as the Palace at Pembroke Dock failed to survive the combination of the Depression and the extra bills impending for sound equipment.[20] But most bigger cinemas were into the fray quickly with talkies, following the worldwide success of Warner's system and the company's part-talkie, **The Jazz Singer** (dir. Alan Crosland, 1927), and Al Jolson's unforgettable gambit, 'You ain't heard nothin' yet.'[21] Queen's cinema, Cardiff – the former Cardiff Cinema Theatre in Queen Street – took the honours in 1928 as the first in Wales to book the film and boast sound. It was in the Capitol by February 1929 when the Queen's was already advertising, as an imminent attraction, 'the first up-to-date talkie programme in Wales', Jolson's full-sound all-talkie **The Singing Fool** (dir. Lloyd Bacon, 1928), and claimed to have equipped the cinema for sound 'at great expense'. Large crowds besieged the building, with long queues for each of the four performances a day, and thrilled to Jolson's tearjerking number 'Sonny Boy'.[22]

The Singing Fool ran to May, then moved on to Cardiff's Pavilion (the former Philharmonic Hall and Panopticon) the following month. This venue advertised RCA sound equipment – 'the first of its kind in Britain'.[23] The Queen's followed the Jolson sensation with Pauline Frederick in Warner's sound feature **On Trial**. Then came **The Home Towners**, which like **The Jazz Singer**, offered 'Warner Bros. Vitaphone' sound, and Raoul Walsh's 'Cisco Kid' Western **In Old Arizona**, billed as '**The Covered Waggon** of the talkies' and 'the first talkie production of the great outdoors'.[24] In September 1929 the Queen's booked the film which above all clinched the appeal of sound in the British public's affections – the first UK part-talkie, Hitchcock's ingenious **Blackmail** 'including John Longden, the Welsh actor [*sic*] and Hannah Jones, a former opera singer from Swansea, touring with Adelina Patti'.[25] The film company had no use for niceties, advertising the film in the *South Wales Echo* erroneously as a 'real British 100 per cent talking picture'. The *Echo* reviewer, appreciating the spartan dialogue, noted, with obvious relief, that 'not a single unnecessary sound has torn the fabric of the picture.'[26]

The Park Hall cinema had previously offered Novello's first sound film **A South Sea Bubble** and the Capitol, after **The Jazz Singer**, played, as their first all-talkie, Paramount's **The Doctor's Secret** with Ruth Chatterton and H. B. Warner.[27] A Capitol advert for another Chatterton film, **The Dummy**, announced: 'The whole cast speaks'; and for a time managers and studios seemed to forget vision altogether. 'Listen to Mary Brian, John Loder, James Kirkwood, Lloyd Hamilton, in the all-talking thriller, **Black Waters**,' the Capitol trumpeted. A local critic noted: 'The voices came out clear and distinct.'[28]

Swansea also took to the talkies, when the Jolson films arrived months after local cinema managers first experimented with sound. The Castle cinema screened from February 1929 a series of British Phototone Sound shorts – produced by Ludwig Blattner at the former Neptune Studios, Elstree – featuring revue artists such as Teddy Brown and Albert Sandler. The Mumbles Cinema booked these shorts, the Blattner Pocket Novelties, the same month, announcing they would be a 'permanent feature'.[29]

An early report of an opera extract – an aria from Puccini's *Tosca* – praised 'the accurate synchronization' and claimed: 'This system needs only a little more volume to bring it to perfection.'[30] But there were rivals, most notably the De Forest Phonofilms using the invention of Dr Lee De Forest. This series of shorts, produced at Clapham and then Wembley, included the nine-minute 'talking sketch' **The Fire Brigade**, starring the inimitable droll Robb Wilton in one of his best-known stage routines. When the film was shown at the Regent, Mumbles, it received 'unprecedented applause' according to the *South Wales Daily Post*. 'The success of British talking pictures is evidently assured,' the reporter enthused. 'The film boasted such clear enunciation that no joke or quip was missed.'[31]

Producer-director Bertram Phillips, alive to every possibility, released a series of shorts under the British Sound Film Productions banner. One featured Bransby Williams reading from Dickens's *Bleak House*. The Regent, Mumbles, and the Elysium screened BSF films for months, some at the Elysium featuring Moore Marriott, later one-third of the Will Hay comedy team.[32] By this time the Albert Hall, Swansea, had stolen everyone's thunder screening **The Jazz Singer** from 1 April 1929, with vocal quartet the Radoms engaged to sing incidental numbers. Within the month it was booked at the Mumbles Cinema – 'Hear the Synagogue Choir!' the advert ran. Not to be outdone, the Elysium screened **Wings**, the Oscar-winning aerial action movie with Charles 'Buddy' Rogers and Gary Cooper, made back in 1927 but now released with sound effects only – 'The finest sound effects picture yet shown in Swansea.'

Many initial doubts about talkies had now been dispelled. In May 1929 South Wales Cinemas Ltd. announced plans to install Western Electric equipment – 'without which the big American talkies cannot be exhibited' – and to screen sound films permanently from July, installing new bioscope boxes costing £500. British Talking Picture apparatus was being installed at the same company's Carlton and Picture House, in Swansea, that month.[33] At Mumbles, the Regent management still felt obliged to remind patrons they were showing real talking pictures, 'NB: not synchronized with gramophone records', and announced they had booked a sound version of the FA Cup Final, 'regardless of cost', so that people could hear 'the roar of 100,000 voices . . . and the community singing'.[34]

By mid-year cinemas were acutely aware of the kudos and profits available from sound films. The Elysium finally pipped the Albert Hall in screening the town's first all-talkie **The Donovan Affair**, and also advertised the first 'all-talkie cartoon' **The Jazz Stringer**. The Albert Hall had spent £7,000 in equipping for permanent sound, and the synchronization and clarity of Warner's Vitaphone system used for **The Singing Fool** were excellent, according to the local press. The movie was reported to be a phenomenal success and 30,000 had seen the film by its third week.[35] In October, the Tivoli (Mumbles) opened – as a talkie cinema using Western Electric sound and pegging its lowest seat prices at 5*d*.[36]

Almost from the first mooting of sound as a commercial proposition, politicians were anxious to capitalize on the new possibilities and capture audiences – with the well-organized Conservative Party machine in the vanguard. In 1928 Stanley Baldwin was 'phonofilmed' and the *South Wales Daily Post* hoped this would 'give stimulus' to a movement for keeping the talking picture in UK cinemas 'confined as far as possible to British manufacturers, British players and British speakers'. British talking-picture equipment was the greatest factor in 'the preservation of pure English from the inroads of American jargon'. In April 1929, the press announced that twelve touring talkie vans were showing films for the Tory Party. By July, the Albert Hall, Swansea, was screening Ramsay MacDonald in a film 'introducing members of the Cabinet', and Lloyd George had featured in a Movietone talkie, shot in his orchard, the previous October.[37]

As the demand for sound cinema became deafening, actors' careers hung on initial reports of their voice quality. The south Wales press cited an anonymous agency reporter who, no doubt responding to favourable publicity from the studio machine, noted that John Gilbert, later the most celebrated alleged victim of these 'quality tests', had taken to talking pictures 'like the proverbial duck to water'.[38] Many early cheap and poor sound systems were rough enough to put more than Gilbert out of business. The most foolproof systems were beyond the pockets of some small exhibitors, and certain south Wales cinema men were naturally unwilling or unable to see the advantages or implications of the sound breakthrough. One unnamed Cardiff theatre manager, after a trade show of

The Palace Cinema, Chepstow, decked out in 1937 for the Coronation of King George VI. Gary Cooper vies for equal billing.

Universal's 1929 **Showboat**, said: 'I came out laughing. Now if that's the best they can do, I should worry.'[39] The columnist noted there was only 15 per cent dialogue. 'All-talkies' proved a different proposition, though some cinemas retained loyalty to silents and certain managers were laggards in realizing the increased box office potential and in coming to terms with the greatest change since the cinema's birth. Cardiff's Central cinema, which advertised British Phototone sound shorts months earlier, did not introduce talkies until June 1930. In March 1930 the city's Imperial was still, with a kind of perverse pride, billing itself as 'the home of silent cinema', while the Globe at Penylan/Roath in the same month claimed it would be a talking cinema shortly. It re-opened in July with the screening of its first sound feature, **The Singing Fool**, almost coinciding with the first anniversary of the Queen's breakthrough with the same film.[40] Cardiff's Plaza cinema also converted to sound as late as September or October, 1930.[41] The *South Wales Echo* noted that it cost £1,000 to £3,000 to wire for sound with the best-known systems – the *Kine Yearbook* estimated normal costs at between £2,000 and £5,000, but, whatever the price, the bulk of exhibitors felt they could not afford to be too tardy in providing apparatus especially when nearby cinemas *with* sound were syphoning off the audiences and reporting record business.[42] The Castle Supercinema at Merthyr, which screened **The Singing Fool** in July 1929, announced spending of £7,000 on talkie apparatus and even then the manager took no chances, providing 'an excerpt from *Pagliacci*' by the famous Italian tenor,

Martinelli.[43] Among front-runners in wiring for talkies was the new cinema at Hopkinstown which advertised itself, perhaps improbably, as the UK's first cinema to install the British Talking Pictures system when it opened in April 1929.[44]

The fate of thousands of musicians was writ large by late 1929. Scores of cinema orchestras and conductors and notable individual artists had enjoyed their heyday in the last decade of silents – in Cardiff alone, Lionel Falkman at the Capitol, Garforth Mortimer at the Park Hall, Lindsay Priest at the Queen's, organist Tom Jenkins at the Plaza and Percy Wheeler at the Olympia, for example. In Swansea, musicians thrown out of work formed a dance orchestra 'to ease hardship' and the local paper felt 'it was the duty of the public to express its resentment' about the fate of the cinema musicians. Mortimer, who played in a 29-piece orchestra at the Cardiff première of the 1923 **Ben Hur**, was still appearing at the Park Hall in the 1930s and obtained a retaining fee until at least 1945. By the early thirties, most orchestras had wound up.

Often the public, deprived of 'live' music, had to suffer distorted sound and the limitations of actors struggling to adjust their technique and styles of delivery to the new medium which was fettered by practical problems, as cameras in soundproof booths remained immobile. Film scenario editor Sinclair Hill complained in a local press syndicated article that: 'Hardly had cinematography reached a decent stage of development before the talkie came and swept the silent cinema off the face of the screen. America jumped ahead and forced the pace. This country followed gingerly.'[45] But the public had few doubts about talkies; attendances climbed, and theatres felt the draught. Repertory crowds dropped – even Moss Empires lost business. A company representative claimed Cardiff, Newcastle and Sheffield were 'the blackest spots' on their circuit.[46] And an actor, Percy Hutchinson, appearing in a comedy at Cardiff's New Theatre, appealed to the audience not to send their 'good money to America to support American films instead of supporting the good English plays'.[47] A *South Wales Echo* columnist, similarly unimpressed by talkies, complained about the inroads of 'yankee flap doodle into normal speech'.[48] Even **The Singing Fool** had not met with unqualified approval. 'Cannot something be done to prevent the invasion of American films interlarded with slop sentiment?' complained a writer to the *South Wales Daily Post*, who resented paying 2s. 4d. to see 'ham actors' in 'Yankee sob stuff' routines.[49]

Some south Wales journalists were becoming increasingly liverish about the talkies and the American influence. 'Mary Pickford's first talkie . . . had failed,' the *South Wales Daily Post* leader writer pointed out, noting, ungraciously, that 'leading ladies sometimes had the countenance of a seraph and the voice of a seagull.' The jazz and flapper age, and the momentum and vivacity of American life were captured on screen in scores of features, even before sound. Talkies merely accentuated the differences in life-styles enough to raise hackles. The *Post* leader writer was swift to denounce the American cinema as immoral – 'not particularly in the sexual sense as in the picture it presents of a so-called civilisation that is hectic, violent, undisciplined and semi- pagan'. Impressionable youths were subject to 'representations of a fantasy life, with no real counterpart in this country but tending to encourage a replica here'. The writer took this tone from the Bishop of Swansea and Brecon who had just denounced 'immoral plays, films and books', but a *Post* reporter leaves us in no doubt of his chauvinism following an Albert Hall screening of Maurice Elvey's British movie **High Treason** (starring Jameson Thomas and Benita Hume): 'How pleasant to hear good English voices . . . Every word is distinct and well modulated. The film is ample proof that the future of the talkies is in the hands of English-speaking artists and that the nasal twang of the Yankee is about as suitable to voice reproduction as a whip to a taxi driver's equipment.' The paper was predictably overjoyed by **Blackmail**, reporting that Hitchcock's film 'has the Yankee productions whacked'.[50] The presence of Englishmen in American movies was enough to induce eulogies in some quarters. 'Clive Brook's voice is great, perfect English and a joy to hear,' ran the Albert Hall advert for **Interference** (1928), also starring William Powell.[51] The anti-sound brigade and dog-in-the-manger xenophobics were drowned out in the acclaim as sound systems improved – even if the films for months betrayed the primitive talkie technology and the lack of confidence by producers who tried to insure against problems by importing Broadway writing talent often ill-equipped to write for movies. Even before talkies, silent cinema was stealing theatre audiences in Wales, and the decline in live drama attendances continued in the late twenties and thirties. Fred Astaire and his sister Adele failed to sell out for a three-week run of **Funny Face** at the Cardiff Empire in 1928 and there was widespread speculation that the Empire could no longer sustain nightly shows.[52] Theatre in Wales continued to lose ground in the thirties when dozens of new 'supercinemas' opened their doors. In 1934 there were nine Welsh cinemas with more than 2,000 seats. Among the biggest was the Plaza in Swansea, from February 1931 with 3,000-plus seats (top price 2s. 4d). The first feature there was **King of Jazz**, a vehicle for Paul Whiteman and his band. The support was Laurel and Hardy's minor comedy, **Blotto**. The cinema boasted an illuminated fountain in the foyer, atop a grand staircase plus coloured glass windows and a metal plaque depicting the Women of Mumbles Head.[53] Later in the thirties the now familiar Odeons opened up throughout Wales, all owned by Oscar Deutsch and his family. Cardiff's Odeon opened in September 1936, on the site of the former Imperial in Queen Street, with Chaplin's corrosive social satire **Modern Times** in which the comedian – resistant to sound even after eight years of talkies – employed music but no dialogue. The Odeon's main competition in the city came from the Capitol and the ABC Olympia, just a few yards away on the former Solomon Andrews hall site. Other Cardiff cinemas to open in the 1930s included the Rialto at Whitchurch, the Tivoli at Llandaff, Rhiwbina's Monico and the County at Rumney.[54]

In north Wales, Rhyl boasted three cinemas with impressive capacities in the 1930s: the 1,408-seat Odeon opened in 1937 with Tim Whelan's British feature **Farewell Again** starring Leslie Banks and Flora Robson and vied for audiences with the Regal (1,600 seats, 1937) and the Plaza (1931). The architect of the last two was S. Colwyn Ffoulkes, noted for his work on cinemas all over Wales. A string of Odeons opened between 1936 and 1938 in north Wales. **Song of Freedom**, starring Paul Robeson, baptized the 1,246-seat cinema at Wrexham in March 1937, and the company's venue at Colwyn Bay – a five-cinema town by 1929 – was launched in 1936 with René Clair's UK comedy-fantasy **The Ghost Goes West**. Chester followed, launching with Tim Whelan's comedy **Two's Company**.[55]

Even those on their uppers in the Depression managed to scrape together a few pence for the more inexpensive seats. A much quoted Carnegie Trust study of unemployed youths in Cardiff, Liverpool and Glasgow in 1936–9 found that cinema attendance was the most 'important single activity' of young men embraced by the inquiry. About 80 per cent attended at least once a week and a quarter of those attended more often.[56] By that time, the cinema, so recently a novelty and a 'turn', had lost any vestige of inferiority.

You never saw working people on the commercial screen as anything but comic characters, idiotic pantry girls and cooks, housemaids who always managed to drop the crockery all over the place. They were never treated seriously.

(Director Ralph Bond, interviewed by the author, London, 1985)

All the dialogue was in general approved by the lads before we started shooting – their advice was of the utmost value . . . and in most cases their suggestions were incorporated into the script. It was their film as much as mine.

(Ralph Bond talking, in 1985, of his film **Today We Live** made with Rhondda miners in 1937)

Alongside the cinemas, enjoying palmy days despite the Depression, an alternative circuit sprang up – slightly improbably – in the miners' institutes and clubs of the south Wales valleys. Since the First World War the institutes had realized the value of picture-shows as an extra source of income: in some villages and towns the miners' cinemas were at least as popular as their commercial counterparts. Ticket prices were adjusted as the fortunes of individual pits changed but the institutes, which tended to book mainly commercial fare until the early thirties, dug deep into their cash reserves to cope when, to their dismay, the face of cinema suddenly changed with the talkies' arrival.

The prospect of installing costly apparatus must have been intimidating to many committees trying to eke out funds on the miners' bare subscriptions. Most adapted, despite teething troubles, and at their peak there were eighty-three cinemas connected with miners' halls in Wales, Bristol and the West – more than seventy of them in Wales. Most were a 'substantial asset' in the thirties and forties – especially as work-men's clubs in Wales were forbidden from holding liquor licences until 1956 (unlike their counterparts in England and Scotland – another legacy of the Nonconformist tradition).[1] Twenty-seven 'funding members' (clubs and institutes) in this Wales and West region formed the Miners' Welfare Workmen's Hall Cinema Association to strengthen negotiating powers with renters over film fees; the miners' halls also benefited from their exemption from Entertainment Tax.[2]

But wiring for sound in the institutes was a slow process. Tredegar, in the vanguard of miners' cinema since the twenties, installed a screen in the revamped Workmen's Institute Hall (opened by their local MP Aneurin Bevan) in 1931, but when the institute introduced sound, members complained about the 'heavy tone' of the British Acoustic system.[3] BA carried out improvements and still held the sound contract four years later, despite challenges from both RCA and Western Electric. Few workmen's halls could rival Tredegar in the intensity of its interest in the cinema. In 1933, the hall committee was asked to hire 'voices' (a choir) for £12 to accompany Cecil B. De Mille's religious epic, **The Sign of the Cross**.[4] A few months later, members balloted for seats at a screening of Frank Lloyd's Hollywood extravaganza, **Cavalcade**. For a showing of Henry Hathaway's **Lives of a Bengal Lancer** (1935) an extra 5,000 handbills were to be delivered in the Rhymney and Pontlottyn areas and a jobless man's services were obtained at £3 a week to act as sandwich-board man.[5] The main part of the institute's central building became a new cinema auditorium in 1936, with stalls seating for 500, plus 300 in the balcony, and from the start attendances exceeded expectations.[6] In 1937, the cinema committee even discussed the possibility of acquiring its own cine-camera to make films. By 1938, the Tredegar cinema was in use seven days a week for months on end, screenings had to be added in a lesser hall and lectures were arranged by experts on film and production. A film society had been mooted there that year but was eventually formed in 1944 showing French, Russian, Italian and 'non-commercial' American films.[7] In 1945, Chancellor Hugh Dalton exempted from income and entertainment taxes all non-profit-making societies doing educational, recreational and cultural work; thousands of extra pounds flowed into south Wales club coffers.[8] And in 1946, the Tredegar Institute even added a Saturday morning cinema club.

Among the first working men's institutes to plump for talkies was Celynnen which opened a cinema in 1923 with the spectacular silent **The Thief of Baghdad** and opted for sound (RCA) equipment in 1930.[9] More typical was Ferndale Workmen's

Hall, Rhondda, which built up cinema audiences slowly after a serious fire there in 1920. The committee experienced problems in obtaining silent films after sound came in – and there was a worrying slump in attendances as neighbouring commercial cinemas wired for talkies – but members could not agree on the best system and the wrangle went on for months. The headaches were worth it. When talkies were introduced there they 'did much to improve revenue'.[10] Mardy had worse troubles. The workmen agreed sound installation for their cinema in 1930, but could not raise the funds through loans. In 1934 they obtained £900 from the miners' welfare, a fund set up after the Sankey Commission recommended a levy on coal-owners of 1*d*. per tonne of output – the miners' 'magic penny' for recreational and social well-being.[11]

District miners welfare associations at Glynneath, Kenfig Hill and Pyle bought out local cinemas as they prospered and Brynamman miners controlled their own cinema for decades.[12] Cinema was also a high priority at Oakdale in Gwent where the institute formed a cinema committee within months of opening the new hall in 1927, and 1,000 handbills were distributed for a showing of **April Showers**.[13] The committee announced plans in 1928 to slash advertising budgets to engage an orchestra for films, changing the hall's name to the Picture House, with Chaplin's **The Circus** among films booked.[14] A 'Madame' Templeman was appointed musical director there in 1929 and the following year eighty-eight applications were received for a cinema operator's job – an indication less of cinema's appeal than the desperate employment position in the south Wales valleys.[15] The Oakdale cinema committee was praised for its 'magnanimity' in granting so many applications for attending films at reduced rates. In February 1931, prices were reduced from 4*d*. to 2*d*. (ground floor) and 6*d*. (balcony) to increase takings – a month earlier prices for the unemployed were cut to 3*d*. and 2*d*.[16]

At Blaenafon, unemployed miners even made their own film in 1928, after obtaining a second-hand cine-camera. **By the Aid of a Rogue** was an eighteenth-century costume drama, featuring an elopement of an aristocrat's daughter and a squire, a pursuit by a jilted suitor and the hold-up of the errant pair's stagecoach by a highwayman, who proved to be the brother of the fleeing girl and helped her escape. It also included a duel in a field near the local railway station and other scenes shot at Llanover Hall. The Blaenafon company was formed by a young engineer W. H. Fleet, who bought the camera, and a Mr J. R. Payne, a Pontypool journalist, was brought in to act as producer and actor and revise an original story written by Mr A. S. Northcote, secretary of the Blaenafon Workmen's Hall. Doris Evans played the heroine and Albert E. Parsons was the blueblooded villain. Production was soured by the death in a mining accident, two weeks after shooting finished, of one actor, Ernest West – but the drama was sold to the European Motion Film Company who intended to run it in aid of 'the distressed miners of the Eastern Valley'. Twelve prints were made: 'Every print, it's hoped, to be accompanied at screenings by a quartet of unemployed singing Welsh miners.'[17] The *Bioscope* reviewer found it a worthy effort in self-help, but damned with faint praise. He considered it a 'simple drama' with no ambitious pretensions which reflected 'great credit on the amateur producers and company'. The film was released and shown in several cinemas, including the Elysium in Swansea; and J. V. Bryson of European even spoke of obtaining world distribution through Universal, though no documented evidence exists to suggest this ever happened. The miners' quartet did appear to publicize the film at the Rialto, London, and at the Rialto, Leeds, where they were banned by a Leeds watch committee who apparently had an aversion to 'fancy dress' and stage prologues before screenings. Prologue entertainments were a feature of movie presentations in south Wales in silent days, and one Tonypandy miner wrote prologues for local screenings of the Rex Ingram 1921 classic **The Four Horsemen of the Apocalypse** and **Dawn**, Herbert Wilcox's 1928 tribute to the British First World War nurse Edith Cavell.

The *South Wales Echo* also announced that an American company had offered to finance a five- or six-reel drama, **The Reckoning**, which the Blaenafon miners planned to shoot in summer, 1929, starring a local beauty queen, but no record has been found of any release.[18] Blaenafon was an isolated example of miners plunging into film production by themselves, but by the thirties many institutes pulled in large crowds for film shows. Ferndale, with seats for 1,000, had only the fourth highest workmen's hall cinema capacity in those days behind Aberaman (1,200), the Parc and Dare at Treorchy (1,100) and Abercynon Hall and Institute (1,026). But workmen's halls at Nantymoel and Ogmore Vale, where films had been screened early in the century, had seating for 900-plus in the 1920s.[19]

The miners' cinemas were to play an important role in south Wales in the twenties and thirties in screening classic European films, especially from Russia, Germany and Spain. These films, often about working men and heavily political in content, were at last reaching the audiences that could readily identify with them and arguably appreciate them most – and they enabled many ordinary families in Wales to place their own plight in the broader international context. Just as significantly, the films introduced to many Valleys communities for the first time some of cinema's greatest work. In the thirties, a group of socially conscious film-makers in Britain also began to produce combative and absorbing documentaries centred on the drama of the miners' protests and hunger marches, and the problems of the coalfields and communities of Wales – and helped to make their presence felt in the beleaguered south Wales valleys . . .

Out of the mainstream: *Today We Live* and *Eastern Valley*

As the Depression deepened and more pits closed, non-mainstream film directors and producers sought to provide a chance for unemployed Valleys men to impress their living and working conditions on the public. One of the most influential figures in the brief heyday of miners' cinema and in the newly formed Workers' Film Society movement in Britain was Ralph Bond (1904–89) – the 'incorruptible left-winger', a former member of the General Post Office film unit, which, under John Grierson, established an enduring reputation for British documentaries. Bond, a London-based communist, lively polemicist and fierce critic of a class-ridden and anodyne British cinema, came to Pentre in the Rhondda to make the Welsh sequences of **Today We Live**, a 1937 documentary produced for London's Strand company by the distinguished documentarist, Paul Rotha. Bond's section of the film centred on the plight of jobless pitmen building their own leisure centre with funds from the National Council for Social Service, an autonomous body with strong government links. **Today We Live** has fascinating echoes and debating points in our own times. It tackles the then-prevailing orthodoxy of a government preparing to create leisure centres for the unemployed and nurture the philosophy and concept of self-help as a placebo – without developing a humanitarian or social and industrial strategy or prevailing upon private pit-owners to keep pits open during the hard times. Bond, paying his first visit to south Wales, was appalled by the poverty and privations of

Ralph Bond

miners' lives, but impressed by their resilience. The conditions made an equally deep impression on Donald Alexander, a Scottish doctor's son and a young Cambridge graduate, who shot one of the film's finest sequences and later allowed some of his undoubted anger and passion to seep into his directorial début film, **Eastern Valley**, made in Gwent (also in 1937) in another area of steep industrial decline. It homed in on a workers' co-operative land scheme, with the unemployed producing goods which the whole community could buy at half normal shop costs.

Neither of these films emerged from a vacuum. For some years, left-wing film-makers – including Bond – had made their own fairly primitive newsreels on peppercorn budgets. A distribution network for radical and classic European films had been developed, aimed at a generation who felt they could no longer remain passive at a time of traumatic social and political change, faced with the tide of international events. The film-makers thought cinema should reflect attitudes and partisan passion aroused by the industrial problems in Britain, the revolutionary activity in Russia (political and cinematic), the strife in Spain and the threats posed by Nazism. For years these film-makers and trade-union leaders in the film business had been engaged in a searching debate about the nature and purpose of film – its possibility as a tool for change. **Today We Live** and **Eastern Valley** emerged from that debate. In some ways, they are artless films made with very basic equipment and containing fairly standard cinematic devices; but they were important precursors of commercial features such as MGM's **The Citadel**, which vividly illustrated the south Wales mining community for film-goers in Britain's more affluent areas.

Both these documentaries, whatever their manifest shortcomings, are important in cinema history as two of the first films fairly widely screened which attempt to present issues from the perspective of working men. **Today We Live**, in particular, dispensed to some degree with narration which mediated between subjects and consumers of films and diluted their political content. There is poetry in these films (particularly in the montage and scene-setting of **Eastern Valley**) but the film aesthetic has never been allowed to override the political message or urgency as it often did in the GPO documentary films, which glorified the mechanics of industrial and social progress and the achievements of the working man without emphasis on individuals or due reference to the economic and social forces around him.[20]

Bond had made only two instructional films for the GPO before making **Today We Live** but he was already a key figure who, in article after article from the late 1920s on, hammered out his credo. He sought to make and circulate work which 'dramatized the lives and struggles of ordinary men' and present them in films shown through workers' film societies in clubs and community halls and centres.[21] 'These alternative films must expose the stupidity and false values' of the commercial film, he stressed; 'we should aim at achieving naturalism and avoiding obscurity. We organise and we attack. That is our purpose.' Bond thought the subjects available were inexhaustible: 'unemployment, victimization, housing, children, strikes, hunger marches, war' – and he believed there was no point in attempting to make films for the major circuits, which had far different values.[22] In a 1935 article in *Plebs*, the National Council of Labour Colleges journal, Bond laid out the ground rules, and spelled out the 'evils' of the successful cinema chains: 'We can and must fight capitalist influences by exposing in a Marxist manner how it [the cinema] is used as an ideological force to dope the workers.' This could be done by 'exhibiting the films of the only country where the workers are the ruling class'.[23]

Bond had attended the opening screenings of the London Film Society, set up in 1925 by the Oxford-educated Ivor Montagu, an aristocrat but fellow communist, who throughout his long career as a director and critic continued to draw the fire of screen pundits and ideologues. The LFS with its 25*s*. annual subscription – when the average weekly wage was 49*s*. – had an élite membership. Over the next few years the society showed films from Russia and Spain which the timorous British censors were loath to allow into the commercial cinema, such as Eisenstein's **Battleship Potemkin** (1925) and Pudovkin's features **Mother, End of St Petersburg** and **Storm Over Asia** (1926–8). Bond was 'overwhelmed by the Russian films – we all were', but was adamant that such works were wasted on the middle classes and an élite who 'wouldn't be seen dead in a fleapit'.[24] He worked with Montagu in helping to launch the Federation of Workers' Film Societies in 1929, with its own 35mm. distribution organization, the Progressive Film Institute, which imported films from Europe, mainly through a company called Atlas. Bond was also heavily involved in the formation of the London Workers' Film Society which cost 13*s*. for a season's subscription and hit censorship trouble with the authorities. It scored a big audience success in showing Viktor Turin's exhilarating Russian film **Turksib** (1929) based on the building of the Trans-Siberian railway. The work was notable for its rapid-fire montage editing and inspirational camera angles which emphasized the heroic stature and dignity of the labourers on this awesome project.[25] The film attracted nearly 2,000 at the British première, which Turin attended, and the WFS reaped the benefits, gaining hundreds of new members in London alone.[26] Bond thought the **Turksib** screening an 'enormous success' – 'after that the Workers' Film Society sprang to life in a big way.'

'Both before and after London's first performance, the Federation of the WFS had been receiving letters from enthusiasts in areas of south Wales and other coalfield districts,' said Bond. In June 1930, he reported the formation of societies in Liverpool, Cardiff and Edinburgh. Cardiff's branch began canvassing that year and the national Federation's first annual conference was held in September. The Association of Cinema Technicians' leader, George Elvin, claimed the society's films were mainly preaching to the converted and preferred the idea of making inroads into commercial cinema.[27] However, Bond saw this as 'a completely unrealistic, romantic view of things' because the great cinema chains and circuits were 'owned by the Rank Organization and others who were in the business to own cinemas and make films for the purpose of making money.' 'They weren't interested in screening films which would undermine that particular philosophy,' Bond stressed. He saw 'no possibility if we made the sort of films we wanted to make of them being shown in the cinemas' and he thought it imperative to form an alternative circuit of audiences, with south Wales a key area of development. British film-makers would then theoretically draw inspiration from the struggles of the working classes presented through Russian masterpieces and the documentaries of the Spanish Civil War. The chance had arisen after 1923 when 16mm. film production and exhibition became possible. Previously almost all films had been on 35mm. standard stock but 16mm. films were non-flammable, so escaped fire regulations under the 1909 Cinematograph Act and avoided censorship. The freedom from legislation did not necessarily preclude police interference, and society screenings met with various forms of harassment from law officers suspicious of departures from the norm. In 1934 a particularly vigilant chief constable in Cardiff ran his own tests on 16mm. acetate (safety) film after claims that it was non-flammable. He found the acetate film would burn slowly and he could not accept registered clubs' exemption from the Act. The police had no power to enter these premises without a search warrant but where clubs allowed entry without a warrant he had withdrawn his objections.[28]

As late as 1939 the Peace Pledge Union and its leader Dick Sheppard ran into trouble when they attempted to show G. W. Pabst's German mining classic **Kameradschaft** in Cardiff on non-flammable 16mm. stock, together with three PPU shorts featuring appeals by Sheppard, former Labour Party leader George Lansbury and Stuart Morris. The chief constable asked for synopses of the films and conducted lively correspondence with the PPU head office. Two policemen and a fireman were present at the show, with the fireman insisting that a sand bucket was available and that the operator should rope off the area around the projector. The 1923 Cinematograph Regulations then enforced related to portable projection use where the enclosure was 'not permanent' – but the Regulations were part of the *1909* Act which did not cover inflammable film.

Bond and others could see the possibilities of a 'circuit' which could show radically different films and, theoretically, circumvent the watchdogs. He saw the commercial cinema in a Britain dominated by Hollywood as impoverished in ideas and hopelessly middle class, and thought it demeaned working people, presenting them as humorous relief.[29] The WFS 'wanted to put on the screen the dignity of labour, the importance of labour and working people to the economic and social life of the country. This was considered to be a total revolution.'[30]

The miners' institutes in south Wales offered, theoretically, a receptive network for political and progressive European 'art' films, particularly from Russia and Germany, though the lack of 16mm. facilities in most halls severely limited their exhibition potential even if there was tremendous interest and goodwill shown by some institutes, notably Tredegar.[31] Aneurin Bevan, the town's MP, was an adviser for International Sound Films (who distributed 16mm. and 35mm. working-class and progressive films in the 1930s) and was also a general council member of the 'alternative' distributors, Kino.[32] The more radical film-makers remained convinced there was a receptive audience for 'heavier more committed work focusing on many aspects of British life totally neglected by the big studios'.

A social disaster

Strand, the London-based documentary outfit run by managing director Donald Taylor with Paul Rotha as resident producer, employed a nucleus of people with common ideas and principles – 'a generally humanist left-wing viewpoint'. Strand gave Bond a chance to put theories into practice by making part of a film dealing with life in a Rhondda Valley of high unemployment. The other half, intended to provide a sharp contrast, would centre on rural life in the village of South Cerney, Gloucestershire. The Welsh segment of **Today We Live** was shot in winter 1936 in

Les Adlam (right) in
Today We Live.

Pentre, Treherbert and Treorchy, and on the slag-heaps of Cymmer and Tylorstown. It centred on unemployed men building the Riverside centre and workshops 'at the edge of a river in Pentre polluted by coaldust'.[33] Bond, seeing the area for the first time, became aware that the pit closures and unemployment levels were 'not only a social problem but a social disaster'. Interviewed in the 1980s he still remembered Pentre's 'desolation . . . because no one was working and the lads were just hanging around on the street-corners, unemployed with nothing to do'. He found the Rhondda Valley and its slag-heaps 'a monumental indictment of the ruthlessness of early mining capitalism' – but was surprised by the cultural life the miners had inherited.[34] His observations seem a touch naïve today.

> The local miners' library had one of the finest collections of books, even better than you would see in some large towns . . . I went into the homes of the miners and I was astonished to see rows of books on their shelves which you very rarely see in other workers' homes, not cheap penny novels, but serious books on philosophy. I even saw the works of Karl Marx and Lenin. [I was surprised] to see those books in those wretched houses which were then the best the miners could get . . .

He saw that pits everywhere in south Wales were standing idle. 'The only contacts miners have with coal are the slag-heaps where sometimes they are permitted at ever present risk to life and limb to scramble for enough to keep the fires burning in their own homes,' Bond wrote in 1937.[35] Donald Alexander had explored the Rhondda in 1935 and had also been taken aback – by the 'beastly houses' he saw on *his* first visits to south Wales.[36]

Today We Live opens by recalling a past when wealth lay in fields and farms. Then Bond cuts to images of explosions, rushing water and steam power. Over shots of homes we hear that 'thousands of homes were built without plan or conscience.' The film dubs this 'The shame of Britain'. The sound of a barrel organ heralds a sequence of men at labour exchanges and factory gates. Crane shots and pans lead us to the key date of 24 October 1929, and the words: 'Breaking point – the Wall Street crash'. An image of pit-head machinery in motion gives way, on a downward pan, to a view of an empty coal truck. This kind of evocative visual language only became a cliché in the next few years causing Graham Greene, in particular, to attack **Proud Valley**.

Bond's film then tells us that Scotland and Wales found themselves 'without a share in the revival of work'. The factories in which men had wished to work had been broken up. 'Bread of Heaven' is heard over the industrial landscape, then come the now-famous low-angle images of men dashing up slag-heaps to salvage coal. In a coffee (*bracchi*) shop sequence a radio broadcast extols the value of funds from the National Council for Social Service for building village halls and occupational centres. Later the unemployed miners are told they must contribute £15 to £20 of their own money to take part in the scheme to build their own centre – and one miner, Glyn Lewis, leaves in disgust claiming it's hard enough to obtain the dole. We see the scheme mainly as it involves three of the miners, Lewis, Les Adlam and Evan Jones. Lewis bristles with anger at the project: 'We can make wirelesses, grow cabbages and do physical jerks until we're blue in the face but it isn't paid work. That's what I mean . . . it isn't real work, not the work that we want.' Towards the end of this piece a shot of the new spick-and-span centre is set against pointed images of miners on their haunches in the street, patently bored, while the commentary winds up reminding the viewer that the trouble 'will not go away' and that out-of-work miners were living on as little as 1*s.* a day.

Strand was sometimes compromised by its reliance on sponsorship and **Today We Live**, beneath its patina of social concern, makes little attempt to analyse or probe causes for the demoralization of the mining community, or place the pits in a wider British economic or industrial perspective. But it does implicitly mount a critique of the government's priorities in pouring money into self-help projects rather than tackling the unemployment problems or the state of the pits more directly. The comments were undoubtedly bold for the day and Bond had no illusions that the National Council for Social Service was merely a 'damage-limitation' outfit.[37] He described it as 'one of those well-intentioned do-good organizations whose main aim was to revive community life in this country which, because of the great Depression of the thirties, and other factors, had largely disappeared'.[38] The National Council, through the Trealaw-based Maes-yr-Haf organization, injected limited cash into projects, such as centres for the unemployed which miners built themselves, and they were intent on promoting their good intentions in the film – so Bond and Alexander were hamstrung to some extent. But they were able to use Glyn Lewis as a mouthpiece. Interviewed in the 1980s, Lewis insisted the government scheme was a sop: 'They wanted to keep us quiet.'

There was little or no spontaneity during the filming. Rehearsals, to avoid using up valuable film, precluded that – but Bond actively encouraged the men to express disenchantment about the centre. 'My part in the film was to criticize the government. They told me I was to be against the whole thing', said Lewis.[39] Les Adlam, another of the trio whose fortunes are central to **Today We Live**, said later:

'They more or less told us what to say but they wanted us to say it in our own way, our own words.'

Bond spent about two weeks in the Rhondda meeting local men, researching local conditions. 'The first thing I did after the research was to rough out a possible script and . . . I invited some of the lads . . . to talk about it . . . much to my surprise and delight they made their own comments and suggestions. These lads felt they were participating in their film and once that sort of rapport has been established . . . with ordinary people you're half way home.'[40] But for all Bond's professed intentions, the miners in **Today We Live** deliver lines by rote and only a little of their frustration emerges on screen. The film-makers wanted – but essentially failed – to preserve freshness in dialogue delivery, while appreciating the need for rehearsal. The budget – below £2,000 – imposed its own constraints.[41] The details, shape, rhythm and editing of the Welsh section were left to Bond. Howard Marshall provided the commentary, from a scenario credited to Stuart Legg.

Les Adlam in *Today We Live*.

Some of the miners had been out of work for years when the film was made – and Adlam also had experience, as a teenager in the 1920s, of scavenging on tips.[42] A miner at Pentre for ten years, he was on the dole when they were building the Riverside centre, and making **Today We Live**: 'We were getting no payment because of the Means Test, you know. They would have stopped our dole. Bloody hard times they were.' Glyn Lewis – also thrown out of work when Pentre, a Cory Brothers colliery, shut in 1934 – had formed the local unemployed club in a local garage, where training in boot repairing and handicrafts took place before the men became involved in the Riverside scheme – 'We were on our uppers. You got 15*s.* for yourself [dole], 10*s.* for the wife, 2*s.* for each of the two children.'

There are, fascinatingly, different versions of how the film progressed and who deserves the most credit. Bond said Rotha's contribution was 'considerable' – 'mainly in encouragement and he kept a close eye on editing'. But Rotha in his *Documentary Diary* claimed he stepped in after the first day when he realized the film would go way over budget and: 'I more or less took over the direction.'[43] 'A sound truck alone cost us something around £100–£200 a day and [Bond] had one in south Wales for **Today We Live**,' Rotha pointed out.[44] He claimed that he intervened for budgetary and thematic reasons, and took an active part in shooting and editing the film. Bond also acknowledged 'sync' sound as a headache. 'The unit had an enormous van with miles of cable and a generator to help light the sets, but lack of proper lighting hampered filming in houses,' he stressed. 'You must remember that documentary was fairly new – it only started as a film form right at the beginning of the thirties. We were all finding our way and learning all the time.'[45]

Great claims were made later for **Today We Live**. Documentary director and film historian Basil Wright thought it 'a brutally frank picture of the bloody capitalists, in particular the coal owners who were one of the wickedest races the country has ever known'.[46] Rotha said he was proud to have produced it and edited the prologue.[47] But he hinted, significantly, that he would have made a stronger film, more critical of the government, if he had been given a free hand: 'Oh yes, had it been my own money or my company's own money. But it wasn't. You can fool a sponsor part of the time but you can't fool him all the time.'[48] For all its technical immaturity seen today, the film 'lived by its passionate desire to be truthful', Rotha insisted. And he praised a now-celebrated sequence shot by Alexander on slag-heaps as the miners searched for waste coal with the dust whipping up around them.[49] These scenes are stunning and constantly appear in TV films using archive footage. 'Bond hadn't shot certain material of the coal tips,' Alexander recalled in the 1980s. 'Rotha asked me to go back and film it.'[50]

The film garnered good reviews and was appreciated when shown to a packed audience at the Grand Theatre, Pentre, and also screened by Maes-yr-Haf at the Parc and Dare, Treorchy. A *Times* review of 1937 claimed the encouragement to the men to 'work out even part of their Salvation' was 'immeasurably more important than, say, the agonizing pictures painted by those serious novelists who have looked on unemployment and despaired'. Rotha, interestingly, later cited the comment approvingly with no sense of irony.[51]

Today We Live, despite its gauche qualities and technical shortcomings, remains one of the very few *contemporary* British documentary films to present any kind of criticism of the social scene in human terms in the 1930s. It was certainly among the very first films to emphasize some of mass unemployment's terrible results in Wales (or in Britain) and also proved one of the most popular of British documentaries in America. The documentary should be considered in the context of Bond's other work around that time. **Winter** (1936), **Advance Democracy** (1938) and **The Big City** (1940), reflected his preoccupation with class and social inequalities and iniquities. All caught the temper of the times, particularly **Advance Democracy**, a film stressing the sacrifices of the Chartists and Tolpuddle Martyrs and extolling the virtues of the Co-operative movement. The film's tack – the abandoning of class divisions to form a popular front against Fascism – is confirmed by the final images of an overhead shot of miners with banners marching alongside people of all occupations and social classes.[52] These documentaries were not subtle but they expressed the mood and will for change among the guiding lights in the Workers' Film Society movement, a large percentage of the dispossessed in Britain and the Rhondda community embraced by **Today We Live**.

Donald Alexander and *Eastern Valley*

London-born Donald Alexander (1913–93) is now best known as the director of **Eastern Valley** – but it was not his first film in Wales. He came from the impeccably middle-class, university or public school background which seemed to breed so many committed documentary film-makers fascinated by what they heard of social conditions in south Wales. Alexander helped organize holiday camps for the unemployed in the 1930s, as his protégé and later fellow director, the south-Walian Jack Howells, was to do in the following decade.[53] As a Cambridge undergraduate Alexander became aware of the great Russian, German and French films and responded enthusiastically when student Margo Heinemann, of the Heinemann publishing family, helped organize a trip to make a film in the Rhondda valleys. The group included Rudolph Messel, Ralph Elton (son of British documentary-maker

Arthur Elton, of **Housing Problems** fame), who had a prized Filmo 16mm. camera, and Judy Birdwood, daughter of Lord Birdwood. She had a Kodak 16mm. camera enabling Alexander to make the 10- or 12-minute short **Rhondda**, filmed in 1935 around Tylorstown and Maerdy and including shots of Rhondda Fawr and poor housing at Ystrad: 'We were very green and I was absolutely appalled by what I found there. It was a devastating experience . . . it [the place] was so cut off.'[54]

Alexander stayed with Rhondda communist councillor Jim Morton and their political discussions stimulated the embryo director and helped involve him with the community. His diary of the time revealed his impressions: 'West to Ferndale, and Maerdy and found very good colliery. Finally the great tip – the landmark and overhanging symbol of the valley. As the sun westered the tip cast a huge and terrifying shadow across the hilltop.'[55] His film featured evocative shots of miners (some silhouetted) scrabbling for coal on a 250ft.-high tip, with the slag thrown up around them, on the road between Ferndale and Llanwynno.[56] Alexander and Judy Birdwood headed for London to see the documentary film-makers they respected, hoping for help in editing their material – 'though we'd edited it pretty well. We knew what was dramatic.' The director claims that the same day – on the strength of the rushes – he was offered jobs by Rotha (then with British Instructional Films) and John Grierson at the GPO Film Unit. **Rhondda**, made for about £30 and filmed in about ten days, was shown in local miners' welfare halls in Wattstown, Pontygwaith and Tylorstown to the pitmen in the film, then edited in London. It was probably the same film distributed by Kino in 1936 and made with a camera supplied to the Alexander–Birdwood group by the Film and Photo League.[57]

Alexander's **Eastern Valley**, for Strand, cost around £1,500 – financed mainly by the Order of Friends and Lord Forester – and it focused on a 'social experiment' in Gwent by the Subsistence Production Society.[58] Surviving prints have poor sound and visual quality but they scarcely detract from this succinct, adroit work which conveys the shifting social conditions and features of the Gwent valley down the years before focusing on the farming and craft schemes run by the society in the Abergavenny,

Trehafod we found a very derelict colliery; and made something of it. Rhondda Fawr, however, yielded little, except a glorious shot of derelict houses ending with a notice-board "This valuable site for sale". After tea we went up Rhondda Fach to Ferndale and Maerdy, and found another very good colliery. We then climbed a hill, lay in the bracken, and made one lazy shot of Ferndale. Finally the great tip — the landmark, and overhanging symbol of the valley. The car took us to the foot, and then I tried to run up the two or three hundred feet of it. The effort — which nearly succeeded — was worth it. The view in all directions is superb. As the sun westered, the tip cast a huge and terrifying shadow along the hill-top. We came down, and made the sun set by our descent. At supper with the Jeffries I was sleepy, but a talk with Jim revived me and it was again after 1 before we broke up. The talk proved a useful one. We straightened out a lot of things. I put my objections to Communism as it appears from the D W, and the speeches of its leaders — mainly the fact that it does not satisfy the full man, only the economic man — and Jim admitted the fault with a readiness that surprised me. He

An extract from Donald Alexander's diary, clearly indicates the emotional impact of his first visit to the south Wales valleys, filming *Rhondda* (1935).

138

Cwmafon and Brynmawr areas. It might be seen as a less subtle precursor to the 1980s film **So That You Can Live** but was a remarkable effort, principally from a two-man team – the director and the cameraman Alf Jeakins.[59] Produced by Stuart Legg, the work contains many Strand trademarks including skilful cutting and lyrical commentary, mainly in the opening section which reveals a surprising political sophistication.[60] Alexander distils the disenchantment of men representing generations who had moved from lives as agricultural artisans and skilled rural craftsmen to become ironworkers and miners. They had hoped for greater rewards and leisure, but found they had sacrificed their freedom to industries which proved only too vulnerable. This obliteration of liberty is conveyed by a right-to-left pan of an 'idyllic' valley – lost in a pall of smoke. Alexander is never content to merely *state* on the sound-track; he uses imagery to comment ironically on the 'legacy' of the industrial boom. 'The houses we built for them were huddled together that the men might be close to their jobs,' states the voice-over, and Alexander cuts to a low-angle view of the pits and slurry, then a reverse shot of a house, seemingly half-buried (from the camera's viewpoint) beneath the tips. The sound-track's emphasis seems almost superfluous. In a telling close-up the camera pans along a line of jobless men, shot from the chest down, all with hands in their pockets.

We later see the success of the Gwent co-operative venture, partly through the eyes of jobless miner Dai Williams as he discovers how the self-help scheme revives pride: 'Men used to the hot clamour of the foundry turned now to the slower, quieter movement of the land,' the narrator informs us. We see how the men work their own farm, produce vegetables and fruit and make and distribute goods from stores in a recently derelict but reconditioned brewery. A butcher's shop and bakehouse is established and beef is provided to families who have not previously been able to afford it. The film also includes shots of men working in their temporary factory making and fitting cloth and suits from wool. **Eastern Valley**, like **Today We Live**, makes clear that the men see their venture as no more than a short-term palliative but it says that each of the 400 men involved has recovered some 'lost values'.

'I reckon what you get out of it doesn't count for much,' says one man. 'The main point is that you have an interest in life.' The valley remains a memorial to an industrial development which had turned the country into a morass, the commentary states – 'But out of decay has been born hope in this one valley of all the valleys of South Wales.' In an epilogue a Mrs Whetton talks to camera about her husband, unemployed for ten years – 'He used to work underground, now he's on a round [for the Subsistence Society scheme] delivering milk and bread to unemployed homes like ours.' She tells of having to rear three children on 30*s*. a week. And **Eastern Valley** ends with an appeal for help for other unemployed men in other valleys who want to mount similar schemes.

The film is flawed. The men on camera seem uncomfortable with their lines – even when the sentiments delivered are obviously heartfelt. But this painstakingly constructed film deserved its accolades from Graham Greene, who said Alexander had learned from the documentary director Edgar Anstey 'the value of direct reporting', and from Basil Wright 'how to express poetically a moral judgement'. Greene also claimed the film showed: 'Life as it once was before industry scarred and mutilated the valley. Life as it is – life as it should be.'[61]

Alexander later played a key role for the film documentarists' group DATA in supplying the National Coal Board's Mining Review films, which featured a wealth of

Welsh material. He was also involved with Paul Rotha Productions Ltd. on one item in the famous **Worker and Warfront** series (No. 14), which focused on the medical treatment of miners and servicemen after injury, and was shot partly at the Caerphilly Miners Hospital and the Talygarn Rehabilitation Centre. Alexander's **Life Begins Again** (1941) had also dealt with rehabilitation in industry and the services. Both pre-dated Cardiff director Paul Dickson's feature on the subject, **The Undefeated**.

Alexander became film adviser for the Steel Company of Wales and also worked with the NCB's Film Unit.[62] He later employed the **Eastern Valley** scenario structure, almost a Strand cliché by then, for a film made in **Scotland – Wealth of a Nation** (1938), produced by Legg with Harry Watt as commentator. After reflecting on harsh industrial conditions of the past, and the terminal decline of heavy industries such as coal, steel and shipping, the film stresses the work of the Scottish Development Council in providing new industrial estates. But Alexander – in advocating a more balanced economy – also emphasizes the gradual return to the Highlands of many crofters and smallholders who by the end of the 1930s had 'greater access to markets and communications'.

Seen together, these works might suggest a rather futile hankering after a rural idyll, but both **Eastern Valley** and **Scotland – Wealth of a Nation** are laced with a healthy cynicism, and suggest the need to revalue the past in terms of progress in the present. Alexander once more demonstrates his ability to present cogent ideas through visuals and economic editing and adopt a film form to match moods. He was undoubtedly a finer technician – more alive to the nuances of editing – than Bond, who was always primarily a motivator and organizer. Bond was certainly the more politically committed and this is reflected in the often naïve excesses of the films he made on a shoestring. He would have argued that points had to be overemphasized to make an impression. He was, after all, weaned on the **Workers' Newsreels**.

The workers' films

Before the Bond and Alexander Welsh films for Strand, miners had been exposed to far less sophisticated workers' movies of little artistic merit but much fervour and political polemic. It is almost certain that many miners in south Wales saw, or were aware of, **Workers' Newsreel Film** No. 1 (1934), produced for next to nothing by the Workers' Film and Photo League and the Communist Party as an 'attempt to present news from the working-class point of view'. It contrasts, sardonically, shots of ordinary peacetime activity with caustic observations on the workers' role in wartime. The tenor of the film is pacifist. Images of aircraft performing stunts and formations at the 1934 Hendon Air Pageant are intercut with successive titles: 'Workers make these machines to destroy workers . . .' (much bigger title) . . . 'And their children'. We are told that the workers are organizing and the newsreel ends with footage of an anti-war congress at Sheffield and anti-war demonstration in Hyde Park.

The second **Workers' Newsreel** (1934) opens with a 'Free Thaelmann' rally (for the gaoled German Communist Party leader), carries anti-Fascist march footage from all over Europe and shots of an international anti-Fascist sports rally in Paris. Oswald Mosley is seen addressing a crowd in Hyde Park, then we see Harry Pollitt, former leader of the Communist Party in Great Britain, and former Labour MP, Fenner Brockway. But the most interesting footage from a Welsh viewpoint is of the disaster at Gresford Colliery near Wrexham, showing the aftermath of the fall, when 265 miners were killed. The film was almost certainly made with the help of writer

Herbert Marshall, the Russian drama expert, a guiding spirit of the left-wing Unity Theatre and co-author of the original story for **Proud Valley**.[63] The item is prefaced by a title stressing that miners risked their lives for low pay. Shots of ambulances and miners dwarfed by pit-head machinery are followed by men in silhouette and a big crowd of workers. The film ends with the rescue party, smoke-blackened, relaxing in trucks – and the ironic words 'Gresford Colliery for all classes of coal'.

Ralph Bond, who helped edit the **Workers' Newsreels** of 1934 and 1935, also worked on assembling the first **Workers' Topical News** magazine (1930) and edited the Atlas Co.'s **Workers' Topical News** No. 2 (1930). This features the march of the unemployed on London and some squibs aimed at the socialist government: shots of hunger marchers at Bolton bear the title 'Underclad, underfed, under the Labour government'. Wal Hannington, organizer of the march and of the NUWM – and its battle against the notorious Means Test – is seen visiting the south Wales men near Slough. A close-up of Tonypandy marchers is shown, with the banner 'SOS – Struggle or Starve'. The film concludes with the May Day rally in London with the Communist Party of Great Britain and various miners' lodge banners prominent, plus women hunger marchers.[64]

Bond edited two hunger marches films between 1934 and 1937 for the Workers' Film Societies: 'We had different cameramen in different parts of the country, each one taking, say, 100 ft. . . .' It is interesting to compare the strategy adopted with the way various groups, including Cardiff's Chapter Arts Centre Video Workshop, combined in the 1980s to produce the **Miners' Tapes**. In **March Against Starvation** (1937, alt. title 'Hunger March 1936'), a title conveys stark information: 'Four and a half million people spend less than four shillings a week on food.' There are warnings of impending cuts from the Unemployment Assistance Board, then we see the 'Wales contingent' including the 'Mid-Rhondda marchers' of 1935. We learn of marchers' demonstrations in Cardiff and see MP Ellen Wilkinson and the Jarrow marchers. A banner – 'Rhondda unites against the Government means test' – is shown. Then other banners declaring 'Llansamlet Council of Action' and 'Amman Valley Unemployed'. A reference to Prime Minister Stanley Baldwin refusing to meet the miners, then agreeing to see a delegation of forty-seven, introduces the somewhat guileless title: 'Man's pressure wins.'[65]

Another short worth noting was issued in 1935. The South Wales Miners' Federation combined with Oxford Trades Council and the Film and Photo League to make the 15-minute **Holiday from Unemployment**, set in a south Wales miners' camp near Oxford. This short film was distributed by Kino in a tour of the mining valleys in October, showing with Pudovkin's **Storm Over Asia**.[66]

The workers' films suffered from lack of money. Their sound and footage tended to make them strident rather than analytical, but at least they were honest attempts to counter the anodyne magazines of the commercial cinemas. And, as researcher Bert Hogenkamp has noted: 'The virulent anti-Communism at the top of the Labour Party found barely an echo at the base where they didn't really care whether the distributor of film was a communist organisation or not as long as the films were useful.'[67]

Regular customers for European 'art' films included local Labour Party constituency branches, trade unions and various co-operatives but one main obstacle militated against the spread of workers' films and political classics from abroad. Miners' institutes generally lacked 16mm. facilities – but the situation improved after the formation of the Progressive Film Institute, to circulate 35mm. features.[68] Yet there was never any question of the miners accepting programmes of political material undiluted – especially when the future of workmen's halls hinged on the success of the cinemas. Bond was pragmatic enough, when helping to promote WFS screenings around the country, to insist on a leavening of commercial fare and comedies – including Chaplin silents – to make them more appetizing. He recognized that miners, for all their commitment, needed escapism to forget the daily drudgery of dole queues and of eking out a living.

Hollywood v. agit-prop

The south Wales miners' cinemas, in particular, were almost unique in seeking to combine Hollywood mainstream with 'educational' and emotive political features such as the Russian anti-Nazi propaganda work **Professor Mamlock** (dirs. Adolf Minkin and Herbert Rappaport, 1938). Some films were appreciated as much for film aesthetics as social content. **Spanish Earth** (director Joris Ivens, 1937) appealed on both counts.[69] For all its radical commitment, it poeticizes the struggles of the peasants, frequently framed heroically against the sky or caught in evocative close-up as they irrigate the land or battle to hold the high road – the only route for provisions between Valencia and Madrid. The film was compelling viewing for south Wales miners, many of them then considering joining the battle, or knowing comrades already in the thick of it. Ivens's film was effective as propaganda because its style, and choice of camera angles, proclaimed a grandeur in the many deeds of ordinary men who had never handled rifles before joining up. The form was also, of course, familiar and palatable to audiences weaned on such romanticized imagery in the commercial cinema.

The Tredegar Institute was just one organization practising what Bond preached, with a judicious mix of Hollywood blockbusters and the often more challenging, socially conscious films. The institute screened traditional newsreels (the **Movietone News**, the **March of Time** series) and swelled coffers with Hollywood money-spinners, from Shirley Temple confections to Hollywood epics. But by the late thirties, it was showing a reasonable quota of films distributed by the Progressive Film Institute and was extremely keen to screen Spanish films as more and more miners went to Spain to fight the Republican cause.[70] The screenings in miners' clubs played an important role in opening up the institute's traditional male preserves to wives, pensioners of both sexes, and children.[71] This lifting of an anachronistic barrier was very important to confirm or recreate a sense of community feeling in the Valleys' mining villages, as Hogenkamp points out.

The alternative circuit of progressive political film began to peter out in the late 1930s after the arrival of sound in miners' cinemas by mid-decade led to a drop in demand for silent agit-prop material, though Kino helped continue circulation of European films on 16mm.[72] The Second World War finally staunched the flow of Russian, and Spanish Civil War films. The surge of interest from Strand and the workers' film movement in presenting more abrasive, questioning material on screen did not, unfortunately, lead to the growth of any film-making group in Wales – or much activity from any other quarter.

Other documentaries and shorts

A handful of other documentaries made in Wales between 1929 and 1936 deserve attention. Very few contained any explicit or covert criticism of the status quo, and all are minor works, though some had undoubted merit. **Great Western Ports** (1929) produced for the Great Western Railway, was a sponsored documentary of some verve and energy, making use of fluent tracking and travelling shots, irises (principally a silent screen device), and graphics. Shots of Penarth Docks and the Queen Alexandra and West Bute Docks in Cardiff give way to footage expressing the docks' role as importers of world cargoes. The film highlights Barry Docks' record of shipping 11 million tons of coal a year, and emphasizes the growth of Swansea, largest of the GWR docks, from a small port 150 years before to the 'metallurgical and anthracite centre of Great Britain'. The film lacks any kind of analysis or reference to the docks slump of the early twenties, strikes, or the vagaries of economic fortunes, but it is an assured documentary within its own narrow parameters and its footage was still readily employed by the new breed of TV documentarists in the 1980s.

There is also a quiet assurance about **Slate Quarrying in North Wales**, made around 1936, apparently as a silent. It is a moving testament to the achievements of the men in the slate mines during their heyday. The camerawork is not always fluent but the use of long shots and startling, low angles places the dangers of quarrying in perspective, and gives some idea of the monumental scale of operations at Dinorwic, near Llanberis, mined for nearly 200 years, and at that time the largest slate quarry in the world, employing 2,500 men. An impressive crane shot into the quarry opens the film. Then a locomotive, which at first sight might be moving across a pock-marked lunar landscape, is dwarfed by rocky outcrops. Slate is shown on journeys by cable car and mountain railway to the higher level of the galleries. Horses pull waste material in trucks to the dumps, the rest goes to workshops and the end product is shown delivered in the quarry's railway to its own port, Port Dinorwic. This purely observational film lacks a human dimension (the workers are seen only from a distance), but the titles are simple and informative and free of the facetiousness and stridency endemic in so much titling of the 1920s and 1930s. The restraint, formal rhythms and the respect shown to the employees by the film-makers give this well-crafted work and its subjects an impressive dignity.

Land of My Fathers (1931) was no more than a short musical entertainment. But **Black Diamonds** (1932), by ex-miner Charles Hanmer, set mainly in Yorkshire, had more substance. It contained newspaper-cutting references to a Rhondda disaster – at Llwynypia – in a low-budget attempt to show difficult and dangerous pit conditions in Britain through the eyes of a would-be film-maker, effectively the film's narrator, who has to be convinced of their cinematic potential. The film ended with a pitfall injuring the film-maker and shots of miners in silhouette, moving across the skyline to a song limning their courage.

A primitive storyline was essayed by the journalist and publicist C. H. Dand in his lone independent film **Men Against Death** (1933), which, apparently, no longer survives.[73] This dramatic reconstruction of Welsh slate-quarrying conditions, a documentary drama shot by James Burger, had a slender story-line but earned praise from John Grierson. The 35mm. sound film, telling of 'the risks taken by quarrymen in their daily work', was given an E rating, which meant it was a British film not eligible for quota and so stood little chance of appealing to cinema managers or surfacing regularly in programmes. It obtained some screenings on the Gaumont-

British circuit but – handicapped by the grade – failed to make enough money to enable Dand, a one-time scenario writer for the Associated Sound Film Industries Co. at Wembley, to continue in production.[74] The film historian Rachael Low is disparaging about the film. She refers to its poor photographic quality and its serious anticlimax, a weak ending fashioned around a rockfall avalanche. The BFI-sponsored *Sight and Sound* magazine claimed that, photographically, it left much to be desired, and editing was for 'effect rather than meaning'. The reviewer 'PR' (Paul Rotha?) complained that Dand should have taken a 'less ambitious approach' and been content with a simple re-creation of daily tasks instead of trying to 'build up a dramatic crisis' which failed to materialize on screen.[75]

A Welsh-language talkie

More significant than either of these last two films was **Y Chwarelwr** (The Quarryman) (1935), the first Welsh-language talkie – made by Sir Ifan ab Owen Edwards, founder of Urdd Gobaith Cymru (The Welsh League of Youth). Edwards, son of the pioneering journalist-educator Sir O. M. Edwards and father of the S4C's first controller, Owen Edwards, worked with the writer John Ellis Williams. Williams's drama company bought a £250 Bell and Howell camera, £100 worth of film, two projectors and a generator and shooting took place at a quarry in Blaenau Ffestiniog. In a throwback to pioneer days, the film was toted by van to rural areas and many venues where there was no electricity.[76] The hero of the film was a young man who, following the death of his father, left school and sacrificed the chance of further education to earn money in the quarries to allow his brighter younger sister to enter college. The theme of choice between pursuing education, staying at home to face up to one's family responsibilities or allowing others to seize chances was to remain at the core of much Welsh work from **How Green Was My Valley** and **The Corn is Green** to **David**.

Y Chwarelwr, costing some £2,900, was shown extensively in north Wales in 1935–6, an average of five times a week, and attracted large crowds, but it does not appear to have been distributed outside the Urdd movement.[77] In a seventies television interview, John Ellis Williams said Sir Ifan had been less interested in reproducing the details of a quarryman's life than in telling a story and producing a 'romantic melodrama'. Yet there is much emphasis in the film on the quarrymen's lunchtime recreation in their on-site 'cabin' where they stage their own light-hearted Eisteddfodau, competing with songs and accordion. The film-makers obtained free use of the locations and Ellis Williams recalled that only one actor was paid – 10*s.* for two half-days a week. The film was shot mute and the actors were ferried down to Ealing to record the sound on disc.

Owen Edwards says now that the film was primarily made as propaganda: 'My father thought the best way to get people excited about the Urdd was to make films about it . . . he believed in Welsh as a medium of communication and thought Welsh should be used with modern techniques.' Sir Ifan filmed until the 1950s and captured much footage of Urdd events, including summer camps in Europe. In 1993 some of this material, 'exhumed' by the Wales Film and TV Archive, was screened at the Celtic Film and Television Festival in Brittany.

Despite the birth of Welsh-language talkies, the Strand documentaries and the increased film consciousness of the miners' institutes, the public by the late 1930s had rarely seen truly individualized Welsh characters in either fiction or documentary.

Y Chwarelwr (The Quarryman) made by Sir Ifan ab Owen Edwards – the first Welsh-language talkie.

Even **The Citadel**, King Vidor's version of A. J. Cronin's novel, for all its strengths and insight into valleys ravaged by unemployment, scarcely touched on proletarian characters in its Welsh sequences, apart from Emlyn Williams's sympathetic miners' agent and a few unflattering cameos. But seeds had been sown elsewhere – in the left-wing dramas presented by London's Unity Theatre – for the feature which proved a watershed: in Ealing studios' production, **Proud Valley**.[78] It showed a south Wales mining community riven by class and social divisions, pit closures and disasters and presented, albeit in a tentative way, both racial and worker–management conflict. The **Citadel** and **Proud Valley** showed aspects of urban life which had never reached the screens before – but both these works, as we shall see, were undermined by compromise.

THE CITADEL

In *The Citadel*, the principal obstacles to the miners' health are bureaucracy and the miners' own superstitions rather than the healthy capitalist instincts of the mine owners which carry the weight of blame in Reed's film.

(Raymond Durgnat and Scott Simmon comparing King Vidor's film **The Citadel** with **The Stars Look Down** in Durgnat and Simmon, **King Vidor, American**, 1988, p. 208)

There was little chance of authentic images of Wales penetrating the major circuits in the 1930s. Despite odd exceptions, the larger London-based companies were still reluctant to film on location outside the metropolis and feature film-makers were hamstrung also by the censors' dictum against material centred around industrial disputes or with emphasis on any trade-union activity. These restrictions, plus the tramline thinking of producers who thought their audiences incapable of appreciating anything but escapist entertainment, help explain much of the pap peddled on British screens in the early sound years. Michael Balcon, as we have seen, accepted, in hindsight, his culpability not merely for the undemanding Gainsborough silents, which attempted to feed on 'safe' middle-brow plays and novels, but also later for the smugness pervading some of the lesser Ealing comedies in particular. The mentality of many 1930s British producers was not far removed from that of studio bosses during the First World War who had such a low opinion of their audience's concentration powers that they insisted that even some four- or five-reel films should be released with the publicity slogan 'No padding'. Producers and exhibitors resorted to pussyfooting and safety-first programming partly in response to pressure groups and religious watch-dogs who regularly expressed worries about the effect on morals of the racy American gangster movies and films with their amoral life-styles, psychopathic hoods and glamorous molls. In 1929, even before many cinemas were wired for sound, the National Union of Teachers' Swansea branch asked the local education authority to launch an inquiry into the type of films at local picture houses; and said they 'realised the influence on our schoolchildren of frequent visits to the cinema'.

In 1934, the newly formed, 12,000-strong, Cardiff Board of Catholic Action, the first diocesan organization of its kind, 'declared war on immoral films', threatening to advise parishioners to boycott films they thought unwholesome (*Catholic Times*, 27 April 1934). *Today's Cinema* pointed out that the boycott threat had the Pope's approval following a visit to Rome by the CBCA founder Archbishop Mostyn, and warned that 'unless there is an improvement in the standard of films shown the 90,000 adherents of the Roman Catholic faith in South Wales may be forbidden to attend cinemas.' But these were empty threats compared with the impact of the Hays Code – Will H. Hays's Motion Picture Production Code – which emasculated much American cinema of the thirties, even if witty, resourceful writers and studio heads soon worked out their own codes of sophisticated innuendo and *double entendre* to mitigate the impact of MPPC's strict guidelines. It is, perhaps, ironic that an American company brought to the screen **The Citadel**, which suffered at the hands of censors but proved the first of a series of mining films which was to fix, indelibly, the image of south Wales in the minds of audiences throughout the world. It was also the first 'Welsh' fictional feature of any real significance with a contemporary theme.

Fallow Years

Michael Powell, probably the most talented of all British directors, was not as lucky, or as powerful, as **Citadel** director King Vidor when he made his potboiler melodrama **The Phantom Light** three years earlier and chose to film early sequences near Portmeirion (later the location for **The Prisoner** TV series). Powell, who had spent holidays in Wales, 'loved the scale' of everything in that part of north Wales: 'the little trains, the slate quarries and the mountains'.[1] And he devised the film's entire Welsh opening, breaking away from Evadne Price's stage source material, to present the impressions of the central character, Gordon Harker's lighthouse keeper, on his first visit to the principality. His train journey becomes an odyssey as he leaves behind familiar landmarks to encounter an eerie terrain, in which events seem almost arbitrary. 'I wanted to make a thriller with a sense of another world, an atmosphere of its own, but I really didn't do it until I made **The Edge of the World** in the Shetlands,' Powell reflected later.[2]

The Phantom Light (1935) was the last of a four-film package by Powell for Gaumont-British and the director was already reasonably well established, yet when he presented his chiefs with early footage they told him to shoot the rest of the feature in Cornwall, closer to home: 'They made films mainly in the studios in those days. Films were a kind of cottage industry in England. I'd persuaded them to let me do that opening sequence. They weren't too keen about it, but it's amazing how little they knew about Wales.' Powell was upset by the decision, and rightly made no claims later for the film, a ponderous tale of seafaring and smuggling skulduggery with the visuals in interior shots flat and unimaginative: 'I did what I could given the limitations of plot, mainly . . .'[3] There *is* some effective economical editing but the work presents a typical outsider's stereotyped image of a folksy, quaint Wales viewed through the eyes of Harker's comically blinkered but brash visitor.

It is sad that Powell's later hopes of filming in Wales remained unfulfilled. In later days he could never agree a Welsh project with his writer-collaborator Emeric Pressburger. One idea floated was a film called **Bouquet** with one story from each of the four home countries. Powell suggested a Dylan Thomas short story, probably 'The Extraordinary Little Cough'. Pressburger considered as his contribution 'Gents Only', the 'Rhys Davies work about an undertaker whose wife left him, so he refused to bury any women' ('Very Welsh', thought Powell).[4] This theme of individuals or families exacting petty revenge was later exploited in the 1953 Welsh comedy **Valley of Song**, while a wife's infidelity also triggered obsessions and insular humour in another fifties work **Girdle of Gold**.

Another 'Welsh' melodrama to emerge prior to the Second World War was Irishman Donovan Pedelty's 66-minute feature **Landslide** (1937), made by Paramount British – another 'quota quickie' from an American company anxious to retain a foothold in Britain and cash in on the UK market.[5] It centred on a small fit-up theatre company, the Orientals, touring Wales and playing the (fictional) Llancreigiaucrog Empire. The players are cut off when the venue is all but engulfed by falling boulders and concrete. A murderer in their midst plucks off the cashier, then attacks two other company members. One victim, Dinah (Dinah Sheridan), finds her boyfriend, the company's juvenile lead Jimmy (Jimmy Hanley) is the no. 1 suspect but the culprit turns out to be 'a half-witted stage hand'.[6]

In 1938 Zoltan Korda, brother of the ambitious Alexander of London Films, used Wales to double up for exotic locations in the company's Technicolor production of **The Drum** (1938, from A. E. W. Mason's novel). The metamorphosis of Wales here was as ingenious as cameraman Freddie Young and designers achieved with **The Inn of the Sixth Happiness** (dir. Mark Robson) twenty years later.[7] **The Drum** starred 14-year-old Sabu – and Barry-born actor Roger Livesey, who made a distinctive contribution to most of Michael Powell's finest films in the forties. It was made at Denham – but another work to surface from those studios was to have more durable appeal and influence.

Vidor's film: the background

It is hard to think of a film more suited than **The Citadel** (1938) to herald the most fruitful decade for features reflecting the conditions and turmoil in urban south Wales (the decline of north Wales industries remained curiously neglected). It was the first work to show, or even hint at, the high incidence of silicosis or allied dust and lung disease from the pits. It also broke new ground in the commercial cinema by suggesting the shabby morality of a *laissez-faire* mining industry and health service and, by implication, a whole social system which refused to countenance even the most meagre compensation pay for miners who wished to attend hospitals for tests.

Despite the vigorous attentions of timorous censors, which delayed filming, the work presented a slightly lurid but vivid – and chastening – picture of a pre-nationalization medical profession, top-heavy with miscreants; washed out, overworked GPs; and mountebanks who preyed on the fashionable and gullible in London private nursing homes. Its subject matter caused the two censors serious concern. Mrs N. Crouzet considered 'there was so much that was disparaging to doctors' in the book that it was 'unsuitable for production as a film . . . I think it dangerous to shatter what faith the general public has in the medical profession.' The other BBFC watchdog Lt.-Col. J. C. Hanna suggested 'the faults of the undesirable types of doctors be not presented in such a manner to suggest . . . they are the rule and not the exception'. James C. Robertson, in a detailed study of censorship based on rare access to records, claimed the BBFC 'went in for mutilation on the grand scale' with **The Citadel** and made 'extensive cuts and alterations', but he stressed that BBFC records were too incomplete to evaluate the impact of the cuts in detail. Neither director King Vidor nor producer Victor Saville has been noticeably critical of the censorship but it seems clear that the production was diluted at the scripting stage and, as we shall see, there were other important factors shaping the final adaptation.[8] **The Citadel**'s authenticity was still vouchsafed, for many, by its source – the best-selling novel by A. J. Cronin, formerly a GP in Scotland (an experience which spawned his *Dr Finlay's Casebook*) and in the south Wales valleys in Tredegar and Treherbert.[9] He had also, more relevantly perhaps, acted as a medical inspector for Britain's mines and written a report on haematite pits. His credentials were strong enough for 200 copies of his novel to be circulated at the British Medical Association's national conference in 1937, when a session was apparently devoted to discussing its significance.[10]

The film was one of a trio of features made immediately before the war by MGM in Britain to qualify for British quota. The American director King Vidor was a maverick in Hollywood, enlighted and progressive by the Hollywood mores of his time.[11] Other films he directed explored living conditions, poverty and class issues, notably **Our Daily Bread** (1934) and **The Crowd** (1928) – which for all its compassion and decency in treating the travails of a working man seems reactionary in its exhortation to the audience to settle for anonymity and the status quo, however unpalatable, rather than climb above one's 'station' in life. Fascinatingly, it runs counter to the philosophy of the later films of Roosevelt's 1930s New Deal period which encouraged the notion that any man could reach the top by his own efforts in America's democratic society and make *fundamental changes* to that society. The idea underpins such Frank Capra humanist comedies as **Mr Deeds Goes to Town** (1936) and **Mr Smith Goes to Washington** (1939), and his later **It's a Wonderful Life** (1947). It also lies at the heart of **The Citadel** which reflects Vidor's shift from a fairly radical left-wing position towards the 'populism' subscribed to by the new administration.

Transfiguration . . . Robert Donat as an idealistic Dr Manson in the harrowing childbirth sequence of *The Citadel*.

Vidor obviously saw south Wales in highly romanticized terms and reacted like many outsiders on his first visit. He was 'astonished' to see the miners walking to their homes at the end of the day with black faces, 'not a particle of white skin could be seen.' Though Vidor's comments suggest a certain admiration, even awe, of the miners, there is neither identification with them nor real compassion. The lead actor, Robert Donat (Oscar-nominated for his role), spent some time in Wales observing everything before production began.[12] Yet apart from opening shots at Treherbert – arguably the most evocative in the film – Vidor shot almost the whole feature in the Denham studio with the mine reconstructed on a huge sound stage. Despite this, the pit scenes, including the celebrated sequence in which the hero Andrew Manson performs an improvised amputation, carried great conviction, prompting Basil Wright to compare them with Pabst's superb **Kameradschaft** (1931).[13] **The Citadel** certainly pre-empted much of the dominant mood and many of the key motifs of British mining films in the 1940s.

Manson is a self-educated Scot, a small-town GP and idealist who, unlike David Fenwick, the protagonist of Cronin's filmed novel **The Stars Look Down**, allows himself to be caught up in the corrupt lucrative byways of the profession. Fenwick is enmeshed in the bureaucracy of a Labour Party prepared to break nationalization pledges in the 1920s just as Manson in his later London days is surrounded by mercenary medical charlatans or timeservers. **The Citadel** – the film and the novel – fell on fertile ground with so many members of the medical profession advocating cheaper medicine and some kind of state control of standards, even if King Vidor stopped well short of pressing for nationalization. The film was also almost inevitably diluted by the director's conception of Hollywood demands and even the key casting was revealing (and problematic) and affected the story's treatment. Rosalind Russell who, coincidentally, made her initial screen impact in the 1937 version of Emlyn Williams's play *Night Must Fall* gained the part of Manson's wife Christine – after Donat had exercised a contract clause allowing him to reject the company's original choice.[14] English actress Elizabeth Allan had been announced for the role and it appears that the casting alteration was made after the film company decided to change Cronin's ending to avoid killing off Mrs Manson, the lead female character, in a road accident. Miss Allan, best known as Ronald Colman's great love in **A Tale of Two Cities** (1935), took MGM British Studios Ltd. to court and the case fought by the actors' union Equity became a temporary *cause célèbre*. She was awarded £3,400 with costs, after alleging breach of contract (though the judgement was later reversed), and a different version of events emerged to challenge the brusque reference to the affair in J. C. Trewin's Donat biography in which he confirms acting on the casting-approval clause.[15]

The film's producer Victor Saville, who initially bought the screen rights, said that 'owing to the re-writing of the script it would not be correct on artistic grounds for Miss Allan to play the part.' It is clear that the decision not to kill off the heroine affected the whole political and social premise of the denouement. And the choice of a rising star like Russell imposed its own box-office logic on the storyline. Saville said he had asked Cronin 'why he had killed her [Christine] off in the book'. Dr Cronin said he wanted his hero to go to the heights of medicine unshackled by a wife, but Saville thought that 'a very unfair motive'.[16] Years later, Vidor said that Allan had been signed to play the part 'but after I met her I thought Rosalind would be much better' – though Margaret Sullavan was his first choice.[17] Russell, in fact, gave a first-rate performance, even though she seemed more feisty and modern than the schoolmarm of the novel, and her conception of the role was in strong contrast to Clare Higgins's insipid paragon in the fatally attenuated 1983 BBC TV version.[18] Russell's presence in Vidor's cast, and the deference to box-office needs, no doubt confirmed MGM in its determination to ensure Mrs Manson's survival to the final credits and it is Manson's mentor and amanuensis Denny (Ralph Richardson) who dies in the road accident. The tragedy finally helps bring Manson, who has been seduced into fleecing rich hypochondriacs, back to his senses. Censorship forces probably influenced the decision not to allow Manson the extra-marital affair he enjoyed in the novel.

Tackling social evils

The re-writing caused serious changes in the tenor of the work. It enabled Vidor and the writers, including wife Elizabeth Hill, to place the emphasis in the last reel or two on Manson's individualism and courage rather than (as in the novel) his renewed determination to revive his life by launching a doctors' co-operative with Denny and his coal industry friend (who does not even figure in the film). Elsewhere the casting seems, in retrospect, flawless with Ralph Richardson memorably insouciant as Denny, the embittered doctor's assistant who befriends Manson on his arrival in south Wales and opens the naïve young doctor's eyes to chicanery in his profession and the social and health scandals which need fighting. Rex Harrison as mephistophelean medic Freddie Lawford (the Freddie Hamson of the novel) is the epitome of insidious charm, and Dilys Davies, actually a doctor's wife from Blaengwynfi, made the most of her first screen chance as a GP's unmarried sister and pennypinching harridan who might be a spiritual cousin of her importunate postmistress in **Proud Valley**.

Vidor's style in the film is terse. He is faithful to Cronin's challenging material in the early stages, allowing us to appreciate Manson's intensity and idealism and the force of Cronin/Manson's arguments and researches. Throughout, Vidor and his writers – who also included Ian Dalrymple, Emlyn Williams (credited for additional dialogue), Frank 'Spig' Wead and John Van Druten – telescope events in the original work with intelligence, helped by Charles Frend's exemplary editing.[19]

The film soon establishes Manson's acceptance of the medical doctrines and shibboleths of his college days but also his blazing enthusiasm for his new calling – witness the first admirably concise shots from the train as the steam engine carries Manson into the Valleys. Vistas of terraced houses are reflected in the windows, or revealed through smooth travelling shots. Donat's expression conveys his character's excitement and barely restrained sense of exhilaration, mingled with slight apprehension, moments before his arrival at Blaenelly in the rain. Initially a stickler for doing things by the book, Manson swiftly recognizes the sloth and fallibility of many of his fellow professionals in south Wales and understands the contempt his friend Denny holds for them. The medical men of the valleys are indeed the 'rag, tag and bobtail of a truly glorious profession'. 'Here', says Denny, 'there's no hospital, no ambulance, no X-ray, no anything, if you want to operate you use the kitchen table.'

Denny, despite his hard drinking and bohemian life-style, implicitly shares Manson's concern for humanity and initially alerts him to the health dangers in the Clydach Place wells. Faced with ignorance and tardiness from colleagues during the community's typhoid outbreak, Manson risks his career by joining Denny in a nocturnal expedition to blow up the festering sewers contaminating the water supply. It is interesting that Raymond Durgnat, in his early seventies review of the film, asserted that terrorist groups like the Angry Brigade would be better off directing their passion in exploding bombs on inanimate objects, but made no references to incidents of bombings of 'inanimate objects' in Wales in the thirties and sixties and the conviction of Welsh Republican John Jenkins and his companions for offences involving water pipe and railway-line bombings.[20]

Vidor cleverly presents Manson as an aloof figure, recognizing his Calvinist roots and self-righteousness, and deflates his pomposity when he first clashes with his future wife Christine Barlow, the schoolmistress he threatens to report for failing to keep away from school the brother of a boy absent with measles; she gives him short shrift. In his determination not to be beaten, Manson then saves the life of a baby. He gives the kiss of life when all seems lost, in a sequence far more stylized than any other and superbly choreographed. It owes much to Frend's editing, linked with Louis Levy's music. The heroic nature of the profession is emphasized by holding Manson in low-angle close-up in his moment of triumph and when, alone, he gently offers thanks to God that 'I'm a doctor'. Levy's score matches the increased tempo of the cutting as

Manson strives to keep the child alive, just as the staccato strings earlier on convey his tension and turmoil. At the moment of release for Manson, his looming shadow on the wall both emphasizes his increased stature and presages bleaker times.

These early scenes are undoubtedly the most memorable; from now on **The Citadel** enters much more problematic areas, mainly in Vidor's treatment of the miners, but the screenplay conveys a wealth of ideas about the coal industry and the film is undoubtedly highly critical of the medical profession. By implication Vidor endorses – or does little to refute – Denny's judgement of the local district medical officer Gribley as a 'lazy, evasive, incompetent swine'. The mercenary nature of the profession is first established in the bleakly humorous scene when the fearsome scold Miss Page (Dilys Davies) alleges that cash Manson has accepted for saving the miner Joe's baby should go to her brother Dr Page and berates Manson as 'a dirty thief'. Manson responds by reminding her that he receives one-sixth of the money *they* earn for work he does for them.

Shackled by the anachronistic censorship system which prevented trade-union references, the film keeps its distance from the miners, who have their quota of malingerers. It stresses Manson's zeal in trying to alleviate the damaging effects of dust in genuine illness cases. If the doctors are shown as corrupt or ineffectual procrastinators, the miners are seen as blinkered, almost to a man, in their condemnation of Manson's experiments and refusal to see the pit as the source of their ill health (though Cronin's matter-of-fact acceptance of animal tests would scarcely go unremarked in today's climate). Cronin's apparent cynicism about the working men's intelligence and integrity has attracted some justified criticism, but he adopts a similar jaundiced view of their exploiters. In a pertinent exchange, Manson is warned by a veteran medic Llewellyn Jolly: 'I wouldn't be too difficult about renewing old "unfit for work" certificates. There are a lot of chronic cases here. We don't want to get the men stirred up.'

The miners emerge as unenlightened – Raymond Durgnat describes them as 'hardcore Bible Belters' – and they are prone to manipulation by rabble-rousers such as Ben Chenkin, the burly committee-man who resents Manson's refusal to grant him a certificate for 'stagmus'.[21] The doctor attributes Chenkin's troubles to 'an over-indulgence in malt liquor' and declares him fit for work, though he pursues his suspicions of links between the illnesses of some patients – pit hauliers and drillers – and dust in anthracite pits. It is Chenkin who leads the move to steal Manson's guinea pigs, allegedly to prevent them suffering during experiments. But Manson's findings lead directly to his conclusions that the dust is responsible for the men's coughs. The Scot, railing against the tuberculosis caused by chemical action on the lungs of the silicon in the coal, keenly senses a social injustice. 'I think it's a disease caused directly by the work they do and when they get laid up from it they don't get a penny piece in compensation as it isn't classed as an industrial disease,' he points out in scenes which broke new ground in highlighting mining's toll. Vidor, while allowing the script to make these compelling points, is anxious to sweeten the pill with humorous character foibles.

The care taken over small details gives much of the film's south Wales section credibility. Vidor is not frightened to dispense information about working conditions and economic facts, both in short supply on screen up to that point. That is particularly obvious in scenes when we learn of the Aberalaw Medical Aid Society, who are financed by pitmen giving a percentage of their wages every week. Manson is

soon made aware by the miners' agent Owens (Williams) of the hold the men have over him. Vidor shows how the system which allows the men to choose their own doctors can be misused if the medics become prey to special pleading and pressure groups.

Manson's transformation from south Wales altruist to London money-grubber is effected, in contrast, in a succession of broadly sketched scenes. The film emphasizes the disparity between the vital work and needs Manson encounters in the Valleys and the trivial advice and sometimes fraudulent minor treatment which earns him so much money in London where he falls in with his old friend Freddie and the urbane but inept surgeon Ivory (Cecil Parker). Manson's outburst against Ivory after a botched operation costs Denny his life leads into a stream-of-consciousness voice-over. The scene in which a dazed Manson, after lurching through the streets in a none-too-convincing sequence, decides to carry on with his calling, is unsubtle and leaden – inviting highly unfavourable comparisons with the whimsy of a Frank Capra. This decision might have been more persuasively presented in an altercation between husband and wife, but Vidor had already expended the disenchanted Christine's ammunition in an earlier scene when, in the film's pivotal speech, she sabotages a happy picnic by reminding him of the ideals he once had: 'Your work isn't making money. It's bettering humanity. Don't you remember the way we used to talk about life? It was an attack on the unknown, an assault uphill as though you had to take some citadel you couldn't see but you knew was there.'

Denny's death during Ivory's operation triggers Manson's disgust at the quackery around him and makes him aware that all his tetchiness and dissembling stem from guilt and insecurity. Earlier Manson has scarcely listened to the worries of Mrs Orlando, who runs his favourite restaurant, when she talks of her daughter Anna's poor lungs. After his change of heart Manson makes amends, virtually abducting Mrs Orlando's sick child from hospital and taking her for successful treatment to the outlawed Stillman, an American maverick doctor with an international reputation but no official qualifications in England. Vidor swiftly establishes Stillman's credentials and commitment to his calling when the American expresses appreciation of Manson's paper on dust inhalation and silicosis and says it's a pity the young man hasn't continued with work in the tuberculosis field after his 'brilliant start'.

Lazare Meeson's decor – airy interiors, uncluttered surroundings, pristine walls, bright lights – suggest space, gloss and leisure in the London scenes just as the chiaroscuro lighting helps create a sense of claustrophobia in the miners' homes. One can understand, perhaps, why a small-town doctor suddenly surrounded by such conspicuous consumption and 'sophisticated' friends should find it difficult to resist blandishments, particularly after his encounters with the mean-spirited Miss Page and Ben Chenkin and the dead wood of the south Wales health service.

Manson refuses Denny's offer to join his team of idealists in a clinic of specialists: 'a bacteriologist, ear, nose and throat man, an obstetrician . . .' His dull response – 'Where's the money coming from?' – sums up his new priorities. But the finale, with Manson called before the English Medical Union, rounding on his persecutors and justifying his liaison with the 'unqualified' Stillman is a dramatic *tour-de-force*. Manson throws in the face of his accusers the names of Pasteur and Ehrlich – both vilified in the past as so-called quacks. The speech now has a special resonance, reminding us of the wholesale changes in the medical profession in the 1940s. It is significant that some ideas advocated by Cronin were incorporated and sometimes broadened in scope by the 1948 Health Bill steered through Westminster by Ebbw Vale MP Aneurin Bevan. Manson's credo reflected a little of the Labour government's philosophy in shaking up the service: 'It's high time we started putting our house in order. If we go on trying to pretend everything's right in the profession and everything's wrong outside it will be the death of scientific progress.'

But Vidor significantly departs from the book at the finale when Manson leaves the hearing with his wife – his career apparently shattered. The director leaves open the question of whether Manson will resume his research. Certainly it hardly seems likely to be in the kind of co-operative visualized by Denny; and the finale is a long way from advocating nationalization, rather suggesting that it will take more brave *individuals* to ensure wholesale reforms in thinking. Vidor claimed the book's ending was too much in the literary tradition and would be found wanting unless changed. He said later that he hit on the 'gimmick' of Denny's death to shake Manson's life back on course 'and spur him to return to Wales to resume his work on silicosis research'. This conclusion is not readily apparent from the film.[22] Vidor's quoted statements about the film in later years were extraordinary, betraying a faulty memory. He allegedly claimed, in one interview, that Denny in the book was 'a little tailor who lived in the neighbourhood' and a minor character.[23] His comments certainly beg questions. It is not at all clear from the film that Manson has won the hearing, nor is it established who is to fund any research. At the finale the doctor has retrieved some lost pride and honour but he seems in a vacuum and, with these changes, Vidor has filleted the work of some of its politics and social content. If Denny had lived and Christine Manson died, Manson could equally have decided to change his former life-style (particularly after Christine's speech cited earlier). The avenue to social and political solutions with Manson joining forces with Hope and Denny has been blocked by Vidor and the writers to the detriment of the film's logic. At the climax it seems suspiciously as if Manson has closed his mind to the possibilities of real change and resolved to continue his research in isolation – to fit snugly into Roosevelt's New Deal individualism. Raymond Durgnat even concluded that at the finale Manson 'walks proudly away from the medical profession'.[24] It was a far cry from Cronin's intent, even though by the late thirties he had apparently lost faith in achieving reforms through literature and, after the success of his filmed novel **Hatter's Castle** (1941), he retired from the fray and spent his last thirty-five years in Switzerland.

MGM executives would not have lost sleep over the blurring of the political message and Vidor later contentedly observed that 'the film paid for itself many times over in America.' It ran a few weeks at the 5,000-seat Capitol in New York and also broke box-office records in London, opening at both the Empire and Ritz in the West End, and was the top British box-office film of the year, according to *Kine Weekly*.[25] **The Citadel** was also cited by the *Kinematograph Year Book* as the outstanding film to emerge that year from 'the British side of American organizations'. But in more recent years Raymond Durgnat is just one critic to take exception to the presentation of the miners as 'a mob who wreck Manson's laboratory', claiming it was 'wildly at odds with Welsh trade-unionism and chapel culture'.[26] He pointed out that the doctors' co-operative of **The Citadel** was not a 'paraphrase of a National Health Service but an alternative to it' – 'a demonstration that socialism would be unnecessary if only the medical profession followed "an inspirationalist" change of heart.' He also believed that MGM would never have criticized American doctors and hospitals and he cited what he termed a 'cold feet title card' in America which said the film was not 'intended as a reflection on the great medical profession, which has done so much towards beating back those forces of nature'.[27]

The Welsh historian and film writer Peter Stead has also objected to the miners' depiction as 'essentially idiots' and 'a stupid peasantry'.[28] He points out that the men's medical aid scheme was 'revealed as a rip off'. Stead claims, a little uncharitably, that the film 'fudged every political issue', and in particular that mining trade-unionism had been presented inaccurately and dismissed as a 'restrictive guild or syndicate'.[29] **The Citadel** did at least deglamorize mining and stress the hardships, and legacies, of the pitmen's lives and the iniquities of a health system which failed to provide proper compensation. It also pressed the need for codes of practice and minimum standards in a hidebound, patchwork medical profession. That is no small list of credentials for an engrossing and affecting film. As the American critic, William K. Everson, acknowledged: 'It said more about serious issues of the day than Hollywood was allowing itself to say in the never-never land immediately prior to World War II.'[30] The last word should perhaps go to Durgnat. He considered '**The Citadel** was pretty negative about everything' but concluded that its 'mixture of moral verve and concern spoke louder than the plot's fine print'.[31]

HOW GREEN WAS MY VALLEY – AND THE MINING FILMS, 1938–1949

No picture of a mining district ever seems to be complete without a disaster (we have two in this picture), the warning siren is becoming as familiar as the pithead gear shot against the sky – and that has joined the Eiffel Tower and the Houses of Parliament as one of the great platitudes of the screen . . . Colour prejudice is dragged in for the sake of Paul Robeson, who plays the part of a big black Pollyanna, keeping everybody cheerful and dying nobly at the end . . . the theme dies out altogether at the close with patriotic speeches and crisis posters and miners dying for England [*sic*].

(Graham Greene on **Proud Valley**, *The Spectator*, 15 March 1940)

No worthwhile study of films about Wales can afford to skimp in exploring the handful of fascinating mining features which emerged in the 1938–49 period. Most outsiders asked to define Welshness on film will ransack their memories for the images which have coloured people's perception of Wales for decades: the potent views of industrialized mining Wales and its stoic heroes offered by **The Citadel**, **Proud Valley** (1940) and **How Green Was My Valley** (1941). These films more than any others have borne the weight of Welsh folk-memory and created a mythic Wales unlikely to be easily dislodged from the minds of cinema-goers. **Blue Scar** (1949) also deserves a place in the pantheon, for Jill Craigie's film, more than the others, sought its inspiration in the actual urban Wales of the period (and not some writer's or Hollywood director's fanciful misconception). **The Corn is Green** (1945) and **Last Days of Dolwyn** (1949) discuss the language, cultural tensions and Welsh dependency on England (and vice versa) in the framework of screen melodrama, and explore the ambivalent attitudes to Wales of its creator, Emlyn Williams. All these films offer fascinating, if partial, views of the Welsh industrial experience. Also demanding consideration is **Fame is the Spur** (1947), where trade-union politics and social conditions in the Rhondda, central to a late segment of the book, have been all but excised.

The Stars Look Down (1939), a key work amongst British films and in Carol Reed's *oeuvre* as director, does not deal directly with Welsh miners, but there are obvious parallels between events shown in the North East just prior to the First World War and the breakdowns in industrial and social relations in the south Wales coalfield which led to incidents such as the Tonypandy riots. The sense that scenes in Reed's film have a Welsh feel is reinforced by the film's genesis in the novel by A. J. Cronin, and by the forceful presence in the cast of Welshman Emlyn Williams, playing the most manipulative, disruptive and arguably influential character. This film surely provided *his* finest hour as an actor.

The influence of all these mining films cannot be overestimated. Only one or two mining films set in Wales since – the 1960 and 1976 BBC TV dramatizations of **How Green Was My Valley**, perhaps, and certainly Karl Francis's **Above Us the Earth** (1976) – have proved nearly as persuasive. Yet all the works from the late thirties to late forties, apart perhaps from Reed's, were compromised fatally even if they showed, to greater and lesser degrees, the contradictory forces at work in the coalfield (particularly conflicts of loyalty) or in the battlegrounds of trade-union and party politics. **The Citadel** was diluted by the prevailing political attitudes in the US and director King Vidor's attempts to yoke Cronin's fairly radical ideas (and ideals) to the dominant individualism and ethos of Roosevelt's America. Jill Craigie's **Blue Scar**, which could never have been made without National Coal Board backing, was surprisingly forthright about pitmen's qualms on the realities of public ownership, yet that sponsorship of necessity imposed its own limitations. The two main Welsh films of the forties were both susceptible to outside factors. The original scripted ending of **Proud Valley** – in which miners take over the pit – was changed by producer Michael Balcon in line with the mood of the times and the call for employers and miners to present a common front against the Nazi threat.[1] So pitmen and bosses finally work together at the film's climax to re-open the colliery after a disaster. **How Green Was My Valley**, perhaps the most provocative work of all, presented a heavily romanticized vision of Wales filtered through the imagination of Hollywood director John Ford, a deceptively sentimental man who often dwelt on his Irish ancestry (he was baptized Sean O'Feeney) and drew on its mythology for inspiration. Unfortunately, Ford, who never visited Wales and shot **How Green Was My Valley** on the 20th Century–Fox back lot and the studio ranch near Malibu, was indifferent to the distinctions between Celtic nationalities, a blindness demonstrated when Irish jigs were performed by the Welsh family patriarch Gwilym (Donald Crisp, a Scotsman) at Angharad's wedding. Ford's replies to criticism, 'It's a Celtic country, isn't it?' or 'They're all micks, aren't they?', were revealing. No other film about Wales has raised so many hackles – or produced as much emotional involvement.[2] The director's confection, from Richard Llewellyn's 1938 novel, is anathema to many people despite its five Oscars. It is dismissed by some as a work of blarney which, by glamorizing the lives of people in industrial south Wales and simplifying the turmoil they lived through, betrays a lack of respect and appreciation of their struggles.

How Green Was My Valley

Ford's film *can* be seen as shameless pathos, another attempt to package the past by a director who has never stinted on emotion. In doing this, the argument runs, he has defused a community's politics and problems, robbed pit families (by presenting them through the roseate glow of memory) of their vitality and has created icons rather than human beings. Certainly there is something enervated about **How Green**, and all these complaints and readings have some validity. But the criticisms fail to explain why the film, and the novel in its day and probably up to the seventies, had such a potent emotional charge for audiences and readers within Wales.

The idealized past of the book's earlier sections is a world of certainty and stable values – a world that by 1938 had been torn apart by the Depression, the disputes that had convulsed the major industries, and the uproar and uncertainties in Europe and particularly in Spain, where thousands of miners joined the fight against Franco. *How Green*, and the mining novels generally, mythologized the worker, gave him the heroic stature denied him by employers through the bitter years of the twenties and thirties, and invested proletarian tasks and lives with the kind of dignity directors like Ralph Bond had found so singularly lacking in the British screen's depiction of the working class.

The movie's detractors often seize on obvious incongruities while ignoring deeper shortcomings – ridiculing the sets, the ludicrously out-of-scale miners' cottages with their inflated interiors, the emphasis on miners' songs and, above all, the casting. It is perhaps small wonder that south Wales historian Peter Stead has termed Ford's mining village 'an Irish Shangri-La'.[3] Four Irish players had key roles. Maureen O'Hara played Angharad, Sara Allgood was Beth Morgan, the mother (later eclipsed in popular Welsh memory by Rachel Thomas's performance in the 1960 BBC TV version), Barry Fitzgerald (who never quite shook off the stage dust as he ran the gamut of garrulous Hollywood Irishmen) was Cyfartha, and his brother Arthur Shields the vicious deacon, Parry.[4] Crisp, who played the boy Huw's father, was a Scot who had acted (and co-directed) with both D. W. Griffith and Keaton. Roddy McDowall (Huw) and Anna Lee (Bron), John Loder (Ianto) and Patric Knowles (Ivor), were English. Rhys Williams, as puckish pugilist Dai Bando – and also dialogue coach and (probably falsely) credited narrator for the film – was the only Welshman in a significant role.[5] It remains a paradox that perhaps the most deeply felt performance (ignoring the intrusive accent) comes from the Canadian Walter Pidgeon as the preacher, Gruffydd. Despite the idiosyncrasies of casting, only Morton Lowry's rather dapper teacher, Jonas, is untrue to the *spirit* of Llewellyn's novel – even

Anna Lee (left) and Sara
Allgood in *How Green
Was My Valley.*

if many people refused to take the film seriously from that moment, early on, of the mother's first appraisal of Bron: 'There's lovely you are' (delivered in a strong Irish brogue).

The film's champions argue that literal accuracy scarcely matters, that **How Green** has a deeper, more potent reality, its imagined communal experience reflecting another kind of truth. What counts, they insist, is a recognition of the diverse emotional ties and loyalties which bind both families and workers in Valleys communities. The Morgans are as indomitable, as fundamentally emotionally indivisible, as the Joads in **The Grapes of Wrath**, made by Ford the previous year.[6] Ford's 'Welsh' film also enabled him to summon up a time (however brief or illusory) when the old values of benevolent management control and co-operation between rulers and ruled were seen as immutable. The questioning of employers' priorities and motives by Gwilym's sons is seen to usher in a period of doubt and mutual distrust between the coal barons and colliers.

The writer and historian Jeffrey Richards has described **How Green Was My Valley** as a richly nostalgic and deeply moving view of a mining community: 'Whether or not it is an accurate picture of the life of a mining family is irrelevant for it is life as seen through the eyes of a child.'[7] Ford alerts us to his intentions immediately. As the ageing Huw Morgan (merely a voice-over) prepares after fifty years to leave the valley, now beset by personal enmities and befouled by pit slag, the camera slides out of the windows to present a view of pinched, picturesque cottages winding up to the pit.[8] 'Who shall say what is real and what is not?' asks Huw, the narrator, reflecting in the 1930s on events since the 1890s, a significant period of south Wales miners' militancy. 'Can I believe my friends are gone when their voices are still a glory in my ears?' This adult Huw observes that 'there is no hedge or fence around time that is gone' (in other words, Ford is saying, in this film anything is possible). Indeed, the director makes it clear he is shutting out contemporary realities: 'I close my eyes on the valley as it is today.' The shift from the real world to an idealized past has already begun. From then on the family's life is, as Richards says, 'bathed in the golden glow of reminiscence'. The opening shots are as dislocating as the moment when Dorothy, in the American Midwest, enters her magical other world of Oz. From that first movement of Ford's camera, almost on the word 'memory', we are in a world of selective imagery. The south Wales valleys of Ford's film are a rich country of the mind and they are only as true and real as the protagonists' (or film-goers') memories of them.

Those who argue that Ford's work is weighed down with ersatz sentiment compared to the novel should re-read carefully Llewellyn's more glutinous passages. The novel itself was highly coloured and Ford's treatment of the father's emotions, compared with Llewellyn's, is at times remarkably restrained and free of affectation.[9] But anyone demanding accuracy from Ford's film will be discomforted. In this terrain of the memory, the family, despite rifts, remain bound together unshakeably in Huw's mind's eye, defying differences and any physical separations. Huw's credo and attitudes and the susceptibilities which shape the film's tone, are seen to stem from the attitudes of his parents (pragmatists imbued with the same respect for continuity and hierarchy as Ford himself).

How Green Was My Valley cannot be considered without reference to Ford's other work and preoccupations. The treatment of a tightly-knit community here has affinities with the benign American rural townships of Ford's affectionate **Judge Priest** adventures or his films of Western frontier settlements. And the family's trials in economic adversity once more recall the Joads, whose privations summoned up tales and folk-memories for Ford of the Irish famine.[10] The knockabout humour of the Dai Bando/Cyfartha sequences – especially the glorious comic interlude when Dai avenges little Huw by humiliating and KO-ing his vicious (and racist) classroom teacher – resembles Victor McLaglen's near-burlesque moments in the 'Cavalry Westerns' (and his role in the brawl central to Ford's entertaining slice of Irish flummery, **The Quiet Man**, 1952). **How Green** has some Ford strengths and many of his weaknesses, though the director came late to the project (William Wyler was the original choice) and was not responsible for the fundamental casting decisions which stripped the film of much of its political force. Fox's production head Darryl Zanuck was determined not to create another **Grapes of Wrath**, and wanted to eschew realism in favour of a child's-eye view. Huw's embittered stance, the disenchantment with the work-force's priorities, the emphasis on a breakdown of communal values running through the last section of the book – all are largely absent from Ford's feature. The film is indeed 'emotion recollected in tranquillity'. But it would be churlish to ignore its cinematic qualities and power to affect audiences. Scenes, for instance, showing the growing rapport between Huw and Gruffydd, and the confidences shared as the boy fights his way back to fitness after saving his mother from drowning, are genuinely moving. As Andrew Sarris has noted, 'there have probably been more tears shed over **How Green Was My Valley** than any other Ford film.'[11]

Ford's nous and visual flair, his ability to compress meaning into simple scenes, is best illustrated by those mountainside walks of Huw and his father. In the final shots, father and son are seen walking, then standing, framed against the sky – as one. What matters to Ford are the values and solidarity of the extended family (which embraces Gruffydd). This is clear when he brings his characters back for a roll call at the film's end, presenting the idealized family unit (a device also used in his West Point film, **The Long Gray Line**, 1955).[12] The family's attitudes include a resistance to change. The mother, like the matriarch of Cronin's **Stars Look Down**, despises learning, feeling no good can come of it. Her rejection of new ideas is made explicit in amusing scenes when she guffaws at the seeming illogicality of the mathematics Huw ponders for homework. Gwilym sen., of course, acquiesces in Huw becoming a miner, and distrusts attempts by the men to improve working conditions.

The black-and-white camerawork, the interior lighting of photography director Arthur Miller and his painstaking use of camera angles, all arouse admiration even if the constant preoccupation with formal groupings seems occasionally to drain the film of energy.[13] The darkness of the interiors, the perspective and deep-focus shots, often suggest a womb; and Ford's taste for expressionism, though far more obvious in Joseph August's camerawork for **The Informer** (1935), is evident in the scene when triangular pools of light fall on the Morgans, grieving after Ivor's death.

If Ford had been more sensitive to the nuances of Welsh mining life he might have made Crisp sing a Welsh song at the wedding's festivities, and he might have made more of the class prejudices and aspirations revealed by the teacher, Mr Jonas. Jonas is a mere shadow of the pedagogue of the book in which his every action is a fascinating disavowal of the Welsh language and his own roots. There is also an irritating shift in focus at times from the Morgans to the aborted romance between Gruffydd and Angharad (no doubt in deference to the casting of Pidgeon and O'Hara). But it is the omissions from the film which niggle. The decision to dispense with all Huw's adult life meant that crucial moments of Welsh industrial and political history – including the Tonypandy riots and major coalfield disputes – are lost and the film never does more than suggest, in a few sentences, the extent of Huw's disenchantment with the subversion of the miners' original ideals. When, in the book, Huw, Cyfartha and Dai effectively help the 'scabs' and oppose the strikers by manning the pit's engine against the besieging men, we can see that this action, despite appearances, is not entirely the betrayal it seems. It reinforces Llewellyn's theme of continuity and in a way validates the life of the father. Huw is enslaved by, and inculcated with, his father's values which reassert themselves at the novel's climax. The book opens up issues of loyalty to class or kin and when Huw risks his life to stand up for the past, for pragmatic and sentimental reasons, he also legitimizes the whole of the Morgans' past life as he sees it. It is also significant that the attack on the engine house is led from outside the community by *agents provocateurs*. Ford's failure to grasp the political nettle and bring life to the confrontations between management and men rankles, and he makes less than he should of the mountain of slag as a metaphor for avarice and a darkness or dulling of the human spirit.

Screenplay writer Philip Dunne had no compunction about lopping off much of the crucial political element in the pit scenes – so vital to an understanding of Huw's values and the weight of the past on him. The writer even congratulates himself, in his autobiography, for his expediency in trimming the film to the length required by Darryl Zanuck.[14] The cuts were apparently 'easy' for Dunne because the studio had

Maureen O'Hara, Roddy McDowall in John Ford's *How Green Was My Valley*.

discovered, in Roddy McDowall, a youth who could carry the whole film. Tyrone Power – the original choice as the adult Huw – was no longer needed. The riot scenes become casualties of this decision and Huw is more passive and quiescent than the character of the novel. Ford and Dunne have included as their final setpiece the pit disaster claiming the father's life and have even reprieved Gruffydd who, in the book, has effectively been hounded from the village before the tragedy. In the screen version his leavetaking is interrupted by news of the pitfall, so he is allowed to reclaim his heroic stature by descending in the cage and helping to recover Gwilym sen.'s body. Ford isolates him in the frame, against the pit-head, to reinforce the point. Gruffydd's compassion for the community which has previously rejected him has an irrefutable logic in the film's terms. Gruffydd's values, as much as the traditionalism of Gwilym and his son, endure in the audience's mind at the end, as the minister straddles the two camps, constantly asserting family loyalties yet remaining sympathetic to the men's rights.

After all the criticism of Ford it is interesting to note Dunne's disclosures that most of the actors had been chosen – and his script written with original director William Wyler – before Ford was assigned to the project.[15] Ford may have 'identified' with the material, but he took over the film because, unlike Wyler, he was prepared to accept stringent budget limits.

How Green Was My Valley was a huge box-office and critical success and landed Oscars for best feature (in a year which included **Citizen Kane** and **The Maltese Falcon**), director, photography and supporting actor (Donald Crisp). In view of all the criticism of the seemingly risible, mining-cottage sets it is chastening to note that the best art direction Oscar went to Richard Day and Nathan Juran, with Thomas Little collecting a Certificate of Merit citation for interior decoration.[16] But **How Green** on the screen is less of an odyssey than the novel. It does not convey the gradual emotional transition of a confused boy who uses the statements and behaviour of adults as a touchstone for his own nascent opinions and values, then little by little arrives at maturity, taking his own distinctive stance. The adult Huw's disenchantment has to be taken largely on trust, with the book's vital second half effectively eliminated.

Gruffydd becomes the film's moral centre, his relationship with Angharad made prominent, so the loss we feel at the end is not just for the dilution or destruction of the community but regret that so many romances/loves have been nipped in the bud or shattered by tragedy. Pidgeon delivers a monumental, stoic performance of world-weary grace and the film's creators do all they can to ensure that he is a figure of both admiration and pity as he pines for the love of Angharad, a married woman, locked in loveless union with the mine owner's son Iestyn. Gruffydd, at times, functions as a sort of chorus – an omniscient, forlorn sage. When the men strike, for instance, it is the preacher who interprets events for Huw: 'It means something has gone out of this valley which can never be replaced.' The writer and director have skilfully telescoped episodes so that Gruffydd grows in stature. When the deacon Parry interrupts the wedding revelries at the Morgans' home, he threatens that the preacher will be reported to the deacons for advocating socialism at the gathering. In the novel Gruffydd is reported for merely *condoning* the celebrations. The director also creates a memorable *frisson* and metaphor as Angharad's coach draws away after her marriage to Iestyn and exits the frame. The gap on the screen is immediately filled by Gruffydd, seen among the gravestones at the back of the church, looking on. The image suggests, with beautiful economy, that Gruffydd's life is, from that moment, consigned to stasis and living death.

Ford's ability to suggest a whole value system in an image or two is demonstrated repeatedly. When the father is at loggerheads with his sons about whether to accept the new reduced mining pay scale and he is told that power can only be gained from a union of all the men, Ford frames in the background Angharad holding Huw's shoulder and the mother is seen turned away from the camera. In this vignette, Ford hints that it is the union's industrial strife which will shatter the domesticity and force males of the family for the first time to look outside their home and even beyond the coalfield. For a moment the family is held in polarity with an inimical force for change which challenges those hierarchical values which the older Morgans cherish. As a film about the indestructibility of family loyalties Ford's feature is intelligent and superbly crafted and fits snugly into his canon and world view. But it has failed to capture a seminal moment in Welsh history and to come to terms with the class issues as distinct from the generational conflicts and blood ties.[17] An extra dimension might have been added if **How Green** had presented the Welsh–English language conflicts of the schoolroom and shown Mr Jonas as representative of a whole colonizing regimen. It is tempting to think that Ford, after turning Llewellyn's Welsh miners and families into Americans and Irishmen, was loath to labour the point.

The Proud Valley

Proud Valley, in its very different way, has almost as many claims to distinction as the Fox feature. It was perhaps the nearest Ealing Studios, in their palmy days under Balcon, came to producing a genuine radical film, at least in content. And, with all its inherent contradictions, it remains – with **Blue Scar** and **The Citadel** – one of the most fascinating of the 'Welsh' films. In the original script, miners finally took over running the Blaendy colliery after its closure following a disaster. Production began in August 1939 but war intervened (denuding the crew of key personnel and at least one important actor), and Balcon in the interest of the war effort insisted on taking a milder tack.[18]

Proud Valley is virtually the only British film of the thirties and forties to feature a black actor – Paul Robeson – as a sympathetic working-class lead.[19] Robeson's itinerant stoker is integrated into the local Valleys community and choir, proves his heroism and finally sacrifices himself to free trapped workmates down the pit. In saving young Emlyn Parry (Simon Lack) at the expense of his own life he ensures that his adopted family is kept together, with Emlyn resuming his role as breadwinner. Robeson's hero has a semi-mythical stature (signalled by the name David Goliath – the film's working title). He proves less a catalyst for change than a crucial force for continuity. The film was tailored, largely, for Robeson's vocal talents ('He has a bottom bass like an organ' as Dick Parry says of David) – you only have to consider the number of cut-aways to close-ups of the star – even if director Pen Tennyson was anxious to prevent his dominating to the detriment of the picture.

Proud Valley: Rachel
Thomas, Paul Robeson.

The opening song, 'You can't stop us singing', written by *Welsh Rarebit*'s radio team Lynn Joshua and Mai Jones, might be viewed as a hostage to fortune in view of later events but it emphasizes the plea for stability at the film's core.[20] Those who find the number's facile optimism crude in context might compare it with the similar rousing but equally naïve mining speech on the sound-track of an otherwise much more sophisticated film, **Ms Rhymney Valley** (1985).

Made for around £40,000, **Proud Valley** had a fascinating gestation. It seems incongruous that the film's director Pen Tennyson, great-grandson of the poet and a 'John Bull Englishman' (according to his father) was an old boy of Eton and (briefly) a student at Balliol College, Oxford. He was also a house guest, more than once, of David Davies of Llandinam, heir to the Rhondda pit baron of the same name. Tennyson might have pulled off the 'socialist' ending originally envisaged, but he capitulated readily enough to Balcon's request to change the final reel. Significantly, he could not wait to enter

the war, and months after completion of **Proud Valley**, his third feature, he was killed while serving in the Fleet Air Arm. Yet he was surprisingly radical, given his background. He even wanted the film to be called 'One in Five' – the injury rate in the pits – and he was an active trade-unionist.[21] He joined the film-makers' union, the (then) ACT, in its first year, became secretary of Gaumont's own branch at Shepherds Bush and, in 1936, played a leading role in negotiating the union's first agreement with a British studio.[22] In 1941, in a letter published posthumously by his union journal, Tennyson advocated full-scale nationalization of the film industry – an idea anathema to Balcon. The notion that private enterprise could operate with a state concern and 'ginger it up' was 'a spineless and ineffective' compromise; government and privately run studios could not be bedfellows, Tennyson insisted.[23]

Proud Valley's original story was written by a man from a very different background – Herbert Marshall, an Ealing producer and avowed communist, educated at a Moscow theatre school, a pupil and later translator of Eisenstein and a noted director of Russian drama.[24] Marshall, with his sculptress wife Alfredda Brilliant – produced a detailed treatment as a vehicle for Paul Robeson after directing him at London's left-wing Unity Theatre in the drama *A Plant in the Sun*.[25] Marshall's treatment (which included a song in homage to the revolutionary Joe Hill) was just one of several rejected and he later found himself ousted as associate producer.[26] He claimed that producer Sergei Nolbandov, a White Russian, was instrumental in denying him a direct role in developing the story's ideas, and that Balcon later reneged on promises to allow him to make two films of his own choice if he dropped the **Proud Valley** credit.[27] The final script, part-credited to Louis Golding, a popular left-wing novelist, was thrashed out in regular discussions during the film's development by Tennyson, Nolbandov, and ex-miner Jack Jones of *Rhondda Roundabout* fame.[28] Jones, a wooden actor, has a small but crucial role in the film but his own individual screen treatments were also rejected. Always resourceful, the writer, a communist through the twenties and thirties, revamped the original screenplay and some of his own discarded material and wrote a special Radio Wales version, approved by the studio and broadcast before the film's release.[29]

Robeson had forged a relationship with the miners from the late 1920s. In the 1930s he sang in the south Wales valleys, in Aberdare and Mountain Ash, to raise cash for the Spanish Civil War. From the twenties onwards his magisterial, sonorous singing and authoritative performances made him an international figure, steadily eroding racial barriers despite constant vilification, especially from the presses of Hearst and Beaverbrook. He played major concerts and leads in stage productions of *Othello* and *Showboat* in England between the wars and in the **Showboat** film version of 1936.[30] In the fifties, after his US passport was confiscated in the wake of McCarthy anti-communist purges, he broadcast live from a recording studio on the Canadian/United States border to Welsh miners at an emotional 1957 miners' conference at Porthcawl.[31] The role of David Goliath offered him dignity after the disappointment of his experiences on **Sanders of the River** (1935), made for Alexander Korda when he played an African chief. The film was edited by the Kordas into a jingoistic hymn to Empire and Robeson was so upset he tried to buy up and suppress all available prints.[32]

In contrast, **Proud Valley**, which enjoyed fine box-office business at Cardiff's Empire Cinema, is undoubtedly a film of warmth and affection. The early family scenes with Edward Chapman as the bluff, roguish miner Dick Parry and Dilys Thomas from Barry as his mischievous little daughter have a genial flavour lacking, for instance, in Ford's film. Supporting roles are incisively drawn, from Dilys Davies's sour-apple postwoman to Edward Rigby's incorrigible drifter and busker, Bert, who train-hops around the Valleys singing – or rather massacring – good tunes and forcing the populace to stump up money to force him to move on: 'Art related to psychology', as he puts it; 'These Welsh are daft about music and as open-handed as the sun.' The wandering seaman David Goliath, out of work since his ship landed in Cardiff, encounters Bert when he jumps aboard a freight wagon heading to Blaendy and Bert's comments effectively lead us to the heart of the film.[33]

Proud Valley, by 1990s standards, is cautious and even bland. It may seem coy in its treatment of racism but it broaches the subject openly and courageously enough for the 1940s, even though the film is careful to avoid presenting racial conflict in the wider community outside the mine, or in the Parry home. David's arrival opens up rifts in the mining community, even though he is soon made at home in the Parry family. In one sequence Clifford Evans as the obstreperous miner Seth harangues Dick for bringing a black man down the pit. The tension is defused and Seth deflated by Dick's response, perhaps the film's best-remembered lines: 'Damn and blast it, man, aren't we all black down that pit?'[34] Seth's hostility is manifest in his complaint that Dick has flouted the seniority rule in bringing David into the choir, taking Seth's brother Ben's solo part. David, of course, gradually earns the men's respect and it is no accident that after the final pit explosion it is Seth who atones, keeping vigil over David's body.

The film does not stint on the clichés of Welsh film drama or literature: 'Life in the valley of Blaendy is birth, coalmining, the National Eisteddfod and Death' (as the *Sunday Chronicle* reviewer wrote in 1940).[35] Yet it is still a shock to read some of the harsh contemporary judgements. The *New Statesman* writer complained that the film avoided any point of view and 'shunned reality like a disease', and thought it was likely to prove a disappointment to 'those looking for social significance, an attitude towards mining conditions, approach to the colour question or even to the mere seeker after entertainment'. The *Reynolds News* reviewer thought the miners' march to London to ask the colliery owners to re-open the dangerous pit was 'silly' and the influential American critic Bosley Crowther inveighed against the 'stiff playing' and 'purple acting'.[36] Before **Proud Valley**'s release, the *Western Mail* had opined that, as Clifford Evans and Jack Jones had contributed to the film, 'the dialogue will be the real thing, not an Englishman's music-hall idea of how a Welshman speaks.' But the *Observer* reviewer certainly had reservations about the finished product: 'I should like to have seen this film made entirely in Wales with a Welsh director, a wholly Welsh cast and more singing in Welsh which is, after all, the language of the country.'[37]

The film's observations on colour may seem pussyfooting now but the role of David tells us much about the passable screen limits of the day. He is nominally the film's hero but is never seen as an active force in the decision-making. He scarcely deserves Graham Greene's 'big black Pollyanna' description, but it is hard to disagree with the contention that he merely 'bears witness'. It is Jack Jones – the former pitman playing Ned – who warns of the build-up of gas in the Klondike seam and delivers the stilted key speech urging miners and pit-owners to work together. And it is Emlyn who strives to arrange a meeting of the London-based mine owners and the men. David is never the hub of the family, even after Dick's death, and he is strangely passive in domestic scenes.[38] But he does assume, explicitly, the role of wage-earner for, and protector of, the Parry family and is martyred when he refuses to allow young Emlyn – trapped with him – to light the final dynamite charge which enables them to reach safety.

As present-day critic Richard Dyer has observed, David is never seen to pose any threat. He is stoic in the face of racist taunts and, for example, has no sexual relationship of any kind; there is no friendly intimacy with Mrs Parry (they never feature in any scene alone). But from the first moments David adds his voice from the pavement to the *Elijah* chorus of the Blaendy choir preparing for the Eisteddfod we sense his integration into the community will be a foregone conclusion. It seems strange, in hindsight, that Pen Tennyson, on a 'scouting' visit to south Wales before production, wondered whether the Welsh would object to Robeson's voice being used in the Eisteddfod sequence. The *South Wales Echo* reporter, observing Tennyson's qualms, concluded: 'In any case he [Robeson] is a sensitive soul, the type of man who would not do anything he thought might upset the susceptibilities of Welshmen.' The studio, highly sensitive to possible reaction, unfortunately made him too good to be true. He is not merely anodyne and impossibly understanding, but the writers have also endowed him with a physical strength and courage which ensure his acceptability (just as Sidney Poitier in **Guess Who's Coming to Dinner** (1967) was not merely well groomed, but groaned under the weight of academic and professional qualifications). Dyer, in a 1985 National Film Theatre lecture on Robeson, described his performance in **Proud Valley** as 'akin to the servant role, constantly tidying up after others' – a clever and fairly accurate observation.[39] Certainly, nothing is allowed to alienate the audience. Even when David throws the left hook to KO 'Em' (Emlyn) he has first stressed the young man's family responsibilities. His action is solely to prevent Em being killed in the liberating explosion, and close-ups have clearly signalled David's thoughts and motives to the audience.

Robeson himself was aware of the screen conventions of the day and his role's limitations. As his son said on a 1985 visit to south Wales, Paul accepted that he must wind up as noble victim – 'the Negro going down the chute again' – but he was prepared to accept the compromises (even political) to play a sympathetic Negro in a working-class context.[40] The film's acknowledgement that race was an issue was a step forward, even though it was careful to suggest the novelty of a black man in the pits. Paul jun. says his father regarded **Proud Valley** with **Song of Freedom** (1936) and **Jericho** (US: **Dark Sands**, 1937) as his finest films, and his daughter Susan claims that in retrospect Tennyson's film was his favourite.[41] Robeson sen. certainly considered it a transitional work which treated the black actor as something more than a servile eye-rolling retainer, just a year after Hattie McDaniel had perpetuated the demeaning stereotype in **Gone With the Wind**. He regarded Tennyson's feature as strongly anti-Fascist in offering the prospect of a genuinely homogeneous community in which the colour of skin was of no account, and he thought the racial tolerance theme outweighed the problem of the diluted finale and the failure to hint at final conflict between management and men and to provide a radical solution.[42]

Old Etonian Pen Tennyson discusses *Proud Valley*'s script with ex-miner Jack Jones.

Proud Valley is rather too obviously a vehicle for Robeson's singing talents. Yet although the film is an unduly sentimental patchwork, Tennyson threads the choir numbers and solos intelligently through the film – and the use of 'Deep River', sung at the Eisteddfod as a requiem for Dick Parry, is an eloquent touch. Similarly, Rachel Thomas's own rendering of 'Yn y Dyfroedd' (In the Great Depths) is more moving and less discomforting than you would expect, thanks to Tennyson's direction as she stands with the anxious wives waiting for news of the pitfall. He moves away from a close-up of Thomas into a gentle crane shot which takes us high above the crowd as her voice merges with the other singers.[43]

Ultimately, the film presents little social criticism or real observation of the miners' daily conditions. Even though pertinent points are made about the poverty in the valleys – miners and families living on 'tick', wives avoiding the rent man – they are undercut by comedy. Only Chapman's patriarch really burrows beneath the skin of his character and the film tells us less about the mechanics and realities of mining than either **Blue Scar** or **The Citadel**. The decision to present men and employers operating as a united front also leads to script compromises. Pit-owners' representatives have to be 'well-meaning', for instance. The closure of the Blaendy mine is seen as an act of nature with no human agency involved, and the decision to re-open the pit, by blasting through the sealed area after the men's plea, is taken with almost unseemly haste to satisfy the work-force. The engineer Mr Lewis (George Merritt) who volunteers his services, setting off for Blaendy on the same night with the miners who have marched to London, meets a hero's death throwing himself in front of a runaway truck and pushing a prop in its path, to protect a fallen workman who has been left behind to support the roof.

The miners' decision to march to London is taken not for altruistic reasons but because they desperately need to earn a living, yet their consciousness of the Nazis' inexorable advance through Europe and the threat to London is awakened by a series of newspaper headlines which become progressively more ominous as they near the capital. 'What has Hitler to do with us?' one marcher asks early on. By implication, the miners' growing concern and determination to act together against the Führer lead naturally to their eagerness to pull together with pit-owners when they eavesdrop on a meeting in which the despairing bosses are discussing the impossibility of increasing coal output to meet the government's latest demand. It is significant that the German threat is not broached directly in the film's first half, which opens in 1938, though there is David Goliath's reference to seeking employment in the Darren Valley arms factory. The last sections of **Proud Valley** betray the hasty script revisions to meet the new war situation. Yet the disaster scenes, shot in the studios, and the pit-head sequences where mothers and daughters grieve or wait for loved ones, are handled with sensitivity (and had not yet become cliché, despite the cynicism of Graham Greene's response).[44] It is hard to fault the pacing or handling of the pitfalls, and the moment when a sheet of flame belches towards the camera is genuinely frightening. Tennyson makes effective use of low-angle shots in the pit to generate tension and he confidently uses a swift montage of close-ups as the stranded miner realizes – and Mr Lewis embraces – his fate. Tennyson also uses a rapid-fire montage intelligently at the film's first intimations of a disaster, cutting from Gwen to Emlyn in the pit then to Rachel Thomas crying, 'Dad'.

But the director, still finding his feet, reveals a lack of confidence elsewhere. At least four times he uses pit winding gear in establishing shots. Yet the gear – as symbol – is never used in the dynamic way Carol Reed employs it in **The Stars Look Down**, for instance. There, pit backdrops represent, at various times, the roots of the film's hero David Fenwick, the challenge he faces and the oppressive expectations he has set in train or his father has demanded: 'Someday you're going to do something about this industry of ours.'[45]

In **Proud Valley** the expectations, beyond the miners' desire for work, revolve around education. This was one of the first films to present the aspiring parent with ambitions beyond the colliery, in this case Mrs Owens who is anxious to obtain the leverage for her daughter to avoid life as a 'mere' collier's wife and does all she can to blight her relationship with Em.

The film introduced to the public Rachel Thomas, a Cardiff schoolteacher's wife with no professional stage experience who was chosen reputedly on the recommendation of Jack Jones. Her untutored performance as Mrs Parry drew rich praise from Balcon, the *Observer* film critic C. A. (Caroline) Lejeune and *The Times*. To Lejeune Miss Thomas was 'the symbol of all miners' wives and mothers'.[46] The actress, daughter of an active trade-union miner victimized in the Swansea Valley in the early days of the Miners' Federation, had previously appeared in Jack Jones's stage play *Land of My Fathers*. She was to personify the Welsh Mam after later appearances in **Blue Scar**, **David**, **Undercover** (1943) – a slightly bizarre Ealing drama about the Yugoslav resistance, shot in Brecon and directed by Sergei Nolbandov – and as the prickly, ousted contralto in **Valley of Song** (1953).[47] Rachel Thomas's permanent place in Welsh screen history was assured, however, by her Beth Morgan in the 1959-60 TV version of **How Green Was My Valley**, opposite Eynon Evans.

Proud Valley bought unsolicited praise from Lloyd George in a letter to Balcon. He considered it 'one of the most moving and dramatic films I have ever seen', and thought it 'throbbed with human emotion'. The film had a successful run at the Leicester Square Theatre but its success in Britain was hampered by a vicious campaign from Beaverbrook newspapers, which barely mentioned it after taking exception to pro-communist comments by Robeson. He had also stressed that, in the light of treatment meted out to them, coloured people should feel no obligation to fight 'America's' war.[48]

Gwyneth Vaughan, Emrys Jones – fickle lovers in *Blue Scar*.

In 1941 Tennyson, who had married Nova Pillbeam, star of Hitchcock's original **The Man Who Knew Too Much** (1934) and **Young and Innocent** (1937), was killed at twenty-three during service as a sub-lieutenant. He had made two other features: **Convoy** (1940), a disciplined naval fictional film with a strong documentary feel, which did well at the box office, and **There Ain't No Justice** (1939), a robust boxing drama starring Jimmy Hanley, which captured persuasively the ambience of seedy fight hall scenes. Tennyson's contribution to Ealing was acknowledged by Balcon soon after the director's death: 'British films have lost a craftsman whose achievements were already great and whose promise was greater.'[49]

Blue Scar

Only one Welsh film handled the theme of nationalization in the months following one of the biggest shake-ups in more recent mining history – and Jill Craigie's **Blue Scar** (1949) is among the most important of 'Welsh' films. It was a highly courageous undertaking by almost the only British female film director then working in UK films, and can certainly be seen as a singular warning against viewing the changes uncritically. Craigie is now best known as a campaigning feminist, a historian of the suffragette movement and as Michael Foot's wife, but in a brief career as director she produced an invigorating and cogent screen documentary plea for equal opportunities, a film of real intelligence and wit, **Born to be a Woman** (1950), which was decades ahead of its time.[50]

Blue Scar deals with the impact of the pits on one family, and the tug of emotional and class loyalties facing one miner – Tom (Emrys Jones). There is sourness and cynicism in the film, and an ambivalence in Tom's make-up which helps make it compelling. Both Tom and his girlfriend Olwen (Gwyneth Vaughan) are ashamed of their roots and anxious to discard the past. Tom's feelings stem from his sense of inferiority (he frequently sees himself through the eyes of the English) and Olwen wants desperately to be assimilated into the bourgeois metropolitan culture as an opera singer.

Craigie's film is blighted by crass stereotyping of bohemian upper-class characters in the London sequences. Neither the writing nor one or two inferior central performances do justice to the film's themes, and the romance between Tom Thomas and Olwen, generally poorly handled and strained, tends to dominate the film's more worthwhile elements. P. L. Mannock praised the film's sincerity, but thought it suffered from 'a prolonged thread of romance'. There is no doubt that Craigie was happiest when working on location in south Wales, and the conviction of these Valleys scenes justified her decision to shoot most of the exteriors around Port Talbot and nearby Abergwynfi.[51] Compare the location work here to the awkward mix of studio and locations in **Proud Valley** where the march sequences, filmed partly in Llantrisant, seem to be set in limbo. But **Blue Scar**'s confusion and Craigie's ambivalence about its priorities – the men's attempts to come to terms with the new state industry, or the romance – are never more obvious than at the finale when tacky formula writing takes over. Tom, after seizing a pretext to see Olwen in London, is rapidly disillusioned by the shallowness of her arty friends and returns to south Wales where he suddenly discovers the quieter virtues of a doting village girl, Glenis (Dilys Jones). Glenis is demeaned by seeing herself clearly as second best (he only turns to her when the other romance is extinguished). We are clearly meant to see this as a happy ending with Tom making the right moral choice, yet it seems like a defeat for both parties. It is possible to read in the resolution of this relationship a parallel with the mining industry – a decision to accept a compromise or second best – but this would probably be stretching a point. This other woman's quiescent attitude, her malleability, are not what we would expect from Craigie's feminism. It is tempting to believe that much of the romantic content and the ending were imposed on her by the producer, William MacQuitty, or distributors, and MacQuitty has written of the demands on *him* to supply some romance.

Blue Scar focuses on the mining village of Abergwynfi in the heady run-up to nationalization when many old pitmen savoured the ending of the long fight against the dominance of private mineowners and the prospects of a victory denied them when Ramsay MacDonald and the Labour Party reneged on election pledges in 1929 and watered down their Nationalization Bill. The film centres on the Williams family and its hub, the old miner and silicosis victim Ted (played with great restraint and skill by Prysor Williams) whose perkiness and droll wit give way to increasing fatigue.[52] His gradual enervation seems to symbolize the oppression of the community by the pits and the tempering of the initial optimism and dreams of genuine co-ownership by the men. At the climax, though the miners are emotionally affected by the ceremony of vesting the pits in 1947 with red flags hoisted, the dominant note is pragmatism, as they are forced to realize that things have not changed fundamentally. Misgivings about the quality of management before and after nationalization are evident in scenes when the private pit-owners' representatives (seen as hard and curmudgeonly) press for more tonnage and, later, as one miner makes the tart observation that the pits under the state are 'the same old firm dressed up in a new suit'. The men are forced by economic necessity into the familiar compromises and acceptance. The hope is expressed that future managers – like Tom, who has been elevated to that status by the film's end – will be more enlightened than their predecessors and avoid some of the bitter confrontations of the past.

Blue Scar's view of the mining industry is markedly ambivalent. The pit community is seen largely as a retreat and the miners as a focus for decent feelings, sharply contrasted with the shallowness of Olwen's cosseted artistic coterie in London. But Tom is unhappily conscious of status and of that other social class which he castigates but to which he seems to aspire. These emotions find an outlet in the miners' club scene when Tom, trying to read 'The Socialists' Creed' (a none-too-subtle touch) is distracted by superimposed images, over the text, of Olwen dancing with her new companion Collins. The image suggests Tom's possible rejection of his past as he tries to oust Collins from her affections but the superimposition also conjures up that other life of infinite possibilities. Craigie again uses metaphor, this time to more telling effect, in the sequence when Olwen's father Ted collapses fatally whilst lifting a heavy coal scuttle as he listens to a Raymond Glendenning boxing commentary in which Britain's Bruce Woodcock is battering his opponent into submission.

Tom Thomas, following the same escape route to pit management Emlyn seeks in **Proud Valley**, has by the film's end become a white-collar man reconciled to remaining in the community after severing his first romance. It is implied that his own roots as a pitman and his conscience will help him to improve the miners' lot. Yet the suspicion remains that he has been bought after he agrees finally not to speak up after witnessing the ill-treatment of a miner by the foreman. Craigie seems constantly to cast doubt on Tom's worth, presenting him as an industrious but hangdog idealist, lacking in charisma and even the compensatory moral fervour of that selfless but pallid work-horse Arnold Ryerson in the Boulting Brothers' version of **Fame is the Spur**. Tom pours scorn on his own surroundings and culture and is immersed in self-pity as his own background does not satisfy Olwen after she gains a singing scholarship to the university. When he tries to persuade Olwen to leave London with him after her marriage to Alfred Collins (an 'industrial psychologist'!), he woos her on her terms – appealing to her vanity and mercenary instincts. He says he has been offered a 'house the size of a mountain'. She has told him earlier that with his brains he should land a 'collar-and-tie job', and that she has chosen Alfred partly because 'he's steady, not in and out of strikes all the time'. We cannot really believe that Tom has shed permanently the rancour and disenchantment which finds an outlet in the extraordinary speech at the miners' club when he begins to rail against Olwen, women generally, management and the stereotype of working Welshmen gained by outsiders – 'singing, football, night classes, scum of the earth – that's what they think of us . . . They prefer white-collared workers adding figures' ('subtracting, even better . . .', one miner adds, laconically). Tom's comments seem to vilify his own roots, and reflect his disenchantment with the miners' own values. He emerges as a prig and a moral wimp too, one of the most unsympathetic leads in all Welsh films. Tom's observations seem oddly but fascinatingly at variance with the way miners such as Ted Williams see themselves. They have taken pride in their jobs and accepted

Jill Craigie, the only woman director in British feature films at the time, on set with photographic director Jo Jago for *Blue Scar*.

conditions stoically and have no truck with malingerers. The opposite view is represented by Ted's peppery and fly son Thomas Williams (Kenneth Griffith) who is first seen scanning the left-wing *Weekly Tribune* and soon expresses forceful views about Saturday working: 'If they want the coal they can come and get it.' He stays at home at weekends convinced that Saturday absenteeism will lead to a five-day week. The debate is compelling in the light of such debates in the 1980s.

The pit-owners want the workers' co-operation because they are desperate to raise output – and we see the managers demanding that more tonnage is squeezed from the miners. The clashes between the father steeped in the work ethic and his son (given to barbed digs at Tom Thomas) have a fascinating edge. Olwen and Tom seem more interested in improving their own economic status than the fortunes of the community, despite both delivering polemics (when they seem more cyphers and mouthpieces for Craigie than genuine characters). Yet it is not easy to judge how much Craigie is in sympathy with the criticisms of the mine or the community. The Kenneth Griffith character, the most openly cynical of the pitmen, is presented in the film as something of a loafer, arrogant and irascible; and Olwen, who also rejects Valleys values and seems a vacuous social climber, is not above making emotional capital of the past. 'I'm only one of a million or so brought up on the dole,' she tells her middle-class friend in the dorm. 'Sometimes I wonder if there is a curse on the Valleys.' Craigie seems much more attuned to the values of the old man Ted and certainly his integrity and by implication the integrity of an exploited generation, and she seems to treat Tom Thomas with wary, almost cynical detachment.

The strongest scenes smack of documentary – the confrontations when Thomas Williams tells Ted he should go before the Board for illness compensation, and the discussion on the five-day week, for instance. And the most poignant sequence of all centres on Ted, as – panting for breath – he climbs the hillside to watch an Abergwynfi soccer match and allows his feelings, briefly, to surface in a conversation with an elderly companion: 'I'm not long for this world. I've cursed this place for many a long year but now I'm thinking it's beautiful.' Ted is already nostalgic for a past he sees slipping away. The moments when the men philosophize and reminisce have a raw authenticity; Craigie gives other scenes a pleasing levity – notably in the behaviour of the crotchety old grandmother (Madoline Thomas) with a passion for football pools.

The director makes it clear in two scenes before and after the mine vestment that, fundamentally, things have not changed for the miners. Pit officials instruct their underlings to squeeze the men for 720 tons a week and after nationalization Tom as union representative argues against a manager who suggests lowering the wages and is sceptical about the new rules in the pit: 'Nationalization is too idealistic. Theory is one thing, practice is quite another, especially when practice becomes bureaucracy.' Later a management man, as if to illustrate the point, patronizes the pitmen: 'Those pneumatic picks lighten your job considerably. We'll soon be sending you down with feather dusters.' And in the film's most melodramatic sequence, a tetchy overman rounds on a miner: 'You thought nationalization would put you on top, thought you'd be running the show,' he barks as bosses seek to step up output. His attitude sparks the fight which Tom witnesses. Tom stays silent when his conscience is appeased by the counsel of miner friends who advise him to lie low and allow the matter to be sorted out through new-style democratic union negotiation. Later the overman, with bad grace, admits he was over-hasty. It is noticeable in these passages that while Craigie presents the NCB practices (new negotiating style, improved physical working conditions) she also undercuts them.

The pit and community scenes, though marred by some pedestrian dialogue delivery, contain a wealth of data on mining life and preoccupations which does not figure in other films of the period – and it indicates a real feeling for the more prosaic intimacies of ordinary lives. Spontaneity drains away whenever romance enters the frame. The relationship between Tom and Glenis is novelettish and could have been junked without materially affecting the plot, and the scene when Tom confronts Olwen at her London flat and both try to impress may have some psychological truth but it is excruciatingly condescending towards Tom and by implication his social class.

Your Opinion on

"BLUE SCAR"

This film was made by Britain's only Independent Film Company who will be grateful for your replies to the following questions.

1. Did you like the film?

   Very much indeed.

2. Who did you like in the film?

   Emhys Jones & "Glynis." (Nurse)

3. Would you like to see more films of this type about the real people of Britain?

   Yes.

4. The Producer would be grateful for any further comments you might care to make about the film.

   Held the audience throughout. Fine performances by all players. I personally would rather see a film of this type about real people than films about life as the majority of us will never experience it.

An audience reaction card used at vital previews for *Blue Scar* (from William MacQuitty's collection).

Blue Scar is still, overall, a fine achievement and remarkably outspoken, given NCB involvement. The film cost £80,000, according to Craigie – half the cash from the Coal Board, half from other sources. In his autobiography MacQuitty claims that the original costing was £45,000, with Outlook supplying half.[53] Craigie and MacQuitty, partners in Outlook Films, hired the Electric Theatre cinema at Port Talbot at £1 a day, levelled the floors and ferried coal into the building to shoot the pit interiors and also created a soundproof stage in the cinema.[54] The film was transported every night to Merton Park Studios for processing and miners saw the daily rushes. Finance was easier than distribution. 'We had no clout,' said MacQuitty. 'We couldn't force them to take it. At that time there was a feeling that people wanted only escapism, not reality.'[55]

Craigie's earlier films, **The Way We Live** (1946), presenting plans for the reconstruction of a bomb-blitzed Plymouth, and **Out of Chaos** (1944), featuring the work of war artists, were handled by Two Cities who had access to the Rank circuit. But Outlook, who had gambled, unsuccessfully, on **Blue Scar** obtaining release as a British quota film, could not sell it (the *Daily Worker* suggesting, darkly, that Miss Craigie's offence could only be 'the crime of dangerous thoughts').[56] Outlook wound up showing the film to Harold Wilson, at the Department of Trade, and Alexander Korda, who apparently set up the deal with British Lion, after sneak preview screenings at Uxbridge and Tooting where public reaction was favourable. The film was rejected by all three British circuits before Sir Arthur Jarrett of British Lion accepted it.[57] **Blue Scar** finally gained release as a B film on the 450-cinema Associated British Circuit after Rank turned it down, and ABC released the feature nationally only after a trial in seven towns and cities – including Cardiff.[58]

Craigie's talents probably lay primarily in the documentary field and **Born to be a Woman** was her best film. But, disenchanted by the perpetual struggle to raise funds for worthwhile projects, she bowed out of film direction. She says she hates to think of her past work – 'I really feel I was born too soon' – and she cites the progress made since the 1940s in creating opportunities for women.[59] 'No woman today is regarded as a freak if she enters the cutting rooms or even if she works on the camera. All my male competitors had experience in the cutting rooms and on production before directing. I had no experience at all and had to battle to help raise the money. Much of my energy was expended on promotion rather than direction, which is one reason, coupled with my [lack of] experience, why my films are so bad.'[60]

But **Born to be a Woman**, **The Way We Live** and much of **Blue Scar** suggest that Craigie was a genuine screen talent prematurely extinguished. As she acknowledges, her projects almost had to be *too* ambitious for her to make any kind of impression and counter the pervasive sexism in the industry. Craigie's **Blue Scar** at least evoked the authentic, gritty world of working men and the south Wales valleys. Other films of the forties, which suggested parallels with conditions in Wales, drew the sting from sequences involving serious social and class issues by presenting them in a comic vein, as we have seen with **Proud Valley** particularly. A typical example from the same year was **Love on the Dole** (1941) which, for all its moralizing about unemployment in north-west England, its problems with the censor and the grim picture of Hankey Park offered by director John Baxter and screenwriter Walter Greenwood, cannot resist the temptation to present working-class women as a sort of comic chorus – from Marjorie Rhodes's rancorous Mrs Bull to Mary Merrall's wheedling Irishwoman. They are all seen as Hogarthian habitués of a local pawnshop who take refuge from the grim social conditions in seances and drinking parties. The film conveys the grit of working-class life – and includes some of the fiercest scenes of police brutality ever seen on British screen up to that time. It presents a male lead character at his wits' end through unemployment, and the heroine's mother Mrs Hardcastle reduced to pawning her wedding ring. Yet it is undermined by the patronizing humour – despite fine performances from Deborah Kerr as Sally Hardcastle, a nice blend of the careworn, prim and matter-of-fact, and the Welsh actor Clifford Evans as the conscientious and harassed trade-unionist. The film, which attracted the censors' attention, summons up the milieu of the troubled impoverished area from the moment the opening crane shot takes us over rooftops into backyards cluttered with ramshackle sheds and washing lines.[61] We have the real sense of dropping into a grimmer subterranean world which the British commercial cinema, up to then, had shamefully ignored.

British mining films – other perspectives

Love on the Dole rarely compares as a realistic study of conditions with **The Stars Look Down**, which presents an unequivocal picture of shortsighted pit-owners who conceal mine dangers from the men.[62] Carol Reed's film offers an affecting study of David Fenwick (Michael Redgrave), a principled schoolmaster and former miner riven with self-doubts, fighting – against the tide of his friends' and relatives' boundless greed and ambitions – to rectify conditions within the Paradise colliery, which claimed his father's life. David's battle for his own self-respect, faced with the insults and infidelity of his wife Jenny (Margaret Lockwood), is the core of the film. Fenwick's incorruptibility is thrown into sharp relief by the unhealthy ambitions of his wife, and her tawdry pursuit of status symbols, and the opportunism of his one-time fellow miner Joe Gowlan (Emlyn Williams). It is Williams's avaricious social climber, striking up deals with private coal suppliers and putting the miners' lives in jeopardy, who is seen as the villain of the piece, rather than the mine owner's hunger for profit or the social system itself. Gowlan eventually rises from a menial position in the local steelworks to lord it over the town as an industrial baron, and Williams – in perhaps his finest film role – is marvellously brash and vulpine, cutting a dash with his gall, effacing Fenwick as completely as Redgrave's character Hamer Radshaw obliterates Arnold Ryerson in **Fame is the Spur**.

Reed conjures up the misery of unemployment superbly. The scenes along flyblown back streets with fretting, disenchanted miners mooching around or railing against conditions could scarcely be faulted, and confrontations between the company bosses and men – led by that amiable staple of so many Welsh films, Edward Rigby – are handled with persuasive sensitivity. In early scenes Reed builds up a riveting dossier of ineptitude and greed among the pit-owners. We see vividly how the character of David Fenwick is forged. But the film's force is blunted when – even more than in the novel's later sections – the emphasis shifts away from the employer's culpability to focus on Gowlan's venality. The bosses' decision to re-open the colliery's Scupper Flats seam, despite all warnings, is presented more as gullibility rather than criminal negligence. Reed has also elicited sympathy for the mine owner Richard Barras (Allan Jeayes) as the sacrificial victim of disaster rather than, as in Cronin's book, a man broken in mind by the knowledge that the enormity of his guilt has been discovered by his own son. The film's mining disaster is viewed as the natural result of exploitation allied to ignorance, and the remedies are seen to lie in the idealism of individuals and greater enlightenment rather than collective action or nationalization of the pits – or any avowal of principle by the Labour Party. Reed has cut the element of the book dealing with the systematic betrayal of Fenwick's ideals and principles by the Labour Party who, under Ramsay MacDonald, renege on the coal nationalization plans. There are the usual screen sops to objectivity and balance, and the links between capital and politics and social justice are established more adroitly in the book. In contrast, scenes when the latent hostility is fanned between the shopkeepers and unemployed miners, forced to subsist on credit, are refreshingly direct. The butcher who tells David's mother Martha Fenwick (Nancy Price) that she will have no free meat from him, and turns away a man trying to obtain food for his sick wife, finally prompts the skirmishes and looting (and the scene vividly brings to mind reported incidents in the Tonypandy riots).

In almost all these mining films the pit disaster is seen as a force for change or a crucial element in the film. In **Proud Valley** it forms part of David's rites of passage to martyrdom and heroic/mythical stature and Emlyn's to maturity and the mantle of responsibility. In G. W. Pabst's **Kameradschaft** (1931), the most technically assured and ingenious of all mining films, the disaster was the catalyst uniting two warring nations, Germany and France, in much the same way that the re-opening of the mine to boost Britain's war effort linked colliers and coalowners in **Proud Valley**. The only film in which the disaster is the *raison d'être* is the post-war **The Brave Don't Cry** (1953), perhaps the most honest and austere of all fictional mining films, made by John Grierson's Group Three for just a quarter of the costs of the average feature of the day. Set in Scotland and directed by Philip Leacock, it eschews all obvious dramatics.[63] The pit looms over the village. There is conviction in understatement as mackintoshed men trudge along rainy streets. We hear the small talk of the workers – and then see the close-ups of the porous pit roofs which presage disaster. Seconds later there is a cave-in, fields fall away into the pits and Leacock lets us see the intricacies/mechanics of the rescue operation as the enlightened, almost altruistic employer arrives to help. There is an arresting dramatic development when the wife of a miner guides the men to reach the injured – and generally the scenes which stress the women's involvement (in more than a passive role), and the steady accumulation of small details, give the film its strength. The one death is conveyed in a tacit, sensitive way, with the bereaved wife, in her misery, giving mutual support to the pitman who has to steel himself to bring news of her husband's death.

The Brave Don't Cry was that rarity – a mining film untainted by the whiff of betrayal. **Fame is the Spur**, adapted by Nigel Balchin from Howard Spring's novel, reeked of it. A Labour politician, based loosely on Ramsay MacDonald, gradually sullies all the principles and ideals he once espoused as he pursues a career which leads, inexorably, to the House of Lords. Director Roy Boulting has since compared Radshaw to Harold Wilson: 'I think Wilson is the personification of Radshaw – a man who has an overwhelming vanity and is very persuasive.'[64]

Boulting was forced by his production front office to make drastic cuts and the result coarsens the subtleties of Spring's novel which was much more sympathetic and sensitive in its view of Hamer Radshaw (called Shawcross in the novel).[65] Yet certain sections of the film still work superbly as we follow Hamer from his illegitimate, impoverished roots in Ancoats, Manchester, and – through a nicely judged flashback – learn of the inspiration he derives from tales spun by his grandfather whose girlfriend was cut down decades before by troops during the 1819 Peterloo Massacre.

As the story unfolds, we see how Radshaw uses the sabre with which his grandfather avenged himself. He flourishes the weapon at political meetings, employing it as a symbol of defiance and resistance and ostensibly to remind his audiences of the evils they face at the hands of their upper-class overlords. But gradually we realize how the sword exercises a baleful influence on Radshaw's life, becomes an instrument of self-delusion and a metaphor for his own heroic aspirations and quest for self-aggrandizement. He may often sound altruistic and may feel at times a certain compassion and grievance but his acts are a means to an end. Hamer Radshaw wants to be admired. Boulting uses the sword as a double-edged weapon most effectively in the key scene, filmed at Denham Studios, when Radshaw addresses striking south Wales miners and incites them to riot. The miners shown here are as gullible, and as unflatteringly presented, as in **The Citadel**. Hamer raises the sword aloft and its shadow on the wall looms over Radshaw's fellow platform-speaker Ryerson, the party factotum, who is Hamer's conscience. At that moment it seems as if Radshaw's principles and scruples have been eclipsed. It is the politician's recklessness and empty polemic which stirs up the pitmen to a demonstration ending in a man's death at the soldiers' hands. Much later, when Radshaw, as an elder statesman and government bastion, is sent to the Valleys to mollify supposedly suggestible miners, he is derided by the pitmen (including one of Boulting's stock actors Kenneth Griffith). The scene differs significantly from the book where Shawcross proves persuasive enough (one example of the Boultings' loading the dice against the politician).[66]

It is interesting that Roy Boulting still believes the film was not intended to be harder on Radshaw than the book. 'What in essence he's saying is that you may be moved initially by a theory, later you discover there are better ways of achieving [those] ends. This is his tragedy – that almost imperceptibly, perhaps subconsciously – he makes these moves and people who have a lesser mind, lesser ability . . . are stuck with their blinkers on and regard any deviation from theory as a betrayal of promise and his commitment.'[67] The film still plots a surefooted course into fascinating controversial areas, though it tends to simplify and polarize arguments. Moreover, it omits the crucial passages from the novel in which Radshaw visits south Wales and his eyes are opened by Ryerson to the privations of life in the Rhondda – major omissions for the film of a novel by the former Cardiff-based journalist who had observed at close quarters the harsh conditions of the south Wales valleys.

Fame is the Spur thus becomes the third major feature of the forties – after **Proud Valley** and **How Green Was My Valley** – to be severely emasculated and shorn of significant Welsh political/social content. It telescopes many ideas in the novel well but falls into the trap of concentrating too much on the individual domestic conflict rather than the wider political, parliamentary and industrial arenas. The miners' march to London, ending in Arnold Ryerson's disenchantment and his explosive confrontation with Radshaw, remain fine setpieces.

The Brave Don't Cry, with its refusal to compromise or resort to melodramatic excess, continues to rank with the finest of all British mining films. The dirt, and the sense of cramped stultifying lives, seem to permeate the film. It is the antithesis in some ways of **Kameradschaft** with its wonderfully lit interiors (reconstructed in Germany's UFA studios) and mobile, lambent camerawork. Pabst's film poeticizes the dignity of labour in the same way that disciples of the Grierson school were prone to do in Britain in mining films such as Cavalcanti's **Coalface** (1935) – part-directed by Humphrey Jennings – and the nocturnal pit scenes in south Wales which conclude

Jennings's 1939 **Spare Time** with silhouettes of silent men going about their labours. Jennings's film has atmosphere and its impressionistic, kaleidoscopic images of Britain have a tranquillity out of temper with the times, for all their resonance. Neither is it free of condescension – witness the scenes of the youthful jazz band.[68] And **Coalface** seems a cold, hermetic work which emasculates the men in rendering them so anonymous. There is little sense of political or social awareness in either film, in which form seems in search of content.

Jennings was to make his mark in Wales with **Silent Village** (1943), one of the finest of all British drama-docs (though it contains some of **Spare Time**'s faults) and the Welsh were also to figure strongly in the 1940s documentary work of the Strand company. Strand's *oeuvre* was invigorating and eclectic, and the company was a forcing ground for new film-makers. It was also for a few years to provide a screen voice for one of the most distinctive Welsh creative talents – Dylan Thomas.

. . . I feel at least that we have really begun to get close to the men – not just as individuals, but also as a class – with an understanding between us; so they don't feel we are just photographing them as curios or wild animals or 'just for propaganda'.

(Humphrey Jennings, letter to his wife, Cicely, 14 November, 1942, while making *Silent Village* at Cwmgïedd, west Wales)

Have you seen Wales in snow?

I don't mean on the hills or photographs of Snowdon

I mean on Dowlais Top and the Merthyr Road

I mean the shift that went down in starlight and worked in the dark and came up in the pale fleece of the afternoon.

I mean this man with thumbs in his belt and his old mac blowing with the black

Earth on his face and the white sky on his boots with only his teeth and eyes

Whiter than Wales in snow.

(Humphrey Jennings. Poem and letter from Mary-Lou Jennings (ed.), *Jennings: Film-maker, Painter, Poet*, BFI, Riverside Studios, 1982)

In the war years British cinema acquired far more prestige, with a string of fine films based on service life and the problems of 'ordinary' but generally middle-class families triumphing under duress. Audiences continued to patronize the cinema in healthy numbers after early alarums when the government briefly shut down all venues, then curtailed programmes in the later curfew days. Cinemas in many areas, including Cardiff, were forced to close each evening at 10 p.m. The government's shut-down

precautions against aerial attack proved unnecessary during the 'phoney war' period before the blitz in 1940. Similarly British studio space was soon freed after initial requisitioning for storage. There was film activity in Wales not merely with the mining features but also with dramas like the Associated British spy thriller **Tower of Terror** (1941), starring Wilfrid Lawson and set in Germany but shot partly at Porthcawl and Flat Holm. The hostilities did not stop companies launching new cinemas. Splott (Cardiff) Cinema Co. opened the County at Rumney, for instance, on Boxing Day, 1939, with an Irene Dunne and Charles Boyer romantic soufflé, **Love Affair**. The blitz took its toll on cinemas, of course. Swansea, which took the brunt of bombing, lost the Picture House, High Street, and at least two Cardiff cinemas suffered damage. Welsh audiences generally reacted with fortitude and stoicism. Cardiff Capitol cinema's management praised the calm, sensible behaviour of its audiences during siren warnings, and emphasized in adverts the safety of its air-raid shelter, for 1,000 people in the basement 'with four reinforced concrete floors above' but it also assured customers that during air raids Frank Davison's orchestra would be 'in full swing, rendering popular music' until the all-clear. Most patrons preferred to stay in their seats, watching programmes, rather than dash to the shelter, the *South Wales Echo* noted.[1]

The debate on Sunday cinema openings in Wales was revived again – with applications made for special 'Sabbath' screenings for servicemen, just as they had been for munitions workers in the First World War, with similarly discouraging results. The Welsh Halls Ltd. and Hanbury Electric Theatre Co. had been fined in 1917 at Bargoed in Glamorgan for showing films illegally on Sundays. One prominent exhibitor, Jackson Withers, protested in court against the alleged injustice of denying 'thousands of munitions workers', employed for long hours, their right to relaxing Sabbath entertainment. He added that many Sunday services in chapels were in Welsh and 'couldn't be understood' by the many immigrant workers. Support for relaxation of the cinema taboo had increased considerably by the Second World War, but in 1941 Barry Council voted by just 13 to 12 against a move for Sunday opening, and Cardiff City Council deferred a recommendation by its watch committee to open the cinemas 'for the entertainment of men and women of the services', stressing there had been 'very protracted discussion' on the issue eleven months before.[2]

Cinemas still reported huge business through to 1945, as propaganda features and war movies vied for popularity with weepies and musicals, often featuring a new breed of glamour girl. Cinemas also boasted heavy collections for the war effort, and for providing more Spitfire fighter airplanes in particular. Rita Hayworth and Betty Grable became cinema and service favourites, exuding sex appeal. Grable, in particular, eclipsed at the box office the charms of late thirties stars Alice Faye and Deanna Durbin (whose appearance as a teenager in **Three Smart Girls**, 1937, with Welshman Ray Milland as romantic male lead, had saved Universal from bankruptcy). In Britain audiences preferred the unflappability and almost reticent heroism of Irish-born Greer Garson in her Mrs Miniver roles. There were still odd outbursts in Wales of Noncomformist puritanism faced with more overt female sexuality on screen. In March 1941 at Abercynon court, a cinema at Ynysybwl was refused a Good Friday screening of the Grable vehicle **Million Dollar Legs** (1939). After scrutinizing the synopsis stipendiary magistrate Mr J. Bowen Davies chipped in his two penn'orth: 'Is this the kind of thing you are going to show?' he asked, '. . . something to make your hair stand on end. No, I do not like the look of it.'[3]

Poetic Strand

Even before war broke out British producers were busy making patriotic noises – even if few reacted with the alacrity of Michael Balcon, who tampered with **Proud Valley**'s projected finale to provide an 'acceptable' patriotic ending. As early as 1938 he sent a memo to a government department to suggest the harnessing of films to the national effort and the fight against Fascism.[4] The memo, he said, fell on deaf ears at the time, but other producers and companies were only too eager to tap the emotions and chauvinist passions of the audiences. The Ministry of Information commissioned dozens of films in the war years and by January 1941 claimed to have 'given 300 shows in Wales, some in villages where talkies had never been seen before'. Mobile film units toured the country and there was a demand from some quarters for Welsh versions of the films, though very few bilingual films were made.

In the forefront of war production was the London-based Strand company, run by Donald Taylor, using directors weaned in the Grierson tradition and based in Oxford Street offices formerly occupied by the GPO Film Unit.[5] The films made included, at one extreme, rather smug little eulogies on aspects of national life. These were frequently elaborate symphonies of images and sound which paid homage to elements in our tradition or celebrated the fortitude of individuals and institutions in wartime. There was also a strain of more bellicose, bludgeoning agit-prop in Britain exemplified by the Strand company's **These Are the Men** (1943), a vituperative short attacking the Nazis written by Dylan Thomas. It cannibalized Leni Riefenstahl's extraordinary vainglorious **Triumph of the Will** (1935) and replaced the 'straight' translation of speeches at Nuremberg with the liverish prose of Thomas who presented us with the apparent spectacle of Hitler, Goebbels, Goering and company reeling off their own character defects.[6] The Welshman's links with Strand, no doubt, influenced the tone and occasionally the direction of the company's work, which increasingly emphasized the aesthetic values inherent in British life, even in wartime. After their early pre-Thomas forays into the Rhondda, Strand made two notable documentaries with a strong Welsh content: **Wales: Green Mountain, Black Mountain** (1942) and **Our Country** (1944).

Thomas had fond recollections of film-going experiences in his local fleapit, the Uplands Cinema in Swansea, when money collected for Dr Barnardo's was reputedly used to finance film trips by his gang and he 'shouted and hissed threepences away' at Saturday afternoon matinées. He never lost an affection for the cinema which occasionally found its way into his poetry. His employment with Strand, busy turning out propaganda films for the Ministry of Information, began in 1941, and he worked on at least ten documentaries before leaving in 1945. Much of this was hack work and it is no secret that Thomas did not always take his assignments very seriously, yet he made conscientious attempts to provide lyrical poetry and images to match the visuals in Strand's two Welsh films.[7] He was also capable of providing journeyman scripts for films extolling the virtues of military routines or even industrial processes.

These were clearly churned out to boost the bank balance of the usually impecunious poet.

The best of the Thomas/Strand films is John Eldridge's **Our Country**, a kaleidoscopic impression of a cross-section of British life observed by a sailor on shore leave. It is a felicitous blend of elegiac imagery and Thomas's prose-poetry which in early scenes, and often in a line or two, casts our attention away from the landscape we see – the factory and the city – to the wider world beyond. Thomas uses his familiar sea and bird imagery to advantage, to help charge scenes with menace, and the lines are often a perfect emotional bridge between scenes.

Over a conventional montage of traffic, a bus journey and shots of railways as the seaman arrives in London, Thomas evokes 'the owl sound of the dry wind in the tube tunnels' and the euphoria of the film's matelot, returning home after two years, is summed up by Thomas's spry style as his central character embraces 'a day as lively and noisy as a close gossip of sparrows . . . A day when the long noise of the sea is forgotten'. After platitudes from Burgess Meredith (then of Air Transport Command) on behalf of American servicemen in Britain, the film begins brightly with a crane shot as we see through a mirror the seaman (David Sime) sprucing himself up before entering the city's hurly-burly.[8] A montage of rivers, bridges, spires and domes suggests not merely the sailor's physical surroundings but the rush of memories. Jo Jago's camerawork and the lighting do justice to the architecture of vaulted railway stations; then the screen is ablaze with light as the sailor begins his journey through Britain, embracing a short stay in Wales. Thomas's poetry is purplish and patchy at times as he summons up 'the moon-mauled, man-indifferent sea' and the wind on 'velvet' cliffs, but Eldridge compensates with a splendid telescoping of time and memory as suddenly the sailor crosses fields where tanks lumber and loom as men who were 'late at harvest' stand 'cold and calm and armed on hilltops under the punishing rush of planes'. When he reaches Wales the sailor first peers in at the window of the school where children learn the names of the seasons in Welsh and immediately some florid poetry, referring to the 'grief-fed' country's furnace, wrenches us away into images of town . . . the mining valleys . . . the steelworks of Sheffield . . . The sailor meets his girl and her sense of foreboding sustains the images which follow. As the pair pass jagged, charred buildings we glimpse a war factory. Again, Eldridge cleverly fractures the prevailing mood as the couple burst into a dance contest and a jazz session. These upbeat elements gradually shade into another scene in which the sailor, returning to his ship by train, plays his harmonica. As he stands on the quay, awaiting transit, Thomas again evokes the siren call – the long noise of the sea.

Jack Ellitt's polished editing and William Alwyn's music make their contribution to a buoyant film. It is drenched at odd moments in a spurious romanticism, and glosses over unpalatable realities, but still works well as a coherent, impressionistic and affirmative little essay. Its rather dogged optimism and blinkered approach to realities naturally upset some reviewers – and Thomas's own work received decidedly mixed notices. One critic, comparing the film to Humphrey Jennings's **Listen to Britain**, saw it only as 'an album of wonderful photography' ruined by Thomas's prose-poetry and 'windy self-consciousness'.[9] The *Documentary News Letter* described the film as 'the most notable of the past five years' but admitted that it aroused strong feelings, with some film-makers finding the narrative 'an impediment to enjoyment'. The newsletter considered the film important enough to carry two separate reviews (both uncredited) when first completed. One writer hailed it as the 'sole and most successful

experimental film of the war period', and claimed it said important things in a new way involving poetry and impressionism. The film's continuity was deemed 'specially exciting' with its 'flow of visuals and sounds'.[10] This reviewer described the film as 'a live vision of the inwardness of our daily life though it might best be seen as a yearning for the tranquillity sundered by war. The reviewer praised Thomas for succeeding 'for the first time in wedding and subordinating his style to the needs of the medium'. The second critic was less than laudatory, attacking **Our Country**'s 'vagueness and woolliness' as it wandered 'gracefully and nebulously over Britain'.

For all the reservations, the film reached a much wider audience than the average documentary, enjoying premières at both the Empire, Leicester Square, and London's prestige art house cinema, the Academy on Oxford Street.[11] The polarized reviews indicate the schism in the ranks of documentary film-makers, one writer emphasizing the primacy of imagery, the need for purism in visuals, the other opposing the traditional GPO style typified by director Harry Watt's use of Auden's poetry on the much praised 1936 documentary **Night Mail**. **Our Country** remains a neglected work which, aesthetically at least, stands comparison with all but the very best of Jennings's films.

In **Wales: Green Mountain, Black Mountain**, opening images of castles (the legacy of the old war against the English) and Celtic mists (a dominant strain in so much Welsh film and literature) give way to shots of the clamour of the latest war, overlaid by Thomas's lines. Director John Eldridge manages to hold in delicate counterbalance images of a Wales of unemployment with the pits shut down, visions of an industrious Wales playing its part in the future and pastoral scenes suggesting immutability and an unchanging idyll. The poetry and Jo Jago's camerawork help the film linger in the mind with Thomas exhorting the viewer to remember 'the procession of the old-young men' from the dole queues and the days when depression clamped down '. . . over the blind windows of the mean streets'. But too many lines indicate that Thomas was operating on automatic. Much of the imagery is conventional, the narrative redundant and at its worst the writing is stale and even excruciating: 'The miners of the Rhondda go down like ghosts in black, only their smiles are white.' The hortatory tone, shorn of any real context or persuasive intellectual content, merely sounds foolish: 'The world shall never deny the people of Wales again,' for instance. Yet the film, like **Our Country**, did suggest values worth preserving. One can readily imagine it carried a resonance in wartime which may not be readily apparent in hindsight.

Nothing too contentious escaped the censors during those years but heights of bureaucratic absurdity were scaled when the M.o.I.'s Welsh Office apparently objected to the film on the grounds that Thomas was not a 'real' Welshman, as he lived in London.[12] The work suffered other interference and much attention from government agencies and there were several versions – one or two prepared by the British Council, shorn of the Thomas sound-track. The M.o.I. in London finally discounted its Welsh Office's views and kept faith in the poet's work for their official version.[13] The other versions, while stressing Wales's cultural heritage and the wild countryside traced by George Borrow, wound up with the familiar patriotic call of wartime, pleading with those in coal pit, factory and farm to defend the 'land of their fathers'.

Thomas's declamatory style in the M.o.I. short proved a dry run for **These Are the Men**, in which the poet, at his most splenetic, placed Nazi leaders in the confessional. In a deceptively subdued opening the film counterpoints shots of men at work in bakeries, in the docks and iron foundries with more menacing portents and apocalyptic intimations on the sound-track. The images of men performing prosaic tasks, the world over, in peacetime are succeeded by scenes of men fighting in war, and Thomas's prose, occasionally sliding towards tabloid journalese, summons up a world grappling for survival: 'We are the makers, the workers, the starving, the slaves.'

The tone soon veers from the incantatory to the histrionic:

> 'Who sent us to kill or to be killed, to lose what we
>   love
> Widowed our women, unfathered our sons, broke the hearts
>   of our homes?
> Who dragged us out, out of our beds and houses
>   and workshops
> Into a battle-yard of spilt blood and split bones?'

A baker opens an oven door, flames belch across the screen and there is a dissolve into the Nazi salute. The sounds merge into the 'sieg heil' of crowds and suddenly we are in Nuremberg. But over the sounds of the Nazi rabble-rousers, an English voice is heard with an ersatz translation. Hitler, for instance (in a would-be satirical shaft) imputes to himself neurosis as a child, incompetence as an artist and homosexuality.

> I am a normal man.
> I do not like meat, drink or women. Heil, Heil
> Neurosis, charlatanism, bombast, anti-socialism.
> Hate of the Jews, treachery, murder, race – insanity
> I am the leader of the German people.

Each of these fake-revelations, of course, meets with tumultuous applause from acolytes. Arch-propagandist Goebbels castigates the Jews as editors and publishers who refused to publish his work and impelled him to launch, with Streicher, a newspaper to 'propagate obscene lies' against them. Streicher announces himself as 'a lover of birds and animals, a torturer and murderer of Jews'. Rudolf Hess proclaims his devotion to Hitler and tells of his aborted mission to Britain ending in his prison term.

In hindsight the incorporation of the Nuremberg sequences does not seem as inspired as it might have during the war, perhaps because the power of the imagery of Riefenstahl's original defied the rather glib, coarse satire. It is significant that French director René Clair was so appalled by the power of **Triumph of the Will**'s images after Luis Buñuel had re-edited them for New York's Museum of Modern Art that he advised him never to show them.[14] But *after* the Nuremberg sequence **These Are the Men** produces its most effective melding of images and words. As the Gestapo led by Himmler march across the screen, we hear:

> And these are the men, the young men, the callow boys
> Who have been taught the knuckleduster and the rubber hose [and]
> [Young men like you] have left a slug trail behind you
>   of terror and death.

Even the sympathetic reviewer of the *Documentary News Letter*, though appreciating Alan Osbiston's editing and much of Thomas's verse – 'which frequently cuts like a knife into the pompously bestial affectations of this race of supermen' criticized the finale.[15] The voice shouting that the Nazis could never be offered 'pardon or pity' had 'a suspicion of hysteria', the writer felt. 'Most ordinary people have no intention of forgiving Hitler, Goebbels, Goering, Streicher or Hess and they will be somewhat bewildered to find the Government regarding it as a matter worth announcing so excitedly.' Certainly the film's humour seems leaden and Thomas seems to have strained at a gnat.

The Welshman also provided the scripted commentary for **The Battle for Freedom** (1942), another Strand film with a strong, overt war content. Directed by Alan Osbiston, it centred on the Commonwealth's preparations for the war, and its contributions to agriculture and industry in wartime. This smacked of a dutiful assignment and aroused no great critical interest. **Balloon Site 568** (1942), made at the Women's Auxiliary Air Force Base, Cardington, Bedfordshire, also had no great pretensions. It allowed Thomas to script a film acknowledging the role of women in wartime, but proved a conventional 'short', stiff with platitudes, and the writer was obviously constrained by the film's propaganda role which prevented any genuinely intelligent analysis of women's wider wartime contribution.[16] Thomas was later to script shorts about the rebuilding of Britain after the conflict, notably **A City Reborn** (1945), focusing on the resilience and activity in Coventry after the heavy blitzing. This work, directed by John Eldridge and shot by another of Thomas's regular collaborators, Jo Jago, introduces us to the damaged city through the impressions of a soldier (Bill Owen) returning there for the first time since the bombing. The film, permeated with that unflagging optimism which became the trademark of these dramatized documentaries, then stressed the opportunities for renewal and transformation and the work on replenishing Coventry's housing by providing thousands of prefabricated homes, often made in the city's own factories.[17] **New Towns for Old** (1942), a much slighter Eldridge/Thomas collaboration, again stressed the post-war opportunities to remove the slums and the need to allow ordinary people to play a part in deciding on their future living conditions and surroundings.[18]

Forays into fiction

Thomas later branched out and scripted two 1948 fictional films for British National made at Elstree: **No Room at the Inn**, shot on a peppercorn £70,000 budget, and the abysmal **The Three Weird Sisters**, the nadir of his short screen career in which he uses the central male character as a mouthpiece to criticize alleged Welsh parochialism and backbiting.[19] The result was a poor, toe-curling imitation of the sardonic style of Caradoc Evans. Both the films were directed by the former documentary film-maker Dan Birt who also in the 1940s made a five-minute Verity film for the Ministry of Information, **Dai Jones, Miner**, centring on a south Wales pitman in a rescue squad.[20]

No Room at the Inn, a story of evacuees browbeaten by harridan Mrs Vornay (Freda Jackson), and based on a Joan Temple stage play, earned chequered reviews when released through Pathé. The Joy Shelton character, schoolmistress Judith Droy, alerts the authorities but cannot persuade the council of the cruelty of the evil landlady. Mrs Vornay finally falls down a rickety staircase to her death, after a spat with her spiv boyfriend.

The *Daily Worker* praised Joan Temple's courageous story and, interestingly, claimed censorship of the film had denuded it of a powerful ending 'when the children exacted their own revenge'.[21] But the *Monthly Film Bulletin* was more disappointed that the film balked at dealing with the social implication of the woman's death and found the ending 'curiously ineffective' and abrupt.[22] 'Children are still being turned into delinquents by criminal negligence. Local authorities are still inclined to hide their heads in the sand and people who try to take action against social evils are still called mischief makers,' the reviewer remarked pointedly. The *Daily Mirror* critic was surprisingly squeamish. He was sorry to see Miss Jackson used in a picture about 'such an out of date and sordid side of English life'.[23]

The script, a collaboration between Thomas and Ivan Foxwell, at least highlighted neglect, guilt and official complicity in child abuse cases long before the British documentary cinema had embraced them. Burrells, the billeting officer, knows Mrs Vornay's shortcomings but settles for the easy option when finding a home for the well-behaved youngster Mary O'Rane, who is soon victimized by the landlady. The film is told in extended flashback with events filtered through the memory of the adult Mary, a saleswoman who protects a Cockney woman (Norma) accused of theft. We soon learn the common bond they share as past victims and lodgers of Mrs Vornay but the screenplay soon shifts focus to Norma, a gamine – and a more charismatic character than Mary O'Rane. 'Norma steals the part of heroine from the well-brought-up Mary whose disintegration is supposed to provide the tragedy of the film,' the *Daily Worker* reviewer noted.[24]

Joan Dowling, as Norma, and Joy Shelton, as the schoolmistress, earned plaudits from critics who were generally generous to Freda Jackson. But 'MF' in the *Daily Mail* cavilled: 'In its quieter moments the film is a raucous red-nosed melodrama . . . The horror is so overplayed that it becomes merely ludicrous.'[25] The *News Chronicle* attacked the script, referring to 'the small mystery' of the recruitment of Dylan Thomas as a scriptwriter. His talents were in 'direct opposition to the needs of screenwriting' and his touch was dismissed as 'furiously false'.[26]

Three Weird Sisters, with Thomas, Louise Birt and David Evans sharing the writing credit, is a bizarre Gothic horror story with pretensions, in which the ostensible villains are a trio of extremely strange ladies from a mineowner's family.[27] With its ramshackle, risible script, the film is a disgrace despite a cast including Hugh Griffith and Nancy Price. The motivations and behaviour of characters change from scene to scene, almost from moment to moment, as the script frequently switches tone and tack. Nova Pillbeam played perhaps the most sympathetic role in the picture and remembers it, accurately, as 'a horrid little melodrama'.[28]

The work is centred on a motley trio of fairly incompatible sisters, the Morgan-Vaughans, who plot to kill their dyspeptic half-brother Owen (Raymond Lovell), a character perhaps even more dislikeable than his relatives. Almost comically self-centred, he constantly demeans and criticizes his secretary (Pillbeam). The film is chiefly interesting if seen as a black comedy with symbolic pretensions, and for some startling anti-Welsh speeches by Owen whose hypochondria and love of mollycoddling are fascinating in the light of Dylan Thomas's own character.[29]

In the opening scene, a pitfall claims two or three lives when cottages slip into a chasm as the Morgan-Vaughan mineworkings collapse. The tragedy leads to recriminations from locals about the sisters, 'profitmakers who don't give a damn in hell about the people that make their profit for them'. The sisters, it transpires, are starved of money by Owen (Raymond Lovell) who holds the family purse-strings. The sisters' resentment of Owen is apparently based on class and fuelled by Owen's boorishness and wealth: 'Perhaps it is my common blood which enabled me to make more money than my father ever did,' he suggests. From the outset Owen, whose money from mining apparently keeps the ingrate sisters afloat, dubs them the Three Furies and trades abuse with them, the insults reaching humorous and sometimes childish heights of hyperbole. It gradually becomes apparent that they are plotting to murder him and his secretary (if necessary) but the scheme is (almost predictably) pre-empted by another fatal pitfall. The film is notable only for the scope it allows Thomas to vent his spleen about Wales but Owen's tirades are so unfocused that it is often difficult to tell how much they indicate the writer's real views.

A later spell with Gainsborough Films proved abortive (and failed to yield any features produced by the studio). Various Thomas projects and screenplays remained on the drawing board, others were resurrected unsuccessfully by other companies many years later (including **Rebecca's Daughters**, directed by Karl Francis). But none of the poet's big-screen ventures had half the critical impact of the first BBC TV live version of **Under Milk Wood**.[30]

Silent Village

Thomas's best cinema documentary work remains **Our Country**, but this was dwarfed in significance in 1943 by the most innovative of all wartime reconstruction films, **Silent Village**, made in Wales by Humphrey Jennings for the Crown Film Unit. Jennings's taste for pastorale, his ability to find grandeur in the everyday and his flair for *mise-en-scène* were complemented by Stewart McAllister's bravura editing.[31]

The film, ingeniously transposing the 1942 Nazi massacre in the mining village of Lidice in Czechoslovakia to south Wales, was born of the kind of consultations with south Wales miners initiated in a less ambitious way by Ralph Bond in 1936/7. It was the brainchild of Victor Fisch, Czech Minister of Foreign Affairs. Britain's Ministry of Information – anxious to co-operate – consulted the South Wales Miners' Federation president Arthur Horner, asking about possible locations. Horner had previous

experience of film, by proxy: one Strand documentary, **Coalminer** (1944), had revolved around a radio talk between the miners' leader and a Rhondda pitman, Charlie Jones, about the changing conditions underground, and the role of miners and the new pit production committees in increasing tonnage during wartime.[32] Jennings was introduced to the miners by noted newspaper designer Allen Hutt. Horner advised Jennings and his team to resist the Rhondda and to film in unknown parts of Wales in the western valleys at the anthracite end of the coalfield.[33] That area was more Welsh-speaking, had an agricultural and industrial population and boasted beautiful country, it was pointed out. Horner linked the M.o.I. with the miners' agent at Ystradgynlais, Dai Dan Evans, and Evans and senior NUM colleagues worked closely with the former miners' agent, Llanelli MP Jim Griffiths (later Welsh minister from 1945 and the first Welsh Secretary of State, in 1964). They hit on Cwmgïedd which had both a church wall, for the climactic firing-squad scene, and a cemetery. The decision was made in August 1942, when Jennings was much taken with his first view of the village with its stone cottages and he spoke at length of his love for Cwmgïedd in a 1943 radio talk.[34]

On 21 August 1942, barely two months after the massacre of all 173 male adults then at Lidice, 100 people attended the miners' hall, Ystradgynlais, where a committee of twelve was elected to help with the project. They met once or twice a week during the four-month shoot in the Swansea and Dulais valleys, when the film unit lived in miners' homes.[35] Shooting was wrapped up by Christmas but editing continued until at least May 1943. The people of the area played themselves, using their own names

The men of Cwmgïedd, defiant surrogates for the Lidice massacred, face up to the Nazi firing squad in Silent Village.

192

in the intense registration scene, when the villagers all file past their protector-oppressors and verbally confirm their identities.

The film opens with long shots of Cwmgïedd, somnolent in the sun. Jennings's vision of Wales at the film's outset is idealized, comforting. Men wend their way from the pit singing 'Men of Harlech' and share camaraderie. Jennings cuts to show children in a cinema, enthusing over a Donald Duck cartoon. Then the mood changes as loudspeakers announce the presence of the new 'Protectorate State' after the German invasion. The voices of the occupying Nazis ricochet around the village. Requests to the population soon become imperatives, with the usurpers moving to break up the trade unions, deeming the miners' lodges 'no longer necessary'and exhorting the locals to 'put your trust in the Führer'. Strikes are banned, and in scenes of great economy and understatement, Jennings suggests resignation and quiescence while providing evidence of the welling minority defiance – the miners refusing to buckle under, the production of an underground Welsh-language paper, the shooting of guerillas in the wood, shots of the swelling ranks of resistance men. This passage culminates in the news of Deputy Reich Protector Heydrich's killing given in a broadcast of double-talk: 'He held Welsh workmen in high esteem . . .'

Editor Stewart McAllister's cutting gathers momentum and assumes a new urgency. Remarkably we see very few Nazis: Jennings preferring to represent them through icons/inanimate objects – helmets, swastikas, a radio broadcasting messages from the invader. All gain significance as agents for the Nazi machine.[36] We are soon made aware that the apparent tranquillity of families at home is illusory as broadcast threats increase.[37] A fretful schoolmistress tells her children gently not to forget their Welsh language (and the Welsh songs and hymns also banned). It seems likely that Jennings was aware of historical parallels which could be drawn with the English colonizing of Welsh education through language and of the notorious Blue Books episode.[38] Ordinary people discuss the evidence of reprisals. We hear of a woman shot merely for allegedly laughing at her persecutors. Then the names of those locals killed following Heydrich's death are read in a menacing monotone over the radio. Cwmgïedd is ordered to surrender culprits by midnight, villagers refuse and at dawn the women are driven to a concentration camp and the children transported in lorries to captivity. In one poignant moment the women, as they are herded across the bridge, can look down on the men facing the firing squad. The miners sing 'Land of My Fathers' as they are gunned down.

The film moves to the present. Dai Dan Evans delivers a eulogy, reminding us that the community at Lidice has been immortalized, lying in the hearts of miners world-wide. The scenes of the men meeting their deaths with stoicism and the aftermath shots of the smouldering, charred village carry a powerful charge nearly fifty years on. The strained postscript of Evans testifying the Welsh miners' loyalty to their comrades at Lidice is, as some contemporary reviewers pointed out, something of an anticlimax. **Silent Village** would have gained dramatically if Jennings had gone the whole hog, presented Cwmgïedd actually under threat and eliminated any framing device. It might have generated some of the excitement obvious in Cavalcanti's **Went the Day Well?**; but Jennings's style was essentially reflective and observational. Perhaps the film would have been better served with just an end title, expressing the miners' sentiments. But the *Documentary News Letter* reviewer seemed carping when he asserted that it was 'impossible to say why the film was made . . . the strangely oblique approach robs the film of any direct impact because it might have been

Humphrey Jennings, with
the west Wales miners, on
location for *Silent Village.*

translated into "it might have been like this" not "it was like this".'[39]

It must be remembered that **Silent Village** was released while the war was still in progress and that Jennings suffered constraints, the Ministry of Information expressing early reservations about the script's 'political aspect'. 'The way the miners are picked out at the moment has revolutionary – barricade – implications which we must avoid.' A memo stated frankly: 'I don't like picking the miners out of the rest of the workers as a vanguard . . . I do think the miners must be picked out, for reasons of the film and of increased output, but through the coal.'[40] The memo suggested that great stress should be placed in the film on mining's importance. Coal was the basis of the 'revised state', so those who mined it were 'the fundamental workers of the community'.

Jennings's compromises were minor and, in retrospect, did little to blunt the film's impact. He was clearly affected by his experiences filming in Cwmgïedd. He had 'never thought to see honest Christian-communist principles acted on by a large number of . . . British people living together'.[41] 'We are photographing them as honestly as possible . . . neither like **How Green** . . . too theatrical . . . or **The Grapes of Wrath** . . . too poverty-stricken,' he observed during production.[42]

Silent Village is a small triumph of technique but its limitations are self-evident. Jennings had helped launch the Mass Observation surveys and polls of the 1930s which canvassed ordinary people for their views and produced survey results; in his filming of **Silent Village** he remains too much the outsider, the anthropologist. His people are not sufficiently individualized and the film offers no fresh insights about the community or home life beyond, arguably, the depth of feeling over the Welsh language. Lindsay Anderson, in a perceptive article, praised Jennings's 'affectionate response to simple pleasures' and his 'fond simplicity', but felt he missed the 'necessary sense of conflict and suffering'. Anderson also found the film 'over-refined and under-dramatized'.[43] But it remains a lesson in cogent propaganda with scarcely a redundant image. McAllister's virile editing sustained the narrative drive while Chick

Fowles's incisive camerawork, in the service of Jennings's vision, should not go unnoticed.

Silent Village continues to be a potent – or provocative – inspiration for writers and film-makers. Stage dramatist Edward Thomas, a native of Cwmgïedd, combined with director Marc Evans on an ambitious impressionistic 1993 BBC Wales drama-documentary using footage from the Jennings work but presenting folk-memories of the 1943 filming from the perspective of a writer (played by Richard Lynch), born in the village post-war. In his 1994 stage play *Atrocity* another Cwmgïedd native Ewart Alexander, whose elder brothers were in the film, communicated the mining community's ambivalence to the Crown unit's visit and impact.

Night Shift

The role of women in factory and wartime was not forgotten in other films of the period, and one well-orchestrated and fairly lyrical documentary deserves mention. **Night Shift** (1942) was made by Jack Chambers, of DATA, for Paul Rotha's production company and filmed at the Royal Ordnance Factory in Newport. It focused on the arduous nature of the women's work rather than on technical detail in the gunmaking factory, unidentified in the film. It employed nearly 2,000 women, we are told by the narrator, who introduces us to the workers' tasks.[44] The liberated camerawork, including some very effective travelling and dolly shots, careful interior lighting and resourceful use of overlapping sound help suggest the factory atmosphere and the sense of time slowly passing for girls working ten-hour shifts. The rhythm of the editing picks up as the night progresses.

Chambers impressively builds up banks of sound to convey the hubbub of background talk. This device is repeated during the eloquent canteen sequence in which cross-talk and banter prepare us for a later canteen scene in which workers dance to the music of a woman pianist and a red-hot momma who provides a rousing 'Some of These Days'. As the number concludes, Chambers wraps up the scene with panache. The performer, still singing, moves to the foreground of the screen and begins to clear away plates at now-deserted tables. The song continues over the next shot, on the factory floor, and gradually fades into the noise of the machines. The sequence is a *tour de force* but **Night Shift**'s importance also resides in what it says and does not say about women's self-esteem and prevailing sexual attitudes. A girl seen absorbed at her machine has been doing the work for six months and is as good as any man at her job, we are told. There are odd moments of chauvinism: a male worker with cheery condescension asks a girl machinist, 'What are you trying to do – win the war on your own?' and tells her, 'you need a man about the place.' Later she says she'd rather be firing than making guns. The female narrator tells us: 'While we can't be firing them we're putting all we've got into making them for the men who can.'

In fifties films, including Jill Craigie's **Born to be a Woman** and Ealing's **Dance Hall**, the women on the factory floor were treated with less condescension and were much more assertive – and sure of their identity.[45] British fiction features between 1959 and 1965 explored the sexuality of women and their intimate sexual relationships. In movies starring Welsh actress Rachel Roberts, for example, relationships were expressed with a candour scarcely visualized a decade earlier.

EMLYN WILLIAMS: INSIDER OR OUTSIDER?

One Sunday morning I went to see Cukor and Hepburn. Hepburn wasn't very happy with my appearance. They wanted someone who looked like a miner . . . a young De Niro or Brando type . . . I kept being called back to see Cukor. Two months later Hepburn turned up at my flat one day with two bell weights she'd bought so I could work out and develop my shoulders.

(Welshman Ian Saynor – Morgan Evans in the 1979 screen version of Emlyn Williams's **The Corn is Green**)

The thirties and forties saw dramatic changes in the British film industry. The seminal influence of Balcon, at Gainsborough and Gaumont British, then his even more important tenure at Ealing, shaped much indigenous film output. The brief flowering of Alexander Korda's London films, with such epics as **The Private Life of Henry VIII** (1933) and **Rembrandt** (1936), offered hopes (soon snuffed out) that UK features could make significant and lasting inroads into US markets. But from the forties onwards the dominant figure was undoubtedly J. Arthur Rank, the former Yorkshire flour manufacturer. He gained control of Gaumont-British and Odeon Holdings Ltd., just a few years after dozens of Odeon cinemas sprang up throughout Britain, including thirty-six new purpose-built venues in 1937 alone, all bearing the same uncluttered design, the cream-tiled façades – the trademark of Balcon's former Midlands schoolmate, millionaire Oscar Deutsch. When war came Deutsch was dead, Rank had moved into Korda's ailing former studios at Denham, was running Gaumont-British from Pinewood and major studios at Elstree, and had production/distributor links with the cream of British talent (from Michael Powell, Carol Reed and David Lean to Launder and Gilliat and the Boultings). Rank effectively controlled the most significant strands of British creative film: dramas, documentaries, Ealing comedies – and the Gainsborough costume melodramas. Such confections as **The Wicked Lady**, Britain's top money-spinner in 1946, proved exotic enough to entice American audiences for a spell, even though Rank's dreams of conquering Hollywood had collapsed by the late forties.

SECTION 3

Winds of
Change – The
Welsh Impact
on Post-War
British Cinema

A new realism

Welsh actors and writers contributed much in these years, gaining their grounding through the studios. The career of Emlyn Williams as actor and writer first burgeoned with Gaumont-British and at a watershed period for British film, with the last pre-War gasp of that transient genre, the British musical, and the final years of UK feature films predominantly locked in a time-warp and an upper-class or upper-middle-class milieu. Three films featuring Williams – **The Citadel** (1938), **The Stars Look Down** and Arthur Wood's realistic trucking movie/thriller **They Drive by Night** (1938) – were among those which marked the transition to a more realistic cinema attuned to contemporary life. Rhondda actor Stanley Baker, whose career helped break the mould, established himself as perhaps the first virile artisan, proletarian hero and anti-hero of the British screen. He made his début at fourteen, at Ealing, and graduated to playing leads while on the Rank roster alongside actors like Dirk Bogarde. Both men later gravitated to the films of the blacklisted former Hollywood director Joseph Losey – a man fascinated by the British class system – and gained the critical recognition which had been denied them in routine British productions. Rachel Roberts, from west Wales, through anguished roles anchored firmly in a working-class milieu, also brought the authentic flavour of real life to studios which had previously kept it at arm's length. Baker and Burton, in particular, suggested one strain of Welshness, constantly playing or suggesting the abrasive loner with a turbulent, dark side; but from the forties a more congenial Welshness (to many outsiders at least) found expression at Ealing Studios where actors like Meredith Edwards and, to a lesser extent, Mervyn Johns were among those whose roles established another stereotype of the screen Taffy, likeable but insular, naïve or gullible. Launder and Gilliat, in their British Lion days, and the Boulting Brothers were to reinforce this notion of Welsh parochialism and suggest, through the screen persona of Kenneth Griffith, for instance, other character traits such as sycophancy and duplicity.

This period of British studio films from 1945 to 1962 proved crucial, not merely in establishing a new breed of star, exemplified by Baker and Roberts, but in projecting images of the Welsh which lingered to the 1990s. Actual living conditions in Wales suggested by the Strand films and documentaries by Humphrey Jennings (**Spare Time**) and Jack Chambers (**Night Shift**) rarely found expression in fictional features outside the mining films already discussed, though **Night Shift**'s study of girl munitions factory workers in wartime inspired Launder and Gilliat's **Millions Like Us** (1943). But outside the major documentary studios, John Roberts-Williams produced in Wales **The Heritage** (1947–9), which proved an invaluable record of rural pastimes and preoccupations about to disappear forever with increasing urbanization, while Brunner Lloyd's **Noson Lawen** (1950) reinforced the emphasis on Welsh traditional customs and values. In the fifties and sixties more realistic indigenous work surfaced with the TV documentaries of John Ormond and Jack Howells, rooted firmly in urban south Wales. Through these works, plus the feature-film presence of Baker and Roberts, it was finally possible to gain a *frisson* of real Welsh life and 'Welshness' on screen.

Emlyn Williams as actor and writer

The most riveting and repellent study of working-class evil in 1940s British cinema was provided by a Welshman. Emlyn Williams as Joe Gowlan, the most unscrupulous of the rioters early in **The Stars Look Down**, metamorphoses later into the *bête noire* of the film's decent hero, David Fenwick. In the novel, by unctuous glad-handing and betrayals, he winds up controlling both the steel and coal industries, the lifeline of the community. Gowlan in Carol Reed's 1939 film is never quite allowed the stature of Cronin's original in the novel, but he still epitomizes insidious evil, thanks almost entirely to the nuances of Williams's performance. Gowlan is a fancy dan who thrives on the vacillations and fulminations of the grey men around him and makes a fortune on others' backs. He betrays the film's hero Fenwick publicly – and privately, by disrupting his marriage.[1]

If A. J. Cronin made, indirectly, the most enduring contribution to films of any writer with Welsh connections in the thirties and forties, George Emlyn Williams was among the most versatile of the nation's screen actors in Britain in those decades, and a writer whose works touched fascinatingly on issues of individual Welsh identity and nationalism. Though Williams (b. Mostyn, north Wales, 1905, d. 1987) was always at pains to profess his apolitical nature, his writing sometimes seems to betray him. Born into a Welsh-speaking, working-class family, he was too susceptible for his own comfort to the turbulence of Welsh life.[2] His writing in the theatre and on film – heavily influenced by the dominant stage modes when his career began – was often bound by the parameters of conventional suspense/melodramas and potboilers (though his thrillers, especially the twice-filmed **Night Must Fall** (1937 and 1964), betray some of his inordinate interest in the psycho-pathology of murderers and their victims).[3] But it is the two 'Welsh' films **The Corn is Green** (1945 and 1979), made from his award-winning stage play, and **The Last Days of Dolwyn** (1949) – his sole feature as director – which provide screen evidence of Williams's innate sensitivity to issues such as national identity and the fight for the Welsh language and its use as an index of social status. They also expose, as painfully as his two volumes of autobiography, his ambivalent attitude towards his roots.

In **The Corn is Green**, the central character, miner Morgan Evans, becomes the protégé of a teacher from England, Miss Moffat, who is the tangible manifestation of the increasing encroachment into the community of wider European values. These threaten to swamp vestiges of Welshness as surely as the dam in **Dolwyn** seems certain to swamp the village to provide water for Lord Lancashire in England. It is fascinating that it is Williams himself in another evil incarnation, Robbie Davies, who plots to bury this hitherto idyllic community which reminds him so forcibly of his past disgrace. Williams has constantly revealed through his work his confused reactions to his Welsh background which emerged after he went to Oxford – the precise route taken by Morgan Evans – and on to London, Broadway and Hollywood. His two key screen works reveal more than he possibly intended.

As an actor Williams had a remarkable range; he could play worldly sophisticates, both in period and contemporary work, but was as adept at playing small-time ferrety little hoods or blackmailers. He could be the dyed-in-the-wool villain, or the sage confidante. For almost fifteen years before **The Corn is Green**, Williams was at the peak as a performer in Britain. His first decade in cinema coincided with the re-shaping of the British film industry, after the financial problems encountered by both Gaumont-British and Alexander Korda's London Film Company in the 1930s, and the rise to pre-eminence of J. Arthur Rank, who soon had a stranglehold on production and exhibition.

Williams began with Gaumont-British, but his only film as director, and perhaps his most personal work for the screen, **Last Days of Dolwyn**, was made for Korda. Korda had over-reached himself in the 1930s with his lavish spending on epics, and failed to gain the huge US markets he sought. He left for the States in the early 1940s, but when he returned he was still prepared to take risks in backing idiosyncratic projects such as the Williams feature. The Welshman's screen career had seemed set to take flight as early as 1931, when he made his debut in Edgar Wallace's **The Frightened Lady** made for Balcon at Beaconsfield Studios. He made such an impression repeating his stage role that he topped a *Film Weekly* poll in 1933 for the outstanding British performer of the year (with Leslie Howard and Herbert Marshall in his wake and Ivor Novello – seen in **The Lodger** sound version that year – just gaining a top-ten place). *Film Weekly* praised Williams's 'extraordinary talent'.[4] Success led to a two-year contract as writer-actor for Gaumont-British and his reputation in the industry rose in this period when he furnished scripts and/or dialogue for the intriguing suspense film **Friday the Thirteenth** (1933) and that effervescent musical Evergreen (1934), a Jessie Matthews vehicle – and starred opposite Evelyn Laye in **Evensong** (1934).[5] All three were directed by Victor Saville, later to produce **The Citadel**.[6]

In **Friday the Thirteenth**, written by Sidney Gilliat, Williams and Angus McPhail, the Welshman featured as a vicious blackmailer, Blake, one of several people aboard a bus during a fateful crash. Two die, and the film follows the fortunes of each before revealing the victims' identity. Williams's predator, battening on Frank Lawton's one-time fellow jail inmate, proved to be one of these fated passengers. In the same movie, fellow Welshman Edmund Gwenn features as Wakefield, 'the City Man', who tries to make a killing through oil concession shares and is saved from disaster by his wife's forgetting to make the deal. This portmanteau feature was an expertly packaged, neatly-turned entertainment. But **Evergreen** was much more – a captivating musical, a *tour de force* for director Saville (who displayed a superb talent for choreography) and the perfect showcase for Jessie Matthews. The film *was* predicated on the preposterous notion that Matthews could play a daughter masquerading on stage as

Bette Davis, Emlyn
Williams and (right) the
author's mentor, Miss
Cooke, who inspired *The
Corn is Green* and the role
played by Davis in Irving
Rapper's Hollywood ver-
sion.

her mother (Betty Balfour), but the mobile, liberated camerawork, and the numbers 'Over My Shoulder' and 'Springtime in My Heart' helped smooth over cracks in the plot and the Matthews role was particularly well written.

In **Evensong**, he was unusually volatile as George Leary, a jealous lover and early piano accompanist and manager-mentor of Irish singer Maggie O'Neill (played by Laye) who becomes the prima donna 'Irela', later fêted throughout Europe. Jilted by the girl, who takes up with impresario Kober (Fritz Kortner), Williams throws water over her and even pulls a gun during a performance before thinking better of it. Retribution is at hand. When we last see him he is a virtual cabbage, shell-shocked on army service. The film was intensely melodramatic, and not without its risible moments; but it had style, and Saville handled the characters, ornate decor and musical numbers with *élan*.

By then, Hollywood had already filmed Williams's intense 1935 stage thriller *Night Must Fall*. Many contemporary critics found Robert Montgomery too insipid and debonair as the mysterious and murderous charmer Dan, a role the writer had baptized himself in Miles Malleson's production at London's Duchess Theatre.[7] Dan, who insinuates himself into the household of slothful hypochondriac Mrs Bramson, is a congenital liar with traces of Welshness – his first, professed memory is of Cardiff Docks. His mental instability seems to have stemmed partly from a warped religious upbringing and maternal repression. The part is a showy role but none too convincing, and Williams's writing, while evincing his lifelong fascination with the macabre, lacks the coherence or discipline to present Dan as a credible heavy. The strengths of the play lie in the depiction of the selfish employer Mrs Bramson, the mutual hostility between this old lady and the spinster Olivia, and in Williams's bleak view of the participants' lives. The drama has its misogynistic elements, and at times borders on the seriously unpleasant, but Williams supplies a string of visual coups – using darkness as an enticing cloak near the denouement, and some finely tuned, deliberately incongruous one-line *non sequiturs* which dissipate tension and lull the audience before the next shock effect.

The first screen version of **Night Must Fall**, directed by Richard Thorpe, was adapted by John Van Druten, a popular and highly prolific stage dramatist of the 1930s, and sometime lecturer at University College, Aberystwyth. Van Druten wrote in extra scenes and was responsible for turning the dramatic screw, according to Williams.[8] When Albert Finney played the killer in Karel Reisz's sixties MGM version, he retained the residue of Welshness from the original but telegraphed the character's instability from the first reel. Mona Washbourne was admirable as the threatened old lady but Williams felt Finney would have been 'marvellous' playing the killer with a lighter touch and the kind of charm and flippancy he brought to **Tom Jones** the year before.[9]

SECTION 3

Winds of
Change – The
Welsh Impact
on Post-War
British Cinema

Williams continued to be a major star throughout the thirties, on both stage and screen, and was superb as the hounded murder suspect in the 1938 British thriller **They Drive by Night**, which had obvious plot affinities to Hitchcock's **Young and Innocent**.[10] The Welshman played a bitter little man, Albert 'Shorty' Matthews from Swansea, just released from Pentonville, who stumbles upon his old flame, a dance-hall hostess (Alice), just after she has been murdered. He spends the rest of the film trying to elude police even, at one point, assuming a lorry driver's identity. Shorty is cold-shouldered by his card-playing friends, even though they do not reveal his hiding place; but he is befriended by Molly, a former friend, who is in turn menaced by the actual murderer, Hoover (a splendidly cadaverous Ernest Thesiger). Williams's performance as a wily fugitive permanently on tenterhooks was a pleasant departure. The film is dense in humorous detail, reasonably tense, and showed Saville as resourceful in his use of milieu and detail and tracking shots.

The thirties were, in hindsight, the high point of Williams's screen career and his stock would have risen even higher had Josef von Sternberg's **I Claudius** (1937) not been aborted after rows between the director and Charles Laughton (in the title role) and a serious injury to Merle Oberon.[11] Tantalizing extant footage of the film – in Bill Duncalf's 1965 British compilation documentary **The Epic That Never Was** – suggests that it would have been memorable even by von Sternberg's standards, and Williams was set fair to extend his range playing the ruthless sybarite Caligula.[12]

One of the actor's more bizarre assignments was as the sympathetic Chinaman in London's East End in **Broken Blossoms**, a remake of the D. W. Griffith film with Richard Barthelmess in the role. The 1936 version was prepared by Griffith but actually directed by Hans (later John) Brahm.[13] Williams's Oriental befriends, and sacrifices himself for, the film's heroine (played by Brahm's wife Dolly Haas). The Welshman scripted the film, from Thomas Burke's play, captured the character's innate gentleness and selflessness, and played the part with dignity and restraint even though he was on a hiding to nothing from critics.[14]

The Corn is Green

Williams's more personal concerns surfaced on screen when Hollywood filmed the largely autobiographical **The Corn is Green** (1945), directed by Irving Rapper with his **Now Voyager** star Bette Davis, aged thirty-six, playing Miss Moffat (the part Ethel Barrymore had played, aged sixty-one, to acclaim on Broadway in 1940).[15] Williams based his female protagonist on Miss Cooke, the conscientious teacher who educated him virtually from scratch and motivated him to gain a place at Oxford. Much of his gratitude emerges in the film, even though it is tempered by some regret at his increased alienation from his roots. The quality of dialogue given to the strong-willed schoolmistress, and the play of political, social and feminist ideas blended with comedy, has proved a magnet for an impressive array of performers since Sybil Thorndike first ventured the role, opposite Williams, in the original 1938 theatre production. Flora Robson and Joan Miller played Morgan Evans's amanuensis in BBC TV productions, and Katharine Hepburn starred in the 1970s remake.[16] Davis wanted to play the role even before she was riveted by Barrymore's performance and she persuaded Warner Bros. to buy the film rights. But her box-office leverage enabled her to wield damaging influence on set. She apparently insisted on filming in chronological order even though shooting was held up for days when she was injured. According to one biographer, Charles Higham, the first eleven days' footage had to be re-shot because she decided at a late stage to accept the studio's advice and wear a wig.[17] Davis and Rapper later bickered openly.

The Corn is Green remains Davis's film, though ostensibly it is a study of the education of an inarticulate Welsh-speaking young man in rural Wales by an indefatigable Englishwoman – and based fairly faithfully on the Williams play. The film dealt with a theme popular in modern Welsh literature, the preoccupation with education as a means of career advancement and as an escape route from communities impoverished, parochial or repressive. The theme occurs in different forms in **Blue Scar**, **How Green Was My Valley**, **David** and was also broached interestingly by Elaine Morgan in a 1960 BBC Wales TV six-part serial **A Matter of Degree** in which the partly autobiographical heroine, Pauline, left her mining community home to go to Oxford.[18] Yet the focus of the play and film **The Corn is Green** is not intended to be Morgan Evans at all, but Moffat. It is a homage to the woman who first recognized Williams's own potential; the Moffat character's obsessive desire for his success can be read as a hunger for self-justification – a need to assert herself in a society repressing women and as a sublimation of her own emotional longings. Williams, who did not write either screenplay, does not find it odd that the two film versions have both been developed into vehicles for their heroines – 'The whole play's about Miss Cooke. It's where the focus is' – and that the 1945 version revolved around Davis's shrewd, busy performance.[19]

It is easy to concur with the American critic Bosley Crowther who castigated Rapper's incessant use of close-ups and cutaways which 'often militated against dramatic tension and pulled the characters too often out of the dimensions of the play'.[20] Crowther conceded that 'whenever Miss Davis is permitted to back away from the camera and really act it must be said that her trenchant characterization is a close match to that of the legitimate "queen" [Barrymore].'[21]

More interesting from the Welsh viewpoint is Morgan's alienation from his fellow miners in the village of Glansarno as he is taught by Moffat to shed his Welsh and to cultivate not merely English but other European languages. But our absorption in the meeting of minds and clashes of wills in the Morgan–Moffat scenes is frustrated at times by contrived comic business, and it is not really surprising, given the fitful presentation of Morgan Evans and his aspirations, that the tensions inherent in his peer group of miners just melt away conveniently when Morgan wins his scholarship to Oxford and is borne away in triumph by the very pitmen who minutes before (in screen terms) have vilified him.

The resolution is pat, if dramatically valid, with Morgan capitulating to one Moffat speech and agreeing to let her salvage his threatened university career by assuming responsibility for the care of his illegitimate son by the daughter of housekeeper Mrs Watty. Miss Moffat is still a compelling protagonist, even in such a self-conscious setting, and Davis, though slightly overbearing in the role and certainly more unbending than Hepburn's teacher in the later version, plays her well-born creation with integrity and intelligence. Unfortunately, neither Rosalind Ivan (as the strident Mrs Watty) nor Joan Lorring – despite her Best Supporting Actress Oscar nomination – as her *enfant terrible*, Bessie, seem to be credible in the film's milieu, though much fault lies in the strained attempts at humour and idiomatic dialogue. Bessie, in particular, is one of the playwright's more tiresome creations.

The fairly faithful Casey Robinson/Frank Cavett script adaptation, at a simple plot level, appears to take a feminist tack in celebrating Moffat's triumph over prejudice and male intractability, but here again the story is riven with contradictions. Moffat is only too ready to see her well-bred but vapid assistant Miss Ronberry (Mildred Dunnock) through conventional male eyes as a frustrated spinster for whom new school duties prove a salvation and no more than an acceptable alternative to a sexual relationship. Ronberry buckles down to her educational chores (and her own slow self-improvement) in lieu of finding a man. In the same way, Moffat has resigned herself to spinsterhood and accepted that a career for a woman is incompatible with a relationship. It is interesting how Williams makes comic play of her no-nonsense approach to the opposite sex most of the time, and of her cultivated coquetry when she flatters the squire – pandering, of course, to his chauvinist prejudices in order to realize her ambitions for Morgan. The resolution can now be seen as deeply reactionary, with Moffat's freedom worth sacrificing to allow the male, Morgan Evans, his 'right' to pursue career advancement.

The film succeeds fitfully as entertainment, partly because Davis's breezy assertiveness contrasts so amusingly with the innate caution of her male teacher, Jones (Rhys Williams), with his amusing capacity to regurgitate received ideas. Davis invests her character with such spirit, and just the right suggestions of warmth, that we do not immediately see that her life – largely lived vicariously through Morgan – is almost as constricted as the squire's or Miss Ronberry's. The script ridicules the squire, a benign if hopeless sexist patriarch who makes no attempt to understand the miners and their families or their native language (that 'absurd lingo'). He is presented as a bluff buffoon and Miss Ronberry, Miss Moffat's assistant, as a vacuous racist who unconsciously purveys the values of her genteel class. In fact, legitimate criticism might be levelled at Williams's own attitudes to Morgan's fellow workers, depicted as devoid of individuality and generally represented as rather dim rustics in order to throw Morgan's gifts into relief. Davis, at least, catches the right blend of forthright plain dealing and regal condescension in Moffat – implicit in the play.

Both screen versions fail to make the inferior position of Welsh in this society as clear as Williams did in his award-winning play.[22] In a speech omitted from both films, Jones rails against the prevailing values: 'It is terrible isn't it? the people on these green fields and flowery hillsides bein' turned out of heaven because they cannot answer Saint Peter when he asks them who they are in English? It is wicked, isn't it, the Welsh children not knowing English, isn't it?'

It is significant that Williams set the film back in 'the latter years of the last century' and in a remote Welsh countryside apparently to locate the work in an era of Welsh education more backward than it was when he fell under Miss Cooke's spell. Yet the screen version, set in the 1890s, ignores the 1870 Education Act which made schooling

206

compulsory, and retains anachronistic references to the owners refusing to release the miners for schooling above ground. And Rapper hides his exterior scenes in a permanent pall of Celtic mist as if to emphasize the work's essential unreality. The Wales presented in Rapper's feature is a glossy confection, and the image of the miners is too often insulting, notably when they gambol artlessly near the village water pump.

The American actor John Dall, surprisingly nominated for an Academy Award, never remotely masters the accent and, though adequate in scenes when Evans is at his most gauche and in awe of his teacher, lacks the confidence to impose himself over Davis in the pivotal scene of the pupil's rebellion. When he should be abrasive and bitter, Dall suggests only petulance, and this militates against the scene making its anticipated impact. Seen by his fellow workers as the schoolmistress's 'little dog', Morgan is hopelessly confused about his identity, unable to assimilate the meaning of his new-found knowledge and its implications for his future – and his past. He has become almost as much an outsider in his own community as Robbie Davies, Williams's prodigal, in **Last Days of Dolwyn**. The disaffection of the miners is made more explicit in a scene when Morgan, taunted while penning Latin conjugations in the public bar, winds up brawling with the pitmen.

Warner's 1940s feature, finally, is an unwieldy marriage of social drama, melodrama and comedy with stock characterizations (notably the squire and the reformed thief turned zealous Salvationist, Mrs Watty). We are won over to some degree by Rhys Williams's selfless performance as Jones, who comes to dote on Moffat after his initial scepticism and whom she does liberate in a very real sense. Rhys Williams softens the Jones of the play but suggests in numerous ways the bemusement of a man who has been forced by his Nonconformist upbringing to sublimate his potential. As the squire, Nigel Bruce needed to shed a little more of his familiar Dr Watson persona to be convincing in his caricatured role.

The Corn is Green is too laden with self-conscious theatrical devices to adapt to the screen comfortably, and in his stage dialogue Emlyn Williams shied away from exploring deeper issues and aspects of characterization. The 'stage-convention' artifice at the heart of the play is as obvious in the 1979 film version from director George Cukor. Patricia Hayes is immeasurably superior to Rosalind Ivans as Mrs Watty, but her character and that of her daughter (Toyah Willcox) are hopelessly overdrawn and unconvincing and Bill Fraser's squire is never able to transcend caricature. This film gained more credibility from the casting of the young Welsh actor, Ian Saynor, a native Welsh-speaker born just a few miles from Williams's own birthplace, who suggested superbly the character's initial gaucherie but also a certain independence of spirit and cast of mind.

Hepburn was a slightly less regimented Miss Moffat and the performance seemed more flexible, less bound by the mechanics of the script than Davis's conception. One might speculate that the rapport between Cukor and his female star, built up in eight previous films since 1932, contributed much to the more relaxed characterization. The collaboration proved too much for the screenwriter James Costigan who finally used the *nom de plume* Ivan Roberts because he was miffed with the extensive re-writing by the director with some help from Hepburn, and the replacement of much of his own script with Williams's original dialogue.[23] The film also gained from Cukor's decision to shoot exteriors on locations in north Wales, but this later version, made for television, obtained very few cinema screenings in the States and never had a British theatrical release.

Edith Evans, Richard
Burton (making his screen
début) in *The Last Days of
Dolwyn*, the only feature
directed by north-Walian
Emlyn Williams.

SECTION 3

Winds of
Change – The
Welsh Impact
on Post-War
British Cinema

Dolwyn – and an English jewel

Williams himself conceived **The Last Days of Dolwyn** (US title **Woman of Dolwyn**) as a showcase for the English actress Edith Evans – 'she must be set in it like a jewel in a case' – after seeing her as the Welsh maid Gwenny in his stage adaptation of *The Late Christopher Bean*.[24] Williams, commissioned by Alexander Korda to write a feature for London Films, persuaded Korda to accept a bilingual text which seemed natural given the location yet, paradoxically, helped seduce an English audience which found itself sucked into 'exotic' settings in which even class barriers prove insubstantial.[25]

The film's starting point, the idea of a village flooded to supply England with water, was not inspired – as may be supposed – by Welsh Nationalist campaigners opposed to a scheme to uproot a local community. It took hold of Williams's imagination from a glimpse of a church tower, almost submerged, in a reservoir in north Wales. This potent image is captured in the camera's first slow track after the opening shot of the lake pressing down on the doomed village. After a brief framing device – a modern scene in which tourists ogle the scenery and a sign refers to events in Dolwyn in 1892 – Williams transports us back to the last century. A slow dissolve, a shiver of harps, and we see again that spire – but no longer submerged. This time we are in an unmistakably charmed milieu and a homogeneous community of people at ease with each other and with nature. The establishing shots of Dolwyn place the film close to pastorale and the studio sets also seem non-corporeal, compatible with a legend to captivate that later generation of tourists. The images summon up the world familiar in the romances of Allen Raine, whose writings Williams admired in his youth. But, as in Raine, there are forceful disruptive elements at work.[26]

When Rob Davies (Emlyn Williams) arrives in the village to set in train the fateful events which destroy Dolwyn, he first passes Huw, a shepherd boy, singing 'a Welsh traditional song, light and gay' apparently to the nearby sheep – again shades of Allen Raine. As Rob walks through Dolwyn he sees the rose tree kept by the local policeman, a baby in a pram and the communal well 'with a cat asleep on the rim'. The slightly ostentatious quaintness of the settings soon ceases to jar as Williams, with the help of Otto Heller's ravishing camerawork, builds a persuasive picture of the community. The suggestive music, attuned to the character's feelings and the tenor of events, hints at the menace to come – foreshadowed cleverly as Rob knocks over a child's rocking horse and climbs into the graveyard, peers into the chapel and places one foot negligently on a child's grave with a Welsh inscription. He implicitly condones the observation of a local boy that the 'Welsh Sunday' is dead. Rob will, before the film is much older, trample over the Welsh-speaking inhabitants' lives to gain spiteful redress for the way the villagers pilloried him as a twelve-year-old when caught stealing the chapel collection and drove him away. It is significant (but a heavy touch) that the Welsh preacher in the first sequence is reading, in Welsh and English, the text of John the Baptist's betrayal and Salome's revenge. Rob – 'I'm cosmopolitan' – has not merely disavowed his fellow countrymen after an absence of twenty years from Wales; he also plans to wipe out the village which has shamed him. He represents – as an agent – his employer, coal baron Lord Lancashire (Allan Aynesworth), later to emerge as a genial, protective patrician. But we are told, initially, only that the peer, as president of the Cambrian Water Company, wants to buy up the village and flood it from the dam to take water to towns in his country. Lord Lancashire offers compensation only to leaseholders, accommodation on his new estate in a Liverpool suburb, Hagton, and employment in his cotton mill, which serves it. The peer is also, naturally, chairman of Hagton Building Society.

Williams whets our appetite for a political polemic which presents a conflict between proud, obdurate villagers who do not want to move and the agent for the English landed gentry who have an obvious class ally in Lady Dolwyn. But the author-writer, described in the film's own publicity material as an 'intense nationalist', is not interested in pursuing this tack wholeheartedly or, seemingly, in the political ramifications of the water scheme.

Lady Dolwyn, it appears, has been forced by penury into selling her hall and countenancing the flooding proposals. In a crucial confrontation with the old church cleaning lady, Merri (Edith Evans), she is clearly discomforted by the sale's implications. Merri, with her natural dignity reverses the class roles and dominates the scene. (Merri's moral superiority is implied by judicious use of camera angles). As the film develops, Lady Dolwyn is seen to have an affinity with Merri, a shared loyalty to the village which both women recognize. Merri's adopted son Gareth (played by the young Richard Burton), who significantly finds difficulty expressing himself in English, also finds that Lady Dolwyn's ward Margaret is not as aloof or unattainable as she may appear to be. Williams has set up expectations of class inflexibility in order to confound them. But the film slides away into conventional melodrama when it is revealed that Lord Lancashire had no knowledge that the homes he planned to buy were any more than derelict outhouses – an impression fostered by Rob Davies. The peer, on a visit to the village to oust the troublesome Merri, who has deeds in perpetuity to her property, is won over in a humorous scene which invites the complicity of the audience. We, unlike the villagers standing outside Merri's cottage, know that the sounds of Lord Lancashire's discomfort and pain from within stem not from the fight they fear, but from his lordship's response to Merri's application of her homespun physical remedy for his rheumatism. Lord Lancashire, after this meeting, rounds on Davies and confirms that the village will not be drowned and the water will be diverted via another landmark, the Horseshoe, even if this alternative is more expensive. From this moment the Emlyn Williams character is perceived by the villagers as the potential enemy – and not the English; so Williams defuses the politics. It seems mealy-mouthed (and perverse) of Williams not to see the question of the water's destination in national terms. The only disparaging comments heard about the community re-location scheme are aimed at Liverpool's lack of flowers and greenery; the only questioning comes from Merri: 'Why can't the Lancashire English make do with what's on their own doorstep?'

Williams sustains interest with the glimpses he affords of local foibles, the banter of the inhabitants (which has a sublime logic all its own) and the volatility of their reactions. He builds up an affectionate portrait of the village with its part-time preachers, jacks of all trades, comforting chapel ethos and taproom camaraderie. The bond uniting the village men is hinted at when publican Caradoc (Roddy Hughes) and the local bobby Septimus conspire in some harmless poaching. The locals are initially unable to comprehend the idea of moving to Liverpool and the promised incentives of swift comparative wealth. When they realize the economic incentives, conscience wars with cupidity.

Merri has a pivotal role in all her scenes, dictating their moods by her actions or stasis (as when her adopted son relays news of the impending exodus). In a well choreo-graphed scene, Williams points up Merri's dislocation when she feels she must say goodbye to Dolwyn. She leaves her well-scrubbed, spartan cottage at dawn and takes leave one by one of the surroundings and landmarks, she cherishes. She pulls the well rope, as if remembering childhood days, caresses the bridge wall, and an empty creaking children's swing. (These moments obviously recall Garbo's homage to her surroundings after her romantic interlude with John Gilbert in **Queen Christina** (1933), but the film is scarcely the worse for that.) There is an almost pantheistic strain to the scene in which Merri asks Gareth to read the Bible to her for comfort. These passages of the old lady preparing and the villagers coming to terms with their new situation are the most eloquent and heartfelt in the film, but the spell is gradually broken as the script loses its way in the last half hour. The ending was drastically re-written in November 1948, some months after the initial shooting script.[28] In the original, Rob Davies is caught red-handed trying to flood Dolwyn after bribing the dam's night-watchman Ephraim to gain access. He is chased by Septimus and other villagers and finally knocked into the well by the officer, and Merri is left to hide on behalf of the village the evidence of the murder by flooding Dolwyn itself. The original ending would have given significance to the first pan to the well and the cat poised on its edge, a harbinger of ill fortune; and irony to the moment when Merri pauses by the well when saying her farewells. But in the final version Rob, after failing to move the dam controls, decides to set the village homes ablaze but encounters Gareth who has returned to find his mother. She has not joined the exodus, apparently deciding to die in Dolwyn after a change of heart. The two men fight, Rob is doused in a spilt can of paraffin and burned to death and Merri, to protect her son from a murder charge, pulls the body into the inn and locks it before flooding the village. This seems as an ending less plausible and less psychologically astute than the first version. Merri's love for the village is so acute that her decision to flood it, rather than find an alternative way to save her son, negates much of the subtlety with which Williams has built up the character. The finale, in any case, is much less interesting than much that has gone before.

Richard Burton, with the
villagers, near the climax
of *Last Days of Dolwyn*.

Richard Burton, with the
villagers, near the climax
of *Last Days of Dolwyn*.

Last Days of Dolwyn ultimately falls into that category of films described rather too
disparagingly by Scottish critics as 'Kailyard, a world concerned only with its own
cabbage patch' in the context of their own national cinema.[29] But, though it contrasts
the close-knit eccentric, rustic community with the urbanity of the outsider, the film
is never condescending to the locals, apart from in a few snatches of dialogue.
Williams manages to suspend disbelief until the last reel. It is only when he sacrifices
characterization and psychological truth to plot mechanics that the film goes awry.
But it remains one of the most distinctive post-war contributions to the cinema of
Wales and it is regrettable that Williams was not inveigled into directing again –
though he always acknowledged the help he received in making the film from Russell
Lloyd, a noted Welsh film editor (born Swansea 1916).

On the strength of his work on second-unit direction in Venice on Julien Duvivier's
1947 version of **Anna Karenina** (with Vivien Leigh) Lloyd was singled out by
Alexander Korda to advise Williams on technical matters and took over much of the
direction of **Last Days of Dolwyn**, allowing the actor to concentrate on the
performances.[30] After **Dolwyn**, Lloyd was second-unit director on **Treasure Island**
(1951) before returning permanently to the cutting room. He helped shape a clutch
of John Huston films including **Moby Dick** (1956), shot partly at Fishguard
Harbour, and edited **Bitter Harvest** (1963), Pete Graham Scott's cautionary film
about a Welsh girl (Janet Munro) lured into a life of depravity in London.

Williams himself remained a strong presence, mainly in cameo roles in British and
American films up to the early seventies, though his appearances were limited by stage
commitments, particularly his one-man shows as Dickens and Dylan Thomas. He
also found time for much writing, including his two volumes of autobiography, issued
in 1961 and 1973. He played Mr Dick in Delbert Mann's **David Copperfield** (1969),
made with TV screenings in mind, but it was pilloried by critics as mind-numbingly
dull, despite a stellar cast including Ralph Richardson as Micawber, Ron Moody,

Edith Evans and Megs Jenkins. Williams also played Emile Zola in José Ferrer's **Dreyfus** (1958), with Ferrer as Dreyfus defended by Zola against treason charges in the notorious *cause célèbre* – but this Cinemascope production scripted by Gore Vidal met with a lukewarm response.

After many years off the screen, Williams achieved a triumphant swansong in the year before his death with a superb performance, employing all his professional craft and guile, as Edward, an incorrigibly mischievous resident of an old folks' home, in Richard Eyre's 1986 BBC TV drama **Past Caring**, written by Tom Clarke and screened at the London Film Festival. Williams teamed up with Denholm Elliott's gleeful maverick to cause happy mayhem. In retrospect, it seems a great pity that (after **Dolwyn**) neither Williams – nor Russell Lloyd – produced in Wales another cinema film of distinction.

SECTION 3

Winds of
Change – The
Welsh Impact
on Post-War
British Cinema

THE WELSH AT EALING

I got out at Ealing at 5 a.m. I met Leslie Norman [the producer] and Charles Frend [the director]. Frend asked me where I came from. Of course I come from Rhosllanerchrugog, near Wrexham, so I spelt it for them, and I thought . . . I've got to walk like a collier and even extend my Welsh accent which was pretty thick then. I did the collier walk right out of the gates.

(Meredith Edwards describing his first visit to Ealing after Hugh Griffith recommended him for a part in **A Run For Your Money**, interview with the author, 1985)

If Ealing, in the interests of the war effort, were keen to stress class unity – as in **The Proud Valley** – they were also anxious to bury national differences within the UK. The studio sought to project images of a homogeneous Britain and Michael Balcon's own brand of cosy egalitarianism or paternalism. In the heyday of Ealing Studios a token Welshman, as George Perry and Charles Barr have noted, was almost obligatory in their films, alongside an Englishman, Scotsman and Irishman.[1] In film after film his ordinary folk (who, as often as not, were pretty extraordinary) closed ranks against the threats of interlopers or outsiders whether they be officious American businessmen (**The Maggie**, 1954), the Nazis (**Went the Day Well?**, 1942) or bureaucrats. Communities sank petty differences to ward off outside interference (**Passport to Pimlico**, **Whisky Galore**, both 1949).

SECTION 3

Winds of
Change – The
Welsh Impact
on Post-War
British Cinema

Welshmen were usually stereotyped. They were good-hearted but gullible miners in **A Run For Your Money** (1949), parochial wiseacres given to dispensing local saws (such as Meredith Edwards in **The Long Arm** (1956), or, often, the epitome of the little man so beloved of Ealing and usually exemplified by Mervyn Johns (most notably as the Welsh POW in **The Captive Heart**, 1946).

The Welsh characters were often musical of course – remember Edwards's impromptu singer and Hugh Griffith's itinerant harpist in **A Run For Your Money**? – and sometimes they assumed the role of choirmaster in the company (Johns, again, extemporizing in **The Captive Heart**, and Edwards with his police songsters in **The Blue Lamp**, 1950). They were also homebodies and nature-loving and generally law-abiding. The only villainous 'Welsh' character in Ealing's canon is played by Johns in **The Next of Kin** (1942) and he is a rank imposter, a Nazi spy. Johns of course played the ubiquitous murderer taunting incompetents Will Hay and Claude Hulbert in Basil Dearden's Ealing comedy **My Learned Friend** (1943); his fireman in the studio's **The Bells Go Down**, made the same year, had a dubious light-fingered past.[2] But in both these films he played Cockneys – curious because Johns, on screen, never lost the intonations and speech rhythms of his native west Wales. If we exempt Johns's agent of dubious lineage, no Welsh character in Ealing's output is even devious or particularly aggressive (give or take the odd moment of angry bluster from Meredith Edwards). It is as difficult to conceive of a broody, volatile actor like Stanley Baker in Ealing films as it is to visualize Richard Burton in one of the **Run For Your Money** leads – though Clifford Evans suggested him. (Director Charles Frend thought Burton was 'pockmarked, bandy-legged and had no sex appeal'.)[3]

Ealing had no truck with angst. They specialized in benign caricatures and presented a Britain more or less at ease with itself. The Welsh were treated no more condescendingly by the studio than anyone else but they *were* patronized: even when they displayed native nous and their integrity enabled them to triumph over alien skulduggery we were left in no doubt that it was a victory for innocence and a fundamental lack of sophistication. It is interesting that there was no moral toughness, deviousness or shading in the miners' characters in **A Run For Your Money** comparable to the defiant Scots in **Whisky Galore**. However they were presented on screen, the Welsh played a primary role in Ealing's fortunes during the Balcon years – as actors, writers and musicians – and a more detailed study of their contribution should show precisely how they were characterized and stereotyped.

A Run For Your Money

Features based on Wales or the Welsh by British studios in the 1940s and 1950s tended to be simple genre films, escapist suspense fare or, more interestingly, movies depending for their individuality and richness on the idiosyncrasies or foibles of humorous 'types' or archetypes. Examples include the Associated British feature **Valley of Song** (1953), perhaps the most endearing of all Welsh comedies, and **A Run For Your Money** – a forerunner of films like **Rattle of a Simple Man** (1964) and, more relevantly to Wales, of BBC's **Grand Slam** (dir. John Hefin, 1978).

A Run For Your Money (working title **The Lark**), directed by Charles Frend from an original story by Welsh actor Clifford Evans, was unfortunately released at the fag end of a year which proved the high-water mark of Ealing humour; critics tend to make unflattering comparisons between Frend's feature and the other key 1949 films – **Passport to Pimlico**, **Whisky Galore** and Robert Hamer's incomparable **Kind Hearts and Coronets**. Considered on its merits, **A Run For Your Money**, though markedly less ambitious than those other works, is a lively study of two gauche Welsh miners, up in London for an England–Wales rugby clash at Twickenham, falling prey to distractions sexual and alcoholic – just as Harry H. Corbett's slightly simple Northerner was seduced by Diane Cilento's warm-hearted hooker in Muriel Box's **Rattle of a Simple Man** (1964), and Hugh Griffith and Windsor Davies and co. were diverted by Parisian nightlife in **Grand Slam**.

Twm (Meredith Edwards) is led astray by Huw, Hugh Griffith's wonderful drunken sot of a harp player, an exiled Welshman now reduced to busking. Dai (Donald Houston) is waylaid by Moira Lister's confidence trickster – one of those women who, in the miners' parlance, 'paints her toenails' (the description might be compared with the miners' jokey reference in **Valley of Song** to 'painted Jezebels in London'). Frend's film, with location shooting at the Parc and Dare Colliery, Treorchy, and at Cwmparc, contrasts the honesty and candour of the miners with the hypocrisy and dissembling they encounter in London. It is interesting to speculate how much more astringent the movie might have been if Dylan Thomas, involved in early script conferences, had been given free rein to adapt material. Thomas worked on an outline script with Clifford Evans but producer Leslie Norman did not like some of their ideas.[4] Evans was inspired by a Rhys Davies short story, 'King Canute', in which miners visit London for a soccer match, hit the bottle and miss the game: 'One of them is found in a lavatory at Paddington Station sitting on a shoeshine box tight as a lord in water up to his ankles. Ever afterwards he's called King Canute and can never lose the tag even when he moves house.'[5]

Just as the locals in **Passport to Pimlico** and **Whisky Galore** were at odds with bureaucracy and austere establishment figures, Twm and Dai find themselves perpetual outsiders in London. Dai is beguiled by Jo (Lister), the antithesis of Bronwen, the girl he left behind in Wales, and by Jo's male stooge Barney, a petty thief and 'fence'. The miners' honesty and innate good manners lead to mutual incomprehension on their London visit – and the film is cast in Ealing's amiably iconoclastic mould as the pretentious and the entrepreneurial classes become the butt of humour. Amusing parallels are drawn between Davies, the windbag paternalist pit manager who tells the two miners they have won a free trip to London in a newspaper competition, and the paper's editor. The script satirizes gleefully both men's tendency to bluster and launch into flowery speeches and gestures while forgetting more salient matters. Davies: 'Boys, you do not know it, but today we are

SECTION 3

Winds of

Change – The

Welsh Impact

on Post-War

British Cinema

famous. Famous from Lands End to John O'Groats. Up there in London, the hub of
the universe. What are the newsboys shouting this January evening?
Hafoduwchbenceubwllymarchogcoch.' It is Davies who entrusts Dai with his hat as a
'sacred symbol', a reminder of his girl, and the fate of the titfer becomes almost a sub-
plot and a marker of his fidelity. The *Weekly Echo*'s editor is as histrionic as the mine
boss. He is seen in true colours when Twm and Huw, plus harp, blunder into his
offices while he is rehearsing platitudes for a speech on the good relationship between
press and public. Told of their presence, he immediately orders bouncers to throw
them out.

Another slightly affected character, Whimple, the gardening correspondent (Alec
Guinness as a sort of cutprice William Boot),[6] suffers the worst come-uppance. He is
attached, somewhat incongruously, to the miners as a guide and chaperone, winding
up in gaol after a series of mishaps, while Jo goes free to continue acting as bait for
her henchman's malpractices.

There is more than a tinge of condescension in the script, finally credited to Frend,

Richard Hughes and Leslie Norman (with Diana Morgan cited for 'additional dialogue'). This is noticeable in the simple gratitude of Twm and Dai on learning of their win and the supposed rapport between management and men – even if some tilts at the parochiality of both the Welsh and the English amuse. From the first scene, the film tends to treat the Welshmen as more simple than guileless, and certain moments when they reveal their vulnerability to the London wide boys are undoubtedly irritating. The patronizing tone is implicit in the opening voice-over: 'This is the story of how Welsh Wales came to town.'

Most people remember best the scene when the miners arrive at Paddington, and Whimple has only the scantiest notion of how to find them. 'They'll be wearing leeks,' he tells his photographer. Whimple then compounds the idiocy by having a loudspeaker announcement made: 'Will Mr Thomas Jones and Mr David Jones report to the station manager's office,' and the script builds on the obvious gag in a series of reaction cutaways as a gaggle of Joneses respond to the call. Whimple later inevitably loses Dai in the Tower of London while swapping anecdotes with a green-fingered Beefeater (Edward Rigby).

At the finale Twm and Dai return to their homebound train wiser men, and the camera pans along the carriages to discover Huw and his beloved harp also returning to the bosom of his own community after years as itinerant and wastrel in London. The implication is that he can be liberated again back in a nation which can properly appreciate not merely his talent – which once won him an Eisteddfod prize – but also his peccadilloes and, above all, his taste for life. The honesty of the Welshmen, particularly Dai, even disarms Lister's predator, inspiring a (probably short-lived) moral regeneration (as Harry H. Corbett reforms Diane Cilento's hooker in **Rattle of a Simple Man**).[7] **A Run For Your Money**, in equating London with falseness and superficiality, a repression of natural feelings and 'pernicious anaemia of the soul', echoes Craigie's **Blue Scar** released months before. In a typical scene Twm is scandalized by a 'No Music' sign in a pub: 'Music by licence only – what a country.' He also castigates a penny-pinching pawnshop owner for his lack of a musical ear in preferring radio to live music and allowing Griffith's harp – in hock – to gather dust there.

Frend and his editor Michael Truman move the comedy along with broad, deft strokes. When Huw and Twm win the singing contest, as the other key characters all converge on the venue for the dramatic finale, the rhythm of the cross-cutting creates both tension and humour. The victory earned by Twm's rendering of 'All Through the Night' in Welsh naturally leads to uproarious anti-climax. The leads are fine foils for each other. Edwards's Twm – based loosely on the actor's father, a former miner at the Hafod and Bersham collieries in north Wales – is querulous and awkward but alert; Houston's Dai is more trusting but a little too gauche.

Some English-based critics have sharpened their invective on the film, seeing it as a failed attempt by Ealing to 'wring some laughs from the Welsh way of life'; Terence Pettigrew claimed it sent up the Welsh as timid, mindless yokels by presenting 'two likeable Welsh dimwits on a big city jamboree'.[8] One perhaps might have wished that the Welsh trio had been as sharp and shrewd as their Celtic counterparts in the other Ealing films of that year; certainly the performance of the raw-boned, north-Walian Edwards, blustering as Twm flounders out of his depth, occasionally inclines towards parody.[9] And though containing comment on social mores (the anti-English banter of the miners, for instance) the film settles too easily at times for clichés and asinine comedy. Yet despite its shortcomings, **A Run For Your Money** remains one of the most convivial and memorable of 'Welsh comedies' and is still frequently revived on television.

Two of the film's four writers were Welsh: Richard Hughes (1900–1976), author of the best-selling *High Wind in Jamaica*, and the more influential Diana Morgan, who gained credits on six of the studios' films between 1941 and 1950 and provided ideas and lines for quite a few more. Morgan certainly did not think the film condescending – and she wrote much of the dialogue in the scenes involving the miners, especially the arrival in London. She thought she deserved a much bigger credit than for 'additional dialogue'.[10] 'I was put on the film when they were in a mess,' claimed Morgan. 'I re-wrote the script more or less. The dialogue needed putting into shape. "Dickon" Hughes was a lovely man but he wasn't a scriptwriter – he dealt in words not pictures, he just did not see it.' Morgan also wrote much of Moira Lister's dialogue in the London sequences, and the Welsh writer certainly imparted some broad humour. Yet there is little room amidst the chases and plotting for the class and culture clashes which are such an engaging feature of **Whisky Galore** and particularly **The Maggie**, where supposedly 'simple' Celtic seafarers strip Paul Douglas's slightly pompous American authority-figure of dignity.

SECTION 3

Winds of
Change – The
Welsh Impact
on Post-War
British Cinema

Edwards and Houston

Meredith Edwards's appearance in Frend's film led directly to an offer to play the Welsh PC and zealous conductor whipping George Dixon (Jack Warner) and the station's police choir into shape in Basil Dearden's **The Blue Lamp**, the top British box-office film of its year.[11] Edwards (b. 1917), whose sunny disposition in the film belied his pugnacious appearance, was used as the butt of canteen humour. And his musical obsession, which the audience could infer was typical of the Welsh, was the source of predictable gags. Crimes and call-outs were seen by Edwards's PC Hughes as unnecessary interference with choir practice. Equally predictably, perhaps, Hughes – the most engaging of the minor characters – was slugged at the finale by Dirk Bogarde's sweaty-palmed young hood who then pumped the fatal bullet into Dixon, who then extended his career into a BBC TV series spanning twenty years.

In **The Long Arm** (dir. Charles Frend), the last film actually made at the Ealing Studios and shot partly in Snowdonia, Edwards enjoyed a humorous cameo as an insatiably curious tittle-tattling Welsh garage owner and taxi driver who almost unwittingly helps out Jack Hawkins's world-weary detective. Again the Welshman was a target of humour – for his insularity (he cannot for the life of him understand why anyone should want to go to Chester).[12]

For **Dunkirk**, Leslie Norman's 1958 feature, Edwards insisted on delivering the last words of his character, lying shot in an orchard, in Welsh. 'Who the hell's going to understand?' Norman asked when Edwards sought permission. 'I have a feeling that when someone is dying they go back to childhood – and if I went back to my childhood it would be the Welsh-speaking one,' said Edwards later.[13] So Edwards expired in Welsh after John Mills, stoic as ever *in extremis*, told him the men would have to leave him and push on.

The Welsh actor appeared primarily in small roles in Ealing films, though he was prominent, once more, in one of the studio's lesser comedies, **The Magnet** (dir. Charles Frend, 1949), a children's adventure which failed to repeat the success of the studio's **Hue and Cry** (dir. Charles Crichton, 1947). Edwards's only lead in a British feature, apart from **A Run For Your Money**, was in the 1952 **Girdle of Gold** (a non-Ealing film), despite Balcon's hint that he was destined for bigger things: 'The secret of his appeal is that he is an ordinary sort of fellow. It's because he's so ordinary that he's out of the ordinary. He might be the fellow you meet everywhere, his tie out of place, his clothes never too well pressed.' [14] The gawky, balding actor's penchant for playing rather stagey Welshmen probably militated against his landing more serious parts for Balcon (though Harry Watt used him as support for beefcake leading man Anthony Steel in the studios' surprisingly commercial 1951 African wildlife feature **Where No Vultures Fly**). But within comedies, his natural forte, Edwards was capable of rich variations (witness his post-Ealing, starchy bookworm cleric in the Launder–Gilliat **Only Two Can Play**, 1962).[15]

Rhondda-born Donald Houston (1923–91) had already made a huge impact on screen before the Frend film – opposite Jean Simmons as the young lover marooned on an uncharted island in Frank Launder's **The Blue Lagoon** (1949) based on Henry de Vere Stacpoole's 1908 novel and shot in Fiji. It proved to be Launder and Gilliat's biggest box-office hit. The actor was never to repeat that success, even though he continued to play worthwhile cinema roles through much of the sixties. In his other Ealing appearance he was unsympathetically cast, and more than a little dull, as the jealous wet-blanket and sexist husband Phil in **Dance Hall** (dir. Charles Crichton, 1950) alienating the affections of wife Eve (Natasha Parry) and almost driving her into the arms of Bonar Colleano's predatory serviceman. Houston wound up slugging it out, successfully, with Colleano's devious home-breaker in a muddy car park. The Welshman's screen charm was allowed to flicker in Jack Clayton's influential **Room at the Top** (1958) where his penchant for playing clean-living, rather self-righteous characters made him a useful foil to Laurence Harvey's odious social climber Joe Lambton in a powerful version of the John Braine novel.[16] Houston was the unappreciated office friend, Charlie Soames, doling out killjoy homilies in one of the New Wave films which brought a bracing dash of reality to the airless British cinema.

Ealing, in common with other studios, failed to make use of Houston's prime asset in many stage productions – his fine speaking voice, with its superb cadences. It is not surprising, perhaps, that the actor achieved his most enduring success re-creating his stage role with the 1957 BBC live TV version of **Under Milk Wood** in that first decade when Welsh actors made their presence felt on the small screen.

Mervyn Johns – an Ealing stalwart

One Welsh actor in particular played a significant role in Ealing's fortunes. It is small wonder that Mervyn Johns has been described by a noted studio writer, T. E. B. Clarke, as 'the cornerstone of the Ealing repertory company'.[17] Johns (b. 1899 in Pembroke, d. 1992) imparted to his roles an edginess and bemusement, and his clipped delivery somehow suggested inner tension. The abiding image of the actor is as the perennial timid little man – a British equivalent of Hollywood's Donald Meek or Elisha Cook jun. Yet his dignified bearing, self-effacing style and ability to communicate to an audience a sense of unease, singled him out as Ealing's favourite choice as narrator and anchorman for their two related exercises in fantasy, **Halfway House** (1944) and **Dead of Night** (1945). Johns was also highly effective when cast against type – witness his chillingly phlegmatic Nazi spy in Thorold Dickinson's cautionary **Next of Kin** (1942). The protagonist was nasty enough to lay low Nova

Pillbeam's rebellious Dutch refugee with a right cross, then leave her to die in a gas-filled flat after first incriminating her as a murderess.

In **Pink String and Sealing Wax**, Robert Hamer's first feature (1945), Johns was decidedly unsympathetic as a heavy Victorian father but certainly not helped by a script which gave him no chance to soften the role or render it less of a caricature. His Edward Sutton is a man hardbitten enough to brave his children's wrath about keeping guinea pigs for his own private experiments and to turn his daughter Victoria out of the house rather than allow her to pursue a musical scholarship: 'Singing as a female social accomplishment is one thing. Professional singing is another. Singers are invariably persons of dissolute life and habit.' Victoria later successfully defies her father, and is encouraged by the Welsh-based opera singer Adelina Patti (Margaret Ritchie), who is impressed by an impromptu per-formance for her benefit.[18] In dealing with his children, Sutton frequently

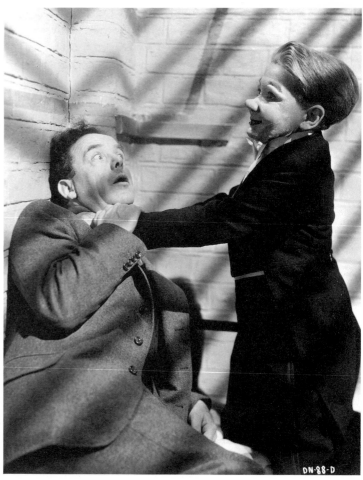

invokes God as his right-hand man: 'Love and fear is [*sic*] inseparable but we're taught to fear him.'

Mervyn Johns and the malevolent puppet in *Dead of Night.*

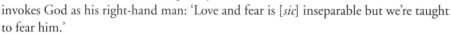

Yet at the finale it is this arid little man's trust in his son (Gordon Jackson) and faith in the values he has inculcated which enable him to divine and nail the lies of Googie Withers as the adulterous wife who poisons her husband and tries to pin the blame on Jackson. The contemporary audience must have been thoroughly bemused by Johns's metamorphosis into hero at the climax. It is a pity that the writing lacks the irony and variety to make the Sutton household more convincing; some of the playing is decidedly erratic (notably by a young Sally Ann Howes). It is difficult to take the film or its sour-apple patriarch too seriously from the moment he complains about giving his maid one half-day off a month: 'I do not pay her £12 a year to have you do the washing up,' he tells his wife. But the direction, the photography and ingenious use of studio sets convey a pervasive sense of cramped lives, repression and simmering tensions, and even the more improbable characterizations and strident melodramatic touches could not entirely destroy that.

Johns, a graduate from Tom Walls's Aldwych stage farces, made a handful of cameo appearances in thirties films, including **Pot Luck** (1936), directed by Walls for Balcon at Gainsborough, and Hitchcock's **Jamaica Inn** (1939).[19] But he moved swiftly out of bit parts (such as the ship's mate in Pen Tennyson's 1940 feature **Convoy** at Ealing), and almost invariably played leads or prominent supports for the studio in a six-year spell, from 1940 to 1946, embracing twelve films. He was an actor of fairly limited range, which seemed accentuated by his inordinate immobility on screen in certain roles. It is difficult to think of a major actor of his period whose screen movements were so economical (even stiff on occasion), yet it was his stillness and inscrutability which lent his Nazi in **Next of Kin** and his pedantic public analyst in **Pink String and Sealing Wax** such a sinister aspect.

No Welsh screen actor could convey as well as Johns the sense of a man harassed and cowed by pressure. His characters usually suggested that their roots lay in corseted parochial communities. An exception was his insidious killer Grimshaw in **My Learned Friend** (1943), an intriguing dry run for one of Ealing's classic comedies **Kind Hearts and Coronets**. The films significantly shared the same co-writer, John Dighton. **My Learned Friend** is notable for a finale featuring Johns struggling on the face of Big Ben trying to blow up the House of Lords. The ending, with all three lead characters dangling from the minute hand at one stage, owed much to Harold Lloyd and **Safety Last** (1923) and was cribbed shamelessly for Don Sharp's 1978 British re-make of **The 39 Steps** with Robert Powell. Will Hay played William Fitch, a dubious lawyer. It is soon established that he helped send down Grimshaw, a manic little forger, for ten years. The criminal, released for good conduct, sets about systematically wiping out those responsible for his incarceration. Johns pretends his murder threat is a joke but he cannot resist promising to 'save until last, the fellow who made such a beautiful fiasco of my defence'. Grimshaw soon litters the screen with corpses and pops up disconcertingly to dispense cryptic clues. This 'pop-eyed soft-boiled egg', as one gangster calls him, is mild to the point of invisibility at times – but looks splendidly creepy. He even turns up with walrus moustache at a bar to prompt the fracas and diversion which enables him to eliminate a hood, 'Safety' Wilson, and he later appears in beret and overalls as Claude Hulbert's (unsolicited) house decorator. The Jekyll-and-Hyde transitions, capped by his final incarnation as giggling psychopath on Big Ben, are frequently unconvincing and Johns, never happy in wildly extrovert roles, sometimes fails to hit the right note in scenes requiring comic menace. Welsh actress Maudie Edwards, incidentally, appears in one frenetic setpiece as an over-ripe stage Aladdin reduced to tears by the unscheduled stage interventions of Hay and Hulbert.

Much more compelling was **The Captive Heart** (1946), with Johns as a loving family man, Private Dai Evans, in an often bleak study of life in a prisoner-of-war camp. In an early scene we see him stumbling along roads, with other captives, recalling (in flashback) the words of his wife Dilys (Rachel Thomas) when he asked her why she married him: 'You – with that wicked tenor voice', she joked. And again Johns, as 'the Welshman' is used as the conductor of the prisoners' choir, leading impromptu male singsongs, notably of defiant choruses of 'Roll Out the Barrel'. The film touches on notions of decency and loyalty but has a pervasive sense of displacement and longing, with Redgrave's hero – a Czech masquerading as a British officer – and the Johns character, Dai Evans, both pining for a return to domestic happiness. Dai has a passion for gardening – just as Meredith Edwards in **The Blue Lamp** was only too keen to discuss compost on a visit to George Dixon's home – and he is also a born conciliator, and the only one quick to defend the Red Cross when parcels fail to arrive on time. The constant references to his wife are like a thread of domestic sanity running through the film – severed abruptly when we learn that Dilys has died in childbirth. The birth sequence was filmed but did not survive the cutting room. It was deemed out of true with post-war priorities on the film's release when the government was anxious to encourage a baby boom.[20]

Mervyn and Glynis Johns
– ethereal figures in a landscape – in *Halfway House*.

SECTION 3

Winds of
Change – The
Welsh Impact
on Post-War
British Cinema

The Captive Heart offered Johns little more than a sensitive support part, but his best roles (in **Next of Kin**, **Halfway House** and **Dead of Night** alone, would be enough to confirm him as the outstanding Welsh contributor to Ealing in the Balcon era (1939–58). In the portmanteau chiller **Dead of Night**, Johns plays Walter Craig, an architect with the gift of clairvoyancy and troubled by premonitions of death, who finds himself in a country house with strangers who have already peopled his dreams.[21] Craig, a deferential unprepossessing man, somehow conveying an acute sense of foreboding, soon commands centre stage as he fascinates fellow guests with his foreknowledge of events. Each guest tells a story of other-worldly experiences; the episode featuring Michael Redgrave as a ventriloquist taken over by his dummy is justly celebrated, and obviously inspired the Anthony Hopkins role in Richard Attenborough's 1978 film **Magic**. After these anecdotes, handled with deft flashbacks, Craig wakes to receive a call from a client. Soon he is driving on a stretch of road – and looking across once more at the familiar house of his imaginings . . . This riveting film, with its internal dream logic, remains perhaps the finest of all British screen fantasies.

Next of Kin, made for the Directorate of Army Kinematography, mushroomed into a feature from a planned 20-minute training film on the theme 'Careless Talk Costs Lives.' It was made after the government belatedly accepted Balcon's offer to produce films supporting the British war effort.[22] Johns played Davis, a German agent and erstwhile businessman, who insinuates himself into the confidence of unsuspecting groups of British civilians and officers. A poster on screen, proclaiming 'Keep It Under Your Hat', encapsulates the film's message. We first see Davis in England flicking through a salacious 'girlie' magazine, the epitome, seemingly, of the slightly seedy nonentity or family man with a taste for the prurient. But the newsagents' business is a front for the spy's contact (played with nicely judged menace by Stephen Murray). Davis's unremarkable appearance and polite deference lulls the British into complacency. He has taken the identity (cribbed from the 'St Barnabas parish magazine, Cardiff') of a nondescript businessman. Later he is described by one of his hosts as 'a very nice little gentleman, bombed out of Cardiff'. Dickinson and his writers skilfully establish the chain of unsuspecting betrayals which render British planning useless and cost many lives in a raid on a German naval base. As the critic C. A. Lejeune wrote, 'This pleasant, pathetic little person, medium size, medium colouring, medium everything, goes right through the film collecting his scraps of information.'[23]

Dickinson was determined not to flaunt star names which would enable the audience to make cosy connections. But to gain maximum impact at the cunningly constructed finale he used Basil Radford and Naunton Wayne (the quintessentially British blimps Charters and Caldicott from **The Lady Vanishes**, 1939, and **Millions Like Us**, 1943), who are seen in a railway compartment blithely swapping military information. A hand reaches out to proffer a light and Davis is then revealed, sitting back contentedly after squirrelling away yet more secrets.

Johns appeared for the first time on screen with his South African-born daughter Glynis (b. 1923) in **Halfway House**, set in a Wales of the imagination.[24] In the war's final years and the later grim days of British rationing and austerity, Ealing provided a nourishing diet of whimsical and wish-fulfilment comedies and fantasies which had the saving grace of irreverence and iconoclasm. The prevailing sense of unreality was a short step from the world created in Basil Dearden's film. Produced by Cavalcanti, it exploited a 1940s vogue in the arts for juggling time and space and focused on travellers who arrived in wartime at a hotel in rural Wales run by the strangely ethereal Rhys (Mervyn Johns) and daughter Gwyneth (Glynis). Little feeling of any real Wales emerges in the film – hardly surprising as it was shot mainly in the studio, contains some very obvious process work and artificial backdrops, and the premises used as the Halfway House itself were on the Devon–Somerset border. Dearden and his writers, Diana Morgan, Angus McPhail and T. E. B. Clarke, sought to inject local atmosphere mainly through a train journey into Wales in which passengers sing 'Sospan Fach' and reminisce about aunts in Mumbles and dentists in Llandrindod. Again the specific Welsh elements emerge through comedy. National characteristics are sent up and parochiality satirized as in films as disparate as **The Blue Lamp** and **The Long Arm**.

Wilkie Cooper's camerawork makes great play of patterns of light to heighten the drama and create the feeling of a twilight zone; we become aware that the hotel itself is in a sense a figment, a staging post outside time, offering the possibility of renewal to characters who, after a sojourn there, will resume their lives in the ordinary world. Rhys tells his guests that 'time stands still here in the valley' but the guests' suspicions that he might mean it literally are only alerted after a chain of events following the embezzler Fortescue's discovery that the hotel is not on any map. David Davies (Esmond Knight), a celebrated conductor, tells them he thought the hotel burned down twelve months before. Mrs Meadows, a serviceman's wife, has been driven to spiritualism after her son's death and she is particularly susceptible to believing in the occult; when she notices that Rhys leaves no reflection in the mirror, we suspect her hyperactive imagination. Later Fortescue discovers that Gwyneth also casts no reflection (the scene recalls, powerfully, the chilling mirror episode in Ealing's **Dead of Night**). The true horror of the situation dawns when Davies is heard on radio in a live broadcast from Toronto, performed a year before . . .

A strong cast included, as Mrs Meadows, the French actress Françoise Rosay who starred in numerous Gallic romances including Julien Duvivier's elegant **Un Carnet de Bal** (1937).[25] Her husband, a retired sea captain, was well played by Mervyn Johns's old stage sparring partner, the Aldwych *farceur* Tom Walls. But **Halfway House** suffered a little from colourless performances by Alfred Drayton and Guy Middleton as the rogues Oakley and Fortescue. Author Jack Jones popped up as a Welsh porter bemused by the eccentricities of the English.

The film has interesting things to say, in passing, about Welsh insularity and chauvinism and, particularly, the concept of nationhood in wartime. The hotel visitors, for example, include a young couple whose nascent love affair is blighted because the man, from Eire, refuses to accept that his country should enter the war. But the film no more than flirts with the issues of Irish neutrality so central to Launder and Gilliat's **I See a Dark Stranger** (1946). For all its shortcomings, **Halfway House** beguiles, thanks to the central performance, Michael Relph's art direction and a script which ekes out tension shrewdly by feeding clues gradually to its audience.

SECTION 3

Winds of
Change – The
Welsh Impact
on Post-War
British Cinema

Johns also featured for Ealing as a gloomy toper (Wicker) in **Saloon Bar** (dir. Walter Forde, 1940). He also had a lead role outside Ealing in Launder and Gilliat's nineteenth-century drama **Captain Boycott** (1947) and was a natural choice as the timorous but big-hearted Bob Cratchit, cowed by Alastair Sim's intimidating employer, in Brian Desmond Hurst's 1951 **Scrooge**. The good roles petered out in the late 1950s but Johns played the commander of a Welsh Outward Bound Trust training school in Aberdovey in John Grierson's Group Three production **The Blue Peter** (dir. Wolf Rilla, 1955); and he was back in familiar hangdog guise as the victimized newspaper-seller Alfie Barnes, who commits suicide when menaced by Peter Sellers's gang, in John Guillermin's **Never Let Go** (1960).[26] But it was as an Ealing stalwart that Johns made an indelible impression on the screen – even though he never figured in any of the classic comedies which have become the studio's hallmark.

Hugh Griffith and Clifford Evans

After **A Run For Your Money**, that larger-than-life actor Hugh Griffith (b. Anglesey 1912, d. 1980) was to make one further memorable foray into the West London studio's canon. He played one of the more comically headstrong backwoodsmen resisting a branch line closure in Charles Crichton's **The Titfield Thunderbolt** (1953), only a few years before the Beeching axe fell and made the film seem even more of a diverting period piece. Griffith, playing an engine driver and covert tippler and poacher, was amusing in a work which set the virtues of the past firmly against the present. When told the railway line they run is in profit, George Relph's businessman says: 'This is dreadful. The next thing we know we shall be nationalized.'

No Welsh actor conveyed self-reliance and stolidity on screen better than Clifford Evans, who played the lead in one popular Ealing film, **The Foreman Went to France** (1942), and, of course, an important cameo in **Proud Valley**. Even in British National's **Love on the Dole** (1941) as Larry Meath, the street-corner firebrand amidst the Lancashire cotton mills, Evans's tone is essentially placatory despite his left-wing credo. Larry appeals to common sense and reason; the object of his wrath – living conditions at Hankey Park *c.*1930 and the poverty of its residents – is self-evident as the camera pans over hovels, cramped back-yards and middens. The Evans character, despite his financial situation, is obviously a sensible theoretical choice as a

Hugh Griffith footloose in London in *A Run For Your Money*.

potential spouse for the film's heroine, the spirited, hard-nosed Sally Hardcastle (Deborah Kerr). But there is no place for reason in the squalor of Hankey Park; Larry is never able to fight his way out, and finally dies in a pitched battle between the working men and police with truncheons, the most graphic scene of social/industrial unrest in British film at that time. Evans's stature and dignity in the Meath role gave this scene a *frisson* rare in British cinema in the early forties. Meath is described as Welsh in studio publicity but no attempt is made to point up his origins, just as the hero's Welshness counted for little in Cavalcanti's **Foreman Went to France**;

Michael Relph's Ealing film **Davy** (1957) similarly made nothing of national identity in Harry Secombe's title role.

Evans (b. Senghenydd, Glamorgan, 1912, d. 1985), reinforced his image as a strong, resourceful loner in Cavalcanti's **Foreman Went to France**, the story of a company boss, Carrick, forced to rescue his firm's equipment from behind enemy lines. The film was based on actual incidents in the life of Midlands businessman Melbourne Cooper. Evans proved a solid foil for the Constance Cummings heroine but his performance, all fortitude and resilience, seemed grey in the context of explosions, aerial bombardment, family traumas and excavations. It also sat oddly with the comic behaviour of the two British 'tommies' seeking to escort the two principals to safety – Tommy Trinder (relentlessly mugging) and Gordon Jackson (as his gauche echo).

Roles of stature were Evans's forte – men difficult to faze or deflect from the course they plotted, as in British National's 1941 **Penn of Pennsylvania** when, as the Quaker leader, he was again teamed with Kerr. Around this time Evans might have built an American career for Warner's. He claimed to have been offered roles in two Paul Muni films, but the war prevented him travelling.[27] On television, the Welshman was given more latitude to convey his versatility. The early characteristics of his screen leads, an independent spirit and wilfulness, seemed to have hardened into intolerance in his later roles. He cut a prepossessing figure as a steely autocrat in TV's **Power Game** series, and as the pragmatic go-between warning Welsh patriot John Jenkins against precipitate use of violence in Richard Lewis's early eighties BBC Wales drama, **The Extremist**. Evans, a noted stage actor and sometime theatre impresario, spent many of his last years in a vain attempt to create a Welsh National Theatre. In view of Evans's screen *gravitas* it is ironic that he made a significant contribution to Ealing through comedy – as the creator and co-script writer of **A Run For Your Money**. He was also, of course, an admirable straight foil for the humorous family squabbles in a non-Ealing feature, **Valley of Song**.

The Welsh 'repertory company'

Johns, Evans, Donald Houston, Edwards and Griffith were the main Welsh performers at Ealing, but there were other members of the 'repertory company'.

In Balcon productions, Roddy Hughes, a roly-poly, florid-faced actor with a penchant for avuncular or bumbling roles, figured down the cast list. He was in regular employment in British films through the thirties and forties often as the nominal Welshman, sometimes merely dubbed 'Taffy' – as in John Baxter's **A Real Bloke** (1935) and Oswald Mitchell's **Cock o' the North** (1935). For Ealing he appeared in two 1941 Will Hay comedy vehicles, **The Ghost of St Michaels** and **The Black Sheep of Whitehall**, as a medic in **Saloon Bar** (1940) and as Tim Linkinwater in Cavalcanti's **Nicholas Nickleby** (1947).

Ronald Lewis (b. 1917) and Glyn Houston (b. 1926) were Welsh actors regularly employed in British pictures but, with the film industry contracting alarmingly in the mid-fifties, they never became stars. Lewis played a Welsh boxer, Eddie Lloyd, one of six fighters whose careers were charted in Basil Dearden's Ealing film **The Square Ring** (1953), which took a cynical look at backstage ambition and corruption.[28] Lewis's mother was played by Welsh actress Madoline Thomas (b. Abergavenny, 1890, d. 1989), who also enjoyed a substantial role in the studio's **Painted Boats** (1945), Charles Crichton's study from a 'Tibby' Clarke script of canal life spanning several generations.

Buxom singer 'Two Ton' Tessie O'Shea (b. 1917), glimpsed in **The Blue Lamp** as the singer who unwittingly helps provide Bogarde with an alibi, also featured as comic relief playing a friend of Peter Finch's swagman hero in one of a small group of Ealing Australian films, **The Shiralee** (1957).[29]

The only Welsh-born actress to play leads for the studio under Balcon was Peggy Cummins (b. Prestatyn 1925), who featured in two lesser studio comedies the anti-TV satirical squib **Meet Mr Lucifer** (dir. Anthony Pelissier, 1953) with Stanley Holloway, and **The Love Lottery** (dir. Charles Crichton, 1954) with David Niven. Her career began auspiciously in Hollywood as the gangster's doxy in Joseph H. Lewis's much acclaimed B movie thriller **Gun Crazy** (1950), but her progress as leading lady soon fizzled out in unambitious British comedies, though she appeared as Dana Andrews's lover, terrorized in Jacques Tourneur's atmospheric chiller **Night of The Demon** (1957).

Outside Ealing, the English-born Megs Jenkins, round-faced, plumpish and fretful, was another familiar player of Welsh roles from the forties to the sixties. She was prominent for Ealing in two non-Welsh parts, in Basil Dearden's Technicolor period piece, **Saraband for Dead Lovers** (1948), and in Thorold Dickinson's **Secret People** (1952) – but many will remember her best, in typically maternal vein, as the friend of Patricia Roc's heroine in the prestigious morale-boosting **Millions Like Us** for Gainsborough. She played Gwen Price, formerly at 'the University of South Wales' who was permitted the odd colourful reference to her Valleys background: 'Dad's a miner. A wonderful time we had on the dole. I was brought up in a distressed area, lovely damp patches of fungus blossoming on the wallpaper and a bath in the zinc tub in the kitchen on Saturday nights.' When Gwyneth Vaughan made a similar speech in **Blue Scar** it sounded self-pitying and affected. When Megs Jenkins said it you believed it, though Launder and Gilliat were as prone to stereotyping as the Boulting Brothers. If exiled Welsh characters referred to their backgrounds they invariably evoked a grim Valleys scene of dole queues and straitened living conditions. Jenkins also had a pivotal Welsh part in the Launder–Gilliat independent film **Green for Danger** (1946), as Nurse Woods, unjustly suspected of spying and murder.

Writers and musicians

Welsh contributions to Ealing were not confined to actors, of course. Composer Ralph Vaughan Williams, from the border country, whose work often reflected his deep feeling for Welsh culture and history, was used by Balcon to bolster Charles Frend's epic **Scott of the Antarctic** (1948) – which featured James Robertson Justice, no less, as petty officer Taffy Evans. Vaughan Williams also provided the score for Frend's **The Loves of Joanna Godden** (1947), and the 1950 Australian drama **Bitter Springs** (dir. Ralph Smart).

Richard Hughes, apart from helping write **A Run For Your Money**, received co-scriptwriting credit on Charles Crichton's **The Divided Heart** (1954), a tug-of-love drama centred on a battle for custody between a German family and a Yugoslav mother, an Auschwitz survivor.

Diana Morgan's influence was much more central and pronounced. She worked closely with the former editor Angus McPhail and directors like Charles Crichton and Robert Hamer, who spent much of his childhood in Wales. Cardiff-born Morgan, a former Cochran girl and actress brought up in a bilingual family, made notable contributions to **A Run For Your Money** and helped John Dighton and McPhail on Cavalcanti's **Went the Day Well?** (1943), based on the tantalizing conceit of a raid on a Gloucestershire village by an advance party of German invaders. The script presents the women of the community as bracingly pragmatic initially, and more than eager to help the men meet violence with violence at the climax. As the film goes on, the womens' gung-ho attitude seems both funny and grotesque. Thora Hird's character even talks of 'keeping the score' as the females take pot shots at the enemy. It is hard now *not* to read the film as a condemnation of the pervasive brutalizing of war but the script was laced with delicious black humour. Morgan's chief influence was perhaps as a writer often asked to 'present something from a woman's point of view' or supply the distaff 'angle' on a script and it is fascinating to speculate on her exact influence in **Dance Hall**, for instance, which showed assertive women and their problems in the workplace. Morgan was required to write key lines to clarify Donald Houston's character's feelings and motives and his despair on trying to force his wife to share home and hearth rather than disappear, however infrequently, to the local Palais. Something of Morgan's own scepticism about the protagonist's macho attitudes crept into the writing.

Morgan herself had to fight for respect in the male ethos of Ealing. It was tough for the relatively few women in creative roles in the predominantly masculine film business in the 1940s, as Jill Craigie found. 'But everyone mucked in and collaborated so the final credits are often misleading,' Morgan said later. 'We helped one another – for instance I did a lot of **The Foreman Went to France**. There was no sense of rush, drama or stars at Ealing and we had wonderful discussions. We argued, and I just had to fight. Nancy Mitford, a gorgeous writer, went to Ealing and lasted two weeks because she just couldn't cope with the boys.'[30]

It was significant that Morgan received the main scripting credit for a film centred on a strong-willed heroine, perhaps the most unsympathetic in the studio's *oeuvre* – Googie Withers's murderess in **Pink String and Sealing Wax**. The film was noteworthy for the performance, her candid characterization, and the clever use of claustrophobic interiors. Morgan's lone venture into comedy apart from **A Run For Your Money** was **Fiddlers Three** (1944), co-written with director Harry Watt, a ponderous satire on screen epics and Ancient Rome, shot through with deliberately anachronistic humour and starring Tommy Trinder, Sonnie Hale and Frances Day. Morgan claims she wrote all the musical numbers – including 'Caesar's Wife', accompanying images of the emperor's spouse bathing in asses milk.[31]

Harry Watt, better known as a documentary director, was to shoot in Wales one of Ealing's most distinctive achievements, the 1943 **Nine Men**, made on a peppercorn £20,000 budget. He demonstrated courage and ingenuity in doubling Margam Sands as the North African desert where a lost British patrol is besieged. The work's intensity, the palpable sense of heat and the performances of a largely amateur cast headed by the professional Jack Lambert, made the feature a memorable addition to Ealing's dramatic canon.

SECTION 3

Winds of
Change – The
Welsh Impact
on Post-War
British Cinema

In the studio's later films – after Morgan's departure following **Dance Hall** – the Welsh connections became increasingly vague, as Balcon saw less need after the war to project a cosmopolitan Britain of consensus. In the cumbersome **Davy**, Harry Secombe's variety-act trouper Davy Morgan, agonizing over whether to quit the family comedy act 'The Mad Morgans' to embark on an opera career, alludes only briefly to his Welshness. The film ends in true Ealing style when, despite a successful Covent Garden audition, he opts not to rock the family boat and rejects the lure of the 'outsider'.

Less typical of the studio was its last UK-based production, Seth Holt's broody 1958 thriller **Nowhere to Go**, written by Holt with theatre critic Kenneth Tynan. Wales becomes the backdrop for the denouement when, after a botched crime, a runaway burglar (George Nader) takes refuge with a comparative stranger (Maggie Smith). Holt never allows us to draw too close to his characters, and their motives and connections remain largely unexplored. Why does Smith help hide out Nader, especially on the estate of her uncle, who just happens to be a chief constable; and what is the source of the bond between Nader and his brutal henchman? This strangely elliptical work never lived up to its opening nocturnal prison escape scene but proved memorable for its confident use of low angles and long shots, its fine editing and Holt's aloof stance towards his hoodlum rather than for any sense of the rural Welsh landscape or a sheltering community. It eschewed the familiar Ealing camaraderie.[32]

In the studios' nineteen years under Balcon, the Welsh made a worthy contribution to creating Ealing's reputation, but even avid followers of their output would have gleaned little knowledge of Wales save as a land of coal miners, singing and usually ingenuous pitmen (**Proud Valley** only partially subverted the image); and of family men out of their depth outside – or hankering after – their own communities. And, though Welshmen like Meredith Edwards were used to provide light relief, the studio (with the second-rate **Davy**) had botched its one attempt to make use of Wales's most versatile comic. **Proud Valley**, at least, had provided some sense of a mining area's communal spirit and concerns and glimpses of the economic hardship in Valleys life with work ill paid and precarious and debt-collectors at the door. There was still a long way to go before any feature film-maker could claim to have captured, consistently, the essence of industrial Wales.

THE WELSH IN GENRE FILMS (1948–1962) CHAPTER 13

There are many things you can say about a Welshman but never be rude about his larynx. That seems to be the message of *Valley of Song*.

(Milton Shulman's review, *Evening Standard*, 4 June 1953)

SECTION 3

Winds of
Change – The
Welsh Impact
on Post-War
British Cinema

With the odd exception, films set in Wales in the immediate post-war years were rooted in mining communities and class, industrial or national conflicts. Even **Halfway House**, with its emphasis on fantasy and suggestibility, explored issues of national loyalty and language. It was set in a Wales even more amorphous than the Celtic-Gothic limbo conjured up in the amusing Hollywood curio, **The Old Dark House** (1932), James Whale's horror-comedy. This was the first Hollywood sound feature set entirely in Wales (though made in the studio) with Melvyn Douglas (as one of a motley group of travellers stranded in a rural mansion one foul night), Charles Laughton, Raymond Massey and Boris Karloff. It was co-scripted by R. C. Sheriff but based, intriguingly, on a novel by J. B. Priestley, whose writing had inspired the vogue for the device of characters finding themselves outside time, or in a time-warp – much as the characters seem to be in **Halfway House**.[1]

Boris Karloff, Gloria Stuart in Universal's *The Old Dark House* (1932), the first Hollywood sound film set in Wales.

In the 1950s industrial issues and problems of national culture and language were largely abandoned as the British cinema, its lifeblood partly drained away by TV, retrenched and concentrated on genre films and cosy undemanding certainties, to hold on to audiences. (There was a perhaps understandable harping on British wartime heroism, for example.) With cinemas closing down apace, most companies were unprepared to tackle more contentious issues. It took the injection of American finance towards the end of the 1950s to ensure a short-term revival. In most UK films from the late forties to mid-fifties there is little sense of post-war austerities, or the optimism and sacrifices of ordinary people in those heady days of the welfare state in Attlee's Britain. Features set in Wales by the British studios, apart from mining films – arguably a genre in themselves – tended to be simple formula hackwork (mainly thrillers or suspense movies), screen diversions focusing not on any broader issues but on the idiosyncrasies and foibles of humorous Welsh types or archetypes.

Of the Welsh post-war big-screen comedies, three – **A Run For Your Money**, **Valley of Song** (1953) and **Only Two Can Play** (1962) – are still frequently revived and stand up almost as well as any contemporary British features in the *genre*. Other British comedies offer sharp, sometimes bruising, characterizations of the Welsh. All the humorous films to be discussed here make more interesting attempts to stereotype – sometimes with protagonists who become the butt of affectionate jibes, notably Rachel Thomas's ousted contralto standing on her dignity in **Valley of Song**. Other characters, like Richard Attenborough's self-important quasi-poet and cynosure of the theatrical coterie in **Only Two Can Play**, and Kenneth Griffith's wheedling nark in **I'm All Right Jack**, are presented more caustically. It is easy to see some of these performances and images as demeaning to the Welsh; some might even seem sickeningly patronizing. The problem lies not in the presentation of these particular images – after all, caricatures of supposed national types were staples of music-hall and variety acts and the comics long before film. The difficulty is that these images of the national character or 'types' were almost the only ones presented in the commercial sound cinema, outside the mining films until the 1970s (Losey in his Stanley Baker films, of course, went deeper). One might have wished that other images, apart from a plenitude of heroic miners, might have emerged in those years, or types much more difficult to categorize or label on screen. Not the least reason for welcoming such films from Wales as **Above Us the Earth**, **The Happy Alcoholic** and **One Full Moon** in particular, in the last eighteen years, is their willingness to subvert stereotypes and to present characters infinitely more complex. These characters do not merely offer themselves up as sacrificial victims. Between the forties and sixties two or three films, as we shall see, offered far more vigorous images of the Welsh than the other genre movies emerging in that period.

The thrillers: from *The Small Voice* to *Tiger Bay*

Two 'Welsh' thrillers emerged around the turn of the decade: **The Small Voice** (US title, **Hideout**) (1948) and **Circle of Danger** (working title, 'White Heather') (1951). The credentials of **The Small Voice** production team were impressive. Anthony Havelock-Allen, producer of the noted British wartime dramas **This Happy Breed** (1944) and **Brief Encounter** (1945), had teamed up to form the small Constellation production company with Fergus McDonnell, editor of the 1945 features **The Way Ahead** and **Way to the Stars**.[2] Their 'Welsh' film, from a Robert Westerby novel, won acclaim despite its more melodramatic passages.[3] Its central character, a crippled playwright (James Donald) and his wife (Valerie Hobson) living in Wales with a housekeeper and two children, are forced to shelter three escaped convicts. The basic idea became familiar in serviceable Hollywood films, particularly the Bogart features **Key Largo** (1948) and **The Desperate Hours** (1955).

Havelock-Allen's feature, eligible for British quota, certainly impressed *Observer* critic C. A. Lejeune who compared it with **The Petrified Forest** (1936), starring Bogart, and warmed to the actor's enthusiasm and the cat-and-mouse games played by a sardonic dramatist (Donald) to unnerve a gunman and obtain medical attention for a child dying of meningitis.[4] She also admired the film's ability, within the straitjacket of format, to suggest how a couple whose marriage is on the brink of a break-up find their differences vanishing at the wrong end of a gun. The movie is perhaps notable today not for its portrayal of the Welsh but for the screen début, as a hood with fatal conscience pangs, of Howard (then Harold) Keel, from the London stage production of *Oklahoma!* Miss Lejeune noted, with prescience, that he was so clearly set on a dazzling Hollywood career that 'it is only a matter of months' before he will be on 'the cover of all the movie magazines'.[5] Richard Winnington of the *News Chronicle*, perhaps the most distinctive daily critic of those years, chose **The Small Voice** and Carol Reed's **The Fallen Idol** as his only two British fictional films in a list of seventeen outstanding features in 1948. He thought Havelock-Allen's feature defined 'the bedrock standard on which commercial British film-making might properly base itself . . . Films like this can confidently meet normal Hollywood competition.'[6]

Circle of Danger was made by Jacques Tournier, a Hollywood director of great visual flair: witness four films made between 1942 and 1957, his horror features **Night of the Demon** and **Cat People**, his thriller **Out of the Past** and the grossly underrated **Stars in My Crown**. But he brought nothing distinctive to **Circle of Danger**, set partly in Wales, partly in Scotland. It has a certain curiosity value and irony in providing Ray Milland (b. Reginald Truscott-Jones, 1905, d. 1986), the most durable of all the Welsh stars in Hollywood, with his first role in his native country.[7] It revolves around the attempts of an American, Clay Douglas (Milland) to find out the truth about his brother's death. As he moves through Britain and a labyrinth of deceit, the visitor is bemused by the hostility and life-styles of the Welsh miners and his Scottish hosts. The film has superficial similarities to Fritz Lang's rather muted Expressionist thriller **Ministry of Fear** (1944), when Milland again played a confused outsider – in this case a man wrongfully arrested who is released into an alien Britain of shadows, paranoia and Nazi plotters. Tourneur's work, containing scenes shot in Welsh pits, made fewer ripples despite a good cast including Marius Goring, Welshman Naunton Wayne, Marjorie Fielding and Edward Rigby, and a plot which seemed to offer the prospect of a critical anti-military stance. Clay Douglas, whose brother served with the commandos and was reported killed in action, has his suspicions fuelled by information gleaned from members of the raiding party on that fateful mission. He discovers that his brother was shot by his commanding officer, Major MacArron (Hugh Sinclair). But the reasons provide the plot's ironic punch line. Douglas's desire for justice is matched by his desire for a girl who is the major's friend. As he is about to shoot the apparently vacillating officer, it is revealed that the brother had been killed for disobeying orders, thus defusing any potential iconoclastic plot elements and tying up loose ends. A similar theme to **Circle of Danger**'s – this time of a man retracing the circumstances of his father's death and finding the truth about his Fascist involvement disturbing and unpalatable – was handled with far greater skill and subtlety in Bertolucci's **The Spider's Stratagem** (1970). The *Monthly Film Bulletin*, castigating Tourneur's film for its absence of tension and improbable plot, noted a trifle wearily that Milland portrayed with 'naïve good faith the type of American for whom all English girls are supposed to fall'.[8]

Another 'Welsh' film, **Tiger Bay** (1959) is perhaps best seen not as a thriller at all but as a character study of an independent young girl with her own fierce notion of loyalty. The film, based at the now defunct Beaconsfield Studios, was made for producer Julian Wintle whose enthusiasm for the project was fired by the huge success of his feature **The One That Got Away** in Germany in 1957 when Hardy Kruger, as the Luftwaffe pilot of the title, provided box-office insurance. Kruger's appeal persuaded Wintle to cast Horst Buchholz in the lead for **Tiger Bay** rather than Rank contract players such as Michael Craig and Dirk Bogarde.[9] Directed by the American J. Lee Thompson and superbly shot and lit by British cameraman Eric Cross, the film is undoubtedly well crafted, and lifted out of the common run by the complementary performances of John Mills as a painstaking police officer and Hayley Mills, in her screen debut, as the little tomboy Gillie, who inadvertently witnesses a killing in Cardiff's dockland. Then, with an engaging blend of innocence, loyalty and bloody-mindedness, she conceals the murderer's identity from the law . . . The film's lineage is fascinating. Seven years earlier Thompson directed **Yellow Balloon** in which a small boy, mistakenly believing he had killed his friend, was hounded by a murderer. And in the same year, Wintle backed Charles Crichton's thriller, **Hunted** (US: **The Strangers in Between**), focusing on a runaway boy who strikes up a rapport with a killer, a seaman played by Dirk Bogarde, who finally gives himself up to protect the boy. Both of these films, as the *Monthly Film Bulletin* noted, were probably influenced by a 1949 Ted Tetzlaff second feature **The Window** where a small boy (Bobby Driscoll), given to crying wolf, sees a murder, is believed by no one, then is terrorized by the killer (Arthur Kennedy). The inspiration of this work was master storyteller Cornell Woolrich (of **Rear Window** fame).

Ideas from all these films found their way into **Tiger Bay** which builds up gradually,

Hayley Mills – an overnight star after *Tiger Bay.*

and with no spurious sentiment, the relationship between Gillie, a girl disoriented in her docks landscape, and Korchinsky, a Polish seaman (Buchholz), in which both ease their loneliness and achieve new stature. The early scene in which Gillie observes through a keyhole the fatal quarrel between the sailor and his girlfriend (Yvonne Mitchell) is well shot and orchestrated. Gillie's chief traits – impetuosity and bravado – are used shrewdly to generate suspense (witness the chapel scene when she cannot resist gaining kudos with her youthful peers by allowing a choir boy a sight of the murderer's gun she secretes). Gillie is no winsome poppet; she has gall and cunning. Her resolution and sullen defiance add a welcome abrasiveness to her verbal skirmishes with John Mills's Supt. Graham, who finally dupes her into disclosing the murderer's whereabouts but cannot loosen her tongue about his guilt.[10] Near the finale, it seems that Gillie's stalling tactics have enabled the Pole to escape to the sea beyond the three-mile limit. Graham

intercepts the ship but Gillie's recalcitrance seems certain to win the day until she tumbles overboard and Korchinsky dives in to rescue her. He forsakes all hope of freedom – but fully rehabilitates himself in the eyes of the film's audience.

Hayley Mills, performing with local dockland children with no acting experience, delivered a versatile, unaffected performance which won her a Silver Bear at the Berlin Festival and a British Film Academy Award. Her performance owed much to her father's solid presence and the confidence instilled by two actors in minor roles, Megs Jenkins (as her aunt) and Meredith Edwards. Hayley, then at ballet school, was chosen after Lee Thompson auditioned hundreds of boys and finally suggested testing her after a visit to her parents' Sussex home. (The scene with Buchholz in the church was significantly chosen as the test setpiece.)[11] 'I wasn't under great pressure making the film and didn't try to be anything other than I was and this made it such an enjoyable experience,' Mills said later. 'I wasn't giving a performance. I was just doing what came naturally. It was all great fun. It was natural, spontaneous . . . it was all the things you try to get back to later.'[12]

Tiger Bay gains much from location work in the Bristol Channel and the docklands (with Newport, and its docks suspension bridge, sometimes doubling for Cardiff), and around Talybont-on-Usk. Aided by Laurie Johnson's appropriate and often wistful jazz score, which might almost have its roots in the area's own clubs, the film ranks among the finest British suspense thrillers of the fifties and is even more eloquent as a study of childhood. The feature may have glossed over or ignored many of the unsavoury aspects of the milieu but the location shooting, while rarely doing

233

more than service the fast-moving plot, caught something of the docks legacy, the grandeur of the mercantile buildings and Cardiff's Mount Stuart Square, for example, in busier days. The film's appeal for many south-Walians now has little to do with its obvious qualities as a taut little drama. Its chief value for them resides in its glimpses of Butetown (the area known as Tiger Bay) and docks landmarks now gone. Yet the Welsh people in the film – the local inhabitants, the actors in cameo roles – are never quite distinctive enough to leave an enduring impression. There are obvious echoes of Lee Thompson's film in Bryan Forbes's **Whistle Down the Wind** (1961) in which the Hayley Mills character befriends a convict (Alan Bates), and in the Welsh screen dramas **The Evacuees** (1982) – in S4C's 'Joni Jones' series – and **Elenya** (1992).

SECTION 3

Winds of
Change – The
Welsh Impact
on Post-War
British Cinema

Wintle and his associate Leslie Parkyn soon backed another project with a strong Welsh flavour – the X-rated **Bitter Harvest** (1963), with Janet Munro as the ingenuous daughter of a south Wales mining village shopkeeper. It is a cautionary story, updated from a Patrick Hamilton novel, of a girl who winds up in London after a drunken night in Cardiff, and is sucked into a morass of drugs and debauchery. Peter Graham Scott directed and Ted Willis scripted this strident film – the visual equivalent of those tawdry sex stories which were grist to the *News of the World* and *Empire News* mill in the late fifties and early sixties. Graham Scott hated the film and thought the script was rubbish: '. . . all those middle-aged people trying to be with it in the world of swinging London and miniskirts. It was a bogus Cinderella story – it [the experience] crystallized everything I hate about the British film industry . . .'[13]

Valley of Song

Of the comedies, **Valley of Song** is distinctive in its casting of Rachel Thomas, the archetypal Welsh 'mam'.[14] In this Associated British film, directed by the Scot Gilbert Gunn, she is presented as a fractious matriarch Mrs Lloyd, undertaker's wife. She is spiteful enough to take away all her personal copies of the choir's score, after losing her place as contralto, for the forthcoming Eisteddfod performance of the *Messiah*, to her shopkeeper friend Marged Davies (Betty Cooper). The film, shot mainly around Llandeilo and Carmarthen and at Elstree Studios, also features in a memorable screen début Rachel Roberts, incorrigibly curious as Bessie the Milk, unfailingly cheerful while foraging for crumbs of gossip. The humour focuses on the choir and chapel, the hub of the community. Disruption in the choir (as in Tennyson's film) leads to wider hostilities.[15]

Valley of Song presents at the outset the impression of a happy homogeneous community – Clifford Evans as successful choir conductor is backslapped by all and sundry on his return to Cwmpant. But this Utopia is soon a comic battleground as the village divides into two camps; loquacious biddies in the street purr comfort, as the wind lists, to each side in turn. The rift between the two seemingly intractable forces widens even at a meeting of reconciliation called by the minister (Mervyn Johns) with chapel elders and deacons. It is only resolved with the emotional intervention by the young and inevitably wholesome couple Cliff (John Fraser), scion of the battling Lloyds, and his girlfriend Olwen (Maureen Swanson), the daughter of Mrs Davies, Mrs Lloyd's arch-rival. The couple, who had eloped to Cardiff in an abortive attempt to marry, return to appeal to the better instincts of the families and ask them to bury their differences, so they can be married 'here among our people and our friends'. The olive branch is seized and Rachel Thomas's humorous speech would have struck a chord with many women taken for granted: 'None of you could ever know what it means to me to sing that part. All the year round it's cooking and washing and mending, I am. But when *Messiah* came around I stopped being Mrs Lloyd undertaker. I was Mair Lloyd – contralto.'

Director Gunn is at pains to show in the opening scenes just how seriously Mrs Lloyd regards her choir role, as she almost drives husband Gwilym (Hugh Pryse) to distraction practising scales in the front room. The film, based on a Cliff Gordon radio play, *Choir Practice* (itself inspired by a legend, 'The Devil Among the Songsters'), never appears stagey even if the solution with Mrs Lloyd and Mrs Davies sharing contralto duties is both pat and slightly implausible.[16] The humour at least bubbles up naturally from character foibles, wittily and incisively drawn, and the indelible impression given of a community living in each other's pockets, knowing every flaw and peccadillo.

The choir's importance in future events is hinted at from the opening images as 'Land of My Fathers' is heard over a tracking shot along the railway line. 'Sospan Fach' fills the sound-track as we see Geraint Llewellyn (Evans), soon to be choir conductor, peering out of his carriage as he returns from exile. Even his reunion with the local miners in the street is accompanied by their lusty singing, and Geraint joins in to emphasize his (spiritual) return. This impression of the reforging of old bonds is completed when the choir's rendition of 'And the glory – the glory of the Lord shall be revealed' accompanies the camera's pans and dissolves to Geraint, for the first time since his return, then ascends the hill near the schoolroom to view once more the countryside around. The more amusing possibilities of the villagers' obsession with the choir are exploited, irresistibly, in a brisk cyclical montage when Mrs Lloyd's vocal exercises are followed by glimpses of Davies, the plumber, singing with gusto as he combs out his beard; then the camera moves deeper into a bedroom where a couple harmonize; another choir member sings in his bath. The sequence finally gives way to shots of the choir rendering 'All Through the Night', which we've seen Mrs Davies singing earlier. The moment of truth for Mrs Lloyd, when Geraint announces his choice for contralto, gains much from Gilbert Gunn's low-angle shots favouring the scandalized erstwhile star. Rachel Thomas achieves a splendid hauteur in this scene.

The digressions from the main narrative and the rather dull romantic sub-plot are always diverting, from Bessie's barrage of tantalizing titbits to the backbiting of the women in the street. The artless one-liners often have a charm (and irrefutable logic) of their own, and Gunn and original writer Cliff Gordon always stay on the right side of crude caricature and treat their characters with neatly judged sly affection. Mrs Lloyd (to her husband): 'Many there?'; Mr L: 'Didn't see anybody who wasn't.' Aunt Mary (Madoline Thomas) amuses when she recalls the choir visit to London to perform *Elijah* and one woman's comments on meeting Ianto Moses Lloyd in a Paddington tea shop: 'A foreigner he was . . . from Swansea.' Only comedy scenes involving old, bedridden Ebenezer Davies regressing into childhood with his space comics seem forced. But even he has one of the film's more felicitous moments when his reverie of a dignified funeral is ruined by the thought that he will have to be carried in Lloyd's hearse.

The performances of Clifford Evans, as the punctilious choirmaster, and Mervyn Johns, who gives off his customary whiff of stealthy paternalism, serve to throw into relief the gleeful vignettes of the two families exacting revenge for slights suffered (real and imagined). Rachel Thomas had been in the original radio version, with Ivor

Novello as the choirmaster, and a live 1949 TV version – from Alexandra Palace – in two episodes.[17]

Girdle of Gold and *The Happiness of Three Women*

Both **A Run For Your Money** and **Valley of Song** trade on mainly fictional stereotypes and models but avoid the worst excesses of condescending caricatures found in some TV series or dramas as recently as the 1980s. The BBC's appalling **The Magnificent Evans** (1984), for example, the brainchild of its star Ronnie Barker, contrived to be laughably anachronistic and woefully sexist with Sharon Morgan as Barker's photographic assistant, the victim of most of the crudities and *double entendres*. Even the filmed dramas by younger directors often seemed to strike the wrong note. Another 1980s work, **Slowly Does It** (dir. Emlyn Williams), invited us to appreciate the stolidity and dumb sagacity of an old farmer, and share his contempt for the pomposity and pedantry of his would-be suitors, yet chuckle at his ignorance of words of more than one syllable.[18] The line between condescension and genuinely funny satire is often similarly narrow in comedies of the 1950s.

Girdle of Gold (1952), a British quota feature, has many of the stock ingredients of Welsh stage and television comedy. Meredith Edwards combines two stereotypes in his role of Griffiths the Hearse – doleful undertaker and village tightwad with a W. C. Fields-style antipathy to banks. The thrift and ingrained pettiness of Cwm Tallin's sole funeral director rebounds on him when he hides his money, unknown to his wife, in her stays. He is naturally thunderstruck when he discovers her plot to elope with Evans the Milk (Esmond Knight) who is finally accused of stealing the girdle. Gwynneth Griffiths (Maudie Edwards), before fleeing with her lover, has sold the stays to a friend who has been driven in the hearse to be married that morning. Griffiths and Evans later sabotage a local choir practice in their hunt for the undergarment.[19]

Edwards himself described the film as 'very Welsh' and enjoyed tapping the possibilities in his characters' venal nature: 'Whenever this fellow met someone he measured them up and down with his eyes.' But he thought the work marred by the prolonged chase sequence. The actor, in deference to his Nonconformist preacher father, refused to play the scene in the script which called for him to pull his wife behind a barrier and strip her: 'They gave me the day off. They shot Maudie Edwards alone with the discarded clothes appearing from behind the bush. I was furious and rang them up and said they'd double-crossed me. When I saw the local minister, of course, he said "I liked that scene best of all." '[20]

The Happiness of Three Women (1954), drawn from Caerphilly writer Eynon Evans's play *Wishing Well*, featured the dramatist in unhappy tandem with Brenda de Banzie.[21] Maurice Elvey directed, with Evans – who co-scripted the comedy – as Amos, an ingratiating postman whose blend of curiosity and altruism shaped the plot. His energies are directed mainly towards solving the problems of a group of women, including Jane, the Wishing Well innkeeper he loves (de Banzie). Gradually the women succumb to his advice and charm. Ann (Patricia Burke), an unhappy widow, learns to be less self-centred, Amelia (Gladys Hay) is able to shed the psychological burden of the fortune she has inherited and Irene (Patricia Cutts), a disaffected wife, is won back for her husband. But melodrama intrudes when Ann and a chauffeur (Glyn Houston) contrive to shock Jane's paralysed son John Price (Donald Houston) out of his wheelchair by faking an attack/attempted rape on his girlfriend, Delith (Petula Clark).

The *Spectator* praised the writer-star: 'Precariously balanced between Puck and Santa Claus, Mr Evans walks his sentimental tightrope with considerable skill and, rather in the manner of Barry Fitzgerald, forces one against one's will to be charmed . . . in real life it would be a miracle if Mr Evans's tricks came off – but there is something about the soft look and lilting voice of Wales which makes magic and charm acceptable.' The *Financial Times* writer was less impressed, finding the Evans character 'execrably glutinous' and claiming danger signs should be put up 'for those with no wish to drown in molasses'.[22]

Evans (1904-89), who much preferred working on the stage version with Lupino Lane and Glyn Houston, was later highly critical of de Banzie whom he thought woefully miscast, too strident for the part and prone to gratuitous scene-stealing.[23] De Banzie could, of course, be overpowering – witness her hysterical aircraft passenger in a Stanley Baker film **Jet Storm** (1959).[24]

Only Two Can Play

Only Two Can Play (1962) is undoubtedly the funniest of all Welsh screen comedies, a coruscating, almost sardonic view of Welsh insularity and punctured male vanities, culled from Kingsley Amis's novel *That Uncertain Feeling*. It did not dissect the same social strata as his jaundiced look at academia, *Lucky Jim*, also filmed, with Ian Carmichael in the lead, in 1957; but it gave most of its characters the same dusty treatment, reserving its more barbed shafts for social climbers, literary poseurs and dim martinets.[25]

The film's chief target is the odious versifier Probert (Richard Attenborough) seen in early scenes reciting to his admirers the dreadful lines of his play 'Thomas Bowen, the Tailor of Llandeilo' ('The Martyr' in the novel). Many of the belly-laughs are reserved for the ill-fated production, which literally wrecks the theatre and leads to the come-uppance of Peter Sellers's philandering lead character – a minion of the local library and occasional theatre critic for the *Aberdarcy Chronicle*. The film is equally harsh on those sycophants unable to separate the elevated from the ersatz, who, by implication, sanctify bad or mediocre poets. Other pet Amis targets (in **Only Two Can Play** and **Lucky Jim**) are obscurantists, those who pursue some inconsequential hobby horse or the minutiae of their profession, dullards who fade into the woodwork of stale committee rooms as decisions are railroaded through, or cling to the coat tails of socialites or careerists in the hope of preferment.

The satire in **Only Two Can Play** is frequently amusing but less acute than the novel and much criticism of the Welsh *crachach* in the Amis book has been diluted in Bryan Forbes's screen treatment. Short of using a voice-over to provide the equivalent of the novel's first-person narrative, it would have been difficult but not impossible to convey the thoughts of the book's central character John Lewis (Sellers) (who might almost be Amis at one remove). But the film still retains many of the novel's provocative qualities, for instance it treats the Welsh language and the minority cultural scene with an almost cavalier disdain.[26] This is illustrated in the interview scene when Sellers and Kenneth Griffith face an intimidating panel in their quest for the sub-librarian's post. In the novel Amis has a sly dig at what he sees as a Welsh phenomenon, the passion for committees. During Lewis's interview, one panellist,

Jones, a bluff self-made man, cannot resist trotting out all his committee affiliations. This passage has been excised from the film but Forbes and the directors, Frank Launder and Sidney Gilliat, have added the clergyman panel member (Meredith Edwards) who is scandalized when Lewis has not heard of his own pet Welsh literati, including 'Revd Treharne Williams, of "History of the Rhondda Baptists" fame – our greatest author'. (Sellers sticks the boot in further, telling him only 'foreigners' ask for Welsh-language books.) Forbes cannot resist the rather cheap gag at the Griffith character's expense after he reels off all his Welsh names to ingratiate himself with the committee. 'Are you Welsh?' he is asked. In the book, Lewis merely amuses himself by speculating on such a dialogue – the change inevitably coarsens the comedy.

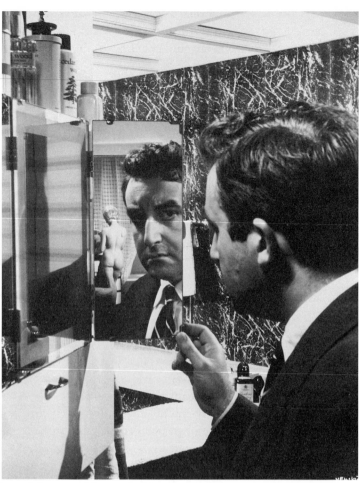

Peter Sellers and Mai Zetterling (or body double) irritating the censors in *Only Two Can Play*, the first X-certificate film set in Wales.

John Lewis is bored with his library job, his newspaper criticism and his marriage, though he is still emotionally bound to his pragmatic wife (Virginia Maskell). His saving graces as he agonizes over his lot and seeming impending adultery are his sense of humour, often self-deprecating, and an awareness – beneath the bluster – of his own limitations. Lewis is the most sympathetic character because, unlike everyone else with pretensions in the film and book, he has a sharp sense of irony and the ridiculousness of his situation. Wife Jean, for the most part, tolerates his peccadilloes and amorous horseplay at parties. But Lewis and his job rival Ieuan Jenkins (Griffith) are only superficially different. Ieuan is a henpecked homebody with a wife who seems to be sick throughout the film and is seen only as a dread vision behind the upstairs window. Both men are riddled with guilt (Lewis both about his amorous fantasies and his failure to act on them) and Jenkins who is forever thinking about his wife's ailments. Both men need the money offered by possible promotion to the vacant sub-librarian's job. Sellers and Griffith play superbly in tandem – and not only here. Devotees of British screen comedy will cherish that moment in **I'm All Right Jack** when Ian Carmichael, playing the chinless *ingénu*, is identified as a management stool-pigeon by Kenneth Griffith's nark, Dai, who dotes on Sellers's one-eyed union leader, Fred Kite.[27] Griffith saw Dai as a 'mentally deficient creep' but thought the film 'very prophetic about the unions'.

But much of **Only Two Can Play** revolves around the inner world and aspirations of John Lewis and his sexual obsession for Elizabeth Gruffydd-Williams (Mai Zetterling), a steely Norwegian-born socialite and wife of the town's libraries committee chairman. In the book, the affair is consummated on a beach at a nocturnal drunken party. In the film, the nearest Sellers comes to seduction is the amusing scene when the couple are interrupted, while undressing in her bedroom, by the premature return of her hubby and his council cronies; Lewis can escape from the house only by masquerading as a plumber, under the baleful eye of a suspicious guest (John Le Mesurier). Lewis, though not oblivious to the contemptuous way Elizabeth treats her male admirers, is prepared to use her influence to land the library job, but balks at her revelation that the interview itself has been fixed. At the book's climax, Lewis resolves to keep trying 'not to be immoral' in the hope that 'to keep trying might turn into a habit', and he settles for a job in the coal sales department at a local colliery. In the film, slightly less convincingly, Lewis and his wife open a mobile library of their own. He still ogles women customers but his spouse is always in attendance to make sure flirtations are stillborn.[28]

Forbes has eschewed some of the novel's characters, such as Ken Davies, the teddy-boy son of Lewis's landlady, and removed some of Amis's diatribes against Welsh life and culture. The director has created broader comedy, much of it around the performance of Probert's play, with Jenkins playing Death and inadvertently setting fire to the stage set and theatre. The recriminations are hilarious, with Lewis unaware of the conflagration until his wife, at the breakfast table, points out the discrepancy between her husband's eulogy of a review and the paper's front-page highlighting the blaze that gutted the theatre.

Amis was unhappy with aspects of the script, particularly the scene when Elizabeth and Lewis are marooned in their car in a field of cows after leaving the theatre during the fateful performance. It seems to belong to a different film: 'I thought when I saw it, "No please, not a farmer with a shotgun".' Perversely perhaps, Forbes in his autobiography, *Notes for a Life*, cited it as one of the funniest scenes.[29] Amis was also disenchanted with what he saw as the 'contrived Welshness of the film: Welsh eccentrics were crawling all over the thing.' But some Forbes touches undoubtedly worked. The script conveyed persuasively the gap between Lewis's aspirations and his drab home life. The stags on his bedroom wallpaper give him nightmares with their suggestions of sexual lubricity: 'Three coats of House and Garden and they're still rampant.' (Later a painting of a stag at bay adorns the ante-room in which Sellers is closeted before his job interview.) The film relies overmuch on running gags (Lewis's ripostes to the landlady, the lugubrious Jenkins's vain chase for buses, and Lewis's enthusiasm for women with large breasts – from the sweater girl he glimpses through a ground-floor door in an early scene to the buxom woman on the bus each morning). But they serve to underline the repetition in Lewis's life.

Launder and Gilliat have managed to suggest the parochiality of a certain stratum of Welsh society and its concomitant pettiness in a way which would win Amis's approval, though Maudie Edwards's prying landlady is more in keeping with the music-hall/comic-postcard view of the breed than any anti-Welsh disposition in the scripting.[30] Gilliat, around that time a non-executive director of the Cardiff-based TWW independent television channel, had made one previous film set in Wales, **The Constant Husband** (1954), from the Somerset Maugham novel. It features Rex Harrison as a bigamist who wakes up one morning to the babble of strange tongues, thinks he is in the Mediterranean and turns out to be in New Quay. He has to explain his memory lapse to Cecil Parker's baffled hospital psychologist.[31] But **Only Two Can Play** – made in Swansea, Llanelli, Neath and Briton Ferry – attracted more attention. It was the fourth biggest UK box-office hit of the year and the only X-rated work in the British top ten after incurring the censor's displeasure with its nude mirror-shot of the Mai Zetterling character and – relatively mild – sex scenes. It grossed £500,000 in Britain alone and was, according to Gilliat, the 'single most profitable film British Lion ever made', and the only BL feature to recover its production costs in the West End alone.[32]

Amis and Forbes obviously have some affection and sympathy for Peter Sellers's lecherous but perennial 'little man' who fantasizes romance and exotic adventures but always feels guilt nibbling away quietly at his innards. Griffith, as his hapless friend in the Aberdarcy library, is hilariously hangdog as he battles with Sellers for promotion. Many will cherish Griffith's comic business in **Only Two Can Play**: one arm which dangles at his side usually swings free once he is outside the front gate; he also wipes the muddied path with his hanky – under his wife's basilisk gaze behind the lace curtains.

SECTION 3

Winds of
Change – The
Welsh Impact
on Post-War
British Cinema

A former lecturer at University College, Swansea, Amis sought to bring out a certain deviousness: 'which doesn't mean dishonesty. The Welsh are no more dishonest than the English but they cheat you with a smile. They're more cheerful, hospitable and have a great sense of irony.'[33] The author had considered *Under Milk Wood* 'a little bit of an insult to the Welsh', and full of stage mannerisms. He thought Thomas was 'selling Wales short to the English and Americans'; and he despised all those 'phoney novels and stories about the wry rhetorical wisdom of poetic miners and the boring myths about the wonder and the glory and the terror of life in the valley towns – all those canonizations of literary deadbeats, charlatans and flops . . .'[34] And he had more to say about Welsh sycophancy and clay-footed Welsh literary lions, and many genuinely perceptive observations to make about the nature of male camaraderie in his novel, *The Old Devils*.[35]

Gilliat rated **Only Two Can Play** among his favourite projects. But it was not easy to make. The atmosphere on set was sometimes tense, and neither Launder nor Gilliat warmed to Sellers who demanded that Virginia Maskell should be fired after a private reading conducted for him behind Gilliat's back. 'He didn't take to Maskell and said he couldn't play a scene with her,' said Gilliat. 'He wanted her fired. All she'd done then was the scene when she comes through the door and picks up the milk.' Sellers, working assiduously to perfect a Welsh accent, was worried about Maskell's ability to handle the voice requirements. It was agreed she'd do it for two weeks and I heard no more about it but it was uncomfortable. Maudie Edwards acted as unofficial voice coach for Virginia.'[36] Gilliat believed Sellers had initially turned down the idea of filming the book, which the producer and director had optioned, but Forbes prevailed on him to do it.[37] Sellers was certainly anxious to perfect his characterization, and worried about the accent, but Gilliat admitted that even after the film began neither the directors nor Sellers had any clear idea of the character: 'I think he had a natural feeling of insecurity and that made it a bit worse. I don't think it helped that he hadn't got the make-up to hide behind. He would arrive on the set in a state of melancholia, and he became more depressed as he saw each day's rushes.'[38]

Amis was disappointed to see the main parts going to English or non-Welsh actors, though he is at pains to emphasize that his attacks on a certain parochialism were not aimed specifically at the Welsh. Mai Zetterling was not satisfactory, he felt.[39] 'My whole point about the character was that, though she had a veneer of sophistication and Anglicization, and was well-dressed and that sort of thing, at heart, she was a nice little Welsh girl with her own kind of simplicity – a rather troubled, bothered,

Welshwoman.' He thought Zetterling acted without humour. However, many film-goers, and particularly feminists, will appreciate her wry deprecating stance towards the male loutishness and sycophancy around her, and towards Lewis's more boorish sexual overtures. Gilliat accepts Amis's criticisms that the Mai Zetterling character was 'not developed enough. The problem was finding a really sexy British actress. **Room at the Top** had Simone Signoret. I wanted to use Deborah Kerr but she said "I'm too old to do that kind of sexpot" . . . We sent a script to Mai Zetterling, asking her to do a test because we didn't know about her as a comedienne. Wendy Craig was also tested, seemed OK but didn't project on screen.'[40] Maskell seems slightly affected but no more than many other female leads in the wake of the Rank 'charm school' influence, and Launder and Gilliat felt vindicated when she was nominated for a British Film Academy award.

Despite Forbes's tendency to rely on gags and broad comic situations (rather than the subtleties of Amis's characterization) and his fondness for parody (as in the job interviews), **Only Two Can Play** is frequently trenchant and perceptive. It remains an amusing tilt at the incestuous Welsh cultural scene and the literary dilettantes who hang around the periphery, lionizing the second rate. This comedy was to be the last one of substance set in Wales for more than a decade. When the BBC decided to dramatize it in the late eighties as **That Uncertain Feeling**, they also plumped for non-Welsh leads in Dennis Lawson and Sheila Gish. Lawson proved unable to provide the same comic touches and suggest the same dedication to lechery (at least in the mind) as the Lewis of the film and book, and one or two actors in cameo roles mugged furiously as if trying to compensate. The drama's shortcomings made one long once more for more genuine home-grown Welsh contemporary comedy features or single dramas.

The strange thing is I've never taken a picture in my life and I've been a television producer . . . but I could think in pictures. There were no Welsh-language films around at all . . . and I thought it was a good idea to make a film to show life as it existed in the parts of the world I knew best. It has recorded something which can never be recorded again. That's not what we intended to do. It was providential – just a lucky accident. People are conditioned to believe things will always be as they are now.

(John Roberts Williams, speaking of his film **The Heritage**, interview with the author, Cardiff, 1987)

The Heritage – Yr Etifeddiaeth

As British studios made their occasional foray into Wales in the 1940s a few indigenous directors struck out to make 'shorts' on meagre budgets. No one had seized the baton from Ifan ab Owen Edwards to carry on Welsh-language film-making in the 1930s. But the most significant film-makers in Wales in the immediate post-war years were the journalists John Roberts Williams, editor of the weekly Welsh-language newspaper, *Y Cymro,* and his colleague, the cameraman and editor Geoff Charles.[1] Just as Edwards felt impelled to provide a record of Urdd activities for posterity and to champion the language through film, Williams (b. Llangybi, north Wales, 1914) set out to provide documentary evidence of the countryside around him, only partly conscious that he was recording, in the late forties, the disappearance of an essentially pre-war culture. He also sought to film working-class experience with parallels to his own and also ensure that key artistic Welsh voices could be heard and seen on screen by future generations. Williams's early independent films made with pitifully few resources are very variable, but his pioneering work gives him an assured and honourable place in any pantheon of Welsh film-makers. His most distinctive, and personal, work was **Yr Etifeddiaeth** (**The Heritage**) an invaluable record of life in part of north Wales, as revealed to a young black wartime evacuee from Liverpool. The boy, Freddie Grant, was one of three children who attended Williams's former primary school at Llangybi on the Llŷn Peninsula and learned Welsh, as the local children spoke no English. 'They hadn't even heard there was such a place as Wales before they came here,' Williams said. 'They were ordinary working-class kids. I based the film on a child: not quite how events would seem to a Welsh boy; rather as they could be explained to an English boy.'

The Heritage, shot mute on 16mm. over more than two years from 1947 to 1949, was made mainly at weekends using a CineKodak Special, and photographed by Geoff Charles (b. Liverpool, 1909, but brought up in Brymbo).[2] But, with its overlaid commentary, it is far from the primitive exercise you might expect, as both Charles and Williams reveal a flair for *mise-en-scène* and employing camera angles shrewdly to serve the Welsh-language commentary narrated by the poet and archdruid Cynan. The film was released in two versions – with English or Welsh sound-tracks. The film-makers travelled from a base in Oswestry to shoot over a wide area of the Llŷn Peninsula and neighbouring Eifionydd (from Porthmadog to Aberdaron). They filmed events at a hiring fair in Pwllheli where employers acquired their menservants and farm labourers; **The Heritage** also included footage of a well-known local preacher, Tom Nefyn Williams, sermonizing in the street, a fair at Cricieth, the recently opened Bettws chapel at Pwllheli, sheep-shearing, work in a wool factory and the Trefor granite quarry (now closed) and of children competing in an Urdd festival. It ended on a cautionary note, with the newly built Butlin's Holiday Camp towering over the skyline. 'We captured the end of an era – the last legacies of pre-war life. The farm labourers hired would live in the stable lofts above the houses. That would be their condition. We filmed a labourer living in a stable loft near Bodfel. You'll never see this again.'[3]

The film is remarkable, considering the privations. The pair had no editing machine, for instance. 'We edited by projecting the film on the inside wall of my office at night. It was rather crudely cut. I made an error, through lack of experience,' Williams said much later. 'I crammed the commentary – it's too overpowering. It doesn't stop – it goes on and on. The film is full of technical errors. There was no

budget at all, only the expenses from the paper which engaged us. The film was made for nothing, and nobody had a penny out of it.'[4] Certainly Cynan's narrative can seem tautologous, given the quality and clarity of the imagery, and his sonorous, florid delivery often appears at odds with the homely content and flavour and the film's intimacies. But the narrative never mars the film, beautifully lit by Charles, who helps create many memorable vignettes of Welsh country life. It is unfortunate that Williams could not find a way to integrate the youngster Freddie more smoothly into the narrative, allowing him to take a more active part in events. We receive very little idea of the impression made on the boy by a life-style totally alien to his Liverpool experiences. But Williams, while showing familiar events of Welsh life, generally avoids presenting them in clichéd travelogue style, and the freshness of observation is still disarming.

The film was shown at Dolgellau, during the 1949 National Eisteddfod, and gained high praise from the press, national and local.[5] The experiences of families with evacuees during the war continued to fascinate later Welsh film-makers, inspiring 1980s work as varied as Rhydderch Jones's BBC drama **Gwenoliaid** and **The Evacuees**, perhaps the most notable of the episodes in Stephen Bayly's S4C drama series **Joni Jones**.

Tom Morgan, a photographer and working colleague of Williams, toured **The Heritage** around Wales (as he had earlier ferried the Urdd shorts of Ifan ab Owen Edwards to rural outposts) and it played the main cinema at Pwllheli and in public halls and even chapel vestries.[6] The director was anxious to create a 90-minute 'roadshow' with the film and made other shorts to accompany it: one centred on the production of *Y Cymro*, his newspaper, another, **Tir Na Nog** (Land of the Young), on the life of the people of Galway (1949), which focuses on the routines and rituals of rural life. The third film, made in just a week and partly in colour, recorded a visit of a choir from Coedpoeth, near Wrexham, to Madrid, and includes shots by Charles of bullfighting in Spain, but compared with **The Heritage** it seems stilted and ordinary with little sense of any visual style or feel for the material that the pair had shown within their own culture.

Williams went into TV news production, occasionally making documentaries and helping to ensure that key figures of Welsh cultural life were available to posterity. He shot the first BBC Wales colour documentary, **Cynan – Llanc o Lŷn** (**Cynan – The Lad from Llŷn**, 1970). The poet was very ill throughout shooting and died before the film was completed. The 45-minute work, inspired by Cynan's use of place-names and locations in south Caernarfonshire, was virtually a monologue to camera with the writer in his wheelchair near the sand dunes at Pwllheli reflecting on his surroundings and past life and work. Williams then shot a similar film on the poet T. H. Parry Williams – **Llanc o Eryri** (**The Lad from Snowdonia**). The director also made a workmanlike series on the North Wales Newspapers group publications – including *Y Cymro*. Most of the imagery was common to all these journalism films, with local-interest shots inserted in each to satisfy individual audiences.[7] The vivid imagery of **The Heritage** stands up well today but the value of Wlliams and Charles's other work is now, inevitably, mainly historical, despite eloquent camerawork.

David

> Through the simple, yet flexible narrative method – the reminiscences of the narrator and of Dafydd himself – the film gives a remarkable impression of place, atmosphere and character. Paul Dickson here gives expression to human qualities rare in present-day British documentary.

> (*Monthly Film Bulletin*, June, 1951)

One of the finest films ever made in Wales emerged in 1951. Paul Dickson's **David**, the Welsh contribution to that year's Festival of Britain, was a leisurely, unusually reflective but engrossing, study of an elderly Ammanford school caretaker, Dafydd Rhys, who distils his crowded memories of his dead son, Gwilym, into a poem which takes second place at the National Eisteddfod.[8] The film is largely autobiographical and the old man is played with muted eloquence by D. R. Griffiths, brother of Wales's first Secretary of State, Jim Griffiths. D. R. Griffiths, in his late sixties, playing himself and telling his own story, is observed lovingly through the eyes of a schoolboy, Ifor Morgan (John Davies).[9] Dickson skilfully blended amateur and professional actors, with Rachel Thomas and Sam Jones (best known as a BBC radio producer in north Wales) as the boy Ifor's parents.

The Cardiff-born director, trained at Pinewood as a battle cameraman with the Army Film Unit, found great scope for personal expression in this story of a man whose history of suffering and self-sacrifice gave the lie to his unprepossessing life-style and the prosaic everyday events of his later years. The film is based on the Griffiths/Rhys experiences at the former Ammanford county school, filtered through the boy Ifor's memories. It begins with the protégé's childhood under the caretaker's wing – 'he seemed to like me better than the teachers' – and burrows further back in time to embrace the old man's youth. We learn that Dafydd's poetry, written when he was a miner, sold door to door, earned the money to send another collier through college; and that the sports-mad son he doted on died of tuberculosis just a year after kicking a celebrated goal in a school rugby match. The relationship between Dafydd, this resilient, spare custodian of the school's moral values, and Ifor Morgan is etched with great precision and feeling, and the film has the tranquillity of reverie. In flashbacks

D. R. Griffiths in the 1951
Festival of Britain film
David.

and gentle fade-outs, we learn of the fatal breakdown in health of Dafydd's own son,
Gwilym. An emphasis on continuity permeates later sequences when Dafydd meets
his future wife Mary (Gwennyth Petty). In one extraordinary moment, Dickson's
cutting links the birth of their child (filmed at D. R. Griffiths's home in
Ammanford), and the pit-gas mining explosion which maims Dafydd. The departure
from Dickson's normal self-effacing directing style is understood best if we see these as
the moments when the old miner begins to live vicariously through his son and his
youthful school charges (a similar link between birth and death, literal or
metaphorical, is used by Karl Francis in **Ms Rhymney Valley** and **The Angry Earth**).
The value of tradition is stressed when the Revd Gomer Roberts (playing himself),
the miner-protégé who has earlier gained from Dafydd's generosity, returns to the
school as a clergyman and eminent historian and is present when Ifor himself receives
his exam prizes *en route* to a scholarship.

David has one or two ordinary scenes which fail to create the intended *frisson* mainly
due to awkward playing in cameo roles, but it interweaves many traditional facets of
Welsh life with a pleasing affection, maturity and tolerance. Dickson, a former scriptwriter for the Crown Film Unit and also once with Paul Rotha, employs the familiar
icons of Welsh film (the Eisteddfod and its choirs) to suggest sources of strength and
comfort, but the director always avoids using them as easy shorthand merely to carry
the emotional weight of his film. Dickson provided a superbly organized, succinct
script of acute psychological perception; and the music from Grace Williams and
Ronald Anscombe's fine monochrome photography added to the persuasive
atmosphere. It was no surprise when the work earned rich praise, especially from key
figures in the documentary movement.[10] Each small revelation has the force of shock,
making us look more closely at what lies behind seemingly mundane events. The taste
and reticence are affecting, especially in moments when Dafydd (after sharing his
grief in bereavement with his wife) resumes his school duties scrubbing floors, and is

SECTION 3

Winds of
Change – The
Welsh Impact
on Post-War
Cinema

observed in long shot by Ifor from the balcony above. After Dafydd returns alone to the school, following his abortive mission to find a cure for his son, little is said, but Ifor – our narrator – observes quietly that 'he no longer cared about us. It seemed as if all his sons were lost to him.' Dafydd plunges into writing the elegy for his son to purge his own grief and he gradually picks up the pieces of his life, telling Ifor of his first day in the mine at twelve years old when he travelled two miles through the mountain to the coalface. He also talks about his seven shillings a week which helped to keep the family of ten.

Cardiff's Paul Dickson (behind camera), director of *David*.

In one scene, the caretaker points out to Ifor family pews in the chapel passed from generation to generation and speaks of his miner colleagues who read books down the pit to better themselves. And in the old man's mind's eye are those happy times when the circus visited Ammanford: 'We were more of a family than a town.' The stress laid in **David** on continuity and enduring values within home, family and community recalls the emphasis placed on family fidelity and roots in **How Green Was My Valley** and **Proud Valley**. Perhaps the finest moments centre on the caretaker's visit to the Eisteddfod, when he loses his prize narrowly but his work is commended. Dickson introduces some sly humour with the banter of the north- and south-Walian spectators but the dominant mood of the sequence is pathos. Dafydd finally wanders slowly away and Dickson leaves us in no doubt that here is a man whose defeat 'has the quality of victory'. 'He was capable not of acting or affecting his emotions, but directing his attention to the recalled events,' Dickson said later. 'What was important was the stature of the man's spirit. What is success – is it adapting to the environment you're in? He [also] seemed to live life at another level – he was inviolable . . . D. R. Griffiths was a marvellous, simple profound man, a saintly person. How he lent himself to my demands on him! The stature of his spirit I remember, he was content to work as a caretaker, but it's the quality of his belief [in the material] which makes *you* believe it.'[11]

Dickson had originally established himself with **The Undefeated**, a 1950 semi-documentary about the rehabilitation of the disabled, made for the Ministry of Pensions under Hilary Marquand, father of Cardiff-born film director Richard Marquand, and scripted with Ted Willis. Produced by James Carr's World Wide company, it centred on a man with both legs amputated above the knee. Leo Genn voiced the dialogue for Gerald Pearson of the Parachute Regiment who played Joe Anderson, a glider pilot whose plane crashed on the Rhine crossing of March 1945.[12] Dickson followed Joe's progress through hospital and rehabilitation, with some scenes shot at Cardiff's Rookwood Hospital, others at Queen Mary's Hospital, Roehampton, and at Stoke Mandeville. We see his fight to overcome disabilities and regain respect, and the growing camaraderie of the hospitalized victims is conveyed with tension and humour. The pace only flags when Dickson spends an inordinate time showing us the nitty-gritty of the pensions operations in Blackpool.[13] The film revives when we see men who have resumed their normal work despite crippling disabilities, and Dickson brings off a neat ending when the reason for the central character's temporary speech paralysis is revealed. He encounters once more the co-pilot he thought was dead and the shock brings back Joe's speech. Dickson sought to introduce suspense by concealing the narrator's identity as long as possible: 'I used the **Lady in the Lake** technique early on with point-of-view shots to conceal the identity of the man [Anderson] who is effectively the film's narrator, and also to delay telling the audience that the storyteller was also disabled. The sticks came into view, then we panned and the audience realized who'd been telling the story.'[14]

The Undefeated, with its blend of professional and amateur performers, is pedestrian at times, but Dickson, despite constraints imposed by his sponsors, still managed enough inventive touches and fluent camerawork to alert us to his potential talent. The film was judged British Film Documentary of the Year, gained an Oscar nomination and earned high praise from director Fred Zinnemann who had recently completed **The Men**, starring Marlon Brando and centred on the plight of paraplegics.[15] When the major circuits were reluctant to book **The Undefeated** it was championed, in typically forthright style, by Richard Winnington who described it as 'the year's best documentary from anywhere'. Pointing out that its box-office chances were bound to be hit by **The Men**, he described the film as 'sincere, competent, free from sentimentality and irresistibly moving'. And when the film finally opened as a second feature in London's West End, some critics compared it favourably with the Zinnemann film.[16] It was probably on the strength of this work that World Wide were approached by the Central Office of Information with a brief to 'show Wales to the World' – a remit which led to **David**.[17]

Dickson's career began to stutter badly when he made (now little-known) British features for the Danziger Brothers at Riverside Studios and at MGM at Elstree in the 1950s.[18] After a short spell with Canada's National Film Board, he embarked on an interesting period as dialogue director, initially for the director Anatole Litvak, in British studios, working on films such as **Anastasia** (1956), with Ingrid Bergman, and the film version of Terrence Rattigan's **Deep Blue Sea** (1955), before directing episodes of TV series, including **The Avengers**.[19] He returned to his first love, making sponsored documentaries – notably the award-winning **Stone into Steel** for United Steel (later British Steel) in the 1960s – and directed commercials before joining the National Film School as specialist acting tutor. He became head of the direction department in 1980–1, playing a leading role in a decade when students included embryo British film-makers Michael Radford, Julien Temple and Bill Forsyth. He has since retired from the NFS but still lectures at the London International Film School. **David**, a masterpiece in miniature, remains Dickson's finest legacy.

Stanley Baker was the revelation this time. Losey drew out of him, and at the same time refined, his aggressiveness, turning it into the prickly ambiguities of a man whose nature it is to hurt others, manifesting in jokey but jealous ways a myriad mean flicks of animosity.

(Alexander Walker writing of Baker's performance in **Accident** in *Hollywood, England*, 1974, p. 368)

The most successful Welsh actors before the 1950s were chiefly noted for quintessentially 'English' roles and mannerisms. Remember Edmund Gwenn, the perennially deferential husband or little man, capable of the odd dubious sleight of hand? Naunton Wayne was usually the dapper, sometimes dyspeptic and frequently bemused sidekick (notably to Basil Radford); and Roger Livesey, with his booming nasal delivery and straight-backed military bearing, is best remembered as an avuncular or autocratic figure, a representative of the English upper or professional classes. Ray Milland, an ex-Guardsman, was adept at playing American or British heroes but usually only if they occupied the higher social rungs. He was equally comfortable as Stanford White, the multi-millionaire architect involved in a *cause célèbre* in Richard Fleischer's **The Girl in the Red Velvet Swing** (1955), the 'anyone for tennis' *ingénu* of Anthony Asquith's **French Without Tears** (1939) and as Sapper's troubleshooter Bulldog Drummond (1937). Of significant Welsh stars and leading actors, only Emlyn Williams, Hugh Griffith and Mervyn Johns played Welshmen on screen in this period. Gwenn and Milland, of course, spent much of their careers in Hollywood, but the truth is that before the Second World War regional or provincial accents were rarely heard in the British cinema, except in comic roles. In uniting classes for the war effort, Ealing and Gainsborough democratized the cinema but Welsh roles remained thin on the ground. When Hollywood attempted to present a Welsh milieu, as in Roy William Neill's 1943 Universal feature **Frankenstein Meets the Wolf Man**, it cared little for authenticity – and the effect could be disastrous. Lon Chaney jun.'s character, who is frequently transformed into a werewolf, is recovering in a Welsh hospital – a location belied by the babble of Irish and Scottish accents, supposedly Welsh, around him.[1]

The Welsh actors of the thirties and forties who achieved stardom or status as front-rank character players all had distinctive talents but they tended to play middle-class roles. The arrival of Stanley Baker, Richard Burton and Rachel Roberts coincided with a more trenchant, acerbic British cinema, focusing on the factory and solid working-class backdrops, with fairly raw idiomatic language the common coinage. That new cinema, for a few years anyway, bristled with the anger of a generation straining at the leash, determinedly iconoclastic and aggressive, intent on eroding class distinctions so lovingly perpetuated through three decades of sound cinema. Burton's role of Jimmy Porter in the screen version of John Osborne's **Look Back in Anger** (1959) may have enshrined this disaffection but Baker, bullnecked and abrasive – on screen at least – was consistently the most dynamic Welsh representative of this new breed. If Gwenn's ingratiating screen persona sometimes reflected unconsciously the desire to please of so much British and Hollywood cinema, Baker's volatile loner at odds with himself and others suggested a Britain – and a British cinema – in flux, questioning entrenched attitudes.

Lindsay Anderson (**This Sporting Life**, 1963), Jack Clayton (**Room at the Top**, 1958, **The Pumpkin Eater**, 1964), Tony Richardson (**Look Back in Anger**, 1959, **Loneliness of the Long Distance Runner** (1962), Karel Reisz (**Saturday Night and Sunday Morning**, 1960) and John Schlesinger (**A Kind of Loving**, 1962), all made problem films with a real sense of immediacy and invigorating ideas. Throughout Europe the cinema was reflecting new mores. During the forties and fifties, neo-realistic work of directors like De Sica and Visconti broke with the predominantly literary or spectacle films of Italy's cinema past and centred on proletarian lives, heightening the drama to give their problems and tragedies universality. And in France, the Nouveau Vague (New Wave) of film-makers headed by Jean-Luc Godard,

SECTION 3

Winds of
Change – The
Welsh Impact
on Post-War
Cinema

François Truffaut, Claude Chabrol, Eric Rohmer and Louis Malle thumbed noses at the studio-bound film-makers of the past. They used lighter, cinematic equipment to create a cinema flexible in technique and ideas, acutely sensitive to the worries, problems and fashions of their contemporaries. The American cinema also placed greater emphasis on realism, with the impact of new Method actors, such as James Dean, Brando and Montgomery Clift, and the arrival of directors like John Frankenheimer and Arthur Penn who had cut their teeth in one of the hardest proving grounds of all, live TV drama; young directors such as Elia Kazan and Nick Ray were not afraid to tackle and give a new inflection to current social problems. Suddenly even the self-consciously stylish British cinema of David Lean and Carol Reed seemed light years away.

Edmund Gwenn

Edmund Gwenn was an outstanding product of the earliest sound era. His career began in silents but took off in the 1930s. He was splendidly overbearing as Hornblower, the frank, uppity Northern industrialist shattering a rustic idyll, clashing with local gentry landlords, and ousting tenants in the Hitchcock 1931 version of Galsworthy's **The Skin Game**, repeating his part in the 1920 film (dir. B. Doxat-Pratt). Gwenn delivered his role with chutzpah, flirting with audience sympathies even when revealing an outrageous philistinism. His comic candour almost succeeded in persuading us of the justice in his arguments, especially as the local autocracy was seen as benign but inert and almost anachronistic. You could sense the irresistible energy of the *nouveau riche* interloper – and you almost felt sorry when he received his come-uppance.

He was even better in Victor Saville's **The Good Companions** (1933), the first screen version of the Priestley novel, as Jess Oakroyd, the doting father-figure living vicariously through the effervescent showgirl played by Jessie Matthews. The choreography and animation of the dance scenes was a delight and Saville, as usual, revealed a real grasp of *mise-en-scène* in following the fortunes of the Dinky Doos, the touring concert-party group. Oakroyd, a one-time mill carpenter, was one of Gwenn's more memorable henpecked characters, hounded from home and employed as stagehand, counsel and dogsbody to the stage troupe. Yet his working man had mettle. In an early scene he was sacked for backchat to his boss after an accusation of idling when he was actually embroiled in a demarcation dispute – surely one of the first oblique references on the British screen to trade-unionism. He was resilient enough to shrug off the theft of his wallet on the road and to stress the need for the performers (later revamped as the Good Companions) to persevere – faced with disastrous takings in venues such as Rhyl 'in a heat wave'.

Gwenn seemed less comfortable in Saville's **Hindle Wakes** (1931) as Chris Hawthorne, compassionate but often ineffectual father of feisty Jenny who flouts moral conventions to spend a weekend with her boss's son in Wales. 'In Llandudno – of all places – I'll never be able to go there again,' says her outraged mum. Gwenn, often the butt of his dreadnought spouse (Sybil Thorndike), was fine in the scenes of domestic discord and moments when the father's natural solicitude for his daughter overcame his timidity, but he was a little too unctuous as cap-twirling supplicant to his mill employer Nat Jeffcoat. Chris Hawthorne was the stereotype of the little man who had rejected his one chance to make something of himself.

Gwenn also appeared, as a flustered City man, in Saville's well-constructed portmanteau drama **Friday the Thirteenth** (1933) with Emlyn Williams, and also appeared to advantage with the Irish comedian Jimmy O'Dea in Walter Forde's 1939 Ealing film **Cheer Boys Cheer**. He was one of the Nazi sympathizers threatening Joel McCrea, in Hitch's **Foreign Correspondent** (1940). But in his last appearance for the director, in the quirky comic suspense thriller, **The Trouble With Harry** (1955), he slipped into caricature as the retired seasalt, smitten by Mildred Natwick's widow, and party to attempts to secrete a dead body. He was much better in the two Fox films which brought him Oscar recognition. He won the Best Supporting Actor award for his Macey's store Santa helping allay eight-year-old Natalie Wood's scepticism and making dreams come true in George Seaton's **Miracle on 34th Street** (1947) – even if the saccharin threatened to silt up the celluloid. An Oscar nomination followed for his improbable forger in Edmund Goulding's **Mister 880** (1950). Gwenn's Skipper, an old junk man with a hand barrow whose inept counterfeiting baffled the US treasury for a decade, was a war hero fallen on hard times. He had worked out that it would cost the state far more in taxes if he stayed in a home than if he made a dishonest living passing dud cheques, for nominal amounts, scarcely harming anyone else. His naïvety, and frankness when brought to book, predictably discomforted Burt Lancaster's zealous treasury sleuth.

Gwenn, a ruddy-faced bull terrier of a man in appearance and a master of the exaggerated double-take, was always at his best in gentler roles, laced with humour. He left behind a gallery of genial husbands and relishable rough diamonds.

Roger Livesey – and other stalwarts

The apogee of Barry-born Roger Livesey's career was surely the cruelly challenging role of Major-General Clive Candy in **The Life and Death of Colonel Blimp** (1943). In the opening scene, Livesey (1906–76) cuts a ludicrous figure, ageing and bloated and caught literally with his pants down in a Turkish bath by military tiros who have broken the usual code of conduct to outwit Candy's men in a Home Guard exercise. Gradually, during this monumental film, our feelings change. The director–writer team of Michael Powell and Emeric Pressburger reveals Candy's growing cantankerousness and dogmatism as his past life is revealed in a series of flashbacks. Yet the film-makers tacitly endorse his values. The work becomes an elegy for a vanished code of brotherly regard for fellow officers in enemy camps – shades of Renoir's 1937 classic **La Grande Illusion**. Candy, despite his lumpen behaviour at times, is seen to possess a grace in adversity and an altruism which, with his endearing simplicity, renders him a strangely heroic figure.[2] Few actors of his generation could have given 'Blimp' such authority.[3] Livesey's burly frame, slightly lurching gait, the timbre of his voice, made him a distinctive presence in films; he could also place a whole scale of values in doubt with a quizzical tilt of the eyebrows.[4] Churchill took steps to ban the film's production as detrimental to the morale of the army. His reservations no doubt owed much to the impact of Livesey's *tour de force* performance, recreating so accurately a character built up in two decades of newspaper-cartoon lampooning, and in 'ageing' some forty years on film.[5]

Livesey was a member of a screen dynasty. He was the son of actor Sam Livesey (b. Flintshire, 1873, d. 1936), a familiar figure in UK features in the 1920s and 1930s. The young Livesey made his screen début as child actor in **The Old Curiosity Shop** (1920) and played a lead role in the Stoll company's 1921 version of A. E. W. Mason's

SECTION 3

Winds of
Change – The
Welsh Impact
on Post-War
Cinema

Roger Livesey, dignified under duress, in *The Life and Death of Colonel Blimp.*

The Four Feathers.[6] He later filled the principal male role in the Gracie Fields vehicle **Keep Smiling** (1938) and enjoyed a strong supporting role in Ealing's **Midshipman Easy** (1935). He achieved wider prominence as one of Korda's bright young actors in **Rembrandt** (1937) and another Mason adventure **The Drum** (1938), but his contributions to Powell and Pressburger films between 1943 and 1946 clinched his screen reputation.

Livesey was an astute actor of great personal magnetism, usually in paternal and genial roles (the fruity chuckle was always a feature), and he invariably suggested a deeper intelligence burrowing away beneath the surface of his characters. In the Powell–Pressburger **A Matter of Life and Death** (1946) he took the pivotal role of the solid doctor Reeves, confidant and *deus ex machina* for David Niven's airman who thwarts death in a crash and then stands trial in heaven to justify his right to remain on earth and consummate his new love affair. Much of the action, it can be assumed, takes place in the hero's head as he fights for life and enjoys only fitful spells of lucidity. Reeves's initial brusque scepticism, confronted by a pilot with an unlikely tale to tell and prone to apparent visions, is disarmed. He becomes comforter, mentor, and finally celestial advocate to the airman whose sanity depends on the successful resolution of the ethereal inquiry. Livesey's bluff cheerfulness and common sense helps to anchor the film and maintain the right balance between fantasy and whimsy. The god-like power to be vested in Reeves later is presaged in the scene when Livesey, perched high in his camera obscura, is seen watching the street below.

In the same team's **I Know Where I'm Going** (1945), set on the Western Isles, Livesey played Torquil McNeil, a principal character in an exploration of Celtic mythology and faith and its collision with feminine pragmatism and a prosaic monetarism (represented by Wendy Hiller). Livesey could not obtain release from a theatre role but Powell was so insistent that he play the part that he 'doubled' Livesey in all the location scenes and featured him only in the studio.[7] The links with Powell, the finest British director of the period, were Livesey's most profitable, though he rarely failed to make an impact in roles even when his character parts dwindled in size in the 1950s. He was particularly memorable as the retired music-hall veteran, Billy Rice, retaining the dignity denied his son Archie in **The Entertainer** (1960).

Larger than life . . . Hugh Griffith as Squire Western in *Tom Jones*.

Livesey's brother Jack (1901–61) was a staple of mainly unremarkable British features in the 1930s, including a series of films for Landslide director Donovan Pedelty and Balcon's Gaumont-British production, **The Passing of the Third Floor Back** (1935).

Naunton Wayne (b. Llanwynno, Glamorgan, 1910, d. 1970), began his theatre career in concert parties at Barry Island and established himself as a stage actor before gaining wider recognition on screen in the 1940s as a vapid but affable and querulous man-about-town. With his high-pitched voice he was often especially humorous in moments of irritability when lesser mortals refused to obey the principles of *noblesse oblige*. As Charters – one half of the cricket-mad pair who went through the late thirties and the war years seemingly oblivious to the nation's plight – he was the perfect foil and seemed quite unable to grasp the obvious, as in Hitchcock's **The Lady Vanishes** (1938) and Carol Reed's **Night Train to Munich** (1940). Wayne and Radford were also in tandem in **Crook's Tour** (1940), Ealing's **Dead of Night** (in the least successful – occult golfing – episode), and as bureaucrats tangled up with irreverent Burgundians bent on independence in **Passport to Pimlico**. Wayne was also memorably truculent in **The Titfield Thunderbolt** (1953), as a village lawyer somehow cajoled into siding with a seemingly hare-brained scheme by locals to run their own railway line.

The career of Hugh Griffith (b. Anglesey, 1912, d. 1980), also flourished post-war after a slow start in films. He was at something like his best as the carousing harpist in **A Run For Your Money** and as the quizzical college principal in the Boulting Brothers' **Lucky Jim**. He was often relied upon by directors to deliver telling cameos in just one or two scenes as in the 1951 British comedy **Laughter in Paradise** (dir.

Mario Zampi) where the idiosyncratic legacy demands of his dying eccentric forced relatives into acts foreign to their natures. He gained the Academy Award for Best Supporting Actor as the extrovert Sheikh Ilderim in William Wyler's **Ben Hur** (1959) – a part praised for its boisterous and cunning comic relief – and garnered a string of fine notices as the bibulous, roistering Squire Western in Tony Richardson's ebullient British film **Tom Jones** (1963). Griffith, larger than life on and off stage and screen, was an engaging, unpredictable performer who probably made his greatest contribution in the theatre and on TV, and, like Gwenn and Roger Livesey, he was splendid playing extroverts (as in the BBC Wales comedy **Grand Slam**, 1978) and mischievous roles with a disarming twinkle.

Ray Milland

Perhaps the most enduring Welsh-born star of these years was Ray Milland (b. Neath, 1905, d. 1986) who professed a continuing affection for Wales, viewing it through the rosy filter of the exile. He rarely worked in Britain after his Hollywood career began in 1930. He saw Wales as a land of music, mountains and mystery and, in his autobiography, vouchsafed that the Celtic mind 'in its lonely moments is a tumbling sea of love, compassion and romanticism and neurotic hates'.[8] 'In Welsh villages you will always see a curtain move as you pass. And the salt of their [the villagers'] life is gossip and intrigue,' wrote Milland, whose own experiences of Welsh village life were limited. After an upbringing in Neath and private education in Cardiff, he enjoyed a stint as a Royal Guardsman where his reputed prowess as a marksman earned him work as an extra at the BIP studios at Elstree on Arthur Robison's original version of O'Flaherty's **The Informer** (1929). For most of his screen career, spanning around 120 films and more than fifty years, Milland was an urbane lead or second lead, often in action adventures and romantic comedies sometimes of the drawing-room variety. His looks, authority and a certain hauteur combined with a fine comic timing (and a voice not unlike Cary Grant's) to keep him in constant employment in popular studio films for two decades (often opposite charismatic female stars, such as Jean Arthur, Claudette Colbert, Ginger Rogers, Marlene Dietrich and Paulette Goddard).[9]

After early excursions for Warners (in the 1931 **Blonde Crazy** with Cagney and Joan Blondell, for example), MGM and odd trips back to Britain for routine screen assignments, Milland worked almost exclusively under contract for Paramount for twenty years. He was regularly cast in prestigious studio work ranging from comedies to thrillers (such as Frank Tuttle's version of Dashiell Hammett's **The Glass Key**, 1935) and adventure 'epics' (William Wellman's **Beau Geste**, 1939, and Cecil B. De Mille's 1942 sea drama **Reap the Wild Wind**). His faintly patrician stamp often led to casting as officers, servicemen or soldiers of fortune, notably in Mitchell Leisen's films, **Arise My Love** (1940) (with Colbert and from a Billy Wilder script), **I Wanted Wings** (1941), and the 1947 **Golden Earrings** (where he appeared in drag with Dietrich). Leisen also directed a string of humorous vehicles featuring Milland, most notably the anarchic **Easy Living** (1937), with Jean Arthur, written by the incorrigible iconoclast Preston Sturges. Milland appeared with Rogers in Leisen's **Lady in the Dark** (1944) and he was prominent in the same director's **Big Broadcast of 1937**, a showcase for the studio's formidable star roster. He was also considered urbane and dashing enough to do service – just once – as Sapper's hero, in **Bulldog Drummond Escapes** (1937).[10]

But overall, during his earlier years, Milland was regarded, at least by critics, as little

SECTION 3

Winds of
Change – The
Welsh Impact
on Post-War
Cinema

Ray Milland on the
Bowery *en route* to his
Oscar for *The Lost
Weekend*.

more than a personable contract player and staple of Hollywood confections (much like Tyrone Power for most of his career, and John Payne).[11] His stock rose, spectacularly, for a time after he linked up with Billy Wilder, first as a debonair and wittily condescending officer falling for a supposedly twelve-year-old schoolgirl (Ginger Rogers) in **The Major and the Minor** (1942), and, most successfully, in his Oscar-winning performance as the alcoholic writer in **The Lost Weekend** (1945).[12] His study of burned-out disoriented author Don Birnam is chilling enough without the inspired special effects (the bat devouring the mouse in the wall still grips) and the travelling shots of the alcoholic's sallies around New York on Yom Kippur day trying to pawn his typewriter to obtain liquor. The performance undoubtedly gained credibility from Milland's own visits to the Bowery for research and the ingenuity of Wilder and cameraman John Seitz in shooting the film with hidden camera – with holes cut in the top of a delivery truck and in following the actor in one marathon day's filming, as he lurched along Third Avenue from 55th Street to 110th.[13]

Milland's films of that period also included the highly rated thrillers **The Uninvited** (1944) and John Farrow's **The Big Clock** (1948), with Charles Laughton and Maureen O'Sullivan. But for most of that decade he appeared in studio films of generally ephemeral appeal, notably **Alias Nick Beal** (1949), John Farrow's political thriller re-working the Faust legend. By the fifties he was working in low-budget independent productions, though he was convincing enough as the treacherous tennis-professional husband plotting wife Grace Kelly's death in Hitchcock's only 3D film, the slightly stilted **Dial M for Murder** (1954). As offers dwindled, Milland began to direct, shooting five films between 1955 and 1967 ranging from the Western **A Man Alone** (1955) to the cautionary Cold War nuclear thriller **Panic in the Year Zero!** (1962), marred by its right-wing siege mentality. He also directed a thriller, **The Safecracker** (1958), based on a short story by Welsh writer Rhys Davies.[14] Milland changed tack again from the early sixties as the haunted hero of two Roger Corman horror classics for American International Pictures. His poached-egg eyes and doleful mien were perfect for the hypertense, over-reaching boffin in **The Man With X-Ray Eyes** (1963). Despite inane moments and some special effects it had more than a few disturbing moments, and the Welshman conveyed the character's self-destructive impulses and an awareness of his own weakness which made the various stages of his metamorphosis the more terrifying. But **Premature Burial** (1962), Corman's resourceful version of Poe, was much superior, containing some of the more potent images in the horror genre up to that time, especially the point-of-view shots as Milland's artist, Guy. He is prescient enough to live his life in terror that one day he will be entombed alive, and has his fears realized thanks to family skulduggery. He screams silently from a coffin's interior as earth is hurled over him . . .

Milland's slight air of melancholy when playing talented men unable or unwilling to avoid their destiny added resonance to films which depended on performances with more restraint than those habitually provided in the Corman–Poe films by Vincent Price. In his last screen years, unfortunately, Milland was less choosy over his horror-film material and appeared in a succession of tawdry potboilers. His later performances in more conventional screen dramas such as **Love Story** (1970) became increasingly inexpressive and stolid.

Stanley Baker

Few actors of the fifties could stoke up anger with the conviction of Stanley Baker (b. Ferndale, 1927, d. 1976). He seemed to feed, and thrive, on tension. His protagonists left ripples of unease in their wake. In film after film his character was eaten up by guilt, envy or avarice; his screen roles persistently whittled away at the confidence of his closest associates, needling them or pushing them towards indiscretions or actions which would turn the direction of their lives. His combustible characters set off a chain reaction of small explosions as they pushed events inexorably, often prematurely, to a conclusion. The British New Wave cinema, inspired partly by writers like John Osborne and Alan Sillitoe, seemed tailor-made for him as they homed in on fierce class loyalties and schisms. In fact, he worked with none of the newer directing tiros associated with the movement. It was ironic that it was an American, Joseph Losey, with his fresh post-war view of the British pecking order, who was to make the most of Baker's talents.

You could sense every small resentment festering in the Baker screen persona. Inaction was anathema – though he could often, in these unsympathetic roles, play the waiting game; the sight of him chafing under the bonds of responsibility or social niceties lent a pleasing, unpredictable quality to much of his best work (for Losey, for example). Baker was born for the screen. He seemed to carry into his roles the tetchiness, restlessness and defence mechanisms developed in his harsh early years as a miner's son in the Rhondda Valley. He could always, with great economy, suggest the warring emotions beneath the hard shell. Even when playing tough nuts as in **The Criminal** (1960), he provided a disciplined, forthright performance free of the tics and histrionics which have ruined more versatile players. He was never at his best portraying chameleons or characters of violently oscillating disposition, but in **Accident** he conveyed the vulnerability beneath the mask of a conniving, adulterous opportunist who attempted to brazen his way through life. The character's areas of deep insecurity surfaced in behaviour which seemed occasionally inconsistent on screen. In **Eve**, he was intense, uneasy, as the Welsh writer who had stolen his brother's ideas but was unable to bring total conviction to the writer's flamboyant, egregious excesses, yet it was fascinating to watch him playing second fiddle to Jeanne Moreau's capricious *femme fatale*.

SECTION 3

Winds of
Change – The
Welsh Impact
on Post-War
Cinema

Baker conveyed such intensity and belief that he often emerged relatively unscathed after delivering adequate performances in unworthy vehicles, especially in his early studio-contract days. If he occasionally produced a one-note performance, the fault generally lay in the writing. He was more credible than most in roles calling for demonstrations of overt or innate class consciousness and there seems no doubt that, at least in his middle years, he saw himself as the artisan, the Valleys boy outside his natural *métier* but determined not to be overawed or to kowtow. His screen characters often compensated for their insecurity by aggression and they had a short way with perceived enemies. Both Baker and Richard Burton were masters of the sardonic put-down, never better on screen than when out-doing rivals or pretenders. But where Burton would draw blood after a few feints and disarming banter, Baker's approach was more brusque and bluff.

It is intriguing that Losey, the expatriate American blacklisted by McCarthy, a socially conscious director with an often distracting and paradoxical taste for the baroque, should choose Baker so often as the epitome of the hard-nosed realist school of British acting, but also to represent heroes driven by class consciousness and inner confusion. Losey thought Baker was 'always exceptional' in his films and, through him, he filtered much of his own disenchantment and vicarious fascination with Britain's social divisions in the Cold War and the first flush of the 'never had it so good' Macmillan era.[15] The actor's screen persona was an elemental force battering away at ossified social structures – and he was never better than in **The Criminal** and, particularly, **Blind Date**. If Losey's predilections for visual flourishes and éclat sometimes bothered audiences and diluted the politics of the director's work, Baker certainly helped anchor his ideas in a recognizable, if desperately uncertain, world.

Baker's screen career began as a boy patriot in the 1943 **Undercover**, a curiosity shot by Ealing in Breconshire but set in Yugoslavia. He played a clutch of minor roles in undistinguished features before establishing himself as a working-class anti-hero before the term became fashionable.[16] In typical roles he played potentially assertive men rendered impotent by circumstances. He was a boxer inveigled into a bank robbery attempt and finally shot in the back by Laurence Harvey's suave gangleader in Lewis Gilbert's **The Good Die Young** (1954); and an ex-con trying to reform in the lively trucking movie **Hell Drivers** (1957), directed with some style by Cy Endfield (another Black List victim) who was to become Baker's collaborator on his cherished Zulu project in the 1970s.

The Welshman was wasted as the level-headed captain battening down the emotional hatches on an aircraft hijacked by Richard Attenborough in **Jet Storm** (1959). The film itself was hijacked by Brenda de Banzie's overbearing performance. Baker enjoyed a more taxing role as the doting father (of child star Mandy Miller) on the run for suspected embezzlement in **Child in the House** (dir. Charles deLatour, 1956). He was in more familiar territory as a splenetic hood in Ralph Thomas's motor-racing drama, **Checkpoint** (1956), but he was a two-dimensional villain as the Welsh jerry-builder Morgan, Dirk Bogarde's *bête noire* in **Campbell's Kingdom** (1957), Thomas's melodrama from a Hammond Innes novel. Morgan built a cheapskate dam on Bogarde's land in the Canadian Rockies, concealing plans revealing oil there, and died when the dam collapsed – a fitting come-uppance for skimping. Baker made more of an impact as the CID man fighting juvenile delinquency in **Violent Playground** (1958), notable for its location work in the rougher areas of Liverpool. He delivered one of his finest screen performances and elicited sympathy, despite his overt bullishness, as an overworked local policeman dogged with domestic problems in **Hell is a City** (1960).[17] His tough-drinking, passionate reporter Beddoes, who falls for Jean Seberg's young painter in Robert Parrish's flat and clichéd romance, **In the French Style** (1962), prefigured a more rewarding, and disturbing, performance as an alcoholic psychiatrist in HTV's **Graceless Go I** (1974), opposite Rachel Roberts, when he disintegrated frighteningly and was convincing despite a slightly uneven script redeemed by flashes of mordant humour.

For many, Baker's most satisfying role outside the Losey canon in the fifties and sixties remains his bullying officer in Charles Frend's **The Cruel Sea** (1953), the Second World War naval drama scripted by Eric Ambler from the Nicholas Montsarrat novel. But it was Baker's work with Losey in **Blind Date** (1959) which stamped him as distinctive in a long-moribund British cinema beginning to stir into life with the influx of American talent and money. From the moment Baker's embittered Inspector Morgan arrives at a singularly chintzy residence to find Hardy Kruger's obvious proletarian Van Rooyen paying court to the lady of the house (who has just – unknown to the Dutchman – been murdered), his cop's antennae probe clues to confirm his perceptions of the man's guilt. As the film develops, Losey reveals Morgan's unease and innate sense of inferiority to Kruger, and also turns his shortcomings to advantage to goad the suspect – a Dutch painter – into revealing his own flaws. The film, more than any other, illustrates what Losey regarded as Baker's blend of 'machismo and puritanism'; the director thought Baker had the right qualities of sexual and class aggression for the role.[18] Morgan's edginess and independent cast of mind emerge in opening scenes of exemplary economy. Baker, as a working-class junior officer, had caused an impact in **The Cruel Sea** with his coarse gibes to married officers just returned from shore leave – *risqué* at the time in British cinema. There is an echo of this boorishness in Morgan's verbal fencing with the stunned suspect who genuinely has not realized there is a corpse in another room. Morgan takes pleasure in announcing that he is no gentleman; a clear sense of displacement is achieved as he baits Van Rooyen into near-violence with comments which project onto the other man many of his own feelings and resentments. Why should a woman with such obvious expensive tastes think a relationship with Van Rooyen worthwhile, he asks. Morgan's class fixation, his resentment at the hierarchical structure of 'the force', becomes more obvious as he prowls the murder victim's rooms, gleefully seizing on apparent anomalies between the elegant woman of the suspect's recollections, and her garish taste in household designs and furnishings (a working-class prerogative, in his mind, seemingly) – 'You'd be surprised how often that kind end up in the morgue.' The script brings out his own fastidiousness with his constant Benzedrine-sniffing, to help him over a cold, and his insistence on drinking only milk on duty. Baker and Losey created these little bits of business to help illustrate the man's almost obsessive dedication.[19]

Morgan is so prone to brandish his proletarian roots that Kruger feels obliged to recite his own credentials – an upbringing as a miner's son – and Losey points up in flashbacks the young man's social incompatibility with the woman who became his pupil and an art lover. 'The poor are vulgar,' she tells him. 'It gives you a certain clumsy charm.'[20] Morgan, alert to nepotism and the tangled skein of the old-boy network, becomes more combative when aristocrat Sir Brian Lewis (suave Robert Flemyng) arrives as go-between to ensure Sir Howard Fenton of the Foreign Office (the woman's sometime lover) is not incriminated. The inspector by this time is beginning to harbour real doubts about Van Rooyen's guilt and reveals his growing unease with barely perceptible gestures and pauses, while still bombarding the suspect with questions. Sir Brian then ups the ante with veiled blackmail threats. 'You need more than a constable's mentality to reach the top,' he tells Morgan, whose interrogation gambits and ideas about rigid class stations, and his notions (despite his own cynicism) that the upper classes are somehow incapable of acts of brute murder, threaten to be Fenton's ally and Van Rooyen's downfall. But the inspector's tenacity and cynicism win out as he pieces together the jigsaw in a finale marred slightly by melodramatics and plot improbabilities and Losey's misguided attempts to milk the ending for pathos. Morgan cannot suppress his elation on finally nailing Lady Fenton but the emotions are linked with his ideas of how people of rank should behave. It is Baker's playing you remember from **Blind Date** as his character's obduracy and bludgeoning approach are gradually tempered and a certain reticence takes over. It remains the performance of his career in the cinema.

Losey's **The Criminal** (1960), is a more arresting film visually and contains many more bravura directorial flourishes and some highly effective setpieces. Yet Baker's central character Johnny Bannion is a stereotype to an extent, despite Losey's attempts to introduce religious guilt in his make-up. Baker is still riveting, suggesting the man's psychosis, barely suppressed rage, and latent power. The scenes with Bannion in the world outside are the least impressive. Based on an original story by Jimmy Sangster, **The Criminal** boasted the first script for Losey by Alun Owen, the Liverpudlian later based in Wales. Owen's work for TV in the late 1950s and throughout the 1960s – often in Wales – established him as one of the more original of the post-Osborne 'kitchen sink' dramatists. Only token attempts are made to soften Bannion's hard-boiled image or furnish him with some sort of valid past. He is an Irish Catholic and a rather clumsy line in the script establishes that he is *persona non grata* with his church. Bannion, the archetypal recidivist harbouring a fistful of grudges, is thawed out a little by his relationship with his new girlfriend Suzanne (Margit Saad) during his brief freedom from prison, and, in gaol, by his odd affinity with the simpleton Paul (Brian Phelan). The love scenes between Suzanne and Bannion, containing so much latent aggression, are among the most erotic in 1960s British cinema.

The Criminal is a film of jagged edges and seething tensions; Losey emphasizes this with the bursts of music which punctuate the action, from the caustic calypsos of the black gaol inmate to the jazz of John Dankworth and Cleo Laine. Bannion's own combustible personality provides the tinder box in scenes with his strident first girlfriend Maggie (Jill Bennett), and with Patrick Magee's sadistic chief warder, Burroughs, with whom Bannion has a sinister, symbiotic relationship. The link is confirmed when Burroughs, in a mixture of impotence and half-crazy exultation, bangs his chain on the rails to dull the sounds of the jailbreak he senses will be Bannion's undoing. His 'hear no evil, see no evil' policy makes Burroughs an implicit collaborator, both in the riot scene and when Bannion arranges the beating up of a

SECTION 3

Winds of
Change – The
Welsh Impact
on Post-War
Cinema

'stoolie' Kelly (Kenneth Cope). Later, Burroughs turns a blind eye to the likelihood of violence when he allocates Bannion to a cell with a psychopath. One scene, in and around a night club, though unconvincingly frenetic, indicates succinctly Bannion's alienation from his fellow hoodlums – and particularly his associate (Sam Wanamaker). Losey emphasizes this by regularly isolating the Baker character within the frame.

The critical seduction scene with Suzanne emphasizes Bannion's 'loner' status. He is more suspicious than flattered when he finds this enticing girl in his bed, and even when he succumbs, it is grudging. When he is shopped and returned to gaol, she declares her love, but Bannion can only reply: 'If I could say it I would.' There is no comfort to be gleaned by a self-absorbed man who has lost the ability to express honest emotions. When Bannion meets his fellow conspirators at an empty park bandstand to plan a racetrack haul, the editing and Losey's subtle camera positions emphasize the lack of camaraderie between the crooks. The scene prepares us for **The Criminal**'s eventual betrayal when he is sprung from gaol so he can – unintentionally – lead the others to his stash of gold buried in a field. After his escape, Bannion finds he has been snared by new-style corporation hoods – just as Lee Marvin's heavy becomes an anachronism in John Boorman's thriller, **Point Blank** (1967). 'Your sort do not fit into the organization,' Bannion is told in a scene climaxing in the final car chase. Wounded, he stumbles across a snowbound field to his buried hoard, but is shot like a dog before he can reach it and dies, delirious, declaiming mumbo-jumbo prayers to the God he feels has deserted him. The Baker loner frequently feels cut off from a past he has partly renounced, yet alienated from 'allies' in different social strata (elements which figured strongly in his most personal project, **Zulu**). Bannion seems crippled by his Catholicism. The religious element might seem almost gratuitous if it did not also render him an 'outsider', a misfit even in prison society.

The problem with the film is that Losey seems afraid to let the temperature drop and to shade in small details which might have made us care more about what makes Bannion tick. The club scenes, with their hollow *bonhomie*, demonstrate Bannion's tenuous relationships with his so-called 'friends' well enough, but carry less significance for him than his umbilical links with the Church, which weigh down on him just as Welsh Nonconformism bears down on Baker's character Tyvian in **Eve**. For all the felicities of the prison scenes, and the careful build-up of violence, Owen and Losey pull us only periodically into the criminal's psyche. Baker's performance, though, is creepily intense, despite the impressionistic nature of much of the script and Owen's failure to flesh out the predators who surround him after his final release.

SECTION 3

Winds of
Change – The
Welsh Impact
on Post-War
Cinema

Eve (Italian title **Eva**, 1961) is the least convincing of the Baker–Losey films, perhaps because it was slashed by the producers Robert and Raymond Hakim from 2hrs. 30mins. to around 2hrs. 10 mins., and re-dubbed.[21] But it is a fascinating portrait of a Welsh protagonist's duplicity and desire to inhabit a different world. Baker's character Tyvian, after claiming credit for a book written by his miner-brother, finds that *la dolce vita* in Europe is a chimera. **Eve** – from a James Hadley Chase novel – remains interesting for what it reveals of common perceptions of the Welsh and their preoccupations, and for its attempts to convey the exile's sense of dislocation. Both Tyvian and the enigmatic Eve (Jeanne Moreau) are self-regarding. Losey set out to use Baker's Welshness to present the character's 'machismo . . . none too attractive personality, his aggressiveness, his gentleness, his awareness, and his comparative lack of education'.[22] Yet all the characters in the film seem bogus, as if distorted by the Welshman's value judgements. The views we are offered are always highly subjective, as Tyvian builds up a spurious picture of his past, and attempts to live up to an assumed role, while dancing attendance on Moreau's mercurial courtesan.

In the opening voice-over, Tyvian harks back to his Welsh days. We soon discover he is addressing friends in an Italian tavern, assuming a pose, and trading on the Europeans' romantic/clichéd views of Wales: 'This bowler hat had to serve for funerals, weddings, important union meetings and all the gatherings at chapel – and chapel was very important to my father, a very religious man.' Tyvian's tone becomes almost hectoring, as he adopts the Valleys' speech cadences, talking of his brother who was 'mother and father to me' and 'in his spare time he did happen to be one of the best bloody coal miners in south Wales.' This risible bombast is typical as he jabbers about the past, employing lurid imagery, and the music develops an urgent jazz rhythm. And Losey begins to move between present and past. During one Venice Film Festival celebrity circus, we meet a coterie of friends and hangers-on. The film producer, Branca, working with Tyvian on a screen project, is clearly not enamoured of the writer and needles him when the writer passes up a drink: 'I had gathered that the Welsh were a great drinking people, Mr Jones.' Tyvian's ripostes acknowledge the stereotyping: 'And all Italians are great lovers' – and immediately Losey has established the film's central concerns as he flirts with notions of myth, sexual politics and power games, national imagery and self-image.

Losey introduces us to Eve as an interloper in Tyvian's flat. Her function in the plot as catalyst, devil's advocate and confidante who disrupts the writer's life and flushes out all his lies and deceit is signalled in these early scenes, when Losey makes much of her sensuality and narcissism. Tyvian's wish to establish rights over Eve leads to his malaise and unhappiness. In an early scene, Losey cuts from Baker to the object of desire – a huge close-up of Moreau's face inclined to camera, as she lies sideways on the bed. The choice of shot hints that Eve is not merely an object of lust. She has become the repository of all his hopes; he projects on her all his desires. From this moment, Moreau dominates the film. Tyvian is aggressive and direct in his overtures but, at first, she resists and Losey surrounds Eve with a strong aura of sexuality. The director also introduces religious icons into sets, and in one club scene, when Tyvian and the courtesan touch fingers, the writer is clearly seeking support and faith. Losey's main characters are obsessed with how others view them – a point made explicitly in Losey's frequent use of mirror and goldfish-bowl imagery.

As Tyvian builds up his chequered relationship with Eve, Branca reveals his suspicions about the authorship of Jones's best-selling novel, and before long, Tyvian is almost betraying himself to Eve. 'Once the chapel's in your blood, it's a devil to get rid of it. You just can't forget,' he tells her, then reveals that despite trading on the success of a book based on mining experiences, he only spent six weeks down the pit. Eve mocks the Welshman's intensity, and the switch of control in their power games is made manifest in a reprise of his earlier attempted seduction of Eve. She delivers the line he has shot at her in his first clumsy overtures: 'Let's see what you can do.' The moment when Eve taps Tyvian's chin with her foot now suggests the erotic gambits of Moreau's character Celestine around foot-fetishism in Buñuel's **Diary of a Chambermaid** (1964). Tyvian is constantly reminded of his shortcomings in social class. At the bar later, he explodes: 'Can't you stop playing your bloody games for one night,' earning a rebuke from a foppish English voice: 'You're not in a pub in Swansea now.' When Losey finally cuts to the present, Tyvian talks about hearing the bell toll the past two years (more chapel guilt), and his full-time exile 'in my Babylon'. In a further flashback, we see that Eve has apparently rejected him, leaving for Greece, and more lucrative prostitution, with the parting shot: 'Bloody Welshmen.'[23]

Losey's film, while tackling important areas of 'Welshness', never has the assurance of tone needed to address those issues in a consistently provocative way. We are never sure of the realities of Tyvian's feelings, mainly due to some pretentious writing. We understand his guilt, but the dialogue, deliberately 'literary', rarely rings true. In its longest extant version, the film is overladen with metaphor but underplotted and finally seems fatally schematic, for all Losey's technical skills and visual flourishes.[24] Baker conveys the character's innate sensitivity and sense of inferiority and his obsession with Eve in quieter scenes, but seems less comfortable with the mood-swings and the frequent switches of tone, which probably owe much to the final editing. Baker certainly disowned the 2 hr. 10 min. film and never felt happy about the work later.

In **Accident** (1967), his last venture for Losey, Baker was cast as an abrasive Oxford don opposite Dirk Bogarde, as his suave colleague, in a study of regret, longing and petty jealousies festering beneath the surface of academic life. As in **Eve**, bells toll the reflexive actions of memory and the onset of guilt. Harold Pinter's elliptical dialogue gnaws at characters' nerve ends. Losey shuttles back and forward in time as he homes in on a supposedly respectable mature quartet: Stephen (Bogarde), Charley (Baker), Anna (Jacqueline Sassard), and a young student, William (Michael York), and shows them lacerating each other. Anna's baleful presence proves the catalyst for a serious examination of social and personal morality and group loyalty. Baker's importunate philanderer, an unwelcome house-guest of Stephen's, suggests both guilt and bitterness about the rift in his marriage, but his sexual voracity and fierce competitive instincts draw him into rivalry with York's student for Anna's attentions. Charley's earthy passions and forthright small talk lead to clashes with Bogarde's fastidious, slightly puritanical don. Much of the film takes place on a sultry Sunday in Oxford where, during a long meal with much drink, enmities surface. The tensions in the Baker and Bogarde characters spill over into general animosity, and Baker's ability to convey inner turmoil and unease and the character's innate selfishness was one of the film's pluses. He gained fine reviews for **Accident**, which climaxed a productive few years after his career seemed to hiccup in 1959, when Rank wound up his long-term contract.[25]

SECTION 3

Winds of
Change – The
Welsh Impact
on Post-War
Cinema

Losey made the Rhondda actor a bankable international star, but as early as 1960 he was Britain's no.4 box-office actor and became the highest-paid actor to work for BBC TV in Wales, commanding a £1,000 fee as an ageing mine-roof repairman – painfully conscious of his waning powers and athleticism – in **The Squeeze**.[26] The greatest satisfaction for Baker was the success of his pet cinema project, **Zulu** (1963), which he produced with Cy Endfield for his own Diamond Films and mounted after two years of research. Made for around 1.5 million dollars, it had grossed 12 million dollars world-wide by 1976.[27] **Zulu**, from a John Prebble story, is an unabashed celebration of 105 men of the South Wales Borderers (B Company, 2nd Battalion, 24th Foot), who were largely wiped out but held Rorke's Drift, scoring a pyrrhic victory against 4,000 legendary warriors of Chief Cetewayo in 1879. Eleven VCs were awarded after the battle, which ceased only when Cetewayo called off his men in deference to the bravery of the survivors and fallen. The film might easily have been just another xenophobic epic, long on action, a paean to selfless British courage, emphasizing the barbarity of natives revelling in the favourable odds. But although the film, released by Paramount, celebrates valour fairly conventionally and is crammed with stock types, from tetchy disciplinarian (Baker) to hell-raising maverick (James Booth), it manages to avoid the worst elements of national self-glorification. It does this admittedly partly by ignoring the strategic value of the stand itself and presenting it as a piece of bloody-mindedness on the part of Lieutenant John Chard (a non-Welshman played, paradoxically, by Baker).[28]

Endfield filmed the action scenes with panache, employing sweeping pans and lateral tracking shots, and eked out tension by excising natural sound in key scenes (notably as Cetewayo's men are poised to attack, then breaking the silence with the rattling of spears and the interaction of the men). But much of the film's interest stems from the tensions between the two central characters as Chard's dogmatism throws him naturally into conflict with the cavalier Lieutenant Bromhead (Michael Caine), a seeming upper-class dilettante. Baker's performance, one of his finest, suggested a self-critical, driven man, conscious of his fairly proletarian roots and susceptible to the baiting of the younger officer. Yet Baker's Chard *is* malleable, despite appearances, and at the finale, severely wounded, he voluntarily relinquishes command of the garrison to his former *bête noire*, Bromhead – by now almost his protégé.

Baker and Endfield are careful to introduce a specific Welsh dimension very early on, reminding audiences where the men hail from, and of their memories. Later, as tension increases, the script is laced with humour. Private Owen (Ivor Emmanuel), with a penchant for song, tells Bromhead that every Welsh regiment has its choir. Then another soldier, seen caressing a calf, recalls his own similar animal 'back home in Merioneth'. Later, there is a reference to the number of Joneses in 'a company with some foreigners from England'.

In the film's concise pre-credit sequence, the Zulus attack Lord Chelmsford's forces on the slopes of the Isandhwana mountain. The Swedish minister Witt (Jack

Stanley Baker (centre),
Michael Caine (right) in
heroic mood for *Zulu*.

Stanley Baker (centre),
Michael Caine (right) in
heroic mood for *Zulu*.

Hawkins) then risks his life to warn the soldiers after he hears of the massacre of 1,000 men at Isandhwana and of Cetewayo's impending arrival. The incipient friction between Chard and Bromhead surfaces when Bromhead opposes standing their ground with 100 men and suggests leading a column into the hills to ambush the Zulus. Chard retorts by issuing even the 'walking sick' with rifles to defend the garrison and its hospital, and even commandeering Witt's wagons. As the men's optimism gives way to sullen apprehension, a note of wry wit is struck when a wistful Merioneth man opines that 'this country's not as good as Bala and the lakes. No moisture in it – nothing to hold a man in his grave.' The comment seems prescient a moment later when thousands of Zulus approach to the south-west. Later, the soldiers observe that the chanting warriors have 'a good bass section but no top notes', a comment typical of the Welsh penchant for ironic humour under duress.

Significantly, only Bromhead and the malingerer Private Hook (Booth) question Chard's tactics. The British drop sixty warriors in the first raid. The film's tendency to decry violence while basking in it – or accepting its inevitability – is reasserted when the surgeon Reynolds (Patrick Magee), awash in the gore of brave men at the casualty station, damns Chard and 'all you butchers'. As the warriors finally attack again under bloodshot skies, the men sing 'Men of Harlech' ('in English, why not Welsh?', as critic Alexander Walker asked later) but Endfield intercuts sound and visuals to provide a rhythmic and dramatic climax.[29] As the Zulus attack again, it seems the defenders cannot survive, and the aggressors wind up saluting fellow braves and call off their siege (one of the most shamelessly emotional moments in all such action adventures).

The film received its world première in Johannesburg. Distributors Embassy later denied that the South African government invested in the film, but admitted it supplied manpower and animals. The hundreds of Zulus in the film were banned from seeing it, as the Publications Control Board of South Africa deemed it 'unfit for black African consumption'.[30]

After his last appearance for Losey, Baker concentrated, from his early forties, on his own venture, Oakhurst Productions, with Michael Deeley. For Oakhurst and producer Joseph E. Levine, the actor starred in **Robbery** (1967), a well-crafted thriller directed by Peter Yates, a fiction film patently based on the Great Train Robbery four years before. Baker played the leader of a gang plotting to raid the night train to Glasgow.[31] Oakhurst's later productions included **The Italian Job** (1969) with Michael Caine (but no Baker), and **Where's Jack?** (1969), when the Ferndale actor co-starred with Tommy Steele (improbably cast as eighteenth century highwayman Jack Sheppard).

Perhaps Baker's most challenging roles from the late sixties were in television: as a TV programme chief resisting the blandishments of a Minister (George Sanders) in order to obtain a revealing interview in HTV's **Fade Out** (1968); as the alcoholic psychiatrist in Harlech's **Graceless Go I**; and, most notably, playing the father in BBC's **How Green Was My Valley** (1976), opposite Siân Phillips, when he was already desperately ill with cancer. As the loving but firm patriarch, he was in his element, drawing on memories of his miner father for the role. For the big screen, Baker played a corrupt bank manager seeking to outwit his employers with a heist in Peter Hall's urbane but lightweight **Perfect Friday** (1970, one of those egregious caper films of the period), and the lead as the fretful, ageing secret agent in Peter Collinson's **Innocent Bystanders** (1972).[32]

Baker remained true to his roots and fiercely loyal to his background, and in the 1960s talked on Labour electoral platforms of the privations – and privileges – of his Rhondda upbringing. His status as actor and icon among Britain's first authentic virile working-class screen heroes has never been properly acknowledged, possibly because Losey's style sometimes obscured the actor's contribution from critics anxious to attach easy labels and unable to see the significance of performance outside a proletarian action-film context. The tensions Baker suggested – and which his characters often failed to sublimate – made him for almost two decades one of the most compelling of British male performers.

Richard Burton

For years before the end of his career, Richard Burton (1925–84) was mainly incarcerated in gung-ho potboilers, though even in this later wilderness there were grace notes – his Machiavellian O'Brien in **1984** (Michael Radford, 1984), for example, and his dignified lead in Losey's persistently undervalued **The Assassination of Trotsky** (1972). Any assessments of his contribution to cinema in Britain, or Wales, are, if anything, more problematic. After his screen début in **Last Days of Dolwyn**, Burton never appeared in another cinema film with a Welsh context save Andrew Sinclair's woebegone **Under Milk Wood** (1971) when he seemed uncharacteristically subdued and out of sympathy with the film's ideas. But Burton – with Baker, a director of HTV – occasionally lent both weight and distinction to television films from Wales, even though he felt occasional twinges of guilt about his failure to fulfil moral obligations to HTV and appear in work the channel originated. As the poet-narrator of Jack Howells's Oscar-winning short **Dylan** (1962) (made years into Burton's Hollywood sojourn), he displayed an unforced roguish charm which must have made many regret the years away from Britain. And his sonorous but unemphatic narration added considerably to John Ormond's BBC documentary/ screen essay **Borrowed Pasture** (1960).[33]

SECTION 3

Winds of
Change – The
Welsh Impact
on Post-War
Cinema

Burton appropriately penned a eulogy to Baker when the actor died, describing him as 'the authentic dark voice of the Rhondda Valley', 'with a face like a determined fist', and recalled his bitter humour and 'the look from the eyes when somebody was boring the marrow out of him'. For Burton and Baker shared some of the more physical characteristics, a certain sensuality and volatility on screen, and they have come to represent the darker broodier side of Welshness more than any other performers. As Wayne Drew noted, Baker personifies 'a certain notion of Celtic masculinity'.[34] At times it seemed as if both men, often suspicious and truculent on screen, could never believe their good fortune in being there and were always expecting someone to pop up at their shoulder to call in the debt. Burton, on film, was much more cerebral, his persuasiveness more insidious, even his outbursts seemed somehow premeditated. His insults often seemed designed more to goad into a corrosive counter-attack than to devastate. His more ambivalent characters delighted in verbal sparring and the acrid riposte. The Burton character would take refuge in a sardonic sally, merely preliminary to the next skirmish. Sometimes, as in **Who's Afraid of Virginia Woolf?** (1966) and **Look Back in Anger** (1959), he would attack by proxy, inculcating views via a third party who would, as likely as not, become an unconscious or unwilling ally. But the Welshman's screen bile was actually often directed at his own fictional character and seemed merely displaced.

In his first screen role, in **Last Days of Dolwyn**, he was perversely cast as Edith Evans's shy, inarticulate, adopted son, painfully conscious of his lack of 'the English' and grammar. The actor opted for a sort of staccato stage Welsh accent, and later dismissed his performance as 'lamentable'.[35] Burton, a protégé of his former school-master, P. H. (Philip) Burton (later a BBC Radio Wales producer), soon began to garner praise from stage critics, particularly in Shakespeare and work by the verse-dramatist Christopher Fry. He appeared in four British films (including an Irish terrorist role in **Now Barabbas was a Robber**, dir. Gordon Parry, 1949) before his first American feature, a version of Daphne Du Maurier's melodrama of suspense and paranoia, **My Cousin Rachel** (dir. Henry Koster, 1952), set in Cornwall. The Welsh prodigy, then on loan to 20th Century–Fox, played opposite Olivia De Havilland in a film deemed sufficiently torrid by censors to warrant script cuts. It gained him his first Academy Award nomination and Fox's publicity hyperbole insisted that with this performance he had 'taken his place amongst the greatest of contemporary screen actors'. The critic C. A. Lejeune was certainly captivated by a Burton 'so closely resembling a fiery young Laurence Olivier that he is bound to set Hollywood ablaze'.[36] But his fifties films were not good enough for that.

He starred as Marcellus, a bibulous, but moralistic Roman converted to Christianity and destined for martyrdom, in the first wide-screen Cinemascope feature, the Biblical epic **The Robe** (dir. Henry Koster, 1953), which did phenomenal business in Wales as elsewhere in Britain. However, for much of the 1950s he consolidated his stage reputation in Shakespeare while coasting through screen biopics which drew indifferent or hostile reviews. He acted in Robert Rossen's **Alexander the Great** (1956), for example, which seemed like a haven for the Welsh, with Stanley Baker and William Squire also employed. As Shakespearean actor Edwin Booth, brother of Lincoln's assassin, in **Prince of Players** (1955), Burton was directed by Phillip Dunne, who wrote the screenplay for both **The Robe** and, twelve years earlier, **How Green Was My Valley**.[37]

Burton at last found a role he could readily identify with as John Osborne's vitriolic mouthpiece, Jimmy Porter, in **Look Back in Anger**. Ironically, his lodger and mediator in marital squalls, Cliff (Gary Raymond), played the stereotyped but good-hearted Welshman and became the butt of many of Jimmy's more sulphurous comments. Burton was at his best in screen personas allowing him to express not merely dissatisfaction with his lot, but the sense of a thwarted (if not always focused) ambition – a man looking for a rewarding niche, or incentive which has eluded him. He essayed the Porter role in Tony Richardson's film when he was thirty-three (already too old, said some critics), but he brought to it the right amount of virility and bemusement at his inability to contain or channel his anger consistently. The strengths of Osborne's play, hardly vitiated by the film, are the contradictions in the Porter personality. He recoils from his bluestocking wife's innate snobbery, yet admires, however grudgingly, his élitist, patrician father-in-law, already anachronistic with his moral certainties which elude Jimmy and (by implication) a whole generation of young men devoid of 'good brave causes' in the 1950s.

SECTION 3

Winds of
Change – The
Welsh Impact
on Post-War
Cinema

Richardson's roots in the Free Cinema movement and his liking for liberating location camerawork are evident in the opening moments set in a jazz club and have a conviction rare in British cinema at the time. Yet the liberated energy of Jimmy, expressed in his music, seems to contrast too abruptly with his frequent enervation at home. There Jimmy turns his self-hate (his sense of having betrayed his class by marrying out of it) into a sustained verbal attack on his weary wife Alison (Mary Ure). Jimmy inwardly seethes but lacks the moral courage to break up his marriage. It is his nature to rail impotently, a tacit acknowledgement of his own compliance with the values he overtly reviles. It is also typical that once his wife leaves him and Jimmy has achieved freedom he should immediately plunge into a relationship with Helena the house-guest, a woman from the same social class as his spouse, and place himself in a double bind. Jimmy needs an audience *and a reason* for his invective as much as he needs a lover.

Burton always seems a little too self-aware, with not quite enough of the rough edges we expect from Osborne's anti-hero. But Richardson, after all, did soften the character considerably with scenes showing Jimmy's attachment to his surrogate mother, Ma Turner (Edith Evans). Burton often prospers when allowed to dominate the frame, as in pub scenes in which Richardson, through careful compositions, gives Jimmy precedence on screen over Ma Turner and Alison. Yet the actor lapses into staginess when asked to rant in close-up as the director finds no cinematic way of complementing the verbal anger – notably in Jimmy's outburst after Helena's arrival in the marital home, his diatribes against the church bells, and his tirade when his wife attends church with Helena. The film still gave satisfaction to Burton, who had virtually abandoned the stage to embrace more lucrative screen work, and perhaps was already aware that the bridge back to 'legitimate theatre' would be hard to rebuild. He was to enjoy another fruitful collaboration with Osborne and Richardson when playing George Holyoake, a radical nineteenth-century schoolmaster prosecuted for atheism in **A Subject of Scandal and Concern**, a 1960 BBC TV Sunday Play. Osborne used the Burton character as a mouthpiece for his own defence of individual freedom and expression. The actor again gained kudos from his performance as the martyred Archbishop in **Becket**, made for Hal Wallis and Paramount in 1964 (director Peter Glenville) when he acted in tandem with Peter O'Toole (as Henry II). He was also impressive as a disenchanted Haiti-based diplomat, again for Glenville, in MGM's **The Comedians** (1967) from Graham Greene's novel.[38]

Burton's finest screen performance, with Elizabeth Taylor, in *Who's Afraid of Virginia Woolf?*

It is possible to read elements of his performance in **Who's Afraid of Virginia Woolf?** as autobiographical. The focus of Albee's stage play and Ernest Lehmann's faithful script is Burton's academic, eaten away with self-loathing – (which, as in **Look Back**, is induced partly by what he sees as an opportunistic and emotionally sterile marriage). Burton, as an instinctive actor with intellectual pretensions, often expressed aspirations for the academic career he might have had if he had pursued the Oxford scholarship he gained through Philip Burton's tutelage. It seems likely that his feelings about a wider academic world gave an intensity to his performance that he was rarely able to sustain elsewhere. Perhaps, also, he was only too aware of the hermetic world he had entered as highly paid screen consort to Elizabeth Taylor (b. 1932) in a series of films following his Mark Antony in **Cleopatra** (dir. Joseph Mankiewicz, 1963), which placed him in the category of stellar earners.[39] Nothing in Burton's subsequent performances matched his achievement in **Virginia Woolf** where his adroit, and sometimes stunning, stage timing dictates the pace, and carries the emotional weight of the film. His George is trapped in marriage to Martha (Taylor), strident daughter of the university president, and only able to escape into alcohol or relentless role and game playing (the similarities with Jimmy Porter's plight are obvious). During a long, woozy evening the couple play host to a pair of young marrieds (George Segal and Sandy Dennis), and their fears, illusions and skeletons surface as George and Martha slug it out after using their guests as sparring partners. George finally forces his wife to accept publicly that the child she fantasizes about does not exist.

Burton is superb as the burned-out history lecturer, still sharp enough to deflect Martha's taunts and home in, with his own acerbic jibes, on her frailties and the naked ambition of the Segal character. Director Mike Nichols makes effective use of unflattering close-ups. Martha's features are bloated, ravaged by years of heavy drinking; George looks gaunt and shell-shocked, especially in the long outdoor scene by the swing when he regales Segal with a story of the traumas of his boyhood friend which may be as fictional as Martha's 'recollections' of her son. Burton nudges nuances from every scene in a performance of extraordinary assurance in which he veers from punchbag to predator. He is at his best when George reveals the full extent of his self-hatred in appearing to acquiesce in Martha's judgement of him. The Burtons were never again to appear together so effectively, and it was fitting reward when Burton gained one of his seven – unsuccessful – Oscar nominations. Taylor benefiting hugely from her husband's advice and encouragement, took the Academy Award as Best Actress for the second time, following her success with **Butterfield** 8 (1960).

Throughout the sixties Burton received rewarding roles. The Welshman was at his most dissolute as the defrocked priest in John Huston's version of Tennessee Williams's hothouse world in **Night of the Iguana** (1964), a part which allowed him to be astringent, maudlin and amusing by turns.[40] His self-critical former cleric turned coach-tour guide managed to be oddly touching in scenes when he established a rapport with Deborah Kerr's spinster, or seemed mortified by his fractious relationship with his former love (Ava Gardner) – and Burton savoured the cadences of the Williams lines. He was also convincingly robust and ebullient in Zeffirelli's lively if superficial version of **Taming of the Shrew** (1967). But the finest of his late 1960s roles was undoubtedly the angst-ridden John le Carré anti-hero of **The Spy Who Came in from the Cold** (dir. Martin Ritt, 1967). Burton's hard-drinking fated victim Leamas, living a half-life in London and concealing his real role from his new love (Claire Bloom), is one of the outstanding portraits of the entire spy genre. The film effectively deglamorizes the agent's profession, with Leamas constantly harping on his ordinary qualities. He sees himself merely as a technician 'who doesn't believe in either God or Karl Marx'.

A filmed record also remains of Burton's New York stage performance as **Hamlet** (1964), in John Gielgud's production, when the actor acquitted himself well, delivering the lines with great authority, and playing action scenes with aplomb. Unfortunately the film itself is cheap and technically inept, with a fixed camera often at the wrong angle to do justice to actors or text and unable to capture, during two live performances, enough key close-ups. One can still see why Burton had made such an impact in the role at London's Old Vic ten years earlier.

Burton became a director of HTV in the late 1960s, but his television appearances – on any channel – were disappointingly few. There was one disastrous and embarrassingly bland 1974 Central TV revival of **Brief Encounter** (dir. Alan Bridges) with Burton cast opposite Sophia Loren, a pale shadow of the actress who played with such feeling in De Sica's **Two Women** (1960). Bridges later claimed Burton showed scarcely any interest in the project.[41] But as the narrator of the BBC's **Borrowed Pasture** back in 1960, Burton was commendably self-effacing and the clarity of the diction, the familiar, almost sepulchral, tones, did justice to John Ormond's prose-poetry. He was even more effective in Jack Howells's short **Dylan** (1962), catching in his performance much of the melancholy and wry self-deprecation of the poet's public persona.[42]

In 1969, Burton delivered a conscientious performance in a personal project helping Professor Nevill Coghill at Oxford to realize a cinema production of **Dr Faustus**, (with Elizabeth Taylor in a cameo as Helen of Troy). The film was neither as passionate nor as terrifying as the Marlowe play warranted. The Welshman earned an Oscar nomination the same year, as Henry VIII in the Hal Wallis production of **Anne**

of a Thousand Days for Universal, and there were two ambitious homosexual roles in Stanley Donen's two-hander, **Staircase** (1969) from Charles Dyer's stage play, playing opposite Rex Harrison, and the title role of Michael Tuchner's disappointingly histrionic London gangster movie **Villain** (1971). Burton's most worthwhile later performances were probably as the mellowing, if still tetchy, doomed Russian revolutionary hero in Mexican exile in **The Assassination of Trotsky** with Alain Delon as the icepick killer, and as Peter Firth's psychiatrist-mentor in the screen version of Peter Shaffer's stage play **Equus** (1977).[43] He was convincingly menacing opposite John Hurt's Winston Smith in **1984** but the most taxing performance in later films was undoubtedly in the title role of Tony Palmer's nine-hour **Wagner** (1983).[44]

Burton's one cinema venture into Wales in his later career, playing the First Voice and Guide in **Under Milk Wood** (1971), proved desperately disappointing, despite director Andrew Sinclair's avowed admiration for Dylan Thomas, and especially after Burton's success in the radio version. Sinclair had cherished the project for years and was anxious to preserve fidelity to the externals of Dylan's 'play for voices'. The casting was remarkable in the climate of a commercial British production of the time, harking back to the fifties Welsh comedies with its emphasis on indigenous actors. The budget was only £300,000, with the National Film Finance Corporation chipping in £100,000 and Burton and O'Toole each pocketing £10,000 expenses in lieu of salary. The film was shot in Fishguard and other Thomas stamping grounds in just five days.[45] 'This is a 90 per cent Welsh production which is as it should be,' Sinclair said during production, and critic David Wilson described the cast – with Peter O'Toole (Captain Cat) and Elizabeth Taylor (Rosie Probert) the only significant 'outsiders' – as 'almost like an Eisteddfod rollcall'. But the film's flaws were prefigured in another statement from Sinclair during shooting: 'The play is an incantation to imagination. But what I'm doing is to make concrete what is imagination.'[46]

Sinclair admired the opulent visual style of director Max Ophuls with its 'continuous fluid' camera movements, and he sought to evoke nostalgia by shooting through gauze to produce muted or softened colours. The limitations of this approach are exposed in the scenes when Captain Cat revives memories of Rosie Probert (the soft fuzzy edges of the frame serve to nullify rather than create any sense of magic). The presence of Ryan Davies as a ubiquitous silent watchdog trooping along in the wake of Burton's narrator, perhaps representing the writer's conscience, seems a laboured and unnecessary scripting device. Sinclair described Thomas as a 'people's poet' and considered himself a 'populist', but his attempt to render literally on screen the shenanigans of the dramatist's characters seems dismally prosaic and the director is unable to give them any extra dimension divorced from Thomas's poetry.[47] In one sequence, Burton seduces an all but anonymous girl in a barn, while Davies looks on. It is a crude, ineffectual attempt to convey the earthier, sensual elements of Dylan's work. The stylized pub dance of Ray Smith's Mr Waldo near the finale, another gratuitous screen invention, also indicates Sinclair's failure to register the characters as individuals with their own endearing foibles rather than as crude types. The scene looks like a laboured Bacchanalian interlude and the Burton/Davies frolicking around the Bethesda graveyard is equally irksome. The film, shown at the Venice Film Festival, had a justifiably rough reception from critics and audiences.[48] Sinclair's approach was distinctly heavy-handed. He seemed to lack confidence in and appreciation of the unwitting humour of Revd Eli Jenkins's ingratiating exhortations and eulogy on nature, insisting – to the disgust of actor Aubrey Richards – that the speech should be capped with the words 'Thank you, God, for listening to me', the better to win a cheap laugh.[49] Sinclair then shot the character's key scene, inexplicably, in long shot. All the scenes featuring a miscast Victor Spinetti as Mog Edwards were shoddy and frenetic.

Burton, rendered speechless in the film with his First Voice only heard in voice-overs, rambled through Llareggub looking morose and lost; the miming and carousing scenes added little. Compensations included pleasing cameos from Glynis Johns as Myfanwy Price, Vivien Merchant (Mrs Pugh), Siân Phillips (Mrs Ogmore Pritchard) and Angharad Rees as a voluptuous but virginal Gossamer Beynon. **Under Milk Wood** was another example of a project initiated by an outsider coming to grief, and it certainly lacked the popular appeal of the 1950s TV version which proved a first-rate example of ensemble acting from a team which had lovingly nurtured their roles through stage productions and which benefited from the exuberance and boyish zest of Donald Houston. Siân Phillips summed up Sinclair's film: 'The director, who had written the screenplay, was besotted with Dylan and very knowledgeable, but perhaps he tried to rationalize everything too much. Just one voice [as narrator] would have done. I don't know how you make a film of it. It's, as Dylan said, a play for voices.'[50]

Rachel Roberts

A Welsh actress was to make an enduring impression in New Wave sixties features – in raw and hard-edged working-class roles. The familiar screen persona of Rachel Roberts (born Llanelli 1927, d. 1980) is a middle-aged woman living on her nerve ends, unable to conceal her sense of inadequacy but sucked inexorably into damaging relationships or desperate situations. As time went on the roles began to mirror the vicissitudes of her own life.

Roberts, an earthy, bold actress, adept at conveying a ripe or repressed sexuality, was the outstanding female screen presence in the so-called 'kitchen sink' dramas of the fifties and sixties. Off the screen, in late Californian exile, she was always ready to emphasize her Welsh roots (even when not playing Welsh characters she could hardly restrain the sing-song lilt in her rapid delivery). She used aspects of her background for her riveting working-class portraits and, to the end, retained the cadences of her home area.[51] Her roles sometimes reflected aspects of her own problematic personality: in HTV's **The Old Crowd** (1978), for example, as a lusting, mercurial theatrical in Lindsay Anderson's version of a slightly obtuse Alan Bennett work bemoaning the decline of Britain into moral decadence. And, increasingly, Roberts was cast in roles which, in hindsight, seemed to prefigure her fate as an alcoholic and suicide. Her strained psychiatrist's wife in HTV's **Graceless Go I**, opposite Stanley Baker (a teaming never to be repeated), and her repressed, toping schoolmistress Mrs Appleyard in Peter Weir's Australian feature, **Picnic at Hanging Rock** (1976), sliding towards self-extinction, became, in retrospect, painful to watch. Her triple role in Lindsay Anderson's **O Lucky Man!** (1973) included a section as a Welsh homebody obsessed by her failure to cope with life, and who kills herself after dutifully completing her chores. The episode, devised by Anderson as a satire on her role in **This Sporting Life**, was excised on the film's American release.[52] Roberts became increasingly difficult to employ in the late 1970s, as her private life fell apart and her obsession with the failure of her marriage to Rex Harrison proved a crippling career distraction.

Rachel Roberts – perhaps
the most talented of Welsh
screen actresses.

Her stature hinges on her redoubtable British Film Academy Award-winning performances as the exploited mistress of Albert Finney's cavalier Arthur Seaton in **Saturday Night and Sunday Morning** (dir. Karel Reisz, writer Alan Sillitoe); and as Mrs Hammond, the landlady offering bed and board to Richard Harris's rugby league player Frank Machin in **This Sporting Life** (written by David Storey, and directed by Anderson).[53] There is a marvellous scene in a graveyard, in the latter movie, when the actress's Welshness surfaces with dialogue expressing her shame about her kept-woman status. Roberts is unforgettably tense in the more intimate household scenes, caught between her devotion to her dead husband, her sexual guilt and unacknowledged feelings for Machin, who attracts her but repels with his arrogance. In both films, Roberts played a woman striving to maintain her defences and finding it difficult to accept her emotions – but the mask of stoicism was constantly slipping. The role is undeniably affect-ing, if slightly passive. It is somehow a relief that we can also remember her cheerful extrovert in **Valley of Song** and that she also left on screen a TV version of E. A. Whitehead's stage hit, **Alpha Beta** (1973), a very different performance as a long-suffering wife – this time vituperative and foul-mouthed and trading rancorous revelations with Albert Finney as the spouse. She was also memorable as a predatory Northerner lusting after Nicol Williamson's vengeful businessman in Jack Gold's thriller, **The Reckoning** (1960).

Roberts's Appleyard, with her awful bun wig and clenched features, in **Picnic at Hanging Rock**, and her joyless Teutonic traveller in **Murder on the Orient Express** (1974), seemed almost to caricature aspects of her former roles, but she had a more rewarding opportunity as the understanding confidante of the young lovers (Lisa Eichhorn as her daughter, and Richard Gere) in John Schlesinger's **Yanks** (1979), which landed her a British Film Academy Best Supporting Actress award. Roberts and Baker remain the true Welsh working-class stars of the British cinema, and it is to be hoped that the Wales Film and TV Archive, as it develops, will acknowledge and house their legacy.

SECTION 4 TELEVISION AND A WELSH FILM 'MINI-BOOM'

Here lies a shoemaker whose knife and hammer

Fell idle at the height of the summer,

Who was not missed so much as when the rain

Of winter brought him back to mind again

He was no preacher but his working text

Was See all dry this winter and the next

Stand still. Remember his two hands, his laugh

His craftsmanship. They are his epitaph.

(John Ormond, 'Lines at his father's grave',
Requiem and Celebration, Christopher Davies, 1969)

The television era, which began in Wales in 1952/3, soon led to the demise of the B movies.[1] By the sixties many of the cinemas themselves had disappeared. Nothing quite compensated for the shutdown of picture palaces (or the creative impoverishment of British films in a declining industry through the fifties) but there were a few obvious benefits in TV's arrival. Indigenous drama, plays written by the Welsh for the Welsh, at last reached the screen. A repertory company of performers could be developed, including some of the casualties when the flow of B movies dried up; writers (such as Alun Owen, Elaine Morgan and – a little later – Ewart Alexander) were encouraged.

More significant, perhaps, for the majority audience was the opportunity to see events in Wales unfold almost as they happened, via the television news and current affairs services. These soon removed the *raison d'être* of the major cinema newsreels, Pathé and Gaumont, which invariably presented Welsh items with a marked time delay and tended, even up to the late 1950s, to dwell on soft news/human interest stories presented in a relentlessly patronizing or facetious tone, or to feature events (ceremonies/exhibitions) which were as predictable to see as to stage. Wales had been served best by the newsreels as long ago as the 1920s, in the years either side of sound when the Topical Budget, a twice-weekly London-based cinema magazine, for years under newspaper magnate Sir Edward Hulton, offered lively competition to the 'big two', even if it featured in only a minority of Welsh cinemas. The Budget certainly concentrated more heavily on British material, though much was innocuous. National emergencies at least drew blood with proprietors showing their hand. One notorious Topical Budget issue, bearing the title **The Greatest Menace of 1921**, bore heavily-loaded intertitles: 'While the mines were flooding, miners watch Cardiff play Nottingham Forest' . . . '3000 gallons pouring in at Llwynypia but 25 men have been permitted to pump' . . . 'Types of the pit ponies which were left to drown in some of the mines'.[2]

Much of the newsreels' coverage of sport was of a high standard but the blandness of much of their material perhaps accounts for their assiduous pursuit of the 'Welsh Wizard' David Lloyd George who featured in 25 per cent of the Welsh material from Topical Budget. TB and the big two scrambled for footage in the silent early twenties concluding that even a dumb Minister of Munitions and, later, Prime Minister, offered better entertainment than many of the soporific hardy annual events. Lloyd George was the most charismatic and camera-conscious of the politicians, though Bonar Law trumped him by inviting Topical's camera into Downing Street for shots of the new Cabinet after the Manchester-born Welshman's coalition crumpled in 1922. Much TB footage of Lloyd George, from around 1915 on, survives in London's National Film Archive.[3]

In the 1920s the Eisteddfod was a fixture of the newsreel, and for three years at least (from 1927 to 1929) Topical even shot the Llandudno May Queen celebrations. After the company folded in 1931, the service to Wales was much thinner, until the Mining Review films, produced by the National Coal Board, appeared regularly in the commercial cinemas from the 1940s onwards. Though these were often generous in tribute to the miners, they were patently filleted of potentially contentious material.[4]

Television obviously had much greater immediacy. Effective service only began in Wales in February 1953 when the country shared an outside broadcast unit with the West of England. BBC drama in Wales flourished from the mid-fifties and into the sixties as D. J. Thomas (a pioneer with Dafydd Grufydd) built on his reputation as producer of the live **Under Milk Wood** (ironically shot at Lime Grove). The creative film and drama contribution of independent television in Wales was always more problematic, though south Wales cinema exhibitors were right to be sufficiently worried by the advent of commercial TV to send a deputation to Westminster.

TWW (Television Wales and the West), with studios at Pontcanna, Cardiff, had a mere eight hours of programming for Wales each week (some in Welsh) when it went on air in 1958, though this had increased to 11 or 12 hours by the mid-sixties. Few works of merit in drama or documentary emerged in those years – certainly little attracted the interest of the networks. As the Welsh comedy writer Peter Tinniswood pointed out: 'When it lost the franchise in 1968, only **Land of Song** [a Welsh entertainment programme trading on stereotypes] had been a network success, though TWW had produced one or two well received documentaries.'[5] The channel gained kudos from screening the Welsh Oscar-winning documentary **Dylan** (1962), and topped £2 million profits in its last year. But its demise was generally unlamented, with Welsh MP Ness Edwards, former Labour spokesman on broadcasting issues, complaining that the channel had ignored the social and political life of Wales and dismissing the amount of locally originated programmes as 'small and trivial'.[6] The neglect of important contemporary issues was stressed by Welsh Labour MPs to Lyn Evans, ITA officer for Wales, months before the axe fell on TWW. Certainly, expectations that some emphasis might be placed on Welsh films or drama might have been raised with Sir Ifan ab Owen Edwards and British film-maker Sidney Gilliat (later to make **Only Two Can Play** in Swansea) on the board and £50,000 of TWW money invested in British Lion, the company set up as a consortium of directors – including Bryan Forbes and the Boulting Brothers. TWW chairman Lord Derby said investment would give TWW 'a strong interest' in any move by British Lion to make television films. More of the channel's cash was also tied up in West End theatres – impresario Jack Hylton was a TWW board member. But, in retrospect, no one could have expected the channel to encompass the realities of Welsh life when it was capable of the crass and sexist pronouncements which accompanied the decision to oust women TV newsreaders in 1963. 'It's a distraction for viewers when attractive young women have to put over unpleasant news,' said Wyn Roberts, then TWW production controller, later Welsh Office Minister. 'Some girls are likely to be emotionally involved, particularly when tragedies involving children have to be announced.'[7]

The language lobby had grown increasingly vociferous after a TV conference in Cardiff in 1959 created the momentum leading to the launch in 1962 of a short-lived Welsh-language channel, Teledu Cymru (Wales, West and the North), based in purpose-built studios at Western Avenue, Cardiff. Directors included Plaid Cymru leader Gwynfor Evans (later to play *the* crucial role in establishing S4C); John Roberts Williams, the film-maker, was news editor. But the venture had lost £220,000 by May 1963 and ceased to provide local programmes after failing to reach financial targets. Roberts Williams claimed ' . . . a brave dream has gone down in a maze of technicalities and finance – it has taken away the pleasures of the little people – those thousands who don't speak a word of English from one week to the next.'[8] Various reasons were advanced for WWN's demise, including failure to estimate revenue positions and to erect and operate transmitters on time. The *South Wales Echo*, never a friend of the language, considered the problem of reviving interest in Welsh was 'massive' and concluded, perhaps a trifle prematurely, that it could not possibly on

CHAPTER 16

Teething

Troubles –

and the

Documentary

Poets

this evidence 'be solved through the medium of television'.[9] TWW absorbed Teledu Cymru and continued to supply some Welsh programmes until its disappearance.

More hope was invested in Harlech when it took over the franchise from TWW in 1968 and bought the Pontcanna studios. Journalist and producer John Morgan and broadcaster Wynford Vaughan-Thomas became driving forces in the launch, with Vaughan-Thomas as programme director, but a crucial element in the company's bid was the presence on the board of Stanley Baker and Richard Burton and the promise of appearances from Harry Secombe and Welsh baritone Geraint Evans. Burton and Elizabeth Taylor had their own production company and would supposedly make films in Wales; Baker and Burton would appear in occasional 'spectaculars', and Baker would star in an adventure series, the local press announced. Vaughan-Thomas claimed the company had assurances from the two male stars that 'they want to work in Wales for a considerable proportion of their time'. Their presence would ensure international appeal and overseas sales, and HTV had provided a stable base by linking up Wales with a West Country consortium, headed by the *Bristol Evening Post* chairman Walter Hawkins. Vaughan-Thomas was scathing of TWW efforts, deriding their claim to be charting new territory in Wales, and stressing the lack of creative input from inside Wales. 'Pioneers, hell', he said. 'They were plush white settler.' The main TWW shareholders had included the *News of the World*, Imperial Tobacco and Lord Derby.[10] But any promises made – if they *were* made to HTV by the actors – soon sounded hollow as other commitments meant Baker and Burton rarely appeared on the screen after their presence at the opening night spectacular.

The new channel, under chairman Lord Harlech, commissioned new dramas from Alun Owen and Ewart Alexander; Colin Voisey as head of film produced a few fine documentaries; but through the sixties and seventies the Welsh studio's contribution was persistently overshadowed by Bristol's, and their networked creative programming and its drama output was relatively small, on the admission of HTV Wales controller Huw Davies, who made most of the best-remembered works himself as a tiro director.[11] There were dismal fallow years before a partial revival of drama in the 1980s, when all the channels were forced to respond to some degree to the arrival of S4C, which traded on home-grown talent but more importantly raised the level of debate about programme content and made the other Welsh studios more aware of the need to cater for their own people. These needs have never been met satisfactorily, as the following pages will show, but S4C was adventurous enough to usher in a surprising mini-boom of independent film companies and to raise the Wales profile internationally, instigating and/or backing films which reached the major festivals (and achieved West End openings) – and creating an animation industry. In the initial TV years, though, the greatest single contribution to film in Wales came, from the late fifties, in the documentary sphere, where two outstanding directors emerged, focusing more sharply on aspects of their homeland than anyone previously operating in the area of Welsh factual cinema.

Ormond and Howells: two spellbinders

In 1990 Wales lost two distinctive, and distinguished film-makers who did perhaps more than anyone else to forge a national documentary tradition. The deaths of John Ormond (b. 1923) and Jack Howells (b. 1913), who lived their last years a few hundred yards apart in the Canton/Pontcanna areas of Cardiff, reminded us forcefully of

John Ormond – a distinctive voice in documentaries for almost three decades.

the impact both made from the 1950s to the 1970s with their stimulating personal films, biographies and character studies. Both had strong literary leanings (Ormond was one of Wales's finest published poets) and a tendency towards the lyrical on screen, but much of their strength derived from intense identification with their subjects. The two film-makers also had links with news and television reporting which enabled them to produce work of contemporary significance, rooted in the local community. The routine efforts of Wales's sponsored documentary journeymen paled by comparison.

Jack Howells, a former schoolmaster with something of the pedagogue lingering in his approach to material, was more obviously in the Grierson/Harry Watt tradition. His work revealed a strong visual sensibility and a taste for impressionism allied to a penchant for equally resonant verbal metaphor and wit which proved his saving grace. After making major cinema compilation films at Pathé, he shot a string of sponsored documentaries before regaining his personal voice with some strong, highly individual television shorts springing from his own Valleys experiences. As a BBC 'insider', John Ormond, a former *Picture Post* magazine journalist, was more prolific, producing a score of rich studies for television in Wales through the years. He was less prone than Howells to intercede in his work between the subject and viewers, much more willing to let his characters/interviewees speak for themselves. His best works have a powerful thematic coherence and reveal a sharp understanding of his characters' lives. The tensions and *frissons* in his work derive, in part, from his refusal to take a stance towards his protagonists; his **Borrowed Pasture** (1960) is so effective and ultimately poignant because it is neither didactic nor an unequivocal celebration of the stoicism and fortitude of its characters, two ex-Polish soldiers farming arid land in west Wales.

Before these two directors, most documentaries or drama-documentaries in Wales, from the mid-1940s on, had been largely unquestioning. There were occasional wartime screen ventures into rural Wales, sponsored films from government departments, or shorts offering idyllic glimpses of the Welsh countryside: works like **Around Snowdonia** (dir. Duncan Robbins, 1937), a north Wales travelogue, and **The Hidden Land** (dir. Hayford Hobbs, 1937) showing the gradual changes in the Welsh culture and landscape. W. B. Pollard's 1943 **Land of the Dragon** presented a broad canvas of life featuring obvious tourist scenes – Conwy, Caernarfon, the Snowdon railway, cockle-gathering and coracle fishing – with only token references to mining and unemployment.[12]

CHAPTER 16

Teething

Troubles –

and the

Documentary

Poets

Much more interesting were two films, still revived today, made in north Wales by the Brunner-Lloyd company.[13] Mark Lloyd directed **Noson Lawen – The Fruitful Year** (1950), filmed in both English and Welsh for the National Savings Committee. It was based on an original story by Sam Jones, the BBC's north Wales director, and featured characters from a radio programme there. Scripted by John Gwilym Jones, it portrayed a Welsh rural family and the rhythm of life in a small village: the harvesting, chapel-going, baking and, inevitably, life in the local post office. It made no attempt to invest its fictional villagers with glamour, even if episodes were linked by a slight narrative from the son of the family who had worked his way through the University College of North Wales, Bangor, gaining a first-class honours degree. Education as a means of social mobility was very much a preoccupation of the Welsh and their film-makers. The short ended with a *noson lawen*, a party of song and dance.

The *Monthly Film Bulletin* reviewer was impressed. The film might be 'slight and anecdotal' but captured its people with 'real sympathy and refreshing informality'; 'that authentic human approach' was much more important than occasional 'technical roughness'. 'The English version is as acute in its flavour of north Wales as **David** is of the south,' the reviewer considered, and he thought the two versions were far removed from 'the correct hygienic style' of so many run-of-the-mill sponsored documentaries. The film was low-key and unpretentious and had charm – even if it was less ambitious and far less distinctive than **David** – and it played to good houses in certain Welsh cinemas.

John Gwilym Jones also scripted the company's **A Letter from Wales** (1953), made by George Lloyd for the Children's Film Foundation and focused on the world of childhood. It showed us a small boy boating, fishing and rescuing a lamb. Again the film reflected an untroubled but essentially ordinary family life, and was made in the intimate narrative style of Ifan ab Owen Edwards's 1935 film **Y Chwarelwr/The Quarryman**.[14] George Lloyd's short should not be confused with **A Letter to Wales** (dir. Tony Thompson, 1960), one of two British Transport documentaries featuring Donald Houston. The Houston character's fond memories of Wales, as a London exile, unfold in flashback as he places his letter aboard the night mail train from Paddington. The film includes footage of Snowdonia and its railway, the holidaymakers of Holyhead, spectacular shots from a north Wales quarry railway at Llanberis, and the launch of the Tenby lifeboat. It is permeated with the narrator's *hiraeth* and also embraces symbols of progress: the new refinery at Milford Haven and hydro-electric projects. Use of colour in the Wales sequences, breaking up the monochrome, merely emphasized the sentimentalism of some laboured narrative contrivances. Lack of fluidity in the editing and inappropriate soundtrack music also jarred.

Every Valley (dir. Michael Clarke, 1957), with Houston as narrator, centred on the life of the industrial south Wales valleys from daybreak to midnight. Houston provided narration between orchestral interludes from Handel's *Messiah*. A similar 'outsider's' view was projected in **Letter from Llandudno**, a 1968 Connaught Productions film distributed by MGM, which presented the north Wales resort through the eyes of an American girl on holiday.

A compelling 'amateur'/independent film to emerge from the immediately post-war period was Evan Pritchard's **The Island in the Current** (*c*.1947), a tribute to the fishermen and people of Bardsey Island, off the Llŷn Peninsula, north Wales. Pritchard, an amateur film-maker, captured the essence of island life and its primitive economy with an affectionate eye. The film showed methods of farming now long abandoned, with liberal use of horse power; Pritchard, using colour, even provided a montage of the people, as if conscious of recording them for posterity. The film has rough edges and betrays its low budget, but Pritchard uses fades and cuts, and by intercutting conveys the powerful presence of the sea in all in inhabitants' lives. There are effective sunset shots of hardy, uncompromised figures moving over the landscape.

Some of these films were fairly anodyne programme-fillers – creative dead ends. When Howells and Ormond arrived on the scene, one was aware immediately of a more critical eye at work, and their editing skills were well honed before they began directing.

Jack Howells

Howells served his apprenticeship with Donald Alexander at the Documentary and Technicians Alliance, mainly writing, and in Pathé's cutting rooms in London.[15] DATA – in London's Soho Square – 'was an offshoot of Paul Rotha and in direct line from John Grierson. You couldn't get more purist that that,' Howells said later. Under Alexander, who was chairman and producer for a spell in the 1940s, DATA launched the twenty-five years of **Mining Review** magazine films – with many items shot in Wales. But Howells felt that Alexander and his fellow documentarians – 'middle-class Englishmen' – had a far too sentimental approach to Wales and the Welsh miner and were 'very earnest about it all'.[16] Yet Howells and Alexander had much in common, believing it was important to show 'the world the ordinary man lives in, and what he does'. Howells himself conceived his film role as teacher, preacher and wit, and it was his fidelity to the nuances of Welsh working-class speech and idioms that led him to break with DATA and Alexander, whose screen dialogue, to the Welshman, had a 'schooly, middle-class ring and often sounded incongruous in context'. In the 1980s, however, Howells still acknowledged his debt to Alexander who had advised him to 'sculpt from within, not try to superimpose'.[17]

The Welshman moved to Associated British Pathé, where he learned the editing craft on compilation documentaries, notably **The Peaceful Years** (1948) and **Scrapbook for 1933** (1949). He joined the newly formed Pathé documentary unit under editor Peter Baylis, who had already been fêted by critics for his 1947 compilation film **Scrapbook for 1922** (based on the successful radio series inspired by Leslie Bailey).[18]

Despite its meticulous craftsmanship and undoubted entertainment value, Howells's first film, **The Peaceful Years**, written with Peter Baylis, seems oddly bland now – though Howells claims the title was deliberately ironic. The dialogue is read by cosy, middle-class actor-commentators (Maurice Denham, James Hayter, Stuart Hubbard), whose tones alone seemed a placebo for those willing to forget the 1914–18 war or regard it as little more than a hiccup. There was no denying the film's technical skill, but it *was* unduly ingratiating and only barely touched on the darker side: the years of misery for many and the international conflicts (Spain, for example). Employing found footage, the film opens with 'the blast of war' and images of the conflict and 'millions dying for a mound of earth', but the downbeat note seems merely token as the positive mood is struck: 'The great thing was to be back in one piece', announces the narrator (Emlyn Williams) before early titles announce 18 million dead, 21 million maimed. Shots of the return of the Unknown Soldier and images of crippled soldiers give way swiftly to scenes of a world many thought shattered for ever by the

CHAPTER 16

Teething
Troubles –
and the
Documentary
Poets

Great War – punting on the river, a sea of racetrack toppers. Howells's puckish humour surfaces early on and his taste for metaphor surfaces in the narration over images of Versailles: '. . . once mighty empires lay ground in the dust and from the broken earth fertilized with blood new creeds were germinating, – creeds that were to spread their vines across all frontiers.' The Fascist Blackshirts' entry into history and footage of Lenin appear in the following montage. The facts of unemployment are accepted, but the treatment is schematic. The Pathé team attempted to pace the film for variety, slowing it down with graphics accompanied by what Howells conceded was 'a rather portentous but semi-poetic commentary'.[19] Scenes are developed piecemeal and are often included for curiosity value rather than to make thematic points, so the more serious rhetoric sounds increasingly hollow and fake. The device of multi-voice commentary is used (an idea culled from Carol Reed's wartime documentary **The True Glory**) but the working-class voice-overs seem ostentatious and condescending over shots of the Great Wembley Exhibition of 1924.

Occasionally, the film makes pertinent and unexpected political points. There is a slow camera pull-away from a peace dove on the League of Nations building to gargoyles representing, as the narrator informs us, 'nationalism, jealousy and suspicion'. Suddenly a wheel stops and a quickfire assembly of shots – of empty railway stations, building sites, silent docks – suffices for the General Strike. Repeated shots of an hourglass are a hint that the film-makers are always aware of the need to convey the transience of peace and happiness. But just one sentence – 'There was one machine he could not master – the economic machine he had created' – hardly seems sufficient introduction for scenes of the Wall Street crash. References to south Wales problems are sketchy: 'Things were very bad for us in south Wales, too' prefaces a shot of Edward VIII's visit in 1936; ' "Something must be done," he said – "and meant it".' The more ominous images are so few they scarcely justify the warning near the film's conclusion: 'The seeds had long been sown and all the land was waiting for the harvest.' Then a montage of church bells, cottages, cathedrals, coastlines and silent long shots of London accompany Chamberlain's voice declaring Britain at war. The voice leads into sirens over an overhead view of the capital, an ending envisaged by Howells and Baylis even before they embarked on the script. The final sequences, impeccably edited for emotional effect, demonstrate Howells's great strength, and the film, capturing much of the flavour and atmosphere of false hope of those years, stands up well in technical terms (and was undoubtedly an invaluable exercise for a relatively young film-maker). It contains a wealth of information and impressions and sweeps us along. But its vacillation in the face of dissent and schisms within Britain, and failure to examine economic and social reasons for the inevitability of further war remain omissions – even allowing for the need to appeal to mainstream cinema audiences. Howells was more intent on striking emotional chords and orchestrating responses in film-goers than probing for the undercurrents of the day. 'I have this Welsh trick of writing and cutting which is going to affect people, reach them, and get an emotional response – and I'm a showman too,' he said in the eighties.[20]

The Peaceful Years still managed to please audiences and critics. Even the *Documentary Film News* critic thought it 'serious enough to make people look into their daily news and wonder if we haven't already started another 20-year march to some bigger catastrophe'.[21] 'To set people thinking is unusual enough for a film in an ordinary cinema programme,' this writer said. 'To do so without grinding an axe and with real humour and wit is an even rarer achievement.'

Asked to devise another compilation film, Howells and Baylis hit on **Scrapbook for 1933**, the year Hitler seized power and Roosevelt arrived at the White House with the resonant quote: 'The only thing we have to fear is fear itself.' Howells wanted the film to 'start in lovely sunshine and end with the Burning of the Books'.[22] The film – an Edinburgh Festival entry in 1950 and given a London second-feature opening at the Odeon, Marble Arch – places heavy emphasis on sports stars and leisure distractions, and features a running gag with Maurice Denham as a peevish newsman sent to find the Loch Ness monster (the style of these scenes and their narration is facetious, but the work generally contains some of Howells's most evocative, droll writing). The 'scrapbook' also includes a passage on Welsh unemployment and – briefly – signs presaging later tragedy. Dilys Powell noted the work's 'truth . . . gaiety and warning undertones', and claimed it 'beautifully recaptures the feeling of an interlude before the major horrors'.[23]

Campbell Dixon of the *Daily Telegraph* found Howells's commentary 'satirical, eloquent and witty'. But Richard Winnington, always a useful ally, complained that, as before, a first-rate editing job was dolled up with 'portentous, facetious or colloquial commentary' from a variety of actors. He found this 'madly irritating but not destructive'.[24] Dixon thought Howells's solo compilation film **Here's to the Memory** (1951–2), made after Baylis's departure from Pathé, had less of the 'glancing wit' of its predecessor and considered that producer Howard Thomas and the writer-director had allowed themselves to preach a little and demonstrate a 'slight tendency to breast-beating'. He still found the work 'uncommonly good' though superficial 'as history in headlines is bound to be'.[25] Howells, then working as a freelance commissioned by Howard Thomas, attempted to embrace fifty years from Victoria's death. He wove into his kaleidoscopic footage evocative Second World War shots of the tube shelters and now familiar images of Dame Myra Hess playing concerts at the National Gallery, London. The director took eighteen months to make the film: 'It almost killed me. There were two editors – one had a nervous breakdown, the other spent six months in hospital afterwards.'[26] The director thought Dixon's criticisms were pertinent and sound, 'but when you have the same length of time to embrace fifty years as one year you haven't much time for glancing wit.'[27]

Howells also wrote much material for Associated British Pathé's quarterly series of two-reelers **Wealth of the World** and commentary for some Pathé Pictorial magazines at a time when the company produced two newsreels a week.[28] He was prolific in these years and also contributed the commentary read by Richard Todd for **Elstree Story** (1952), a montage of memories from the studio films since 1927. He also claimed to have written – uncredited – a section of the screenplay for the 1950 version of Novello's **The Dancing Years**.[29] In 1953, Howells demonstrated his versatility by furnishing the screenplay, with Jay Lewis, for a British Lion journalism drama, **Front Page Story**, starring Jack Hawkins as a news editor. Howells claimed he wrote every line of dialogue for the film directed by Gordon Parry (from a Robert Ganes novel), and the screenplay is humorous and affectionate, notable for its accuracy of detail and attention to the routines of the newspaper day. Despite melodramatic story-line elements and stock characters, the film suggests persuasively the pressures on a newsman who strives for the 'middle way' and objectivity, and to mollify his proprietor while retaining a healthy cynicism. The same year, Howells scripted Don Chaffey's Children's Film Foundation feature **The Skid Kids**, about a youthful cycle-racing gang foiling thieves (shades of **Hue and Cry** and **Emil and the Detectives**). The Welshman then formed his own company, working for sponsors,

CHAPTER 16

Teething
Troubles –
and the
Documentary
Poets

and in 1965 made for ESSO **The World Still Sings**, a documentary on competitors at Llangollen, not dissimilar to John Ormond's **A Small Town in Tuscany**. Howells concentrated on choristers from Leeuwarden in Holland and Le Havre in Normandy.[30] The film was warm and heartfelt, but suffered from a risible commentary of rather stale journalese and a preponderance of tilted lens shots in Festival platform scenes.[31]

Three far more personal television films were the high-water marks of Howells's later career. **Penclawdd Wedding** (1974), a 27-minute film for HTV, recorded village festivities at the marriage of Judith Preston, a local girl, and her Geordie husband John, then a Swansea-based policeman. Howells appeared before camera with his crew and later made little attempt to conceal their presence, interviewing villagers, and the local cockle-shelling community of Penclawdd, on the Gower Peninsula. This material is threaded through footage of the wedding couple as they move towards the moment when they stand before the pastor. Ken Gay, in *Films and Filming*, praised 'this superb colour documentary's human understanding, grace and charm', and said it 'brought a lump to the throat'. He thought 'the film followed the best of documentary tradition.'[32]

Jack Howells with his awards for *Nye!*, judged the best Welsh TV production of its year and the best Welsh television documentary.

Return to Rhymney, a mix of black and white and colour, focused on the history of the director's home area, the coal and steel industries, and the pride of the people reflected through the poetry and imagery of Idris Davies.[33] Howells, born in Abertysswg, left the Rhymney Valley at twelve, but retained a great affinity towards the area, and the film also features his former school, Lewis Boys, Pengam.[34]

Nye!, Howells's film on Aneurin Bevan, was affectionate and admirably detached – and displayed the director's eye for the revealing quote and the ability to ransack recent history for material which polarized views on the politician. If the documentary, with its resourceful use of stills, is finally a victim of its own ambivalence towards the subject, it remains a remarkably stylish and disciplined work containing much resonant imagery. It highlights the appalling housing and health conditions which Bevan sampled at close quarters in Tredegar, with shots of middens, slag-heaps and a huddle of colliery houses. The film is carried along on the tide of the director's enthusiasm and polemic, and skilful juxtaposition of damning quotes and eulogy. In a voice-over which opens the documentary, Howells asks whether Bevan was, in Churchill's words, 'a squalid nuisance . . . brilliant, bitter, proud, a dangerous fellow with every intention of tearing down the pillars of society'; or was he, he asks, the most charming of men, the most principled of politicians, 'clean and magical, a man of chivalrous gaiety and wit'?

Howells lets us know exactly where his feelings lie, in deeming Bevan worthy of such sympathetic scrutiny, but he maintains a scrupulous balancing act, hinted at in his commentary: 'You didn't have to be left wing to love him or right wing to hate him.' In relying upon the commentary and the quotes down the years of newspapermen and politicos, Howells succumbs to the obvious dangers and renders Bevan too much of an abstraction – there is not quite enough variety or vibrancy in the film to bring the MP to life. But the director pulls out the emotional stops. Over the still of a cottage (not Bevan's – long since demolished) we learn that 'in a cottage not unlike this in Tredegar his father died of pneumoconiosis,' before the days of compensation. Howells is able to vent his socialist spleen on the sound-track, and remind us that these were the days when the companies could still dock miners' pay for the time spent carrying home the body of a dead friend. In its final minutes the film becomes increasingly schematic and anecdotal, relying heavily on the politician's more memorable put-downs: of Ramsay MacDonald, 'A pitiful Micawber waiting for something to turn up'; of Fascism, 'The future refusing to be born'. And Howells does not void the more over-heated descriptions of Bevan, including Churchill's 'a gamin from the Welsh gutter'

CHAPTER 16

Teething

Troubles –

and the

Documentary

Poets

The later years, in particular Bevan's Health Service transformations, are skimped. We learn little of the various factions and political arguments within the Labour Party which finally drove Nye into implacable opposition to the leadership and exile from the party; or of the tenor of world opinion which culminated in Nye's eventual re-absorption into the fold and his fateful speech on unilateralism.[35] Even the final shot of a bust of Nye in profile against the books of the miners' library seems ambivalent. It might render him as merely a part of history or an icon but could also emphasize his continuing influence on education within the party. Howells's failure to attribute quotations is also irritating: acting as omniscient narrator, the film-maker denies us knowledge which might enable us to make the judgements the work seems to demand.

Howells will always be best known for the Oscar-winning film **Dylan**, which took two years to mount and make. Its success, while clearly enhanced by Richard Burton's performance, demonstrated Howells's powers to move an audience. As a 'surrogate' Thomas, the actor resisted any temptation to imitate but displayed some of the reckless charm, perhaps, which attracted Thomas's coterie of admirers. Yet the slightly sepulchral voice sets up a somnolent mood early on as Howells's camera roves over Swansea and 'the smug, snug' suburb of the poet's youth. The images of Cwmdonkin Park, for example, tend to be subservient to the text rather than yield insights of their own, though Howells uses light meticulously to make the landscape appear more ethereal. The film, handsomely mounted, is predictable enough until Dylan goes to a London 'paved with poems' and the camera tracks in on Burton in a club bar. He reads Dylan's own description of himself: 'about medium height for Wales, five foot, six and a half inches, mouse-brown hair, bombastic, a gabbing, ambitious, mock-tough, pretentious young man.' The camera pans from a close up of Burton to the rather morose drawing of Dylan by Augustus John, which suggests fleshy dissipation. Burton manages with a curl of the lip to suggest the relish of the true sybarite.

Howells, who throughout fuses text and image with intelligence, admittedly cribs ideas from *Under Milk Wood*. What has become of him? asks Burton; the word 'dead' is intoned several times. Images of choppy seas follow, a cross is lit up after the words 'Do not go gentle into that good night', and the film ends with the poet's defiant flourish: 'Death shall have no dominion.' Charges of pedantry can be levelled, but in some ways the film represents a summation of the director's career achievements, knitting together images for maximum emotional effect and demonstrating his ability to hold an audience. Touches such as the use of storm effects in a Cwmdonkin Drive scene, and emphasis on Dylan's self-critical stance to mollify or offset some of the criticism of him (implicit in the John portrait), are evidence of a strong directorial hand. **Dylan** is much more arresting, for instance, than **Poetry of Landscape – The Wales of Dylan Thomas**, a bland British Tourist Association work in which the poetry has been gutted to serve the Tourist Board notion of a photogenic, homogeneous Wales.[36] Endless shots of lush 'Fern Hill' and windy platitudes from Wynford Vaughan-Thomas contrast incongruously with the often abrasive poetry on the sound-track (read by Donald Houston). This film contrasts interestingly with Karl Francis's laborious attempts to give Dylan's work a political and partly industrialized context in **Mouse and the Woman**. **Poetry of Landscape** chooses to emphasize Thomas's apathy towards the 'strange world going about its business' outside the sea-town of his childhood; shots of coal-mine chutes inserted here are the film-maker's idea of the world Thomas chose to ignore. The diversion is almost an apologia for the film's unwillingness to relate Thomas to any real context. Repeated use of a young boy seen gambolling through the greenery (representing Dylan's lost innocence, or the peripatetic Muse) seems symptomatic of the film's lack of fresh ideas.

John Ormond

Jack Howells won the 1962 Academy Award for Best Short, but some of the more interesting programmes on Dylan came from fellow poet John Ormond, who has displayed greater faith than Howells in allowing subjects to make their own statements and send programmes on an often diverting, sometimes disconcerting, tack.

Much, perhaps too much, of Ormond's output was concerned with paying tribute to fellow artists: Dylan Thomas, R. S. Thomas, Ceri Richards, Graham Sutherland, Josef Herman; plus Edward Thomas and W. B. Yeats, in his **Poems in Their Place** series. Ormond's work is rarely ingratiating or unduly deferential but this stress on traditional documentary perhaps accounts for his comparative neglect outside Wales. The film-maker was often at his most impressive when depicting ordinary working-class people, or refugees in straitened circumstances. Eugenius Okolowicz and Vlodek Bulaj, the old men of **Borrowed Pasture** (1960), living in primitive conditions in west Wales, seemed as resilient and intractable as the land around them. In **Once There Was a Time** (1961), an altogether more ambitious work, the observations of two pensioners, based on decades of life in the Rhondda and an education provided by miners' libraries and Marxist or religious discussion groups, allowed Ormond to use the landscape superbly to make his own points and draw analogies. Often working with a single camera on minuscule budgets, Ormond can be seen as the first creative director-producer in Wales to free film from a narrative straitjacket. More chasteningly, perhaps, he was the first film-maker since William Haggar to build up a significant canon of work in his own country, using a regular crew and – invariably – outside locations. The work of BBC producers D. J. Thomas and Dafydd Gruffydd should not be under-rated in any assessment of the Welsh contribution to film. They trained for TV a school of actors and actresses who otherwise, from the early 1950s, would have had next to no scope outside the shrinking B-picture market.[37] But the major contribution to creating a BBC film aesthetic in Wales came from Ormond, who, after a grounding in TV news inserts, reporting and directing, was appointed films producer for Wales in the early fifties and helped set up the principality's first documentary *cinematic* unit. Yet he never saw himself as propagating a Welsh screen culture or consciousness. 'In my poetry, my first duty is to create a poem in the English language. If there's to be a Welsh element that will look after itself.' So with his films which, naturally, also gained much from the poetry of the narration.[38]

The BBC Welsh Film Unit began with 'one of everything': a camera, an editor, assistant cutter, general lights man, continuity girl and Bill Greenhalgh, 'a marvellous cameraman', according to Ormond. Greenhalgh deserved credit for much of the distinctive atmosphere of Ormond's more personal films. The film-maker began work in two rooms in Cardiff's Park Place under BBC Wales programmes head Hywel Davies. A 30-minute documentary for the series **Second Inquiry**, about the depression in the steel and tin-plate industries, hinted at the industrial malaise to come in Wales. A further programme, **Men to Spare**, shot in Llanelli, centred on the misery of unemployment.[39] For **Second Inquiry** Ormond worked to obtain the mood he later demanded in all his filming, seeking to build up feeling and texture through images rather than a rote recital of text or information. His *Picture Post* training in the vintage years under editor Tom Hopkinson was invaluable, impressing on him the importance of a sequence of pictures (or film montage and structures). He frequently referred to his film direction as 'making my mosaic'.[40] Interestingly, Ormond rarely shot with a full-blown script, preferring to make notes on envelopes or rely on a rough outline. He bargained on the lucky accident which, when viewed in the cutting room, chimed in with the initial notion of the treatment; and he depended on telling imagery, or a cadence of speech, to work on the eye and the ear – 'a kind of gentle branding'.[41] Ormond imposed the film's visual style: 'I have, 95 per cent of the time, directed the cameraman setting up the shot, looked through the lens and decided every cut in the picture.'

Ormond's first full documentary feature, **A Sort Of Welcome to Spring** (1958), was made under rudimentary conditions for just £400: the director recalls 'tearing twigs off conker trees' and forcing them against the office radiator to 'get an atmosphere of fuzz and fur', then using a microscope to shoot the images.[42] The director supplied his own verse-commentary for the film, shot at Three Cliffs Bay, on the Gower Peninsula, and Cardiff's Roath Park Lake. Editing took less than two weeks, and he scrawled the opening and end titles in chalk on a brick wall. These early privations might account for the ingenuity of his later films, which often bear the stamp of the independent rather than an orthodox 'in-house' talent.

The work was Ormond's sole creative feature before **Borrowed Pasture**, the film which portrayed the grim hardships and spartan comforts of two Polish Army war veterans struggling to make a living from sixty-five 'sullen' acres of barren land in the hills north of Carmarthen.' These men who had killed to escape the Siberian camps were now living on the edge of subsistence. The farm they found 'was cheap because unwanted', the narrator (Richard Burton) tells us. 'The house roof was falling in, it was absolute squalor but a kind of dignified squalor.'[43] In the words of the commentary: 'The men borrowed rough pasture from the alien land and coaxed small comfort from decrepitude.'

Ormond spent time building the old men's confidence. The odd day would go by

CHAPTER 16

Teething
Troubles –
and the
Documentary
Poets

without a single shot in the can as the crew performed odd jobs on the farm and in the farm house. Much of the film was shot silent, with sound added later.[44] As usual, the director attempted much more than a traditional character study of the men, linking his subjects' progress to the passage of seasons, stressing the slow encroachment of time on their lives. The men grow almost palpably older during the film as we feel for them in their arduous battle, yet shooting was from autumn to late winter only, climaxing with a snowstorm: 'They could see time moving over them, they were mocked, they were immobile.'

The director was fascinated and touched by the store these men placed in ritual and convention and by their innate sense of propriety and sensitivity towards each other's feelings. (They invariably addressed each other as 'Mr' even though tensions between them might have been exacerbated through their reversal of roles. The elder man had been the younger's commander in army days but now relied on him to shoulder the bigger, physical burden of farm labour, and the heavier responsibilities.) Ormond asked the men to sing lullabies of their own country, then had Arwel Hughes set them to music.[45] He also experimented with form, (as he was to do again, stunningly, in **Once There Was a Time**): 'There are four fades in, four fades to black and it's in four movements, each representing a season.'[46] In the winter of the filming, five of the six cows died. Ormond revealed the spare details of the men's lives only as they revealed themselves naturally, Greenhalgh's camera and close-ups of the farm mechanics helped contrast elemental with more modern forces, and Ormond turned to creative use every discovery. The older man, we are told, has student songs in his head. 'To him the present is interchangeable,' says Burton. A few religious icons are in the men's possession and a handful of books are 'a token of contact with the outside world'. Ormond observes unobtrusively, squirrelling away shots to encapsulate for ever the integrity of these lives in miniature. The older man is seen reading his English grammar book in a corner. When the men retire to bed (with one observing due religious ceremony), the younger writes to his wife, unseen for two decades, giving a formal blessing on his daughter's marriage, 'a letter across twenty years of love'.

Ormond uses everyday farm sounds, an axe chinking on milk churns, a grinding machine sharpening implements, building both a visual and aural montage. And finally, heart-rendingly, we hear the men's voices on the sound-track: 'All this life, you know, is trouble. Without trouble life is nothing. Without the farm I am nothing, I am the farm and the farm, you know, it is me.' **Borrowed Pasture** was Ormond's own favourite work. It has odd *longueurs* and the characters perhaps move us more as individuals than symbols of durable man under duress. The film, perhaps, relies a little too much for its effect on the power and cadence of the director's narrative, and Burton's persuasive reading. But it remains the most perfect fusion of words and image in Ormond's *oeuvre*. After the BBC screened the film the public donated cash to enable the younger man to be finally reunited with his wife after twenty years.[47]

Once There Was a Time (1961) again featured two old men as protagonists – both from Treherbert, Rhondda – one William Thomas, an avowed Marxist, the other Teifi Jones, a committed Christian whom Ormond had discovered at a prayer meeting. The men had never met each other before the programme, but the film-maker spent hours talking to both so he could later suggest ideas for discussion, which bore fruit on camera. He used the men's discourse to present not merely the conflicting religious and Marxist traditions in the Rhondda Valleys but also 'an argument on the power of history on men's lives – to change and to temper'.

CHAPTER 16

Teething

Troubles –

and the

Documentary

Poets

Ormond's shooting ratio was astonishingly low at three to one.[48] He used only one camera and his faith in the use of talking heads in close-ups, and the unconventionality of presentation and content, apparently led to a clash with Leonard Mayall, head of the BBC Talks Department which had overall responsibility over film.[49] The documentary was made with a crew of five, plus the director, and shot in ten to thirteen days. It was another exemplary low-budget achievement. The team, including Harley Jones, the youngest film cutter (at eighteen) appointed by the BBC, was based in a shack by the River Taff, near Cardiff's Empire Pool. This team was later joined by Chris Lawrence, the editor who was to help shape some of Ormond's best work – and many of the finest films in Wales.[50]

William Thomas tends to dominate the exchanges, which slightly reduces the impact of the film, though Teifi, serene in his beliefs and tolerance at times, seems the perfect foil for Thomas's dry humour, weathered by years of hard graft and deprivation. 'Some colliery owners were holy men,' says Teifi, reasonably, at one point. 'They wanted a lot for a shilling,' William ripostes. The camera lingers on the men in close-up or moves across slag-heaps and mountains and rows of terraced houses as Ormond cross-cuts to make forceful analogies. The rough-hewn irregular stone of the cottages gives way, almost seamlessly, to embossed wall paper, linking exterior landscape with intimate family life – and then to the lined face of a miner. The editing also makes ironic points. The men quote from the seventeenth-century poet Robert Herrick and Shakespeare to make philosophical arguments, and express their credos. William cites the line: 'He owns my life who owns the means by which I live.' Then Ormond almost immediately shows a miner ordering a cheap romance novel at the library. The scene might be making a point about the gradual decline in taste, the debasement of miners' culture. But it also helps leaven a film which just occasionally slips towards the pretentious.

Ormond daringly yokes past and present in a vignette of a young couple linking hands under a tree, then over a gravestone; a pan over chimney smoke leads into the men's reminiscences of First World War experiences. Teifi's anecdote of how a phrenologist forecast correctly that he alone of three friends would return from the war serves again to set his faith against William's pragmatism. As the men speak of soldiers' experiences in bordellos, a series of jarring focus-pulls suggest the miners' disorientation as young men facing their new experiences in Europe. The film subsides towards a tranquil ending as William and Teifi talk of time passing more quickly with age, and Ormond again presents the past impinging on, and informing, the present. Photos on walls, spanning different generations, make the point. 'Life is a series of farewells . . . The only thing I can see constant in life is perpetual change.' The camera panning over craggy Rhondda hills seems to mock the point, but the men's conversations reverberate in our minds. Ormond is not always able to relate the dialogue comfortably to either the setting or main themes. There is some meandering – as you might expect from two veterans caught in conversation for half an hour – but even the dissonance is affecting as the camera wanders over an area revealing a landscape more diverse than you expect. In these moments, it seems as untrammelled as the men themselves as they ransack their memories.

Ormond's ability to use locations to distil the essence of the film's subjects was seen in two more works. **From a Town in Tuscany** (1963), again edited by Harley Jones, was shot in the city of Arezzo. It highlights the life and culture of a community which provides a choir for the Llangollen Festival. The film as a whole never quite lives up to the promise of early scenes as the camera moves restlessly over the town's buildings and mysterious alleyways. The photography, for once, often looks self-conscious; made against a tough deadline, the film obviously taxed Ormond's ingenuity, especially the shooting of a scene of a Sunday morning mass in a local church 'where you could hardly see your hand'.[51] Cameraman Russ Walker shot inside the church, but it was much too dark to photograph the murals. He obtained single picture postcards of them all, placed them on a wall, filmed the actual murals and sought to make the postcards double as the real thing: 'We cooked the negative a bit longer in the bath to get the images for the mass. I put a nylon stocking over the lens front when I shot the postcards to degrade the quality of the pictures,' said Ormond later.[52] The camera creates intrigue early on: catching inhabitants in silhouette, offering glimpses of Roman headstones in passageways. There are frequent low-angle shots of church walls, parapets and frescos, and Piero della Francesca's painting of a Corpus Christi procession. Overall is an abiding sense of decay. Among these buildings we see the choir at practice and individual musicians in their normal workplaces – a railway yard, a welding shop, a farm. The film has any number of arresting images. It ends with its *raison d'être*, the conductor urging on his choir.

The Desert and the Dream (1963), winner of the *Western Mail* award as Welsh Television Production of the Year, took Ormond to Patagonia to celebrate the impending centenary of the exodus of Welsh emigrants in a tea clipper in 1865 to seek a new world. It traces the shrinking of the Welsh community in Patagonia, the decline of the chapels there, the gradual erosion of the dream. The documentary crew made four half-hour programmes in Welsh from Patagonia and just one in English: 'that had always been the intention, as the people weren't fluent in English.' Ormond eschews commentary for some time, using only a Spanish guitar over shots of a barren landscape, but the film, though superficial (rather like a terse history lesson), at least conveys a sense of the tribulations of those who fought the land and settled, producing crops and breeding cattle.[53] The director respects the progressive elements of the pioneers' work: the secret ballot, for instance, in which women voted (before they had electoral rights in Britain); the production of newspapers and magazines reasserting national consciousness; the Welshmen's refusal to do arms drill on Sundays in a country under dictatorial military control. Ormond used stills of locomotives resting in sidings to suggest decay, and graveyard shots of memorials to old Welsh heroes. When the film was made, there was just one pastor for a community of sixteen Welsh chapels. The Welsh language is slowly dying in Patagonia and, when the film was made, the area itself had new problems, with saltpetre pushing to the surface of the soil, producing a sterile landscape. The last great wave of emigration to Patagonia was in 1912; the war harvested many young men who might have gone, so that only older folk in Patagonia were fluent Welsh-speakers when Ormond made his film and 'despite their fierce Noncomformist Welshness those who were of any importance at all had taken a Spanish title to show they had achieved some kind of status in local societies.'[54] The film suggests that modern Welshmen are as resourceful as their forefathers: importing sheep from Australia, becoming gauchos and cattle men and hunting wild boars in the mountains. In 1963 there were 5,000 people of Welsh descent in Patagonia where 'the pioneers first possessed the wilderness', the film reminds us. Bill Greenhalgh's photography, with frequent shots of unyielding tracts of land, adds much to the atmosphere. Like **Borrowed Pasture**, **The Desert and the Dream** is about displacement. Ormond saw the settlers' community as a lyric tragedy: 'The effort these men had put into their lives . . . they had tamed the desert . . . and had a dream of preserving the language – after all, the founding fathers had gone to escape the "Welsh Not". But Spanish had taken over long since.' The director felt later that Patagonia is 'not a place I want to go back to' and he summed up his feelings about the barren land in his poem, 'Instruction to Settlers'.

CHAPTER 16

Teething
Troubles –
and the
Documentary
Poets

Ormond's biographical films have tended to complement his features, revealing similar preoccupations. Polish artist Josef Herman, the subject of the director's **A Day Eleven Years Long** (1975), arrived in the Swansea Valley in the 1950s after losing his family in the Warsaw ghetto in 1942. As a man uprooted, his first views of Wales made a forceful impact. He saw miners moving over a bridge at 5 a.m., 'a mixture of sadness and grandeur – caught by a flash of the sun . . .' In one week he did sixty studies of miners. He spent hours drawing at the pits: 'Here I found my inner emptiness filling.' Ormond, who believed BBC Wales as a TV service had an obligation to pay creative dues to the artists within Wales, reveals Herman through the painter's wry reminiscences of his father – a cobbler – and, crucially, through his work with its strong autobiographical elements. Herman reads from *Related Twilights*, his book about his experiences. 'He was a Marxist and his works centred on the dignity of life and labour,' Ormond said later.[55] After fleeing from his homeland with a false passport, Herman painted in the Gorbals before discovering Wales. 'It was as if a chance visit to Ystradgynlais had been invented to heal the artist's wounds.'

Herman's preoccupations square with Ormond's. The artist says, 'the paintings should bring men closer to men.' Herman's worries of repeating himself artistically as he dwells on his later preoccupations with African art, and considers his enforced isolation from the community, are close to Ormond's sense of isolation in what he saw as an increasingly de-personalized BBC in which he struggled to retain an identity after the drama era of Dafydd Gruffydd and D. J. Thomas ended. The film-maker, once a would-be architect and aspiring painter, was able to pay tacit tribute to the artists he admired in his justly celebrated series, **Visions Out of Wales** (1969). He felt particular affinity towards Ceri Richards, born in the same village – Dunvant, near Swansea. Richards's father had succeeded Ormond's grandfather as a deacon in the local chapel. Richards was a child of the chapel and colliery and used his father's background and his own experiences observing and drawing in tin-plate works during the war. In the documentary, he talks of the liberating impact made on him by the Impressionists (notably Cézanne), by poetry (his father loved to declaim Welsh verse), and by music and his love of Debussy. Ormond also demonstrates the impetus the artist derived from the power of Dylan Thomas's imagery.

Graham Sutherland, who worked in Pembrokeshire during the war, was a natural for Ormond's series after his gift of artwork to Wales worth £1 million. The director based his ideas for the piece on Sutherland's own 'Welsh Notebook' slot on TV's **Horizon**.[56] Sutherland is first seen in silhouette, in a wood, clutching a tree: 'This is my raw material, my vocabulary.' His verbal eloquence, the natural grace of his early landscape drawings, and Ormond's restrained but never restrictive style combine to produce an incisive film tribute and shed light on part of the artist's creative consciousness. Ormond observes – literally – the roots of Sutherland's work: his black-and-white drawings of trees, hedges and thorns that inspired his *Crucifixion 1946*, for a Northampton church. The film also highlights Sutherland's pictorial record of the bombings in Swansea, assembled while commissioned as a war artist, and it ends with Sutherland, dignified and introspective, lamenting that: 'my dictionary is not big enough', a statement contradicted by all we have seen.

In **Land Against the Light** (1979), Ormond celebrated landscape artist Kyffin Williams. 'When he set up his easel as like as not he'd be painting in the sun and not with the usual flat effect. Accordingly, I nearly always shot my film against the sun,' said Ormond.[57]

The director, of course, knew Dylan Thomas well and his canon includes several tributes, notably **Bronze Mask** (1969) which related the theme of the poet and the Welsh landscape to Welsh art, and to historical relics preserved in the National Museum of Wales, Cardiff. The film, narrated by William Squire, also sought to provide insights into aspects of the poet's background and personality reflected in his work. Ormond later felt he tried to do too much with his film: 'There are obvious things which seem to be fabricated.'[58] His first Thomas film, **Return to Swansea**, was black-and-white, and composed mainly of stills of the snowbound town.[59] More insights into the real Dylan emerged from **Fortissimo Jones**, Ormond's programme on the poet's confidant and childhood friend, the composer Daniel Jones. Ormond had been a young member of that Swansea circle and thought a tribute was 'long overdue' to a man who had written ten symphonies, an opera, and orchestral and choral works. Ormond moves us back into the past, through anecdotes, shots of old manuscripts and stills, to the days when Jones played piano and composed poems and music as a child prodigy and fell under Dylan's spell after meeting him in the school playground. At Jones's home, Wormley, we see old footage of Dylan honing his skills. 'We tried to write poems together – I wrote one line, he the next,' says the composer. The film uses Jones's Fourth Symphony, written in Dylan's honour, over shots of a wild landscape, zooming out as the music fades, then picking out a man (Jones) seen beside crashing waves as the sonorous music starts up again. Ormond uses stop-motion shots to accompany Jones's Dance Fantasy. Jones's experiments with sound, his admiration for Mozart and Purcell and the poetry of Blake, Donne and Herbert, all emerge from Ormond's film. **Fortissimo** is, undoubtedly, one of Ormond's finest, most deeply felt works.

In Ormond's **I Sing To You Strangers** (1982), the placing of the stone commemorating Dylan in Westminster Abbey proved the inspiration for an inspired, impressionistic view of the poet's career. The documentary skilfully melded interview material and archive footage, and made extensive use of Thomas's lines. It featured Dylan's own readings on the sound-track, stills of landmarks in his life and interviews with Daniel Jones, painter Alfred Janes, composer Elizabeth Lutyens, Dylan's daughter Aeronwy Thomas Ellis, and footage of a 1975 interview with the poet's wife Caitlin, who memorably described their life together, with its many spats, as ' high drama of a low sort'. The director sought to correct the superficial impressions gained from biographies, though he claims they were not wrong. 'Dylan was a tragic man but a major lyric poet,' as he said in his first review of Thomas's *Collected Poems* in 1952.

Ormond's film of R. S. Thomas (1971) was almost too deferential. It was notably austere, in keeping with the priest-poet's life and art, but also more conventional than Ormond's usual work. Yet it brought out the director's prime concerns: the effect of a place and a people on the artist and how the writer responds to the vagaries of life in a hermetic community. Thomas, introduced by Ormond simply as a 'stonehand and a visionary', talks of his experiences on the Llŷn Peninsula and also of his first parish, in Montgomeryshire – 'A sociologist's nightmare to begin with . . . I found nothing I had been taught in the theological college was of any help in these circumstances.' He also talks fascinatingly of the 'rain, spittle and phlegm' of farm life and the 'hard core and harshness of the people'. Ormond uncharacteristically settles for obvious images which merely illustrate the words as Thomas walks through the craggy landscapes. The director sees Thomas's poem 'The Musician' as perhaps the most direct statement of Christian faith. In the film's final sections, Thomas, seen wandering across his own churchyard, expounds on the nature of eternity and, implicitly, the landscape's contribution to his faith and art.[60]

The director rarely ventured into films which professed to provide an overview or study of his own country, but he did write the commentary for **Heart of Scotland** (1961), a heavily romanticized film made by Lawrence Henson, who worked as a film editor, in Cardiff, with John Grierson on Scottish Television's **This Wonderful World** series.[61] Ormond's status as a film-maker has tended to be obscured by his achievements as a poet, and a full assessment of his work, particularly his use of landscape and milieu, has yet to be made. But no creative team in Wales has ever matched the BBC Film Unit for achievement during this period, when Ormond's cameramen included Greenhalgh, John Pike (who shot a memorable sixties James Cameron documentary on India in BBC's **One Pair of Eyes** series), Russ Walker and Robin Rollinson. His sometime editor Chris Lawrence was so affected by **Borrowed Pasture**, as a teenage viewer, that he went to help the old men labouring at the west Wales farm and later claimed that film above all had inspired him to enter television. It was not until the late 1970s, and the rise of the independents in Wales, that other film-makers with regular crews were able to provide similar wide-ranging and regular perspectives on Wales, and turn a critical eye on the nation's life.

CHAPTER 16

Teething
Troubles –
and the
Documentary
Poets

The men could say so much, but I wanted Harri Webb, with his lines about survivors, to suggest the poetry of it. It was a statement about an industry on its last legs. There was one trawler left. It is an allegory for Wales and a lot of its people – they just about survive.

(Richard Watkins, talking of his **Milford Fishermen**, interviewed by the author, Gwent, 1983)

The future of British cinema during much of the fifties and sixties looked gloomy, as venues closed by the score or were converted to bingo. Television lured audiences away from the big screen. British features, after a brief resuscitation in the late fifties with the injection of American finance, fell back into the doldrums. In south Wales the valleys were steadily denuded of pits and picture havens. Ironically, even as cinemas and studios closed in the fifties, film was being taken increasingly seriously in certain quarters in Britain, following the wartime critical success of indigenous documentaries and fictional features. More people saw film as an art form and/or vehicle for possible social change. British audiences were exposed to the best of world cinema, through the widening scope of the Edinburgh Festival (launched in 1947), the London Film Festival (started in 1956), the eclectic fare and retrospectives at London's National Film Theatre, and the growth in the market for more academic film books and magazines. The success of the UK Free Cinema movement, and the poetic realism of films by Lindsay Anderson, Karel Reisz, Jack Clayton and Tony Richardson, proved that the British cinema had a potential for flexibility and virility which critics had scarcely suspected. **Blue Scar** director, Jill Craigie, served under chairman Michael Balcon on the BFI Production Board (successor to the BFI Experimental Film Fund), which helped provide a cash lifeline for ambitious independent young film-makers. The birth of the National Film School in Beaconsfield, Buckinghamshire, seemed to augur well for future UK screen talent. There was even talk of setting up a Welsh Film School, an idea to be resurrected in a wide-ranging report to the Welsh Arts Council some twenty-five years later.

In Wales, the film society movement burgeoned after the war. Some groups, from the outset, mounted ambitious programmes of screenings and lectures. Cardiff Film Society, formed in 1948, doubled its membership from 400 to 800 by 1949–50, and from 1949 showed films at the Park Hall cinema, on 35mm. The critic Dilys Powell gave the society's first annual lecture, and Arthur Watkins, British Board of Film Censors secretary, the second. **Today We Live** co-director, Ralph Bond, spoke in 1950 on the 'role of producer, cameraman and editor'. The CFS even formed a separate study group which received its inaugural lecture from Ernest Lindgren, curator of the British Film Library, and later founder and doyen of the National Film Archive.[1] The future of film was deemed important enough for a nationwide broadcast debate in Cardiff in 1949. On the panel for *Now's Your Chance*, a radio programme allowing consumers to question 'people in power', were producer John Boulting, BBFC secretary Watkins, Wyndham Lewis, 'independent cinema proprietor and managing director of six local cinemas', and Lt.-Col. S. K. Lewis, public relations officer for the 400-cinema ABC circuit.[2] Wyndham Lewis, typical of so many cinema proprietors who used box-office figures as almost the sole criterion in assessing films' worth, thought that there was little potential audience for British features and stressed that cinema-goers much preferred American movies – as they had through the thirties and most of the forties. He pointed out that in 1947 when there was a 20 per cent British quota fixed for renters 'there were 1,100 defaulters out of 5,000 cinemas in Great Britain.' Yet later figures showed that 1947/8 was the one post-war year in which British cinema did relatively better than US movies at the UK box-office.

Newport Film School: the first stirrings

The sad demise of British cinemas and the British studios in the fifties may have reinforced Wyndham Lewis's views. But moves to create a UK National Film School –

reflecting increased interest in film-making after the inspiration of the British New Wave – sparked a fascinating 1966 TV debate in Wales. It involved John Grierson, John Wright, principal of Newport College of Art and founder of the newly formed film department there, London-based BBC documentary department head Richard Cawston and Jerzy Bossak, dean of Europe's leading national film school at Lodz, Poland (the training ground at various times for such directors as Wajda, Polanski, Munk and Zanussi).[3]

Grierson thought a national film school 'not strictly necessary' but 'an advantage' and it was vital, he conceded, to create some 'centre of experiment, to have clinics . . . where people can meet masters or people who have met masters'. The doyen of documentarians also considered it necessary that any Welsh film school should work closely with BBC Wales and TWW to obtain screenings of students' work. Wright obviously took Grierson's advice to heart as Newport students were soon producing work later screened on both BBC and TWW. Wright felt that film-makers should be given similar training facilities to artists and he harboured notions of a Welsh Film School before the Lloyd Committee made its final recommendations to set up the UK National Film School. The mere presence of the NFS served to stymie proposals for an all-Wales school, but the Newport Film School, with relatively limited funding, continued to survive – with some encouragement from the Welsh Arts Council who financed much early work in the face of criticism. A handful of Newport film-makers of talent emerged, to produce a string of documentaries delving into modern social conditions and issues (notably Richard Watkins, Geoffrey Thomas and Fran Bowyer). Fine animation work came from Henry Luttman and Peter Turner, who were to take over main lecturing duties from Harley Jones (b. 1943). Jones, who owed a big debt to John Grierson as a long-established Cardiff-based editor on Grierson's **This Wonderful World**, the Scottish Television series, produced work of some distinction while launching the Newport college's film department.[4] Jones later went freelance and Luttman and Turner became willing mentors for a generation of animators who later entered TV directly or through lively new independent companies.

CHAPTER 17

New Voices:

John Grierson

and the

Newport Film

School

Jones and Grierson, who became a patron and occasional lecturer at Newport, inspired Richard Watkins, perhaps the most talented of the film-makers to emerge from Gwent. So a continuity can be established between Grierson and one strand of Newport's documentary film-making, with the Scotsman's pioneering **Drifters** (1928) clearly influencing Watkins's **Milford Fishermen** (1977).[5] In the mid-1960s John Wright asked Grierson's advice about setting up a film school. 'He wasn't too convinced that there was any need . . . but he hoped that, as other visual arts were being taught in the college, we might succeed.'[6] The school, first opened as the film department, initially ran a one-year documentary course with Harley Jones, on Grierson's recommendation, appointed lecturer in film studies. Students had access to just one Bolex camera between them and Grierson even begrudged them that. 'He said "Give them a box, a cardboard box with a hole in it. You don't need sophisticated equipment. What you're going to say is more important",' Wright said later.[7] The department finally bought a camera and projector, and the newly designated Film School began with Grierson as an occasional visitor and *éminence grise*, even conducting some seminars in local pubs.

Newport students' documentaries in the first years included a study of chest and dust disease complaints in the Rhondda for the Medical Research Council, a short **The Brecon, Abergavenny and Monmouthshire Canals**, **Resurrection**, a film centred on the Barry graveyard for old locomotives, and a short on the **Newport Transporter Bridge**.[8] In 1966, the Newport college launched its first three-year film course and the department moved into an annexe.[9] But there were harsh financial times ahead and, for some years, the school fell back on providing film tuition within fine arts courses. Harley Jones launched another documentary film course in 1975, virtually with one student, Richard Watkins, who was eventually joined by five others. But the course finally ran out of funding, which was channelled for a time into documentary photography at the college.[10] Henry Luttman was brought in as an animation specialist to balance the course's documentary emphasis – in the same way that cartoons by the Poles Walerian Borowczyk and Jan Lenica had balanced the live action footage of **This Wonderful World** – and parallel live action and animation courses developed. The college encouraged, alongside more traditional documentaries, a leavening of more abstract work.

In the Grierson mould

Richard Watkins (b. Swansea 1948), first attracted attention with his second-year student film **Mr Sandman**, made for a mere £200–300, focusing on men working on sand dredgers operating out of Newport. It convinced him that he could become a film-maker and he has remained faithful to black-and-white rather than colour in almost all his works: 'It has more dramatic potential and veracity.'[11] Watkins had been deeply influenced by **Drifters**, and all the qualities and preoccupations he subsequently developed exist, at least in some small measure, in **Mr Sandman** (1976), a 20-minute short shot mainly at weekends with a single camera. The seamen's voices were recorded wildtrack: 'I'd always been fascinated by the sea and the idea of a group operating in adverse conditions fighting the elements.'[12] Watkins, with the dredgermen, ventured for a day at a time into the Bristol Channel from the River Usk, but the film, shot over about five days, spans a day in the men's lives. It begins with stills; there are night shots of the ship, and then we are introduced to the men. The sense of men pulling for each other in these scenes is particularly strong, as we hear their views. Watkins, as interviewer, teases out their interests, and the film also conveys the men's loneliness and boredom: 'I wanted to juxtapose the poetic imagery of their job with the banality and boredom of their lives. I've always hated narration – I don't think it's ever come off,' Watkins said later. 'The documentary film-maker should use the ideas of the people involved with the job he or she's studying.'[13] The men's resentments surface towards the film's end when we hear their disparaging comments about big-beam trawlers with their heavy gear which create dust bowls on the mussel beds, stripping the fishing grounds of stock. Watkins ends on a note of ironic optimism as a jaunty ragtime number plays underneath a freeze-frame.

This raw but resourceful short proved ideal preparation for Watkins's more ambitious and sophisticated work, **Milford Fishermen** (1977), also shot with one camera but threading in footage, possibly dating from 1926/7 of **Trawling Out of Swansea on the Tenby Castle**, made by BBC radio producer Francis Worsley (1902-49) while living in Wales in the twenties and thirties. He was later to become famous as producer of all 310 issues of the radio show *ITMA*, which was evacuated to Bangor during the blitz and was heard from Wales in 1942/3. Worsley shot the 400ft. film – at 16 frames a second, silent film speed – with an Ensign Kinekam on 16mm. film, and it contains some rare and evocative footage of Swansea buildings before the blitz.[14]

In Watkins's Milford documentary – screened by BBC – the director sought to present portraits of five ordinary men and their arduous work but also warned of the decline in the town's trawler trade seen from the men's perspective, reminiscences and anecdotes. Watkins accompanied the seamen on a three-week trip. 'The industry was dying, the owners and the guys on the boat were on the same side. No one was to blame – just the town. The town wasn't interested in a fishing industry and never had been. It was quite a sad story. They were the end of the line – in a few years' time it's doubtful if there will be anything left of it,' Watkins said in 1984. 'It was very touching how these men were trying to keep things going with no finance from the Milford Dock company.'[15] Watkins used Harri Webb's poetry to convey the ecological destruction wrought by foreign trawlers using the wrong sort of nets. Impressed by Harry Watt's use of Auden's poetry in the 1936 documentary **Night Mail**, Watkins asked Webb to provide commentary, and used an original music sound-track by Robert Swain. Harley Jones edited. Under close scrutiny the fishermen revealed a mutual interdependence, and an awareness of each other's strengths and foibles: 'It's the co-operative of the boat that's important. The human respect between the men you notice,' said Watkins later. 'You have to understand – it's dangerous work – and you'd better be good at your job.'[16] Watkins mixed old and new footage with great ingenuity, blending a washed-out grainy colour with black and white for the sea shots. There is a striking moment when a flight of gulls drops suddenly into camera view and later when the birds swoop into water speckled in the sunset to make off with fish morsels. Swain's music evokes just the right atmosphere as the men reflect on their seagoing experiences, their lives and responsibilities to each other. Shots of the old fish market culled from the silent short made by Francis Worsley, are used early on to establish the film's tenor – a lament for times past and a declining industry – though the work is refreshingly free of ingratiating sentiment. We are told there was once a 150-strong trawler fleet; now it is reduced to a handful of vessels. A seaman talks poignantly of his love of trawling, and of his family: 'In a way, it's a wasted life. You blink and they've grown up.' Another rails against the unions. A sense of loneliness seeps in as chilling as any southwester but words written by Harri Webb and read by Ray Smith sum up eloquently, yet tersely, the men's defiance and pride: 'Survivors, that's what we are. What's in our heads didn't get there by correspondence. We've seen them come and go – and proud ships sold for scrap.'[17]

CHAPTER 17

New Voices:
John Grierson
and the
Newport Film
School

The director's fascination with nautical subjects later led him to make **Under the Sea and the Waves** (1981), a Dutch-language film, in the dredging community of the former Zuider Zee in Holland. The film focuses on one family and builds up a persuasive picture of a Calvinist island community living a spartan life unchanged for centuries. It is a fascinating complement to Watkins's earlier work. In his half-hour documentary on **Urk – the Island Under the Sea**, reclaimed under the Polder scheme, Watkins integrated footage from a 1920s print owned by a local. To stress the hardship of life, the director panned over a memorial to all the ships lost at sea in the area from 1920 to the late seventies.

In 1980 Watkins, interestingly, broadened his experience by directing part of **Gone for a Soldier**, for producer Philip Donellan. It dealt with three army recruits from Merthyr and followed them through training in Northern Ireland, then placed their plight as unemployed men entering the service in the historical perspective of the Crimean War, Gallipoli, Aden and Suez. There are echoes of the film's themes in such works as John Hefin's **The Mimosa Boys**, Karl Francis's **Boy Soldier**, and Ken Loach's 1981 film set in Sheffield, **Looks and Smiles**. '**Gone for a Soldier** was an anti-war

Ernest Evans (left) as the
father, Euros Rowlands as
the youthful Gwenallt in
Ar Waelod y Cof, directed
by Richard Watkins.

film basically. It was looking at why these guys were signing on and the whole history
of army recruitment. I was trying to bring out the idea of these army lads turning
into killers for HM Government.'[18] Watkins, credited only for the men's recruiting
sequences, claims to have shot much of the film which caused a furore, with Donellan
receiving death threats. The Welshman was fascinated by the idea of these housing-
estate Merthyr youths with no job prospects, patrolling the same kind of estates in
Northern Ireland. He also edited **The Great Depression**, an Inter-University History
Film consortium work written and directed by Barry-born historian Peter Stead,
which gave the embryo film-maker experience in cutting archive material: 'The film
trained me to look at archive. All the experience gained in cutting that short I now
use.'[19]

The director's most distinctive work is arguably **Memoirs of a Pit Orchestra** (1981), a
45–50-minute allegory of remarkable assurance in which the musicians – 'the guys
always playing along and never able to control their own destiny' – represented
Wales's role within Britain.[20] Swain again composed the music and Watkins used
professional performers. He processed and printed the film himself in black-and-
white and laid poetry by Idris Davies, Alun Lewis and Dannie Abse over the images.
The film presented a potted twentieth-century history of Wales through the eyes of its
Anglo-Welsh writers – and only poetry was used on the sound-track. 'When writers
like Idris Davies were writing about Wales, Isherwood, Spender, all those guys [in
England] were writing about a totally different world. They inhabited a different
country spiritually. The interesting thing about a lot of Davies's work is that the
poetry was dialogue – so you could construct a scene from the dialogue.'[21] Watkins
built a dramatic narrative around a soldier spending his last night before going to the
1914–18 war, and created a silent film-within-the-film accompanied by a cinema pit
orchestra. All the musicians played cowboys in the 'fictitious' film. The main

characters are deliberate stereotypes (the old miner, young miner, man who leaves town), and actors familiar to Welsh audiences – Sion Probert, Gareth Armstrong, Margaret John – were used in emblematic roles. The big scene is a carefully choreographed tango in the town hall, to draw parallels between the 'regimentation' of both leisure and war. 'We had to record all the music first then film the band. We intercut with shots of men going to war.'

The 'live-action' scenes include an extensive reverse track as the soldier (David Lyn) and his wife walk through a narrow gap between houses. Shots revealing the cramped homes and fluttering washing lines testify to the normal life taking place around them as the man takes his leave. There are affecting scenes in which the miner-soldier and his wife wearily mount the stairs on the night before he goes to the front once more. The woman lies weeping on the bed, her face averted as the miner pens lines at the table then seeks to comfort her. Watkins then cuts to a low angle of a train leaving Cardiff and archive footage is deftly employed, showing silhouettes of wagons rolling off to war, accompanied by troops on horseback. Many visual flourishes confirm Watkins as a director of remarkable flair. There is a moment when the camera pulls away from the weathered face of an old miner; the shot remains out of focus a little as if he is returning from a reverie and a line of sound-track is delivered off screen as if reverberating in his head. Then the miner continues reading a poem. In scenes depicting the phoney war before British soldiers leave for France, Watkins wanted to draw analogies with what he describes as the 'silly jingoistic' mood prevalent in some quarters during the Falklands campaign. He used a montage from war sequences at the poem's climax, and intercut a Harri Webb film about Merthyr and the desolation of Wales which drew analogies with the devastation of the economy after the First World War.[22] The juxtaposition of old and new material on **Memoirs of a Pit Orchestra** is often masterly; with the cutting virtually seamless it is not easy to distinguish one from the other, and the images add to the resonance of the poetry – never merely illustrate it – and suggest war as a *danse macabre*. The film, though in English, impressed S4C's hierarchy enough to open doors there and paved the way for another eloquent Watkins work of the eighties – **Gwenallt**.

Watkins's 1983 film **Matador** was commissioned, by S4C, from his own idea. It explored the community and culture of a village, near Seville, home of a bullfighter named Thomas Campuzano. The film-maker drew parallels and ironies from the contrast between the public life-style of the matador and of his father, a herdsman who had no schooling yet taught his son to read and write. The mother spoke of her ambitions for the son, and the local priest was interviewed in a programme which conveyed how the bullfighter's triumphs became a victory for the entire village. Watkins filmed with an Arriflex, on a tripod, and his own hand-held camera. A further, concealed, camera shot slow motion on the combat scenes. The film, made for £25,000, was sold to Spanish state television but when S4C screened it, the priest's narration was cut out: 'They thought it was too complicated – and Welsh poet Dafydd Rowlands was assigned to the project which was slashed by 20 minutes just a week before transmission.'[23]

S4C also commissioned **Marseille–Marseille** (1984), a Watkins film about an anti-terrorist squad in Marseilles, but the director found the brief too limiting and sought to produce an essay presenting distinctive elements of the city and its attitudes to various professions (dancers, law officers and prostitutes were among those interviewed).[24] More ambitiously, he traced unconscious similarities between police

CHAPTER 17

New Voices:
John Grierson
and the
Newport Film
School

routines - almost balletic during arms-training scenes – and the dancing training. Again Watkins found an old photographer who had taken shots of Marseilles and its bordellos in earlier decades and fused them into the film. Watkins was not too happy with the documentary, particularly with the narration imposed on him for the S4C version, but the benefits of the bond forged with Dafydd Rowlands were seen in **Gwenallt: Ar Waelod y Cof** (Deep in the Memory). In this fine work, the director again displayed his penchant for using archive stills for emotive effect, this time linked with dramatized events, setting the poet's life in an international context and showing the experiences which forged the writer, pacifist and Marxist. The film, shot in a lush, striking monochrome by Steve Beer and edited by Pip Heywood, showed Gwenallt's life partly through extracts from a dramatized semi-autobiographical novel featuring a character named Thomas. In the most powerful scenes, Gwenallt/Thomas is gaoled in an English prison as a pacifist and learns at first hand the racist and class assumptions which underlie the prison services (once more the film should be compared with **Boy Soldier**).

Watkins's later works include **Siân** (1987), a portrait of Siân Phillips, which in one memorable scene required the actress to sing the Kurt Weill number 'Surabaya Johnny' at sea, a feat accomplished with some brio. Watkins, constantly searching for new ways to express himself through documentary, is a talent insufficiently recognized in Wales, an individual, radical voice who has constantly avoided routine commercial projects.

Geoffrey Thomas

One of Newport's most promising students, Geoff Thomas (b. 1947), originally from Rhydyfro near Swansea, graduated from the diploma course at the town's Film School in 1969. His first solo film, **Eyes of a Surgeon** (1967), featured surgery in a Newport hospital and he was granted access to operations in adjoining theatres, then cut the film together, and added sound, including the reflections of the surgeon on his work. The director gained valuable experience helping to edit **Just One Lobster** (1968), a BBC TV film made by Newport students on the Isle of Mull under the guiding hand of company executive Aled Vaughan, later Welsh Arts Council film committee chairman.[25] After a period as a TV trainee assistant film editor, Thomas struck out as a freelance, forming the Cardiff-based Scan Productions in 1971. In 1972 HTV screened his documentary, **The Forgotten Village**, based on a legend about a miner hanged in an iron cage in public after a murder in a village near Machynlleth in the 1890s. Thomas then made **They Are** (1976), about working people in Cardiff, with the docks as backdrop, shot for just over £2,300. The film ran into union problems after Thomas, an ACTT member, admitted he had shot, directed and lit the documentary. It was blocked first by his union then the Electrical Trades Union but was transmitted in the mid-1970s after writer-playwright Gwyn Thomas compared it to a Rembrandt painting with the faces 'etched in such pain'.[26] The film proved controversial enough in content alone, with interviews with a middle-aged prostitute and a pederast who talked about his sexual predilections.

In 1978, Thomas's **Your Hand in Mine**, screened by BBC, was chosen for a programme of independent work, 'North of Watford', shown at the National Film Theatre, London. Compassionate and understated, it centred on old people, some in homes for the elderly. Thomas hit on the tantalizing idea of opening the film with a pensioner embarking on a car journey. She is not being taken to a home or visiting

Geoff Thomas, now of Cardiff's Scan Films, one of the more talented of Newport Film School alumni.

family, as we might suppose, but to her marriage at the age of eighty-two to a partner of eighty-five. Thomas sought to show that ageing need not be all sadness if the community is prepared to help – an idea which took root when he saw how the elderly enjoyed three nights out a week at a centre in Cardiff's Splott area. This film led to Scan's **Y Cyswllt Cymreig** (Welsh Connection) series for S4C, six documentaries based on celebrities who arrived in Wales from outside and set down strong roots. Subjects included the Marquis of Bute, the Ladies of Llangollen, Gladstone and William Randolph Hearst. **Mr Hearst and Mr Kane** was a notable launch film for S4C on its opening night in 1982 (as **Citizen Kane a Cynan**), with Orson Welles later providing the narration in English for its Channel Four screening.[27] Since S4C's advent, Scan, with Thomas editing films and his business partner and wife, Fran Gallaher (b. 1950), directing, has become one of the most prolific of the independents with regular contracts with the channel. The interviews in Welsh and English 'conducted back to back' helped set the pattern for other companies anxious to ensure network screenings. In late 1994 the Scan team was working on a biographical feature on the checkered career of the preacher Tom Nefyn Williams.

A guiding hand

Thomas's one-time mentor, Harley Jones, former TWW cutting room assistant, began making films on 9.5mm. as a teenager. He shot a 16mm. short, **Boy in the Streets**, with Robin Rollinson for the self-styled Cardiff Videophone Film Society, and a 15-minute short, **The Boat Builders** (about a Cardiff company), shown on Grierson's **This Wonderful World** which employed Jones from 1963 to 1966.[28] He also made the 15-minute **The Return**, screened by BBC in 1969, centred on a Polish girl wandering around outside her blitzed home and transported into the past after meeting an artist.

Jones, as head of Newport Film School courses, brought in a generation of trainees – helping out on some of their films in the late 1960s and early 1970s. These films included **Perspectives: Pill**, made by student Peter Vass for Newport Borough Council, which focused on attempts to revitalize 'Pwll' (Pwllgenlly), a multi-cultural Newport docks area which grew with the nineteenth-century coal and docks trade and had marked similarities to Cardiff's Butetown district.

Jones also helped direct **Richard Wilson** (1971), Clive Ashwin's handsome if traditional tribute to the eighteenth-century painter, which used the artist's work and Hogarth prints to convey the raucous London society which Wilson encountered before embarking on his European tour which led to the metamorphosis in his art from portraiture to landscape painting. The film demonstrated Wilson's love of antiquity and the classics, reflected through his work on wild landscapes and the stress on light and atmosphere. The narration was unambitious and the token dramatization – a young boy wandering through greenery and dwarfed against the backdrop (illustrating Wilson's love of nature and his painstaking creation of perspective) – seemed stilted. The film also presented Wilson as something of a bohemian and bon viveur, a man whose caustic tongue upbraided and lost patrons, and whose drinking habits wrecked his life. He was, indeed, perhaps the unwitting originator of the self-destructive Welsh artists' or performers' myth.

Jones, for the Welsh Film Board, later made **Capeli** (Chapels, 1974), on the plight of Wales's chapels which had lost their support and emotional hold on local communities, through the years of Depression, war and austerity. The film showed the ingenious ways in which chapels were converted to cope with changing times. The director's **There Was a Time** (1976), backed by the Welsh Arts Council, homed in on the influence of the work of Thomas Hardy on the poet-musician, Gerald Finzi.[29] Jones has worked for his own independent Cardiff-based Celtic Films since 1983, producing television and sponsored shorts and frequently working for S4C.[30]

The Gwent animators

Animator Henry Luttman displayed a whimsical streak with an early student film from the York School of Art – **Moonmen**, a four-minute 8mm. animated diversion featuring aliens on a trip around Earth. At Newport College, he made a string of shorts (including a version of James Thurber's *Thirteen Clocks*), before shooting his first 16mm. film, **Pugh's New Cheese**, a simulated advert delivered by a mouse for a multi-coloured raspberry and strawberry cheese.[31] The rapturous rodent extols the cheese's virtues, then throws up by way of ushering in the company logo. 'I think it was made out of frustration with the commercials of that time – they were very patronizing,' Luttman said in the early 1980s. **Life Track** (six minutes) was an 8mm. colour film, costing just £90. The theme may have been unoriginal – 'that someone damaged at an early age may then damage others for the rest of their lives' – but Luttman attempted, in abstract terms, a corrosive little parable.[32] He went on to the Royal College of Art where he made the playful **Buzz Off** (seven minutes) which was shown on BBC 2, offering 'a fly's eye view of the world'. Point-of-view images of a landscape are presented as the fly moves across it; but the audience is only given an idea of the scale when the fly arrives in dustbins and settles inside the neck of a bottle: 'I wanted to be able to move around objects and move them through perspectives.' It is typical of Luttman's rather cynical humour that the insect is finally sprayed with insecticide.[33]

Luttman returned to Newport as a part-time tutor in 1975 and he animated **Archetype**, one of an eight-episode Bristol TV series, **Animated Conversation**, the brainchild of producer Colin Thomas (later to make an impact on television in Wales with the independent company Teliesyn). Thomas had the intriguing notion of nurturing new talent by encouraging animators to provide visuals for pre-recorded conversations. A similar idea was, of course, the basis of Aardman and Nic Park's success with the Oscar-winning **Creature Comforts**. The five-minute **Archetype** used dialogue between the architect of a shopping centre and its prospective developer, culled from an hour-long talk in the studio about the project. 'They had signed a release allowing any part of the conversation to be used. We were ruthless,' said Luttman. 'They said they'd go for a multi-storey car park as a sop to the con-servationists. We cut it to point up what was happening, so it seemed really appalling that these two guys were doing this. It was very cruel and I regret it now.'[34]

After former student Peter Turner switched from live-action to animation films and joined the college staff, Luttman and Turner introduced animation training alongside the ordinary film course. A two-year film diploma developed. Turner's **Head Rag Hop** (1970), animation set to a blues and boogie-woogie number, gained distribution through the BFI and was screened at the Oberhausen Festival.[35] Turner later traced off photos of horses and nude women by the film pioneer Edweard Muybridge to create another four-minute film. His works since – constantly exploring and dissecting film structure – include **Contract**, a seven-minute documentary on the building of the Newport Museum made with college students, **Bicycle**, which attempted to create a 'strange landscape' by observing the bike through a close-up lens while tracking along the chain, and **Pubism**, a short with every frame recognizably different – '8,000 images in two minutes, with almost a psychedelic effect'.[36] His most ambitious work to date, **Pandora** (1980), took the Pandora's box myth as a springboard for abstract figurative images, and again eschewed linear narrative. It played at Annecy and other festivals, but Turner has never had any wish to reach a wide audience with his personal works, or make 'conventional children's animation'.[37]

Chris Monger

Significant Welsh film-makers also emerged from other colleges. A prominent figure on the south Wales independent scene in the late seventies and early eighties was fine arts graduate Chris Monger. He learned his film-making at London's Slade (after training at the then Cardiff College of Art), before embarking on low-budget features at Cardiff's Chapter Arts Workshop. His first London college film, **Narcissus** (super 8mm.), was a highly personal work, featuring Monger and his brother, which flirted with the tendency – or need – for compromise in film-making, and the conflicts within young artists constantly chafing against their existing surroundings and limitations, and their parents' expectations of them.[38] He then made **Story From a Corner**, based on the traditional prologue to Welsh fairy-tales related by the grey old man in the corner; and his London student film, **Cold Mountain**, about the Chinese Zen poet-philosopher Hon Shan who wrote the 'Cold Mountain' poems or stories.[39] Actor Ian McNeice and Monger then collaborated on **Aesthete's Foot** (1976) with help from the Welsh Arts Council, a comic tilt at structural film-making. A number of narratives were intercut – the main one with McNeice as a huckster who could set up people's fantasies for them. Monger claims he was heavily influenced by Pier Paolo Pasolini, particularly with **Pigsty** (1969), and by Godard's **Vent d'Est** (Wind from the East, same year) – 'which I hated with a passion'.[40]

The director, clearly a resourceful potential talent, experimented with structure within the film, shooting each scene differently, one with emphasis on the *mise-en-scène*, another with the camera pirouetting around the actor, another on the run with a hand-held camera. Monger was constantly testing new ideas, particularly of multi-track recording, and in **Enough Cuts for a Murder** (1977) he employed dialogue in Greek, French, Italian, Welsh and Hebrew: 'We did it all with idiot boards.' In this 55-minute film, costing £5,000 (£3,500 from the WAC), Monger dealt with the limitations imposed by language, different forms of structure and contradictory perceptions: 'I clashed ideas against one another – pornography and feminism, sensitivity and the bomb, house building and de-forestation.'[41]

Many of Monger's ideas, particularly about the flexibility of sound, came together in **Voice Over** (1981), a film with McNeice which was to create a bigger stir than all his

CHAPTER 17

New Voices:
John Grierson
and the
Newport Film
School

previous films put together, but this work (to be discussed later) was to prove influential in helping give valuable impetus to the workshop movement in Wales, which for a brief spell in the late seventies and early eighties, seemed the only hope for the future of Welsh independent film-making. All the various college talents were creating, very gradually, a climate in which experiment in style and technique was being actively encouraged and sought. But for south Wales directors such as Watkins and Monger, and north Wales talents including Wil Aaron and Alan Clayton, there were few distribution outlets and funds as they developed skills with little encouragement from the major TV channels. That was to change, to a great extent, with the arrival of the Welsh Fourth Channel in 1982.

SECTION 4

Television
and a Welsh
Film 'Mini-
boom'

THE WELSH ARTS COUNCIL AND WELSH-LANGUAGE TALENTS

There will be no further developments in . . . Welsh-language film until the BFI is persuaded that the Welsh have as much right as the English to their own celluloid culture.

(Film-maker Wil Aaron in the Welsh-language magazine, *Barn*, October 1976)

The Welsh arts establishment's reluctance to take film seriously only partly explains why it was so slow to fund productions through the Welsh Arts Council. Films *about* art were given approval; others were deemed beyond WAC's scope, with the council placing the onus for funding new work firmly on the British Film Institute and its production board. In the late seventies, Scotland was in the same position, with the Arts Council backing only films about artists and musicians. But the Scots made significant progress in public funding in the following decade while the WAC film budget remained paltry, and a national disgrace throughout the eighties. It is a salutary reminder of misguided priorities that WAC's biggest single investment on any feature prior to 1991 remained £11,500 (including completion money) for Chris Monger's **Voice Over** a decade earlier. That, *at the time*, was about half the budget for a routine half-hour drama on S4C.[1] In the eighties the WAC film panel saw itself mainly as a provider of 'seed' money for scripting productions, rather than as a serious investor in film, but that was a case of cutting the coat. The panel's attempts to fund film-making earlier in the decade had been largely stymied by the low level of Arts Council of Great Britain support for the Welsh Arts Council generally, though film was consistently treated as a poor relation *within* WAC. Film-making grants rose only slowly in the first years from £14,500 in 1978/9 to £41,554 in 1980/1 and by 1982 the *total* allocation *to all* aspects of film in Wales was £94,000 (£55,000 from WAC, £39,000 from the BFI). Things became so bad that, around 1983, Monger waived any claim to a production grant because he felt embarrassed after receiving WAC's biggest individual film-making hand-outs in previous years for **Voice Over** and **Repeater** – a grand total of just over £19,000.[2]

The position contrasted starkly with Scotland. Here film-makers were disillusioned by lack of support from the BFI Production Fund around 1980 and increasingly felt they wanted to be funded by a body closer to home and *au fait* with local concerns and grassroots talent. A Scottish Production Fund, jointly operated by the Scottish Film Council and the Scottish Arts Council film committee, was set up, with a production budget of around £100,000. Scotland had also maintained a film-making tradition and strong network of sponsors and film-makers in the sixties and seventies, thanks mainly to Films of Scotland, and principally its livewire head Forsyth Hardy who worked tirelessly and obtained sponsored commissions for scores of film-makers, even if they sometimes led to unambitious work by young directors who felt constrained by their funding sources. The new Production Fund, designed primarily to provide scripting money, had also been used for training individuals (years ahead of any comparable Welsh scheme) and for part-funding particular films. A £23,000 grant for Charlie Gormley's **Living Apart Together** (1983), was exactly double the highest level for a one-feature grant from WAC.[3]

The Welsh Arts Council's role in film began unprepossessingly with piecemeal investment, and for years almost the only budding directors to benefit consistently from WAC cash injections were students at Newport Film School. Wil Aaron bemoaned the high proportion of WAC grants to student film-makers between 1970 (the year of the council's first broad sponsorship policy for films) and 1975. He found much of their work 'self-indulgent, often revealing a far greater fascination with technique rather than with communication'. Aaron also claimed that no 'excitement' had been generated in the first five years; no WAC film had won great critical plaudits; 'no film-maker made any particular impact.'[4] By 1990 – fifteen years of public subsidy later – the situation had improved, if not nearly as much as one could reasonably have expected. WAC could point to encouraging some talented Newport film-makers already mentioned, to creating a limited amount of interesting innovative work, and to 'hidden' achievements (with many of the film-makers financed playing significant crewing roles on major Welsh TV productions). Other WAC 'graduates' such as Monger and Steve Gough have made an impact in recent years as feature film directors. The council could also claim credit for progression in other areas – the creation of a network of film and video workshops, from the early 1980s, for example, notably through the All-Wales Video Project which spawned a 1984 WAC discussion document and a pledge to encourage the launch of more workshops. WAC films officer Martyn Howells wrote that 'the formation of workshops should be at the core of any policy for film and video.'

But it is hardly surprising, given the peppercorn awards, that comparatively few film-makers of reliability emerged from these workshops in the 1980s: production levels were low and film-makers had to catch the eye of TV companies to gain outlets for their work. By the nineties the energy had drained away from the workshop movement and workshops ceased to gain a separate financial allocation from WAC. Groups such as the Chapter film-makers were thrown back on their own resources, keeping themselves afloat with self-financing courses and weekend schools. Some creative independent directors, outside the workshops, found it difficult to gain acceptance by television, even by S4C. Film-maker Marc Evans, for instance, gained a Spirit of the Celtic Festival prize with the WAC-financed **Johnny Be Good** in 1985 in Brittany, yet the film was not screened by S4C until Evans had produced other work for the channel, and operated closely with them as a member of Stephen Bayly's London-based Red Rooster team. Undoubtedly, the rudimentary attitude demonstrated towards film by WAC in the early 1970s, and the scant support given by the British Film Institute, retarded film development. But during this period, the BFI itself was grossly underfunded by the Arts Council of Great Britain.

The Welsh Arts Council began life as a Welsh committee of the ACGB and helped promote and back **David**, the Welsh entry at the 1951 Festival of Britain. Apart from this impressive but token flag-waving effort, the first official recognition of film seems to have been a joint investment, with the ACGB, in Dudley Shaw Ashton's eight-minute 1961/2 **La Cathédrale Engloutie** (The Cathedral Under the Sea), based on paintings by the Welshman Ceri Richards, and commissioned from London's Samaritan Films.[5] From the mid-to-late 1960s, WAC sponsored numerous Newport Film School shorts and later injected some funding into Gethin Stoodley Thomas's film on Augustus and Gwen John, **The Fire and the Fountain** (1972–4), shot in England. In 1974, the council backed a more ambitious fictional film, Alan Mainwaring's **Never Come Monday**, starring Lisa Harrow and Kenneth Colley. Colley played an extra-mural lecturer embroiled in a lecherous weekend in Porthcawl with dramatic ramifications.

That year the first WAC film committee met under the chairmanship of Keith Evans, Clwyd's deputy education director. It included Charles Roebuck, a stalwart of the film society movement in Wales who had worked as a technician for major French film studios in Joinville and Paris in silent film days, Harley Jones, Wil Aaron, John Ormond and Mik Flood – a co-founder of Cardiff's Chapter Arts Centre which did more for films in Wales than any other centre outside the TV studios in the next decade. The first WAC film sub-committee, with a shoe-string budget of £10,000 from the BFI, spent about £7,500 on film production in 1974–5.[6] In 1975–6, coincidentally during the production of Karl Francis's ground-breaking and independent film **Above Us the Earth**, the sub-committee began to expand operations.

WAC financed the first video films to focus on local Welsh communities and social issues, made by Cardiff Street Television which operated for some time in Cardiff's Riverside area and was later brought under the Chapter Arts Centre umbrella. The Street Television included such embryonic talents as Terry Dimmick, a driving force of the Chapter Video Workshop throughout the eighties, and Steve Gough, later a graduate of the National Film School and writer of Kevin Billington's BBC Wales film **Heartland**, starring Anthony Hopkins, in 1988.[7]

Another step forward came in 1977–8 when the now fully-fledged WAC film committee or panel distributed an extra £20,000 grant from the BFI and another £37,000 from the Welsh Arts Council (though only a small proportion went on production).[8]

A language breakthrough

An important early initiative was the formation of the Welsh Film Board (Bwrdd Ffilmiau Cymraeg), originally the North Wales Film Board, spawned after a discussion at Gregynog near Newtown, in July 1970, initiated by Glyn Tegai Hughes.[9] The board began in 1971, when Welsh-language film was virtually non-existent, and first made its presence felt with a showing of its productions on the Eisteddfod field in Rhuthun in 1973.[10] Within a year the territory of the board, based in Bangor, embraced all Wales, even though the bulk of initial finance came from the North Wales Arts Association. By 1975/6, twenty films in Welsh were available for hire and the board's own output had been supplemented by BBC films in the language, such as John Roberts Williams's tributes to the poets Cynan and T. H. Parry-Williams.[11] By 1980, the board had produced eight original features, four shorts and nine films for children.[12] The output was generally poor in quality and quantity in its fifteen years, but it gave initial opportunities to work in the language to film-makers who, prior to S4C, had no other significant outlet. When the Welsh Fourth Channel came along, the board – soon in deep cash trouble following over-spending on the feature **Madam Wen** (1982) – found much of its *raison d'être* had disappeared. The board was always at pains to stress its priority of preserving the language and its members were primarily interested in literary/linguistic applications of Welsh. This perhaps militated against any real concern for film aesthetics or techniques. Wil Aaron, at one stage almost the only film-maker on the board, thought it perceived its role as 'a sword in the battle for the language'.[13] Yet hopes that the board might attract support from the giants of the literary world reckoned without the intransigence of some of its luminaries. An early board minute recalls that Saunders Lewis – perhaps the greatest of all Welsh playwrights – spurned involvement in one project, telling Emyr Humphreys, 'gwell gennyf neidio o ben pier Penarth ar ben llanw' (I'd rather jump into the sea from Penarth Pier at high tide).[14] Certainly in the eyes of the BFI the Film Board was 'essentially a language activity rather than a film activity'.[15] It was grossly underfunded and lacked film equipment or editing facilities of its own. In the board's first five years the BFI provided a meagre £3,250 and as late as 1976 it had no full-time director. In 1979, four Welsh Arts Council film committee members – including Chris Monger – resigned because they felt the council could not continue supporting the board without 'adequate funding from the BFI and Welsh Office'. The Film Board *was* later backed directly by the Welsh Office who, ironically, constantly provided more money for the Welsh-language films than the WAC film panel could squeeze from its benefactors for films in English *and* Welsh. The BFI fuelled disenchantment by claiming the Film Board did not make films good enough to justify Institute support – a curious statement, considering some of the more opaque, self-regarding BFI-backed features of recent years. Welsh Office money, naturally, created another anomaly and a bone of contention as some film-makers – especially non-Welsh-speakers from the south Wales valleys – felt they were at a financial disadvantage. Some recent film-makers have expressed serious concern about the kind of images which were projected via organizations such as the board and much Welsh language TV (essentially bucolic, with much emphasis on myth and legend), and stressed the cinematic terrain left unexplored. Wil Aaron complained: 'The board has no expertise, no experience of film,' though overall, he thought it accomplished much, with little.[16]

Wil Aaron

Wil Aaron and Alan Clayton (later head of HTV drama) were by some way the most distinguished talents nurtured by the Film Board (cynics might say it was vice versa) and in recent years Aaron's Caernarfon-based company Ffilmiau'r Nant has become one of S4C's most prolific independent suppliers of films. In their early work on the long-running **Almanac** series both Aaron and his colleague Alun Ffred Jones re-created with skill and resource, and within a limiting format, key social developments and moments in Welsh history. Aaron, from Aberystwyth, worked for five years for the BBC current affairs programme **Heddiw**, became a film director in 1963 and later a news photographer for **24 Hours** – often working with journalist Max Hastings, sending film back from the world's trouble spots, including Vietnam.[17] The Welshman's work for the board began after he went freelance in 1971 and claimed to be the sole independent film-maker trying to earn a living in the language.

His **Hen Dynnwr Lluniau** (The Old Photographer), a dramatized tribute to the now almost forgotten Cardigan-born photographer John Thomas, and made for around £3,000 in 1973, is an understated work of benign, droll humour. We follow the fortunes of the old man, who owned a Liverpool photographic shop and gallery and toured Wales, revealing a critical and sometimes jaundiced eye. Aaron used Thomas's own diaries to help convey the indefatigable photographer's feeling for his subjects; and the extent of his privations emerges graphically in the film. 'JT' is seen using a pig shelter as a dark room during his rural forays and stepping into a newly-dug grave to develop his photos. Thomas tells us of the killings he made taking religious pictures and portraits of the 'best' Welsh families in Liverpool: 'They were more worried about the quality of the frames than the pictures.' Aaron uses tableaux to good effect and Thomas's own photographs help to build up a vivid amusing portrait of an individual who took valuable shots of the high society of his day, of residents in the Elan Valley – about to be swept away by the creation of a lake – and the denizens of Liverpool hovels.

The director's second board film **Scersli Bilîf** (Scarcely Believe) (1974) was much less successful. It is a primitive knockabout comedy, with much elephantine humour, about the Welsh working-class character Ifas Y Tryc – created for Radio Wales by Wil Sam Jones. The director is dismissive of the film: 'It was made cheaply, for about £7,500–8,000, and looks it.'[18] Aaron travelled with the film around the country – a throwback to the pioneering days of Ifan ab Owen Edwards. The operation offered its own eloquent commentary on the state of Welsh film and its distribution facilities before S4C.

Aaron was back to form with **Gwaed ar y Sêr** (Blood on the Stars) (1975), which was shot in just ten days, a punning title for a spry, broad comedy – cheerfully artless. In lesser hands the humour might have been a disaster, but the film is amusingly scripted by Dafydd Huw Williams. Aaron delivers the robust gags, the shameless ironies and the shocks with such gusto that we enter into the spirit of the pantomimes and rough magic shows we surrendered to in our youth. The film's villain, Shadrach, is the village choirmaster, an old man with his face half burnt away and a limitless supply of death curses, murderous schemes and also his own 'devil doll'. These lay low, in turn, a string of Welsh male contemporary heroes (actual and fictional) such as Barry John (blown up as he punts a mined rugby ball), the DJ and broadcaster Hywel Gwynfryn, Welsh folk pop performer Dafydd Iwan, and even the eponymous Ifas y Tryc. That film cost £6,000 – and even Aaron's undoubted talent could not always conceal the pennypinching. It was clearly unreasonable to expect film-makers to produce consistently high standards on such budgets. In 1974/5 Aaron made **Dyma'r Urdd** (This is the Urdd), a £50,000 sponsored documentary, before forming, in 1978, his own Caernarfon-based company Nant. S4C's launch gave the company impetus and a market and freed the director to some extent from the cash constraints hampering his previous personal films. Alun Ffred Jones and Robin Evans, both from HTV, joined Nant in the early 1980s as the company began to explore areas of Welsh life, history and politics rarely screened before. They have been strangely reluctant to venture into the kind of contemporary documentary areas in which Aaron first developed his skills, but his company helped act as pathfinders for a whole generation of young film-makers in indicating the rich indigenous material to be mined. **Almanac** programmes tended to be anecdotal rather than analytical but the 30-minute format largely precluded development of ideas.

One of Aaron's first efforts televised by S4C was **O'r Ddaear Hen** (From the Old Earth) (1981), again centred on a curse, this time visited on a Welsh family by an old stone head. It proved to be a well-executed thriller. The main character William Jones (Charles Williams) releases evil Celtic spirits when he discovers a stone head in his garden, and dies in a car crash and explosion. Some direction is over-emphatic but the film is a work of undoubted flair with Aaron making intelligent use of slow motion, hand-held tracking shots and concise cutaways which often give mundane objects an eerie, unnatural quality.

Alan Clayton

Alan Clayton's **Newid Gêr** (Changing Gear) (1979) was a lively action 'mini-feature', forty-five minutes long. It was also a compact, sensitive study of a slowly developing romance between a widow and her husband's long-time friend and business partner – a survivor of the crash which killed her spouse. The men had been involved in rallying and the film made superb use of rigorously edited travelling shots as cars hustled around country lanes. It also boasted an unusually thoughtful and sympathetic script – by Euryn Ogwen Williams who was later, as S4C's programme editor, to encourage the channel's first wave of independent film-makers.[19] The widow (Sue Jones-Davies) and her husband's mate (Dewi Morris) grope their way towards mutual trust and love. One pub scene in particular, with silences stretching out as eloquently as words, was particularly involving and plausible, with interesting changes of pace.

Glyn Houston and Alan Clayton at the Monte Carlo International Film Festival with Houston's Best Acting award for HTV's *Better Days*.

Clayton, from near Wrexham, employs flashbacks of the fatal crash with the character trapped in the car, fighting for air, and involves us in his gradual rehabilitation as he begins to drive at speed again and finally wins a solo race. The tight cutting adds much to these sequences, together with drivers' point-of-view shots. In the euphoria of after-race celebrations the hero is preoccupied, but he takes his trophy to the woman, who resists his overtures with a curt, but not unkind, 'Don't spoil the day,' and they arrange a meeting for the morrow. He drives off but the car crashes and explodes. The catchpenny, unnecessary ending ruptures the mood and seems at odds with the rest of the film, so acute in its psychological perceptions.

The board had wanted a B film costing around £28,000 and Clayton felt they expected 'an adventure film with movement' and a very basic story to accompany on release the main feature, Gareth Wynn Jones's **Teisennau Mair**, with its £56,000 budget.[20] But, in **Newid Gêr**, Clayton tried to explore the relationship of the driver and the widow: 'What interested me were the tensions they created in each other which they weren't able to resolve.'[21] He sought to avoid the usual love story and show the way pressures in a small-town community and the tensions of bereavement all control the pace and rhythm of new relationships, forged in such extraordinary circumstances. The film was shot in Llanilar, a village eight miles from Aberystwyth.

Clayton later developed a script with actor Michael Povey for an S4C feature **Aelwyd Gartrefol** (A Friendly Home/A Homely Hearth) about the return of a young man who left Wales after university to live in London and New York and put his Welshness behind him. The work explores a collision of values between this man – now pursuing a career in art film – and a young woman activist and language campaigner, the fiancée of a college friend. The relationship proves abortive as the pair test each other and find language, cultural and philosophical barriers between them which could prove insuperable. **Aelwyd Gartrefol** contains a strong semi-autobiographical strain, says Clayton.[22] There are thematic links with **Newid Gêr** as the man develops romantic notions about the girl, who is on the brink of marriage. She sleeps with him but denies to herself that any deeper relationship exists.

Clayton was later to emerge as a forceful director in English-language work, in tandem with the south Wales writer-actor Robert Pugh. Their HTV dramas range from **Ballroom** and **Better Days** to **We Are Seven**.

Other Film Board features

The convoluted extravagant Edwardian period piece **Teisennau Mair** (1979) catered for the Welsh predilection for folk tales. This feature (from a script by Iwan Meical Jones) of thwarted love, dimming ambitions and marital infidelity has some striking imagery, good moments and a certain tension, but the narrative seems secondary at times as Gareth Wynn Jones lards his film with metaphor and symbolism. Scenes are bleached in red at regular intervals, presaging tragedy and spilled blood; flames that appear apropos of nothing, early on, presumably indicate passion; there is even a fast montage sequence of a lone hawk diving on another preparing us for the relationship between the predatory, capricious heroine Mair (Marged Esli) feeding on the misery of the boyfriend (Cefin Roberts) she rejects in favour of a respectable marriage and stability. At the film's climax the bride entices the lover to her home then poisons him with cakes just before her husband turns up. The spouse has previously forced the truth from his wife, vowing revenge on the ex-boyfriend, a local blacksmith's groom. (Glowing molten metal at the forge prefigures the later passion and the denouement.) The murder of the boyfriend leads, inexorably, to more guilt and tragedy. The film is spiced with melodrama: the husband slices off his finger with a knife as a riposte to his wife's claim that her infidelity is only a little indiscretion. Jones elsewhere seeks to create a Gothic horror mood with sonorous music, lush landscapes – a scene as the lovers languish by a tree recalls Pre-Raphaelite paintings – but the director overplays his hand, repeatedly signalling the girl's character and intentions in close-ups. Despite the rash of visual metaphors, only odd moments have a genuinely disturbing *frisson*.

John Pierce Jones and Marged Esli in the profligate *Madam Wen*.

Jones's blackish **O.G.** (1981), shot in and around Caernarfon in about three weeks from a Wil Sam Jones script, is a similar uneasy blend. It reworks some of the same ideas in a modern setting – again a husband is cuckolded by a sensual wife. The film's sluggish pace and poor editing only emphasize the paucity of ideas in a story-line which could barely sustain a 30-minute TV drama but is stretched out, interminably, for 90. The central character, O.G. (John Pierce Jones), is a burly coach driver and workaholic, and the conductor of a local women's choir. His wife, Bet (Elliw Haf), spurned in bed by her tired husband, is seen ruminating on the humiliation of forcing herself upon him and soon seeks solace with the lecherous Huw Handi-Twls (Huw Handy Tools). O.G., who remains convinced of his wife's loyalty despite increasing gossip, finally has a heart attack, is crippled and reduced to dependency on Handi-Twls (Dafydd Hywel) who runs his business for him, with every sign of showing remorse for his deceit. When O.G. is run over by one of his own vehicles while working underneath it, the accident prompts confessions. Again Jones cannot resist symbolism and metaphor which is risible at times. In early sepia flashbacks a girl and boy are seen playing with a cart and the boy falls off (prefiguring O.G.'s disability); a rotten apple falls in the gutter. The film is about innocence, represented by O.G. and his doting choir, and corruption – illustrated by the crude chauvinism of the dialogue and the repeated casual fondling of the wife by both her lover and a lascivious old man. But it is stilted, and studded with redundant scenes, and the plot dawdles until any potential drama is lost.

Emlyn Williams, another young director, also graduated from WFB films to S4C. His **Y Dieithryn** (The Stranger) (1976) is intermittently arresting, occasionally almost surrealist; it is a short study of alienation and a cry for individual freedom and against loss of identity. It suggests that city values, involving the erasure of individuality, are contagious. The swift economic cutting is noteworthy but the subject matter and treatment are, for the most part, depressingly familiar. Again the film is laden with shots of birds on the wing (a moratorium on the use of bird symbolism and funeral scenes might not have gone amiss at the board in those days). In **Y Dieithryn**, a bespectacled young man catches a bus from Llanbedrog to Pwllheli. He is next seen merging and jostling with the crowds in London before flinging himself from a blitzed building, a scene indicative perhaps of the rubbish and detritus of city life. The film virtually ends with a primal scream. It is an interesting diversion, made with some skill, but slightly marred by uneven performances.

By 1980, with the imminent creation of S4C, the Film Board's functions were being questioned. Wil Aaron thought it 'should not be making films to compete with independents'. He considered its primary role should be in touring S4C work around villages and making films for the new channel but crewing them up mainly with technicians who could gain experience of different, more advanced roles. The films should have a strong training element, he felt.[23] A discussion paper presented to the WAC asked, pointedly, if the board's existence was justified. Was there still a need to provide films mainly for showing in theatres and halls which might then be screened on TV?[24] By that time it was obvious any future board films would be competing for skilled personnel, not merely with TV companies but a clutch of Welsh independent companies – and its production costs would soar. The paper suggested the board might serve as an archive, broaden media education by producing films and video presenting a wide canvas of Welsh life, work on Wales's screen heritage, or venture into experimental Welsh-language films – serving as a 'nursery' for technicians. The non-commercial rules of the Association of Cinema and Television Technicians (ACTT) and other unions could be employed to crew up films cheaply. The paper also suggested the body could appoint a director and produce popular features to give young film-makers 'a chance to establish themselves'. The Bwrdd Filmiau duly appointed as virtual full-time administrator Gwilym Owen, but disenchantment with its role increased and it was wound up in mid-decade. Losses on several films and Owen's own alleged profligacy in shooting **Madam Wen** way over budget helped hasten its demise.[25] The adverse publicity surrounding the film's costs was a big disappointment for S4C, which could hardly have had a more unpromising start.

FILM AND THE WELSH FOURTH CHANNEL:

EARLY MISTAKES – AND SUCCESSES

There was so little to base a film policy on. We had to create the environment where people would begin to think . . . of film rather than the old regional television programmes . . . The second stage was to get that film industry recognized outside its own community and culture. With *Coming Up Roses* and *Boy Soldier* we were able to put in the shop window two Welsh-language films that could hold their own with a cinema audience.

(Euryn Ogwen Williams, S4C programme controller, interviewed August, 1987)

S4C was launched in 1982 in fraught circumstances after a long, bitter fight by activists and, finally, a threat to fast to the death by Plaid Cymru leader Gwynfor Evans. It took Welsh-language programmes off BBC and Independent TV channels, but even some language campaigners felt the new channel created a ghetto. Many monoglot English-speakers saw it as an irrelevance or a sop to the Welsh establishment. Others, with no axe to grind, felt a separate channel within Wales should have catered for a significant number of English-language Welsh-produced programmes. It was vital, to disarm critics, that S4C made a good early impact – especially in its more creative drama or documentary slots.

Yet S4C's opening feature films betrayed a fatal lack of confidence and ambition. It was sad that an outsider, Yorkshireman James Hill, was chosen, for instance, to develop the most significant of these flag-waving productions – **Owain Glyndŵr**, (Owen Glendower) – the St David's Day production of 1983 – when much Welsh talent remained relatively untapped, and that no one at the new channel saw the subject itself as an opportunity to produce a provocative and stirring adult production with reflections on nationhood and analogies with the present. Hill, by his own admission, knew little of Welsh politics.[1] He ran into problems when he discovered that the original plan to make a series of dramas on Glyndŵr had been abandoned in favour of a feature film and he conceived it as nothing more than a children's work.[2] Hill blended three scripts together quickly just before shooting. Even though celebrated cameraman Wolfgang Suchitzky made the most of broody landscapes and a spectacular quarry location near Betws-y-coed, and Hill used the outdoor settings to maximum visual effect, the film's English-language version, in particular, was woefully simplistic with ludicrously anachronistic modern colloquialisms. J. O. Roberts in the lead, though stately (not to say monolithic), lacked the charisma to hold our attention or send the viewer back to reading more subtle alternative versions of history. The film seemed fatally torn between subscribing to the 'Glyndŵr as action-hero' myth and hinting at the character's more sober credentials as a lawyer. It contrived to reduce fifteenth-century politics to tiresome domestic or internecine aristocratic squabbling, and Glyndŵr's persecutor Lord Grey (Hugh Thomas) to the pawn of a harridan mother (played by Hugh Griffith's sister, Elen Roger Jones). Little sense emerged of the political, social realities of the day or of ordinary life.[3]

S4C's programmes head, Euryn Ogwen Williams, later acknowledged that **Owain Glyndŵr**, conceived merely as 'entertainment', did little for Wales or the channel and 'wasn't substantial enough', and the choice of Hill may have been a mistake. He also claimed that this kind of film 'wasn't really part of the Welsh psyche'. Welsh film-makers were into 'developing small intimate ideas, set in local communities, with a local theme', he insisted. The revealing remarks hinted, perhaps unwittingly, at a fatal parochialism and a resistance to genre features which Wales badly needed to establish itself internationally as a significant film-making country. Hill's feature also threw up more significant problems which other directors aiming for TV network acceptance were to encounter later in the decade. He auditioned 200–300 actors in English and Welsh but some performers found difficulty in adapting to the English-language version in the back-to-back shooting. The Welsh-based director Stephen Bayly was to find it even more difficult when he shot **The Works** in two different versions and discovered the contrasting speech rhythms of the two languages led to fairly severe editing problems.[4] Back-to-back shooting had economic advantages but directors working on productions made simultaneously for Channel Four and S4C, with the same casts doubling up, found themselves restricted by the limited pool of Welsh actors – especially when some found it difficult expressing themselves naturally *enough* on screen in English. Hill and Bayly, both non-Welsh-speakers, brought in veteran stage director Wilbert Lloyd Roberts to direct the actors in Welsh.

Owain Glyndŵr merely compounded the sense of disappointment felt after the première, in 1982, of **Madam Wen** (White Lady), a film entertaining on its own unambitious level but scarcely original or inspired enough for the vanguard of a channel carrying such high hopes and launched after highly emotive campaigns and a series of political convulsions. It was significant that the two major dramas in S4C's early days were both set in the distant past. They epitomized too much of the channel's dramatic output in the 1980s. It was not, arguably, until Gareth Wynn Jones's **Ysglyfaeth** (Prey, 1984) and Karl Francis's **Yr Alcoholig Llon** (The Happy Alcoholic) – screened on S4C's second anniversary – and his 1986 Northern Ireland film **Boy Soldier**, that the channel presented the kind of provocative, steely contemporary dramas its original champions had a right to anticipate. **Madam Wen** did arouse fierce discussions, but its artistic merits and treatment seemed almost incidental during the row that developed around its budget. The film, S4C's first Boxing Day offering, and scripted by Dafydd Huw Williams, was conceived as family entertainment – according to its producer Gwilym Owen who became director of Bwrdd Ffilmiau Cymraeg in 1980. Owen had been asked for a 'blockbuster' by Ogwen Williams who was 'anxious that the first dramatic feature should come from independents'.[5]

Owen wanted to make 'Helynt Coed Y Gell' (Trouble at Coed Y Gell), a smuggling tale, based on a story by G. Wynne Griffith and set off Anglesey's north-east coast. That would have involved few locations and a small cast.[6] But the sea scenes were deemed a problem and S4C decided instead to shoot the legend of **Madam Wen**, the mysterious seventeenth-century robber, a Robin Hood character also reminiscent of sixteenth-century Welsh folk hero Twm Sion Catti. Owen said later that Williams was anxious to have a Welshman based in London to direct 'rather than the Aarons and Claytons' in order to demonstrate S4C's willingness to lure proven professionals back to Wales. Owen thought Williams was right to go for something non-political and 'a period piece adventure with love, romance, beauty . . .' – but he denies there was any negative thinking or fear of embracing a more contentious subject after the flak the channel had already taken from some MPs and critics who feared S4C would be 'a gravy train for Welsh-speakers'.[7]

Owen's first choice as director was Geraint Morris, an experienced TV drama series hand then working in Scotland, but he was unavailable and the assignment went to London-based Pennant Roberts (b. 1940, Weston-super-Mare, of Welsh parents) who had made episodes of **Dr Who**, **The Onedin Line** and **Juliet Bravo**. Roberts brought his own production team down from London and it was apparently accepted that the whole crew would be on standby for six weeks. Above all, the team lacked an experienced accountant on set, and this was to cost S4C and its credibility dear in ensuing weeks as the budget soared out of control, even though Roberts wrapped up shooting within schedule. There were also fundamental miscastings, with John Pierce Jones playing the male lead Morys, scarcely the romantic figure envisaged in the 1930s book of *Madam Wen*. Owen would have preferred John Ogwen for the lead but Ogwen had just appeared as the hero in BBC's similar **Hawkmoor** series about Twm Sion Catti.[8] The final choices forced script changes to emphasize the pathos of Morys, forever hankering after an unattainable romance, and his awkwardness and limitations as a potential lover. Marged Esli, though personable and efficient as Madam Wen, rarely suggested the glamorous enigma conveyed in the script.

Originally budgeted at between £240,000 and £270,000, according to Owen, but commissioned officially for £335,000, the film finally cost between £500,000 and £550,000. It also placed at risk the future of its producers, the Welsh Film Board. The feature *needed* reasonably lavish spending so it was perhaps crass to think of making it for the original sum. It could also be argued that the movie should have been made on 35mm. rather than 16mm. The 135-minute feature was shot in six weeks and some actors were on location the whole time when needed only briefly, though Roberts claimed he kept a minimum crew, except for the beach and ballroom setpieces.[9] Owen himself, with roots in literature and journalism, had little experience with film or large budgets. There were swift repercussions as the overspending became a *cause célèbre*. With as many as 150 people on set, costs escalated but Owen only 'saw the light' after five weeks: 'I told S4C we were in trouble.' Costs might have been higher if the production team had not skimped on extras – they used only twelve cavalrymen, for example, and completed model shots cheaply at the old Hammer Studios in Bray, Berkshire.

'We were working in absolutely new conditions,' Owen said later. 'Certainly I was to blame for some of the things to happen, but only some. We should have taken on board all the location costs. I should have had an accountant on set and I should have questioned things more – but I was so excited by the possibilities.'[10] Owen was fired from the film during the editing – feeling he had been made a scapegoat – and Dafydd Huw Williams took over as producer, amidst much unfavourable publicity and with S4C attempting 'damage limitation' by issuing statements condemning the overspending and expressing grave concern.[11] Roberts later claimed the channel did not 'sell' the film afterwards – 'having created a *bête noire* they did not want to publicize it.' In the prevailing atmosphere, it would have been surprising if **Madam Wen** had been impressive enough to disarm S4C's opponents and forestall further criticism. At least the finished product looked polished enough to reflect the production values, even if the editing of swashbuckling beach scenes at the finale seemed confused.

Madam Wen is established early on as a local aristocrat on Anglesey's west coast, who charms the bluebloods around her – even Englishman George Price (Ian Saynor), a cold-fish military martinet. One of her victims is Morys, a local squire in her social circle, who bemoans the loss of his rent money to highwaymen. Madam Wen in her highwayman's guise is seen as a masked, elusive figure materializing suddenly in a white dress on a white horse, at night or in the shadows, to taunt the gentry with raids for rent money, which she later tosses away to poor tenants. But the bandit leader is troubled by the dissension within her gang's ranks and the criminal forays by a faction led by one follower, Wil. Finally Wen's loyal followers and Wil's renegades clash by the beach but Wen's party escapes. When Morys finally learns the identity of his female scourge, he arranges to help her flee across a lake to her cottage retreat. The film has a pleasing uniformity of colour on interiors and a persuasive wintry feel to exteriors, but it never overcomes the casting flaws, and merely skirts the political issues and national and economic divisions of the day. The feature made little impact with the public or critics after the ballyhoo during its gestation.

Owen stayed on to complete his year's contract with the Film Board but the organization, already suffering budgeting constraints, was severely embarrassed by the incident, and certain of its films, which might have brought in income from TV screenings, were shown free on S4C as a part of a *quid pro quo* deal after the budget problems.

Madam Wen seemed to set the tone and establish the direction for much early S4C drama, with its frequent emphasis on myth, legend and fable, also epitomized by the Gareth Wynn Jones feature **Macsen** (1983) in which Geraint Jarman played a troubadour, 'a king of song obsessed with the vision of a maid', in a work rooted in the potent *Mabinogion* folk tales.[12] S4C also made a brave stab at **The Mabinogi** (1984), thanks to the combined talents of co-directors Chris Monger and Geoff Moore, and the skills of Moore's drama and performance company, Moving Being. The stories, though heavily condensed (with the film, made in English and Welsh, culled from twenty-three hours of filmed material), had an irresistible lyrical quality, captured by the outstanding location filming at Caernarfon Castle and music by Robin Williamson, of Incredible String Band fame, and Geraint Jarman.

Coming up roses – at last

S4C was perhaps more grateful in its early days for the competent film-makers who delivered the 'drama-doc' series which became a staple of its weekly diet. Cardiff-based Scan (Geoff Thomas and Frances Gallaher) made the first favourable impression, with the ingenious **Mr Hearst and Mr Kane** (1982).[13] Gallaher even induced Hearst's *bête noire* Orson Welles to provide the English-language narration for the Channel Four version in a notable coup, and the film-makers were audacious enough to attempt a reprise of **Citizen Kane**'s introductory shots establishing the newspaperman's lair at Xanadu. Gallaher shot part of the film at Hearst's former sumptuous Californian home, San Simeon, but the film centred mainly on Hearst's retreat at St Donat's Castle in South Glamorgan, telling of his visits – accompanied by silent-screen star Marion Davies – with welcome wry wit. Gallaher at one point even essayed a visual equivalent of the key moment in **Citizen Kane** when the paperweight tumbles down into the foreground of the frame. The S4C film had a pleasing lushness of style, fascinating testimony from old castle retainers and rare archive footage with Hearst and Davies in California playing host to guests including Chaplin and Garbo.[14]

The film-makers again used locations enterprisingly in another programme in the same series (**The Welsh Connection**). **The Rich Man in his Castle** centred on the Marquess of Bute, a man with the patrician values of a chieftain. The programme sketched his singular relationship with the extraordinarily talented architect William Burges whose ornate, eclectic designs transfigured Cardiff Castle's interior and created the Victorian Gothic folly at Castell Coch, Tongwynlais, Mid Glamorgan, beloved of film-making crews. The Scan film attempted to capture the sweep of Burges's imagination – a tall order – and the visual pyrotechnics and swooping camera movements, more pronounced here than in other films by the team, somehow did justice to the grandiose ambition of the subjects. These two programmes alone made the series worthwhile even though others were, in comparison, disappointing. **The Ladies of Llangollen** was routine and inert and the Gladstone programme suffered from lack of old film footage and/or photographs, and became mired in clichés, especially in reconstructed London scenes to dramatize Gladstone's interest in fallen women. The London material was surprisingly given precedence over the Home Rule question – reduced to a few diatribes by letter writers and one or two cartoon diversions.

Richard Love, Iola Gregory in *Joni Jones*.

S4C's most compelling material in the first eighteen months to two years tended to be in half-hour series such as **Almanac**, looking back rather than forward. It was clear that Welsh history needed a more caustic eye: and one which dwelt on issues and not on the gallant deeds of great and remarkable men. S4C's more pungent critics stressed its failure to find creative focus in a Wales becoming progressively de-industrialized with pit closures on the scale of the 1930s. Even the channel's first significant 'discovery', Stephen Bayly, a former architect from Baltimore, did not, initially, buck the trend – though his period pieces, made with Swansea-born Linda James of the Aberystwyth-based independent company Sgrin '82, immediately announced him as a considerable talent. Bayly, a former National Film School student, had already revealed a flair for buoyant editing, humour and observation of human foibles in his splendidly robust NFS short about trainee dancers, **Smile Until I Tell You To Stop** (1979), shot partly at Denham Studios.[15] In 1982 Bayly made, for S4C, **Joni Jones** – five 33-minute films drawn from short stories by R. Gerallt Jones and superbly shot in Wales by Richard Greatrex, who made striking use of landscape and light without sacrificing reality for the easy picture-postcard image.[16] The series, centred on the adventures of a schoolboy during the Second World War, engaged audiences with its humorous and sympathetic observations of social life, and sensitive use of period detail. Bayly was prepared to let key events develop at their own pace, to present the subjective viewpoint of the boy Joni (Richard Love). The half-hour format occasionally appeared too restrictive for Bayly's style but some episodes, at least, conveyed with remarkable assurance the loneliness and durability of the boy. Love, with an almost permanent frown, caught superbly Joni's self-absorption in a performance free of the usual child actor's 'cute' affectations. One episode, 'The Evacuees' – the first Welsh-language drama to be screened at the London Film Festival – was outstanding. It told of two boy evacuees from Liverpool bullying and causing havoc in Joni's local community with random acts of cruelty. The programme had a moral toughness and unblinking honesty which few films made in Wales had approached. It made **Gwenoliaid** (Swallows, 1986), also focusing on evacuees, seem a little too soft-centred for all its overt charm and the writer Rhydderch Jones's integrity and painstaking re-creation of period and familiarity with the milieu.[17] The dialogue of 'The Evacuees' had a rawness which rang true and there was no attempt by Bayly to soften the edges of his characters, even though Iola Gregory as the mother was a stoic loving presence and comfort throughout.[18] Nor did the drama offer solutions (the evacuees, described by one local as 'savages without shame', were eventually packed off in disgrace, and the killing of a pet pig by the new arrivals led to mutual incomprehension between the villagers and strangers). Bullying scenes in the episode when Joni leaves home to go to school miles away were also well handled, usually avoiding cliché. Another programme in the series, 'Y Ffoadur' (The Fugitive), in which a German prisoner of war (Alfred Molina) was recaptured after a brief friendship with Joni also refused easy options at the climax.

Much credit for the achievements in **Joni Jones** must go to the screenwriter, Sussex-based Ruth Carter, Bayly's contemporary at the NFS. It was scarcely surprising that Joni Jones should transcend the language barrier and in 1986 became the first Welsh-language series shown (with subtitles) on BBC2. A feature-length version followed later. Even 'The Evacuees' scarcely prepared us for Bayly's first feature comedy **Aderyn Papur** (**And Pigs Might Fly**, 1984), also the first UK feature to offer, within a fictional format, a critical view of a blighted north Wales quarry community. The ability of Bayly and Carter to build on gags and situations and link them with great precision, while fleshing out minor characters, helped to maintain momentum and take us inside the lively mind of an eleven-year-old boy who must become 'very old very young' in adversity.[19] Freckle-faced Alun (Richard Love again) believes, wrongly, that two Japanese visitors are preparing to revive his village by creating a local industry there. He hopes this will provide employment for his jobless father and unite his family after his mother's defection to Liverpool. Brother Idris, a sour unemployed skinhead, hints darkly at joining the army, but Alun believes the slate quarry will soon boom again – thanks to demand for material for snooker tables. His perambulations around the village trying to sell the place's attractions to the bemused Orientals, who cannot understand his language, are both amusing and touching. The combination of Bayly's witty, restrained direction and Carter's sensitive script enables us to sympathize with the two visitors – too good-natured to query the point of the boy's strenuous efforts – yet revel in the youngster's ingenuity. The father's bitterness gives the film an asperity lacking in most Welsh comedy and the film does not lack piquancy, either, as we sense that Alun, wide-eyed in some respects (especially when he quizzes his grandfather about the past), is approaching the end of innocence. **And Pigs Might Fly** goes awry only in an unduly cute scene, which probably read better than it plays, when the community (now with an eye to the main chance) stage a Japanese night, with all the trimmings, at the local pub.

Bayly's next film **Y Gwaith** (**The Works**, 1984), set in an Aberdare factory, was a comparative disappointment. It had obvious affinities with **Smile Until I Tell You To Stop** in its emphasis on manipulation – in this case of a gauche youth by his first employers who encourage him to spy on colleagues. Bayly asked questions about the quality of life through the boy's rites of passage. The youth does not have the nous, initially, to stave off the wiles of the female deputy managing director (Iola Gregory). He finds himself gradually picking his way through a minefield of moral choices, after exposure to the liberating views of a wide-boy shop steward (splendidly played by Dafydd Hywel) – 'the anarchist-saboteur type'.[20]

Bayly said **The Works** tried to show the 'alienating effect of much modern industrial practice in Thatcher's Britain, the meaninglessness of tasks and the lack of rapport between workforce and bosses'.[21] Kerry Crabbe's script of 'a young man's voyage' provided the basis of 'a pageant rather than a narrative film' and might have been designed for Lindsay Anderson 'in the **O Lucky Man** mould', the director said later.[22] He thought the script was 'intelligent and politically spot on' but felt the budget was never big enough to cope with its ideas. Attempts to pare the material down to meet resources may be responsible for the uneasy mix of documentary realism and comedy and more impressionistic scenes, and the frequently disconcerting tempo switches. The film often gives the impression of a half-realized project, lacking narrative drive. Bayly later acknowledged the dangers implicit in presenting a central character who is too passive. Pitched one way or the other by events, the boy never imposes himself. 'One flaw . . . is that you don't see the change in him or his attitudes,' the director conceded.[23] The central character is tugged emotionally between the polarized views of Miss Puw (Gregory), who represents a hardline management obsessed with profitability, and Sam the shop steward (Hywel). One represents an abnegation of life, the other spontaneous forces.

Bayly was pleased with the art direction, photography, and art design but less satisfied with the revised script after material was excised to meet the tight five-week schedule for shooting in both Welsh and English – 'back to back'. This was a disastrous experience, the director later admitted.[24] There were forty-five speaking parts; with available Welsh-language talent spread very thinly, actors were under-rehearsed and the early English takes were done first to enable Bayly to explain to actors the interpretation. Differences in rhythms and pace between English and Welsh speech presented editing problems and the need for a large cast forced him to complement actors with cabaret performers.[25]

After these problems, Bayly confirmed his high promise with **Rhosyn a Rhith (Coming Up Roses**, 1986), another fruitful collaboration with writer Ruth Carter.[26] The film, made for just £400,000, mounted an unambiguous critique of south Wales valleys life under the Tories in the eighties, within an intimate British comedy in the forties and fifties vein. It appeared to owe something at plot level to the Margaret Rutherford–Peter Sellers feature **The Smallest Show on Earth** (dir. Basil Dearden, 1957), though the director only saw that film at a special screening he arranged on location at Aberdare during production.[27] The earlier work drew most of its comedy from the idiosyncrasies and resilience of Rutherford as the cinema's ubiquitous cashier and usherette in a 'bijou' cinema, Sellers as the hard-drinking projectionist intent on saving his beloved fleapit and Bernard Miles as the near-geriatric factotum and eventual saviour. Bayly cast Dafydd Hywel, used to macho roles, against type as the timorous divorced projectionist Trev, whose natural diffidence is cancelled out by the tenacity of usherette Mona (Iola Gregory) when their cinema the Rex is jeopardized by a probable sell-out to major developers. The entrepreneurs are merely interested in making a killing on the cinema's bric-à-brac but the local council want to turn it into a car park. They reckon without the resourcefulness of Mona, who brings out in Trev his latent bloody-minded qualities. After embarking on the film's least successful element, a scheme to grow mushrooms for profit in the darkened, derelict cinema, the pair eventually persuade the council to plump for restoration. The pair also raise enough cash to erect an eloquent memorial to the cinema's old owner, Eli Davies, and pay off a debt of honour. The cinema becomes a metaphor for the plight of south Wales, and the economic privations are demonstrated graphically by the financial plight of Dave, Trev's former wife's boyfriend, and *en passant*, as the harried Trev travels around town seeking cash help.

Coming Up Roses has its fey scenes but usually when the humour strays towards whimsy it is saved by the Bayly–Carter sense of irony. The film is also replete with the small details of eighties life. Mona's daughter leaves her baby with granny while she goes off to pursue (abortively) a Youth Opportunities course in the Midlands. Trev's timidity inspires fine comic moments, and his brand of self-effacement and bruised dignity is seen at its best when he is affronted by the suggestion that, with the cinema facing closure, he might become a security doorman for a while. Yet Mona and Trev are as much survivors as Dave, whose HP goods are whittled down as his economic fortunes dip, and the ice cream lady cajoles her reluctant friend into fighting back to woo the developers and the sniffy Valleys bureaucrats.

Bayly and Carter again work superbly in tandem, trading on the director's obvious affection for the cinema's past. The first half of **Coming Up Roses** is wellnigh flawless, with its screening of the Rex's last cinema show, a tacky gorilla monster film – a clever touch recalling **King Kong** and, by extension, the brave struggles of a creature fighting extinction in the same way that the cinema 'stands against' progress and the old-style Valleys life struggles to survive pit closures and the shifting demands of industry. Carter, a former newspaper 'agony aunt', proves once again to have a discerning eye and ear for banter and foibles, and much of the screenplay's structure is exemplary (apparent throwaway lines or asides early in the film are invariably shown to serve a purpose later on).[28] She builds the structure while Bayly orchestrates with adroit pacing – sometimes extemporizing and slipping in dialogue. The feature won widespread praise and the *Observer*'s Philip French found it 'a funny, observant film' and, making the obvious comparison, 'less patronizing than Ealing'.[29] Lauded at Cannes, it won prizes at the Chicago Festival and the comedy festival in Vevey (Chaplin's adopted home town in his last years) and later opened in New York.[30] In 1987, the two Welsh-language films, **Coming Up Roses** and Karl Francis's **Milwr Bychan** (**Boy Soldier**), made history, opening in commercial West End cinemas, the first such showcases for Welsh–English bilingual films. The critics' response generally augured well though S4C, after commissioning both as 16mm. films, seemed surprised by the success of Bayly's feature. Both had to be blown up to 35mm., with inevitable slight lack of definition on the big screen. S4C subsequently determined (at least in theory) to make prestige film productions in future on 35mm. with an eye on theatrical release and co-production deals, and the channel's programmes director Euryn Ogwen Williams talked enthusiastically of building up a shelf of S4C films and indigenous Welsh-language features to help 'my successors fill their schedules'. He also expressed hopes that S4C could, in future, make two films a year for the cinema.[31]

In October 1987 Bayly announced an appetizing new project: four one-hour programmes based on the north Wales quarrymen's strike of 1898 and the infamous behaviour of employer Lord Penrhyn. Barry Hines of **Kes** and (more pertinently) **Days of Hope** was assigned to the project. Hines submitted several treatments but none was satisfactory, according to Ogwen Williams. In 1989 Bayly's Red Rooster announced that the film had been abandoned – a sad blow, as the project, and Hines's astringent, polemical style, might have provided a welcome leavening of combative, committed work, a contrast to the worthy and intelligent but all too often anodyne view of Welsh history purveyed elsewhere by the channel.[32]

S4C's other coup in early days was **SuperTed**, the animation series (from Cardiff's Siriol company) launched in 1983, conceived by Mike Young and animated with great panache and splendid use of colour by former commercials director Dave Edwards.[33] **SuperTed**, screened on the channel's opening night, proved an instant hit with audiences and a spectacular success for S4C after HTV had rejected it, apparently fearing the character might infringe DC Comics' Superman copyright. Edwards's animation of the lively (often extra-terrestrial) adventures of the bear, able to defy gravity thanks to rocket boots, placed heavy emphasis on inventive backdrops. The films also owed much to the resourceful storytelling of Robin Lyons. SuperTed and his friend Spottyman and their adversaries,

SuperTed and Spottyman – created by the Siriol animation company.

especially the dumb-ox Western heavy Texas Pete, all helped draw encouraging audiences for the series on both S4C and BBC. Derek Griffiths provided SuperTed's voice in English with Jon Pertwee as Spottyman, Victor Spinetti as Texas Pete (a part written for him by Lyons), Roy Kinnear as Bulk, and Melvyn Hayes as Skeleton. Geraint Jarman voiced SuperTed in Welsh. The film-makers and S4C soon claimed sales to forty countries, and were cock-a-hoop in 1984 when **SuperTed** was bought by Disney's cable channel. It also gained a BAFTA animation award.

Siriol's success – and the activities of Cardiff dockland-based companies like Teliesyn and the internationally renowned, but relatively short-lived, John Cross dubbing studio ECO – finally brought some life to Cardiff docklands and Mount Stuart Square after the abortive attempt to create a Welsh Assembly in the former Coal Exchange building there (a plan scuppered by the referendum vote against devolution). Siriol also made another successful children's series, **Wil Cwac Cwac**, based on the published children's stories by Jennie Thomas and J. O. Williams broadcast on radio in the 1950s. Edwards then consolidated his reputation with **Sion Blewyn Coch (A Winter Story)**, a half-hour film also culled from stories by the same two authors, based on a fox's attempts to purloin a Christmas turkey. The film was notable for its unfussy animation, delicate colours, narrative flair and black humour, especially in its unflattering treatment of the human protagonists.

Wil Aaron

S4C's drama-documentary strand was well served by companies such as Wil Aaron's Ffilmiau'r Nant, who made thirteen half-hour programmes for the **Almanac** series and followed with four further series of a dozen each. They included a 1982 programme on the Great Plague at Haverfordwest (well shot and lit by Dafydd Hobson) and an episode devoted to the 1935 *cause célèbre* play *Cwm Glo* (Coal Valley) by J. Kitchener Davies, banned from the Eisteddfod for its presentation of a fairly explicit sexual relationship between a miner's daughter and her father's overseer. The play was described as a libel on Wales, and three adjudicators who voted it the best play were against it being performed. Aaron interviewed actors from the original production and re-staged the most controversial scene.

Aaron's own choice as the company's outstanding early **Almanac** was the drama **Dau Frawd** (Two Brothers), directed by Alun Ffred Jones about two siblings who were the last members of a chapel congregation in the Llŷn Peninsula. These men, one a deacon, lived together but never spoke to each other.[34] Nant concentrated on true, often bizarre, stories, notably **Y Chwarelwr** (The Quarryman) about a man who suspected his wife of infidelity, stole dynamite to blow up his imagined adversary, then found, too late, that the supposed seducer was his own daughter. As he ran away after the discovery a slate fell, decapitating him. Another programme dealt with Joanna Southcott, the West Country prophet and religious leader who, in her sixties, believed she was pregnant by the son of God, an episode recounted in his diaries by a faithful follower, the Merionethshire writer and publisher William Owen Pughe.

Four early **Almanac**s were sold to BBC Wales, including a recreation of the fateful 1911 strike in Llanelli scripted by Gareth Miles. Some of Nant's programmes were fine achievements, given the low S4C budgets of £20,000–30,000 per half-hour. The company often switched from film to video in mid-series to trim costs. Each **Almanac** episode had a meagre five-day shooting schedule, and Nant often shot virtually two at a time – back to back.[35] The company later developed the series **Hywel Morgan, Ustus** (Hywel Morgan, Justice) (dir. Alun Ffred Jones, 1984), which focused on a local magistrate and allowed the film-makers to say much more about the class barriers blighting Welsh society in Victorian days. Nant also dipped toes in contemporary community politics in a video based on a Theatr Bara Caws satirical review about housing problems in Sgubor Goch in Caernarfon, and local audience reaction to the stage production. The programme integrated interviews with residents suffering health or housing problems.

By 1984, Aaron was already convinced that there was more exciting work possible for S4C than for the Welsh Film Board. 'But I wouldn't have survived without the Board. They've kept a few of us alive,' he acknowledged.[36]

Docklands success

Prominent among S4C contributors from the outset was Teliesyn, run as a co-operative, with everyone involved in the company taking an equal share of profits. It was formed by Colin Thomas, a committed socialist who had learned his skills as part of John Boorman's BBC documentary team at Bristol, and Paul Turner. Thomas (b. 1939) had resigned from the BBC after interference on two documentaries he made in **The Irish Way** series around 1978, and both men also felt they wanted to work within a structure offering freedom from bureaucracy and which allowed them to make occasional films which reflected the 'kind of society we wanted to see'. Teliesyn honed the skills of these film-makers, provided scope for new talent, including Cardiff-based director Emlyn Williams and Richard Pawelko, and soon established itself as a producer of series and 'drama-docs'.[37] Early work included in 1982–3 Paul Turner's **Chwedlau Serch** (Welsh Love Stories), made for S4C only, and a package of six Anglo-Welsh stories, **Tales from Wales** (**Arswyd y Byd** in the Welsh-language version), which was pre-sold to BBC 1 and 2.[38]

Cornish-born Turner, formerly a BBC film editor (notably on John Hefin's 1981 series **The Life and Times of David Lloyd George**), first emerged as an independent with a personal work, **Trisgel** (1981), an ambitious romance, without dialogue and steeped in folklore and mythology. It revealed his eye for almost tactile imagery and a flair for telling stories through visuals. The film, made after a £5,000 WAC grant, centred on the themes of sexuality and sexism and the concept of 'possession' in relationships within Celtic mythology, and opened with a poem by Dafydd ap Gwilym. The film – focusing on a woman's feelings trapped in a relationship and freed by the arrival of a mysterious stranger, a second woman – has been accused in some quarters of its own insidious sexism. Yet Turner was anxious to explore the dichotomy in men's attitudes to women, placing them on a pedestal as love goddesses and symbols of purity or treating them as chattels. The director later felt the complex form of his hour-long film was far too ambitious.[39]

For Teliesyn Turner (b. 1945) worked on the later 'Love Stories' series with writers like Geraint Jarman, Dwynwen Berry, Dorien Thomas and Margaret Griffiths, and sought to remind viewers of an indigenous history and culture largely lost. The director's visual flair and the skill of cameraman Ray Orton were obvious in one programme in the series, **Llyn y Morwynion** (The Lake of the Maidens) an ancient folk story, based around a lake in Merionethshire, about the kidnapping of three women including a chieftain's daughter, by a trio of young bucks who discovered their own village had been ransacked and their females carried off. Bloody retribution followed after a chase through north Wales beauty spots and two of the three women were drowned, even though they were in love with their captors by this time. Turner made the most of moors and wintry landscapes. He also dealt with Celtic myth – this time in Ireland – in **Ar Groesffordd Ofn** (At the Crossroads of Fear) in which holidaymakers unwittingly disturbed ancient burial grounds and paid the price.

Paul Turner on location in Australia for Teliesyn's feature *Realms of Gold*.

Turner also directed the hour-long drama **Wil Six** (1984), a project long cherished by the veteran actor Meredith Edwards. The story of a schoolboy Wil Jones in a village school strict on discipline was filtered through the memories of Edwards's elderly narrator.[40] The school atmosphere, a curious but engaging blend of outmoded authority and bucolic gusto, is captured beautifully in the opening minutes when a group of boys including Wil, a freckled ginger-haired lad (Llŷr Hughes), are caned. When an HM inspector arrives, the head warns the children – in Welsh – that he will give them signals when to revert to the approved English language, which he is constantly trying to promote in vain. 'It's a very witty script – the interplay between the languages. The film makes the point very clearly that to get on you mustn't speak Welsh – that would be a disadvantage,' said Turner later.[41] The points made recalled **The Corn is Green**, set more than four decades earlier.

Turner later directed **Dihirod Dyfed** (1986–7), a dramatized series based on actual murders in west Wales – but budgets were tight. Two **Tales from Wales** films from Rhys Davies stories were made for £70,000 in total. **Wil Six**, which realized Edwards's ambition in screening a radio play he had heard decades before, cost £55–60,000.[42] Operating on minuscule funds Teliesyn worked fast, making dramas in ten shooting days. It was inevitable that the co-operative should plump to work much of the time with pre-existing scripts or literary works rather than original screenplays, but gradually mere professionalism gave way to slightly more lavish productions made with some style.[43] Welsh companies such as Nant and Teliesyn were determined to

Llŷr Hughes in *Wil Six*, directed by Paul Turner.

prove themselves the equal of English independents, and Teliesyn from the beginning shot back to back with English and Welsh productions, using the same actors on the same locations.[44] 'The Welsh industry will be better if we do things ourselves bilingually rather than allow dubbing in the country of purchase,' the co-operative's secretary, Richard Staniforth, said in 1984.[45]

Teliesyn's **Tales from Wales** included **Where There's a Will** (1983), from a Clifford Evans story, with the Cardiff-based Emlyn Williams directing. The work is heavy-handed at times but relishably droll occasionally and it revolves around two farming sons who attempt to defraud a third son of a share in the father's legacy. They invite a cobbler to take part in the ruse to gull a solicitor by impersonating the father on his death bed. The shoe repairer (Charles Williams) outsmarts them all by ensuring that he inherits the £1,500. By the mid-1980s, Teliesyn had expanded into feature film international co-production with Turner and Colin Thomas in the vanguard. The company's fare included the spirited, slightly frenetic but witty documentaries and drama-docs of Richard Pawelko, who shot the international six-day **Enduro** rally film – which went out on cinema circuits – and **Enka** (1983), with music by Geraint Jarman.[46]

Carmarthen-born Thomas had announced himself in Wales with **And Dogs Delight (Fel Ci i Gythraul)** in the **Tales from Wales** series, shot on the greyhound track at Aberbargoed, about a greyhound racing fanatic out to catch a wild dog which could outrace his own champion. Thomas built the drama around an actual race meeting, worked mainly with amateurs and found himself fascinated by the area 'shading between drama and documentary'. He was to establish himself later with a series of documentaries featuring the historian Gwyn Alf Williams. After the pair's initial success, with Wynford Vaughan-Thomas as Williams's co-narrator on **The Dragon Has Two Tongues** (1985) for HTV, they made a significant impact with Channel Four's 1988 **Cracking Up** series which allowed Thomas to dramatize events in the lives of heroic figures linked with revolution. The pair also teamed up on a series of smaller, less ambitious documentaries which had a strong political perspective. In 1986 Thomas directed back to back for S4C and BBC Wales **An African from Aberystwyth (Yr Affricanwr o Aberystwyth)** in which Williams paid homage to David Ifon Jones, a Welsh-born Communist Party member and preacher who became a crucial influence on blacks in South Africa after emigrating there, and was buried in Russia in the early 1930s. The subject was ideally suited to Gwyn Alf's polemic and verbal pyrotechnics, and his metaphors helped spark the programme to life as he stomped Jones's trail from Cardigan to the Soviet Union. Thomas's flair for weaving archive material into 'live' footage and his pragmatic approach to the material allowed Williams his head, ensuring the documentary's success. The pair also made for S4C and BBC Wales **Lest Who Forget (Y Llygaid Na All Agor**, 1985), when Gwyn Alf Williams celebrated the anniversary of Russia's contribution to the Second World War, and **Back to Barcelona** (1988), a record of south Wales miners' revisiting the Basque capital for a reunion, celebrating their heroic Spanish Civil War efforts.[47] They began the nineties as they had finished the eighties with another fine documentary **Hughesovska** (1991) tracing the career in Russia of the Merthyr industrialist John Hughes, and using rare and rich archival footage. The apogee of the Thomas/Williams achievements came in 1992/3 with the ingenious drama-documentary on Saunders Lewis in the **Writing on the Line** series when Williams confronted an actor playing Lewis and examined some of his more controversial statements on class and race. The style was barbed, astringent and bracing.

Storm clouds

Despite some challenging individual works homing in on contemporary issues, S4C faced constant criticism in its early years that its fictional features and drama-docs were too often rooted in the past or in rural backwaters. In 1983, Stephen Bayly was able to assert that S4C material was 'essentially bucolic and folkloric'. The criticism came when there was increased disenchantment with the standards of all channels in Wales, reflected later in an impassioned speech by Gwyn Alf Williams at the National Film Theatre, when he made it clear that HTV had no room for complacency despite the success of **The Dragon Has Two Tongues**: 'You would need a microscope to find the programmes about Welsh life on the major channels as both have failed to fill with suitable Welsh material the slots left vacant with the transfer of material to S4C,' he said. At the same NFT seminar Plaid Cymru president Dafydd Elis Thomas also criticized the channels for their lack of Welsh-based material. Wales 'was too often represented in films and television through the eyes of "outsiders",' he claimed.[48] Certainly, S4C could no longer justify the early dominance of material from north and mid Wales when most of the industrial turmoil, political dramas and employment problems (affecting the bulk of the population) were taking place further south. Euryn Ogwen Williams's comments that 'you're more likely to find Welsh communities in rural areas' suggested a parochialism that came under fire from S4C's detractors increasingly as the decade wore on and suggested that sustenance of the language remained the channel's *raison d'être*.[49]

Ogwen Williams indicated worries over audience satisfaction in an interview in 1987: 'There's a tension between the English and Welsh-language programmes. Half a million people speak Welsh . . . We rely on our judgement – after all the language was part of the creation of S4C. But you can't restrict directors like Karl [Francis] to [making films with] a fixed maximum percentage of dialogue in English.' It was not good enough to try to forestall criticism or mitigate the effects of the geographical imbalance of material by setting soaps in south or west Wales, or shooting the occasional crime thriller series in Cardiff. From the mid-eighties there was a growing realization within S4C that a broader span of drama features was needed to confront social and political themes and hold up to ordinary people in the Valleys some kind of mirror to their lives. Ogwen Williams thought the channel should not be 'so inward-looking' and he encouraged the idea of English-speaking directors making films in Welsh.[50] He began to approach film-makers who had not previously worked for S4C (notably Karl Francis who delivered **The Happy Alcoholic**). The critical success of Francis's later S4C film, **Boy Soldier** and Bayly's **Coming Up Roses** was a massive boost to S4C's image. But it scarcely hid the realities of its first few years. Dramas produced for the channel rarely dealt with key issues confronting a country in flux and in the throes of industrial crisis.

Ogwen Williams could point to encouraging certain indigenous talent which might never otherwise have surfaced. He cited Alun Ffred Jones of Nant and Paul Turner among the film-makers developed. And, late in the decade, S4C was more active in promoting Welsh Arts Council work by independents, screening (belatedly) Marc Evans's **Johnny Be Good** (1985), a genial, amusing study of youthful yearnings for liberation from family constraints, clashes in language and life-styles and the impact of the juke box and its music on rural life in the shadow of the Preseli mountains.[51] Yet the limits of S4C's willingness to experiment can be gauged from Williams's comments that much WAC product was 'too esoteric' for transmission. Few would argue with his statement that quality rather than themes or emphasis on particular issues should dictate S4C's feature film and drama content but it was still disappointing that the first of the 35mm. films to emerge, Endaf Emlyn's **Stormydd Awst** (Storms of August, 1987), proved a throwback to the naïve, simplistic comedies of the Welsh Film Board. The subject matter could have been intriguing: the emotional turmoil of a jilted youth who, almost from peevishness, exposes the hypocrisy and cant of a north Wales seaside town already divided by the impact of a local newspaperman's campaign against the advent of TV in the 1950s. Emlyn's lively programme on the pop group Bando in **Shampŵ** won the Celtic Film Festival Spirit of the Festival prize in 1983, two years before **Johnny Be Good** carried off the same prize. Emlyn also made a prestige S4C film **Y Dyn Nath Ddwyn y Nadolig** (**The Man Who Stole Christmas**, 1985, with Michael Povey as a crook intent on wiping out all festivities); and, **Y Cloc** (The Clock, 1986), a tantalizing but uneven, overambitious and frenetic exercise in nostalgia with time-travel elements straight out of **Dr Who** and a cautionary subplot owing something to Dickens's *Christmas Carol* and the whimsy of Frank Capra's 1947 James Stewart movie **It's a Wonderful Life**. A more significant Emlyn film was **Gaucho** (1983), an enterprising, meandering quasi-Western set in Patagonia.[52] But **Stormydd Awst**, shot in Pwllheli, was anything but progressive, the broad humour was thinly spread and the film larded with caricatures. It was hard to see the film having any appeal outside Wales. This type of feature has been described (in a more general context) by Deryk Williams, S4C's programmes director, as 'Fair Isle TV – drama in rural backgrounds with everybody in woolly jumpers. It's a fair criticism of our first ten years that we concentrated too heavily on the past.'

The same vein of rural nostalgia was also tapped in Emlyn Williams's Nant movie **Gwynfyd** (Paradise, 1992), which followed the adolescent rites of passage of a north Wales girl (Luned Gwilym) in the late 1950s, and the impact on her of a Nonconformist upbringing, its moral tenets contrasting sharply with the gleefully lascivious comments of her more worldly-wise 'best friend'. Williams had confirmed a talent for comedy with **Dyddiadur Dyn Dwad** (Diary of an Incomer, 1992), with Llion Williams as a north-Walian radical tiro journalist stirring up a hornet's nest in Cardiff.

North Wales talents

Bucolic features with a strong feeling for milieu and locale became the stock-in-trade of Ffilmiau'r Nant's Alun Ffred Jones, the Caernarfon film-maker and sympathetic collaborator and screen interpreter of the work of veteran radio playwright Wil Sam Jones (b. Caernarfonshire, 1920). Typical was **Y Dyn Swllt** (Shilling Man) (1989), adapted from a Wil Sam short story about a clubman cycling around the district, thwarted at every turn in his bid to collect insurance arrears from hard-pressed but often cunning villagers. Wil Sam, perhaps best known for his character Ifas y Tryc, often celebrated local eccentricities. His use of colourful, idiomatic language was again demonstrated in **Plant y Tonnau** (Children of the Waves, 1986). The same pair collaborated for **Sgid Hwch** (Bad Move, 1992), in which a garage-owner's search for a motorcycle became a metaphor for the pursuit of Wales itself. This film, from a partly autobiographical script by Wil Sam, also reflected the author's sharp concern about the future of the Welsh language.

Alun Ffred linked up with writers Mei Jones and Michael Povey on **Deryn** (1985) a six-part drama series set in what the director described as the 'demi-underworld' of Anglesey. This spawned another eight-part series (1987) and a feature **Deryn Dolig** (Christmas Bird, 1989). There was humour in **Rhew Poeth** (Hot Ice, 1987), which homed in on youths in an ice-cream selling war in the Llanberis area. The series had been apparently inspired by anecdotal reports of factional in-fighting among Italian families but might have owed something to Bill Forsyth's **Comfort and Joy** (1984), a work of wry comedy with similar feuding in Glasgow as the backdrop to the central character's career and marital problems. By the early nineties, Alun Ffred was seeking to create more work relevant to contemporary Wales, but was adamant that his forte lay in working-class dramas. He produced **Cylch Gwaed** (In the Blood, 1992), for instance, which dealt powerfully with the plight of a young garage mechanic (Rhys Richards) caught in a vicious circle as a lowly, not particularly successful, pro-boxer trying to fight his way out of the poverty trap. The film, directed by Timothy Lyn, son of actor David, was noted for its fractious family relationships, earthy dialogue, superbly shot fight scenes and unrelenting view of characters who rapidly became shorn of all illusions. The film won the Best Drama prize at the 1993 Celtic Film and TV Festival in Lorient, Brittany, and Richards gained the 1994 BAFTA Cymru Best Actor award despite competition from Anthony Hopkins and Huw Garmon. Alun Ffred's comedy series **C'Mon Midffild** (C'Mon Midfield) (five series, 1988–94) for S4C was a sharp contrast, with its robust humour, and play on loveable soccer stereotypes. The series involved local amateur players and referees and the community in a resourceful, positive way – and it was no surprise that this series also ultimately yielded a feature-length drama **Midffild** (1992).

Another director to switch his attention to modern drama was former Welsh Film Board stalwart Gareth Wynn Jones, driving force of another north Wales independent company, Ty Gwyn. Jones has specialized in recent years in genre films, particularly in thrillers such as series **Cysgodion Gdansk** (**Shadows of Gdansk**, 1986), focusing on a renegade British spy (J. O. Roberts) finding refuge in Anglesey; and one-off dramas like **Blumenfeld** (1988), a somewhat confused tale of German terrorist groups and British secret service machinations, with Philip Madoc in a dual role. Another Wynn Jones drama, **Barbarossa** (1989), sought to capture an audience increasingly concerned with ecological and global environmental issues and pollution. The villains were a group of clandestine neo-Nazis spreading worldwide tentacles to take over Antarctica and its mineral wealth, and gaining footholds in respectable research organizations.

The director's earlier S4C work, **Ysglyfaeth** (Prey, 1984), was compelling in its presentation of character and weaving of Welsh social, language and cultural issues into the fabric of a lively political suspense film. Scripted by Harri Pritchard Jones, the film starred Tom Richmond (later known as Dafydd Dafis) as a Welshman in the SAS who falls for the Irish girlfriend of his IRA target. Jones maintains tension superbly, while drawing parallels between the background of the hit man, Non-conformist from a poor, working-class slate-quarrying family in the Nantlle Valley near Caernarfon, and his prey, another victim of internecine bigotry, a Catholic from

Catherine Tregenna in the title role of *Blodeuwedd*, directed by Siôn Humphreys.

the Isle of Arran. Jones, filming in Derry, Cork and Arran, gave due weight to the force of nationalist pride and feeling, and scenes between the Irish girl and her boyfriend and his family arguing the pros and cons of sectarianism and violence were particularly powerful. The film pre-dated **Boy Soldier** and handled the love affair across sectarian divides with equal sensitivity, though the girl's final acquiescence and virtual complicity after the fact seem a little too abrupt and summary and to undermine, to some extent, the depth of honest feeling and intensity of the movie's political and ideological discussions. But Jones handled the action and the ideas in the script with dexterity, and the film is permeated with a sense of fatalism which finds bloody expression at the climax. Jones also demonstrated his grasp of period atmosphere and wartime intrigue and of *mise-en-scène* in **Sigaret** (1991), his claustrophobic version of Saunders Lewis's play. The work suffered a little from some slackening of tension during prolonged domestic scenes, but conjured up an alienating world only half-understood by the central character who is given the onerous job of killing a former political associate of his wife's father. Jones used spare settings, ellipses and muted colours to fine effect.

Another north-Walian, Siôn Humphreys (b. 1951), son of Emyr, continued through S4C's first decade to provide an eclectic range of drama, often derived from plays or scripts by his father and he revealed a strong feeling for text, landscape, metaphor and painstaking framing. Humphreys, who runs his own company Bryngwyn, near Caernarfon, has tended to go his own way since his film-making début drama, **Y Gosb** (The Punishment) (1982), a study of a Nonconformist minister imprisoned in a campaign for a Welsh-language TV channel and who suffers sexual abuse in gaol and discovers the hatred felt for chapel dogma. Humphreys's work tends to be intense and reflective, with passion contained or repressed, and to rely on atmosphere, sometimes at the expense of narrative drive. Occasionally he can seem downright perverse, notably with his version of Saunders Lewis's **Blodeuwedd** (1989) – set in a photogenic quarry – which scarcely uses camera movements at all, except pans around the characters as they deliver slabs of text in close-up. The film, while also making experimental use of colour filters, lost the essential magical elements of the play, but Humphreys wanted to concentrate people's minds on the text as a feminist work, and to re-interpret the play to make Blodeuwedd more sympathetic than normal, a child of nature exploited by her masters rather than simply a vengeful, unfaithful wife who betrays her creator. 'The magic didn't interest me as much as the manipulation and the way the manner of Blodeuwedd's creation mirrored the society around her,' the director said later. The film, hampered by a short shooting schedule and low budget, still seemed like a missed opportunity and was not well received by the public or the higher echelons of S4C.

Another introverted work was **Barcud Yn Farcud Fyth** (Once a Kite, Always a Kite, 1992), starring Dyfan Roberts as a stolid, strait-laced English teacher who dreams of small rebellions but is too timorous to challenge his usually dismissive head. The teacher finds himself increasingly aware of his own shortcomings, especially in a key confrontation with an aggressive former pupil who taunts him in the local pub about his worthlessness and the superfluous nature of his work. The film was too slow and mannered, despite effective and intriguing use of screen space and metaphor. More gloom and introspection characterized **Byw yn Rhydd** (Living Freely, 1984), with an ageing man, Jones (Mei Jones), reflecting on a failed life of soured relationships and missed opportunities.

Humphreys used highly stylized, theatrical devices in **Ac Eto Nid Myfi** (And Yet Again Not I, 1989), from the drama by John Gwilym Jones. The director employed split-level stage sets, lighting and alienation effects and monologues, often to pleasing effect, in a study of a young man's thraldom to three generations of women against a backdrop of Nonconformism. The drama centres on the relationship of Huw Jones (Llion Williams) with his mother, grandmother and pregnant girlfriend as he reflects on his failure to slough off the influences of his parents or to transform a fundamentally stunted life. Humphreys resisted opportunities to open up the story with cinematic techniques – only once startling us by sudden use of flashback – and it seemed that here, as elsewhere, he had decided to maintain fidelity to the dramatic, literary structure of a work without adapting it, overtly, to his own chosen medium. In his films generally Humphreys seems to make conscious decisions to efface himself to service and keep faith with the literary source material, which clearly means much to him. But **Ac Eto Nid Myfi**, though persuasively claustrophobic, seemed a little too slight to justify the tone and deferential treatment – even though it was a film central to Humphreys's concerns as a director. It revealed his fascination with exploring the psychology of characters forced into situations alien to their nature and also with continuity and the force of a past impinging (often destructively) on the present.

Much more arresting were two films starring Iola Gregory. The first, **Teulu Helga** (Helga's Family, 1985), centred on a schoolteacher desiring to create a school élite, in the manner of Jean Brodie's *crème de la crème*. Her dangerous views open a Pandora's box. Once more, as in **Gosb**, the pedagogue finds his/her beliefs challenged. Personal relations sour, tragedy intervenes and a former idyllic state of grace gives way to long periods of isolation. A cluttered narrative rather blunts the film's impact, even if there are tantalizing scenes revealing the psychological complexity of relationships with suggestive, impressionable pupils. In **Yr Alltud** (The Exile, 1989), Gregory played a German countess living out her life in a north Wales village and seeking to bury the past as the wife of a leading Nazi. Her friendship with a doting local girl, though fraught with tension, provides her only emotional sustenance in a suspicious community riven by petty jealousies. The past cannot so lightly be shrugged off, as she discovers in a finale which provides a test of loyalty before the inexorable tragic climax. Humphreys conveyed depth of emotion in the interaction of the countess – the familiar mentor figure of his films – and the protégée, who constantly seeks the approval of this 'outsider', even when clashing with her implacable will.

Iola Gregory has become a familiar figure in Humphreys's work, playing Siwan in the S4C Welsh-language version of the Saunders Lewis play (1986), and then Kate Roberts, the novelist, in Siôn Humphreys's **Triple Net** (1987, Channel Four), a biopic which was not particularly ambitious cinematically but told us much about the formative influences on the writer and her reflections on the role of Welsh culture and language. Gregory, who was also seen to advantage in Paul Turner's powerful, claustrophobic lesbian tragedy **Tra Bo Dwy** (1984), played important roles in Humphreys's **Twll o Le** (A Dump of a Place, 1986) and **Dŵr a Thân** (Water and Fire, 1991). The first, from a Wil Sam story – shot in and around the quarry at Dinorwig – focused sharply on a north Wales community drained of life by the decline of the slate trade. Men forage in the mine for good stones to sell, and the *ennui* is well captured by the director. A young man, Mostyn (Bryn Fôn), is sucked into crime by his straitened fortunes. The only jobs available are menial and Gregory's character, a headmaster's widow, bemoans her daughter's attempts to find work as a cleaner in the very school where the girl's father was head. Guto Roberts plays Taid, an old man ruminating on the demise of the community, the frustrations of the young who are 'like animals looking for an open door', and the cynicism of modern times. But he is prepared at least to act, on behalf of a newly formed Unemployed Workers' Union, and finally to use his skills to build the house which will help in the rehabilitation of Mostyn and – symbolically – the community. Unfortunately the film's would-be affirmative ending is at odds with the tenor of previous scenes, and the expressed hope that Mostyn's predicament and fall from grace might somehow bring the community to its senses seems whimsical. Humphreys's characters appear to function in a vacuum, and a work always strong in atmosphere finally smacks a little of complacency about problems, and lacks irony and political thrust.

In **Dŵr a Thân**, Humphreys uses a meeting of Polish and Welsh couples at a Breton holiday camp to examine issues of individual and collective responsibility, the durability of memory – and guilt. He frames his characters, typically, with great precision, on what seem to be stage sets, and frequently links them with slow lateral tracks. In the Polish family is a daughter anxious to be freed from the constraints of 'party' bureaucracy, and an old man, half-deranged with his fragmented recollections of driving trainloads of Jews into the Treblinka camp. Gregory's lawyer, in conversations with her teacher husband, argues the primacy of justice and reason over emotions, love or 'sexual impulses'. Much of the dialogue is stilted and the film, for all Humphreys's attempts to liberate the camera, never seems cinematic enough. Humphreys, in a career of more than twenty films, has always been prepared to confront serious issues, and treat them intelligently, but, in regarding his literary influences and sources with perhaps too much fidelity, his own creative voice has sometimes seemed muted.

After S4C's first ten years the suspicion remained that the channel had no coherent policy on film. Siôn Humphreys complained, for instance, that S4C had shown little interest in screening European movie classics with Welsh subtitles – a development which he saw as vital in the creation of an awareness, especially among young people, of the broader trends of screen culture, and range of film technique.

Blazing a trail

It was irritating that so few new home-based works (commissioned or bought in) dealt with salient issues of the late eighties and presented them in a progressive style which might signal the way forward for film in Wales. The channel's most significant contribution had been in animation where it continued to build on the reputation forged by the original Dave Edwards/Robin Lyons Siriol company, encouraging short films from independents (notably the new workshops within Wales) and commissioning longer works. This culminated in plans for the country's first animation feature **The Princess and the Goblin**, which finally emerged in 1991 co-directed by Les Orton and co-produced with Hungary

for Robin Lyons's company. S4C executive Chris Grace, the man who snapped up **SuperTed** for just £20,000, also played a key role in making Cardiff a major focus for

animation film in Britain. The city first acted as hosts for the British Animation Awards in 1989 and 1991, then Grace helped bring together a sponsorship package to lure the 450-film International Animation Festival to Wales and Cardiff for the first time in 1992 and take the event away from Bristol.

But, just as significant as either of these stimulating developments, was the emergence of Cardiff-based film-maker Joanna Quinn as one of the UK's independent animators. She gained a spectacular triple award at the leading international animation festival in Annecy, France, in 1987 with **Girls' Night Out**, which offers an intelligent look at sexism in the Valleys by reversing male and female roles. It focuses on a middle-aged woman factory worker who enjoys herself at a hen party, ogling a male stripper – while her hubbie is seen slumped before the TV.[54] The brash characterization and incisive editing, with forceful use of close-ups and amusing earthy Valleys vernacular, was a tonic and an antidote to so much esoteric or elliptical animation work. S4C was quick to sponsor Quinn's follow-up, **Body Beautiful**, a more overt attack on macho values featuring the same middle-aged roly-poly heroine, Beryl, who humiliates a narcissistic male bodybuilder. Quinn's were the first 'political' cartoons from Wales – necessary antidotes to previous animation which had been unproblematic, unchallenging in content, merely interpreting literary work, supplying lively juvenilia or reinforcing preconceptions about Wales. Her **Tea at No. 10** (1987), with its slogan 'Eat a Tory before he eats you', prefigured the biting satire of Quinn's anti-Thatcherite, award winning **Britannia** (1993).

S4C and/or Channel Four also provided a showcase for two other Welsh-based independent animation talents: Clive Walley and Phil Mulloy. Their abilities were recognized in the BBC Wales series **Statements** – one of the few worthwhile arts-based TV programmes to emerge since the seventies in Wales – and by WAC and S4C who ploughed money into a feature about Walley's work and methods. Mulloy (b. Wallasey, Cheshire, 1948), with a studio in a converted cowshed near Carmarthen, created extraordinarily fluid, assured comedies, using silhouette animation and drawing inspiration from comic strips. His **Cowboys** series for Channel Four explored character foibles and universal themes. In his later 1993 movies **The Sound of Music** (an 11-minute virtuoso piece) and **Thou Shalt Not Kill**, the foibles of his vulpine, predatory creatures (similar to those peopling his **Cowboy** films) reflected a world bereft of all reason and justice. Here was an unbridled but formidable talent with a taste for the grotesque and for assaulting his audience's sensibilities. Painter Clive Walley (b. Chester, 1943) made one WAC-backed short in the 1970s, then broke a ten-year animation silence when S4C came along to resurrect his career. His 1993 films **Divertimento No. 2: Love Song** and **Divertimento No. 4: Life Study**, shown at the International Animation Festival held at Cardiff the following year, confirmed his penchant for abstract imagery allied to vivid colours and eclectic musical soundtracks. David Usher's blues harmonica added much to the texture of **Divertimento No. 2**.

Animation successes helped appease S4C's critics. Yet, by the early nineties, there was a groundswell of feeling that no channel targeted for a mere 500,000 Welsh-speakers could hope to fulfil the needs of viewers throughout the country. Film-makers in urban south Wales, in particular, increasingly felt that an English-language television showcase was also needed to bring their work to international attention and give Wales the cachet internationally of Scottish film-makers like Bill Forsyth (**Gregory's Girl**, **Comfort and Joy**) and Bill Douglas (with his autobiographical trilogy of youth beginning with **My Childhood**) and of Ireland's Neil Jordan (**Angel** and **The Crying Game**), Pat O'Connor (**Cal** and **Ballroom of Romance**) and Jim Sheridan (**My Left Foot** and **The Field**).

WORKSHOPS AND THE 'INDEPENDENTS'

Chapter Film Workshop got its political conscience late in life, but that may be not such a bad thing. If the predominant mode of Chapter output since its beginning could be defined, it would be something like 'experimental narrative', a concern with finding new forms to say new things. However successful or futile, significant or trivial these films may have been, the workshop has had a whole history of trying to find new ways of working with images and techniques without much preciousness or fear of not making films the right way.

(Article by Roland Denning, the workshop's co-ordinator in the organization's journal *One Eye*, no. 2, August/September 1984)

The birth of the workshop movement in Wales was potentially almost as important a development as the new opportunities for independent film- and video-makers opened up by the launch of Channel Four and S4C. Film workshops, such as those at Cardiff's Chapter Arts Centre, grew up as embryo film-makers felt the need to learn and collaborate in experimenting creatively, free of commercial pressures. They crewed each other's films and individuals switched roles for different projects as part of their development. The collective group methods bore fruit – at least in the early eighties – in a succession of invigorating and combative low-budget works. The standard of individual work varied immensely in these years as Chapter, and similar film-making organizations, struggled to find an identity. Chapter workshop co-ordinator Roland Denning stressed that the centre's creative and experimental impetus came from the success of groups like the avant-garde, iconoclastic London Film-makers' Co-op, though – as he acknowledged – Chapter's base was broader than that might imply as the centre had its roots equally in community film-making through the impact made by Cardiff Street Television (launched in 1975), and the forerunners of Chapter's Video Workshop. The workshops produced stimulating work at first, then came a hiatus as the public subsidy well ran dry. From the mid-eighties it was Chapter's video, rather than film, workshop which, while rarely essaying new forms, produced the more stimulating work, casting a caustic eye on social injustice and the forces in south Wales causing rapid and often damaging community or industrial change. The Welsh Arts Council, with limited funds, deserve some credit for promoting workshops in the 1980s, notably through the All Wales Video Project, which linked Cardiff's Chapter Arts Centre workshop with groups in Brecon and Powys.[1] The project enabled video-makers to hone their skills and gain experience working with, and for, communities, with tapes on vital social issues. Chapter later acknowledged that these bonds between the three workshops were always loose as they failed generally to find much common ground, but some of the livelier debates on film and video and their role in Welsh society came from the workshops in the mid-1980s, even if these forums tended to be ghetto-ized and given only limited attention at such forums as the Celtic Film Festival – financed and controlled by the major TV channels.

In the late 1970s and early 1980s, the Chapter workshop became a lively focus of new talent with young directors such as Chris Monger, Tim Thornicroft, Mick Stubbs and Caroline Limmer in the vanguard. Many of the film-makers were from England and produced often idiosyncratic, highly personal works which owed little to modern Welsh life but more to the individual vision and often eclectic tastes of the directors.

Chapter film-makers

Chris Monger (b. 1950, Church Village, Glamorgan), drew on the French New Wave (Nouvelle Vague) directors and particularly François Truffaut's 1973 **Day for Night** for his first significant feature **Repeater** (1980), a work shot partly in France and distinctive enough to gain a screening at both the Edinburgh and London Film Festivals. Monger constantly made the viewer aware of the artifice of film-making (notably with a stage set doubling as a police station) and the film delighted in highly contrived, sometimes incongruous effects while operating as a diverting, loosely structured suspense thriller. Monger used an amateur (Chris Abrahams) in the lead role of a glacial, enigmatic beauty who confesses to a killing but may be a mere fantasist. 'I wanted to lock people into a detective story of sorts and then take it apart to show the artifice of things,' Monger said later.[2]

He sought to jolt the audience, challenge their passivity and involve them more in the narrative process. Later, in **Voice Over** (1981), Monger demonstrated, spectacularly, his predilection for experiment with banks and layers of sound. The eventual breakdown of his protagonist radio-show host Fats Bannerman (Ian McNeice) is signalled in the confusing babble of noises on the sound-track on his show and visually when he is entangled in a mass of sound tape. The film – though often raw in execution, especially in contrived party scenes shot in Chapter itself – was more sophisticated at narrative level than almost any other film to emerge in Wales at that period.[3] It certainly aroused more controversy after a final scene in which Bannerman repeatedly knifes Bitch (Bish Nethercote), the stray, catatonic girl he has treated and nurtured after she was victim to a vicious attack. Fats's inability to cope with women is demonstrated early on. He is only happy when they are contained safely within a radio show and past social values. The inspired device of a radio serial, 'Thus Engaged', presented by Fats, set in a Jane Austen milieu (where women are twirled around fashionable spa ballrooms by young gallants) gives the final scene of the film, the stabbing during a dance, a vicious irony. An ending with Fats, now obviously deranged, dancing and circling a floor with Bitch in a grotesque parody of the ballroom sequence created on radio might have been poignant or pat. A stabbing or act of violence was necessary to demonstrate the extent of Fats's alienation/self-disgust. Repeated knifings were bound to be more contentious. Whatever one's final reservations, the mental and sexual confusions and ambivalence are superbly built up; the anodyne romance of the serial shades into Gothic horror, as his mental state deteriorates. And Monger juggles subplots tantalizingly.

McNeice is splendidly bloated and baleful in the lead and the director uses imaginative editing and employs music with sensitivity to create surprising nuances. It is unfortunate that **Voice Over**'s merits tended to be ignored after protests at the two major British festivals by feminist distributors the Cinema of Women, who thought it contained 'brutal misogyny' and heckled the director at public screenings. The South Wales Women's Film Co-op, based at Chapter Arts Centre, criticized the final killing as 'gratuitous' but argued for its screening as a powerful tool in the debate around screen representation of women.[4] Both Monger and his female producer Laurie McFadden defended the work from the platform in Edinburgh and at the National Film Theatre's London Film Festival screening. It also found an unlikely champion in British film censor James Ferman who stood up from the stalls at the NFT to praise the work of 'a highly promising young film-maker'.[5]

Monger later offered a detailed and fairly persuasive description of his motives and the film's genesis, though conceding that his writing the script for a male actor undoubtedly 'coloured' its content and led to projection of 'a male view'.[6] 'I don't have a problem with that, for it seems valuable to me that men make movies that show their fears and ambitions. I can't think of a more exciting thing for male film-makers to do right now.' Monger insisted Fats was sexist but not a misogynist: 'He does not hate women, he idealizes them and cannot cope with the reality of women when they refuse to fit his romantic stereotype.' The director stressed his wish to create sexual ambivalence (and, possibly the hint of 'latent homosexuality') in the Bannerman character, and expressed his hope that 'the final murder would be seen as the ultimate confusion between Fats killing a character and a real person and a part of himself . . . In the repeated stabbing motion I wanted it to be ambiguous whether he was stabbing Bitch or his own groin . . . . It is obvious from the ensuing furore that it wasn't that simple. I tried to make the death a simple stab whilst in an embrace . . . followed by a repeated stabbing of the body as if he was trying to deny the personality by disfigurement.' Monger saw the film as a 'perfect paradigm for power between the sexes' and (initially at least) a 'feminist movie'.[7] He was not to return to problems of sexuality until **Just Like a Woman** (1992) and then only in a pasteurized comedy, with more combative issues and conclusions effectively fudged by Rank, the distributors, and the producer.

But challenges to macho assumptions and male prejudice were preoccupations of Chapter film-makers (and other Welsh independents) during the previous decade, in work as diverse as former Newport student Frances Bowyer's **Here Comes the Bride** (1982), Yorkshire-born Lynn Skipworth's **Lips** (1980) which contrasted cosmetic images of women manufactured by the media with the messier realities of female sexuality, Laurie McFadden's robust 1980 shorts **Tits for Tat** and **Made Up** (which explored female stereotypes with caustic wit), and Penny Stempel's humorous **A Certain Mr Smith** (working title, 'How Do You Explain This?') (1987). **Here Comes the Bride** was warm and amusing but Bowyer (b. Sydney, Australia, 1957, of Scottish parents) offered a cautionary view of marriage, comparing the realities with the euphoric image of connubial bliss peddled by women's magazines. Its high spot proved to be interviews with two girls, one almost comically pragmatic and worldweary who, while accepting the inevitability of marriage, sees it in anything but the glamorous terms of the myth-makers. The other dreams only of playing women's football at Wembley and scoffs at the idea of a traditional female/family-homemaker role.[8] The film's pithy put-down of the marriage 'industry' disarms but Bowyer failed to integrate animation (by another former Newport Film School student Linda Jennison) smoothly enough, and statistical inserts (of divorce rates, for example) were primitive. Yet the work has a buoyancy and conviction sometimes sadly lacking in subsequent Chapter work of the eighties.

Ian McNeice as the disintegrating radio personality in Chris Monger's *Voice Over.*

One lively talent at Chapter was Tim Thornicroft (b. Loughton, Essex, 1953) whose **Walter Ego** (1980) was a pastiche of pulp private-eye movies made with affection, and an eye for the incongruous and the lurid hand-me-down scripts of much B-movie fodder. It also boasted a third-person voice-over which added to the quirky appeal and helped debunk its hero's Walter Mitty fantasies.[9] Thornicroft revealed a similar streak of humour in **Debased** (1984), lampooning film stereotyping and screen narrative styles while focusing on the life of an agonizing and self-pitying composer who uses his women friends as sounding boards for his soul-baring.[10] Roland Denning, Chapter film workshop co-ordinator (b. London 1951), in his **Another American Movie** (1981), betrayed the fondness of a certain strand of the centre's film-makers for kitsch, pulp and soap opera by presenting, with genuine wit, a rag-bag of images from the screen during a weekend spent watching American TV in his hotel. In **Lager 11** (1981), Les Mills (b. Barry, 1942) (a later Chapter Film Workshop joint co-ordinator) artfully mixed live modern footage of a now-derelict camp for

German POWs, near Bridgend, with period German cabaret sequences simulated with panache. Paul Jackson used his knowledge of reporting for the *Western Mail* to produce **Reporter** (1981) a strong, amusing semi-documentary look at local journalism, contrasting the reality of hackwork, with the myths propagated by editors.

The influx of English-born film-makers into the workshop in the early eighties created an imbalance. Most members were more preoccupied with experiments in form than content (perhaps understandably) and it was some years before the films generally acquired any kind of recognizable Welsh identity. Severe cash shortages militated against expensive location work and continuity of production, even if some of the rookie directors did tilt effectively at society's mores in early films, though often from an 'international' or general perspective. Certain women film-makers at least provided a distinctive (if slender) body of committed work. By the mid-eighties the decade's new arrivals were confident enough to home in on specific Welsh subjects (when budgets permitted), and began to confront and debunk myths. Graham Jones (b. London, 1960) and

Dane Gould in Mick Stubbs's *Contortions* – winner of the Best Workshop Film in the 1984 Celtic Film and TV Festival in Cardiff.

Jeremy Bubb (b. 1960) in **It Ain't Necessarily So** (1986) contrasted the respective public and private personas of Ray Milland and Paul Robeson and challenged received perceptions of the actors, placing particular emphasis on Robeson's political influence and crusading activity. Later Jones and Bubb in the uneven **The Joke Works** (1991) became virtually the first Chapter *Film* Workshop members to feature workplace protest and demonstrations as a backdrop to events – itself a significant comment on the odd detachment of the centre's film-makers from Welsh life and issues in the past.

The Chapter film most successful in reflecting dominant moods in a Wales of high unemployment and class and social divisions was Mick Stubbs's cynical yet playful **Contortions** (1984), which fused a realistic style with bold innovation in mock interview scenes and focused on a jaundiced youth's attempts to obtain work, and his brushes with potential employers. Scenes of relishable humour emphasized the prevailing indifference of management and, by implication, the middle classes. Stubbs (b. Welwyn Garden City, 1958) tilted at a media seen as generally uncomprehending, and those who glamorized industry in Wales without acknowledging the impact of an unemployment rate of around 30 per cent in some west Wales areas by the mid-1980s. Points were made with asperity about the numbing nature of so much shop,

347

store and factory work, with the film's central character reciting with deadpan wit his shelf-stocking chores as a minion.[11]

Contortions, a thoroughly deserving winner of the Best Workshop film award at the 1984 Celtic Film Festival in Cardiff, gained much from a droll script (credited to two or three Chapter members) and a striking po-faced performance in the lead by Dane Gould (b. Cardiff, 1960), who made his own directing début with **Eyeballs Against the Windscreen** (1984), a rambling inchoate film about avarice, obsession and zealotry which contained some striking camerawork. A later Gould

work **The Smell of Human** (1991), a short, impressionistic and subjective study of a frightened individual hiding and under house siege from police and tracker dogs, was much more effective, resourcefully mixing live action with graphics and employing slow-motion camerawork with some ingenuity. His 1993 work **Love Bites**, a study of a disintegrating relationship, was remarkable for a bravura dinner-table scene containing foul-mouthed tirades and painful home truths, and a fine performance from Athena Constantine.

Athena Constantine as the troubled, vituperative wife in Dane Gould's *Love Bites.*

An early Chapter influence was Steve Gough (b. Gwaelod-y-Garth, Mid Glamorgan, 1948), whose work in his later National Film and Television School (NFTS) days disclosed a preoccupation with form, particularly through narrative, lighting and long takes. Gough twice won the director's prize at the Tours festival in France with NFTS works, **The Secret Life of Fish** (1979), a study of the adverse impact of the recession and a man's early retirement on his family, and his 42-minute graduation film **Day of Atonement** (1984), an elliptical, though oddly highly charged piece about guilt, bureaucracy, persecution and alienation, making imaginative use of a derelict railway station location, artificial lighting and sound. The latter film suffered a little from sub-Pinter dialogue and a certain pretentiousness, not entirely relieved by snatches of humour, but it was impressive enough to indicate the arrival of a new, provocative talent, and was shot and lit immaculately by Gabriel Beristain, later the cinematographer on Derek Jarman's startling homo-erotic feature **Caravaggio**.[12] Gough, London-based for most of the eighties, maintained only tenuous links with south Wales, despite regular funding from the Welsh Arts Council whose earlier generosity was at least partly vindicated when he provided the powerful script for BBC Wales's networked drama **Heartland** (1988), which stressed some of the concerns of his early video work – the value of the community and continuity.[13]

The female experience: Red Flannel

Outside Chapter, but developing from it, the most influential Welsh workshop was undoubtedly the Pontypridd-based all-women film and video co-operative Red Flannel (formed 1984) which soon became an enfranchised workshop under ACTT and Channel Four conditions. Prominent among its film-makers were Michele Ryan (later to direct episodes of the Channel Four **Cracking Up** series), Carol White and Fran Bowyer.[14] The co-operative's first film, **Mam**, perceptively blending found footage with interviews, scrutinized the potent image and the actual pivotal role of the mother in Welsh life. It also stressed radical recent changes which have, in many cases, created a gulf between that image and the actualities of life for women increasingly less house-oriented and more involved in work/unionism. It ended with a trenchant comment on new economic forces in the Valleys, highlighting the life-style of former Nantgarw miner Gary Thomas who, since redundancy, had taken the full-time role of housewife and babysitter, while his wife worked as breadwinner.

The later work **Special Delivery** was a combative, cohesive film stressing the right of women to choose home births. It suffered from stilted dramatized sequences but gained much from the passion of its articulate interviewees – professionals and mothers who talked of their experiences during pregnancy. In 1991, Red Flannel was commissioned by Channel Four to make a documentary on women in national politics, with crew members visiting Latvia, Bilbao in the Basque country and Ireland to gather varied experiences. While this documentary was being prepared the film-makers proved their versatility, and softened their daunting image as makers of partisan or fractious social documentaries, with **Otherwise Engaged**, an affectionate glimpse into women's invasion of Valleys clubs which once shut their doors against them. A camera crew was stationed in the 'Ladies' to obtain lively and occasionally ribald anecdotes and reflections on life from women, ranging from teenagers to a group of defiantly energetic septuagenarians who insisted they were on the prowl for men. The humour and resilience of so many Valleys women was captured with rare sympathy, thanks to self-effacing interviewing, and the fine editing of Fran Bowyer, Andrea Williams and Eileen Smith.[15]

Throughout the 1980s, women film-makers trained through Chapter continued to make an impact. Caroline Limmer (b. Norwich, 1958), with **Press Me Slowly, Crease Me Quick** (1981) and **True Love, Dare, Kiss or Promise** (1984) revealed an ability to create superb editing effects and played around with screen form and jump cuts, upsetting audience expectations. Her films were never quite as good as their parts, but usually visually arresting. She later honed her skills helping edit TV features. Former Newport Film School student, north-Walian Mali Evans (b. Pwllheli, 1954), used her own experiences as an anorexia victim in **Taxi** (1981), and, in a work again noted for its dexterous editing, succeeded in evoking a world of private fears, even if the film did not always maintain narrative tension. Angela Ungoed Hughes (b. Bangor, Gwynedd, 1957), with **Pa Un Wyt Ti?** (Which One Are You?, 1981) also drew on personal memories for a genuinely distinctive work with peculiarly dreamlike qualities, exploring the nature of sibling rivalries. Christine Wilks (b. Leeds, 1960), who had revealed a talent for montage with her college films **The Machine** and **Self-Portrait** (both 1982), made an enterprising low budget sci-fi film **Zombie UB40** (1988), a prickly and visually pleasing political parable in which teenagers were transformed into the walking dead by their local dole office. The odd scene failed to gel, the quality of performances was uneven, but Wilks made intelligent use of varying camera angles and hi-tech to create her effects.[16]

Indigenous works on social injustices, aspects of women's fight to combat sexism, and the plight of distressed or run-down pit communities had been largely absent from the work of mainstream TV film-making in Wales until the early 1980s (apart from references in current affairs or news programmes). Then independent film- and video-makers, including many committed left-wingers who made no pretence to balance and objectivity, began to challenge myths and stereotyped imagery of the past and produce subjective documentaries or fiction films to provide for those previously denied any say. The growth of the workshop movement was potentially the biggest single development in creating this alternative strand to the main TV companies' in-house productions and the work of the larger independent companies.

By 1984, both Chapter film and video workshops had made the breakthrough with television, gaining commissions

Pa Un Wyt Ti? (Which One Are You?), a Chapter Film Workshop short from Angela Ungoed Hughes.

and sales. The film-makers were commissioned that year to make four shorts, on 'fringe sports' with a total budget of £10,000 from S4C; the video-makers gained TV screenings for works including **Ceiber** and **Rumours at the Miners' Fortnight** (part two). The film workshop had already produced an encouraging variety of work, much of it challenging (perhaps more in form than content) and harnessed a score of talents who were to make contributions crewing up – and occasionally directing, editing or shooting – some of the more interesting TV work by independents in Wales through the decade. But when a certain inertia set in as WAC funding dried up, it was often the Chapter centre video-makers, with roots in Cardiff Street TV or the community, who seemed more prepared to draw on the experiences around them to provide a pungent flavour of Welsh urban life.[17] After a few works made for local groups on housing and health issues, notably **Would You Live Here?** (1979), about poor housing conditions in Cardiff's inner city (Adamsdown and Splott), the video workshop – based permanently at Chapter from 1983 and centred initially around Terry Dimmick (b. 1951), Steve Gough and Eileen Smith (b. Scotland, 1951) – made **Miners' Strike 1981** (1981), a record of the three-day strike by south Wales miners to fight pit closures, and broke new ground with **Rumours at the Miners' Fortnight** (1981).[18] Miners on their two weeks' annual leave with their wives were buttonholed on the beach and by their caravans on Trecco Bay near Porthcawl and encouraged to talk without inhibition, and often amusingly, of the failing coal industry and their concerns.[19] They regaled viewers with shrewd observation, received opinion, and trenchant put-downs of the 'bosses'. The vox-pop treatment had a raciness and candour often missing in conventional news and magazine programmes featuring industrial disputes. It allowed old miners themselves to make the kind of comparisons with other disputes and life in the Valleys in earlier decades which were often laundered or erased from TV documentaries. Three years later, in the wake of industrial strife and numerous pit closures, Chapter made a sequel when comments naturally were more cynical and disenchanted and the video-makers' approach was more astringent. By this time the workshop was operating on bigger WAC budgets and the much praised second film was co-produced with the London-based Television History Group.[20] The video workshop also produced a worthy and revealing look at alleged sex discrimination in the Hoover

An essay in political/social horror – *Zombie UB40*, directed by Christine Wilks.

factory in Merthyr, in **Political Annie's Off Again** (1982).

Between 1984 and 1987 the flourishing video group attracted £300,000 in non-Arts Council grants – mainly from television – at a time when total annual Welsh Arts Council film money for *all* clients failed to reach £100,000.[21] The group became a party to the ACTT union workshop declaration and was able to fund eight full-time employees between 1984 and 1988. Chapter film and video members helped shoot some of the **Miners' Tapes**, in 1984–5, joining forces with other workshops – and miners – around Britain to provide an 'alternative' view of the pit strike. The centre's video-makers, with George Auchterlonie effectively replacing Gough as the set-up's co-ordinator, also produced the lively and well-argued **The Case for Coal** (1984) (co-directors Chris Rushton and Penny Stempel) and **Ceiber** (1984–6) a work contrasting the realities of pit closure at Penrhiwceiber, in the Cynon Valley, with the initially optimistic National Coal Board forecast of the pit's longevity and productivity prospects. In **Burning Burning** (1989) co-directors Chris Rushton and Richard Davies used travelling shots and the caustic comments of locals effectively in a film examining the grandeur of the south Wales landscape and the industrial imperatives causing massive change and social dislocation.

Chapter's video workshop occasionally dealt with wider concerns, notably in the passionate if bludgeoning **Programme for the Destruction of a Nuclear Family** (1982–3) made with Bridgend CID. A broadside against Mid Glamorgan's decision to build a bunker, and a tilt at ludicrously condescending (and inaccurate) Civil Defence propaganda, the film ended with a bomb dropping on Bridgend with an eleven-year-old girl reading her poem, 'Will Someone Please Tell Me Why?'[22]

The 'realism' or 'socially conscious' school within Chapter included, for a time, Susan Twizzy Evans and Liz Forder, whose videos on wife-beating and the traumatic effects on the family – **Crying Inside** (1982) and **The Break** (1983) – provided powerful evidence of social problems long hidden. Both tapes were financed by Welsh Women's Aid, which employed Evans and Forder as communications workers on the project.[23] Evans alone completed the trilogy with **Living Without Fear** and her tape landed her an HTV film-maker's award which earned her the right to work on a project with a commercial crew. The result, **No Place Like Home**, did not quite focus, as Evans intended, on the male role in violence, but it encapsulated themes and experiences touched on in her earlier work, bringing them to a wider audience.[24] It had force and a pleasing unity, and Evans, without exploiting her subjects, conveyed vividly the impact of violence on the women and their children. The programme was a little short on facts – a fault of many more partisan works emerging from the independent sector – though increasingly, from mid-decade, polemic was sustained and bolstered by liberal and intelligent use of statistics. The **Case for Coal**, for example, marshalled arguments and figures to press for more investment in the coal industry, and pits' continued productivity and worth.

The outsider's view

Two of the most significant low-budget independent documentaries on contemporary life in Wales in the seventies and eighties came from London.

Women of the Rhondda, directed by Esther Ronay and made in 1973 by the London Women's Film Group, focused on elderly women and their memories of the 1930s and the General Strike, and allowed the interviewees to expand on the roles of women generally in their community. The film, though modest in ambition and rudimentary in technique, has a directness and integrity rarely seen in the more slickly edited works tailored for TV consumption in Wales at that time. Women recall taking potato sacks to fill with coal during strikes and then selling some coal off. An interviewee, with brothers in the pit, speaks of feeling like a 'slave' burdened with chores at home and appreciating that her brothers were equally slaves to the mineowners. A female health visitor remembers miners' homes where women deprived themselves of meals to make sure their families were fed. We hear how an interviewee's mother kept her wedding ring in pawn during the strikes, pledging that all the arrears would be paid off when the men went back. The film's scope gradually broadens to embrace the role of women outside the home, focusing on the role of the Co-operative Women's Guild in encouraging women to develop independent interests. One woman, denied a college education, tells of enjoying armaments factory work. After the war, she reveals, she had the confidence to form a trade union branch. The strength, solidarity and insularity of the communities all emerge in the women's testament but, above all, the film presents startling anecdotes of deprivation and human resilience, and is admirably devoid of sentiment. Those who broke strikes, snubbing the loyalty of all around them, have never been forgiven, or accepted: 'We've always looked on them as scabs.'

More ambitious was the London-based Cinema Action's **So That You Can Live** (1982) which pivots on woman trade-unionist Shirley Butts and her family and recalls her fight for equal pay at the GEC factory on the Treforest Estate, near Pontypridd.[25] It attempts a disquisition and dialectic on the changing nature of the Valleys, the process of industrialization, the importance of retaining a sense of history, the increasing economic contribution of women and the sexist stance of male-dominated trade unions. The work leans heavily for ideas on the work of novelist, socialist and cultural historian Raymond Williams, particularly *The Country and The City* (1973) and his novel *The Fight for Manod* (1979). The film's symmetry and formal style – with travelling and tracking shots over terraced homes sequing into images of shelves of miners' library books – sets up resonances. It makes points about political, social and historical continuity, and the visuals often express the meaning and values of local community life as eloquently as the script. Historian Hywel Francis talks poignantly about the growth of the miners' institutes and claims: 'There is no comparable political culture anywhere else in the world.' In the libraries of these institutes, the camera pans over the political texts which have nourished generations of Welsh working men, but we hear of the decline of the institutes in the 1950s as they lost their educational role to television.[26]

So That You Can Live, championed by the influential British cinema magazine

Framework, which described it as 'one of the most important films of the decade', was a brave attempt to create a dialogue around the quality of Valleys life which went far beyond the usual management v. workers, urban-industrial wealth v. agrarian idyll debates. It captured the changes in pit community life more vividly than any documentary set in Wales since John Ormond's **Once There Was a Time**. Yet the film attempted far too much and its message was muted by its slightly oblique, theoretical approach and occasional ponderousness. It also failed fully to integrate the Butts' lives into the discourse: some scenes, notably an embarrassing passage with the daughter, Diane, reading Williams's work while scarcely suggesting that she understood it, smacked of film-makers imposing their own theories from 'outside' over the heads of the documentary's ostensible subjects. The film-makers saw the region as 'always ruthlessly exploited' (in the past) or 'deliberately discarded by market forces, respective economic models and a dominant metropolitan culture', and they viewed Shirley's struggle to assert herself as a microcosm of 'a continuous conscious effort' by the working class 'to grow, to learn, to teach'. One sensed that the Cinema Action team were not altogether willing to acknowledge the more ambivalent nature of Shirley's life as wife and trade-unionist – revealing, unguardedly, at times the limits of her emancipation, as when she talks of her gratitude that her husband 'lets' her go to union meetings.

The documentary ends with Williams's assertion that we need to move confidently towards very complex societies to defeat capitalism. The film only suggests in broad terms the malaise which afflicts present industrial society and it fails to present cogent solutions beyond the rather pious hope that men and women should be prepared to control their own destiny. But it also stresses that valid change is not possible without some knowledge and appreciation of past vicissitudes – both of the nation and of organized labour. For all its shortcomings, **So That You Can Live** is a brave work which provides a distillation of, and discourse on, past experience and offers a vision (however vague or amorphous) of the future. It is sad that, with rare exceptions (such as Karl Francis, Colin Thomas and Stephen Bayly) later Welsh film-makers, as opposed to video groups, have been (generally) unprepared to provide works as combative or cerebral, with provocative analysis of the need for change and a positive attitude towards the future while not neglecting the greater virtues of the past.

Women's views featured increasingly strongly in Welsh independent documentaries in the eighties and the tendency of more politically aware women to use film to highlight their concerns was reflected in much of the best work. A Penarth-based group, Boadicea, including the feminist historian Deirdre Beddoe, produced a spirited documentary **I'll Be Here For All Time** (1983) drawing on archive material, particularly stills, to present a kaleidoscopic and affirmative view of women's political struggle and history, from protests against soaring corn prices in the 1790s to unemployment marches and peace protests in the 1980s. The film featured testimony from the feisty former Young Communist Dora Cox, wife of ex-*Daily Worker* editor Idris Cox, on her experiences on the 1934 Hunger March from Tonypandy to London. Cox was also (at 88) the subject of one programme in a Red Flannel series on courageous but essentially 'ordinary' Welsh women, **Time of My Life**, made for S4C and BBC in 1993. Cardiff-based Beata Lipmann helped to film and exhibit valuable smuggled film from South Africa and directed **Rita Ndzanga** (1984), about a black South African trade-unionist. The South Wales Women Film-makers Group or Co-op (formed 1982) made its presence felt as the decade wore on, with Fran Bowyer, Michele Ryan, Carol White and Clare Richardson all making strong creative

353

contributions to Red Flannel. The group itself produced the half-hour **Something Else in the House** (1984), which centred on miners' wives support-group activities and militancy during the 1984–5 miners' strike.

An animation breakthrough

Another stimulating development was the rapid progress made by the newly formed Chapter Animation Workshop, operating within the arts centre. Outstanding among the younger Cardiff-based animators working out of Chapter was Alison Leaf (b. Wetherby, Yorks., 1962). Her short, **Systems** (1987), made arresting use of photo-montage and graphics to contrast aspects of capitalism and the consumer society with socialism. Former Newcastle Polytechnic and St Martin's School of Art student Candy Guard (b. 1961), with deliberately primitive but sharply drawn, unfussy animation (in the European tradition) allied to wily dialogue, announced herself as a promising arrival in Wales with work such as **Moanalogue**, featuring a woman's railing and bemoaning aspects of her life to her boyfriend, and **Alternative Fringe** (1988), a very funny study of a garrulous, preoccupied female hairdresser blithely ignoring her customer's wishes and finally reducing her to tears. Guard's **Wishful Thinking** (1988) – an amusing study of disparate party-goers and their hang-ups – and **Fatty Issues** (1990) also focused sharply but sympathetically on feminine concerns and paranoia. Her influences were comic strips and women comedians.[27] **Fantastic Person** (1991) was another witty study of domestic angst centred on a lay-a-bed woman failing to fulfil plans hatched in a drunken euphoria the night before. Louise Forshaw also made enterprising shorts, including a caustic and pithy look at male violence to women, **Hammer and Knife** (1987). Rachel Calder (b. Sussex, 1965) impressed with the witty **Not Waving But Drowning** (1990), and Jane Hubbard (b. Newport Pagnell, Bucks., 1962) co-directed (with Gerald Conn) **The Black Lagoon** (1988), a trenchant short satire in the guise of a horror spoof – on the Bay Development scheme and plans for a Cardiff Barrage, one of the more controversial projects in the city in recent years. In 1988 Chapter animators combined on a well-choreographed 12-minute film **Century City**, a lively playful look at capitalism, consumerism and the power of numbers. It was commissioned by S4C for younger teenagers.

By 1987 Chapter Animation Workshop, thanks largely to advice and tuition from Cardiff-based animator Joanna Quinn and workshops by visiting luminaries such as American avant-garde veteran Robert Breer, had begun to build confidence and a small, but impressive, body of work.[28] The young film-makers' successes suggested they could have a vital and challenging role to play as S4C wooed animators in the early 1990s.

DRAMA ON THE SMALL SCREEN

We have tended to choose the safe short story or novel and not concentrated in the past twenty years on new work or the structure of TV or film. There was [in this period] very little original writing for theatre, TV and film, so one compromised – took what there was more of: Welsh literature, novels, short stories in magazines, classics . . . There was a sense of reality in those decisions but what was lacking was boldness, really – we should have invested more in encouraging original writing.

(John Hefin, BBC drama head in the 1980s, interviewed, Cardiff, 1990)

In the early 1980s, a marked change could be detected in the direction of BBC Wales drama. After a barren creative period in the seventies, the BBC began to respond to the issues and social upheavals of the day in new work which also, occasionally, drew political parallels between past and present. The best work (**Mimosa Boys/Penyberth/ Ms Rhymney Valley**) seemed increasingly relevant to contemporary life. HTV Wales, though constrained by its poor-relations status outside the 'Big Five' in independent television's power structure, also managed from the mid-eighties to acquire a national reputation for its often trenchant and well-researched current affairs programme **Wales This Week**, and went just a little way towards reviving the comedy-drama genre in Wales. Both channels were spurred on by the competition from Channel Four but HTV perhaps found the renewal of independent TV franchises in 1992 helped to concentrate the minds of executives. Certainly, marginally more of the filmed dramas produced around the turn of the decade were relevant to Wales and the lives of its consumers. But there was still a desperate shortage of space and hours for indigenous drama on HTV Wales as the nineties began, and a woeful lack of ambition in planning, generally, in both the Culverhouse Cross studios and in Bristol. All channels gained much from commissioning the work of independents. If HTV feature-film programming and its overall standards through the seventies and the early eighties were abysmal, its stock rose in mid-decade when 'independent' talents were imported: Karl Francis, for his highly charged but amusing drama-doc **Merthyr and the Girl**, and Claire Pollak for her study of unemployed youth and boxing, **Turning Pro**. HTV's reputation – with a mere ten hours' drama on the network per year – hinged on the work of just one or two talented directors and writers, notably Alan Clayton and Bob Pugh, who provided a hat-trick of successes with the feature-length dramas **Better Days** and **Ballroom**, and the series **We Are Seven**. But their high profiles, in a sense, served only to underline the paucity of indigenous talent unearthed by HTV or lack of opportunities for new young film-makers.

As the nineties neared, the move towards international co-productions (by the two major channels in Wales and independents working for S4C) allowed bigger budgets, enabling film-makers to slough off some of their past inhibitions, film in exotic locations, and widen their creative range. In 1991, for instance, BBC went abroad for **Filipina Dreamgirls**, a spirited comedy by Cardiff's Andrew Davies; HTV linked up with New Zealand for their comedy, **Old Scores**. The following year Steve Gough's film **Elenya**, set in Wales, was shot mainly in Luxemburg with German money, with the BFI and S4C joining forces to help mount the project. Just as enterprising, perhaps, were Teliesyn's ventures into co-partnership deals and filming in Russia and Australia – and the work it produced was challenging and combative. Some of the international drama co-productions elsewhere in Wales were, almost inevitably, dismal hybrids which seemed tailored to the needs of an international cast itself dictated by multi-national sales markets rather than to logical dramatic narrative or emotional truth. But increasing efforts were at least being made to produce better work able to rank alongside the most creative UK TV dramas. It seemed a contrast to the creative drought of the seventies when HTV, for instance, produced few distinctive fiction films, despite all the promise held out when the company touted the arrival of Baker and Burton as directors after gaining the franchise from TWW. Too much BBC Wales production in that decade was also essentially either sterile or safe, with emphasis on fidelity to classic novels and dramas rather than original work, much emphasis on the single drama on one or two sets, and a lack of ambitious exterior shooting. BBC Wales *did* deserve credit for bringing to a wider audience the

Welsh screen stalwarts –
Aubrey Richards (left),
T. H. Evans and Emrys
James in the 1959 BBC
Wales production of *A Car
in the Thicket* by Wil Sam
Jones.

works of Welsh playwright Saunders Lewis (frequently in productions by George
Owen and Emyr Humphreys). The discursive style and powerful arguments of even
Lewis's 'period' dramas had startling relevance to our own day.

BBC Drama – from Richard Llewellyn to Dennis Potter

An awareness of cinematic possibilities *per se* was lacking in too much of the pre-
1980s output. There was a preoccupation with conscious 'filmed theatre or novels'
and work chosen for its literary properties rather than the visual challenges offered. A
certain lack of imagination could be detected in the early BBC Wales TV feature-
comedies and the regular choice of uncomplicated, if robust, plays by the former
Caerphilly bus driver and actor Eynon Evans, notably **The Prodigal Tenor** (1957),
The Bachelor Brothers (1960) and **Jubilee Concert** (1961). Evans's plays were even
more prolific on radio where he also scored a huge success with his character Tommy
Trouble in **Welsh Rarebit**.[1] The same popular audience which enthused over Evans
often enjoyed the unsophisticated humour of the Brecon writer T. C. Thomas,
another product of the amateur stage, whose series on the south Wales railway
signalman Davey Jones proved memorable in the mid-1950s, bringing wide acclaim
to experienced radio performers such as Jack Walters (who played Davey) and Aubrey
Richards, as his assistant.

Much drama tended to be respectable but unadventurous – epitomized to some
extent by the repeated reliance on the plays of Emlyn Williams (though **Wind of
Heaven**, with its religion and redemption theme, was a tragedy out of the common
run). More common were warhorses like Richard Llewellyn's derivative thriller **Poison
Pen** (1956) based on a thirties stage play.[2] But producers David (D. J.) Thomas and
Dafydd Gruffydd still accomplished much good work on short commons in poor
conditions in the BBC Wales studio in a former chapel vestry in Broadway, Cardiff,
and the novelist Emyr Humphreys completed a trio of significant productions by the

sixties. Gruffydd's **How Green Was My Valley** (1960), with Rachel Thomas and Eynon Evans, compared favourably with any drama series of its period. And, from London's Lime Grove studios, D. J. Thomas, who had never even *seen* TV when appointed BBC Wales's sole TV producer in 1952, directed the now legendary live drama production of **Under Milk Wood**, watched by nine million viewers, in 1957.[3] This fluent, ebullient version, with much enterprising mobile camerawork and with Donald Houston as an appealing narrator, set new standards and garnered ecstatic national reviews, even though it was produced in fairly primitive conditions, by today's standards, and a camera failure caused a 20-minute breakdown.

The Saunders Lewis plays were invariably 'events'. One of his best works, **Siwan** (dir. Emyr Humphreys, 1960), an invigorating study of expediency, political and internecine power games and private and public loyalty, was given a riveting English-language production with Siân Phillips as the Queen imprisoned after an affair with a military commander (Peter O'Toole). Clifford Evans was an admirable foil as the agonizing cuckolded monarch. Other Lewis productions televised included **Blodeuwedd**, brought to the screen with a cast in birdmasks by producer Emyr Humphreys.

In the decade from the late fifties, a new breed of Welsh dramatists – writing mainly for TV rather than the stage – also began to emerge, reflecting the increasing realism evident in the cinema. These dramas presented their human dilemmas against contemporary backdrops and were laced with contentious issues. Some playwrights, like Rhydderch Jones (b. Aberllefenni, Merionethshire, 1935, d. 1987) and the former teacher and later BBC script editor Gwenlyn Parry (b. Deiniolen, Caernarfonshire, 1932, d. 1991), worked mainly in Wales. Others, such as Elaine Morgan (b. Hopkinstown, Pontypridd, 1920) and Ewart Alexander (b. Cwmgïedd 1931) moved easily between Wales and London.[4] Foremost among the new medium's neophytes and in demand by both BBC and the ITV companies was former 'Bevin Boy' Alun Owen (b. Menai Bridge, 1925) who spoke only Welsh in his early years and gained equal inspiration from his youth in Liverpool and his early childhood and roots in Wales. A former stage and TV actor – who wrote **The Criminal** for Joseph Losey – he demonstrated through his theatre and TV writing the preoccupations and dilemmas of a man absorbed in two cultures. Owen, who still describes himself as a Liverpudlian and a Welshman, explored notions of individual and national identity through idiomatic, often lyrical dialogue which often revealed more than the (generally proletarian) characters intended of their motives and prejudices, often rooted in the past. Most of his work first appeared on the stage, sometimes at London's Royal Court during his most creative period.

Among his early plays seen on the small screen was **The Rough and Ready Lot** (BBC, 1959, dir. Caspar Wrede/Michael Elliott), a period piece about a battle of wills between a Welsh atheist but rigid puritan, Morgan (Alan Dobie), and a fanatical Irish Nationalist and Catholic (Patrick Allen) in South America – an antagonism which ended in tragedy. **Progress to the Park** (dir. Christopher Morahan, 1960), a contemporary drama set in Liverpool, centred on male camaraderie with, at its hub, a Welsh writer living in London. The writer, Teifion (played by Roy Kinnear), consciously plays parts, buttering up superiors for career advancement, but he is astute enough to know his limitations and laugh with his friends about his chameleon nature and role-playing. His companions include an Orangeman's son (Sean Lynch), but Teifion usually distances himself from his Irish friends – until the intervention which provokes the denouement.

Owen's celebrated 'Liverpool trilogy' for pioneering producer Sydney Newman and ABC's Armchair Theatre (all directed by Ted Kotcheff) earned an enduring reputation for **No Trams to Lime Street** (1959), which explored the battle of wills and ideology between an old hard-drinking seaman (Eynon Evans) and his son, a Nonconformist puritan and teetaller (Alfred Lynch). Estranged for years they are brought into contact again, by coincidence, when the boy enlists for his father's ship. The drama was based on actual incidents in the lives of Owen's grandfather and father. D. J. Thomas later directed another 1960s version for BBC starring Tom Bell and Mike Pratt. Owen, of north Wales parentage, explored some of his own ambivalent feelings about his Welshness and confusions about nationality in the second part of the trilogy **After the Funeral** (1960), which also aroused much interest with its fierce family passions and exploration of issues of Welsh identity. Morgan, one son in the drama, is a nationalist, converted to the Welsh language with all the passion of the zealot. He wants his bilingual grandfather to live with him to impress his own Welsh credentials on his sceptical university colleagues. 'There have been times when I've tried to be as Welsh as I could possibly be to impress, and as an actor I've not found it difficult playing a role,' says Owen. Morgan in **After the Funeral** and Teifion in **Progress to the Park** obviously expressed facets of this experience, and in **Funny** (Yorkshire TV, dir. Barry Davies, 1971), Owen enjoyed himself creating a drama in which a Welsh couple in London deliberately played roles to discomfort an English couple after inviting them on a vacation at their Welsh cottage. Judicious use of the Welsh language was an important element in that unease. ('The English are paranoid, always suspecting the worst if the Welsh talk to each other in their native language, in *their* presence,' says the dramatist).

Lena, O My Lena (1960), which completed the trilogy, was again preoccupied with class. Billie Whitelaw's factory girl is torn between Peter McEnery's raw recruit and Scott Forbes's burly Welsh womanizer and long-time boyfriend. The drama said

359

much about conventional social expectations in a working-class milieu. Owen dealt with issues even closer to home in his drama, **The Ways of Love** (dir. Ted Kotcheff, 1961), in which a Welsh writer in London struggles to retain his integrity but proves fatally flawed and self-deluded, and capable of the kind of literary compromises which his friends deem unacceptable. The 1968 BBC Wales production of Owen's partly autobiographical **Dare To Be A Daniel** – a play first directed on TV by Stuart Burge for Southern – was an early experiment in back-to-back filming in English and Welsh by director John Hefin (b. Aberystwyth, 1941). It centred on a successful businessman (James Villiers) returning to his Alma Mater to avenge himself on his headmaster-persecutor (Clifford Evans).[5]

In **The Stag**, directed by David Thomas for BBC, Owen explored family loyalties and the relationship between two brothers. The elder brother (played by Tom Bell), returning home to west Wales from America for the youngster's wedding, finds himself at odds with the home life he left behind and is disturbed by the prospect of the stultifying domestic vista facing his brother. The film handles the dilemma of this returned exile, cleaving to his roots almost despite himself, yet rejecting the suffocating ties of home and a mother (Rachel Thomas) who still insists on cleaning his shoes. D. J. Thomas also directed Owen's BBC work **A Little Winter Love**, a play about a hitherto staid Welsh lecturer (Jack Hedley) who is drawn into an affair with the wife of his new college principal from America, and opposes the new broom's methods and philosophies.

Elaine Morgan, after landing a BBC scriptwriting prize with her second performed play, **Wilde West** (1956), a fictionalized account of a visit Oscar Wilde made to America, proved a prolific talent in the next three decades. Her work included biography (**The Life and Times of David Lloyd George**, 1981, for director John Hefin) period pieces (**The Tamer Tamed**, 1956, was derived loosely from *The Taming of the Shrew*) and serial adaptations: **How Green Was My Valley** (1976); **A Pin to See the Peep Show** (1973, dir. Raymond Menmuir); Vera Brittain's **Testament of Youth** (1979, dir. Moira Armstrong), a hugely successful dramatization, and **Off to Philadelphia in the Morning** (1978, dir. John Hefin), based on Jack Jones's novel about the struggles of the Welsh composer, Joseph Parry.[6] Morgan's original dramas were eclectic by any standards, ranging from plays about the massacre of the Holy Innocents by Herod (**The Soldier and the Woman**, 1960), to work on pertinent issues of the day in Wales. Her play **11-plus** (1957), set in a school staffroom, aired many doubts then rife about the wisdom of testing children at the age of eleven. Among more personal work was **A Matter of Degree** (1960), a six-part serial which focused on a girl (Anita Morgan) from a south Wales background who won a place at Oxford, then fretted that she would be alienated from her family and roots – problems Morgan had confronted after going up to Oxford from the Valleys. Morgan herself never had any doubts about her wish to remain in Wales where she often drew inspiration from issues of fierce local concern. Her drama-documentary, **Black Furrow** (1958), written while living at Abernant, Aberdare, gave vent to her own anger over opencast mining pollution in the area.

Ewart Alexander, then a west Wales teacher, was inspired to write by the new talent emerging through BBC TV's Wednesday Play (from London) and ABC's weekly Armchair Theatre. 'North of England playwrights like David Mercer and Alan Plater made a big impression on me. There was a feeling that radio and TV was at last opening up, that drama now embraced the whole of society.' Alexander made his début with **Dial Rudolph Valentino 1** (dir. Gareth Davies, 1968), a whimsical comedy script sent on 'spec' to BBC in London. To his amazement three of his plays were transmitted within a year, the Valentino piece as a Wednesday play, the others by London's Rediffusion. The dramatist's success soon interested BBC Wales who commissioned **A Touch of Willie in the Night** (1971, dir. John Hefin) a drama of gallows humour set in a mental hospital and celebrating the triumph of faith over bureaucracy and scepticism. It centred on two patients, determined to fly, who built their own wings. One man fell off the roof and died, the other remained with his face upturned to heaven for the rest of his days – expecting his friend to return. When he died, affronted staff turned the coffin upside down, so he was facing the ground, but the coffin turned turtle at the graveside. Hefin also directed **The Return** (1971), a modern Good Samaritan parable. Alexander explored the limits of faith when tempered by pragmatism in **The Leaning Virgin of Albert** set on the Somme in 1916 – but his script for **Omri's Burning** (1969, dir. Marc Miller), commissioned by HTV Wales programme controller Aled Vaughan but made in Bristol, marked a significant departure. It was an intense, downbeat work, focusing on a hopeless, obsessive alcoholic (Ian Holm). The dramatist has since slipped easily between genres (especially the comedy and thriller) and between series, single plays and literary adaptations, such as **Heyday in the Blood** (dir. Huw Davies, 1979) for HTV and **That Uncertain Feeling** for BBC (dir. Bob Chetwyn, 1986). He is perhaps most proud of **Maybury** (1980), a thirteen-part BBC 2 series from his own pilot drama about psychiatrists and their patients which involved intensive research working in hospitals. He wrote several of the first series, and a few in the second (1981). Alexander's experience scripting police series dramas – from **Softly Softly** to **Juliet Bravo** – could be discerned in his **Tell Tale** (1993), a three-part drama which might in other hands have been just another buddy-buddy cop movie but proved with its subtle wit and cryptic, edgy dialogue an eloquent and shrewd exploration of character and camaraderie under duress.

From the late 1950s on, other writers and directors emerged to focus squarely on the grittier realities of Welsh life. **The Rescuers** (1956), an Islwyn Williams play based on a nineteenth-century pit explosion at Tynewydd, Rhondda, proved forceful enough to win the Best Drama and runner-up for Best Film in Wales during the *Western Mail*'s short-lived sponsorship of annual screen awards, and boasted a fine cast with Glyn Houston, Jack Walters and John Robinson. Harry Green's play **The Squeeze** (1960, dir. David J. Thomas), a vehicle for Stanley Baker, and co-starring Jessie Evans, centred on an ageing miner reluctant to admit his fading prowess.[7] It is a pity that much of this work no longer survives for objective assessment.

In the late 1960s, BBC drama from Wales began to embrace more location filming of contemporary subjects. One startling work still extant from this period is the 1966 **Where the Buffalo Roam**, an early play from Forest of Dean dramatist Dennis Potter, a daring work of gallows humour. It seems extraordinarily prescient in the light of the Hungerford massacre.[8] Gareth Davies's film yanks us into the world of Hywel Bennett's fevered imagination from the opening moments when, as the camera patrols one of those roller-coaster Valleys streets, a Wild West-style shoot-out is heard on the sound-track. We first see the half-baked fantasist Willy (Bennett), dressed all in black, shooting bottles in a bar. His 'Western' *alter ego* can be seen with hands aloft in the mirror as Willy twirls his gun. He dubs himself 'Shane': a poster of Jack Palance looks down from the bedroom wall. The sound-track of Western music in Willy's head and musak on the radio played by Willy's mother (Megs Jenkins) merge. He menaces her with a carving knife, jokingly, and harbours fantasies of his probation officer (Glyn Houston) as a dude in a fancy waistcoat. Willy is as much in thrall to his comic book and celluloid heroes as his grandfather (Aubrey Richards) to First World War memories.

Potter, as usual, provides rich and dense allusions, with much emphasis on the sacred and profane (an incendiary has cracked the local church bell). The illiterate Willy's sense of failure is fuelled by a harridan of a teacher (Dilys Davies, typecast again). He only assumes dignity by escaping into fantasies of violence, nourished by repeated visits to the local

Shane Lives . . . Hywel Bennett as the fated fantasist in the 1966 BBC production of Dennis Potter's *Where the Buffalo Roam.*

cinema to see the Western, 'Ambush at Abilene'. His class teacher (Richard Davies) is a cynic who has given up on his charges, refusing to accept their potential or the responsibility for channelling their enthusiasms. Potter reveals that Willy was repeatedly beaten in childhood for his inability to read, developing a stutter which prefigured his retreat into a world of imagination. Houston recounts Willy's history to Davies and the two develop a camaraderie resolving to help, if possible, but both are unaware of the full extent of Willy's traumas as they reminisce with a casual brutality on the pulp novels they loved as youngsters – secret complicity with Willy in admiring those Western screen heroes. The film develops into a study of crippled lives. The Houston and Davies characters cannot break free of bureaucratic shackles and tramline thinking, and are unable to provide Willy with the support he needs; Willy's mother, hopelessly reliant on her husband, has never asserted herself after his death. As the film's tension builds, inexorably, we sense an unhappy resolution but scarcely expect the explosive climax. Willy is thrown out of a cinema showing a Western, after disturbing the audience; shots of his demeaning ejection are skilfully juxtaposed with images of triumph on the screen. Then he shoots his grandfather and mother. A news bulletin reveals details of the search for a twenty-year-old unemployed labourer, and Potter overtly links TV and violence. This film can be seen as central to an *oeuvre* in which Potter – as in **Pennies from Heaven** and **The Singing Detective** – has constantly explored the impact of clichéd images and popular songs on the suggestible, the harmful effects of visual and literary exploitation, and the play of memory and imagination on *immediate* reality. He has also used and subverted glamorous/romantic stereotypes to powerful ironic effect. The finale, with Willy taking pot shots, unable to distinguish between cops pursuing him and the villains of his imagination, is superbly orchestrated. As firemen and police (shouting instructions) and a crowd converge on a building Willy is finally shot and in the last disturbing image is seen trussed, hooked and swinging. The scene is oddly reminiscent of the shock ending to **Public Enemy** (1931), with Cagney's corpse wrapped up as a mummy. 'The Streets of Laredo' plays over the final chilling images of **Where the Buffalo Roam**. Potter's film is an indictment of the wanton disregard for individual life and a plea to wake up to people's problems and society's ills before it is too late.

Work like Potter's was relatively thin on the ground. The social contemporary dramas of Welsh life were seen at very irregular intervals. We had to wait until the eighties for the home-produced dramas and drama-documentaries to catch the tenor of the times.

The BBC tradition – Richard Lewis and John Hefin

Richard Lewis, after mounting a number of biographies including **The Revivalist** (1975, an intense, claustrophobic study of that fearsome Nonconformist bible-thumper, Evan Roberts, played by Gareth Thomas), **Dylan** (1978) and **Nye** (1982) – all scripted by Paul Ferris – dealt with more pertinent, contemporary issues in **The Extremist** (1984).[9] It centred on the activities of the Welsh Republican John Jenkins, jailed for his role in the radical campaign of violence surrounding the Prince of Wales's investiture in Caernarfon in 1969. The film appeared at a time when police concern about the activities of radical nationalists was at its height, with numerous arrests in arson cases following damage to 'holiday homes' in Wales. It was also intriguing material, given the language and the nationalist campaigners' penchant for attacking TV and radio transmitting stations. **The Extremist** contained a chilling performance from Dyfed Thomas as Jenkins and fine support from Clifford Evans as a pragmatic sympathizer urging caution, but it was too conventional in style to make a major impact outside Wales – especially on those unfamiliar with the extremist campaigns. Only its content distinguished it from any other worthy 'in-house' drama productions.

Richard Lewis later directed **Babylon Bypassed** (1988), which focused sharply on the unresolved emotional conflicts and residual bitterness of a failed thespian (Ray Smith), the implied atrophy of a community split by a motorway and the relationship between an unemployed youth and aspiring actor (Richard Lynch) and a girlfriend with itchy feet anxious to avoid stagnating in marriage within this community. Michael Povey's script was rich in contemporary resonances but failed to draw all the strands together or integrate the personal dramas with the wider issues, and the film was also marred by gratuitous and outmoded special effects.

Overall, both **The Extremist** and **Babylon Bypassed** made less impression than **Penyberth** (1985), produced by John Hefin. It centred belatedly on the arrests and trial for arson at an RAF station of the great Welsh playwright, Saunders Lewis (then president of Plaid Cymru), the pacifist Revd Lewis Valentine, and teacher D. J. Williams. They attempted, in 1936, to raze to the ground buildings on an RAF bombing range at Penrhos in the Llŷn Peninsula. All three were indicted and jailed after a re-trial in London following a hung-jury stalemate in Wales. **Penyberth** was notable chiefly for its high-quality script by William Jones, which allowed exploration of all the crucial moral arguments, and for the intensity of its performances, particularly from Owen Garmon who presented Lewis as a dry ascetic, humourless and off-putting in his detachment and single-minded objectives.[10] The script did emphasize, with some subtlety, the chilling precision of the men's plotting, the integrity of the central characters and the different forces and social passions working on them during their historic campaign. The film was directed in fairly routine style by the actor Meredith Edwards's son Peter Edwards inspired by the book *Tân yn Llŷn* (by Dafydd Jenkins) which made extensive use of court transcripts. Scriptwriter William Jones was fascinated that 'these three men really stood and challenged the system in the thirties, well before the popularity of protest . . . They weren't students, people without family commitments.'[11] He was also intrigued by Lewis's lack of a smooth public persona: 'he was a popular figure but not a good public figure, certainly very shy and not a "natural".'[12]

The film makes much of the natural qualms of D. J. Williams (John Phillips) – the eldest of the trio and the most innately conservative – voiced at the dinner before the three men embarked on their raid. Williams cautioned against the effect the act might have on young people, possibly leading Plaid Cymru in the wrong direction. 'Many people who admired DJ wouldn't have liked him shown in that light before the raid but I wanted to show the natural heroism of a man in his fifties who kicked over the traces for the first time for a passionate belief, and was prepared for prison even though he was the kind of gregarious man who would suffer most.'[13] Jones himself has said that he does not feel in tune with the right-wing nationalism of that time – 'it was bordering on Fascism, actually' – but his doubts and reservations add tension and bite to the film's philosophical arguments. Jones plays devil's advocate through the character of a Pwllheli shopkeeper who voices his hostility to Valentine (Dyfan Roberts) with some of the most persuasive dialogue, taking the populist stance.

John Hefin later directed **The Mimosa Boys** (1985) which examined and challenged the official version of the bombing of the *Galahad* and the loss of life of Welsh soldiers in the Falklands campaign. Salient questions were raised, though hardly answered, about the culpability of senior military in leaving soldiers unprotected. The attack climaxed a film which focused largely on the lives and attitudes of four young men immediately before embarkation to the Falklands.[14] **The Mimosa Boys**, based largely on interviews with survivors, was a creditable attempt to provide an unblinkered account of a foray which turned into a tragedy for the soldiers, though Hefin hedged his bets on occasion. There was uncertainty at the core of Ewart Alexander's script about its stance: was it a radical critique of tactics or a homage to the bravery and honesty of men who were too easily labelled as bigots or innocents who did not comprehend the nature of their work?

Hefin, as BBC drama chief in the eighties, became increasingly aware of the need for more original films and plays as the decade wore on. He acknowledged that, for much of the past two decades, Welsh directors had 'done almost too much' to bring good literature to the screen. He himself had drawn extensively on the talents of writers like Kate Roberts, Rhys Davies and Idris Davies, for example – but opportunities for new writers from the seventies on had been limited.[15]

HTV – and the Independents

HTV through the sixties and seventies had neglected Welsh film-making and new drama. Periodically it dipped into the huge store of native literature for inspiration – but employed bright new adaptors. One sixties project was a series of three 'Border Country' dramas: **Country Dance** (dir. Huw Davies), scripted by Julia Jones from a Margiad Evans novel, **Heyday in the Blood** (written by Ewart Alexander and directed by Huw Davies) from Geraint Goodwin's novel, and **The Shining Pyramid** (adapted by Emyr Humphreys from a short story by the renowned Gwent-born horror writer, Arthur Machen, and directed by Gareth Davies).[16] Huw Davies, later head of HTV Wales, also directed a series of Welsh-language drama-docs for the channel. **Y Gwrthwynebwyr** (The Opposers) focused on historical figures who challenged established thinking and suffered for their beliefs, from Irish Troubles heroes Pádraig Pearse and James Connolly to Trotsky and the Spanish Civil War poet-victim

Federico García Lorca. Hopes that drama output would improve when Harlech gained the independent TV franchise from TWW proved short-lived. Neither Stanley Baker nor Richard Burton did much drama or film for the new channel, though Baker and Gwyn Thomas had earlier appeared recalling old times in an unambitious but affectionate TWW documentary **Return to the Rhondda**.

Better Days

HTV began to provide more credible drama or drama-docs in the eighties. Notice of new intent was served when they commissioned from Karl Francis **Merthyr and the Girl** (1989), a powerful dramatized version of a local actress's struggles. They also gained, from the late eighties, from the creative collaboration of another Valleys talent, Penrhiwceiber-born writer, Bob Pugh, with director Alan Clayton. The most consistent of the films by this team was undoubtedly **Better Days** (1988), which offered Glyn Houston scope for one of his finest performances in years as Edgar, a retired miner taking stock of his life and clinging to his identity and pride after uprooting from the Valleys to live with his snobbish lawyer son in Cardiff. Beautifully written, the drama dwelt on aspects of the generation gap and made trenchant observations on the priorities in a Thatcherite Britain and on the human casualties of the prevailing mores. The minor characters were not always convincingly drawn, but there were beady-eyed portraits of the affected and bored daughter-in-law and her husband, and a superbly drawn cameo of an old miner friend who represented Edgar's one link with his former community. Edgar's decision to reject his son's offer of an old people's flat in the arid gentility of Porthcawl and to return to his beloved valley and perennial skirmishes with nosey neighbours, seemed inevitable. In the best scene of all Edgar, after enduring much patronizing, finally (literally) knocked his son's nose out of joint, after delivering withering home truths.

Ballroom (1988–9), a more challenging and ambitious work, presents a Valleys family with much internecine strife. The humour is almost mordant and the language, especially from a wife (Beth Morris) suspecting her husband's fidelity (wrongly, as it turns out), helps to give the film a pleasing authenticity. It hardly offers a flattering portrait of women. Morris's wife is presented as a tiresome scold, her mother (Gwenllian Davies) as an embittered harridan, yet this defiant old biddy is a memorably affectionate portrait etched with biting wit in a performance which ensures the character is much more than merely the epitome of the caricatured mum-in-law. William Thomas as Dick, the long-suffering husband, who wishes to enjoy no more than a night out ballroom dancing with brother Ellis (Glyn Houston), plays the role with welcome shading. He is slow to anger and often hangdog when faced with his wife's whiplash tongue, but asserts himself with some dignity, especially in the attempted reconciliations. Yet the tolerance and his compromises to keep the family home together begin to seem increasingly masochistic faced with the wife's repeated outbursts. The film makes discomforting points about the insularity and limitation of Valleys life (mainly through the observations of Robert Gwilym's character, after his return from university, and of his girlfriend who has felt the full brunt, as a single parent, of parochial prejudice). Pugh's astringent comedy, though meandering at times and containing too many characters, captures the tensions in Valleys life of the eighties with so many people instinctively loyal to, and protective of, the traditions of the past yet uncertain about the future.

The first series of **We Are Seven** (1988), based on a Una Troy play set in Ireland (and filmed for the cinema as **She Didn't Say No** in 1958) scarcely seems like the work of the same Clayton–Pugh team. The drama, centred on a village scandalized – and galvanized – by a woman with seven illegitimate children by six different men, is a throwback to the days of the more robust if finally irredeemably coy screen comedies of the forties and fifties.[17] One sensed Pugh was less at home with the material and the situation than with more acerbic treatments of contemporary issues, yet the drama is lifted out of the common run by the quality of the performances. When Ken Horn directed a sequel to the networked series in 1991, it was noticeable that the humour was more hard-edged and effective. Pugh was able to concentrate more on the disparate lives of his villagers rather than the extended family of the central character.

Glyn Houston (left) and William Thomas courting disaster in *Ballroom*, directed by Alan Clayton, written by Bob Pugh.

Pugh's talent for creating colourful cameo roles and revealing character through vernacular and the colloquial – and his love for the incongruous – gave his writing an energy rare in Welsh televised drama and held hope for the future. There are many more satisfactory avenues to explore in his kind of indigenous dramas than in financially expedient visiting productions such as HTV's **Mistress of Suspense** series (1989–92) (based on thriller writer Patricia Highsmith's work), and BBC works like **The Vision** (1987) which merely used Wales as a convenient location.

Drama-docs and Kenneth Griffith: maverick and gadfly

Kenneth Griffith is the bane of those bodies whose main purpose in life is to tie a nice neat label on the left leg of each and every one of us.

(*South Wales Echo*, 22 March 1975)

It has been well said that upon seeing his apparently eccentric films one is persuaded that he could play, or would like to play, **Gone With The Wind** singlehanded.

(*The Times*, 1986)

The BBC over the last two decades has provided a regular outlet for Griffith's fiercely partisan documentaries and maverick talent. He has attracted some opprobrium and ridicule with his tub-thumping, hectoring style as presenter but has focused in a highly individual way on political iniquities and particularly the injustices and anomalies of colonialism and colonization. He has championed rebels and underdogs and debunked historical heroes. It is paradoxical that an actor who spent much time playing devious or woebegone comic Welshmen on screen and reinforcing Welsh stereotypes – in Boulting Brothers and Launder and Gilliat comedies, for instance – should devote his later career as a director to defending the colonized. He sees nothing inconsistent about his personal films supporting subjugated peoples and his performances as timid, henpecked or humourless Welshmen kowtowing to authority of one kind or another (**I'm All Right Jack**, **Only Two Can Play**), or Bible-bashing puritans (**Heavens Above**). But then Griffith's whole stance could be seen as a paradox. He describes himself as a 'radical Tory' and tends to punctuate his public comments and TV appearances (on HTV's 1986 film history series **The Dream that Kicks**, for example), with unsolicited attacks on trade-unionism. It is ironic that in **Blue Scar** Griffith played the young miner who read *Tribune* and criticized the exploitative mineowners and their attempts to introduce a six-day week. He was also chosen to deliver the passionate lines of Idris Davies in **Bitter Broken Bread**, one of the more striking programmes of the Dai Smith **Wales! Wales?** 1984 six-part series.[18]

In the mid-1980s Griffith (b. 1921) defied his own union, disappearing to South Africa, intending to make a sympathetic portrait of General Kruger, scourge of the British in the Boer War. This programme was aborted, but later he indicted politicians and sports officials for wrecking the athletics career of the South African runner in **Zola Budd – The Girl Who Didn't Run** (1989), a documentary which contained some distasteful harassment of interviewees when he abandoned all pretence at objectivity.[19] Griffith is almost cavalier in rejecting the tendency of so many broadcasters to adhere to the approved tenets of balance and objectivity: 'I would never stoop so low as to be objective about anything,' he once told then BBC head and fellow countryman Huw Wheldon. He is fiercely critical in his programmes and in private of the British imperialistic role (in India, South Africa in the past, Northern Ireland now).[20] It is small wonder that opinions about his personal films vary widely. Some see them as merely vehicles for his own ego and arid exercises in polemic or rhetoric of little cinematic merit. They find his florid, button-holing presentation off-putting, his dogmatic defence of his heroes tiresome, and reject as simplistic his view of history as a seemingly interminable procession of great men bending nations or armies to their will. All these criticisms have some validity – Griffith, like writer-director Jack Howells, has never been ashamed of showmanship. Yet his work, fascinating in its iconoclasm, can never be written off. He has consistently focused, with a rare and infectious passion and integrity, on aspects of British history so often ignored or circumvented in textbooks and official screen biographies. Two of his films, **Curious Journey** (dir. Gareth Wynn Jones, 1977) which contains interviews with IRA veterans remembering the 1916 troubles, and **Hang Up Your Brightest Colours** (dir. Anthony Thomas, 1973), his combative defence of Michael Collins, were banned from television and only shown in the 1990s.

Curious Journey was shelved by HTV and resold to Griffith for £1 on condition that the company name never appeared in the credits. The Collins programme was axed by Sir Lew Grade at ATV – a ban debated later on the Thames networked programme **The Public's Right to Know** (dir. Silvio Narizzano, 1974). Sir William Deedes, on the programme, implied that the Collins work was treasonable, using the argument (once marshalled against Michael Powell's **Life and Death of Colonel Blimp**) that Griffith had 'committed an offence' by producing material which might encourage British soldiers to doubt the rightness and validity of their work in Northern Ireland. Griffith claimed for the loss of overseas sales and ATV finally settled out of court.[21] **Curious Journey** featured survivors of the Troubles, seven men, two women, who later became bastions of local society – both Free Staters and Republicans. Griffith, for once, did not appear on camera, but the programme was riveting with its passionate testimonies from old folk of events which they re-lived almost daily in the memory. 'I think it was banned for the simple reason that if the case made by the IRA was too responsible, too sound, ordinary people might ask, "What are we doing there if we've done that to them?" ' said Griffith later. He sought to make people aware that 'these were old people of great quality' and to suggest they were telling the truth. The film says that 'Imperialism is the foremost criminal activity.'

The Welshman was an unashamed admirer of Michael Collins and his homage was intense and highly subjective, though none the worse for that. From his opening gambit, quoting the remark, 'There is no Irish problem only an English problem,' Griffith champions Collins. He traces the roots of his alienation from the British back to and beyond Lloyd George's role in suppressing the Dáil (Irish parliament), 'putting spies and informers into Ireland' and allegedly turning a blind eye to the bloodshed in Ireland after Churchill formed the pro-Loyalist Ulster Voluntary Auxiliaries. He also condemned Lloyd George for being 'grossly dishonest about the border', by claiming there would be no permanent partition.[22]

Kenneth Griffith – bane of the establishment, writer-presenter of a string of stimulating, combative TV drama-documentaries, and a winner of the BAFTA Cymru Lifetime Achievement award.

Griffith's expressed conservatism would seem at odds with one of his best-remembered films for BBC – on the left-winger, Tom Paine, the eighteenth-century author of *The Rights of Man*. But Griffith will have none of that: 'Paine was a devil for the work ethic and standing on your own feet, who would be appalled by much of the state machinery and the philosophy of present-day union leaders.'[23]

The programme provided a compassionate, intense if impressionistic study of Paine which, in typically bullish fashion, he titled **The Most Valuable Englishman Ever** (dir. Michael Pearce, 1982). Paine appealed to Griffith as the English Enlightenment personified, 'a man with absolutely steadfast beliefs in the importance of equality in human society'. Paine's lowly birthright, unprepossessing background, courage and role in the French Revolution were all seized on by Griffith, the romantic, who felt Paine's philosophy and influence made him the real architect of Jefferson's Declaration of Independence. But he was also drawn to the hero's wit and tolerance of other's foibles, which allowed him as an actor to deliver pithy, resonant dialogue. Griffith came into his own in this programme, larding his presentation with gleeful asides, his voice swooping through the registers. As an actor with a penchant for fruity rhetoric, he also identified closely with his biopic of one of the most charismatic of stage actors, Edmund Kean – tippler, womanizer, tragedian. **The Sun's Bright Child**, directed by David Munro for Thames, sought to convey the experience of those who described Kean's performance as 'like watching Shakespeare by flashes of lightning'. It proved robust, if self-indulgent, entertainment. Most of Griffith's later screen biographical ventures were prefaced by **Bus to Bosworth** (1976), a totally contrasting, gentle BBC Wales comedy. He played a headmaster and history teacher stressing the Welshness of Henry Tudor to his pupils, yet seeking to prevent one embryonic schoolboy nationalist from too readily adopting the monarch as a Celt or rejecting traditional notions of history. Griffith's comic vacillations in the role are a delight and the teacher's boyish enthusiasms are disarming and contradict his assumed objectivity. In this film, produced and co-written by John Hefin, both the boy, who talks passionately of Owain Glyndŵr, and the teacher (Rachel Thomas), affectionately humouring and chiding the head, might be seen as mouthpieces for Griffith.[24] His spirited school head stands humorously on his dignity but communicates his enthusiasm to his charges. The actor provides one of his more amiable character studies, tolerating the pupils' peccadilloes and small rebellions and even picking the 'nationalist' boy for the plum role of Henry Tudor in a re-enactment of events spread over the various actual locations on their day out. The script managed to suggest, without didacticism, that Welsh history could be taught palatably and with the right catholic approach. Henry's own role in allowing children to be taught Welsh is stressed and Griffith, with undisguised relish, delivers a few lines about the English regarding early Welsh poetry as 'most dangerous and disruptive'.[25] The drama, a likeable study of an eccentric, is not as lightweight as it first appears and humour is sustained well despite some obvious padding and incongruous music towards the climax when it appeared shortcuts were taken to accommodate the film within its half-hour format.

Griffith had made his first personal drama-doc after overtures from both Huw Wheldon and David Attenborough. Wheldon eventually gave him *carte blanche* to make a film in South Africa.[26] During the visit, Griffith developed deep sympathy towards the Afrikaaners: 'About 340 years ago they became a white African tribe with no retreat to anywhere else. They have fought for their way of life, their standards, more against the British than the blacks.'[27] His brief was to 'communicate my enthusiasm' and **The Widow's Soldiers** (1972) – a feisty defence of the Boers – opens with bravura aerial shots travelling east to west along the Tugela River, effectively drawing battle lines between the British and Boers, with the camera settling on a distant figure (Griffith) seen on the mountain dividing them – the Spion Kop.[28] Griffith soon clashed with the director Lawrence Gordon Clark over the lapel-grabbing style which was the presenter's distinctly subjective forte – but he intended his first personal film as a counterblast against 'those who have found in South Africa comfortable pariahs, people they can point the finger of scorn at – or feel superior to – on behalf of black people'.[29] The climax, Buller's success in relieving Ladysmith, presented an unflattering picture of British hostility towards the South African farmers who 'just happened to be sitting on the largest gold deposit the world has known'.[30] The film left Griffith dissatisfied after Clark had the final say in ordering the material following BBC reservations about the actor's personal style.[31]

Later, directing and presenting **Sons of the Blood** (1977), interviews with Boer veterans, Griffith developed his philosophy about colonialism in Africa, and his next film **A Touch of Churchill – A Touch of Hitler** (1980) was a corrosive attack on Cecil Rhodes and the politicos and industrialists who fuelled British jingoism: 'It really was the most obnoxious collection of Englishmen.' This feature, directed by Anthony Thomas (of **Death of a Princess** fame) was 'the only film I've made where, instead of being the devil's advocate, I'm the prosecution'. Griffith claims to have placed great emphasis on Rhodes's 'few redeeming features', including his loyalty and capacity to forgive friends and his placing of the failure of the Jameson Raid squarely on Jameson. Griffith describes the film now as 'straightforward, subjective, committed storytelling'.

His detailed studies of South Africa's history led Griffith to make **Black as Hell, Thick as Grass** (dir. Michael Pearce, 1979), a study of the Zulu Wars with an unpopular anti-British slant. Not content with appearing as British officers, Griffith also played various Zulus. Issues of national identity were again explored in **Napoleon: The Man on the Rock** (dir. Michael Pearce, 1975), a study of the final years on St Helena, with the presenter naturally playing the 'Pocket Emperor'. **Clive of India** (1981) was another critique of colonialist attitudes and their roots rather than a diatribe against the East India Company. Later he was in India again shooting **I Have Promises to Keep** (dir. Alan Birkenshaw, 1987), a documentary tribute to Pandit Nehru – a visit hampered by official bureaucracy.[32] The film, apparently first commissioned by Indira Gandhi, was completed but allegedly suppressed by the Indian government.

Perhaps Griffith's most ambitious film is **The Light** (dir. Michael Pearce, 1988), a sprawling study of David Ben Gurion, which encapsulates most of the Welshman's preoccupations. The film, after sketching the history of the Jewish people, mixes in newsreel footage and re-creates key incidents of Ben Gurion's career. As one might expect, it devotes a critical section to the culpability of the British and the ramifications of the declaration by Foreign Secretary Balfour pledging the establishment of an Arab state in Palestine to combat what he saw as a carve-up of the Middle East by the British and French. The British are indicted for tardiness in reacting to the Mahdi's slaying of the Jews from 1936 onwards and the various pogroms. The film is also highly critical of the 1939 declaration – when Colonial Secretary Malcolm MacDonald effectively reneged on Balfour's promises – and of Britain's vacillations over Suez.[33] Griffith as usual delivered breathless narration, trenchant punchlines, a grab-bag of seductive facts and anecdotes, and played a bewildering variety of roles from a notorious Turkish interrogator to Ben Gurion himself, as he scuttled from one locale to another. His commitment was undeniable but the programme might have gained if polemic had been offset by statements defending the British or by political opponents of Ben Gurion, and the ending seems a trifle complacent in failing to confront the realities of present-day Lebanon.[34]

In recent work Griffith has returned to the Irish theme with **Roger Casement – Heart of Darkness** (dir. Michael Pearce), a typically emotive and spirited defence of the Protestant and British diplomat executed as a traitor by the British in the First World War, screened in BBC 2's **Timewatch** series in October 1992. That programme's executive producer, Roy Davies, later became head of BBC Wales TV documentaries and was responsible for the eventual BBC screening in Wales in 1993 of the Michael Collins movie.

The influence of Griffith has been profound: the polemical styles of historians Gwyn Alf Williams (**The Dragon Has Two Tongues**, 1985) and Dai Smith (**Wales! Wales?**, 1984) acknowledge, however unwittingly, his ground-breaking work in bringing the past vividly to life with subjective, combative narration. Griffith continues to act – occasionally – in TV or feature films for others but he is much more committed to presenting personal movies – and acting all the parts. He is certainly no blushing violet – how many men have played Christ, Hitler and Napoleon in their careers! Despite their manifest flaws (some of his drama-docs are too frenetic and flat visually) Griffith's films provide a jolt to complacency and force us to re-assess received opinions. Irritated by the hectoring style, you begin to play devil's advocate yourself against the presenter's bellicose pronouncements. The façade should not blind us to his ability to reach the core of his subjects and the arguments around them and to turn the spotlight on unsavoury aspects of nationalism and human personalities which do not fit snugly into accepted notions of history. His *best* films display a surprising catholicism and ability to see problems 'in the round' – even if his final verdicts are unequivocal.

Realism, Roger Graef and Claire Pollak

The BBC had gained considerable kudos from the work of John Ormond in the documentary field, and if much work in documentary was routine in the sixties and seventies, other film-makers (sometimes from outside the area) were able to prove that Wales was still a fertile source of inspiration. Perhaps one of the most influential of all the 'Welsh' BBC documentaries of the seventies was, ironically, made by a London-based team headed by the New York-born *cinéma-vérité* specialist Roger Graef whose fly-on-the-wall studies of British life proved major talking points with the public and among professionals intrigued by his methods. His beady-eyed view of Cardiff's city-centre planning problems in **Is This the Way to Save a City?** (1974) forced the city council and ratepayers to ask searching questions about a planned co-financing deal between the city council and a multi-million pound Ravenshead development company. Graef later claimed his team had 'done their homework' and proved the city could not benefit financially. The documentary, which featured the writer Christopher Booker, among others, talking to city officers, effectively 'stopped the redevelopment of Cardiff', along the lines originally proposed by the authorities, Graef claimed later.[35]

The BBC also responded to the decline in the south Wales mining community with one or two forceful dramas or drama-docs during the eighties. As pits in the area continued to close, confirming the scepticism and, what had seemed to many, the wild prognostications of miners' leader Arthur Scargill, BBC West in Bristol produced **The Last Pit in the Rhondda** (1984). Shot by Chris Cox, the programme homed in on the closure of the Maerdy Colliery, Rhondda, and provided a vivid impression, with much resourceful camerawork, of life below ground and a colourful, deeply felt testimony by miners talking about a way of life which would soon have vanished. It also placed the shutdown in the context of general industrial decline. In 1913 there were more than sixty pits in the Rhondda, employing 41,000 men, the film tells us.

Much of its interest, beyond the versatile camerawork, stems from what is revealed about the miners' self-image, sense of loyalty and a certain masochism: 'When you go down you become a man, it changes your character because it's something you experience that you've never experienced before.' One interviewee talks of watching his father at work on the coalface at sixty-five and says he felt like crying. 'He's been there fifty-one years. My father ended up with £200 – he thought it was a fortune.' Testimony to the miners' pride, obduracy and idealism is mixed with analysis, as they reflect on the changing nature of the industry, the new schisms forming under duress in each pit, and the generation gap which often divides men in any union struggle to keep a pit open. The men's bemusement at the implacability of management and decisions which renege on earlier pledges, is well conveyed. The film, shown in two parts on TV, centres on the miners' struggles and attitudes during the last desperate attempts to keep the pit open. The signs outside shops, advertising special rates and reductions for miners, offer sharp reminders of the continuity of Welsh industrial and communal experience.

One of the most disturbing drama-documentaries based on actual events in Wales was made for BBC by **The Singing Detective**'s director, Jon Amiel, from a play by Marjorie Wallace, based on fact. **Silent Twins** (1986) centred on two mutually dependent sisters with a psychopathic disorder who were finally committed to Broadmoor after acts of arson and physical violence. The film was claustrophobic, fairly unrelenting and ultimately unnerving.

Harlech had found no natural successor to Jack Howells in the documentary field, but by the mid-eighties HTV was more conscious of the need to reflect urban Wales to its people. It began to take tentative steps to encourage independent film-makers and was rewarded with **Turning Pro** (1986), one of the most affecting and thoughtful of all Welsh documentaries focusing on aspects and repercussions of unemployment. Director Claire Pollak explored the motivations and backgrounds of south Wales youths lured into boxing by penury and straitened family circumstances, as so many Valleys boys had been in the past. But it also ventured into other fascinating areas: corruption or mismanagement in the fight game, and wife battering. The analysis of these interrelating themes gave the film a rare depth even allowing for Pollak's previous impressive track record as an independent. It also contained striking fight sequences shot by Tony Impey. Pollak obtained candid interviews – notably at ringside when one boxer claimed his opponent had been switched on him at the last moment. The interviews, something of an unwitting scoop for the director, contrasted favourably with the anodyne quality of much conventional sports reporting.

Pollak, who gained early experience as a sound recordist on National Film School shorts, first emerged working in tandem with friend and NFS graduate Kim Longinotto on a startling and superb documentary **Theatre Girls** (1979), which probed the lives of derelict, generally fairly elderly, women living in a Soho hostel.[36] It eliminated the traditional distance placed between documentary film-makers and their subjects (as Howells had done in **Penclawdd Wedding**) and Pollak and Longinotto, while embracing aspects of the *cinéma-vérité* style, made no secret of their presence behind the camera. They were both seen in shot occasionally and deliberately retained on the sound-track their questions to interviewees. Both lived in a flat above the hostel for three months, gaining the confidence of their subjects before starting filming. The resulting candour and lack of inhibition by the women justified the film-maker's style, though Pollak later had qualms (probably justified) about a distressing sequence when the camera remained, unblinking, on an addict shooting up in a toilet with a friend's help.

The film won a prize at the Mannheim Festival and the same team later made **Cross and Passion** (1981) in West Belfast, shot on a Catholic estate (Turf Lodge).[37] It presented the frustrations of women's lives in the ghetto and drew analogies between the repression of wives on the estate and Catholic girls conditioned by their church upbringing. Much play is made of church rituals and the subjugation of women suffering both sectarian harassment and the constant, worrying presence of the British forces. This film, made with Radio Telefis Eireanne and part-financed by the BFI Production Board, was slightly looser in structure than **Theatre Girls** and lacked its incisiveness. Yet it once more explored feminist, national and political issues in an astute, compassionate way and was undoubtedly more ambitious than the earlier work.

In the 1980s Pollak was joint co-ordinator of Cardiff's Chapter Film Workshop and worked with Frances Bowyer on **No Place to Hide**, a partisan but journeyman study of the Bridgend bus driver and peace campaigner Ann Thomas, and then directed solo a four-part HTV series **The Dream that Kicks** (1986) which focused on the history of films in Wales and the attitudes of communities, directors and film technicians involved in their making. That series demonstrated Pollak's continuing concern with the impact of outside economic, social and political forces on ordinary lives – a preoccupation reflected in the director's further TV series **Working Women**.

The Pollak style, generally devoid of narration, and giving priority to the subject's/protagonist's viewpoint, was in contrast to Dai Smith's **Wales! Wales?** BBC series in which the historian sought to demolish some myths about Welsh urban life and adopted a no-nonsense, partisan stance. Yet both approaches stemmed from a desire to project radical ideas and a critique of prevailing mores.

A new view of history

HTV also – perhaps in riposte to **Wales! Wales?** – produced its own series analysing the traditional images of Wales presented in literature, history textbooks and films.[38]

The Dragon Has Two Tongues (1985), directed by Colin Thomas, offered views of Wales from protagonists at opposite poles: Wynford Vaughan-Thomas, arch-apostle of the Welsh Romantic tradition, and the volatile Marxist professor Gwyn Alf Williams. They clashed on a bewildering variety of locations, and offered contrasting explanations and interpretations of the genesis of Wales and its culture, with Williams constantly setting his face against the folksier notions and relating developments to industrial and social imperatives. Colin Thomas's hyperbolic visual style, with the camera often swooping on or prowling around the protagonists, often matched the sound and fury of the presentations, which included some engagingly energetic perorations by Williams down coal-mines and atop hills. The style at times was not far removed from Kenneth Griffith's customary rumbustious approach. The series garnered large audiences and, as with **Wales! Wales?**, the stimulating ideas in the script alone would have made the project worthwhile and proved there were viewers willing to analyse their own response to the 'Wales' often presented on screen, and to challenge accepted TV notions of Welshness.[39] Some episodes managed to compress an impressive amount of information, ideology and passion into the limiting half-hour format.

Teliesyn's Channel Four series, **Cracking Up** (1989), fronted by Williams and produced in the bicentenary year of the French Revolution, attempted to analyse the impact of revolution and rebellion on influential historical figures (including the Welsh myth-maker Iolo Morganwg) and vice versa. The Morganwg study proved the least visual and most disappointing of the series but there were impressive programmes devoted to Sylvia Pankhurst (dir. Michele Ryan) and the ardent feminist Mary Wollstonecraft, mother of Mary Shelley (dir. Sue Crockford). The pick was undoubtedly Colin Thomas's programme on Goya (played by Jack Shepherd) which blended the painter's work with dramatization and animation (by the outstanding Joanna Quinn). Superbly edited by Pip Heywood, whose skills garnished Richard Watkins's films in the 1980s, it conveyed the flavour of the times – despite the deliberate alienation devices built into the programme, with the actors, while playing the parts, regularly confronted by the historian, Williams. The Goya documentary, placing due emphasis on the painter's views on the church, his iconoclasm and anti-war engraving, demonstrated Thomas's increasing sophistication and confidence as a director. The series's flaws stemmed from script rather than directorial defects and the tendency to fit lives into preconceived and convenient patterns to demonstrate Gwyn Alf Williams's eloquently expressed theories.

Teliesyn gained more kudos in 1989 with **The Enemy Within**, the last testament of journalist and film-maker John Morgan who was dying of cancer. The film, recording his final days, was directed by J. David Hutt, and landed Britain's Grierson Award for Best Documentary. The Teliesyn co-operative, also striking out into the area of international co-production with feature work, were a fine example of a company with a clear appreciation of its strengths and a commitment to producing work embracing the contemporary issues in Wales and the patterns in the nation's past impinging on the present. There seemed no danger, even if its boundaries continued to expand, of Teliesyn settling for bland hybrid productions of little relevance to 'home' issues, certainly while Gwyn Alf Williams remained as a forthright, often acerbic, pivot.

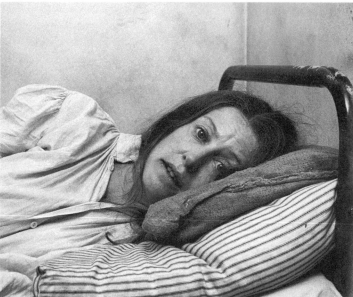

Sharon Morgan as the heroic suffragette in *Sylvia Pankhurst – Thursday's Child*, directed by Michele Ryan for Channel Four's *Cracking Up* series.

But it was patently obvious by 1990 that more sense of purpose, more commitment to content and to independents was needed by the main channels' in-house programme-makers and executives at a time of fierce satellite and cable competition, and a recession which was beginning to eat away at programme budgets. HTV, in particular, was to face even bigger problems after winning a renewal of its franchise in 1992. Its commitments to meet national yardsticks co-incided with heavy losses on advertising revenue (leading to job cuts). These threatened to drive policy-makers back into the trenches to rely on the safety-first, often lowest-common-denominator, broadcasting which had proved anathema to many in the seventies and eighties.

Many films fail because the accountant fell in love with the film . . . caught film fever . . . and the director was able to persuade the accountant that it didn't matter if he spent another 10 million quid. Of course it matters. You have no right to spend 10 million on a film, or half a million, when people are starving. It's evil. In Britain, *My Childhood*, which is one of my favourites, was made for peanuts. *Above Us the Earth*, which I think is a very good film, was made for nothing.

(Interview with Karl Francis, Cardiff, 1987)

Karl Francis has been the most powerful, distinctive and combative voice in Welsh film-making for almost two decades. In film after film (from **Above Us the Earth** in 1977 to his 1991 short **The Committee**) he has mined a rich seam of industrial/urban life and confronted the contemporary social and economic dilemmas and predicaments of his country. In much of his work during the years of demoralizing pit and factory closures, Francis has focused on his native beleaguered south Wales valleys, most notably in the richly detailed mining trilogy: **Above Us the Earth**, **Ms Rhymney Valley** (1985) and **The Angry Earth** (1989).[1]

Francis (b. 1942) has explored all manner of injustices and concerns in his films, including local-government corruption, TV and government censorship (in **Giro City**), feminist issues and sexism (in **Ms Rhymney Valley** and **The Committee**), class divisions (central to **The Mouse and the Woman**), the damaging impact of addiction (in **The Happy Alcoholic** and **Morphine and Dolly Mixtures**) and nationalism/culture divisions (notably in **The Mouse and the Woman** and **Boy Soldier**). His best features are patently the work of an insider (operating from within a community or – as in his critical explorations of the media – as a director familiar with TV's inner workings and machinations). They are the creation of someone who cares, and shares the worries of his subjects/protagonists. No outsider could have made **Above Us the Earth** with such controlled anger or concern for detail, or captured as honestly the stoicism and defiance inherent in dwindling mining communities. Few other Welsh directors could have brought the same warmth and sense of camaraderie to **Ms Rhymney Valley** (1985), a drama-documentary primarily about women's role in the 1984–5 miners' strike and the campaign opposing the closure of the pit in his home village of Bedwas, Mid Glamorgan.[2] His films *in toto* provide a vivid, unparalleled screen record and impression of the often disquieting realities of south Wales life since the 1970s.

Francis has made his own political statements in focusing so relentlessly on life in the Valleys. He believes his urban communities are under-represented (and mis-represented) by the official media in Wales and he remains angry that the only specifically Welsh channel, S4C, is in the Welsh language – effectively 'disen-franchising' most of the population. A middle-class media may, ultimately, be unable to change the injustices suffered by the working class, but it has a duty to go on trying, he believes. Francis's films articulate powerfully his concerns and, though rarely pessimistic overall, they present a world of disintegrating marriages, families and communities brought to breaking point by outside or internal pressure. Yet he is an instinctive optimist who emphasizes repeatedly the resilience of the communities he knows, mainly in Mid Glamorgan, Gwent and west Wales, and their ability to adapt, even to traumatic change. At times the message of hope he delivers beneath his films' abrasive surfaces seems like wishful thinking and at odds with much we have seen before (as in the closing scenes of **Ms Rhymney Valley**). There are innate contradictions in his work, which seem to stem from the paradoxes within Valleys life itself (for example, his ambivalent attitudes to the pit in **Above Us the Earth**).

The director's work is unashamedly personal, gaining much from repeated use of an unofficial 'stock company' (headed by Dafydd Hywel and Sue Roderick). In private he can be a prickly customer – he does not suffer fools or fence-sitters gladly. His films are periodically strident but the faults are due often as much to an excess of passion as an unduly blinkered approach or any failure of technique.

Sexism under siege – and the confrontational approach

Subtlety is not Francis's forte, though his work is never short of ideas and the features have a habit of yielding more on each successive viewing.[3] His films are confrontational, often have a barbed edge and are unashamedly partisan as he champions communities in thrall to economic exigencies, and charts the decline (physical if not necessarily spiritual) of Valleys townships and villages, and the infringing of civil liberties and social and artistic freedom. He also repeatedly stresses the need for a macho Valleys society to readjust to current socio-economic mores (his films have a strong feminist streak, for instance – from **The Happy Alcoholic** and **Giro City** onwards).

In **Ms Rhymney Valley**, he confronts sexist issues with great humour, focusing on a beauty contest planned by miners during the 1984–5 pit strike.[4] He gently mocks entrenched attitudes and suggests that men and women must pull together if the Valleys are to retain their life and heart. Francis pays out enough rope for Abe, the chauvinist organizer of the contest, to hang himself. Yet the tone is affectionate and sympathetic rather than superior and admonishing, and he makes it clear that Abe, unashamedly sexist, is fighting a vain rearguard action especially during a miners' strike in which so many women played decisive roles.[5] Sexism is also under siege in Francis's **Forty Minutes** series film **Rough Justice** (1980), in which shop steward Dilys Hardacre waged a campaign for women to use a male-only pool table; and in **Boy Soldier** (1986) it is the Welsh squaddie's Irish girlfriend who has the nous and objectivity to end their relationship, given the combustible political climate.[6] The only unsympathetic woman in Francis's *oeuvre* is the predatory Gilda, the coalowner's wife, in **The Mouse and the Woman** (1980). She is exposed as a sham – but even she is more a victim of social forces than a virago. For all her stance as a new woman and her dilettante tilts at photography (in which she seeks to 'control' the working class – and her husband's employees – by freezing them in shot) she falls back into an expedient, loveless marriage to the mineowner rather than pursue her supposed drive toward independence. More typical of the central roles of women in Francis's productions are Glenda Jackson's politically committed TV producer in **Giro City** (1982), and Sue Roderick's earth mother and miner's wife in **The Angry Earth**.[7]

Concerns and shortcomings

In much of his work, Francis is preoccupied with the role of the family and its continuity, the tug of memory and tradition, the rifts between generations and the need, above all, to learn from the past. At times the director's features cannot quite sustain the burden of ideas, and he occasionally lays himself open to the charge of opportunism – that he is merely latching on to cult or trendy left-wing issues. This accusation trivializes the depth of his commitment to changing society and ignores the many hints in his films that communities themselves must re-examine all aspects of their lives in order to avoid being erased, or bypassed, by history. The works frequently centre on the nature of individual and collective responsibility or expand the duties of the press and broadcasters (and by implication film-makers) to reflect accurately the society around them. In **Ms Rhymney Valley**, for example, Francis contrasts, tellingly, the realities of the picket line during the miners' strike and the mass media's limited perceptions of the dispute. In **Giro City**, the TV reporter's attempts to expose political corruption in south Wales local government and provide a broadcasting platform for an outlawed Irish 'terrorist' both prove abortive. In **Boy**

Soldier the military collude with the government and the press to defuse a potential political scandal.

At their worst, Francis's films are hectoring and two-dimensional. He still has a tendency to polarize, too glibly, views and characters, and protagonists on the 'wrong' side of the political fence are sometimes set up too readily as Aunt Sallys or presented so schematically (or uncharitably) that serious points are blunted. Yet Francis, almost alone of Welsh directors, deals repeatedly with crucial issues in Wales *now*. He refuses to take refuge in the past or to be satisfied with using historical incidents as metaphors for the present.

Early days

Francis's preoccupations were in evidence in his first film as writer only, the 45-minute **A Breed of Men** (1971), an account of the right-wing 'scab' Spencer Union which grew from the 1926 General Strike – and attempted to break the South Wales Miners' Federation. Directed by Euryn Ogwen Williams and made as a drama-documentary (with Stanley Baker as narrator) for HTV, the film is based partly on the reminiscences of Francis's father and grandfather who worked in the Bedwas Colliery during the lock-out. The Spencer episode later fuelled ideas for scenes in **The Mouse and the Woman** and is recalled, graphically, in **Ms Rhymney Valley** by Ernie Bailey, an old miner at Bedwas bitterly antagonistic towards the black-legs of more than fifty years before. The dramatized episodes, featuring the 1920s leader of the SWMF, Arthur Cook, and George Spencer and William Gregory of the 'scab' union, are presented with passion and humour, and the film's wealth of ideas and invigorating forthright writing impress. Twenty years later it stands up well and is overdue for revival.[8]

Francis's first directing assignments were for Granada and on Thames TV's current-affairs programme **Thames Today**, and also on a BBC further education series **Factfinder. A Man In His Place** (1971), a series of BBC 2 half-hour documentaries on the class system he made for producer Peter Jarvis, included a mining film shot in Easington, Co. Durham. Its re-screening, coinciding with the 1972 pit strike, excited some media attention.[9] The director then joined LWT's **Weekend World** and between 1973 and 1975 was a producer for BBC 2's arts programme **Second House** when subjects included Chekhov, D. H. Lawrence and film itself – but his abrasive personal style and desire to experiment led to numerous clashes with employers over these years. Francis complained that the internal TV censorship of ideas, content and artistic creativity had reached 'unbelievable proportions' with programme-makers under 'impossible' pressure to compromise. Interference from above spurred him to go it alone as an independent – and led him ultimately to focus on internal censorship in **Giro City**.[10]

Above Us the Earth

The film-maker's career took a crucial turn in 1975 when he began making **Above Us the Earth**, in his own community of Bedwas and Fochriw. The project was to drag on for two years, but proved a riveting and disquieting study of the pit closure at Ogilvie Colliery and the political pragmatism at work within the Labour Party and the NUM. It presented a mining community in thrall to dramatic historical forces, and miners more resigned and bemused than overtly heroic during the kind of closure repeated so many times in south Wales during the 1980s.

Windsor Rees, the central character in *Above Us the Earth*.

Francis received £5,600 completion money from the BFI for the film, after he ran out of cash midway. Certain dramatic sequences of miners' reactions were finally reconstructed a year later and slotted into the 'documentary' material. They included the wryly humorous scene where a miner sees Joe Gormley on the TV news virtually administering the *coup de grâce* to Ogilvie by accepting the economic arguments for shutdown. The local miner reacts, apparently spontaneously: 'I don't think that bloke's a friend of ours.' The miner was, in fact, watching a video a year after the news bulletin, and this technique of re-creating events within a supposed documentary drew fire from critics of Francis's 40-minute **Rough Justice** film and led to an exchange of letters in the quality press about the ethical issues involved.[11] It was no accident that Francis appeared himself on screen in the later **Mister Perks** to validate his documentary and pre-empt public moral qualms about his role in filming an alcoholic released from jail. Francis continued to meld factual and re-created footage in ways which frequently confused and sometimes angered observers, as in **Merthyr and the Girl**, and has dubbed these films 'documentary narratives'. Generally, the re-staging does not affect the main thrust or tenor of his work and excites serious objections mainly from purists.

CHAPTER 22

A Rich Seam –
a Rough
Diamond: the
Work of
Karl Francis

In **Above Us the Earth**, part of the story – the involvement in the pit closure of the lead actor, Windsor Rees (playing himself) – is fictional, though the personal dramas are constructed against a painfully real backdrop. Francis was rewarded with a performance of great truth and stoicism from Rees (of Craig-y-Rhacca, Machen). His miner's heaving shoulders and contorted features in pain-racked close-up bespoke a lifetime gasping for breath underground. Rees was a collier in earlier life, but was later a publican at Trethomas, and was never at Ogilvie, yet he was a victim of pit dust – and this gives the film added poignancy.[12]

Above Us the Earth offers a salutary view of a numbed mining community in a state of confusion and flux. Its portrait of taciturn miners left out on a limb by union leaders contrasts sharply in tone with the comradeship manifest in much of **Ms Rhymney Valley** a decade later. In the wake of so many other pit closures (notably the colliery at Bedwas), the earlier film remains a piquant social and human document. Most of the protagonists are now dead: Rees himself, Gwen Francis, the director's mother who played the miner's wife, and Evan Jones, the hard-working lodge secretary, who tries to appease the men and stoke the fires of optimism. Jones was left jobless after the closure but later, ironically, worked for the NCB as an industrial relations officer. His fretting, chafing and cajoling dominates the film, even if the images of Windsor Rees are the ones we remember.[13] In the film's most harrowing shots, Rees, in a paroxysm of coughing, slumps forward unconscious in an outside privy. The camera peers from above – recalling the old miner's last moments in Jill Craigie's **Blue Scar**. Earlier, the camera lingers on the face of Windsor Rees as if trying to out-stare him. He seems too ill to avert his gaze. It is a shot which burrows in the mind.

Francis presents a workforce genuinely unable to see a way forward, clutching at tawdry consolations offered by union big-wigs and politicos. Michael Foot's meeting with the miners – featured in the film – was less squally than the MP expected, given Foot's tacit acceptance of the pit's fate, Francis says. 'The deep-seated loyalty he'd built up over the years helped him to get away with it.'[14] Later, in one of the most trenchant scenes, Ted Uzzell, a miner from Deri, berates his workmates for 'listening to the lies' he claims have been spoken by Foot and others.

Timmy and the Experts

Francis's next personal film **Timmy and the Experts** (1977) concerned a seventeen-year-old (Down's Syndrome) boy and a clash of wills between his parents and a local social services department hell-bent on switching Timmy Jones from a private residential home in Bedfordshire to a day-care centre closer to his home in Solihull. The documentary, made for BBC 2's **Inside Story** series, adopted a sympathetic stance to the devoted parents. Mrs Jones, the mother, even suffered a breakdown during the ordeal and needed psychiatric treatment, and the marriage itself almost snapped. The Joneses were convinced that Timmy was happy where he was. The officials, determined to reduce bills, were intent on removing him from a home costing ratepayers around £5,000 a year and placing him in a centre where he could enjoy the council's under-used care facilities. Francis was present during case conferences and the final tense meeting between the social workers and parents, and he captured briefly a sense of the residential home director's jubilation and relief after the decision to leave Timmy where he was for an indefinite period. The film allowed the social workers to reveal themselves and the workings of the bureaucratic channels in numerous scenes when discussions and conferences descended into jargon and almost meaningless verbiage.

The film appealed to reviewers across the spectrum. The *Morning Star* described it as 'quite exceptional' and the *Daily Mail* acknowledged it 'a considerable achievement . . . to at least begin to break down the wall of suspicion and fear that isolates the mongol from the rest of us.'[15]

Francis and continuity

The director's experiences of one film have invariably triggered ideas for another. There are echoes of **Timmy and the Experts** in films like **The Committee** and **Giro City**. The TV confrontation between the IRA leader Flynne and journalist O'Malley in **Giro City** (1982) were inspired by an interview Francis conducted with the ex-Provisional IRA chief David O'Connell in 1972 when the director was a producer with **Weekend World**.[16] His own battle with alcoholism in the 1970s helped him identify with **Mister Perks** (1983), a **Forty Minutes** documentary which remains chilling in its objective treatment of a liquored-up lag, Bernard Perks, a personable man when sober. Perks had made thirty court appearances on drink-related offences in the previous fifteen years. Within forty-eight hours of release from Cardiff prison (captured in the film), he was drinking again. That film in turn sparked **The Happy Alcoholic** (1984), a moral drama, almost perversely anachronistic in form, about the devastation of lives by drink which Francis managed to render both convincing and affirmative.

Rough Justice's scenes providing an insight into sexism in the Valleys were reworked to fine comic effect in **Ms Rhymney Valley** and in a slightly more muted way in **The Happy Alcoholic** (1984), when the central character's wife 'trespasses' in the male domain of the club and hurls a spoiled dinner at her feckless hubbie. In **Merthyr and the Girl**, the sex war is fought again when the male majority in a local club prove to have a blinkered idea of entertainment and vote with their feet faced with the music of actress Donna Edwards and her friend; and the battle is joined once more in **Mr Chairman**, where a male working-men's club committee reveal ignorance and prejudice against a women's group.

Issues of communication and language were raised in **The Mouse and the Woman** (working title, 'Afternoon of War'), where a soldier about to be shot reverts to his native Welsh tongue and is told brusquely by his commanding officer to speak in English. Language divisions led to alienation again in **Boy Soldier** when raw military recruit Wil, now in jail after shooting an Irishman who killed his friend, tells his colonel that his father 'doesn't use English much'. Wil is asked immediately if the father is a nationalist, and is forced to translate his father's letter into English, a demeaning experience. Elsewhere in the film Wil frequently uses Welsh, revealing in these passages his state of mind while concealing emotions from non-Welsh-speakers. The allegorical tale of the seashore Wil spins to his Irish girlfriend is delivered in English, but more pertinent observations revealing his own guilt about deceiving her over his true identity and role are made in Welsh, forming a kind of subtext. Wil's observations about his loyalty to the army are in Welsh to the sympathetic Welsh sergeant (Dafydd Hywel) and hidden from the English superior officers who have made his life purgatory. He can similarly insult his persecutors verbally by taking refuge in his own language. A Welsh soldier abused by his English superior on the parade ground in Paul Turner's **Hedd Wyn** (1992) similarly retorts with abuse in his native language. Francis is fascinated by the way 'Welsh can conceal as much as it can reveal' and his films are an argument for a rapprochement, a benign bilingualism which precludes division.[17] He feels English directors suffer from S4C's language policy and that dramas/documentaries in each language must be given space on channels within Wales. As he said in 1986, 'English is a Welsh language too and that's denied by the people who run Wales.'

CHAPTER 22
A Rich Seam –
a Rough
Diamond: the
Work of
Karl Francis

The Mouse and the Woman

From the 1940s on, certain films set wholly or partly in Wales had tackled the economic and class tensions between the Welsh working class and English pit-owners or gentry (for example **Blue Scar**, **Last Days of Dolwyn**, **Fame is the Spur**). **The Mouse and the Woman**, from the Dylan Thomas prose-poem, is perhaps the first Welsh film to handle, albeit almost *en passant*, the cultural and linguistic divisions of the English and Welsh, through the central character's brush with the English military in the First World War. It is also in many ways the least satisfying of Francis's early works. Set in west Wales, it embraces the turmoil of the immediate post-war years – up to around 1924 – and the problems caused by scab workers in a rural community and in the mines. But the film is fundamentally a story of a fated romance across the class barriers. The bounty-hunting pitmen from 'away' are as destructive as the colliery owner's wife Gilda (Karen Archer) is to Morgan, her lover. She sees the miners as forever trapped in a historical mould she does not want to break. Each one, including Morgan (Dafydd Hywel), is representative of his class.[18] She lusts for Morgan, captures him (on camera) and seduces him (while her husband is at war),

Karen Archer, Dafydd
Hywel – the tragic denouement of *The Mouse and
the Woman*.

but the miner is no more than a sop to her vanity – establishing in her own mind her credentials as a woman of innate sympathies with the working class. Francis shows, in the best scenes, the destructive nature of her dilettantism and her reliance on the comforts, the crutches even, of a class she affects to despise. Her independent-woman stance is exposed as a brittle façade by events emphasizing her failure to confront the consequences of her affair with Morgan after its novelty value is played out. But Morgan's passion, once stirred, cannot be so easily quenched. The film moves inexorably towards its tragic denouement, when Morgan murders the woman he loved on the seashore.

Gilda, the *femme fatale*, is imbued with conventional notions of heroism and patriotism and helps goad Morgan, against his better judgement, to volunteer 'for Kitchener' in the war which crippled her own husband. This results in Morgan's disgrace and loss of self-respect. Complex ideas about exploitation underpin Francis's film, which is diluted as drama by the director's perhaps misguided decision to yoke the social problems and antagonisms to an abstract Dylan Thomas work in order to force a re-assessment of Thomas's concern about economic conditions in his own country and his strong feelings for his 'dirty little home town', Swansea. The innate pacifism of Dafydd Hywel's central character reflects Thomas's own views on the Second World War. The plight of a writer taken up by elements of London-and-American high society and in danger of being seduced from his roots suggests parallels in the film as Morgan is temporarily dazzled by Gilda and the vision of another world opens up. Francis proved unable to weave all these elements into a cohesive work or to integrate Thomas's poetry smoothly into the text. When Morgan expresses his love in the metaphorical terms of the poem, while in bed with Gilda, the scene seems highly contrived. It is significant that Hywel felt awkward delivering the lines and never thought they worked in a dramatic context. The film's treatment of the relationship between Morgan and his sister Bran was more successful, suggesting something unspoken in the past, tied up perhaps with the sister's illegitimate child.[19] But the impact of **The Mouse and the Woman**, shot in Narberth, Pembrokeshire, is always vitiated by the director's uncharacteristically tentative approach to his material. He fails to find an appropriate tone or visual style. The scenes of a brawl in the local pub involving miners and scabs are shot in soft focus and seem almost perfunctory.

The film unravels, in extended flashback, through the poet's fractured memories as he is incarcerated in military prison or asylum. He recites poetry of a sensuous, tactile nature – harking back to his doomed relationship with Gilda. These exposition scenes, however episodic the style, convey the idea that the poet is an intuitive character who trusts his senses rather than his intellect. This is explicit early on when Morgan seems to be recalling his affair in the third person: 'He remembered the oval of her eye, the pitch of her voice but not what she said.' Gilda, on the other hand, experiences life at one remove – framed in her camera lens. She intellectualizes about her role in society but cannot break the shackles of class. The social and cultural divisions between the poet and Gilda, as their relationship develops, are sketched with economy. Morgan and his sister are revealed early on outside the church grounds at Gilda's wedding, for instance, clearly excluded by their class. Edward, Gilda's new spouse, patently officer class, is seen helping Kitchener's recruiting drive and mouthing the right patriotic platitudes. Morgan balks initially – 'We're all out of our minds – going to volunteer for oblivion' – but then, wishing to impress Gilda, he follows Edward's lead and volunteers.

In the war scenes Morgan is seen cowering behind a wall, his nerves shot. He is warned that he could face a firing squad, but is given five years' hard labour. When he refuses to join a shooting party to execute deserters he is beaten up by a group of military men, from whom he is divorced, fundamentally, by language.[20] Francis's frequent assertion of the poet's Welshness helps us identify later on with Private Jenkins, the soldier facing execution. The ambivalent role of the Welsh fighting for the British (English) superiors is stressed when the captain of the shooting party demands that Jenkins speaks English if he has anything to say before execution. Jenkins tells him, 'I've killed twelve Germans in the past three years. Am I to be put down like a sick dog?' The line ensures the audience's sympathy and demonstrates where Francis's own feelings lie.

The growing bond between Gilda and Morgan is sealed after a rift with her husband illustrated on screen when she rails against his drunkenness and alleged promiscuity abroad and continues to attack his drinking habits when he returns from war, bitter and paralysed, in a wheelchair. Gilda enjoys the thrill of Morgan's pursuit from the first tentative tryst. 'I'll have to keep an eye on you,' she says. Often that 'eye' is the camera lens, as she seeks to acquire Morgan as another 'possession'. 'What have you done with that?' he asks when she first photographs him; 'Captured you,' she replies. The fragility of the new relationship, even when consummated, is indicated with body language and by his speech: 'I am in your left hand, the hand on your breast. Don't make a fist or you'll crush me.'

Gilda is soon alienated by Morgan's puritanism and guilt, revealed by his poetic references to 'unclean nakedness'. She finally reveals to Edward her infidelity and

CHAPTER 22

A Rich Seam –
a Rough
Diamond: the
Work of
Karl Francis

pregnancy – 'the mouse will out'. Morgan, beaten up in a pub fracas with black-legs, is later made aware of Gilda's diminished feelings for him as emotional and industrial battle-lines are drawn. Edward orders the breaking of the strike and, to compound Morgan's misery, Gilda aborts the baby: 'I had a new life inside Gilda. She's killed it, she's killed me.' As he wanders through the empty mansion after Edward and his wife move away, all that remain are Gilda's photos and the mice which scurry out as he lifts a dust sheet ('The mouse will out'). In the final beach scene Morgan strangles Gilda (dressed in red) and is arrested as he walks out to sea to 'purify' himself.

The film, well shot by Nick Gifford, is rigidly schematic in its equation of the working class with honest feeling and natural emotion and the upper class with oppression and opportunism. The scripting of most later scenes, despite all the fresh perceptions, is shallow and the film rarely builds Thomas's imagery and poetry effectively into the narrative. There were still enough ideas and distinctive moments to arouse anticipation about Francis's next project. The director's main achievement lay in the performances, especially from Hywel, Patricia Napier as the sister, and Karen Archer as Gilda, though Alan Devlin's Edward was a caricatured, petulant villain.[21]

Chekhov in Derry

Francis's concern with the artist's responsibility to his own country surfaced fitfully in **The Mouse and the Woman**. His sense of a duty to reflect national preoccupations and schisms possibly drew him to Ireland to make his 1982 Channel Four documentary **Chekhov in Derry** (1983), which followed the Field Day theatre company, including actor-director Stephen Rea, writer Brian Friel, and actors Ray McAnally and James Ellis, as they performed Chekhov's *Three Sisters* against the turbulence of a Londonderry background (a bomb exploding a few hundred yards away stopped filming at one point).[22] The Field Day venture aims to stress the non-sectarian nature of art and the drama's capacity to break down geographical and spiritual obstacles. Francis's empathy with the company's commitment is obvious in the emphasis placed on the intensity of actors in rehearsal, and particularly on a dispute between Rea and Friel about changes in the material. Friel argues for cutting twenty minutes from the script, and Rea insists that the writer cannot be allowed to massacre his own adaptation. Speeches within the film make pertinent points about Northern Ireland. It is no accident that, in such an affirmative film, Francis isolates the *Three Sisters* speech: 'Our suffering won't be wasted. Our frustrations are a preliminary to better times.'

Much of the director's own philosophy is embedded in this documentary and the sentiments expressed by the protagonists off and on stage. Friel cites, approvingly, W. B. Yeats's comments that, 'You can stay on your island, speak to your own people in your own voice and find some completion in that.' In **Chekhov in Derry**, Friel describes merely touring a play around the North as 'a political gesture', but Francis allows no didactic note to creep in, no overt sectarian stance to intrude, even though the exteriors all provide telling glimpses of the everyday world the actors inhabit. From the 'Free Derry' signs on the roadside to the flurries of activity as people are hustled out of the Guildhall after the car bomb warning, to the British soldiers hurrying across the road and ordering people back, we are aware of the background turmoil, and regular rifle shots over the images provide staccato accompaniment. The film – which also features Irish poet Seamus Heaney – has a density which may not be obvious on first viewing. Francis weaves in footage of TV's **Scene Around Six** about the huge strike at the Maze prison and the local elections, even an item on the explosion which curtailed filming at Spencer Road, Londonderry. The documentary lacks some unity and the performers' discussion on the need for fidelity to the text occupies too much screen time. But the issue of censorship, particularly self-censorship, has preoccupied Francis since his early television days. It was touched on rivetingly in **Mister Perks** when Francis appeared on screen to remonstrate mildly with his subject drinking himself into oblivion just after release from prison. Francis was stressing the limits to the distance that a director of commitment should maintain with his subject, and also accepting, tacitly, the moral responsibility every film-maker has when privy to private traumas.

Giro City

Censorship issues were at the core of **Giro City**, the film in which Francis took up cudgels against vacillating TV middle-management and executives, government mouthpieces, corrupt local politicians and businessmen and a straitjacket legal system which can militate against presentation of the truth.[23] The director drew on his own experiences on **Weekend World** in presenting tensions and altercations within a TV company current-affairs team riven by internal and external pressures.[24] The team hit intractable problems when trying to expose a local councillor's complicity in a plan to strip a tenant farmer of his land as part of a power station scheme; and in seeking to present, without cuts, a speech from an IRA man on the run.

Giro City's scattergun style, in trying to hit all manner of targets, irritates slightly, but the film has intensity and authenticity, thanks to Francis's refusal to soften the central characters. The protagonists do not pontificate on the insidious corruption around them – they merely seek to reflect it in their programmes (abortively, as it turns out). Francis tells us little about the characters' inner or private lives. The journalist Sophie (Glenda Jackson) has split up with her husband who could not cope with her career aspirations – this much is revealed in a morose *tête-à-tête* with the reporter O'Malley (Jon Finch). He is even more enigmatic – we are offered only glimpses of his domestic life. Sophie and O'Malley are committed to ferreting out the truth which proves, here, obstinately elusive. The film's tenor is established when the arch-compromiser, Martin, the programme producer (Kenneth Colley) counsels caution in presenting the Irish material pursued by O'Malley. The dangers implicit in filming in Ireland are also suggested in a terse sequence when O'Malley meets a contact in Dublin; a message is left for Sophie in church and an interview with the IRA quarry on the spot is curtailed by the impending arrival of the authorities. This is succeeded by a brief scene when the military stop O'Malley's car at night, but the vital film taken is concealed in the car seats. O'Malley is then seen interviewing Flynne, the IRA man, on screen as Martin watches. But Flynne has subsequently been arrested and the dead hand of the government and timorous TV executives soon drops on the programme. The minister demands a spot to answer allegations and Flynne's claims that the majority of the Irish want British troops out of Northern Ireland. It is Joe, a tame lapdog at the station, who finally interviews the minister. After the programme O'Malley is beaten up by enraged Irish contacts for his 'betrayal'.

O'Malley's early sentiments indicate the film's main thrust: 'I don't start with the truth – all I know is that when we suppress the truth we create the violence.' Sophie, in turn, ruminates on the role and morality of the media: 'We visit the natives once a week. We placate our liberal consciences.' The impossibility of overcoming red tape and government interference to film true situations in Northern Ireland has its corollary in later scenes focusing on attempts by the TV team to flush out a scheme involving Greater Northern Holdings – subsidiaries of a German firm manufacturing nuclear war containers – and the local council's planning committee led by corrupt councillor Tommy Williams (Emrys James), who has received pay-offs. Clandestine film is taken of Williams himself accepting a package (an obvious back-hander) in a car on wasteland after leaving a choir rehearsal – a tilt at the cant of Welsh public life.[25] Francis, while establishing the trust built up earlier between Sophie and the kindly, if brusque, farmer, Elwyn Davies, continues to make salient points about the treatment of women in the media. Sophie frequently clashes with her boss, Martin, and has to persuade him to honour an equal opportunities pledge by allowing a minor member of the team, the researcher Brigitte (Karen Archer), to carry out the crucial incriminatory interview with Tommy Williams's son John.

Glenda Jackson, Kenneth Colley in *Giro City*.

GN Holdings, after trying to stop the programme, decide to sacrifice Tommy Williams, ensuring his arrest will make the whole issue *sub judice*. (Francis rather glibly glosses over the ramifications of the arrest which will undoubtedly produce massive court publicity at a later date . . .) At the film's climax, Sophie and O'Malley rail impotently against censorship. An old man we have seen periodically spraying anti-Fascist graffiti on walls enters with evidence of anti-Semitic atrocities. Sophie listens, but her wan smile betrays her feelings that the cycle will be repeated, the subject will never be screened. **Giro City** is a cynical film, constantly commenting on the nature and manipulative elements of news-gathering and on TV itself. The farmer, Elwyn Davies, finding his own programme has been dropped, is not in the least mollified to discover its replacement is 'Death of a Pit' (Francis here commenting on what he sees as Welsh parochialism or apathy to what he patently considers as everyone's fight). And a documentary on starving children in Africa seen on the Davieses' TV is presented so that one is alive to the incongruity of the programme's glossy packaging and its juxtaposition with other routine and vacuous 'entertainment'.

All kinds of social concerns jostled together in **Giro City** and occasionally the film's focus blurred but, despite some pat and not entirely convincing investigative work by the TV crew, the film's conclusions were far from facile. **Giro City** was Francis's most satisfying work since **Above Us the Earth**, not least for the scripting and Jackson's down-to-earth performance as the wry, self-deprecating journalist.

Yr Alcoholig Llon (*The Happy Alcoholic*)

The Happy Alcoholic (made in Welsh for S4C) was in some ways the director's most unconventional and certainly least fashionable film. Yet, in the context of his *oeuvre*, it can be seen to embrace his central concerns. The issue of Welshness and the role of the language in 'belonging' is confronted head-on here. Dafydd Hywel's reformed toper Alun, who loses his wife (Eluned Jones) and child before conquering, at least temporarily, his addiction becomes (at times almost embarrassingly) a conduit for the director, most notably when he berates a friend who has become a famous conductor and part of the establishment. Hywel's miner-husband emphasizes the alleged phoneyness of the world which has assimilated the musician (David Lyn) and of that other world outside the Valleys – of Eisteddfodau and bards. Yet he feels intimidated by the ubiquity and durability of all these trappings of nationhood, even though he cannot accept their relevance.

Once more Francis highlights the place of women in a male-dominated society, and makes Alun's wife the focus of sympathy. We understand why, after one drunken beating which he cannot remember the following day, she packs her bags to go. We identify with her resistance to his subsequent overtures, even if our feelings are much more ambivalent when he is denied access to their child.

The film is fascinatingly structured. The director removes all elements of suspense by showing us from the outset that Alun, though still technically an alcoholic, has come to terms with his condition and, as far as can be guaranteed, lost the craving for drink and become a 'respectable member' of society again – witness his acceptance by the choir. (Francis himself appears in an Alcoholics Anonymous scene in the film.) The events unravel in flashback – the device Francis also favours in **The Mouse and the Woman**, **Boy Soldier** and most notably in **The Angry Earth**.

The film is intimidatingly, relentlessly, downbeat – it is not a pleasant film to watch – even allowing for any tentative optimism. But it *is* dramatically effective, especially when Francis latches on to issues which engage him as an English-language film-maker in a country where, in the eighties at least, most significant subsidies went to Welsh-language directors and where much past output has ignored the complexities and problems of urban south Wales. When Alun rails against the 'baggage' of the Welsh establishment and itemizes the sacred cows he considered outmoded and irrelevant to Valleys life, 'Calon Lan, the Eisteddfod, Llewellyn', the opposition of forces is reinforced aurally: he plays modern music or ordinary sea shanties. His mother (Gwenllian Davies) loves the Welsh tenor David Lloyd who died of alcoholism – an extra layer of irony.[26]

Francis spares his audience little in showing Alun's plight – almost as degrading as the real life traumas of **Mister Perks**. The flashbacks unfold after a brief scene in which Alun leaves a choir practice to help a drug/alcohol addict. After an early wife-beating scene, we see the extent of Alun's past reliance on liquor, his subterfuge (he is seen retrieving a bottle from behind a washtub hanging on an outside wall) and his belated contrition. Loss of his wife is the husband's first humiliation. He is then sacked when caught drinking on duty by his boss and rejects the help of his union. Finally, his philandering with a member's wife at his workmen's club sparks a public brawl. After rejecting AA he is forced to accept their help and Francis does not stint on the realities of addiction, presenting Alun shaking and crying self-pityingly as he craves drink, before winding up in a special hospital unit. Only when his binge with his

CHAPTER 22
A Rich Seam –
a Rough
Diamond: the
Work of
Karl Francis

friend Dic ends with the latter's death is the hero stunned into accepting his dependency – the first step to cure.

The Happy Alcoholic conveyed the character's twilight world with precision and honesty. Dafydd Hywel's pivotal performance was his most powerful yet for the director. It was not surprising that the work landed the top prize at the Celtic Film and TV Festival in Brittany in 1985.[27]

Ms Rhymney Valley

Ms Rhymney Valley places feminist issues in the context of the 1984–5 miners' strike and suggests that they should be confronted within the class struggle itself. It presents a vivid, impressionistic picture of a mining community pulling together under duress, but also confronts the question-begging and contradictions implicit in the idea of holding a conventional beauty contest at a time when women were joining their men on the picket line. Made for the BBC, the film is shot through with humour and the finale is charged with an optimistic polemical fervour which might be seen as running counter to the realities of the miners' situation in Bedwas where they were forced back to work and defeated in the dispute. The pit itself closed soon afterwards.[28]

The film concentrates on the men and women's fight to keep the mine open and the implication of this solidarity on future sexual politics in the Valleys. But there are less obvious radical elements in the work which could easily escape the viewer from outside Wales when it is re-screened in the nineties. The key event of the movie, the beauty contest, was abandoned and the competition transformed into a reward for women helping the community during the months of the dispute. But it also raised cash for the miners jailed following the death of David Wilkie, the taxi driver transporting strike-breaking workers to the colliery – though the film only refers to a collection for imprisoned miners. Francis also persuaded the organizers to postpone the event until Neil Kinnock could attend – therefore suggesting implicitly Kinnock's tacit support for all the indicted miners. It is paradoxical that Francis came under fire, not for stage-managing aspects of the **Ms Rhymney Valley** event, but for engineering reactions on the picket lines (the director had no compunction about placing microphones on the clothes of demonstrators at actual protests).

The film points out that in Wales in November 1984 less than 2 per cent of the miners had crossed the picket line, and **Ms Rhymney Valley** can be seen as an uncritical celebration of the miners' solidarity and resilience. It opens with TV news footage of the Wilkie killing and NUM south Wales spokesman Kim Howells describing such a tragedy as inevitable in the prevailing climate and Kinnock himself, according to the bulletins, expressing 'complete horror'. The film briefly introduces a strike activist Charmaine Nind, granddaughter of Bill Nind, the leader of the Unemployed Lodge in south Wales during the 1926 strike – then abruptly changes tone.[29]

Ray Davies, a left-wing Mid Glamorgan county councillor, is seen speculating on the 'aggro' the men will face from the girls if they press ahead with the beauty contest. We then meet burly Abe, the chairman of the Bedwas and Trethomas Labour Party branch and the mouthpiece of the traditional 'reactionary' males of the Valleys. Francis, who sees Abe as 'a bit of a dinosaur', presents him with unstinting affection, even when it is clear later on that Charmaine, fiercely opposed to the contest, holds all the moral cards.[30] Francis teases out the humour and suggests the mutual affection

Neil Kinnock chats with director Karl Francis on the set of *Ms Rhymney Valley*. Abe Roberts is in the centre.

between Charmaine and Abe which stems from their unity in the struggle against the NCB. But Francis artfully suggests sexism may be ineradicable in the scene when Ray Davies, Abe and other male judges spend most of the time spinning jokes during the acts or putting down the performers; the judges' attention is held only with the appearance of one group fronted by an attractive female singer. Francis never allows the contest to distract from the strike itself and the rapid filming – fifteen days' shooting over nine weeks – helped give the narrative the necessary immediacy. But the film's real strength stems from the sharp contrasts Francis makes between the material impoverishment of the area during the strike and the community's emotional richness and diversity.

The director constantly cross-cuts between scenes of conflict (the picket-line skirmishes and the beauty contest policy squabbles), and quieter moments when old stagers reflect on past disputes, for example, or NUM leaders in Wales handle aspects of the strike. We are reminded, in the film, of Scargill's warnings of a pit 'hit' list, the union's discovery that 'scab oil' was allegedly handled at Avonmouth and their suspicions that the CEGB were running down the Aberthaw power station so mines lost output. And, throughout, Francis implores his viewers to take note of the lessons of history and the idea of the past living on in the present. The concept of continuity is most apparent when we see the birth of a baby to striking miner Brian Attwood and his wife, Jacqui.

The director threads images of the women on the picket line protesting at the impending closure of the Bedwas pit, and demonstrating outside the Abercwmboi Phurnacite plant, into increasingly lighter scenes in which arguments over the contest are resolved. Ups and downs in the miners' fortunes are charted largely through Charmaine's reactions. She is seen recovering the Bedwas miners' banner from the old workmen's hall and cinema for a consecration ceremony, but any celebrations are undercut by scenes of the crisis overtaking the pit in February 1985. Francis observes with compassion the stunned reaction of the NUM lodge chairman who claimed to have been given no forewarning of plans to shut the pit. The film ends with Kim Howells talking of links binding the community into an indomitable force, insisting that ordinary pitmen are the guts of the NUM and the Labour movement. The triumphalist sentiments appear hollow in retrospect as later developments vindicated Scargill's warning and its implications for the Valleys.

Those who accused Francis of vacillating in **Above Us the Earth** in his attitude to the miners' predicament could hardly indict him for pussyfooting in **Ms Rhymney Valley**, though the film lacks the intellectual rigour of the earlier work. It fails to provide an adequate framework for us to take a stance on the Wilkie affair and finally surrenders to an emotionalism which undermines the weightier pragmatic arguments of the NUM local leaders for keeping the pits open – the statements about the need for coal for power stations and details of the coal reserves at Bedwas, for example. **Ms Rhymney Valley** *does* convey what Francis describes as 'the changing face of Welsh Valleys politics with women creating miners' support groups which are continuing and becoming a major force in the Labour party and in politics generally'. He has forcefully defended the film's stance: 'I think I made the right choices – not to make the film about the whinges of the week. It was about the whole colour of the strike, the strength of it . . . People have a way of resisting the power of the state. A lot of people came forward in the strike and they're not going to go away.'[31]

Milwr Bychan (*Boy Soldier*)

The director wrote the script for his highly charged next feature after spending a year working on **The Monocled Mutineer** (1985) for BBC. That riveting First World War drama raised the hackles of influential critics with its jaundiced view of the military. But it was perhaps a blessing in disguise that the Welsh director was taken off the Alan Bleasdale script by a new producer during a hiatus when the BBC were trying to raise more cash for the project.[32] While the programme was in limbo, Francis – in a six-month period – conceived and wrote **Boy Soldier**, **The Happy Alcoholic** and **Ms Rhymney Valley**.

Boy Soldier turns a critical eye on British Army officers. Francis's Welsh 'hero', a nineteen-year-old who volunteers for service from a Welsh working-class background, is savagely ill-treated by his superiors after his arrest following a killing during a routine patrol. The film is a powerful, claustrophobic work examining the teenager's increased alienation from an army which makes him a scapegoat – and his affinity and identification with Celts subjugated (it is implied) by the occupying British forces. It was perhaps only a matter of time before Francis, in a film for S4C, felt impelled to treat the problem of national identity and Welshness as a central concern. In **The Mouse and the Woman** he hinted at the predicament of a Welsh soldier alienated from the class-ridden British Army and in **Boy Soldier** he was to present the ambivalent attitudes of a Valleys boy facing the moral conundrum of serving in Northern Ireland for a force he comes to recognize as the potential aggressors.

The film shuttles backward and forward in time. After a glimpse of the realities of a military house raid, Wil Thomas (Richard Lynch) softens and relaxes in his uncle's farm retreat and through the love of his new Irish girlfriend Deirdre (Emer Gillespie). But, languishing in prison after the killing, Wil recognizes how he is used by a force whose objectives are not his own. He feels far more affinity for the Irish than for his fellow squaddies from England, or their military superiors. Just as the poet and the executed soldier asserted their Welshness through language in **The Mouse and the Woman**, Wil acknowledges his language roots, which in turn cut him off from most of the other squaddies. He is ordered to read a letter in Welsh from his father to his commanding officer, Lt.-Col. Truscott-Jones (James Donnelly) – but it is only after his girlfriend discovers his true identity and after she has been tarred and feathered by her friends that he accepts his shift of camps to the 'colonized'. He is then able to see the condescension and xenophobia implicit in the attitude of superiors like Roberts (Bernard Latham), the violent RSM (Robert Pugh) and Truscott-Jones himself.[33] Wil, destined to face a murder charge after the death of a civilian, is as much a victim of the British forces as the Irish people he helps to subjugate. After his naïve love affair is broken up, he has no sympathy for the way his colonel, almost unwittingly, talks disparagingly about the ordinary Irish people. 'As far as I'm concerned there are no

Micks any more,' Wil tells him. It is the Welsh Sergeant Crane (Dafydd Hywel) who becomes surrogate father to Thomas, teaching him with a crude moral pragmatism how to play the 'army game'. Crane acts as confidant, sounding-board and conspirator, sharing his antagonism towards prevailing hypocrisy within the Army. There is a mutual recognition of the impossibility of treating as the foe people who live 'only thirty miles from Liverpool', as the sergeant observes. The film argues that ignorance is the great barrier: a captain (Ian Saynor) bemoans the undermining of the soldiers' hostility in the recent past through relationships with Irish girls.

Wil's offence, finally shown quite late in the film, is the act of an inexperienced boy genuinely terrified by the advance of a youthful mob upon him in an alley and by the death of his friend (Timothy Lyn). Wil's killing becomes a *cause célèbre* as the Army takes the course of expediency in trying to appease the Ulster authorities, first laying a murder charge while seeking to hush up the affair and spirit Wil away from Northern Ireland. Pressure increases when the victim is seen as the son of an influential figure in Ireland, but the charge is reduced by degrees as the Army seek presumably to compromise between the government's wish to play events down and the Ulster authorities' desire for justice. Wil's own refusal to wilt in the face of harassment and the Army's apparent retreat when forced to reduce the charge is seen by Sergeant Crane as a victory for the Welsh soldier's courage, but the ending is far from satisfactory. It is not obvious whether we are meant to accept the victory at face value (a conclusion suggested by the emphasis on Wil's rebelliousness and his 'Dare to be a Daniel' refrain) or as irony, as Francis has established (a little shakily perhaps) the pervasive hold the politicians have over the military. Any victory is clearly that of the faceless establishment over the Army and the more bellicose Ulster political factions.

CHAPTER 22

A Rich Seam –
a Rough
Diamond: the
Work of
Karl Francis

The presentation of the Sergeant Crane character seems a trifle confused. He appears to harbour a distaste for the ugliness of the Northern Ireland campaign and the role of soldiers as pawns, but also condones many of the military's values and methods of conducting the occupation and the dishonesty of double-think. Francis's screenplay also reveals suspiciously late in the day that the victim's father is important in Irish politics; furthermore it is not clear, beyond suggesting a build-up of pressure on the military, what significance this disclosure has, if any. **Boy Soldier** is least satisfactory in schematic scenes when a government agent/minister, a Machiavellian figure played by Bernard Hill (inexplicably in dark glasses) insidiously pressurizes the Army with instructions from above to let the reverberations from the killing just fade away. Failures to flesh out the Hill character or fill in the detail of the agencies manipulating him are obvious. Francis also tells us little of the background of the boy killed or the machinations beyond the barracks.

The film works best when Francis attests to the possibility of a romance beyond the sectarian barriers, while undercutting optimism with constant reminders that relationships in such an emotional battlefield are often built on dishonesty and hypocrisy. It is hard to fault the emotional validity of the bedroom scene when Deirdre recoils from Wil after discovering his military status and is accused by her uncomprehending lover of rebuffing him merely because of his disappointing sexual performance. The flashbacks suggest Wil's confused state of mind and his attempts, as he juggles images, to make sense of a world which suddenly seems strange and threatening.

Francis, while acknowledging Deirdre's genuine love and compassion for her man, refuses her any soft options. The confrontation scene in which she discovers his 'true'

identity has genuine power because we do not believe her protests that she hates him. It is the *situation* that she loathes – and its socially demeaning implications for her – not the soldier himself. The film is compelling when Wil and Deirdre are most themselves. There is a potent moment when Wil is seen blubbering outside his mother's south Wales flat after his rift with the girl.[34] But there is also crude power in prison scenes of Wil's harrowing ill-treatment, even if the film's failure to make his persecutors more than two-dimensional is irritating. It is not easy to believe in their hatred for Wil (surely it is not all predicated on a hatred for the language and the feeling that Wil is not 'one of them'?).

Superbly shot by Roger Pugh Evans, the film opened to generally favourable reviews after enthusiastic audience reactions at the London and Edinburgh festivals. Ian Christie of the **Daily Express** described it as an 'admirable human document, a tribute to personal courage and resilience'. And Derek Malcolm thought it 'a *tour de force* of memorable proportions . . . I can't think of another British film-maker with this kind of certainty and passion, with the possible exception of Ken Loach . . . It is the best and most resonant thing Francis has done.' Yet by 1993 – six years after release and its S4C screening – **Boy Soldier** had still not been screened by Channel Four which continued to procrastinate, conscious of its military sensitivity.[35] When the film was about to open in London, Francis acknowledged the problem. He praised the courage of S4C for backing his £250,000 film and allowing him to make it. 'Channel Four wouldn't put up the money and it's doubtful whether I would be able to get the cash for the project in Wales if I started it today in the present political climate.'[36] The situation is no less sensitive in the mid-nineties.

Francis strongly denied that his new work was lurid or sensational: 'The sort of thing that happens to Wil in the film happens every day in Northern Ireland, and it's no use telling me that violence isn't inflicted on people in military prisons where nobody knows what's going on.'[37] He wanted to make important points about colonization. 'The Welsh soldier in the British Army may feel like the Gurkha or the Maori soldier, for example – an outsider. I think people join the Army out of poverty rather than patriotism. Loyalty to the Army is pretty thin, under pressure. I have sympathy for young soldiers [from Wales] who don't know what they're getting into, of course I do – but everyone who dons a uniform has to face responsibility for violence and killings in certain situations.'[38]

Merthyr and the Girl

Francis next made a film about actress Donna Edwards, comparing her public image as a star of the S4C soap **Dinas**, with her turbulent home life.[39] It would not be unreasonable to suggest that Francis, in this disturbing, often fraught work, intended to contrast the glossy domestic dramas of much S4C work with the earthier realities, which he deemed S4C should be tackling in more of its programme slots. The film follows Edwards's chastening attempts to introduce drama to south Wales clubs and halls and convince her own family that she is not letting them down by doing club and stage work in the Valleys rather than in London or on national 'telly'.

Merthyr and the Girl (1989) embraces some popular Francis themes such as alcoholism and feminism but, almost perversely, glories in the individuality and bloody-mindedness of its characters. The film is laced with gallows humour – though the laughter often sticks in the throat, as we sense the quiet desperation behind some of the dialogue. Francis moves into highly problematic areas. Edwards is presented as caring and passionate, if sometimes blunt and strident in dealing with friends and family. In the most brutal and moving scenes she remonstrates with an alcoholic male friend who expresses a wish to die and a belief that life is 'continuous hell on earth'. At the film's end the man who has earlier seen his heavy drinking only as a side issue of his troubles, seems partly to be coming to terms with his problem. But he died soon after the movie was completed and the death raised serious questions about how far film-makers should go to capture reality. The film also led viewers to believe the relationship between Donna and the dying man was much closer than it actually was – though most other aspects of her life were treated with fidelity. **Merthyr and the Girl** also re-creates real events, but is most effective in its fly-on-the-wall sequences with family bickering and soul-baring. Edwards obviously had courage in exposing her private life to the camera. The result was compelling, gritty and at times painful watching. Francis's concern to present Valleys life as it is rather than as more self-conscious image-makers (or local residents) might wish it to be, was reflected in often amusing scenes when Donna and her friend Kath tried vainly to impress family and friends with their planned drama extracts.[40] The domestic scenes yield memorable moments, with Francis exposing tensions between Donna's mother, brother and father as they cope with physical and social disabilities.

Running through the film is Donna's desire to continue working close to her roots – even if the real money lies elsewhere. Francis was not unaware of the dilemma as he continued to work in Wales rather than seek more lucrative pastures which might remove him from the most fertile source of his inspiration. **Merthyr and the Girl** is an examination of the plight of the artist, to place alongside the director's earlier **Chekhov in Derry**.

Llid y Ddaear (*The Angry Earth*)

In the most piquant scene of Francis's S4C drama **Llid y Ddaear** (**The Angry Earth**, 1989), Gwen (Sue Roderick), herself a miner's widow, agrees to lay out the corpse of a 'scab' pitman killed in an accident after defying workmates to break a strike.[41] The widow is so impoverished that she cannot refuse the work – or what she calls 'dirty money' – but as she enters the dead man's home she runs the gauntlet of other, hostile wives. Yet Gwen is tearful, performs her duties conscientiously, reliving her own pain through flashbacks, which reveal that her first husband Emlyn (Robert Pugh) died in a pit fall. Her spouse was a union man loyal to his fellow colliers, but as Gwen cuts off the dead man's boots to reveal his bloodied feet, and tends him gently, we appreciate her mettle and indomitability, and her simple, humane feelings which transcend any political disagreements. The scene is crucial to an understanding of Francis's work, conveying once more his ambivalent feelings about the south Wales pits which have blighted so many lives and inspired such conflicting emotions. He also believes that local life is about much more than the pit and any vested interests (however sympathetic). There are shared experiences which bind even those who have taken different paths. Gwen may chide the dead man's widow for failing to distinguish between a strike and lock-out in a miner's fight to obtain better safety conditions, but the bonds of sympathy are unshakeable.

The Angry Earth spans nine decades of Gwen's life as, wheelchair-bound in hospital, she celebrates her 110th birthday as the oldest person in Britain. Outside, a nurses' strike emphasizes the continuation of the industrial struggle. As her past life unspools, we confront all the disasters she has overcome since orphaned at sixteen – including the later death, in another disaster, of her second husband Evan (Dafydd Hywel) and son Guto. The film, embracing the times of the Tonypandy Riots and the Senghenydd pit disaster of 1913 has courageous bravura flourishes even though it too often veers towards cliché. Francis, one suspects, seeks to make points – too insistently and obviously – for a wider audience. Near the climax he invites us to see Gwen, who has lived in the Rhondda Valley since she was thirteen, as a stoic Mother Courage forced to uproot from her home with her goods and chattels in a truck. Her struggles have assumed an epic grandeur. As usual, Francis also finds a physical metaphor for the continuity of the south Wales miners' lives and their resilience. Gwen is raped by English soldiers and traumatized but she recovers, just as the mining communities have been 'raped' yet in extremity always recovered and adapted.

The film is rich in detail. Many outside Wales will be shocked to learn that, years ago, more compensation was available when a horse died in the pit than was provided to women widowed in pit falls. But the telescoping of south Wales mining history into one woman's life has limitations – events of the twenties and thirties are skimped, and at times the film descends into heavy-handed melodrama, hustling from one trauma to another. Guto's revenge for Gwen's rape seems highly improbable, for example. Characters become mouthpieces for the director, but there is a warmth and passion in the work to help compensate for most of the film's shortcomings. Scenes of mother and daughter washing down the corpses of their loved ones provide images of loss, resilience and durability as eloquent as any in Francis's *oeuvre*.

In 1990, Francis paid tribute to a man he had long admired. His Channel Four film, **Raymond Williams: Journey Of Hope**, provided a dense, rich documentary embracing many of Williams's preoccupations and weaving together interviews with dramatized extracts from the novels, including *The Fight for Manod* and *Border Country*, often to underline Williams's more trenchant philosophical writing, and his credo. Kim Howells, Dai Smith, Gwyn Alf Williams were more familiar faces paying homage but Francis also featured Raymond Williams's former colleagues at Cambridge, whose views, *pro* and *con*, on his work created a dialectic, and a *frisson* at the often arid intellectual climate in which the Welshman had sown his left-wing, egalitarian theories.

Morphine and Dolly Mixtures

The director's fascination with lives ravaged by alcohol and drugs found its most chilling outlet in **Morphine and Dolly Mixtures** (1990), his BBC Wales feature based on the childhood ordeal of the Penarth writer Carol-Ann Courtney.[42] His films **The Happy Alcoholic**, **Mister Perks** and **Merthyr and the Girl** centred on men unwilling to acknowledge their own dependency on drink, but rarely focused on their damaging impact on others (apart from the battered wife in **Alcoholig Llon**). In **Morphine**, set in the 1950s, there are two main victims: Terence (Patrick Bergin), a toping, schizophrenic father with lung cancer and addicted to the drug, and his daughter, 'Caroline' (the young Carol-Ann), who is beaten and placed under appalling emotional pressure, following her mother's death from a brain tumour. Francis shows how the father displaces his own guilt – about his treatment of his wife, his own drug craving – onto the daughter, by maintaining the fiction that she was responsible for the fall which allegedly caused the mother's death. He even fabricates, on a typewriter, a death certificate. The action rarely moves outside the family home (London in reality, Wales in the film) as Francis builds up a persuasive picture of a man with a dual personality haunted by his own shortcomings. The director uses close-ups of Bergin and dialogue pauses to good effect, and the sense of children trapped in a volatile, dangerous milieu is emphasized, rather than dissipated, by the presence of Sue Roderick's blowsy mistress (superficially pleasant, but fractious and uncomprehending when trouble develops). The grandmother (Gwenllian Davies), who constantly snipes at her son-in-law, also creates dissension in the home. The screenplay is a little too thin to sustain the weight of emotions at play and the father's mood-swings do not always convince – yet the film holds our attention, thanks to the force of fraught domestic scenes and the performance Francis has drawn from teenager Joanna Griffiths, who suggests the youngster's bemusement and paralysing

CHAPTER 22

A Rich Seam –
a Rough
Diamond: the
Work of
Karl Francis

fear (especially in a taut sequence when she has her first period and vainly tries to hide soiled underclothes). Once more Francis suggests that the ostensible victim is a survivor. In a climactic scene, when Caroline's brothers and sisters are seized by the authorities, her bearing never suggests defeat. There is an innate resilience and dignity which provides an unexpected affirmative finale.

An HTV trilogy

In 1991, Francis directed three 'shorts' in a lighter vein than all his previous work. He is dismissive of his 1991 HTV documentary trilogy **Mr Chairman**, **A Night Out** and **The Committee**, claiming the programmes were made as relaxing diversions. But he did want to make films with humour to counter critics who had drawn increasing attention to the lack of levity (or, sometimes, of any kind of relief) in his films (**Ms Rhymney Valley** was the most obvious exception).[43] It is also conceivable that he wanted to test his abilities in handling humour prior to his first feature comedy, **Rebecca's Daughters**.

The most successful of the three is undoubtedly **Mr Chairman**, despite its uneasy meld of fiction, drama, didacticism and slightly laborious special pleading. It is a thinly veiled satire on men's clubs in the Valleys, shot in the Bedwas Working Men's club (which gave it added trenchancy). Abe Roberts, the Labour Party backwoodsman of **Ms Rhymney Valley** plays a club boss who lays himself open to ridicule as he airs his anti-homosexual prejudices. Francis enjoys sending up sexual roles in a scene in which the boss, uncharacteristically in a hairdressing parlour, rails against gays. One committeeman, his nephew Kevin (Robert Hale), already established in the film as a homosexual, tells the Roberts character he would not know a gay if he saw one – and we know this is true. This is rather obvious knockabout fun but there are serious points made about the petty tyrannies of officialdom, and repression of both men and women (who feel bound by the conventions of their peers). Francis stresses the mores of a male-dominated community which stifles expression. The committee prevaricate, for instance, over whether to allow a women's group into their club – then admit them only on sufferance. The group is banned later on the blatantly hypocritical pretext that they have been discussing sex too loudly, despite a bitter reminder from one woman about the local wives' positive role in the miners' strike. 'Where's the unity now?' she asks. The plight of many women in the Valleys is illustrated when a tearful victim of her husband's violence stresses her reluctance to make the decisive break with him. But elsewhere, in a scene shot in the Ruperra club, we see women enjoying a degree of liberation once inconceivable in this macho community – watching, and bantering with, a male drag artist.

The Committee has fewer pretensions, Francis merely allowing a clutch of pundits to air their often shrewd and amusing views about the Welsh passion for committees and the lack of accountability of *ad hoc* bodies. Once more he catches hall committee minions on the hop, to expose mindless bureaucracy. In one scene a man emerges from S4C offices and complains about the lack of accessibility of English speakers to the channel, a rather contrived (and mischievous) interlude in which the speaker was clearly acting (however unwittingly) as the director's mouthpiece.

A Night Out is a record of an evening's entertainment at Mountain Ash rugby club, observed affectionately by the director who managed another gentle tilt at bureaucracy with his emphasis on the entertainment secretary warning earthy singer-comedienne Stella King to eschew 'blue' jokes. The film manages to say much about the innate vulgarity and good humour of Valleys club life, and the routines of professional comic Colin Price, especially salvos against the conservative Nottingham miners, often echoing the director's feelings.[44]

Rebecca's Daughters

Francis had previously returned to drama and proved his adaptability to handle conventional thriller narrative in **1996**, written by G. F. Newman – in which elements of the Stalker affair were transposed (on the director's initiative) from Northern Ireland to Wales, or 'the much-troubled Welsh province'. Newman's dogmatic approach and the lack of shading in characterization, soon palled and the abrupt about-turn of the Stalker figure, Jack Bentham (Keith Barron), finally undermined the film, even though Francis did his best to insert bridging scenes or dialogue which might have made the transition more credible.[45] Constantly seeking to extend his range, the director visited America in 1990 to work with Oakland police in California and blur the division between reality and fiction even further in a lively drama-documentary which involved the lawmen playing themselves in actual and re-created scenes.

It was perhaps only a matter of time before he handled a more overtly commercial subject. Few could have predicted a period comedy, but he was approached by Chris Sievernick, (producer of John Huston's **The Dead** and Wim Wenders's **Paris, Texas**) to make **Rebecca's Daughters**, a £3 million cinema film, from a forgotten screenplay written by Dylan Thomas for Gainsborough in 1948, published, but never shot.[46] The film dealt with an episode of Welsh history curiously neglected on screen – the Rebecca Riots which began in west Wales in 1839 when farmers, some of whom donned female guise, smashed and set ablaze toll gates in protest against charges levied by English landowners. Shot in summer 1991, the feature starred Joely Richardson, Peter O'Toole and Welshman Paul Rhys. Francis was able to make salient political points about the social class which produced, in the same decade, the Chartists. But, surprisingly perhaps, the film misfired. The final script, from Guy Jenkin (writer of the much-praised **Drop the Dead Donkey** TV series) but adapted by the director and comedian Dewi Morris, was a patchwork, with most of the better gags and interesting incidents in the first half, when Peter O'Toole (in an over-ripe performance) was given too much leeway. The film petered out in tiresome farce and scenes lacking conviction, though the director drew a fine performance from Paul Rhys as youthful lead, the aristocrat who led the rioters. The work was savaged by some critics and had few screenings but Francis then changed tack again to make the 1992 BBC Wales networked TV drama **Civvies**, when he proved once more his ability to handle action in a convincing context. The series – violent and caustic – was primarily the work of the novelist and scriptwriter Lynda La Plante, whose idea it was to home in on six ex-Parachute Regiment men who serve in the Falklands and Northern Ireland, become misfits back on Civvy Street, and gain little help from the Army in making the crucial adjustment to domestic life. Most become pawns of a London gangster (played again by O'Toole). Francis made noticeable contributions to the scripting, persuading La Plante to re-locate the second episode from Ireland to Wales, for example, a switch which recalled his intervention at the pre-production stage of **1996**. Francis was also able to develop one or two themes from **Boy Soldier**, hinting at the ruthlessness of the Army machine and links between Army recruitment

CHAPTER 22
A Rich Seam –
a Rough
Diamond: the
Work of
Karl Francis

and unemployment. Both the director and La Plante, in interviews, stressed the moral obligations of government and the possible traumatic social implications, when 65,000 soldiers released through defence cuts find themselves on the employment market in the mid-nineties. The situation stirred a collective folk memory of Lloyd George's infamous broken pledge to house the soldiers after the Great War. In 1993 Francis was working for HTV again with an ambitious four-part comedy drama **Judas and the Gimp**, which attempted to blend robust humour centred on local conmen's schemes to defraud the government into paying out false benefits to a 'fictitious' estate, and religious allegory, with the community of the notoriously down-at-heel Penrhys Estate, Rhondda, staging a miracle play as backdrop to the villains' machinations. Francis said he hoped the film would be seen as a humorous antidote to the gloom surrounding estates like Penrhys – which had attracted bad press with its housing conditions and social problems in the past – and help people understand that the difficulties here were essentially similar to those experienced on countless estates. 'Judas', an unemployed youth, nagged by his sister, has no confidence and has a poor opinion of himself – until he is galvanized by the schemes of the local fly boy (Karl Johnson).

Whatever his future ventures – and it seems inconceivable that he will work long outside Wales – Francis's body of work has remained without parallel in his native country. He has turned an unwavering eye on the major social forces at work in south Wales and examined the root causes of much industrial and social malaise. Who knows what he might accomplish working more regularly with TV budgets comparable to those of his London-based counterparts?

OUT OF THE PAST: STEPHEN WEEKS

I have always been interested in industrial archaeology. There is something that strikes the imagination about some places, buildings which were once busy and are now empty. One seeks these haunting . . . marvellous images of dereliction. The *Marie Celeste* sailing along with the kettle still boiling . . . wonderful houses once lived in, with grass growing through the staircases.

(Stephen Weeks, interviewed December 1984)

If Karl Francis's films have been almost obsessively preoccupied with the present and with urban life, Gwent-based Stephen Weeks has regularly taken us back to a medieval or imperialist past, or a misty Celtic world. Weeks (b. 1948) is almost certainly the only British director living in a castle – Penhow, an eyrie perched above the old Newport–Chepstow road, and a refuge he has restored to much of its medieval splendour.[1] The home could hardly be more suited, for Weeks is riveted by bygone events, 'lost worlds' and their echoes and reverberations in our own day. Still only in his forties, he has completed four cinema features, from **I, Monster** (1971) to **Sword of the Valiant** (1982), plus a handful of early shorts and two first-rate TV documentaries – and all his significant work has been set, or emotionally anchored, in the past. Even **Ghost Story** (1974) his one feature film set in the present century was shot in an India resonant with reminders of the eighteenth- and nineteenth-century Raj and opened out adventurously to embrace life in a Victorian madhouse. Weeks's **Gawain and the Green Knight** (1973) was the first known film version of the epic fourteenth-century poem, among the most influential of early rites-of-passage adventures. And Weeks was so fascinated by the poem's cinematic challenges that he filmed it again almost a decade later – as **Sword of the Valiant** (1982).[2]

The director has virtually lapsed into silence in recent years after a precocious start in the precarious British film industry of the 1970s, with three features completed by his late twenties. His career has been littered with abandoned or aborted projects, fraught with arguments and stand-offs with producers and financiers. He has done no significant film work since 1986, when his project 'The Bengal Lancers' was aborted in acrimonious circumstances during shooting. Weeks has seemed preoccupied with conservation and tourism issues in recent years, and it is small wonder, perhaps, that he is thought of, by some of his fellow film-makers in Wales, as some kind of dilettante, not quite successful or busy enough to be considered a mainstream commercial film-maker, yet definitely divorced from the camp of the active 'independents'. Yet the director's cinema and TV work up to the mid-1980s, though uneven in quality, is clearly worth detailed consideration, revealing strong thematic threads and a certain clarity and consistency of vision. His fascination with Britain's military traditions and notions of war inform all his early documentaries from the short **Owen's War** (1965) to his finest work **Scars** (1976), an elegiac celebration of those – including the Cardiff PALS – who fell in French and Belgian fields in 1914–18. The film is still exhumed every few years by HTV for Armistice Day screenings.[3] Weeks's love of Kipling and respect for the writer's values is manifest, not merely in his S4C documentary **Kipling Country** but in his choice of fictional material (the fated project on the Bengal Lancers). Of modern British directors, perhaps only Weeks would have hit on the notion (partly as a cost-cutting expedient) of filming **Ghost Story** in an India which has never thrown off the shackles of the past in order to evoke a rural England between the wars when, for some, time appeared to stand still.

The director's fondness for pastorale and stories which weave elements of the inexplicable into historical events stems partly from his enthusiasm for the novels of Rosemary Sutcliff, the children's writer who collaborated on both **Ghost Story** and **Gawain and the Green Knight**.[4] He has also displayed an almost inordinate affection for photogenic Welsh locations (particularly castles, symbols of English colonization) and Arthurian legend. It is precisely this absorption in Celtic material or romantic allegory and legend which makes Weeks worth study. The Arthurian terrain has been explored *ad nauseam* in commercial features. John Boorman's **Excalibur** (1981) is perhaps the most celebrated example, but Celtic and specifically Welsh myth have most regularly been thrown into focus by feature films or series made for S4C – from **Owain Glyndŵr** and the truncated **Mabinogi** to much more recent legends of Madam Wen and Twm Sion Catti – and by directors such as Wil Aaron and Paul Turner. No film-maker apart from Weeks has focused on Wales – *specifically* – as the setting for Arthurian adventure. Even Eric Rohmer's **Perceval Le Gallois** (Percival of Wales) (1978) was set in a strange limbo-land of contrived stage sets, and proved a work of arid formality, a discursive exercise of almost Bressonian austerity. Notions of knightly courtesy and chivalry, and the importance of the quest for the Holy Grail, were explored through tableaux vivants.[5]

Weeks's struggles to mount projects are also worth recounting, as a salutary reminder of the problems and compromises almost inevitable for an independent trying to make cinema films within Wales, or with British finance. Budget, distribution and production problems have undoubtedly had a debilitating effect on the director's creativity.

Early work

No Welsh-born director of fictional features had achieved even limited success in the British cinema since John Harlow (born 1896, Ross-on-Wye) whose career blossomed briefly in the 1940s as a maker of low-budget crime potboilers, mainly for British National but occasionally for Warners.[6] His material ranged from formula programmers (**Meet Sexton Blake**, 1945) to risible and pretentious melodramas such as **While I Live** (1947), reissued in 1950 as **Dream of Olwen**. He garnered some good reviews with the 1946 thriller, **Appointment with Crime**, starring William Hartnell and Robert Beatty, when he explored the world of gang violence and spivs also embraced by Welsh novelist Richard Llewellyn in his stage and screen play for **Noose** (dir. Edmond Greville, 1948). But Harlow was already a back-number by the mid-fifties and it was to be another twenty years before a director based in Wales – Stephen Weeks – emerged to make commercial features (latterly with his own small studios). Weeks was born in Gosport, Hampshire, but the bulk of his work has been produced in Wales.

Weeks began his TV and film career with **Owen's War**, a five-minute short made for Southern Television when he was sixteen, using schoolfriends as actors and presenter Tony Bilbow reading Wilfred Owen's poetry over evocative images of desolation. A derelict railway station with weeds growing through the sleepers held emotional associations with troop trains carrying men now grown old or long gone. Here indeed 'the past was almost tangible' to the director, who later regretted taking the easy option in using Owen's poetry and rendering the images necessarily subservient to the verse. These early stamping grounds offered his imagination free rein with their frequent reminders of old army hospitals, cannon foundries, transit camps used before the wartime cross-channel push and all the flourishing activity of the dockyards. **Owen's War**, an evocative, gentle little film, was shot around the mudflats at Gilkicker, Hampshire. This was also the scene of his second film, **Army Camp**, made initially as part of a Southern TV series but later extended with Weeks's frequent musical collaborator Ron Geesin providing sound effects.[7] Weeks – with a lecturer friend Brian Cox – then made **Deserted Station** (1965), which echoed and crystallized earlier themes. Passengers are shown entering a station, supposedly in the thirties; no train comes; the camera pulls back to reveal the station as disused. Once more, past and present fuse in the imagination and the film has a deceptive poignancy. **Victorian Church** (1967), continued the fascination with dereliction and mortality. The central character (Brian Crocker) shelters in the building during a storm and becomes possessed by the spirit of past events, including baptisms and funerals. The experience was to serve Weeks well as inspiration for the test sequence from **Gawain and the Green Knight** which impressed producer Carlo Ponti and led to the film's distribution.

Weeks joined the J. Walter Thompson advertising agency in 1966 and conceived the idea of **Flesh** (1967), which drew analogies between meat in butcher's shops and markets with tawdry strip shows and sexploitation acts.[8] The notion of parallels between meat and human exploitation was popular in the early seventies, notably in Warhol's film **Flesh** (1971)and Michael Ritchie's **Prime Cut** (1972) – and lingered later, as in John McKenzie's London thriller **The Long Good Friday** (1981), when villains dangled from meat hooks (shades also of Dennis Potter's BBC Wales drama **Where the Buffalo Roam**). Weeks used repellent huge close-ups for shock effect, notably in juxtaposed scenes of flesh and rotting meat, and repeated shots of a giant eyelid clamping down as a device to link scenes.

The First World War provided the inspiration for Weeks's first longer film **1917**, shot (mainly in monochrome) in a disused Swansea zinc works doubling as a no man's land and the trenches. The story, of a soldier egged on to kill a German corporal, is permeated with wry humour. It was made for Tigon for £20,000, shot in six days in December and based on the anecdote of an old soldier Weeks met in a St Dunstan's Blind Home.[9] Co-written by the director and Derek Banham, the film cleverly builds up interest in the character, aspirations, small triumphs and frustrations of a little German corporal, Willy (Timothy Bateson). Tension is generated by allowing the audience the privileged position of knowing poor Willy is in the firing line of the British military who have spotted him between the sandbags. A couple of old sweats bet a recruit that he is too scared to shoot Willy the next time he passes them. The man *does* shoot, and the Front erupts once more after a brief hiatus. Weeks adds to the piquancy by revealing Willy's fears, tastes and fantasies (of deserting, for instance). Another flashback in colour centres on the English recruit's dreams of cleaning up the Boche single-handed. Weeks intercut between the two dreams and reality with aplomb. This short, given commercial release as the second half of a double bill, marked the start of a productive relationship with cameraman Peter Hurst. It also helped pave the way for Weeks to enter feature-film production.

I, Monster

According to Weeks, Christopher Lee showed **1917** to Amicus producer Milton Subotsky, then trawling promising talent to find a director for an ambitious planned 3D version of the Jekyll and Hyde story. It finally emerged as **I, Monster**.

Weeks, who claims he was the fifth director offered the film, says the 3D process was never a success and was abandoned half-way through the production, co-financed by the National Film Finance Corporation and the Boulting Brothers (who were then partners in British Lion).[10] Neither financier read the script beforehand, according to the director, who claims it was 'very poor, larded with half-baked Freudian ideas'.[11] Weeks found himself mainly confined to Shepperton Studios, working on a tight budget between £166,000 and £174,000, and spent much time working on the set

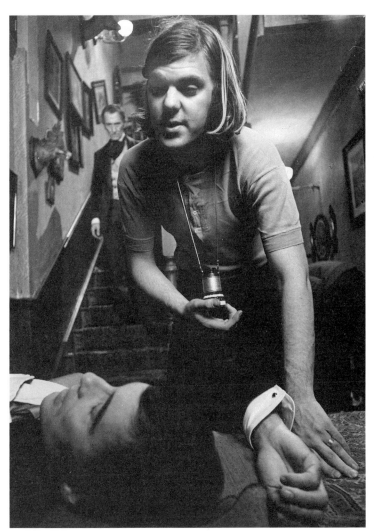

Peter Cushing (rear) and Stephen Weeks on the set of *I, Monster*, the director's first feature.

used for **Oliver!** (1968) and **Anne of a Thousand Days** (1970). He later said that Subotsky had insisted the camera should move all the time from left to right, but art director Tony Curtis thought it would work only if everyone moved from right to left, so the sets were built with the left side of a corridor only.[12] 'There was no way it was going to work if Subotsky's theory had been applied. Halfway through, Subotsky was accusing me of ruining the film.' Weeks insists that the Boulting Brothers decided the process should be abandoned after he was forced to use superfluous corridor tracking shots to demonstrate the process.[13] **I, Monster** looks desperately stilted today but has some deft moments, notably in transition scenes when the victim (Lee) falls prey to habitual drug-taking. Weeks managed to light and pace the exterior scenes well but the opening club scenes jar, with their apparently odd choices of camera angle and garish lighting. Lee himself looked suitably dissipated and wild-eyed, despite the disconcerting beatific smile, and he ensured the effectiveness of Weeks's close-ups of his schizophrenic shooting-up.

Weeks lost interest after the rushes were re-cut each morning before he saw them and the film was finally released, cut by nearly thirty minutes (to 78), and won some guarded praise.[14] The specialist sci-fi film magazine *Cinefantastique* claimed the producers had not bargained for the fact that their young, inexperienced director would be allegedly unable to master the 3D technique and then when scenes were shot incorrectly and filming fell hopelessly behind schedule the idea of releasing the film in three-dimensions was abandoned. **I, Monster** finally appeared in commercial cinemas in a double bill with **Fright** but as Mike Raven, one lead actor, observed, 'They'd done some extraordinary things. They'd re-edited it so much that at one point my actions weren't corresponding with the sound track.'[15]

Ghost Story

After this chastening experience, Weeks did not return to the horror genre until **Ghost Story** – a superior haunted-house thriller, replete with chilling *frissons*. The past cast an insidious spell on the present, as a rural idyll in Britain around 1930 turned sour for an ill-assorted trio of university undergraduates. The film, originally titled 'Asylum', was scripted by the director, Rosemary Sutcliff and Philip Norman. Weeks chose to film in India, with no loss of atmosphere or credibility.[16] In **Ghost**

Story, the house's former associations are tangible and exert a malign and almost fatalistic influence on its visitors, Talbot and Duller, and the host McFayden, an initially supercilious and laconic leader (played by Murray Melvin). The butt of most of the eerie events, which soon disrupt the group's holiday, is Talbot (Larry Dann), the archetypal 'silly ass'. Talbot is ensnared by a medium, an innocuous-looking doll, which propels him back in time to confront the only-too-naturalistic shades of a neurotic family which once lived in this mansion. Talbot suffers nightmares but is powerless to arrest the course of past events. He witnesses scenes in a madhouse where Sophy (Marianne Faithfull) has been incarcerated by a brother (Leigh Lawson) plagued by thoughts of incest.

Weeks's direction is remarkably disciplined, apart from over-flamboyant asylum scenes when he resorts to tilted lens and fish-eye shots, and the pervasive atmosphere of encroaching evil about to overwhelm the unwitting holidaymakers is persuasively conveyed. The director also contrasts well the darkness of the interiors where the past holds sway, with the glare of the exteriors, the dusty country roads and refreshing glades. Weeks also leavens his film with humour, pushing characters towards caricature as they seem more and more like affected dupes. The deliberate jokiness of certain scenes has baffled some critics, but Weeks wanted to make a film which owed something 'not only to M. R. James but also P. G. Wodehouse'.[17] Marianne Faithfull's own drug problems at that time meant she identified readily with the Sophy role. The film also gained credibility from the presence in the more fraught scenes of Barbara Shelley, a staple of so many 1960s horror films, as the asylum matron.

Screened at the Edinburgh Film Festival, **Ghost Story** – with its splendid Gothic feel – won major prizes at sci-fi and horror and fantasy film festivals and was described with memorable hyperbole by *Financial Times* film critic Nigel Andrews as 'like Citizen Kane in colour'. Yet the film never gained a theatrical release after at least three potential distribution deals fell through.[18]

Gawain and the Green Knight: Tolkien or Disney?

Rosemary Sutcliff began her collaboration with Weeks on the dialogue of Gawain and the Green Knight, the first of his forays into Arthurian romance. The director, long interested in medieval chivalry, handled the action setpieces with brio, despite a cheese-paring budget and a compromised script which passed through several re-writes. He remained faithful to much of the poem's narrative line and alliterative lyricism (as translated by Tolkien) to create an admirably fluent, picaresque tale.[19] He also sought to use imagery of a Pre-Raphaelite flavour, evoking the paintings of Burne-Jones and Rossetti, bathing the screen in pastels, blues and russets.

Weeks was fascinated by the medieval story with no known author, 'the archetypal legend, the parable of life. You know you're going to die but you go through the adventure nevertheless, half-hoping you can cheat your fate.'[20] To emphasize Gawain's rites of passage, Weeks created a much younger hero than the knight of the original poem. The screen hero is merely a squire until knighted by Arthur at the film's opening. The story of Gawain has a winning simplicity and its vivid imagery – of chivalric splendour and the passing of the seasons – makes the story a natural for the cinema. Gawain (Murray Head), 'a beardless boy' and callow or 'green' youth, travels over Wales to settle a debt of honour in what seems a certain tragic rendezvous with the importunate Green Knight (Nigel Green) who is endowed with magical powers and intimidating sagacity. The Green Knight has visited Camelot earlier and thrown down the gauntlet to Arthur's jaded men. Only Gawain responds and grudgingly accedes to the Green Knight's demand that he take a free axe-blow at the visitor's head. The knight's head duly tumbles but he is able to replace it. Gawain must now reciprocate, allowing the knight a similarly free blow in a contest to take place a year later in the Green Chapel.

The film becomes a protracted odyssey with Weeks using Wales as the setting for Gawain's journey which holds a succession of pitfalls and tests to prove his manhood. Gawain's travels through the landscape mirror man's ageing as the seasons move from spring to winter. He takes part in jousts against doughty opponents (some may be the Green Knight, to judge from tell-tale odd glimpses of plumage) and faces an even more severe test of valour – an attempt to seduce and disgrace him by the knight Bertilac's wife. Weeks shifts the emphasis of the poem to stress the youth's increasing maturity. He discards the ending in which Gawain returns to Camelot and confesses to failing (in his terms) the test of chivalry by accepting the lady's girdle as a token. But the spirit of the poem, with Gawain emerging to maturity with honour, after facing the Green Knight, is retained, even though Weeks thought the script suffered considerably from United Artists' changes which excised most subtleties.[21] Yet the film benefits from shrewd casting, particularly of Nigel Green's sardonic protagonist, a striking, saturnine figure with straggly black hair and a deep mocking voice. Robert Hardy was similarly authoritative as Bertilac, and two Weeks regulars were memorable foils – Ronald Lacey as the robber baron Fortinbrass and Murray Melvin as his son Senechal, a languid sybarite borne everywhere on a red bier and dressed in crimson.

Weeks employed his locations well, including Caerphilly Castle, Castell Coch (the 'red castle' overlooking Tongwynlais near Cardiff) and Cardiff Castle (doubling for Camelot). They were south Wales locations familiar to Hollywood audiences from director Tay Garnett's disastrous and unintentionally hilarious venture into Arthurian romance with **The Black Knight** (starring Alan Ladd) in 1954. The scenes in the fantasy land of Léonesse where Gawain meets his love Linnet (Ciaron Madden) have welcome *frissons* of the fantastic, especially when Gawain returns to cobwebbed battlements to find everyone frozen in time.

The film is a creditable action-adventure (at the very least), but its troubled history offered Weeks a taste of the frustrations he was to encounter in subsequent projects. He initially made six minutes of the film – of Gawain reaching a church during a colourful mass, stepping inside and finding it empty save for wind-blown leaves. Then Weeks sent it to Carlo Ponti who was sufficiently impressed to back the project and offer the feature, as a bargaining counter in a package deal, to United Artists when UA wanted Ponti's wife Sophia Loren for the musical **Man of La Mancha** (1972).[22] Weeks later disowned **Gawain**, claiming the company had transformed the hero from a 'parfit gentil knight' of valour into a 'real macho killer' capable of tossing men from battlements – at a time when most films were preaching pacifism.[23] He accused UA of re-shaping the screenplay from a 'Tolkienesque piece' to a sub-Disney Prince Valiant adventure and particularly resented the tampering with the tone of the film.[24] He was also upset with UA's decision to abandon music by the Gryphon group and some pilot material by his usual collaborator Ron Geesin in favour of a Ron Goodwin score. The budget, a meagre £200,000–250,000 for a three-month shoot, forced the curtailing of special effects.[25] The ultimate blow fell when Nigel Green committed suicide before the film's release. Yet the finished film, though much longer on spectacle than characterization, has a winning gusto and zest; the jousts – though an all-too-predictable way of replacing spiritual and emotional tests of honour (and nice distinctions of courtesy) by the physical and visual – are handled with no little skill. Opening scenes, as Gawain's youthful ebullience contrasts with bleakly humorous images of an Arthurian court of knights fast running to seed, memorably encompass the film's theme – of age acceding to youth. The denouement is splendidly eerie, with Green's tormentor transformed with the touch of Gawain's blade, into a greybeard, before becoming one with the elements.[26]

Weeks may now regret his decision to remake the film and wish he had heeded his own words of years ago. He told the writer David Pirie, then, that he thought budgets could be lower and directors could gain from restrictions imposed by the industry. Then he offered a hostage to fortune.[27] 'If someone said tomorrow that I could have all the money and all the time I wanted I would still make **Gawain and the Green Knight** on £120,000 and in six weeks.'

Sword of the Valiant

He was given the opportunity to remake the film by Golan and Globus of Cannon but **Sword of the Valiant** had an inflated budget and suffered even more mixed fortunes than its predecessor. The first setback occurred when Weeks was apparently told by UA in 1980 that all out-takes of the original production had been junked (without the 'correct people's permission', according to the director). It was impossible to restore it and Weeks pondered on the possibility of making another medieval legend but could not find another story he wanted to do as much as the Gawain myth: 'None had that archetypal legend, the parable of life . . .'

The second version cost between six and eight million dollars, had a token south Wales première at Cardiff's Monico Cinema and limited screenings around the country. Weeks wound up taking legal action against the moguls, claiming loss of potential profits and demanding full disclosure of Golan–Globus' budgets for the film.[28] Sean Connery was paid one million dollars for his Green Knight role, shot in France only, reputedly the highest fee for just one week's work in cinema history at that time.[29] The film, with American Miles O'Keeffe playing Gawain and French actress Cyrielle Claire as Linnet, was patently geared to an international market, with attendant problems of credibility and continuity. Trevor Howard also enjoyed a one-week Gallic stint, conveniently near his home at Avignon, as a dyspeptic King Arthur in a sprawling, strangely lethargic production which rarely came to life despite an effective early scene of Connery bursting into Camelot in an explosion of green smoke (and dry ice). The film was a curious patchwork, and the distribution delay meant **Sword of the Valiant** – conceived by the audience as just another sword and sorcery film – was at the fag end of the cycle of films so popular in the early eighties. The Green Knight loses his head more spectacularly than in the earlier screen incarnation and the return to Léonesse is singularly more impressive visually. Ironically the changes made by Weeks to create a gutsier adventure story to suit the times and a Gawain more bellicose than earlier, were never radical enough to justify all the extra spending. The director's idea – to create a riddle focusing on Gawain's journey through 'heaven and hell, light and darkness' – never really worked and the film finally bore the hallmarks of a chaotic production repeatedly halted by bad weather and labour disputes.[30] Weeks later acknowledged the weakness of this kind of

Miles O'Keeffe in *Sword of the Valiant*.

packaged film-making. O'Keeffe was Cannon's suggestion: 'That was simply a part of the mechanics of deal-making, to use a young American actor who had some identity as an action star.' He had a voice coach on set but both O'Keeffe and Claire were finally dubbed.[31]

There were elements of the original to satisfy Weeks that he was remaining true to his vision. By shooting in France he was able to convey much more strongly the exotic flavour of Léonesse, but Cannon decreed that for an American audience Claire and Lila Kedrova must shed any trace of foreign accent. The sage was played for laughs with the casting of David Rappaport from **Time Bandits** (1981). The budget did allow more scope for the climactic battle scene with Ronald Lacey and Peter Cushing and their men against Gawain and his aide (Leigh Lawson), and Weeks also provided an extra character, Vosper (Brian Coburn), a kleptomaniac monk who, in the film's most memorable setpiece, is submerged in sand with 400 rats scampering around him. Veteran cameraman Freddie Young, who shot one of Connery's Bond films (**You Only Live Twice**), was brought in to film French sequences after Peter Hurst photographed the Welsh scenes. Young, in Cannon's eyes, was eminently more bankable, and a fortune was spent on special effects with Tim Rose from the Frank Oz team creating a toad into which the villainous Morgan le Fay (Emma Sutton) is transformed.[32]

But the film wound up on video without UK cinema distribution and gained only limited theatrical release in the US. The bigger budget of **Sword of the Valiant** failed to ensure that Cannon's film eclipsed artistically the earlier UA feature and it is significant that Weeks has produced better, more inventive, work when restricted by the schedule and finance.

Scars and *Kipling Country*

The director was on much firmer ground with two TV documentaries **Scars** (HTV) and **Kipling Country** (S4C), which recall the days of British military grandeur.

Scars (1976), inspired by Richard Attenborough's **Oh What a Lovely War**, recalled events partly filtered through the memories of members of the Cardiff PALS who fought at Mametz Wood and of other old soldiers who recalled the slaughter of Ypres and the ordeal of the Somme. The film was shot on and around battlefields at Ypres, Passchendaele, Arras and Verdun. Weeks and editor Dave Camps skilfully threaded poetry, eye-witness accounts, roll calls of the dead and evocative music by Ron Geesin, including a march for the slain, through footage of the battlefields and mile upon mile of gravestones. It was an admirably restrained, mature work which paid sturdy tribute, with dignity and without embellishment, to those ordinary men who answered the call in 1914–18. But Weeks also turned a caustic eye on the present and our trivializing and exploitation of suffering (factories at Verdun make chocolate bombs, for example, which explode – showering people with gifts). Shots of kitsch mementoes were held by Weeks long enough for us to react with distaste or anger and he insisted on music in these passages, emphasizing the cheap and tawdry. The film arouses particularly ambivalent feelings in the glimpses it offers of the Hill 62 Museum at Ypres.

For **Kipling Country** (**Cynefin Kipling**, 1983), Weeks and his team travelled to the North West Frontier and through the Khyber Pass. At Darra, in the Kahat region, they discovered an armaments factory in the hills where tribesmen religiously copied weapons, including the old British .303 rifle – complete with British War Department markings – and other ammunition from the Second World War. The director discovered children working in Dickensian factory conditions, risking lead poisoning as they squatted among machines in alleyways and in tiny factories fronted by arms shops. Weeks also found in Abbotabad a camp 'just like Aldershot in the 1890s', where the PIFFERS, the Punjabi Irregular Frontier Force Expeditionary Regiment, still did British Army-style drill, to the swirl of bagpipes: 'They were an extraordinary group of people, more British than the British Sandhurst types, even though none of them had ever been to England.'[33] This often gently amusing film also featured a Lord Chief Justice of Pakistan who said he 'only made his decisions after closing his eyes for a second and thinking of Britain and what they would do in the same situation'.[34]

The nostalgic appeal of **Kipling Country**, shot in just a fortnight, and its predominant mood of longing and reverie, was established in the opening shots of graveyards which Weeks intercut with images of rugged terrain before we encounter the barracks and the regimental badges of the Raj – the Scottish and the Gordon Highlanders. Jokey music, suggesting the Heath Robinson elements of Home Guard preparations, was overlaid on images of Darra tribesmen. Then a bygone era of pukka Brits was brought vividly to life with Weeks's facetious treatment of the 'Pimms set' – the Bashawar Club, and its tennis players and amateur actors (recalling the world of early Ray and Ivory films). The gap between this incongruously anachronistic world and the harsher realities of past British rule was amusingly underlined in the dissonant music and the prosaic entries in military logs regarding deaths from suicide, cholera, dysentery. A rather arch touch was the rendering of 'Oh Mr Porter' over shots of steam locos in yellow livery. The pervasive influence of Western/British culture was evident and the film concluded with the judge's reminiscences, and shots of soldiers and bugles which indicate that on the North Western Frontier, at least, the values beloved and celebrated by Kipling are imperishable. Both **Scars** and **Kipling Country**, though steeped in nostalgia and a mood of homage, are shot through with cynicism and a certain healthy disdain for those who would re-write history for their own ends.

Weeks was able, with S4C funding, to combine shooting on the documentary with touring locations for his next big cinema feature, **The Bengal Lancers**. Culled from Sutcliff's book *Eagle of the Ninth* it proved fraught with problems. The film had a compelling story-line centred on the disappearance of a regiment in 1877 on the North West Frontier. The central character was the son of the commanding officer who, twenty years later, retraced his father's steps with an American journalist.

Weeks planned a short filming schedule of eight weeks and cast his usual 'repertory company' including Ronald Lacey, John Rhys Davies (also in **Sword of the Valiant**) and Leigh Lawson. But **Bengal Lancers**, long mooted by the director, had shaky foundations as a project, despite a £9,000 grant from the National Film Development Fund. The Rank Organization pulled out after a contretemps in 1978–9, and the film was not developed fully at script stage until 1980 – only to go on ice as the director became embroiled in **Sword of the Valiant**.[35] The project was resuscitated in 1984 when shipping entrepreneur Mahmud Sipra offered to provide finance with loans from the Johnson Matthey Bank (after already bailing out one British feature, **Jigsaw Man**). Weeks and his unit shot 27 minutes of film in two weeks and were astonished when news filtered to India from London that Sipra was dissatisfied with the rushes' quality and had pulled the plug on the production, which was suspended indefinitely. Sipra had also amazed Weeks by insisting on a part in the production and sending telegrams with suggestions about his role to the scriptwriter Lorenzo Semple.[36] The producer had also outraged everyone on the project with well-publicized allegations that the camerawork by Walter Lassally (a past Oscar-winner) was unsatisfactory.[37] Weeks later said only six of 200 camera set-ups showed faults in the shots and only 3 per cent of the film betrayed a slight camera defect which was impossible to detect without seeing rushes available only to Sipra's men and the laboratories in London.[38] The near-collapse of the Johnson Matthey bank then led to House of Commons allegations about Sipra's financial dealings. The Bank of England wound up Sipra's shipping empire and he fled, apparently to Pakistan.[39] Weeks instigated legal proceedings against Technicolor Ltd. Laboratories, London, alleging that reports about the print's standard had been knowingly falsified by an employee. He claimed 'wasted expenditure' for the loss of a share of estimated proceeds from the film's exploitation and for liabilities incurred during the film's abandonment, and in re-scheduling the picture.[40] Sipra later announced he was making his own version (working title 'The Khyber Horse') with a John Goldsmith script, and in August 1985 Weeks insisted that the shipowner had already spent three or four million dollars on this alternative film without producing any footage. It later emerged that a crew sent by Sipra arrived in New Delhi to make his own film, then called **The Khyber Rifles**, which reputedly had a large part for Sipra as a prince – almost a carbon copy of the character 'introduced' by the magnate into Weeks's aborted movie.[41]

The director's original footage survives and in the late 1980s he was still talking of remounting the project from a script co-written with Lorenzo Semple. Since then Weeks has opened his own studio near Penhow Castle, but his film career seems in abeyance. Proceedings against the labs continued until 1993 but hearings proved inconclusive and it was reported that Sipra had gone to ground somewhere abroad. The director's unrealized projects from earlier years include a tantalizing scheme to film a life of the traitor Lord Haw-Haw (William Joyce) with a Christopher Hampton script and Cardiff civic buildings doubling as Nazi HQ in Berlin. 'Black Cat at the Castle Gate' – a projected nine-part series on the Penhow Castle cat through the ages – was never completed, but scenes of a prospective pilot, for a potential American cable sale, were shot, in the eighties.[42] Weeks also made a jokey televised film on the castle itself, playing various historical luminaries while acting as a guide in a pell-mell tour of the grounds and interior.

The director has yet to fulfil his potential but it would be premature to write off a film-maker of undoubted energy and no little flair, capable of work as distinctive as **Ghost Story**, **Scars** and **Kipling Country**.

....
SECTION 4

Television
and a Welsh
Film 'Mini-
boom'

....

FUELLING THE DEBATE

The resources presently at the disposal of the [Welsh Arts Council Film Committee] for production are barely sufficient to sustain a credible programme . . . where the WAC is the sole or main funder . . . The typical budget for these productions, even when inclusive of extra funding to the grant award, is *often smaller than the average design budget for a simple television studio programme.*

(Marc Evans, *In Media Res* – a report to the Welsh Arts Council, 1989. My italics.)

Two outstanding films produced between 1988 and 1991 **On the Black Hill** and **Un Nos Ola Leuad (One Full Moon)**, provided stirring examples of work with a Welsh perspective which transcended national boundaries – and demonstrated how a Welsh screen identity and culture might be forged through the 1990s. They were followed by **Hedd Wyn** (1992) and **Gadael Lenin (Leaving Lenin**, 1993) which demonstrated new-found confidence that indigenous, distinctively Welsh material could have an appeal way beyond UK cinema culture. These last two films – one an elegiac but never eulogistic tribute to a north Wales poet of the First World War, the other using a contemporary south Wales school trip to Russia to examine such issues as international class kinship and the artist's moral responsibility – proved that the best Welsh features could more than hold their own with critics and public, in a British cinema where even London-based directors were forced to rely for budgets on television and co-productions. The films confirmed the status of their directors Paul Turner and Endaf Emlyn at the head of Welsh-language cinema and also gained unprecedented success. **Hedd Wyn** became the first Welsh-language film nominated for Hollywood's Foreign Language Oscar in its 38-year history and gained the Royal Television Society Best Drama award. **Leaving Lenin**, apart from gaining West End commercial cinema screenings, was rated by National Film Theatre audiences the best British film at the 1993 London Film Festival – an honour which had only narrowly eluded **Hedd Wyn** a year earlier.

The last few years of the first century of film in Wales also saw the country release its first animation feature co-production, **The Princess and the Goblin**, and the first animation feature made entirely in Wales, **Under Milk Wood**. These years also confirmed the arrival on the international scene of a trio of independents: Joanna Quinn, Phil Mulloy and Clive Walley – all wooed by festivals around the world.

There is in the mid-nineties, enough evidence, one might think, to justify much more serious funding of film in Wales. Yet any optimism about the future can only be guarded, with the current achievements set against a chastening backdrop. HTV's long-term survival was in the balance when this book went to press. S4C's films were grossly under-funded, with co-production the only means of retaining some of the high standards set. In animation there were increasing signs in 1994 that S4C was in danger of sacrificing independent talent – and even its principal companies – in ploughing all its energies into prestige series (of Shakespeare, opera and Bible films) which relied heavily on talent from outside Wales and even outside Britain. The level of public funding via the Wales Film Council and its main paymaster the British Film Institute (itself in a penurious state) continued to be abysmal. Only BBC Wales offered some (limited) encouragement, with relatively new heads of drama, youth and arts, and documentary, showing they were prepared to launch new talent, even if hamstrung to a large extent by the centralized policies of a monolithic organization. The BBC continued to take its values and priorities from the metropolis, while paying only lip service to many of its regions.

Despite all the doubts and fears it was possible, by 1994, to see that a platform *had* been created on which Welsh film-makers could build, through co-productions, increased budgets from Europe; and with the formation of Screen Wales, the industry had at least some machinery for taking Welsh films into the marketplace and exploiting the nation's resources (locations, crews), internationally.

A new consciousness

Neither **On the Black Hill** (1988) nor **One Full Moon** (1991) gained a commercial cinema release. Each was backed by TV money and depended for wider distribution on television – but the films showed what would be possible from directors confident of their own identity, the worth of Welshness and the importance and merits of source material which could be re-worked cinematically while retaining fidelity to original themes and ideas. Both films, emotionally complex, full of repressed passion, compared favourably with almost any films of their kind produced in the UK in the same period, but they gained immeasurably from the directors' familiarity with the milieu and its people. The timing of the release of both films was fortuitous, given the increasing focus and debate on the notion of a national cinema. There had been reflections on, and celebrations of, past work – in the Welsh film season at the National Film Theatre (1985), the Images of Wales season in Cardiff and in the HTV series **The Dream that Kicks** (both 1986). All these initiatives, in a sense, related to and clarified some of the wider issues of nationhood and national expression explored in the TV series **Wales! Wales?** and **The Dragon Has Two Tongues**. The critical anthology, *Wales: The Imagined Nation* (1986), helped to fuel aspects of the debate as essayists – including active participants in film and TV – fired broadsides in a thorough-going examination of perceptions of the Welsh held by both outsiders and insiders and reflected through the arts. In terms of cinema, none of these initiatives was more important than *In Media Res* (1989), the broad-ranging report on the future of film in Wales commissioned by the Welsh Arts Council and written by Marc Evans, then officer for BAFTA Cymru (the Welsh branch of the British Academy of Film and Television Arts). The report dealt with the malaise of WAC's fallow years from the 1970s and then made a forceful case for developments across the spectrum including the need for distribution and film networks and the formation of a Welsh National Film School.

On the Black Hill and **One Full Moon** tackled issues of identity head-on and embodied many ideas of Welshness, roots, nationhood and longing (*hiraeth*) at the core of the debate. The first film, directed by Cardiff-born, London-based Andrew Grieve from Bruce Chatwin's novel, is a riveting study of the lives together of twin brothers spanning eighty years, and also of rural life and mores in the border country between England and Wales, Brecon and Radnorshire, with Hay-on-Wye doubling as the 'Rhullen' of the book. The film's narrative, unravelling in extended flashback, is a stimulating, dense web of ideas around questions of social class and national dependency and loyalty, individual will and pride, symbiotic relationships and sublimation of ambition and ego. Grieve (b. 1939), who earlier made a TV version of Hitchcock's **Suspicion** (1985), and acted as second unit director on **Young Sherlock Holmes** (1986) for Steven Spielberg's company Amblin, spent much of his early life in west Wales and in Blackwood, Gwent, and returned there over the years. His familiarity with the heartland of the work, the Black Mountains of the title, undoubtedly helped to distil the essence of Chatwin's novel, to create its own powerful visual and psychological *frissons* and convey tensions inherent in the community.[1]

One Full Moon was directed by Endaf Emlyn (b. Pwllheli, 1944), whose emotional identification with, and knowledge of, the Snowdonia of Caradog Prichard's novel enabled him to realize (and release) the many layers of emotion in a deeply personal work.[2] Emlyn pulls us immediately into the tortured world of the protagonist. The film deals with the last days of a man riven with guilt all his adult life after a fatal aberration in youth. He feels guilty not only for the violence which led to a girl's death, but his failure to prevent his unhinged mother from entering a mental institution. He returns to his home village to complete the cycle by seeking absolution through his own death, and the use of woods, hills and barren landscapes in sharp juxtaposition with claustrophobic looming interiors which hem in the protagonist, can scarcely be faulted. The film gains immeasurably from fine editing and the beautifully modulated performance of Dyfan Roberts as the man moving, inexorably, towards atonement and suicide.

These films had as much to say about the human condition as about Welshness, just as **Old Scores** (1991), Alan Clayton's infectious comedy – operating at a much less ambitious level – provided a fine example of a genre Welsh film which did not depend for its appeal on one's knowledge of Wales or love of rugby (the characters' ruling passion). It gained from director Alan Clayton's ability in teasing out national characteristics and idioms, even though the script was prone to glib stereotyping. Tristram Powell's three-part BBC TV version of Kingsley Amis's Booker prize-winning novel **The Old Devils** (1992) also said as much about ageing as about Wales, despite some mordant reflections on the state of a nation caught between eras, heavily influenced by transatlantic values and too prepared to disavow past virtues. Powell, while unable to render Amis's material cinematically in a studio-bound production, or flesh out the ambiguities of the opportunistic central character, was at least true to Amis in debunking the stereotyping and some superficial assumptions about the Welsh.

On the Black Hill

Grieve's film is at every level richer and more satisfying as a screen work and uses imagery of flight as a leitmotif and metaphor for the inner desires of Lewis Jones (Robert Gwilym) who wants to explore further afield in his thirst for new experience but remains on the family farm, The Vision, all his life, out of loyalty and love for his twin Benjamin (Mike Gwilym). The flight imagery is also employed effectively as a bridging device, indicating the passage of time and dividing the brothers' lives into segments. Newspaper stories of air pioneers fire their imaginations when young. Later the 'flight' of a free-wheeling camera conveys the exhilaration of a youth spent running in the hills. A biplane, jet aircraft, then a children's kite, link various episodes. The longer Lewis remains on the Black Hill the more his chances of, and wish for, freedom recede. He is linked almost by osmosis to Benjamin, but confused by the tug of ambition and his attachment to family roots. In the film's most painful scene of suppressed emotion he expresses, haltingly, his feelings to a German traveller, Lotte Zons, who might provide his means of escape, functioning almost as a *deus ex machina*. The moment when he proffers love to this comparative stranger is impelled by the kind of desperate loneliness which earlier drives his female friend and neighbour, Rosie, to take a lover. And when he is rejected with tenderness Grieve, sensibly, tactfully, observes the moment from a respectful distance, as if unwilling to intrude. The bond between the brothers can only be broken by death: Lewis's in a tractor accident. Grieve is less reticent in the film's early scenes, viewing the tantrums of the brothers' father Amos (Bob Peck), a volatile, unyielding man, ever conscious that he has married an Englishwoman (Gemma Jones) of a different social station and increasingly unhinged as economic pressures mount at his farm. Amos equates his

Brothers Robert Gwilym (left) and Mike Gwilym as the twins bonded forever in Andrew Grieve's *On the Black Hill.*

415

wife's desire to save their farm (lost after an auction) as complicity with the English landlords and indicts her for patronizing him. The film tells us much, often through subtle understatement, about ancient feuds and residual antagonism between the English and Welsh.

Gemma Jones, the Dyfed-born actress, conveys, admirably, a wealth of stoicism as the mother of the brothers and of a daughter, Rebecca, who is banished from the home by Amos after becoming pregnant. If Bob Peck's father – a fundamentalist who resents his wife's literary tastes – and his feuding Welsh farmer neighbour, Tom Watkins, are overdrawn, there are compensations in both writing and direction as Grieve elects to use images and compelling silences rather than words to indicate the protagonists' stronger feelings and the legacy of their cramped lives.

SECTION 4

Television
and a Welsh
Film 'Mini-
boom'

The film suggests inherited traits: Benjamin at times reveals his mother's capacity to endure and soak up pain, at others he explodes as his father did, and hints at the same kind of mental anguish. Benjamin cannot bear to be parted from Lewis and there is a painful sequence when they are prised apart in the First World War: he is sent to serve while Lewis is granted immunity as a farm worker (a decision which confirms Amos's hostility and hatred for the gentry who have a hand in such 'illogical' decisions and who renege on promises and break trust). Benjamin also is brutalized in a Hereford training camp. But the brothers remain linked symbiotically. When Benjamin seems certain to perish on the hills in a snowstorm, Lewis can literally feel his discomfort and saves his life in a sequence which is a *tour de force* of strong, concise editing. The void in the brothers' lives, which neither is readily prepared to acknowledge, is filled by the arrival of their long-dead sister's grandson, Kevin, who becomes the apple of their eye and their heir. We can exult in the pair's tearful emotion when they first see him – winsome and smiling as Joseph in a local Nativity play – just as we feel exhilarated when Benjamin, initially intimidated by his eightieth-birthday present from Kevin – a trip in a private aircraft and spell at the controls – begins to loosen up and savour the moment and the view far below of The Vision, proud, mysterious, the repository of their life's hopes.

The Neath-born Gwilym brothers, seven years apart in age, are perfect in the roles. Mike, clenched and taciturn as Benjamin; Robert gangling, sensitive, more mercurial and able to effect Lewis's difficult transition from brash young hopeful to confused middle age, then mellowing dotage. Grieve's fidelity to the novel was unsurprising given his admiration for Chatwin's work and feelings for the area: 'If you read the book and you're not in love with the men by the end, then you can't have any feelings.'[3] The passing of the seasons and the play of light on landscape was captured, memorably, by Thaddeus O'Sullivan's camerawork, and impressive aerial photography back-up. The film, made for only £600,000 with British Film Institute and Channel Four backing, gained a limited cinema release just before its TV première – an increasing trend as television and big screen companies combined to erode old boundaries.[4]

Un Nos Ola Leuad (*One Full Moon*) and *O.M.*

Endaf Emlyn's feature toured Welsh cinemas following its Edinburgh Film Festival screening. It was also shown at the London Film Festival and the BFI distributed it to regional film theatres in 1992. The film's quality raised, briefly, the credibility of its short-lived backers Ffilm Cymru, a body set up by BBC and S4C in 1989 to make a

string of features by 1992. Hampered by funding problems, the organization produced just two before it was absorbed into the newly formed Wales Film Council. The first, **O.M.** (1990), was a disappointing Welsh-language dramatization of the family life of writer and educationist Sir O. M. Edwards, grandfather of S4C's Owen Edwards and father of film-maker Ifan. It certainly went further than many expected in presenting an idol with feet of clay but, paradoxically, never began to convey the man's unique contribution to Welsh education and journalism and his charisma, and even the hints of serious domestic infidelities seemed pussyfooting. The film, based largely on research by Edwards's biographer Hazel Davies, sought to show that Edwards's obsessive drive to improve the nation's knowledge meant sacrifices and suggested that his neglect of his wife and his relationship with another woman led to his spouse's suicide. Bryn Fôn played the part conscientiously and conveyed O.M.'s slightly chilling dignity, but

Dyfan Roberts as the tragic protagonist of Endaf Emlyn's *One Full Moon*.

Emlyn Williams's film somehow diminished him by focusing so single-mindedly on his domestic life. The work's form, despite fine handling of the setpieces, was never arresting enough to sustain interest in O.M.'s emotional entanglements.

The second Ffilm Cymru feature, **One Full Moon**, was in a different class. Emlyn pulled us immediately into the tortured world of a protagonist suffocated by memories. The resolution is at one level ineffably sad, but the ending could also be read as strangely affirmative, with a restless soul at last finding peace of mind. Emlyn melded in the flashbacks with great skill – there seemed scarcely a redundant or random image.

Films of merit: *Heartland* and *Elenya*

Other compelling Welsh films surfaced around the turn of the decade. There are interesting echoes of **On the Black Hill**'s central concerns in Kevin Billington's **Heartland**, (1989), a BBC 1 drama set in Wales which could be seen as a metaphor for Welsh loss of identity.

Anthony Hopkins, renewing his commitment to Wales following years in Hollywood, played Jack, a west Wales dairy farmer driven to desperate measures by an EEC milk quota which threatens to wipe out his livelihood and strip him of his land after he spends heavily on modernization. Jack has bowed grudgingly to family pressure in providing new equipment; he is seen essentially as a man fighting a rearguard action against the forces of change and new types of farming. But other issues in the film are fundamental: the value of continuity, stability and roots, the need to resist

417

standardization and the emphasis on social dangers implicit in technology and production methods which often seem to discard human feelings and worth. Steve Gough's screenplay, drawing material from the local news headlines, asks most of the right questions and exposes shrewdly the moral tensions threatening to split the family. Jack is a combustible disciplinarian, a taxing role which requires Hopkins to mellow gradually as the farmer reconciles himself to change – only to be infuriated by the seeming injustice of his plight and his impotence and inability to affect his fate by legal means. The build-up to the final eruption of anger, with several volatile exchanges between father and sons succeeded by bouts of brooding from Hopkins's farmer, is painstakingly orchestrated and Hopkins's matter-of-fact demeanour makes his final 'unreasonable' act – the kidnapping of two EEC officials – all the more chilling, and futile. **Heartland**, reflects concerns about wider questions of Wales's involvement with Europe rather than merely examining the implications for the nation's farmers. The same preoccupation with the swallowing up of national culture/individuality can also be discerned beneath the surface drama of one of the best Irish films to emerge in recent years, Jim Sheridan's **The Field** (1991).

Steve Gough's directing début feature, **Elenya** (1992), the first joint production of S4C and the British Film Institute, had an unusual genesis. The German state TV ZDF were the first to express interest in Gough's initial treatment from his own short story. The work was eventually backed by a Frankfurt-based company and shot mainly in Luxemburg (doubling for north Wales) to take advantage of that government's generous financial support and guarantees. The film, about an old lady reflecting on her wartime experiences as a girl hiding an injured German parachutist in her local woods, might have been a hotch-potch in other hands. Gough suffered some post-shooting problems which resulted in the editor's resignation, but the director produced – at least in English – a cogent, intense work which takes us into the mind of a girl effectively orphaned, with her father disappearing into the war, and left in the care of a resentful aunt (Sue Jones-Davies) who harbours incestuous feelings towards her brother. Gough conveys, beautifully, the girl's introverted nature and her odd blend of fear and jubilation in looking after someone who needed her love, and in concealing his presence from others. The film is partly about the girl's first experiences of both power and responsibility. Gough – for a film made in two distinct versions (Welsh and English) shot back to back – coaxed a riveting central performance from Pascale Delafouge Jones, a bilingual schoolchild who had never acted in anything beyond school productions and who somehow against the odds managed to bear the emotional burden of the film (just as the young Joanna Griffiths had done with **Morphine and Dolly Mixtures**).

Hedd Wyn

The hero of Paul Turner's feature **Hedd Wyn**, the farmer-poet Ellis Evans (played by Huw Garmon), was killed in almost his first taste of combat in 1917. He became the first to be awarded the Eisteddfod bardic chair after death in war – an event which ensured his immortality in Welsh culture and folklore – and he spoke openly of his failure to understand both the nature of the conflict and his friends' involvement in it. Evans (or Hedd Wyn, his bardic title) was conscripted against his will, but this fine intense work made it clear that he was an ideological rather than a militant pacifist: he did not want to kill but did not oppose the war and wrote, at least at the onset of the action, poetry of a conventional heroic stamp. The film uses the empty chair,

418

covered in a black cloth in honour of the posthumous hero, as a potent symbol of the war's lost youth and talent. The image of the chair at the opening and closing of the film frames Hedd Wyn's story, told via a further stream-of-consciousness flashback as the poet lies dying near Passchendaele.

The film is remarkable for its supple handling of structure, and seamless blending of poetry into the narrative by Evans's biographer Alan Llwyd, a fellow poet. Llwyd and Paul Turner are never afraid to use metaphors, visual and verbal, to provide layers of meaning and to clarify, as far as possible, the vacillating nature of a north Wales proletarian – bemused by the war, antipathetic to the general patriotic fervour – who became a hero almost despite himself. His unresolved relationships with local girls prompted his expressions of romanticism and the humanitarian ethos of his work. Ray Orton's probing, fluent camerawork serves the poetry and the landscape impressively and the final re-created war footage – with the last, fatal rush from the trenches – has a downbeat, deeply affecting lyricism of its own. John Hardy's music is the perfect complement to Llwyd's never intrusive use, in voice-over, of poetry which, ironically, reflects on the nature of heroism – a preoccupation of Hedd Wyn especially in the last months when friends died at the front and before his own decision to enter the war rather than allow his younger brother to take his place. The film, which went through eleven draft scripts, is the perfect example of a writer and director working as one.

Hedd Wyn became one of the body of films (including **Gwenallt** and **Boy Soldier**) offering different perspectives on the feelings of Welshmen fighting the British cause in wartime yet at odds with aspects of the conflict and the priorities of a Westminster government. Both **Elenya** (made in English and Welsh) and **Hedd Wyn** (made in Welsh with subtitles) played the London Film Festival and gained limited cinema release, and it seemed probable that Turner's film would enjoy wider circuit exposure in the immediate aftermath of its Oscar nomination.

Gadael Lenin (*Leaving Lenin*)

Endaf Emlyn's previous films had been rooted in the north Wales communities he knows best but **Gadael Lenin** (**Leaving Lenin**) ventured into new territory. A south Wales secondary school visit to St Petersburg proved an arresting vehicle for the director to explore notions of individual responsibility – domestic, marital and artistic. In the framework of a comedy, there were two distinct strands: the relationships of art teacher Sharon Morgan with her husband and an old flame; and the desire of one disaffected gay student (Steffan Trevor) to embrace new artistic ideas, coupled with his problems in acknowledging his sexuality when meeting a Russian student attracted to him.

Sharon Morgan, and Wyn Bowen Harries reconcile past and present in Endaf Emlyn's *Gadael Lenin* (*Leaving Lenin*).

Emlyn, who co-scripted with Siôn Eirian, had originally planned to make the movie in Paris and the Louvre, but his eventual decision to settle on St Petersburg was inspirational. The iconographic Russian paintings added not merely visual richness to the film but provided the potent metaphors he needed to allow us to grasp the subtext investigating the moral choices of the main protagonists. Emlyn also took advantage of another fortuitous development: the discovery of a firework party on a bridge enabled the director to incorporate celebrations into the film and to suggest a link between the future and past and the gay student's decision to slough off his former life-style. The friction between the two male teachers on the trip, and their growing rapport under duress as they footslog through the countryside after a series of accidents, was the least satisfactory, most hackneyed element of a film of impressive depth and assurance and optimism for the future of a society in flux and confusion.

The concerns of **Hedd Wyn** and most of these films, the fierce pride in tradition, and the social and/or cultural legacy, were issues increasingly dear to film-makers in the early nineties as they considered a future of growing reliance on multinational co-productions and international financing. Would Wales be able to provide – consistently – a body of work which reflected national preoccupations, revealed distinctive traits of the Welsh character and illuminated the Welsh experience to the rest of the world? Or would too much of the future work produced for TV, for instance, be hybrid, with locations and narrative reflecting not so much script inspiration as budget sources?

The actor's dilemma – and Anthony Hopkins

As these issues were debated, fine Welsh actors such as Dafydd Hywel, Sue Roderick, Iola Gregory and Dyfan Roberts continued to work in Wales, often in films and TV or stage dramas which remained largely unseen outside the nation's boundaries. Hywel, in particular, was employed prolifically within Wales, occasionally in powerful networked dramas, such as the BBC's **Out of Love** (dir. Michael Houlday, 1988), where his country worker, suffocated by a possessive father and unable to break with the past and old values to find happiness with his new love (Juliet Stevenson), finally

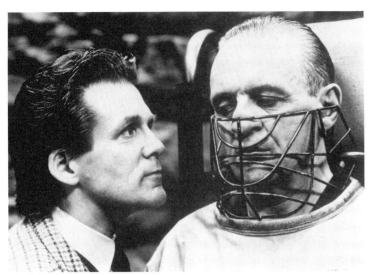

Anthony Hopkins as Hannibal Lecter in *Silence of the Lambs.*

commits suicide. This slow-burning drama, shot through with ironies and suffused with melancholy, was a powerful work of almost unrelieved intensity, with a sure sense of an uncompromising rural landscape.

In the last decade, as UK film production has shrunk, only a handful of Welsh actors have been able to find regular employment in significant roles on the big screen. Towering above all others in reputation and recent box-office clout is, of course, Sir Anthony Hopkins (b. 1937). Hopkins grew in stature from the early eighties on, gaining his profession's ultimate acclaim with the Hollywood Oscar and British BAFTA Best Actor awards for his performance as Hannibal 'the cannibal' Lecter, the psychopath/psychiatrist toying with Jodie Foster's earnest but spunky FBI recruit in Jonathan Demme's **Silence of the Lambs** (1991). Which image of Hopkins will be most remembered in future? The daunting stillness of Lecter in his prison still able to mesmerize interlocutors and warders alike? Or his sly, tortured Captain Bligh jousting verbally and clashing wills with Mel Gibson's Fletcher Christian in the re-make of **The Bounty** (dir. Roger Donaldson, 1984). Will it be his equally impressive single-minded, fretting surgeon, Frederick Treves in David Lynch's **The Elephant Man** (1980), or self-effacing droll Frank Doel, the shop manager rationing his emotions in an austerity-hit London, but befriending Helene Hanff's insatiable American bookworm in **84 Charing Cross Road** (dir. David Jones, 1986)? It is certainly difficult to imagine that two post-Oscar roles will fade much in popular memory and acclaim. The essence of all the actor's screencraft and intuition was distilled into his fatally blinkered butler, regretting lost love, in **The Remains of the Day** (1993), and his C. S. Lewis, freed gloriously from crippling self-absorption by altruistic devotion to the dying Joy Gresham, in Richard Attenborough's cinema version of **Shadowlands** (1994).

Opinions may vary about these performances but Hopkins has an ability to engage an audience given to few screen actors of his generation. His career after **Silence of the Lambs** was only approaching its summit following a period from the mid-seventies to early eighties when he was hampered by poor vehicles and personal problems, and his mannerisms – dry staccato delivery, over-emphatic pauses – came perilously close to affectation. Hopkins has since revealed a consistent ability to communicate despair, broody introspection and a coruscating and self-deprecating humour. Much of the reflective side of his performances seems to stem from his nature and upbringing (in Taibach, Port Talbot) as a youth with a strong sense of isolation. At times his reticence off screen suggests he does not realize just how good he is, and the moodiness may also be a product of his native environment. The actor has spoken, interestingly, of his feelings for the driven, single-minded characters he has played, detached from, if not exactly insulated against the world – the monstrous newspaperman Le Roux, for instance, his character in the stage *Pravda* (1985), and the speed ace Malcolm Campbell in BBC's **Across the Lake** (1988). As a child, Hopkins often felt he was on an 'offshore island looking through powerful binoculars at the world passing by'. Later, acting was 'therapeutic' to a man who claimed to be aware of certain parallels between himself and Burton – not merely with Burton's career as an actor who had moved away from his roots but also with his state of mind, the guilts, the melancholy. Hopkins even tried to find pathos in his playing of Hitler, as an ageing lonely man, bewildered by the turn of events, in a CBS TV movie **The Bunker** (1980). The actor has done much of his best work on stage but, on screen, he has shown an ability to suggest characters who function beyond the lens, even when his role often relies on concealment of emotions and identity.[5] This talent springs from the Welshman's ability to analyse and reflect on his role, allied to extensive reading of source material. He brought much more to the role of Frank Doel than was readily apparent in the script, suggesting a lifetime of denial and self-discipline. Doel became representative, the physical embodiment, of his class – but Hopkins brought out a certain grandeur in his reticence and fundamental decency, qualities he was also able to bring to his time-and-study expert, touched (despite his innate pragmatism) into identifying with the naïve bosses and warm-hearted work-force in the admittedly confused and flawed Australian movie **Spotswood** (1992).

SECTION 4

Television and a Welsh Film 'Mini-boom'

The actor is also capable of extrovert grandstanding moments – as in one prison scene in **Silence of the Lambs**. Director Demme cross-cuts repeatedly, each successive cut tightening on the characters and suggesting that Foster's agent is being tugged, despite herself, into Lecter's malign emotional ambit. In all his roles, Hopkins now commands attention with the smallest screen 'business' but has the confidence not to over-elaborate. He can suggest undercurrents not always obvious from dialogue, and it is his power to suggest the unfathomable evil in Lecter, and tap into others' minds, which makes the performance so frightening.

Hopkins made an early impression as Richard the Lionheart in **The Lion in Winter** (1968), and played Lloyd George, merely a bit part, in Richard Attenborough's **Young Winston** (1972), but for some time his career failed to take off, despite a long Hollywood sojourn. He seemed at the crossroads after critics fell on his performance as the ventriloquist unmanned by his own schizophrenia and dummy in Richard Attenborough's **Magic** (1978), claiming it was marred by mannerisms. This was only partially true. Much of the fault lay in the scripting by William Goldman, from his novel, and some unsubtle direction. Inevitably, unfavourable comparisons were made with the justly celebrated Michael Redgrave's ventriloquist episode in Ealing's **Dead of Night**.

Hopkins returned to prime form as a crisply authoritative but vulnerable Captain Bligh, unmanned by jealousy and undermined by inflexibility in Roger Donaldson's **The Bounty**. He was effective, as a bitter casualty of the sex war, reduced to disgorging his misogynistic bile by proxy in Mike Newell's slightly risible melodrama **The Good Father** (1986). The Welshman was quietly effective as the seafaring mysterious stranger – an IRA man on the run – in **The Dawning** (dir. Robert Knights, 1989), striking up a tentative rapport with the teenage girl (Rebecca Pidgeon) who might have been his daughter in a film almost too self-effacing for its own good. And he displayed an under-used capacity for comedy in a Welsh role (the wild theatre director, Dafydd ap Llewellyn, more of a born thespian than any of his actors) in Michael Winner's lumbering screen version of Alan Ayckbourn's **A Chorus of Disapproval** (1989). Hopkins's performance, based on what he described as his baker father's volatility and capacity for irrational anger, was the film's one redeeming feature. He again expanded his screen range as the hypocritical self-righteous patriarch of the James Ivory–Ismail Merchant treatment of E. M. Forster's **Howards**

End (1991). The character's assumed mask of liberality (or at least aloof tolerance) slips, chillingly, near the finale. Caught off guard when past indiscretions come home to roost, he blusters, then reveals a vulnerability not glimpsed elsewhere. It is a masterly performance. His Van Helsing, the vampire hunter in Francis Coppola's **Dracula**, proved a somewhat eccentric if fascinating reading of the role, with Hopkins presenting him as a wild, introverted man, comically tactless and unaware of the stir caused by his unorthodox views and methods.

Hopkins was to consolidate his new status in the film industry with, to my mind, his two finest performances. As in **Howards End** and **84 Charing Cross Road**, he was to play English traditionalists, with an innate personal reticence, who are *acted upon* and react to events or characters impinging on their lives. In James Ivory's sensitive version of Kazuo Ishiguro's Booker prizewinning novel **The Remains of the Day** Hopkins managed, in a performance of great nuance and economy, to convey the pyrrhic triumphs of Stevens, a butler who kept house almost to perfection but was blind to, or fearful of, events around him as his misguided aristocratic employer (James Fox) consorted with German diplomats and British Fascists to make reparation for the alleged ill-treatment of the Germans after Versailles. The most effective scenes involved his relationship with the housekeeper Miss Kenton (Emma Thompson) and his burgeoning affection which he continued to deny. The playing of the principals in more intimate scenes, with banal dialogue exchanges often running counterpoint to actions and considerable suppressed emotion, was flawless.

There are fascinating parallels between Stevens and C. S. Lewis in **Shadowlands**. Both are happy in a circumscribed, hermetically sealed world; both men have drawn boundaries around themselves and created their own space; both take inordinate pride in their achievements but are frightened of the unknown. Stevens controls his world below stairs; Lewis is happy to be the cynosure of university gatherings, to control his audiences with lectures and symposiums, to act the omnipotent mentor, unthreatened by his students. Richard Attenborough in a succession of succinct, powerful scenes, drew analogies between Lewis's lifestyle and his fantasy stories for children – he is locked into a world seemingly as immutable as his creations, until released by love and at last able to make the kind of emotional commitment he had always avoided. Hopkins seems to shed years with the discovery of this new bond. He suggests, in one or two playful scenes, a euphoria he can barely control, and extends himself unforgettably in the moments of breakdown after the death of his love Joy Gresham (Debra Winger) with cancer. Perhaps no other screen role allows Hopkins opportunities to play to his strengths – suggesting a burning intelligence, reflective qualities, a wry, if cautious and conservative, sense of humour and, above all, a certain bemusement on encountering such unfamiliar feelings of love and loss. The protracted ending is a little maudlin but generally Attenborough avoids ersatz sentiment, and Gresham's forthright qualities in William Nicholson's screenplay, helped the film maintain its delicate balance. It is interesting to conjecture how much Hopkins's ability to play introspective, broody roles owes to a childhood of insecurity in which control of emotion, the role of reflective observer, became second nature.

Jonathan Pryce (b. 1947), the gangling Welsh actor, seemed to have a promising screen career ahead after playing a callous right-wing reporter and dissembler in **The Ploughman's Lunch** (dir. Richard Eyre, 1983), a savage, if ultimately shallow, dissection of 1980s Britain, with an Ian McEwan script. Pryce was splendidly venal, insinuating himself into the confidence of a socialist writer and her daughter, against

the backdrop of a Tory conference. But the film, despite drawing interesting parallels between the prevailing national mentality during the Suez and Falkland wars, suffered from a lack of subtle character shading. Pryce was prominent again in **Brazil** (1985), but played second fiddle to the sets and special effects, as a baffled Ministry of Information factotum in the surrealist world of Terry Gilliam's opulent but ultimately confused film.

Thwarted love: Anthony Hopkins, Emma Thompson in *The Remains of the Day.*

Opportunities in a near-moribund British film industry proved limited and Pryce's excursion in a belated Freddie Francis screen version of a Dylan Thomas script **The Doctor and the Devils** (1986), made for Mel Brooks Brooksfilms, failed to provide him with the impetus his career needed. Francis's feature, inspired by Burke and Hare's bodysnatching exploits, failed at the London box office and wound up quickly on video without gaining a single cinema screening in Wales's capital city. Pryce continues to develop, with leading roles on television and the stage. He was riveting as the husband racked with guilt and on the edge of a breakdown, in the three-part **Thicker Than Water** (1993) directed with some style by Marc Evans using bleak Cardiff dockland landscapes to mirror the inner emptiness and character's wintery disposition. In 1990 the actor achieved surprising success in a singing role – in the Broadway stage version of *Miss Saigon.*

Timothy Dalton (b. Colwyn Bay, 1946), who made his screen début in **The Lion in Winter**, alongside Anthony Hopkins, seemed to have received his big break when he was chosen as the latest 007 in **The Living Daylights** (1987) – after twice previously turning down the role. But his restrained, understated performance had no real authority and seemed at odds with the persistent jokeyness and the emphasis on gung-ho action in a film which was by no means the worst of the Bond cycle, but demonstrated how far the films had lost freshness and direction since the palmy

Saltzman/Broccoli/Connery days. Dalton appeared to greater advantage as a patient kicking over the traces to provide a fellow terminally ill inmate (Anthony Edwards) with one final fling in **Hawks** (1988). The film was blighted by awkward switches of tone, but Dalton at least enjoyed a few good moments, delivering caustic one-liners. He was entertaining as a camp villain in the even more undemanding but likeable **The Rocketeer** (1991). A more substantial body of work has been built up by Karl Johnson (b. Ebbw Vale) who was persuasively intense as the fretful Paul in BBC's **Sons and Lovers** (1981), and in the title role of Derek Jarman's innovative and mercurial **Wittgenstein** (1993).

'Commercial' directors: the exiles

Welsh-born exiled directors have made a bigger impact in the commercial cinema in recent years than the indigenous film-makers. Terry Jones (b. Colwyn Bay, 1942) graduated from acting in the anarchic and inspirational Monty Python team to co-writing and directing their films **Life of Brian** (1979) and **The Meaning of Life** (1983), both replete with relishable *non sequiturs*, iconoclastic and idiosyncratic humour and glorious sight gags, courtesy mainly of animator Terry Gilliam. He also co-directed, with Gilliam, **Monty Python and the Holy Grail** (1974), the most visually distinguished of these films with its emphasis on the physical squalor and decay of the period. Jones's **Personal Services** (1987), about sex madame Cynthia Payne, contrived to be both coarse and anaemic, with neither Jones nor writer David Leland seizing the opportunity to mount a full-scale satire on the social and sexual mores, cant and moral culpability of the establishment.

Richard Marquand (1938–87), Cardiff-born son of former Labour health minister Hilary Marquand – an influential figure in Wales in the post war era – made **Hearts of Fire** (1987) in south Wales, a vehicle for Bob Dylan, but died before its release to poor reviews. The film centred on an ageing pop singer who gave up the business for farming, and a Welsh rock star living in exile (Rupert Everett) who returns to his homeland during a tour. The film failed to gain any south Wales release, and was issued, with almost indecent haste, on video. This was by common consent among the least satisfactory of the director's cinema features. His first, **Legacy** (1978), was an indifferent, creaking country-house horror film. His **Eye of the Needle** (1981), from a novel by former Cardiff journalist Ken Follett, with Donald Sutherland as a German spy, was adapted from a schematic script and suffered from a meandering narrative and some crude violence.

But Marquand's **Return of the Jedi** (1983), the third completed **Star Wars** film, was rich in invention, visceral thrills, and technical skill and energy. It proved probably the best of the George Lucas-inspired cycle though it was difficult to analyse the respective contributions of the director and producer Lucas. Marquand, a former BBC documentary film-maker, always insisted he had a large measure of creative independence.[6] With **Jagged Edge** (1985), he demonstrated his ability to handle narrative and the thriller genre, creating emotional setpieces built around the characters' psychology. The climax, with Marquand and the writer Joe Eszterhas employing a double bluff as Glenn Close's lawyer is falsely reassured of her client/lover's (Jeff Bridges) innocence, has great power, and the film contains any number of visual flourishes embellishing a taut narrative. Marquand had a posthumous co-writing credit (with Eszterhas) on the Jean-Claude Van Damme action film, a modern Western, **Nowhere to Run** (1993).

Chris Menges (b. 1940), who has been based in Brecon recently after living for many years just the other side of the border, carved a reputation as an outstanding photographer on the features of Ken Loach, Stephen Frears and Roland Joffe, notably Loach's **Kes** (1969) and Joffe's **The Mission** (1986). Menges proved to have a masterful eye for composition and ability to convey emotional states of mind through landscapes. His feature film début as director with **A World Apart** (1988) was a revelation. His control of pace and the subjective use of camera was virtually flawless, as he took us into the mind of the daughter of South African anti-apartheid campaigning journalist and martyr, Ruth First ('Diana Roth' in the film), and communicated confusions of loyalty and tensions between a single-minded woman and a daughter who felt neglected despite her better judgement. Menges also drew impeccable performances from Barbara Hershey and, most remarkably, the feature-film débutante Jodhi May, playing the daughter 'Molly' (the film's screenplay writer Shawn Slovo).[7] In 1994 Menges was making his first film in Wales, a thriller – **Second Best** – with the American actor William Hurt.

SECTION 4

Television and a Welsh Film 'Mini-boom'

One more exile must be mentioned. Peter Greenaway, (b. Newport, 1942) emerged with **The Draughtsman's Contract** (1982) from years as an esoteric art-house favourite. The reputation was forged with a few opaque if clever shorts such as **A Walk Through H** (1978), which drew on his passion for draughtsmanship and ornithology and revealed a quirky, mischievous humour and a cineaste's eye. His **The Falls** (1980) was a whimsical fictionalized description of assorted people's role and fate during an imaginary cataclysmic event in Britain. The film centred around Greenaway's youthful haunts on the Llŷn Peninsula and on Bardsey Island in north Wales. The amusing **Act of God** (1981) purported to show the various ways people had been – and could be – struck by lightning, but nothing he had made previously prepared us for **The Draughtsman's Contract**, a playful, handsome and formalist work which also revealed an unsuspected gift for pastiche and mock-Restoration dialogue.[8] It was a feature of great wit and charm, with a splendid Purcellian score from Michael Nyman. **Zed and Two Noughts (ZOO)** (1985), was obscurantist and hermetic but a more vigorous, accessible humour was evident in **Drowning By Numbers** (1988), which featured an astute comic performance, in just the right over-the-top vein, from Joan Plowright.

Greenaway, in his esoteric early works, created a surrogate character, the bird-fancier Tulse Luper, and the hero of **Belly of an Architect** (1987) was, appropriately, a professional (Brian Dennehy) who identified almost equally with his own idol – an architect. The film focused on marital estrangement, paranoia and psychosomatic illness. Greenaway revealed a new maturity as he introduced pathos and yearning into his work, while making resourceful use of Rome as a backdrop to the action and traumatic events. In his most popular box-office film, **The Cook, the Thief, his Wife and her Lover** (1990), Greenaway followed directors Luis Buñuel and Claude Chabrol in using food as a metaphor for greed in an over-rated and over-heated satire on Thatcherism. This two-dimensional work, despite all the intricacies, metaphors and colour motifs, and a splendid bellicose performance from Michael Gambon as a foul-mouthed villain, seemed a thin and arid affair. Greenaway's **Prospero's Books** (1991), using computer technology and graphics and *The Tempest* as a framework for ideas, confirmed him as one of Europe's more important, if controversial, innovators but seemed to lack heart and spontaneity. He seemed unable to translate the mischievous humour of his earlier work to the needs of lighter passages of Shakespearean text.

In 1993 Greenaway released **The Baby of Mâcon**, an elaborate but chillingly angry study of child exploitation and voyeurism, built around a sixteenth-century stage play with theatre and audience action interwoven. The film, formalistic yet combative, fell foul of many critics who were affronted by its clinical depiction of a mass rape and its gleeful savaging of Roman Catholic hypocrisy and self-righteousness. It stimulated thought and debate but was not entirely free of the pomposity it sought to criticize. Greenaway also announced plans to remake **The Falls**, taking advantage of latest hi-definition imagery and state-of-the-art technology. This time it would be set on locations throughout the world, but retain key passages on Llŷn and Bardsey. In 1993 Greenaway was also awarded the second Welsh International Film Fellowship. The first Welsh Arts Council IFF award, of £5,000, had been awarded to the incomparable Czech surrealist animator Jan Svankmajer. WAC and other bodies contributed around £40,000 in providing exhibitions/displays of the films and art modelwork of the director, and hosted a series of his workshops and courses around local colleges. Greenaway celebrated the fellowship by running seminars and art exhibitions in Wales, building on a growing reputation for his imaginative presentation of art gallery collections, notably with displays at the Louvre in Paris and in Venice.

Inside Wales

While talented film-makers such as Karl Francis, Colin Thomas, Richard Watkins, Endaf Emlyn and Paul Turner continued to beaver away in Wales, other directors who had earlier made their names within the country were striving to make an impact in commercial cinema, with mixed results.

Stephen Bayly's **Just Ask for Diamond** (1988), made at Elstree on a two-million-pound budget for 20th Century–Fox, seemed fated from the moment Bayly's company, Red Rooster, agreed to change the original title 'The Falcon's Malteser' – in deference to the wishes of the Lillian Hellman estate which held the rights to Dashiell Hammett's novel *The Maltese Falcon*.[9] Bayly's film, centred on a precocious schoolboy who helped his rather dumb older brother – a gumshoe – to solve a theft by unravelling a clue in a Malteser box, was based on an ingenious novel for younger teenagers by Anthony Horowitz, patently inspired by Hammett's work. Horowitz's book, which bore the punning title, tapped a rich vein of inventive parody of the pulp/private-eye genre, and the plot had only a slender affinity to the three previous **Falcon** film versions.[10] Bayly's feature contained good work by Patricia Hodge as a steely *femme fatale* and Susannah York as a sympathetic, put-upon *chanteuse* – and an outrageously improbable if diverting denouement. The director once more displayed a shrewd eye for locations which had seen better days – notably an old London bath-house – and paced the action sequences well, but the film suffered from certain compromises to reach a youthful market. The broad buffoonery of the hired guns became tiresome and the young lead, Colin Dale, seemed altogether too knowing, even allowing for the ingenuity of the novel's boy hero, and lacked the spontaneity and timing needed to do justice to the Horowitz ripostes. The film obtained only a nominal cinema release, before winding up on video, but it was deemed enterprising enough to spawn a sequel, this time directed by Horowitz.

Chris Monger, who directed the S4C film **Crime Pays** (1986) – based on an errant Pontypridd taxi driver's actual adventures in Ireland – disappeared to America in the late 1980s, toting scripts around until he struck lucky when Shirley MacLaine expressed interest in one project. **Waiting for the Light** was made in Seattle, Washington State, in 1989. MacLaine played an idiosyncratic aunt who delighted young relatives living in a diner by terrifying a mean-spirited neighbour with displays of legerdemain and chicanery, which also convinced the area she had magical powers. Monger cross-cut mischievously and amusingly between news footage of the Cuban missile crisis and the hysteria whipped up by MacLaine's high jinks. The film, which traded on the actress's avowed interest in spiritualism, also featured Teri Garr as the youngsters' mother, which helped to obtain distribution leverage for the film. It received mixed reviews in the States and, despite acclaim from British critics, was badly handled in the UK by distributors Entertainment, receiving only nominal screenings in one or two towns. Monger remained interested in returning to Britain to make indigenous productions. He submitted a script to Ffilm Cymru, set up with a £6 million budget to make features to be co-financed through deals with companies in Europe or further afield. The film never materialized. But late in 1991 he began production for Rank on another cinema feature, the comedy **Just Like a Woman**, shot in London and Pinewood, starring Julie Walters as a middle-aged divorcee landlady falling for a transvestite lodger (Adrian Pasdar). The film, with guaranteed UK release and a strong cast, offered Monger an opportunity to make some impact in the commercial cinema, but it opened in Britain to lukewarm reviews, despite Monger's sensitivity in handling the subject and perhaps Walters's finest screen performance – as a companionable, compassionate woman adaptable enough to cope with a bizarre situation and give her new lover, a closet cross-dresser, the strength to 'come out' both socially and in the workplace. The mix of comedy and social comment proved slightly unpalatable and the film suffered from a fantasy ending, imposed on Monger by writer/producer Nick Evans, which negated the work's political thrust. Monger was again working in south Wales in 1994 – on a cinema comedy (from his own script), **The Englishman Who Went Up a Hill and Came Down a Mountain**, based on a legend in his home village of Taffs Well but shot in north Wales.[11]

SECTION 4

Television and a Welsh Film 'Mini-boom'

The state of play

For those film-makers and actors working almost exclusively in Wales, two major demands were high on the agenda at the beginning of the nineties.

There was mounting pressure for a Welsh Fifth Channel, catering for English-speaking directors anxious to find more outlets for films (rather than downmarket series) about modern life in urban south Wales. This was still a strangely neglected area on S4C, for example, despite the emphasis on more contemporary films by such S4C directors as Alun Ffred Jones and Gareth Wynn Jones, who both tended to set their dramas in north Wales. And independents were increasingly concerned about the need for a network for minority and art-house films following the spread of arts centres and films and video workshops. The frustrations of many film-makers had been expressed forcefully in the 1980s by Karl Francis, who used seminars, both at the Celtic Film Festival and the National Film Theatre, to stress the need for a showcase for directors who represented the huge Valleys and city population which did not speak Welsh. As early as 1985 he called for the formation of a Welsh Film Foundation to encourage production and distribution in Wales.[12] Francis had long inveighed against the alleged élitism of the language's proponents, and he made headlines in walking out of an S4C programme discussing the media when he found undue emphasis placed on discussions in Welsh. At a writer's circle meeting in Tenby he complained once more of the increasing divergence of the Welsh-language establishment's priorities and viewpoints from the needs of English-language film-makers and those seeking to home in on ordinary contemporary situations – and he claimed a series of 'exclusive clubs' had been created in south Wales broadcasting. He criticized, as insular, and indicative of the establishment's priorities, Ffilm Cymru's decision to launch its production activities with **O.M.**, a feature dedicated to a bastion of that establishment.[13] He also confirmed that his honeymoon period making films for S4C was over, claiming he had not worked for the channel in two years and implying that projects had been turned down during that period.

The problems of independents gaining audiences for their films – in cinemas and on television – were also articulated at workshop sessions in Celtic Festivals, notably by Red Flannel and former Chapter film-maker Frances Bowyer, and were again highlighted by Marc Evans in his 1989 WAC report. It called for more funds for independents and greater investment by WAC and the British film industry, but was issued against a depressing background.

There were some encouraging signs at the turn of the decade in the Valleys, even though major companies continued to fight shy of development in these largely de-industrialized areas. Film-makers and enthusiasts, working closely with local councils and arts organizations, formed parallel networks of Valleys cinemas, re-opening screens long dormant in former commercial venues and in workmen's halls. But cinema provision remained geographically uneven. The closure of the Castle Cinema, Caerphilly, in 1989, for example, run by the Miners' Welfare Trust up to the seventies and later by the comedian and actor Stan Stennett, had meant there was no permanent cinema serving a radius of 40 to 50 miles. Most south Wales valleys were without a cinema through the 1980s. Screen venues in many valleys, towns and villages had long ceased to be a valuable focus of community enjoyment and knowledge as the nineties approached, yet audiences for films were rising in UK cities – an anomalous situation.[14] There was also a frightening disparity between audience response and investment in film production as British big screen products dried up and studios were left empty. The major conglomerates were concentrating their attentions on the cities with both Rank and AMC (American Multi Cinemas) announcing major multi-screen projects. AMC opened a 10-screener at Swansea in 1989 (even though their planned similar multi-screens in Cardiff and Newport were deferred) and Rank opened the 5-screen Capitol-Odeon in Cardiff in August 1991, on the site of the former Capitol.

The Welsh Arts Council, under a new films and TV officer, Mike Sweet, played a central role in a Valleys initiative in reviving cinemas in Wales in the early nineties. Cash was injected by the Welsh Office and local authorities to provide cinemas in obvious population centres, reflecting the increased audience demands in the cities. WAC also financed the appointment of a professional peripatetic officer, David Gillam, to help councils in programming and marketing. The two Valleys schemes (Valleys Pictures and Valleys Cinemas) aimed to complement each other.[15] The Municipal cinema at Pontypridd was one of the first to open as these Valleys schemes began. Both projects hoped to provide a flourishing network for Welsh films in future and even seminars and displays at the various centres. The Welsh Arts Council – again responding, in effect, to the ideas in Marc Evans's wide-ranging report – announced in 1991 their intention to launch touring programmes of film, and also scholarships and bursaries to Welsh film-makers in a drive to make Wales aware of a developing screen culture.[16] Special production awards were given to encourage new indigenous film-makers to make shorts, and the TV and film industry joined forces to finance a £20,000 film – chosen in competition – about art. The award funded a feature paying tribute to the work of north Wales animator Clive Walley.

By 1993 WAC, Ffilm Cymru and S4C had joined forces to create a Wales Film Council, to provide the kind of umbrella organization many felt was badly needed in Wales to co-ordinate and unify screen interests. Its brief was to stimulate film culture, education, training and production. These initiatives and cash injections were welcome but meagre – and other initiatives were clearly needed to realize fully the potential of writers, and directors, within Wales. Ffilm Cymru, under seconded BBC Wales drama head John Hefin, was perceived to have an important role when launched and kindled hopes of a permanent Welsh film industry aiming to make features for the big screen, later to be seen on television. The organization sought co-funding, usually 50 per cent, from Australia and Europe on individual projects designed to make inroads into a common European market after 1992. The provisional roster of films announced showed no great ambition (they included yet more biopics of Dylan Thomas and Richard Burton), but these projects were dropped as snags developed with Australian finance. The revised programme touted at Cannes in 1990 looked more promising. Productions in the pipeline – following the first two films **O.M.** and **One Full Moon** – included **Safe House** (a thriller about rival gun-men, to be directed by the **Johnny Be Good** film-maker Marc Evans from a script by Steve Gough) and **Pestilence** from the prizewinning Welsh novel *Y Pla* (The Plague) by William Roberts. Anthony Hopkins was also reported to be considering scripts for his first project behind the camera.[17] None of these films or projects bore fruit. Ffilm Cymru was integrated into the Wales Film Council and a WFC policy document in 1994 announced production grants of £65,000 with the maximum individual grants of £15,000 – scarcely encouraging, even with small bursaries also on offer.

From the late 1980s BBC (and S4C) individually continued to plough cash and energy into international co-productions. These co-productions were of varying worth and benefit. BBC Wales perhaps gained some reflected glory from providing crews and promotional and production help for three much-publicized eighties features originating in London: the BAFTA-prizewinning **Shadowlands** (1986), with Joss Ackland and Claire Bloom as C. S. Lewis and Joy Gresham; **New World** (1986), the story of the Pilgrim Fathers and the battle for power within the Brethren community, and **The Vision** (1987), a rather improbable and overwrought study of a Fascist group's take-over of a satellite TV station (starring Dirk Bogarde).[18] But all these films were essentially London productions with the same creative team of director David Stone, writer William Nicholson and producer David M. Thompson. One absorbing BBC 2 Wales co-production with Canada was **Going Home** (1987), a fraught study of a 1919 rebellion by frustrated Canadian troops retained through bureaucracy for months after the First World War at the Kinmel Camp near Rhyl. The film, featuring a love affair between William Campbell's Corporal and Sioned Mair as a local schoolteacher, carried strong echoes of **The Monocled Mutineer**.

There was more genuine creative co-operation in a 1987 venture, acknowledging the tradition of film-making in Wales. Ken Howard of London-based independents Landseer Films directed **A Penny For Your Dreams** (**I Fro Breuddwydion**), a dramatized tribute to pioneer William Haggar written by Gwenlyn Parry and the

430

Dafydd Hywel as William Haggar in *A Penny For Your Dreams*.

director and produced by John Hefin for BBC Wales. Howard and talented editor Chris Lawrence found a variety of devices to convey the magic of the new medium in Haggar's day and its effects on the travelling showman and his children. Though attempts to burrow into the byways of Haggar's career, with a crude poaching sequence, for instance, were unsuccessful, the struggles of the film-maker made for riveting viewing and Haggar's loving relationship with wife Sarah was drawn with some sensitivity. Sue Roderick as Sarah delivered a remarkable performance, transforming herself, even within scenes, from harassed, almost haggard helpmate and mother to voluptuous silent-screen heroine.[19]

By 1991, BBC Wales, under drama head Ruth Caleb, was concentrating on the work of comparatively unknown Welsh writers in series like Wales Playhouse, though some of these first films were adapted from other media such as novels and short stories. Caleb, encouraged by an increase of BBC Wales drama hours and by a new Welsh English programmes head Michael Chaplin (himself a playwright), announced a more progressive new Playhouse series (1992/3) with what seemed a perceptive blend of indigenous and outside talent. Big names were brought in to star in work by the most promising Welsh directors (Theresa Russell and Jonathan Pryce, for example, in **Thicker Than Water**, 1993). Evans had proved his BBC credentials with the three-part series **Friday On My Mind** (1992) which dealt with great honesty and sensitivity with a love affair between a war widow (Maggie O'Neill) and the air force pilot sent to sympathize with her and ease her bereavement. The film, shot by a new talent, Ashley Rowe, was spread a little too thinly and the final episode was sluggish, but the movie examined raw emotions unflinchingly and there were fine performances all round. It was a particularly strong achievement as Evans had been drafted in at only two weeks' notice, to take over an ailing project after the RAF's refusal to co-operate, and told he would have to rely largely on found 'library' footage for the flying sequences. He decided to opt for a psychological study of the widow and her battle to learn the truth from a macho bureaucracy. Evans, interestingly, used as his inspiration Bertrand Tavernier's superbly evocative feature film **Life and Nothing But** (1991), which portrayed a woman in a similar situation after the First World War.

The Wales Playhouse series also used new directors like the promising former Chapter Arts Centre film-maker Karen Ingham (b. Nelson, Lancs., 1959) who first emerged as a talented independent in the Midlands with **Binding Love** (1986), a fascinating fusion of the Cinderella fairytale with impressionistic and striking images of female subjugation, notably foot-binding rituals in China. The film, cryptic and quizzical, was edited with great style and assurance and was influenced by the novels of Angela Carter which explore fairytale and folklore from a feminist perspective. Ingham's **Salvation Guaranteed** (1992), a foray into the world of hucksters and Bible-thumpers, shot partly in Texas, surfaced as part of the BFI New Directors' Programme. Her Playhouse work **Crystal Blues** (1993) was shot from her own script, originally submitted as a feature to the BFI. Centred on a clash of wills between a mother, opposed to the occult and mysticism, and her teenage daughter, it dealt compassionately with the repression of the independent spirit in women over three generations.

Caleb also achieved an audience success when Karl Francis's networked serial **Civvies** (1992), about former Falkland and Ireland paratroopers lured into crime on Civvy Street, proved a *cause célèbre*. Its violence, conveyed in scenes of powerful visceral excitement, offended some. War veterans, in particular, commented on its presentation of the paratroopers, though Francis and scriptwriter Lynda La Plante expressed in interviews their concern with the British government's capacity for using up manpower, then throwing young men on the scrapheap. La Plante also devised **Lifeboat**, a follow-up BBC Wales networked series shot around St David's, Pembrokeshire, with Francis and his business partner Ruth Kenley-Letts. The drama, despite strong soap elements, was lively and intermittently involving, and was a valuable mainstream showcase for Welsh actors and its directors (such as Dewi Humphreys, brother of Siôn, who made four episodes, and Emlyn Williams). BBC co-productions of note in recent years have also included Les Blair's comedy **Filipina Dreamgirls** (1991), made with a Philippines company and scripted by Cardiff's Andrew Davies. It took an affectionate view of a motley group of Welsh bachelors seeking romance on a package trip and gained much from acute observation of distinct types such as Ray Gravell's deferential Valleys 'mama's boy' and David Thewlis's swaggering macho ignoramus. The BBC also backed Karl Francis's feature **Rebecca's Daughters**. In theory, this kind of venture, with German producers helping to ensure European markets, seemed mutually beneficial. There was a strong Welsh element in the cast and the emphasis on lively indigenous material was relatively undiluted by international commercial considerations.[20] In fact the film, given a limited cinema release, was a misjudged farcical comedy, which squandered its opportunities for sharp political satire.

Another pointer to future trends was provided when S4C combined with Yorkshire Television on a murder-thriller in both languages – set in Aberystwyth. The 1991 drama, titled **A Mind To Kill** in English, **Noson yr Heliwr** in Welsh, and directed by Peter Edwards, was not particularly original. It centred on serial killings and the police's use of an expert to help track the culprit, *à la* Michael Mann's thriller **Manhunter** (1990) and **Silence of the Lambs**, but it made good use of its locations and university milieu. Philip Madoc gave a convincingly world-weary performance as a chief-inspector and Hywel Bennett was the glib professor and media darling with a strange double-life. The drama led to an S4C series – made with US backing and centred on the Madoc character Noel Bain – which marked the screen-directing début of stage dramatist Edward Thomas. Alan Clayton, HTV drama head, thought these domestic inter-channel links were more likely to bear fruit in future than the broader-based international co-productions, which he thought were only necessary, or valid, with larger-budget projects. Clayton, and the majority of Welsh directors, were wary of creating hybrid, amorphous productions which lacked all local flavour and appeal. Certainly **Old Scores**, his ambitious comedy co-produced with New Zealand, lost nothing. The Welsh characters played by such stalwarts as Glyn Houston, Windsor Davies and Bob Pugh, were all strongly drawn and the humour depended on an appreciation of south Wales vernacular and quintessentially Welsh passions and priorities.

Away from film production there were other encouraging developments. Wales formed its own branch of the British Academy of Film and Television Arts in 1989 and BAFTA Cymru hosted the Academy's British craft awards early in 1991, staging its own Welsh film and TV awards ceremony the same year. The prizes were much-needed incentives in acknowledging the creative contribution of Welsh talent – and instilling pride in indigenous achievement. Karl Francis's drama **Morphine and Dolly Mixtures** won eleven nominations and five awards, including best director, but there was recognition also for such talents as Alan Clayton (**We Are Seven**) and Joanna Quinn (for the outstanding animation film **Body Beautiful**). The 1992 Welsh 'Oscars' were more competitive and stimulating, with five awards (and a record fourteen nominations) going to **One Full Moon**, and another five to Marc Evans's **Friday On My Mind**. It was good to see much independent talent of the early 1980s come to fruition – and equally encouraging that Mali Evans, director of **Taxi** in her Chapter workshop days, should win the Best Film Editing award for **Noson yr Heliwr**. **Hedd Wynn** dominated the 1993 BAFTA Cymru event, taking six awards.

The Aberystwyth Film Festival, launched in a small way in 1989, also gained kudos from mounting a string of British premieres the following year and for the first time the event was billed, rather over-ambitiously, as the Welsh International Film Festival in 1991. It premièred **A Mind to Kill** and **Sigaret** the new S4C version of the Saunders Lewis play (dir. Gareth Wynn Jones). The event continued to expand, screening eighty films and videos the following year and staging archive panels and premières of new WAC-funded shorts in a special showcase. By 1994 it seemed likely to remain the premier festival for years to come, following the fund-raising successes of organizer Berwyn Rowlands. The absence of a major annual festival in the capital still seemed a poor reflection on Wales's film and TV industry when compared to the prestige events mounted by Leeds, Cambridge, Southampton and Birmingham in recent years. Champions of the idea pointed to the increasing number of city-centre screens, the burgeoning of independent production in Wales (mirrored in the growth in membership of TAC – the Welsh independent producers' association) and above all the increase in emphasis on Cardiff as a media centre – with one of the strongest TV industries in Europe. The lack of any capital-city shop window for Welsh talent had been underlined by the failure of British Film Year organizers in 1986 to stage events in the city after a breakdown of communications with Cardiff City Council. Chapter Arts Centre had demonstrated what might be done back in 1982 when film-makers there hosted one of the biggest international festivals of work by women, with more than 100 films and videos.

Animation city

The void in Cardiff was partly filled when the city, hosts for the British animation awards for two of the previous three years, was finally chosen to stage the (British) International Animation Festival in 1992, screening around 450 films in a week. Only Cambridge and Bristol had previously hosted the festival, widely regarded by *aficionados* as second in Europe only to Annecy in France, and the presence of Jan Svankmajer and ex-Warner Bros. animator Chuck Jones added kudos to the event, with Jones receiving a Lifetime Achievement award. The choice of Cardiff was largely inspired by the pioneering work in promoting animation of S4C executive Chris Grace and the outstanding achievements of animators in the city.

In 1991 Robin Lyons's Siriol Productions completed the first feature-length animation film ever made in Wales – a version of **Under Milk Wood**, using the original 1954 radio sound-track with Richard Burton. Siriol also unveiled a co-production with Hungary, **The Princess and the Goblin** (from a colourful nineteenth-century fairytale by George MacDonald) noted for its clarity of animation and story-line and the sharpness of its characterization. Lyons's former partner Dave

Storyboard from Siriol
Productions' *The Princess
and the Goblin.*

Edwards, perhaps the most talented mainstream animator to work in Wales, was engaged on a series of American TV pilots and running his own studio in Cardiff after turning down a Disney offer to launch their British studio. He was also supervising director on a series of Russian and Welsh animation film versions of Shakespeare plays – one of the bolder, if more problematic, ventures in British animation in the last decade – plus a series of operas with the Welsh National Opera Company.

English, Welsh and Russian companies were all involved in the operas, but the only Welsh company to make one of these **Operavox** productions was Cartŵn Cymru (Cartoon Wales) which produced a version of Puccini's **Turandot** after switching operations from Llantrisant to Cardiff. The Edwards studio, due to make Bizet's **Carmen**, was replaced by Pizazz from London in fairly acrimonious circumstances. There was a groundswell of concern that Welsh productions were being by-passed as Grace, striving to lay down a long-term infrastructure for animation in Wales, fought to gain S4C a niche in the marketplace with his versions of classics which he hoped would boost earnings and raise the channel's profile.[21] The six Shakespeare programmes made in Moscow studios and released in Britain (with separate Welsh and English sound-tracks) were made with a wide variety of techniques (**Hamlet**, for instance, by a rare painting-on-glass process). The puppet work tended to be the most impressive in **The Tempest** and in the comic interludes of **Twelfth Night**. The series was designed to familiarize many more children, in particular, with Shakespeare but enthusiasm after buoyant sales figures was tempered by the suspicion that most versions (of necessity, given the scope and format) were hopelessly schematic and devoid of internal logic, natural dramatic development, and subtlety of characterization, and failed to find a fresh way to illuminate the bard's work or do justice to the language. Dave Edwards's company also made a lively version of **The Old Man of Lochnagar** (1993), a 'green' pro-environment short culled from a story by Prince Charles and featuring the Prince of Wales in live-action sequences. Animation director Chris Fenna exploited the humorous possibilities of a delightfully blinkered central character and made pithy points with considerable visual ingenuity.

HTV had achieved little for film in the nineties but a welcome initiative was the formation of HTV's junior drama workshop nurturing new acting talent. Budding Welsh actors appeared on screen in the fairytale **The Snow Spider** (1988) and its sequels **Emlyn's Moon** (1990) and **The Chestnut Soldier** (1991), all directed by Pennant Roberts and starring Siân Phillips. But increasingly the way forward seemed to depend on creative co-productions, private sponsorship and the willingness of the British Film Institute and the Wales Film Council, to pump more money into production at a difficult time of financial cutbacks and redundancies. The TV companies also needed to broaden their horizons in soliciting work from imaginative independents. Individual film-makers and independent companies themselves needed to be less insular, more eclectic in absorbing influences and in learning from the best of each country's products, and gearing their work to audiences (however specialized). Government legislation which insisted on a minimum of 25 per cent of TV

programming from independents was a step forward.

The future

More opportunities are about to open with cable and satellite channels providing new markets. But the need for a channel in Wales creating more air time for English-language films and dramas seems imperative with the HTV Wales allocation of drama hours and opportunities unlikely to change drastically in the wake of their successful franchise application. HTV's serious cash problems, which forced staffing cuts in 1992, bode ill for the future. The TV and film industry and many of its more insular film-makers also need to acknowledge, appreciate and familiarize themselves with the best work of the past before moving confidently into the future. The Scottish Film Production Board set an example in the early 1980s producing an embryo industry around a few talents (Bill Forsyth and Charlie Gormley, for example) and allocating six-figure budgets to specific productions. These initiatives seemed to stem from a greater awareness of the need to correct past mistakes with vigorous new productions. The publication of Colin McArthur's book *Scotch Reels* (1985) and events with the same theme at the Edinburgh and Celtic Festivals had all challenged and focused attention on Scottish film and its stereotypes.[22]

There are certain signs that the TV companies in Wales are also looking not only into the future but acknowledging the Welsh film legacy, with HTV mounting 1991 retrospectives of work by news journalist and producer John Morgan, Jack Howells and Karl Francis.[23] Another crucial development came in 1992 when WAC also pumped £50,000 into creating the Wales Film Archive in Aberystwyth following the successful completion of a three-year pilot scheme – it was hoped that TV money would bring total investment in the archive to around £550,000 within four years. The archive's first full-time officers, Iola Baines and Gwenan Owen, have already made an impact – taking advantage of European funding to restore the films of thirties director Sir Ifan ab Owen Edwards for screening at a Celtic Festival première in Lorient, Brittany in 1993; and, in a venture with Germany, working to restore unique footage of Lloyd George's now infamous 1936 meeting with Hitler. This film, shot by Lloyd George's personal secretary A. J. Sylvester, an apologist for the former PM's gullibility in praising some of the Führer's accomplishments, had languished in the National Library of Wales for years. As BAFTA Cymru's Marc Evans observed in his report, 'archive material is . . . a powerful cultural tool enabling different generations and nations to discover more about each other in ways that were never possible before.' Scotland had once more provided an example of what might be done, launching its own archive in Glasgow a decade earlier under Janet McBain and a job creation scheme. Welsh-based film and TV professionals are beginning to absorb the lesson that an industry without a repository for its past wealth has precious little respect for its own culture. Like the Scots, the Welsh must be prepared to acknowledge former and present errors, have confidence in the value of aspects of the native life and culture, produce much more work rooted in or relevant to the present, and much more original work conceived for the screen. This work should ideally reflect the traumatic changes in, and hopes, for Wales.

Overseas markets must be cultivated but not at the expense of national identity – as this book has attempted to show, that has been surrendered too often to outsiders in the past. Wales has never been short of dramatic material to furnish ideas. What is needed now is the feeling from more quarters of the industry that Wales's problems, transformations and preoccupations can now rivet the attention of Europe – and beyond.

SECTION 4

Television
and a Welsh
Film 'Mini-
boom'

APPENDICES

FILM MILESTONES

Film Milestones

1894	Edison's 'peepshow' Kinetoscope demonstrated at Cardiff's Philharmonic Hall.
1895	(28 Dec.) First commercial (projected) cinema screening by the Lumière brothers in Paris.
1896 – April	Barnet-based Birt Acres shows his own short films on his Kineopticon machine to Cardiff Photographic Society.
1896 – May	First public projected exhibition of films at a commercial venue in Wales. Popular magician Felicien Trewey screens Lumière films on the Cinématographe, at Oswald Stoll's Cardiff Empire. Acres screens his movies at Cardiff's Fine Art, Industrial and Maritime Exhibition at Cathays Park.
1896-June	Acres adds to his films (which include the 1895 Derby), shooting in Cardiff the first moving pictures of the Prince of Wales, later King Edward VII, plus other royal family members including Princesses Alexandra and Maud.
1896-July	Acres stages first Royal 'Command' Performance, at London's Marlborough House after request from Prince of Wales to see the Cardiff film. Acres's 'Royal' film later in year a popular success in London music-halls.
1896 – Oct.	Robert William Paul – Acres's former business partner and the 'daddy of British cinema' – visits Cardiff to show 12 shorts on his Theatregraph (or Animatograph) at Stoll's Cardiff Empire, including two scenes in the city's Queen Street.
1897 – July	First 70 mm. films seen in Wales – at the Cardiff Empire, on the American Biograph, a camera-projector system credited to former Edison employee W. K. L. Dickson and Herman Casler.
1897 – Dec.	Huge interest created by screening of World Heavyweight boxing title fight between Gentleman Jim Corbett and Bob Fitzimmons: '165,000 photographs, two miles of film', shown on the Veriscope at Theatre Royal, Cardiff.
	Edison's latest cinema invention, his projection machine the Projectoscope, features in show at Theatre Royal, Cardiff.
	Rhyl printer and businessman Arthur Cheetham builds his first projector-camera and shows films at the Town Hall, Rhyl.
1898 – Jan.	Cheetham shoots the first known short by a Welsh-based director – of children playing on Rhyl Sands. In the next few months he travels all around Wales making 'actuality' shorts and showing them at various venues, including Rhyl Town Hall.
c.1898	William Haggar, Wales-based travelling actor and showman, screens films at Aberavon on his Bioscope.
1898	Cheetham reported working on his own camera, to take 1,000 ft. of film at a time. **Films Irish Mail Boat at Holyhead,** and other shorts.
1899	Haggar's first regular travelling cinema show, the Royal Bioscope, attends Neath Fair.
1901	At Briton Ferry, Haggar shows 'views' taken with his own camera.
	John Codman, son of a Llandudno Punch and Judy man, has a 'living picture' machine and in next few years makes a string of short films including a (probably re-created) version of the passion play at Oberammergau.
1901/2–8	Haggar makes more than 30 films, many released by Gaumont in Britain and Europe.

One, **The Salmon Poachers** (1905), sells a record number of prints. Another, **A Desperate Poaching Affray** (1903) is one of the first recognized 'chase' films and proves influential in America.

1902	Haggar makes his first real short – **Train Arriving at Burry Port Station** – according to unpublished biographies by children Walter and Lillian.
1903	Arthur Cheetham shoots (surviving) footage of Buffalo Bill on visit to Rhyl.
1905	Haggar makes **Life of Charles Peace**, his best-known surviving film, centred on a real-life murder and execution.
1910–14	The boom in opening permanent cinema halls in Wales.
1911	American-born Charles Urban films in colour (Kinemacolor) the investiture of the Prince of Wales at Caernarfon. Film of Llanelli railway 'riots' shown throughout Wales. Screened at cinema of James Haggar (William's son) in Llanelli.
1913	Forty-minute film of Welsh folk legend of **The Maid of Cefn Ydfa** made by William Haggar jun. and his Pontardulais company (partially restored by BFI, 1984). British and later Hollywood and French silent star Ivy Close (mother of director Ronald Neame) stars in short film **Mifanwy**, a tragedy set in Wales. The Llanelli Cinema among first to screen film of the **Senghenydd Mining Disaster** that year – and held relief performance in October for relatives of the family. Hollywood discovers Wales. **Ivanhoe** shot at Chepstow Castle by America's Imp Co. (forerunners of Universal). Release of first certificated films set in Wales.
1914	Row in Cardigan over screening of Kalem Co.'s Bible epic **From the Manger to the Cross** and the use of local choirboys to accompany the film. Edison's British Company releases **The Foreman's Treachery**, a melodrama made in Wales by Liverpool-born Charles Brabin.
1915	The first American film contract star Florence Turner – 'The Vitagraph Girl' – features in **A Welsh Singer**, from best-selling novel by west Wales author Allen Raine (Anne Adaliza Puddicombe). **A Welsh Singer** was re-released in 1918 and by 1922 was most popular film ever issued by Butcher's distribution company in Britain.
1917	Jimmy Wilde, World Flyweight boxing champion, stars in British fictional feature **The Pitboy's Romance**, for A. E. Coleby.
1918	Feature biopic of Lloyd George is completed but never released following attack, in magazine *John Bull*, on alleged German connections of executives of Ideal, the UK film company involved. Oswald Stoll who ran silent movies at Empire Theatres in Cardiff, Newport and Swansea before 1900 opens film studios in Surbiton, Surrey. In 1921 he launches Britain's biggest film studio, at Cricklewood, north London, with 20,000 ft. sound stage.
1919	Llanelli-born Gareth Hughes begins a 12-year career in Hollywood.
1919–20	Ivor Novello's début on screen, in leading role in Louis Mercanton's **Call of the Blood**. His 16-year screen career included **The Lodger** (1926) and **Downhill** (1927) for Hitchcock, **The Rat** (1925) (a popular version of his own stage hit), **I Lived With You** (1933) and D. W. Griffith's **The White Rose** (1923). Cardiff Mascot Star Company makes two shorts in Wales: **Coals and Courtship** and **Down on the Farm** (both survive).

1920	British silent star Chrissie White makes **Aylwin** in Wales.
1921	The Sherlock Holmes of the silent screen – the Stoll company's Eille Norwood – stars in **Gwyneth of the Welsh Hills**.
c.1926–7	Francis Worsley – later producer of radio's **ITMA** – makes film **Trawling out of Swansea on the Tenby Castle**.
1928	Queen's Cinema, Cardiff, shows the first part-talkie in Wales, **The Jazz Singer**, starring Al Jolson.
1929	Queen's screened the first 'up to date' (all-talkie) film – Jolson in **The Singing Fool**.
1932	First film made in Hollywood but entirely set in Wales: James Whale's **The Old Dark House**, starring Melvyn Douglas, Boris Karloff.
1933	C. H. Dand directs the fictional quarry drama **Men Against Death** in north Wales.
1935	Ifan ab Owen Edwards, of the Urdd movement, shoots the first Welsh-language sound (on disc) film, **Y Chwarelwr** (The Quarryman), in north Wales.
1936	Ralph Bond's section of Strand Co. documentary **Today We Live** shot among unemployed miners in Pentre, Rhondda, with help from Alexander and producer Paul Rotha.
1937	Donald Alexander (two years after his short **Rhondda**) directs **Eastern Valley** in Gwent, centred on self-help scheme for the jobless.
1939	MGM in Britain releases **The Citadel**, starring Robert Donat, Rosalind Russell – from novel by former south Wales doctor A. J. Cronin. Filming begins, near start of war, on **Proud Valley**, co-written by Merthyr novelist Jack Jones, and starring Cardiff's Rachel Thomas opposite Paul Robeson. The first British film to feature a black working-class hero as lead. Humphrey Jennings makes **Spare Time**, about Britain at leisure and work, featuring scenes at Pontypridd.
1941	**How Green Was My Valley**, directed in 20th Century–Fox studios by John Ford, wins five Oscars: best film, art direction, direction, photography (Arthur Miller), and supporting actor (Donald Crisp). Rhys Williams (as Dai Bando) is the only Welshman in a leading role.
1942	Dylan Thomas joins Strand Company as writer; works on such documentaries as **Our Country** and **Wales – Green Mountain, Black Mountain**.
1943	Humphrey Jennings makes **Silent Village** at Cwmgïedd, south Wales, re-creating the Nazis' massacre at the mining village of Lidice, Czechoslovakia. Film made with co-operation of local miners.
1945	Neath-born Ray Milland lands Oscar for his role of alcoholic in Billy Wilder's **The Lost Weekend**.
1947–9	**Yr Etifeddiaeth/The Heritage**, made by Welsh-language newspaper editor John Roberts Williams, in both Welsh and English.
1947	Boultings' film **Fame is the Spur** from novel by former Cardiff journalist Howard Spring. Contains key scene of a Welsh miners' riot. Edmund Gwenn wins Best Supporting Actor Oscar award for **Miracle on 34th Street**.

1949	Jill Craigie directs, William MacQuitty produces, **Blue Scar** – set in Abergwynfi. Focuses partly on the nationalization of the pits.
	Emlyn Williams directs his only feature **Last Days of Dolwyn**, and stars with Edith Evans and Richard Burton.
	Ealing comedy **A Run for Your Money** released with Meredith Edwards and Donald Houston as miner heroes.
1951	Paul Dickson makes drama-documentary **David**, with D. R. Griffiths in lead, as Welsh entry for Festival of Britain.
1952	BBC TV comes to Wales, some Welsh programmes shot from London.
	Richard Burton gains first of seven – unsuccessful – Academy Award nominations, as Best Supporting Actor for **My Cousin Rachel**.
1953	Burton stars in first full-length Cinemascope feature, **The Robe**.
	First BBC programmes made in Wales by outside broadcast unit.
1957	London live TV version of **Under Milk Wood**, directed by David Thomas, starring Donald Houston.
1958	TWW (Television Wales and the West) begins operations in Cardiff.
1959	Hugh Griffith gains Best Supporting Actor Oscar for William Wyler's Hollywood epic **Ben Hur**.
	Stanley Baker begins fruitful four-film collaboration with director Joseph Losey – on **Blind Date** (1959), **The Criminal** (1960), **Eve** (1962) and **Accident** (1967).
	Tiger Bay, starring John and Hayley Mills and Horst Buchholz, shot in Cardiff's docklands and Newport by director J. Lee Thompson.
1960	First television version of **How Green Was My Valley**, starring Rachel Thomas, Eynon Evans.
1960–1	John Ormond makes two of his best-known BBC documentaries, **Once There Was a Time** and **Borrowed Pasture**.
1960–2	Rachel Roberts establishes herself in 'kitchen sink', British New Wave films, and gains BAFTA UK Best Actress awards for **Saturday Night and Sunday Morning**, **This Sporting Life**.
1961	Kingsley Amis's novel *That Uncertain Feeling* filmed as **Only Two Can Play**, in Swansea area, starring Peter Sellers, Mai Zetterling, Kenneth Griffith. First 'Welsh' X-certificate film (released 1962).
1963	Jack Howells gains best short film Oscar for **Dylan**, with Richard Burton.
	Stanley Baker stars in and co-produces **Zulu**.
1965	Newport Film School launched, with Harley Jones running courses, John Grierson as patron (and occasional lecturer).
1968	HTV (Harlech Television) launches programmes taking franchise from TWW.
1970	Welsh Film Board born.
1971	Gwent-based Stephen Weeks makes (for Carlo Ponti) first known film version of medieval romance Gawain and the Green Knight.
	Andrew Sinclair directs big-screen version of **Under Milk Wood**, with Richard Burton, Peter O'Toole, Siân Phillips.

1974	First Welsh Arts Council Film Sub-committee formed – leads to creation of WAC film panel (1975–6).
1976	Second TV version of **How Green Was My Valley**, with Siân Phillips, Stanley Baker.
1976–7	Karl Francis films **Above Us the Earth**, centred on the closure of the Ogilvie Colliery. Establishes himself later in 1980s with **Giro City**, **The Happy Alcoholic** and **Ms Rhymney Valley**.
1978	BBC Wales comedy **Grand Slam**, with Hugh Griffith, proves big popular success.
1982	Sianel Pedwar Cymru (S4C – the Welsh Fourth Channel) launched after 'fast to death' threat by Plaid Cymru leader Gwynfor Evans. One of its early feature films **Madam Wen**, a period swashbuckler, caused its producers, the Welsh Film Board, massive financial problems. But the channel scored swift successes with **SuperTed** animation series and Stephen Bayly's **Joni Jones**.
1982	Weeks remakes **Gawain and the Green Knight** – this time for £12m – as **Sword of the Valiant**, starring Sean Connery, Miles O'Keeffe and Trevor Howard, but film obtains only token release.
1982–92	Wales independent company mini-boom, following launch of S4C.
1984	Cardiff stages much-enlarged Celtic Film Festival and Wales takes lion's share of prizes with Bayly's **And Pigs Might Fly** landing Spirit of Festival award.
1987	Bayly's **Coming Up Roses** and Francis's **Boy Soldier** (both made in Welsh for S4C) make history when shown in London West End cinemas with subtitles. Joanna Quinn's **Girls' Night Out** wins three prizes at the Annecy Animation Festival.
1988	Andrew Grieve's feature **On the Black Hill**, set on Welsh borders, released. BAFTA Cymru (Welsh Branch of British Academy of Film and Television Arts) formed.
1989	Official launch of Ffilm Cymru – Welsh Film Foundation – funded by S4C and BBC. Also two-year pilot project mounted to create a Wales Film Archive (pilot later extended into a third year).
1991	Wales BAFTA stages its first annual Film and TV awards, with Karl Francis's **Morphine and Dolly Mixtures** the winner in five categories. Rachel Thomas gains Lifetime Achievement award from BAFTA Cymru after a screen career spanning more than 50 years. **The Princess and the Goblin**, first Welsh animation feature co-production (with Hungary) completed by Robin Lyons's Siriol Company in Cardiff.
1992	First all-Welsh animated feature – **Under Milk Wood** – completed for S4C by Lyons. Cardiff animator Dave Edwards supervises Welsh–Russian co-production series of animated Shakespeare films. Production work begins on international series of animated opera films, with S4C again involved, with Russian, Welsh and English companies. Endaf Emlyn's **Un Nos Ola Leuad/One Full Moon** feature shares most BAFTA Cymru awards with Marc Evans's three-part series **Friday On My Mind**. Film and TV Archive becomes permanent. Czech animator Jan Svankmajer becomes first holder of Welsh International Film Fellowship award. Cardiff stages International Animation Festival and hosts the event again in 1994.

Sir Anthony Hopkins wins Best Actor Hollywood Oscar for **Silence of the Lambs**.

1993	Formation of Wales Film Council and associated organization Screen Wales.
	Wales Film Council absorbs Ffilm Cymru and main functions of Welsh Arts Council film panel.
	Peter Greenaway receives Welsh International Film Fellowship award.
	Paul Turner's **Hedd Wyn** wins Royal Television Society award for Best Play of the Year, weeks after taking the Spirit of the Festival prize at the Celtic Film Festival at Lorient, Brittany.
1994	**Hedd Wyn** is first Welsh-language film to gain a Best Foreign Language Film Hollywood Oscar nomination and wins six 1993 BAFTA Cymru awards.
	Actor/documentary film-maker Kenneth Griffith gains Lifetime Achievement award, from BAFTA Cymru, after screen career starting in 1941.

THE WELSH FILMS

This section contains a comprehensive list of around 400 documentary, topical and fictional productions – film and video – *released or shown in the cinema*. They are either set (or part-set) in Wales, feature a Welsh central character (e.g. Losey's **Eve**, with Stanley Baker), are works directed by Welsh film-makers and made, or partly made, in Wales – but not necessarily set there – or are of some historical or career significance (e.g. Chris Monger's first feature **Repeater** and Stephen Weeks's **Gawain and the Green Knight** and **Sword of the Valiant**). The list also includes various animation works by Welsh-based directors but generally excludes films merely shot in Wales (by outsiders) yet definitely set elsewhere (for example, Hitchcock's version of **The Farmer's Wife** (1928), John Huston's **Moby Dick** (1956) and **Inn of the Sixth Happiness** (Mark Robson, 1958). A list of some of these movies can be found in **Take Wales** (Wales Film Council/Screen Wales, 1993), together with a condensed filmography of films in this appendix.

Details of fiction films listed include principal members of casts. Running times are approximate, as source material information tends to differ slightly, and in some cases there are various release prints of the same film. Space considerations have precluded such details as the film's gauge (principally 16 and 35 mm.) but sources of archive print availability, for research purposes, have been included where possible.

All known films have been listed for the first decade of cinema, 1896–1906, and almost all documentaries, topicals, news magazine footage up to 1918. The details of documentary/topical footage are then more selective, but I have endeavoured to include all known feature films, and the significant shorter fictional and documentary material released in, or made for, the cinema. Material made specifically for TV has not been included unless tied in to, or given, a cinema release.

My chief sources include Denis Gifford's *British Film Catalogue 1895–1985*, various editions of Halliwell's *Film and Tele Guide*, unpublished research information by Jenny Steele collected for the Welsh Arts Council and Bwrdd Ffilmiau Cymraeg (Welsh Film Board) documents, the BFI publication *Traditions of Independence* (1980), the BFI *Film and Video Library Catalogue* and *The National Film Archive Viewing Catalogue* (1985), *The National Film Archive Catalogue Part 1 – Silent News Films* (1895–1933) (published 1965) and Chapter Arts Centre's literature and records. I am grateful for the help of Martyn Howells, former WAC films officer; and of Geoffrey Hill, the Aberdare-based writer and amateur historian, in collating the Haggar material; and I owe a special debt to Philip Lloyd for his original research and material supplied on Arthur Cheetham.

Abbreviations used in this appendix

CCVW	Cardiff Community Video Workshop
CFW	Chapter Film Workshop (later Filmworks Wales)
dir.	director
dist.	distributors
IWM	Imperial War Museum
MOMA	Museum of Modern Art, New York
NFA	National Film Archive (at British Film Institute, London)
p.c.	production company
WFA	Wales Film and TV Archive, Aberystwyth

CCVW productions, made at Chapter Arts Centre, are sometimes entered here as Chapter Video Workshop. They may be regarded as interchangeable for the purpose of this list.

An asterisk denotes that no *contemporary* evidence has been found relating to these films.

Films indicated by title *only* were shown in south Wales cinemas in the relevant year according to contemporary local newspapers.

The films

1896   **Prince and Princess of Wales at Cardiff Fine Art, Industrial and Maritime Exhibition.** (80ft.) Dir. Birt Acres.

Mounted Quadrille at a Military Display, Cardiff. (50–60ft.) Dir. Birt Acres.

Two Street Scenes of Queen Street, Cardiff. Dir. R. W. Paul. Possibly the same shorts as listed in 1898 R. W. Paul catalogue.

1898   (All these films directed by Arthur Cheetham.)
Children Playing on the Beach at Rhyl. NFA and WFA.

Wrexham High Street. Street scene.

Rhyl Town v. Amateurs Football Match.

Slate-loading onto Ships at Porthmadog.

Comical Scene in Queen Street, Rhyl.

A Diver at Work in the Docks at Holyhead.

Mailboat *Munster* Arriving at Holyhead from Dublin. (77ft.) NFA and WFA.

The Irish Mail Train going through Rhyl Station.

Blackburn Rovers v. West Bromwich Albion Soccer Match. NFA. Copy also in North West Film Archive, Manchester. Advertised by Cheetham as the longest film of any football match.

Llandudno Happy Valley and Minstrel Show.

Colwyn Bay Beach and Black-faced Entertainers.

Horse Fair at Llangollen.

Ladies Boating at Aberystwyth Bay.

Arrival of a Train at Llanrwst.

Rhyl May Day Procession.

Steam Roller in Queen Street, Rhyl.

Also **Shots of Conway Castle.** Travelogue. p.c. American Biograph.

1899   (All films directed by Arthur Cheetham.)
E. H. Williams and his Merrie Men. (120–50ft.) Popular entertainers and minstrel troupe seen performing on Rhyl sands, including a double-dance by Jimmy Charters and Fred Egan. NFA and WFA.

The School – 'the screaming sketch'. NFA and WFA.

Beach Scene. (55ft.) Children paddling at Rhyl Beach. NFA and WFA.

Royal Visit to Conway. NFA and WFA. (A 188ft. film of this visit mentioned in the NFA *Silent News Films 1895–1933* catalogue may refer to Cheetham's film.

*c.*1900   **Street Scenes outside Christchurch and Clwyd Street Schools, Rhyl.** (550ft., approx.) Dir. Arthur Cheetham? NFA and WFA. May be two separate films.

Panoramas of Caernarfon Castle, Church Island, Conway, Train Shots, Conway. p.c. Warwick Trading Company.

1901   **Film of the SS *St Elvies* Leaving Llandudno.** p.c. Warwick Trading Company. (Other footage of the ship was also shot by Warwick, possibly at Llandudno.)

Wales v. Ireland, Rugby International, at Swansea.

Turn-out and Drill of the Cardiff Fire Brigade.

Cardiff Flower Show.

*c.*1902   ***Phantom Train Ride to Burry Port** and ***Phantom Ride Through Swansea.** Dir. William Haggar.

1902   **True as Steel.** (150ft.) Dir. William Haggar. Scene from stage play. p.c. Haggar & Sons, dist. Warwick Trading Company.

The Maniac's Guillotine. (120ft.) Dir. William Haggar. Scene from stage play. p.c. Haggar & Sons, dist. Warwick Trading Company.

Cardiff Horse Show.

Wales v. Scotland Rugby Union in Cardiff. p.c. Warwick Trading Company.

Duel Scene from the Two Orphans. (100ft.) Dir. William Haggar. Knife duel from period stage melodrama. p.c. Haggar and Sons, dist. Warwick Trading Company.

The Wild Man of Borneo. (150ft.) Dir. William Haggar. Drama. p.c. Haggar & Sons, dist. Warwick Trading Company.

1903   **Buffalo Bill and May Day Procession, Rhyl.** (150ft.) Dir. Arthur Cheetham. NFA and WFA. Probably two separate films joined together. Shown on same Cheetham programme in 1903.

***Weary Willie and Tired Tim – The Gunpowder Plot.** (125ft.) Direction attributed to William Haggar, tentatively, by Denis Gifford. Tramps comedy based on the Tom Browne cartoon. p.c. Warwick Trading Company.

Mirthful Mary, a Case for the Black List. (120ft.) Dir. William Haggar. Part of comedy series featuring actress known as Mog. p.c. Haggar & Sons, dist. Gaumont.

Weary Willie and Tired Tim Turn Barbers. (118ft.) Dir. William Haggar. With James Haggar as Willie, Walter Haggar as Tim. Tramps comedy. p.c. Haggar and Sons, dist. Gaumont.

A Desperate Poaching Affray. (220ft.) USA: **The Poachers.** (220ft.) Dir. William Haggar. Chase movie. With William Haggar jun. p.c. Haggar & Sons, dist. Gaumont. NFA.

***Weary Willie and Tired Tim – a Dead Shot.** (150ft.) Direction attributed, tentatively, to William Haggar by Denis Gifford. Tramps comedy-farce. Dist. Warwick Trading Company.

The Tramp and the Washerwoman. (100ft.) Dir. William Haggar. Comedy. p.c. Haggar & Sons, dist. Gaumont.

Musical Drill by Cardiff Telegraph Boys at Military Tournament.

The Tramp and the Baby's Bottle. (100ft.) Dir. William Haggar. Comedy. p.c. Haggar & Sons, dist. Gaumont.

Baden Powell in Cardiff.

Amateur Photographers Walk to Porthcawl.

Accountants Walk, Cardiff.

A Dash for Liberty or The Convicts' Escape and Capture. (300 ft.) Dir. William Haggar. Chase film in five scenes. p.c. Haggar & Sons, for Urban.

Aberdare v. Porth Soccer Match. p.c. unknown, shown on Dooner's Electrograph.

1904

Whitewashing the Policeman. (65ft.) Comedy. Dir. William Haggar. p.c. Haggar & Sons, dist. Gaumont.

*Professor Richard Codman's Punch and Judy Show. Dir. John Codman. Llandudno puppet performance. p.c. John Codman's Enterprises.

Mirthful Mary in the Dock. (115ft.) Dir. William Haggar. Comedy in series. With Mog. p.c. Haggar & Sons for Gaumont.

The Sign of the Cross. (700ft.) Dir. William Haggar. With Will Haggar jun., Jenny Linden, James Haggar. From Wilson Barrett's stage play. p.c. Haggar & Sons, dist. Gaumont.

The Bathers' Revenge. (75ft.) Dir. William Haggar. Comedy. p.c. Haggar & Sons for Urban.

Brutality Rewarded. (75ft.) Dir. William Haggar. Comedy chase film. p.c. Haggar & Sons, dist. Urban.

The Meddling Policeman. (125ft.) Dir. William Haggar. Tramps comedy. p.c. Haggar & Sons, dist. Urban.

Flynn's Birthday Celebrations. (125ft.) Dir. William Haggar. Comedy. p.c. Haggar & Sons, dist. Urban.

The Biter Bitten. (50ft.) Dir. Wllliam Haggar. Tramps comedy. p.c. Haggar & Sons, dist. Urban.

Snowballing. (115ft.) Dir. William Haggar. Comedy with Mog. p.c. Haggar & Sons, dist. Gaumont.

The Waterfalls of Wales. p.c. Hepworth. (Also dated 1907 in some records.)

*Mr. Hughes and his Christmas Turkey. (No length available.) Dir. John Codman. Comedy. p.c. John Codman Enterprises.

1905

*The Miner's Daughter. (No length available.) Dir. John Codman. Drama set in Wales. p.c. John Codman Enterprises.

Turn-out of the Cardiff Fire Brigade. (Possibly same as 1903 film.)

The Rival Painters. (90ft.) Dir. William Haggar. Comedy. p.c. Haggar & Sons for Gaumont.

The Squire's Daughter. (600ft.) Dir. William Haggar. Drama from stage play, with Fred Haggar, Lillian Haggar, John Freeman.

Cardiff-Swansea Soccer Match (c.1905).

The Life of Charles Peace. (770ft.) Dir. William Haggar. With Walter Haggar (as Peace), Violet Haggar, Henry Haggar, Lillian Haggar, Sarah Haggar. p.c. Haggar & Sons, dist. Gaumont. (Extracts in The March of the Movies 1938, Film and Reality 1895-1939 dir. Alberto Cavalcanti, 1942), and HTV's The Dream that Kicks dir. Claire Pollak, 1986). Haggar's film probably completed 1904, though in 1905 catalogues. NFA and BFI Film and Video Library.

D.T.'s or **The Effects of Drink**. (220ft.) Dir. William Haggar. Trick film. p.c. Haggar & Sons, dist. Gaumont.

Fun at the Waxworks. (225ft.) Dir. William Haggar. Comedy. p.c. Haggar & Sons, dist. Gaumont.

Royal Visit to Cardiff and Opening of University Buildings.

Bathing Not Allowed. (145ft.) Dir. William Haggar. Comedy. p.c. Haggar & Sons, dist. Gaumont.

A Boating Incident. (130ft.) Dir. William Haggar. Comedy. p.c. Haggar & Sons, dist. Gaumont.

Bute Garden Party in Cardiff Castle.

Two's Company, Three's None. (75ft.) Dir. William Haggar. Comedy. p.c. Haggar & Sons, dist. Gaumont.

The Salmon Poachers – A Midnight Mêlée. (274ft.) Dir. William Haggar. Chase comedy, with Walter Haggar. p.c. Haggar & Sons, dist. Gaumont.

Mary is Dry (94ft.) Dir. William Haggar. Last comedy in film series, with Mog. p.c. Haggar & Sons, dist. Gaumont.

A Message from the Sea. (420ft.) Dir. William Haggar. Drama. With William Haggar jun., Henry Haggar. p.c. Haggar & Sons, dist. Gaumont. 37ft. fragment of film in NFA.

1906   **Pongo the Mad Monkey**. (535ft.) Dir. William Haggar. Comedy. Tentatively attributed to Haggar by Gifford. Dist. Gaumont.

Cardiff Horse Show.

Opening of Newport Transporter Bridge. Viscount Tredegar performing ceremony. NFA.

Opening of Municipal Buildings in Cardiff.

Royal Visit to Rhyl *c.*1906. Topical. Dir. Arthur Cheetham?

Wrexham v. Rhyl *c.*1906. Dir. Arthur Cheetham?

The Opening of the Fishguard–Rosslare Ferry Route.

1907   **Desperate Footpads**. (360ft.) Dir. William Haggar. Crime. p.c. Haggar & Sons, dist. Warwick Trading Company.

North Wales: The Land of Castles and Waterfalls. (810ft.) Travelogue. p.c. Urban company. (In Picturesque North Wales series).

National Eisteddfod.

Royal Visit to Cardiff and Opening of Cardiff's Queen Alexandra Dock.

The Waterfalls of Wales. p.c. Hepworth. 50ft. section in NFA.

1908   **The Red Barn Crime**, or **Maria Marten**. (685ft.) Dir. Haggar and Sons. Crime drama from stage play. With Violet Haggar (as Maria), Walter Haggar. p.c. Haggar & Sons, dist. Tyler.

*****Luck of a Diver**. (No length available.) Dir. John Codman. p.c. John Codman Enterprises.

The Dumb Man of Manchester. (No length available.) Dir. William Haggar. Crime drama (based on stage play) – with Will Haggar jun., Jenny Linden. p.c. Haggar & Sons.

There may have been an earlier version by Haggar *c.*1901. See chapter on William Haggar.

The Maid of Cefn Ydfa. (No length available.) Dir. William Haggar. Wales-set drama from stage play based on Welsh legend. With Will Haggar (as Wil Hopcyn), Jenny Linden (as Ann Thomas).

The Wreck of the Amazon on Margam Sands.

1909   ***Mr. Troublesome**. (No length available.) Dir. John Codman Comedy. p.c. John Codman Enterprises. National Eisteddfod.

National Pageant of Wales, Cardiff. Dir. William Haggar?

Conway Travelogue. p.c. Hepworth.

1910   **The Clydach Pit Disaster**. p.c. American Bioscope.

Excursion into Wales. (*c.*1910) p.c. Urban. This north Wales travelogue could be the same film as above (see 1907).

Welsh Coal Strike Scenes at Aberaman. (65ft.) Inc. shots of Charles Butt Stanton, miners' agent, later MP. p.c. Pathé. NFA.

Capt. Scott's Ship Terra Nova Leaving Harbour in Cardiff Bound for South Pole. (54ft.) p.c. Pathé. NFA.

1911   **Llanelli rail riots** footage. NFA.

Boxing – Freddie Welch v. Jim Driscoll 1910 Contest.

Flying at Pwllheli. (*c.*1911) (70ft.) Early aviation footage. p.c. Pathé Frères. NFA.

Shipwreck at Burry Port. Dir. James Haggar?

Dock Strike Scenes at Cardiff. Union leader Havelock Wilson addressing the crowd. p.c. Pathé. NFA.

Through Three Reigns. Documentary, contains footage of investiture. p.c. Hepworth. NFA.

Investiture at Caernarfon. p.c. Gaumont. NFA and WFA.

Investiture at Caernarfon. (425ft.) p.c. Charles Urban. (Kinemacolor and black and white versions. Black and white only in NFA).

Investiture at Caernarvon. (135ft.) p.c. Pathé. NFA.

Labour Demonstration, Llanelli. Dir. James Haggar.

1912   **The Belle of Betws-y-coed**. US: **The Belle of North Wales**. (1,015ft.) Dir. Sidney Northcote. With Dorothy Foster, Percy Moran, O'Neil Farrell. Welsh romance. p.c. British and Colonial Kinematograph, dist. Moving Pictures Sales Agency.

The Smuggler's Daughter of Anglesea [*sic*]. (1,090ft.) Dir. Sidney Northcote. With Dorothy Foster, Derek Powell, Percy Moran. Welsh crime drama. p.c. B. and C. Kinematograph Co. (as above), dist. Moving Pictures Sales Agency.

The Pedlar of Penmaenmawr. (860ft.) Dir. Sidney Northcote. With Dorothy Foster, Charles Seymour, George Trumpeter. Welsh drama. p.c. B. and C. Kinematograph Co., dist. Moving Pictures Sales Agency.

The Witch of the Welsh Mountains. (990ft.) Dir. Sidney Northcote. Welsh drama. With

Dorothy Foster, Sidney Cairns, Beatrice de Burgh, Georgina St George. p.c. B. and C. Kinematograph Co., dist. Moving Picture Sales Agency.

Wrexham Parade. p.c. Gaumont (for Glyn Cinema Co.) WFA.

1913   **Senghenydd Pit Disaster.** p.c. Gaumont?

Mifanwy – A Tragedy. (675ft.) (U cert.) Dir. Elwin Neame. Welsh romance, with Ivy Close as Mifanwy. p.c. Ivy Close Films, dist. Hepworth.

The Dustmen's Holiday. (433ft.) (U cert.) Dir. W. P. Kellino. Swansea-set comedy based on stage act, with Albert Egbert and Seth Egbert. p.c. Ecko, dist. Universal.

Royal Visit to Wales. p.c. Gaumont.

1914   **The Foreman's Treachery.** (Length unavailable.) (U cert.) Dir. Charles Brabin. Welsh copper-mine drama, with Marc McDermott, Miriam Nesbitt, Charles Vernon. p.c. Edison.

The Maid of Cefn Ydfa. (3,000ft.) Dir. William Haggar jun. Welsh crime drama with William Haggar jun., Jenny Haggar and Wil Fyffe. p.c. Haggar & Sons. Made 1913/14; 26 minutes of 40 original survive in viewable NFA print.

The People of the Rocks. (1,200ft.) Dir. Dalton Somers. Welsh fantasy with Connie Somers. p.c. Captain Kettle. Reissued 1917, dist. Davison Film Sales Agency.

Wild Wales. (350ft.) p.c. Edison.

A Storm on the Welsh Coast. (275ft.) p.c. Pathé.

Cardiff Victims of World War I. (55ft.) Gaumont Graphic. p.c. Gaumont. NFA.

Rhondda, Carmarthen and Swansea City Battalions Marching Through Rhyl. p.c. Gaumont. Three films joined – Rhondda batallions 84ft. and 61ft. (inc. Swansea), Carmarthen 41ft.

Wales v. Scotland Soccer. Incomplete footage in WFA.

1915   **Jimmy Wilde v. Pal Moore.** (63ft.) Boxing footage. Training camp scenes at Moore's headquarters only. Gaumont Serial No. 867. Footage of World Title Fight: Wilde v. Moore.

A Welsh Singer. (4,640ft.) (U cert.) Dir. Henry Edwards. Welsh romance, with Florence Turner, Henry Edwards, Campbell Gullan, Fred Rains, Edith Evans. p.c. Turner Films, dist. Butcher. Reissue 1918.

Lloyd George Reviewing Kitchener's Troops at Llandudno. (101ft.) p.c. Pathé (Pathé Gazette).

Lloyd George at Cardiff. (51ft.) Topical Budget. NFA.

1915/16   **A Holiday in North Wales.** (1,385ft.) p.c. Kinemacolour Ltd.

1916   **Lloyd George at the Eisteddfod, Aberystwyth.** Topical Budget. NFA (51ft.), IWM (63ft.).

1917   **A Pit Boy's Romance.** (4,000ft.) (A cert.) Dirs. A. E. Coleby, Arthur Rooke. Welsh drama with Jimmy Wilde (as Jimmy Davies), Tommy Noble, A. E. Coleby, Arthur Rooke. p.c. Davidson-Tiger, dist. Film Bureau.

The Welsh Eisteddfod. 'Wonderful scenes at Birkenhead'. Footage from Topical Budget No. 3152, 8 Sept. 1917.

Lloyd George at 10 Downing Street on St David's Day. (57ft.) Topical Budget No. 288/2. NFA.

1918	**Armistice in Holywell, 1918.** Footage held by Clwyd County Record Office, Hawarden.

Betta the Gypsy. (4,100ft.) (A cert.) Dir. Charles Raymond. Welsh drama, with Marga la Rubia (as Betta), Malvina Longfellow, George Foley. Welsh romance, based on opera. p.c. Famous Productions, dist. Butcher.

The Life Story of David Lloyd George. (6,000ft.) Dir. Maurice Elvey. With Norman Page (as Lloyd George), Alma Reville (as Megan Lloyd George), Ernest Thesiger (as Joseph Chamberlain), Douglas Munro (as Benjamin Disraeli). p.c. Ideal. Never released. WFA.

Jimmy Wilde v. Conn fight. (2,500ft.) p.c. Harma.

The River Banks of Wales. (*c.*1918) p.c. Charles Urban.

Cardiff Hospital Scenes. WFA.

1919   **Coals and Courtship.** (20 mins.) Dir. Ernest Edmunds. With Ted Hopkins and Miss C. A. Edmunds. Welsh comedy. p.c. Mascot Star (Cardiff). NFA.

1920   **Her Benny.** (5,900ft.) (U cert.) Dir. A. V. Bramble. Drama, part-set in Wales, with Robert Villis, Peggy Patterson, Sidney Wood. Romance. p.c. Diamond Super, dist. Granger.

The Little Welsh Girl. (5,240ft.) (A cert.) Dir. Fred Paul. Welsh drama with Christine Silver (as Ellen Lloyd), Humberston Wright, Booth Conway. p.c. London, dist. Jury.

Aylwin. (5,485ft.) (U cert.) Dir. Henry Edwards. Welsh drama, with Henry Edwards, Chrissie White, Gerald Ames. p.c. Hepworth.

Torn Sails. (5,000ft.) (U cert.) Dir. A. V. Bramble. Welsh drama, with Milton Rosmer, Mary Odette, Geoffrey Kerr. p.c. Ideal.

By Berwen Banks. (4,900ft.) (U cert.) Dir. Sidney Morgan. Welsh romance with Langhorne Burton, Eileen Magrath, J. Denton-Thomas. p.c. Progress, dist. Butcher.

Down on the Farm. (18mins.) Dir. Ernest Edmunds. Welsh comedy with Leo Lyne, Rita Valee, Esta Latner, H. Woodhouse. Produced by T. A. Glover for Mascot Star (Cardiff). NFA.

South Wales Miners' Dispute and footage of **Unemployed.** Pathé Gazette footage. NFA.

Kidwelly Murder Trial, Carmarthen Assizes. (50ft.) Gaumont Graphic footage. NFA.

The Croxley Master. (3,900ft.) (A cert.) Dir. Percy Nash. Welsh sports drama, with Dick Webb, Dora Lennox, Jack Stanley. p.c. Screen Plays, dist. British Exhibitors' Films.

Land of my Fathers. (5000ft.) (U cert.) Dir. Fred Rains. Aberystwyth-set drama, with John Stuart, Edith Pearson, Yvonne Thomas. p.c. Glen Films. Released 1921.

Gwyneth of the Welsh Hills. (6,470ft.) (A cert.) Dir. Martin Thornton. Welsh romance, with Madge Stuart (as Gwyneth), Eille Norwood, Lewis Gilbert, R. Henderson Bland. p.c. Stoll.

Love in the Welsh Hills. (6,057ft.) (A cert.) Dir. Bernard Dudley. Welsh crime drama, with James Knight, Marjorie Villis. p.c. Harma Associated Exhibitors, dist. Regent.

Wales By-elections. In Topical Budget magazine, Feb. 1920.

1921   **Conway – River of a Thousand Moods.** (772ft.) Documentary. NFA.

1922   **Love and a Whirlwind.** (6,858ft.) (U cert.) Dirs. Duncan Macrae, Harold Shaw. Welsh crime drama, with Clive Brook, Marjorie Hume, Reginald Fox. p.c. Alliance, dist. Cosmograph.

The Last King of Wales. (1,960ft.) (U cert.) Dir. George Ridgwell. With Charles Ashton (as Llewelyn), Malvina Longfellow (as Queen Eleanor), Cynthia Murtagh. Film in British History series.

Welsh National Eisteddfod. Gorsedd and sideshow footage.

1923	**Welsh National Eisteddfod.** Prod. Gaumont Graphic.
1925	**Great Welsh Dam Disaster, Lake Eigiau, nr. Dolgarrog (Conway Valley).** (51ft.) In Topical Budget magazine. p.c. Topical Budget/Hulton's Press. NFA.
1925–6	**The Open Road.** Travelogue series by Claude Friese-Greene shot all over Britain to demonstrate a new two-colour process. Dist. Wardour. Twenty-six reels (26 separate films) with Welsh material in reels 2,6,7 and 8. NFA.
1926	**The Ball of Fortune.** (6,500ft.) (U cert.) Dir. Hugh Croisé. Sports drama, with Billy Meredith (the Welsh soccer star, playing himself), James Knight, Mabel Poulton, Geoffrey B. Partridge. p.c. Booth Grainge. dist. Mercury Film Service.
1926/7	**Trawling out of Swansea on the *Tenby Castle*.** (400ft.) Dir. Francis Worsley. Silent documentary (some footage used in **Milford Fishermen**, 1977).
1927	**With the Aid of a Rogue.** (1,517ft.) (U cert.) Dir. J. H. Payne. With J. H. Payne. Eighteenth-century highwayman drama. p.c. J. H. Payne, dist. European.
	Parry Thomas Killed in Speed Attempts on Pendine Sands. (40ft.) Magazine footage. p.c. Gaumont Graphic (available through Visnews).
1928	**Land of my Fathers.** Series of eight films, inc. **Fair Glamorgan** (Cardiff and Lower Rhondda) and **Forest and Fountain** (inc. Anglesey and Caernarfon). p.c. British Screen.
1929	**A Broken Romance.** (6,854ft.) (A cert.) Silent. Dir. J. Steven Edwards. With William Freshman, Blanche Adele, Paul Neville. Romance about crippled Welsh girl.
	That Lass of Chandler's. (2,000ft.) Silent. Dir. W. J. Sargent. With Doris Ffoulkes Griffiths and J. Adams. Conwy-set romance. p.c. North Wales Screen Productions. ('Amateur film shown professionally', according to Gifford.)
	Armistice. (15mins.) (U cert.) Dir. Victor Saville. With Welsh Guards band and HM Coldstream Guards. 15-minute short of songs of 1914–18 war. p.c. Michael Balcon, production for Gainsborough. Dist. Woolf and Freedman Film Service.
	Great Western Ports. (58mins.) Documentary. p.c. Great Western Railway, short partly in Wales. NFA.
1930	**Along the Cambrian Coast.** (168ft.) Pathé Pictorial (No. 623). Item includes seafront at Pwllheli.
1931	**Land of my Fathers.** (8 mins.) (U cert.) Dir. unknown. Welsh songs and scenes, with the Glanhowy Singers. p.c. BIP (British International Pictures), dist. Wardour.
1932	**The Old Dark House.** (71 mins.) Dir. James Whale. US comedy-drama set in Wales, with Melvyn Douglas, Charles Laughton, Boris Karloff, Raymond Massey, Ernest Thesiger. p.c. Universal.
	Heroes of the Mine. (48 mins.) (U cert.) Dir. Widgey R. Newman. Mining disaster drama

set in Wales, with Moore Marriott, Wally Patch, Terence de Marney. p.c. Delta, dist. Butcher.

1933   **The Good Companions**. (113 mins.) (U cert.) Dir. Victor Saville. Comedy-musical, partly set in Wales. With Jessie Matthews (as Susie Dean), Edmund Gwenn (as Jess Oakroyd), John Gielgud. p.c. Gaumont/TA Welsh/George Pearson. NFA.

Men Against Death. Dir. C. H. Dand. Short drama-documentary. Probably shot at Dorothea quarry, Tal-y-sarn.

1934   **Workers' Newsreel No. 2**. (10–15 mins.) Silent agit-prop/documentary. Includes footage of Gresford Colliery disaster, north Wales. Probably directed by Herbert Marshall. p.c. Kino London Production Group, dist. Workers Film and Photo League/Kino. NFA.

1935   **Holiday from Unemployment**. (15 mins.) Silent documentary. dist. Workers Film and Photo League/Kino.

Slate Quarrying of North Wales – at Dinorwic. (1,200ft.) Photographer: G. L. Hawkins. Silent documentary. In Welsh Industrial and Maritime Museum, Cardiff, and NFA.

The Phantom Light. (76mins.) (U cert.) Dir. Michael Powell. Welsh crime drama, with Binnie Hales, Gordon Harker, Ian Hunter, Donald Calthrop. p.c. Gainsborough, dist. Gaumont-British Picture Corporation. Reissue 1950 (10 mins. cut). NFA.

Y Chwarelwr (The Quarryman). Dir. Ifan ab Owen Edwards. Short Welsh drama. The first Welsh-language sound film. Dist. Urdd Gobaith Cymru (Welsh League of Youth). Incomplete copy in WFA.

Rhondda – Depression Years. (400ft.) (8–10mins.) Silent documentary, sponsored by National Union of Mineworkers. Copy at Welsh Folk Museum. Dist. Kino. NFA. Donald Alexander also made a short in the same year called **Rhondda**, with Judy Birdwood of the Socialist Films Council.

1936   **Workers' Topical News 2**. Includes shots of south and west Wales marchers and footage of south Wales miners' marches. p.c. and dist. Film and Photo League.

March Against Starvation. Alt. title **Hunger March**, 1936.

1937   **Night Must Fall**. (117 mins.) Dir. Richard Thorpe. Drama based on Welsh villain. With Robert Montgomery, Rosalind Russell, May Whitty. p.c. MGM (USA).

Landslide. (67 mins.) (A cert.) Dir. Donovan Pedelty. Welsh crime drama, with Jimmy Hanley, Dinah Sheridan, Jimmy Mageean. p.c. Crusade, dist. Paramount.

Today we Live. (24 mins.) Dirs. Ralph Bond, Ruby Grierson. Mining documentary with Rhondda scenes directed by Bond. With Les Adlam, Glyn Lewis. p.c. Strand. NFA and BFI Film and Video Library.

Around Snowdonia. (950ft.) Dir. Duncan Robbins. North Wales travelogue. p.c. Alba.

Eastern Valley. (17 mins.) Dir. Donald Alexander. Gwent-set documentary on co-operative food scheme. p.c. Strand. NFA.

The Hidden Land. Dir. Hayford Hobbs. Welsh documentary. p.c. Visonor. NFA.

The Midas Touch. (68 mins.) (A cert.) Dir. David Macdonald. Drama about Welsh millionaire. With Barry K. Barnes, Judy Kelly, Frank Cellier, Iris Hoey. p.c. Warner Bros., dist. Warner Bros.

1938	**The Citadel**. (110 mins.) (A cert.) Dir. King Vidor. Drama, partly set in Wales, with Robert Donat, Rosalind Russell, Ralph Richardson, Rex Harrison, Dilys Davies, Emlyn Williams, Cecil Parker. p.c. MGM (Britain). Reissued in Britain 1948. NFA.
1939	**Spare Time**. (15 mins.) Dir. Humphrey Jennings. Documentary, partly made in Pontypridd. p.c. GPO Film Unit. NFA. BFI Film and Video Library.
1940	**The Proud Valley**. (76 mins.) (A cert.) Dir. Pen Tennyson. Working title, 'David Goliath'. Mining drama, with Paul Robeson (as David Goliath), Edward Chapman, Simon Lack, Rachel Thomas, Dilys Davies, Dilys Thomas, Jack Jones, Clifford Evans. p.c. Ealing–CAPAD. Dist. Associated British Film Distributors. (Reissued 1948.) NFA. BFI Film and Video Library.
1941	**How Green Was My Valley**. (118 mins.) (A cert.) Dir. John Ford. Mining drama with Donald Crisp, Sara Allgood, Roddy McDowall, Walter Pidgeon, Maureen O'Hara, Anna Lee, Rhys Williams, Barry Fitzgerald. p.c. 20th Century–Fox. NFA.
	Dai Jones. (5 mins.) Dir. Dan Birt. Mining documentary. p.c. Verity, dist. Ministry of Information. NFA and MOMA, New York.
1942	**Night Shift**. (15 mins.) Dir. Jack Chambers. Armaments factory documentary made in Newport. p.c. Rotha Productions, dist. Ministry of Information and Ministry of Supply. NFA.
	Spring on the Farm. (15 mins.) Dir. Ralph Keene. Farming documentary made in Ross-on-Wye. p.c. Green Park, dist. Ministry of Information.
	Wales. (10 mins.) p.c. Hanover, dist. British Council. Footage may have been taken from **Wales – Green Mountain, Black Mountain**.
	Wales – Green Mountain, Black Mountain. (12 mins.) Dir. John Eldridge. Documentary set in Wales. p.c. Strand, dist. Ministry of Information. Copy in IWM.
	The Next of Kin. (102 mins.) (A cert.) Dir. Thorold Dickinson. War propaganda drama with Welsh spy the central character. With Mervyn Johns, Nova Pillbeam, Reginald Tate, Stephen Murray, Basil Radford, Naunton Wayne. p.c. Ealing/Michael Balcon. Dist. United Artists. Reissued 1954 by New Realm Pictures. NFA.
1943	**The Silent Village**. (36 mins.) Dir. Humphrey Jennings. Drama, set in Cwmgïedd, west Wales, and based on events in Czechoslovakia. p.c. Crown Film Unit, dist. Ministry of Information. NFA. MOMA.
	Frankenstein Meets the Wolf Man. (73 mins.) (H cert.) Dir. Roy William Neill. US horror film partly set in Wales, with Lon Chaney jun., Ilona Massey, Bela Lugosi, Maria Ouspenskaya. p.c. Universal.
	The Dragon of Wales. (20 mins.) Dir. W. B. Pollard. Welsh documentary.
1944	**Our Country**. (45 mins.) Dir. John Eldridge. Documentary panorama of Britain, with Welsh scenes. p.c. Strand, dist. Ministry of Information. NFA.
	Coalminer. (15 mins.) Dir. Charles de Lautour. Mining documentary. p.c. Strand, dist. Ministry of Information, Ministry of Fuel and Power. IWM.
	Worker and Warfront Series No. 14. (10 mins.) Dir. unknown. Includes footage of south Wales mine accident, ambulance and treatment service. p.c. Paul Rotha Productions and Films of Fact. NFA.
1945	**The Corn is Green**. (118 mins.) (A cert.) Dir. Irving Rapper. Drama set in Wales with

Bette Davis, John Dall, Nigel Bruce, Joan Lorring, Rhys Williams. p.c. Warner Bros., dist. Warner Bros.

Halfway House. (95 mins.) (A cert.) Dir. Basil Dearden. Welsh fantasy, with Mervyn Johns, Glynis Johns, Esmond Knight, Françoise Rosay, Tom Walls, Alfred Drayton. p.c. Ealing. NFA.

1946   **Welsh Magic**. (1,470ft.) North Wales travelogue. p.c. Paul Barralet Productions. NFA.

1947   **Fame is the Spur**. (116 mins.) (A cert.) Dir. Roy Boulting. Political drama, with Welsh scenes. With Michael Redgrave (as Hamer Radshaw), Rosamund John, Bernard Miles, Carla Lehmann, Hugh Burden, Marjorie Fielding, Seymour Hicks. p.c. Two Cities, dist. General Film Distributors. NFA.

*c.*1947   **Island in the Current**. Dir. E. E. (Evan) Pritchard. Short documentary shot on the Llŷn Peninsula and Bardsey Island. WFA.

1948   **The Small Voice**. (85 mins.) (A cert.) US title: **Hideout**. Dir. Fergus McDonnell. Welsh crime drama, with Valerie Hobson, James Donald, Harold (Howard) Keel, David Greene, Michael Balfour. p.c. Constellation, dist. British Lion.

The Three Weird Sisters. (82 mins.) (A cert.) Dir. Dan Birt. Welsh crime and mining drama, with Nancy Price, Mary Clare, Mary Merrall, Nova Pillbeam, Raymond Lovell, Hugh Griffith, Anthony Hulme. p.c. British National, dist. Pathé. NFA.

1949   **Blue Scar**. (90 mins.) (U cert.) Dir. Jill Craigie. Welsh mining drama. With Emrys Jones, Gwyneth Vaughan, Rachel Thomas, Anthony Pendrell, Prysor Williams, Madoline Thomas, Kenneth Griffith. p.c. Outlook, dist. British Lion. NFA and NCB Library.

The Last Days of Dolwyn. (95 mins.) (U cert.) Dir. Emlyn Williams. Welsh drama, with Edith Evans (as Merri), Emlyn Williams, Allan Aynesworth, Barbara Couper, Richard Burton, Hugh Griffith, Roddy Hughes. p.c. London–British Lion Production Assets, dist. British Lion. NFA.

A Run for your Money. (85 mins.) (A cert.) Dir. Charles Frend. Comedy, with Donald Houston, Moira Lister, Meredith Edwards, Alec Guinness, Hugh Griffith. p.c. Ealing, dist. General Film Distributors. NFA.

The Fruitful Year/Noson Lawen (25 mins.) Dir. Mark Lloyd. Drama-documentary for National Savings Movement. p.c. Brunner Lloyd, dist. National Savings Committee.

1950   **The Undefeated**. (35 mins.) Dir. Paul Dickson. Drama-documentary. Narration: Leo Genn. p.c. World Wide Pictures. NFA.

1951   **David**. (38 mins.) (U cert.) Dir. Paul Dickson. Welsh drama, with D. R. Griffiths (as Dafydd Rhys), John Davies, Mary Griffiths, Gwenyth Petty, Rachel Thomas, Sam Jones. p.c. World Wide Pictures, dist. Regent. NFA and BFI Film and Video Library.

Circle of Danger. Working title, 'White Heather'. (86 mins.) (U cert.) Dir. Jacques Tourneur. Drama set partly in Wales. With Ray Milland, Patricia Roc, Marius Goring, Hugh Sinclair, Naunton Wayne. p.c. Coronado, dist. RKO. NFA.

1952   **Girdle of Gold**. (66 mins.) (U cert.) Dir. Montgomery Tully. Welsh comedy, with Esmond Knight, Maudie Edwards, Meredith Edwards, Glyn Houston. p.c. Screenplays London, dist. Eros.

Sing Along With Me. (79 mins.) (U cert.) Dir. Peter Graham Scott. Musical drama set in

Wales, with Donald Peers, Dodo Watts, Dennis Vance, J. H. Clifford. p.c. Peter Graham Scott/HH Film Challenge, dist. British Lion.

1953 **Letter from Wales**. (15 mins.) (U cert.) Dir. George Lloyd. Drama-documentary, with Evie Wyn Jones, Katie Wyn Jones, Sam Jones, Vera Jones, Olga Jones. p.c. Brunner Lloyd, dist. Children's Film Foundation. NFA.

Valley of Song. (74 mins.) (U cert.) Dir. Gilbert Gunn. Comedy set in Wales, with Clifford Evans, Rachel Thomas, Maureen Swanson, John Fraser, Hugh Pryse, Rachel Roberts. p.c. Associated British Picture Corporation, dist. Associated British Pictures. NFA.

1954 **The Happiness of Three Women**. (78 mins.) (U cert.) Dir. Maurice Elvey. With Brenda de Banzie, Eynon Evans, Petula Clark, Donald Houston, Patricia Cutts, Glyn Houston. p.c. Advana, dist. Adelphi.

The Blue Peter (US title: **Navy Heroes**). (93 mins.) (U cert.) Dir. Wolf Rilla. Welsh drama. With Kieron Moore, Mervyn Johns, Greta Gynt, Sarah Lawson. p.c. Beaconsfield Studios Group, Group 3, dist. British Lion.

The Black Knight. (85mins.) (U cert.) Dir. Tay Garnett. Arthurian drama partly shot in and around Welsh castles. With Alan Ladd, Patricia Medina, André Morell, Harry Andrews, Peter Cushing. p.c. Irving Allen, Albert (Cubby) Broccoli, Phil C. Samuel/Warwick, dist. Columbia. Reissued 1961 when distributed by Unifilms.

1955 **Room in the House**. (74 mins.) (U cert.) Dir. Maurice Elvey, from *Bless this House*, play by Eynon Evans. Screenplay by Evans. Welsh-set comedy with Patrick Barr, Hubert Gregg, Marjorie Rhodes, Leslie Dwyer. p.c. ACT Films, dist. Monarch.

1957 **The Good Companions**. (104 mins.) (U cert.) Dir. J. Lee Thompson. Remake of 1933 comedy musical, partly set in Wales. With Eric Portman, Celia Johnson, Hugh Griffith, Janette Scott, John Fraser, Joyce Grenfell, Rachel Roberts. p.c. Associated British Picture Corporation.

Every Valley. (20 mins.) Dir. Michael Clarke. Documentary set in Wales, with Donald Houston (as narrator). p.c. British Transport Films. NFA.

Sentence on a Valley. North Wales footage of Tryweryn flooding. Pathé News.

Davy. (83 mins.) (U cert.) Dir. Michael Relph. Comedy about Welsh entertainer with Harry Secombe, Alexander Knox, Ron Randell, George Relph. p.c. Basil Dearden/Ealing, dist. MGM.

1958 **Nowhere to Go**. (U cert.) Dir. Seth Holt. Drama, set partly in Wales. With George Nader, Maggie Smith, Bernard Lee, Geoffrey Keen. p.c. Ealing Films, dist. MGM.

Modern Wales. Documentary of modern industry. p.c. Central Office of Information for Foreign Office.

1959 **Tiger Bay**. (105 mins.) (A cert.) Dir. J. Lee Thompson. Welsh crime drama with John Mills, Horst Buchholz, Hayley Mills, Yvonne Mitchell, Megs Jenkins. p.c. Independent Artists, dist. Rank Film Distributors. NFA.

Blind Date (US title: **Chance Meeting**). (95 mins.) (A cert.) Dir. Joseph Losey. Drama. With Hardy Kruger, Stanley Baker, Micheline Presle, Robert Flemyng. p.c. Rank/Sydney Box/Independent Artists, dist. Rank Film Distributors. NFA.

1960 **Pembrokeshire, My County**. (962ft.) Dir. Ronald Stark. Welsh documentary. p.c. Esso. NFA.

Letter for Wales. (25 mins.) Documentary with Donald Houston as narrator. p.c. British Transport Films.

1962   **Only Two Can Play**. (106 mins.) (X cert.) Dir. Sidney Gilliat. Welsh comedy with Peter Sellers, Mai Zetterling, Kenneth Griffith, Virginia Maskell, Richard Attenborough, Raymond Huntley, Meredith Edwards. p.c. Vale, dist. British Lion. NFA.

Eva (or **Eve**). (135 mins.) (18 cert.) Dir. Joseph Losey. Drama set in Italy featuring fake Welsh novelist. With Stanley Baker, Jeanne Moreau (as Eva), Virnia Lisi, James Villiers. p.c. Paris/Interopa/Robert and Raymond Hakim. NFA.

1963   **A Time to Heal**. (40 mins.) Documentary on Talygarn miners' rehabilitation centre. p.c. Derrick Knight and Partners, dist. National Coal Board.

Bitter Harvest. (96 mins.) (X cert.) Dir. Peter Graham Scott. Drama, set partly in Wales, with Janet Munro, John Stride, Alan Badel, Anne Cunningham, Norman Bird, Terence Alexander. p.c. Independent Artists, dist. Rank Film Distributors.

Zulu. (135 mins.) (U cert.) Dir. Cy Endfield. Drama with Stanley Baker (as Lt John Chard), Michael Caine (as Lt. Ganville Bromhead), Jack Hawkins, Ulla Jacobsson, James Booth, Nigel Green, Ivor Emmanuel, Patrick Magee, Chief Buthelezi. p.c. Diamond, dist. Paramount.

1964   **Night Must Fall**. (105 mins.) (X cert.) Dir. Karel Reisz. Drama, featuring Welsh central character, with Albert Finney, Susan Hampshire, Mona Washbourne, Sheila Hancock. p.c. MGM. NFA.

1965   **The World Still Sings**. (3,385ft.) Dir. Jack Howells. Documentary, Llangollen Eisteddfod, 1964. p.c. Jack Howells Production Co., dist. Welsh Office Film Library, sponsors Esso. NFA.

The Master Singers. (47 mins.) Dir. Robert Vas. Documentary, with Treharris and Aber Valley male-voice choirs. p.c. National Coal Board/BBC TV, dist. NCB.

People and Places – Wales. (25 mins.) Dir. Geoffrey Foot. Documentary in series. p.c. Walt Disney Productions, USA.

1966   **Timetable Blues**. (3 mins.) Dir. Peter Turner. Animation. p.c. British Film Institute, BFI Film and Video Library.

1967   **New Neighbours**. (22 mins.) Dir. Jack Howells. Sponsored documentary. p.c. Jack Howells Productions for Central Electricity Generating Board.

1968   **Letter from Llandudno**. (21 mins.) Dir. unknown. Documentary. p.c. Connaught Productions, dist. MGM.

Land of the Red Dragon. (20 mins.) Dir. Sarah Erulkar. Documentary. Dist. p.c. British Movietone, dist. British Tourist Authority.

1969   **Senghenydd**. (17 mins.) Dir. James Clark. Documentary. p.c. Research Film Productions, dist. Contemporary Films.

Mischief. (57 mins.) (U cert.) Dir. Ian Shand. Drama with Paul Fraser, Iain Burton, Gerald Sim. p.c. Shand, dist. Children's Film Foundation.

1970   **Draig o Dras – The Land of the Proud Dragon**. (23 mins.) Dir. Shirley Cobham. Sponsored documentary produced in various languages. p.c. Spectator Films, dist. British Petroleum Co.

Head Rag Hop. (3 mins.) Dir. Peter Turner. Animation. p.c. BFI Film and Video Library.

1971   **Under Milk Wood**. (88 mins.) (AA cert.) Dir. Andrew Sinclair. Welsh poetic comedy. With Richard Burton (as First Voice), Elizabeth Taylor, Peter O'Toole, Siân Phillips, Glynis Johns, Vivien Merchant, Angharad Rees, Ryan Davies, Victor Spinetti, Aubrey Richards. p.c. Timon, dist. Rank Film Distributors.

The Ballad of Dickie Jones. (24 mins.) (U cert.) Dir. George Bekes. Drama, with Morgan Powell (as Dickie Jones), Eric Francis. p.c. GB Productions, dist. Connoisseur.

Richard Wilson. (21 mins.) Dirs. Clive Ashwin, Harley Jones. Documentary on the painter. p.c. Newport College of Art and Design Film School, dist. Welsh Arts Council.

Danny Jones. (91 mins.) (X cert.) Dir. Jules Bricken. Welsh drama, with Frank Finlay, Jane Carr, Len Jones, Jenny Hanley. p.c. Fon Getz/Oakshire, dist. Cinerama.

Anne and Muriel/Two English Girls (Les Deux Anglaises et le Continent). (108 mins.) Dir. François Truffaut. Drama partly set in Wales with Jean-Pierre Leaud, Kika Markham, Stacey Tendeter, p.c. Les Films du Carosse/Cinetel.

1972   **La Cathédrale Engloutie**. (8 mins.) Dir. Dudley Shaw Ashton. Art documentary. p.c. Samaritan Films, dist. Arts Council of Great Britain/Welsh Arts Council.

1973   **Women of the Rhondda**. (20 mins.) Documentary. p.c. London Women's Film Group, dist. The Other Cinema.

Gawain and the Green Knight. (93 mins.) (U cert.) Dir. Stephen Weeks. Arthurian drama with Celtic settings. With Murray Head (as Gawain), Ciarran Madden (as Linnet), Nigel Green (as the Green Knight), Anthony Sharp, Robert Hardy, Murray Melvin, Ronald Lacey, Geoffrey Bayldon. p.c. Sancrest, dist. United Artists.

Adagio. (14 mins.) Dir. Laurie Davies. WAC-financed.

Free the Six. (20 mins.) p.c. National Film School, for north Wales Committee for the Defence of the Shrewsbury building workers.

Sunstruck. (92 mins.) (U cert.) Dir. James Gilbert. Comedy about Welsh school teacher in Australia. With Harry Secombe, Maggie Fitzgibbon, John Meillon, Dawn Lake, Peter Whittle. p.c. Immigrant/Anglo-EMI, dist. MGM–EMI.

Yr Hen Dynnwr Lluniau (The Old Photographer). (33 mins.) Dir. Wil Aaron. Welsh drama-documentary. p.c. Bwrdd Ffilmiau Cymraeg. WFA.

Along the Way. (57 mins.) (U cert.) Dir. Tom Lyndon-Haynes, John Reeve. Welsh-set drama, with Jonny Ross, George Woodbridge, Nellie Griffiths. p.c. Junia/Barbara Woodhouse, dist. MGM–EMI.

1974   **Never Come Monday**. (50 mins.) Dir. Alan Mainwaring. Fiction. WAC-financed.

Chapels (Capeli). (27 mins.) Dir. Harley Jones. English and Welsh versions. Documentary. p.c. and dist. Bwrdd Ffilmiau Cymraeg (Welsh Film Board).

They Are. Dir. Geoff Thomas. Documentary.

Craftsmen of Dinorwic. (20 mins.) Dir. Romola Christopherson. Documentary. p.c. United Motion Pictures (London), with Central Office of Information and Dept. of the Environment; dist. Dept. of the Environment Film Library, Welsh Office Film Library.

This is the Life. (10 mins.) Dir. Clive Walley. Art film. WAC-financed. Dist. WAC.

| 1975 | **How Green Is My Valley**. (25 mins.) Welsh mining documentary. p.c. Central Office of Information/Norddeutscher Rundfunk, dist. Central Office of Information. |

There Was a Time. (24 mins.) Dir. Harley Jones, Glyndŵr Harris. Biography of musician Gerald Finzi. p.c. Newport College of Art. WAC-financed.

1976 **Aesthete's Foot**. (33 mins.) Dir. Chris Monger. Fiction. WAC-financed. Dist. WAC.

They Evict Gypsies. (25 mins.) Welsh documentary video. p.c. and dist. Cardiff Community Video Workshop.

One Hour to Zero. (55 mins.) (U cert.) Dir. Jeremy Summers. Welsh drama, with Jayne Collins, Toby Bridge, Andrew Ashby, Dudley Sutton. p.c. Charles Barker, dist. Children's Film Foundation.

Milford Fishermen. (38 mins.) Dir. Richard Watkins. Welsh documentary. (Includes footage of **Trawling out of Swansea on the** *Tenby Castle*, 1926/7, see 1927 entry).

Harry Tippin of Rhydyfro. (20 mins.) Dir. Geoff Thomas. Documentary. p.c. Newport Film School. WAC-financed.

Life Track. (6 mins.) Dir. Henry Lutman. Animation. p.c. Newport College of Art. WAC-financed.

The Thirteen Clocks. (20 mins.) Dir. Henry Lutman. Animated fiction. p.c. Newport College of Art. WAC-financed.

Whispers of Fear. (73 mins.) (X cert.) Dir. Harry Bromley-Davenport. Welsh-set psychological sex drama, with Ika Hindley, Charles Seely, William Jones. p.c. Sideline/Ian Merrick, dist. Carnaby.

1977 **Enough Cuts for a Murder**. (75 mins.) Dir. Chris Monger. Fiction feature.

Above Us the Earth. (85 mins.) (AA cert.) Dir. Karl Francis. Welsh drama-documentary, with Windsor Rees, Gwen Francis, p.c. and dist. British Film Institute Production Board. BFI Film and Video Library.

1978 **The Big Pit**. Documentary on Blaenafon mine. dist. National Coal Board.

Perceval Le Gallois (Perceval of Wales). (140 mins.) Dir. Eric Rohmer, France. French film about knight of Arthurian legend, with Fabrice Luchini (as Perceval), André Dussollier. p.c. Les Films du Losange/FR3/ARD/Gaumont/RAI (Italy).

1979 **Loose Ends**. (20 mins.) Dir. Steve Gough. Video. WAC financed. p.c. Cardiff Community Video Workshop, dist. CCVW.

Repeater. (78 mins.) Dir. Chris Monger. Drama. With Chris Abrahams, John Cassady, p.c. and dist. Chapter Film Workshop. BFI Film and Video Library.

Teisennau Mair. (60 mins.) Dir. Gareth Wynn Jones. Welsh fiction. p.c. Welsh Film Board.

The Corn is Green. Dir. George Cukor. Drama from Emlyn Williams's stage play, with Katharine Hepburn, Ian Saynor, Bill Fraser, Patricia Hayes, Toyah Willcox. p.c. Warner Bros., dist. Warners UK/US. (TV film but limited theatrical release in US.)

1980 **The Mouse and the Woman**. (105 mins.) Dir. Karl Francis. Welsh drama, with Dafydd Hywel, Karen Archer, Patricia Napier, Alan Devlin. p.c. Alvicar Films.

Rumours at the Miners' Fortnight. Documentary. p.c. Cardiff Community Video Workshop, dist. CCVW.

Walter Ego. (33 mins.) Dir. Tim Thornicroft. Drama, with Alan Sawford, Laurie McFadden, Chris Monger. p.c. Chapter Film Workshop, dist. CFW.

Your Hand in Mine. (26 mins.) Dir. Geoffrey Thomas. Welsh documentary. p.c. Scan Film Productions, dist. Scan Film Productions. WAC co-finance.

Voice Over. (110 mins.) Dir. Chris Monger. Drama, with Ian McNeice, Bish Nethercote. p.c. Chapter Video Film Workshop, dist. CFW.

The Secret Life of Fish. (39 mins.) Dir. Steve Gough. Welsh drama/fantasy. p.c. Chapter Film Workshop, dist. CFW.

Miners' Strike 1981. (45 mins.) Documentary. p.c. Cardiff Community Video Workshop. dist. CCVW.

Newid Gêr (Changing Gear). (45 mins.) Dir. Alan Clayton. Welsh-language fiction. p.c. and dist. Welsh Film Board.

Lips. (9 mins.) Dir. Lyn Skipworth. Welsh documentary/fantasy. p.c. Chapter Film Workshop, dist. CFW.

The Falls. (185 mins.) Dir. Peter Greenaway. Spoof documentary part-shot on the Llŷn Peninsula and Bardsey Island. 16 mm. copy available through BFI Film and Video Catalogue.

1981

Lager 11. (30 mins.) Dir. Les Mills. Welsh documentary. p.c. Chapter Film Workshop, dist. CFW.

APPENDICES

....

Here Comes the Bride. (30 mins.) Dir. Frances Bowyer. Documentary. p.c. Chapter Film Workshop, dist. CFW.

The Expression of Order at FF. (12 mins.) Documentary about Blaenau Ffestiniog. p.c. Huw Joshua and Gweld Video, dist. Gweld Video/Welsh Arts Council.

Tredegar Health Tape. (27 mins.) Documentary. p.c. Cardiff Community Video Workshop/Tredegar Hospital Action Committee.

Reporter. (25 mins.) Dir. Paul Jackson. Documentary. p.c. Chapter Film Workshop, dist. CFW.

So That You Can Live. (85 mins.) Welsh documentary. p.c. Cinema Action. BFI Film and Video Library.

Brecon Letter. (12 mins.) Video. p.c. Powys Video Project.

Another American Movie. Dir. Rowland Denning. Documentary. p.c. Chapter Film Workshop, dist. CFW.

Taxi. (28 mins.) Dir. Mali Evans. Drama. p.c. Chapter Film Workshop, dist. CFW.

Press Me Slowly, Kiss Me Quick. (15 mins.) Dir. Caroline Limmer. Fiction. p.c. Chapter Film Workshop, dist. CFW.

Snotface. (22 mins.) Dir. Mike Stubbs. Fiction. p.c. Chapter Film Workshop, dist. CFW.

The Green Wall. Dir. Catrin Hughes. Drama with Caroline Limmer. p.c. Chapter Film Workshop, dist. CFW.

Memoirs of a Pit Orchestra. Dir. Richard Watkins. Welsh drama-documentary, with Gareth Armstrong, Margaret John, David Lyn. p.c. Cineclair Films, dist. Welsh Arts Council.

Trisgel. Dir. Paul Turner. Celtic mythology/drama. Dist. Welsh Arts Council.

1982   **Political Annie's Off Again**. Video documentary. Prod. video Cardiff Community Video Workshop, dist. CCVW.

The Machine. (20 mins.) Dir. Christine Wilks. Experimental narrative. p.c. and dist. Chapter Film Workshop.

Programme for the Destruction of a Nuclear Family. Drama-doc. p.c. Chapter Video Workshop, dist. Chapter Video Workshop.

Giro City. (102 mins.) (AA cert.) Dir. Karl Francis. Welsh drama, with Glenda Jackson, Jon Finch, Kenneth Colley, Emrys James, Karen Archer. p.c. Silva Realm for Rediffusion and Channel Four.

Experience Preferred But Not Essential. (80 mins.) Dir. Peter Duffell. Welsh-set drama, with Elizabeth Edmonds, Ron Bain. p.c. Enigma/Goldcrest/Channel Four.

1983   **Sword of the Valiant**. (102 mins.) (PG cert.) Dir. Stephen Weeks. Arthurian drama in Celtic settings and shot in Wales and France. With Sean Connery, Miles O'Keeffe, Cyrielle Claire, Trevor Howard, Peter Cushing.

Wales – Heritage of a Nation. (26 mins.) Sponsored documentary. p.c. Collier-Marsland, dist. Wales Tourist Board/British Tourist Authority.

Contortions. Dir. Mike Stubbs. Welsh fiction, with Dane Gould, Robin Lyons. Dist. Cardiff Community Video Workshop.

The Big Meeting 1983. (45 mins.) Video documentary. p.c. Cardiff Community Video Workshop/Durham Union NUM. WAC-financed.

House of the Long Shadows. (101 mins.) (15 cert.) Dir. Peter Walker. Welsh-set horror, with Vincent Price, Christopher Lee, Peter Cushing, Desi Arnaz jun., John Carradine. p.c. Menahem Golan, Yoram Globus/London Cannon, dist. Cannon.

1984   **The Case for Coal**. Documentary. p.c. South Wales Miners' Video Project/Cardiff Community Video Workshop.

A Coal Mine in South Wales. Dir. Joachim Kreck. Documentary. British/German co-production.

True Love, Dare, Kiss or Promise. (20 mins.) Fiction. Dir. Caroline Limmer. p.c. Chapter Film Workshop.

Yr Alcoholig Llon (**The Happy Alcoholic**). Dir. Karl Francis. Welsh drama with Dafydd Hywel, Eluned Jones. Made for S4C but screened at London Film Festival, 1984.

Debased. (65 mins.) Dir. Tim Thornicroft. Drama. p.c. and dist. Chapter Film Workshop.

Johnny Be Good. Dir. Marc Evans. Drama. With Adam Crockett, Emyr Jenkins. Dist. WAC.

Something Else in the House. (20 mins.) Documentary. Dirs. Penny Stempel, Frances Bowyer. p.c. Red Flannel/Maerdy Women's Support Group.

1985   **I'll Be Here For All Time**. (25 mins.) Documentary. p.c. Boadicea Films, dist. Boadicea Films, Penarth.

Whose Law? (27 mins.) Dir. Penny Stempel, Chris Rushton. Documentary. p.c. South Wales Miners Video Project. Dist. Chapter Community Video Workshop.

The Black Cauldron. (80 mins.) Dirs. Ted Berman/Richard Rich. Animation feature based on *Mabinogion* folk tales. p.c. Disney, dist. Disney.

1986 **A Certain Mr Smith.** Dir. Penny Stempel. Fiction. WAC-financed.

In the National Interest. (52 mins.) Dir. Penny Stempel and Chris Rushton. Documentary. p.c. and dist. Chapter Video Workshop, made with other workshops in Britain.

Ceiber: The Greatest Improvisers in the World. (45 mins.) Documentary. p.c. and dist. Cardiff Community Video Workshop.

Rhosyn a Rhith (Coming Up Roses). (93 mins.) (PG cert.) Dir. Stephen Bayly. Comedy, with Dafydd Hywel, Iola Gregory, Olive Michael, W. J. Phillips. Made for S4C but released through the Cannon cinema circuit.

Milwr Bychan (Boy Soldier). (100 mins.) (15 cert.) Welsh drama. Dir. Karl Francis. With Richard Lynch, Bernard Latham, Dafydd Hywel, James Donnelly, Timothy Lyn. Made for S4C but released on Cannon cinema circuit.

It Ain't Necessarily So. (20 mins.) Documentary. Chapter Film Workshop group production during D. A. Pennebaker residency.

The Original Cowboys Were Welshmen. (30 mins.) Drama. Chapter Film Workshop group production during D. A. Pennebaker residency.

Eyeballs Against the Windscreen. (30 mins.) Dir. Dane Gould. Drama with Dane Gould, Stephen Johnson, Helen Edwards, Debbie Debris. p.c. Chapter Film Workshop.

Man Act. (14 mins.) Dir. Mike Stubbs. Drama based on stage performances. p.c. and dist. Chapter Film Workshop.

Past Caring. Dir. Richard Eyre. Drama, with Emlyn Williams, Denholm Elliott, Connie Booth, Madoline Thomas, Joan Greenwood. Shown at London Film Festival.

1987 **On the Black Hill.** (117 mins.) Dir. Andrew Grieve. Welsh borders drama. With Mike Gwilym, Robert Gwilym, Bob Peck, Gemma Jones. p.c. British Film Institute Production Board/British Screen and Film Four International.

Girls' Night Out. (6 mins.) Dir. Joanna Quinn. Animation. p.c. Middlesex Polytechnic, dist. Chapter Film Workshop.

Goodnight Godbless. Dir. John Eyres. Welsh murder thriller, with Emma Sutton, Frank Rozelaar Green.

Tom Jones the Man. Dir. John Hessey. Drama-doc. p.c. and dist. Chapter Film Workshop.

1988 **Degrees of Blindness.** (19 mins.) Animation/pixillation. Dir. Cerith Wyn Evans. With Michael Clark, Leigh Bowery, Tilda Swinton. dist. BFI.

Pirates. Dir. Julian Richards. Drama, with Simon Foy, Graeme Gordon.

Zombie UB40. (40 mins.) Dir. Christine Wilks. Fiction. p.c. and dist. Chapter Film Workshop.

Soapless. (40 mins.) Dir. Mike Stubbs. Fiction. p.c. and dist. Chapter Film Workshop.

Who Comes First? (15 mins.) Dir. Jill Nelmes. p.c. and dist. Chapter Film Workshop.

Castell Cant (Century City). (12 mins.) (Chapter Workshop group production) Animation. S4C/Channel 4 but some cinema showings.

1989   **I'm British But** . . . (10 mins.) Dir. Gurinder Chadha. Documentary, set partly in Wales, dist. BFI.

1988–9   **Alternative Fringe** (3 mins.) **Fantastic Person** (4 mins.) **Fatty Issues** (3 mins.). Dir. Candy Guard. All animated comedies shown at film festivals. p.c. Channel Four/S4C.

1990   **O.M.** (90 mins.) (PG cert.) Dir. Emlyn Williams. Welsh drama, with Bryn Fôn. p.c. Ffilm Cymru–S4C. Dist. by Ffilm Cymru in cinemas.

Ozone Alert. (6 mins.) Dir. Jane Hubbard. Chapter Film Workshop animation. Dist. CFW.

Body Beautiful. (13 mins.) Dir. Joanna Quinn. Animation comedy. p.c. S4C/Channel 4, but seen in cinemas.

1991   **Un Nos Ola Leuad (One Full Moon)** (98 mins.) (15 cert.) Dir. Endaf Emlyn. Welsh drama, with Dyfan Roberts, Tudur Roberts. p.c. Ffilm Cymru/Gaucho films, dist. BFI.

Elenya. (81 mins.) Dir. Steve Gough, with Pascale Delafouge Jones, Sue Jones-Davies. S4C/BFI/Frankfurter Produktions, Germany. p.c. Gareth Lloyd Williams. Made in English and Welsh.

Rebecca's Daughters. Dir. Karl Francis. Welsh period drama, with Paul Rhys, Joely Richardson, Peter O'Toole, Dafydd Hywel. p.c. BBC and Chris Sievernick, dist. Mayfair Entertainment.

The Joke Works. (35 mins.) Dir. Graham Jones/Jeremy Bubb. Fiction. p.c. and dist. Chapter Filmworks (formerly Chapter Film Workshop).

The Smell of Human. (11 mins.) Dir. Dane Gould. Drama, with G. Brennan Fox. p.c. and dist. Chapter Filmworks.

Return to Paradise. (20 mins.) Dir. Jeremy Bubb. Fiction. p.c. and dist. Chapter Filmworks.

Salvation Guaranteed. Dir. Karen Ingham. Fiction. p.c. and dist. BFI.

Cowboys. (18 mins.) Dir. Phil Mulloy. Series of six three-minute animated comedies for Channel Four. Screened at 1992 International Animation Festival Cardiff. BFI.

1992   **Eyewitness**. (27 mins.) Dir. Christine Wilks. With Alison Redford. p.c. and dist. Chapter Filmworks.

Hedd Wyn – The Armageddon Poet. (111 mins.) Dir. Paul Turner. Welsh, biographical drama with Huw Garmon, Sue Roderick, Judith Humphreys, Nia Dryhurst. p.c. Shân Davies/Pendefig. Made for S4C but distributed in cinemas.

Cylch Gwaed (In the Blood). (70 mins.) Dir. Timothy Lyn. Welsh drama with Rhys Richards, John Ogwen, Nerys Lloyd. p.c. Ffilmiau'r Nant for S4C. Dist. S4C but shown in cinema at festivals.

Sprago, Lago a'r Sunshine Miners. (26 mins.) Dir. Emyr Jenkins. Mine closure documentary. p.c. Emyr Jenkins/Y Gweithdy Fideo (Welsh-language video dept. at Chapter Arts Centre).

Cwm Hyfryd (Beautiful Valley). Dir. Paul Turner. Drama with Philip Howe for S4C but seen in south Wales valleys cinemas.

Dando's Brilliantine. (11 mins.) Dir. Philip John. Drama with Ranjit Krishnamma, John Raphael Jones, Caroline Bunce. p.c. Debbie Pearce/Newport Film School. Dist. Philip John.

Under Milk Wood. (50 mins.) Dir. Les Orton. Animation version of Dylan Thomas's play. p.c. Siriol Productions.

Gadael Lenin (Leaving Lenin). (90 mins.) Dir. Endaf Emlyn. Comedy-drama set in St Petersburg with Welsh characters. With Sharon Morgan, Wyn Bowen Harries, Ifan Huw Dafydd, Steffan Trevor, Shelley Rees. p.c. Pauline Williams/Gaucho Films for S4C (cinema dist. First Features).

The Princess and the Goblin. Animation feature, co-produced with Hungary. p.c. Siriol Productions (co-director Les Orton). For S4C but shown in cinemas at festivals.

1993

Hard as Hell. (10 mins.) Dir. Michael Mort. Animation. p.c. and dist. Newport Film School.

Love Bites. Dir. Dane Gould. With Athena Constantine, G. Brennan Fox. p.c. and dist. Chapter Filmworks.

Cranc. (26 mins.) Comedy-drama. Dir. Rhys Powys, for CYFLE, Welsh directors' training scheme.

Recipe for Success. (10 mins.) Comedy. Dir. Graham Jones. p.c. and dist. Cardiff Filmworks.

Dafydd. (50 mins.) Dir. Ceri Sherlock. Welsh–Dutch co-production drama, set in Holland, with Welsh characters. With Richard Harrington, William Thomas. p.c. Gareth Rowlands for S4C but seen in cinemas at festivals.

Divertimento No. 2: Love Song and **Divertimento No. 4: Life Study** (both 3 mins.) Dir. Clive Walley. Abstract animation films made for S4C but shown at 1994 International Animation Festival, Cardiff.

Sound of Music. (11 mins.) Animation comedy. Dir. Phil Mulloy. Prod. Spectre Films. Made for Channel Four but shown at 1994 International Animation Festival, Cardiff.

Thou Shalt Not Kill. (3 mins.) Animation comedy. Dir. Phil Mulloy. Prod. Spectre Films. Made for Channel Four but shown at 1994 International Animation Festival, Cardiff.

1994

Britannia. (5 mins.) Dir. Joanna Quinn. Animation for Channel 4 and S4C.

Deadly Advice. (15 cert.) Dir. Mandie Fletcher. Welsh-set comedy, with Jane Horrocks, Jonathan Pryce, Brenda Fricker, Imelda Staunton, Edward Woodward, John Mills, Hywel Bennett.

Second Best. Dir. Chris Menges. Drama set on Welsh borders. With William Hurt and Jane Horrocks.

The Englishman Who Went Up a Hill and Came Down a Mountain. Dir. Chris Monger. Comedy with Hugh Grant, Kenneth Griffith, Colm Meaney, Ian Hart. p.c. Parallax.

FILMOGRAPHY

Note

The years for film credits are generally the release dates in the country of origin, but some may be production dates. The cinema credits, listed first, are as comprehensive as possible.

I have relied, chiefly, on *The British Film Companion 1895–1985* by Denis Gifford, various issues of the *Halliwell Film and Tele Guide*, *The International Film Encyclopedia* by Ephraim Katz (1982 edition) and Rachael Low's *History of the British Film* series and credits supplied by actors' agents. Television credits are selective but should embrace most of the individual's important work.

Where two film titles are given in English, the first title is for the British release, the second is for the US release.

This section also includes notes on current availability of films by silent film stars Ivor Novello, Gareth Hughes and Queenie Thomas, and shorts directed by William Haggar.

Actors

Stanley Baker   Undercover (1943), All Over the Town (1949), Your Witness/Home to Danger (1950), Cloudburst (1951), Captain Horatio Hornblower (1951), Whispering Smith Hits London (1952), The Cruel Sea (1953), The Red Beret/Paratrooper (1953), The Telltale Heart (as narrator) (short) (1953), Hell Below Zero (1954), Knights of the Round Table (as Mordred) (1954), The Good Die Young (1954), Beautiful Stranger/Twist of Fate (1954), Alexander the Great (as Attalus) (1955), Helen of Troy (as Achilles) (1955), A Hill in Korea (1956), Richard III (as Henry Tudor) (1955), Child in the House (1956), Checkpoint (1956), Campbell's Kingdom (1957), Hell Drivers (1957), Violent Playground (1958), Sea Fury (1958), The Angry Hills (1959), Yesterday's Enemy (1959), Jet Storm (1959), Blind Date/Chance Meeting (1960), Hell is a City (1960), The Criminal/Concrete Jungle (1960), The Guns of Navarone (1961), Sodoma and Gomorra (Sodom and Gomorrah) (Italy, 1962), A Prize of Arms (1962), The Man Who Finally Died (1962), Eve/Eva (1962), In the French Style (1963), Zulu (as Lt. John Chard) (1963), Dingaka (1965), Sands of the Kalahari (1965), One of Them is Brett (short, narrator only, 1965), Accident (1967), Robbery (1967), Where's Jack? (1968), La Ragazza con la Pistola (Girl with a Pistol) (Italy, 1968), The Games (1969), Grigsby (1969), The Italian Job (1969), Popsy Pop/The Butterfly Affair (France, 1970), The Last Grenade (1970), Perfect Friday (1970), Una Lucertola con la Pelle di Donna/A Lizard in a Woman's Skin – Schizoid (Italy, 1971), Innocent Bystanders (1972), Zorro (1975), Petita Jimenez (Spain, 1975), Orzowi, Il Figlio della Savana (France) (1976).

TV: The Creature (BBC, 1955), Jayne Eyre (as Rochester, BBC, 1956), The Squeeze (BBC, 1960), Return to the Rhondda (narrator only) (TWW, documentary, 1965), The Tormentors (ATV, 1966), Code Name: Hereclitus (1967), Fade Out (HTV, 1968), Graceless Go I (HTV, 1974), The Changeling (1974), Robinson Crusoe (BBC, 1974), How Green Was My Valley (as Gwilym Morgan) (BBC, 1976).

Hywel Bennett   The Family Way (1966), Marito e mio e l'Ammazzo quando mi pare (Italy, 1967), Twisted Nerve (1968), The Virgin Soldiers (1969), Loot (1970), The Buttercup Chain (1970), Endless Night (1971), Percy (1971), Alice's Adventures in Wonderland (1972), The Love Ban (1972), Towards the Morning (short, 1981).

TV: Dr Who (BBC series, 1963/4), Dr Who (BBC serial, one episode only, 1965), Where the Buffalo Roam (BBC, 1966), The Sweeney (BBC, 1975/8, series-guest), Pennies from Heaven (BBC, 1978), Tinker, Tailor, Soldier, Spy (BBC serial, 1978/9), Malice

Aforethought (BBC serial, 1979), Shelley/Return of Shelley (various series from 1979–92), Artemis 81 (BBC, 1981), Frankie and Johnnie (1985), Noises Off (1985), The Twilight Zone (CBS, ITV, one episode, 1985/6), Tickets for the Titanic (1987), Joseph Conrad's Secret Agent (1988), A Mind To Kill (English) and Noson yr Heliwr (Welsh version) (S4C, Yorkshire TV, 1991).

Richard Burton	The Last Days of Dolwyn/Woman of Dolwyn (1949), Now Barabbas was a Robber (1949), Waterfront/Waterfront Woman (1950), The Woman With No Name/Her Panelled Door (1951), Green Grow the Rushes (1951), My Cousin Rachel (US, 1952), The Desert Rats (US, 1953), The Robe (US, 1953), Demetrius and the Gladiators (1954), Prince of Players (US, 1955), Tuesday's Children (1955 short, narration only), The Rains of Ranchipur (1955), Alexander the Great (1956), Sea Wife (1957), Amère Victoire/Bitter Victory (France, 1958), March to Aldermaston (1958, short, narration only, documentary), Look Back in Anger (1959), The Bramble Bush (US, 1960), Ice Palace (US, 1960), The Valiant Years (narration only, Columbia, 1960), A Midsummer Night's Dream (Czechoslovakia, 1961, dubbed voice only), The Longest Day (US, 1962), Cleopatra (US/UK, 1963), Inheritance (1963, short, narration only), Zulu (1963, narration only), The VIPs (1963), Becket (US/UK, 1964), The Night of the Iguana (1964), Hamlet (filmed Broadway play) (US, 1964), The Days of Wilfred Owen (1965, short, narration only), What's New Pussycat? (US/France, 1965), The Sandpiper (1965), The Spy Who Came in from the Cold (1965), Who's Afraid of Virginia Woolf? (US, 1966), The Taming of the Shrew (US/Italy, 1967), Doctor Faustus (1967), The Comedians (US/France, 1967), The Rime of the Ancient Mariner (1968, narration only, documentary), A Wall in Jerusalem (1968, documentary), Boom! (US/UK, 1968), Candy (US/France/Italy, 1968), Where Eagles Dare (1968), Staircase (US, 1969), Anne of the Thousand Days (1970), Raid on Rommel (US, 1971), Villain (1971), Hammersmith is Out (US, 1971), Under Milk Wood (1971), The Battle of Sutjeska (as Marshal Tito) (Yugoslavia, 1972), Bluebeard (Hungary, 1972), The Assassination of Trotsky (France/Italy, 1972), Rappresaglia/Massacre in Rome (Italy, 1973), Il Viaggio/The Voyage (Italy, 1974), The Klansman (US, 1974), Jackpot (US, 1975), Exorcist II: The Heretic (US, 1977), Equus (US, 1977), The Medusa Touch (US, 1978), The Wild Geese (1978), Time After Time (US, 1979), Sergeant Steiner/Breakthrough (West Germany, 1979), Lovespell (formerly Tristan and Isolte, 1979), Circle of Two (1980), Absolution (1981, made 1978), Wagner (1983), 1984 (1984).
TV:	Wuthering Heights (as Heathcliff) (US, 1958), Borrowed Pasture (voice only, BBC, 1958), A Subject of Scandal and Concern (BBC, 1960), The Fifth Column (US, 1960), The Tempest (as Prospero) (1960), Dylan (narrator, short, TWW, 1961), Divorce His, Divorce Hers (US, 1973), Walk with Destiny (as Churchill; US title: The Gathering Storm) (NBC, BBC, 1974), Brief Encounter (ITC, Central, 1976), The Fall Guy (1982), Alice in Wonderland (1983), Ellis Island (1984).
Meredith Edwards	A Run For Your Money (1949), The Blue Lamp (1950), The Magnet (1950), Midnight Episode (1950), There is Another Sun (1951), The Lavender Hill Mob (1951), Where No Vultures Fly/Ivory Hunter (1951), The Last Page/Manbait (1952), Gift Horse/Glory at Sea (1952), Girdle of Gold (1952), The Gambler and the Lady (1952), The Great Game (1953), The Cruel Sea (1953), A Day to Remember (1953), The Conquest of Everest (1953, narrator only), Meet Mr Malcolm (1954), Devil on Horseback (1954), Burnt Evidence (1954), Final Appointment (1954), Mad About Men (1954), To Dorothy a Son/Cash on Delivery (1954), Mask of Dust/Race for Life (1954), Peril for the Guy/Lost Tears for Simon (1956), The Long Arm/The Third Key (1956), Circus Friends (1956),

APPENDIX 3

Filmography

Town on Trial (1957), The Supreme Secret (1958 short, reissued in 1965 as: God Speaks Today), Escapement/The Electric Monster (1958), Dunkirk (1958), Law and Disorder (1958), Tiger Bay (1959), The Trials of Oscar Wilde/The Man with the Green Carnation (1960), Doctor in Love (1960), Flame in the Streets (1961), Only Two Can Play (1962), This Is My Street (1962), The Great St Trinians Train Robbery (1966), Gulliver's Travels (1981).

TV: The Day's Mischief (BBC, 1957), Under Milk Wood (BBC, 1957), 11-Plus (BBC, 1957), One Step Beyond (Associated Rediffusion, 1961–2), The Saint (ATV, 1963–8), Great British Preachers (as Christmas Evans, BBC, 1963), Adam Adamant Lives! (series, BBC, 1967), Brad (Treason) (BBC, 1968), The Inheritors (HTV, 1974), Sky (HTV, 1976), Off to Philadelphia in the Morning (BBC, 1978), The Life and Times of David Lloyd George (BBC, 1981), Y Gwrthwynebwyr/The Opposers (HTV, 1978) Hawkmoor (BBC, 1982), The Angry Earth (S4C, 1989), The Old Devils (BBC, 1992), Gwanwyn a'r Gwin (Spring and Port Wine) (S4C, 1992) Eira Cynta'r Gaeaf (Christmas Stallion) (S4C, 1992), Fallen Sons (BBC Wales, 1993), Tan ar y Comin (Gypsy Fires/Fire on the Common) (S4C, 1993).

Clifford Evans Ourselves Alone (1936), Calling the Tune (1936), The Mutiny of the Elsinore (1937), Mademoiselle Docteur (1937), Thirteen Men and a Gun (UK/Italy, 1938), At the Villa Rose/House of Mystery (1939), The Luck of the Navy/North Sea Patrol (1939), His Brother's Keeper (1939), The House of the Arrow/Castle of Crimes (1940), The Proud Valley (1940), Fingers (1940), Freedom Radio/A Voice in the Night (1941), Love on the Dole (1941), Penn of Pennsylvania/The Courageous Mr Penn (title role) (1941), The Saint Meets the Tiger (1941), Suspected Person (1942), The Foreman Went to France/Somewhere in France (1942), The Flemish Farm (1943), The Silver Darlings (also co-directed) (1947), While I Live/Dream of Olwen (1947), The Twenty Questions Murder Mystery/Murder on the Air (1950), Valley of Song (1953), Escape Route/I'll Get You (1953), The Straw Man (1953), Solution by Phone (1954), The Gilded Cage (1955), Passport to Treason (1956), At the Stroke of Nine (1957), Face in the Night/Menace in the Night (1957), The Heart Within (1957), Violent Playground (1958), Man With a Dog (short) (1958), SOS Pacific (1959), Curse of the Werewolf (1961), Kiss of the Vampire (1963), The Long Ships (1964), Twist of Sand (1967), One Brief Summer (1970).

TV: Stryker of the Yard, The Power Game (ABC, originally The Plane Makers), The Man Out There (ABC Armchair Theatre, 1961), One Step Beyond (Associated Rediffusion, ABC America, 1961–2), Out of This World (ABC, 1962), War and Peace (Granada, 1963), The Avengers (ABC, three episodes between 1963 and 1969), The Prisoner (ATV, 1967), The Champions (ATV 1968–9), The Extremist (1984).

Iola Gregory Rhosyn a Rhith/Coming Up Roses (S4C, 1985, cinema release), Stormydd Awst (August Storms) (S4C, 1987, limited cinema screenings), Joni Jones (S4C, 1982), Ŵyn i'r Lladdfa (Lambs to the Slaughter) (S4C, 1983), Aderyn Papur/And Pigs Might Fly (S4C, 1983, shown in cinemas at festivals), Hualan (Fetters) (S4C, 1983), Tra Bo Dwy (In Two Minds) (S4C, 1984), Byw yn Rhydd (Jones) (S4C, 1984), Y Gwaith (The Works) (S4C/Channel Four, 1985), Teulu Helga (Helga's Family) (S4C, 1985), Siwan (1986), Twll o Le (A Dump of a Place) (S4C, 1986), Ac Eto Nid Myfi (And Yet Again Not I) (S4C, 1987), The Triple Net (S4C/Channel Four, 1987), The Country Girl (BBC, 1988), Yr Alltud (The Exile) (S4C, 1989), Dŵr a Thân (Fire and Water) (S4C, 1991), Fallen Sons (BBC, 1993).

Hugh Griffith Neutral Port (1940), The Silver Darlings (1947), London Belongs to Me/Dulcimer Street

(1948), The Three Weird Sisters (1948), So Evil My Love (1948), The Last Days of Dolwyn/Woman of Dolwyn (as the Minister) (1949), The First Gentleman/Affairs of a Rogue (1948), Scrapbook for 1933 (voice only), A Run for your Money (1949), Kind Hearts and Coronets (1949), Gone to Earth/The Wild Heart (1950), Laughter in Paradise (1951), The Galloping Major (1951), The Beggar's Opera (1953), The Titfield Thunderbolt (1953), The Sleeping Tiger (1954), Passage Home (1955), The Good Companions (1956), Lucky Jim (1957), Ben Hur (as Sheikh Ilderim) (US, 1959), The Story on Page One (US, 1960), The Day They Robbed the Bank of England (1961), Exodus (US, 1961), The Counterfeit Traitor (US, 1962), The Inspector/Lisa (US/UK, 1962), Term of Trial (1962), Mutiny on the Bounty (US, 1962), Tom Jones (as Squire Western) (1963), Hide and Seek (1964), The Bargee (1964), The Amorous Adventures of Moll Flanders (1965), How to Steal a Million (US, 1966), Danger Grows Wild (US, 1966), Marito e mio e l'ammazzo quando mi pare (Italy, 1967), Oh Dad, Poor Dad, Mama's Hung You in the Closet and I'm Feeling So Sad (US, 1967), The Sailor from Gibraltar (1967), Cintura di Castità (Italy, 1967), The Chastity Belt (1967), Oliver! (1968), The Fixer (US, 1968), Start the Revolution Without Me (US, 1970), Cry of the Banshee (1970), Wuthering Heights (1970), The Abominable Dr Phibes (1971), Whoever Slew Auntie Roo? (1971), I Racconti di Canterbury/The Canterbury Tales (Italy, 1972), Dr Phibes Rises Again (1972), The Final Programme (1973), Take Me High (1973), Che?/What? (Italy/France, 1973), Crescete e Moltiplicatevi (Italy, 1973), Luther (UK/US, 1973), Craze (1974), Legend of the Werewolf (1975), Loving Cousins (Italy, 1976), The Passover Plot (Israel/US, 1976), Casanova and Co. (Austria/Germany/Italy, 1977), Joseph Andrews (1977), The Last Remake of Beau Geste (US, 1977), The Hound of the Baskervilles (1978).

TV: Quatermass II (BBC, 1955), Now Let Him Go (ABC, 1957), Clochemerle (BBC, 1972), Grand Slam (BBC, 1978).

Kenneth Griffith Love on the Dole (1941), The Farmer's Wife (1941), The Shop at Sly Corner (1947), Bond Street (1948), Forbidden (1949), Blue Scar (1949), Water Front/Waterfront Woman (1950), High Treason (1951), The Starfish (short, 1952), Thirty-six Hours/Terror Street (1954), The Green Buddha (1954), Track the Man Down (1955), The Prisoner (1955), 1984 (1956), The Baby and the Battleship (1956), Private's Progress (1956), Tiger in the Smoke (1957), Lucky Jim (1957), The Naked Truth/Your Past is Showing (1957), Brothers in Law (1957), Blue Murder at St Trinians (1957), A Night to Remember (1958), I'm All Right, Jack (1959), Tiger Bay (1959), Circus of Horrors (1959), Carleton-Browne of the FO/Man in a Cocked Hat (1959), Espresso Bongo (1959), Libel (1959), Snowball (1960), A French Mistress (1960), Suspect (1960), Rag Doll (1961), The Frightened City (1961), Payroll (1961), The Painted Smile (1962), Only Two Can Play (1962), We Joined the Navy (1962), Heavens Above (1963), Rotten to the Core (1965), The Whisperers (1966), The Bobo (1967), Great Catherine (1967), Decline and Fall of a Birdwatcher (1968), The Lion in Winter (1968), The Assassination Bureau (1969), Jane Eyre (1971), Revenge (1971), The House in Nightmare Park (1973), Callan (1974), S.P.Y.S. (1974), Sky Riders (1976), The Wild Geese (1978), The Sea Wolves (1980), Four Weddings and a Funeral (1994), The Englishman Who Went Up a Hill and Came Down a Mountain (1994).

TV (as actor only): One (Associated Rediffusion, 1956), War and Peace (Granada, 1963), The Prisoner (one episode, 1967/8), The Prison (Thames, 1975), Perils of Pendragon (series, BBC, 1975), Bitter, Broken Bread (as Idris Davies in the 'Wales! Wales?' series, BBC, 1983).

TV (as actor and presenter):	The Widow's Soldiers (BBC, 1972), Hang Up Your Brightest Colours (ATV, 1973, first screened BBC Wales, 1993), Bus to Bosworth (acted and co-wrote) (BBC, 1975), Napoleon – The Man on the Rock (Thames, 1975), Sons of the Blood (BBC, 1977), Curious Journey (HTV, 1977), The Sun's Bright Child (Edmund Kean drama-doc, Thames, 1978), Black as Hell, Thick as Grass (BBC, 1979), A Touch of Churchill – a Touch of Hitler (Cecil Rhodes drama-doc, BBC, 1980), Clive of India (Channel Four, 1981), The Light (Channel Four, David Ben Gurion drama-doc, 1988), Zola Budd (BBC, 1989), The Most Valuable Englishman Ever (Tom Paine drama-doc, BBC, 1982), Roger Casement – Heart of Darkness (BBC, Timewatch series, 1992).
Screen biographies/ documentaries on Griffith:	The Public's Right to Know (Thames, 1974), The Tenby Poisoner (Channel Four, 1992).
Edmund Gwenn	The Real Thing at Last (1916), Unmarried (1920), The Skin Game (silent, 1920), How He Lied to Her Husband (1931), The Skin Game (sound, 1931), Hindle Wakes (1931), Money for Nothing (1932), Frail Women (1932), Condemned to Death (1932), Tell Me Tonight (UK/Germany, 1932), Channel Crossing (1933), Marooned (1933), Smithy (1933), The Good Companions (1933), Cash/For Love or Money (1933), Early to Bed (UK/Germany, 1933), Friday the Thirteenth (1933), Waltzes from Vienna/Strauss's Great Waltz (1934), The Admiral's Secret (1934), Java Head (1934), Passing Shadows (1934), Warn London (1934), Father and Son (1934), Spring in the Air (1934), The Bishop Misbehaves (US, 1935), Sylvia Scarlett (US, 1936), The Walking Dead (US, 1936), Anthony Adverse (1936), Mad Holiday (1936), Laburnum Grove (1936), Parnell (1937), A Yank at Oxford (1938), South Riding (1938), Penny Paradise (1938), Cheer Boys Cheer (1939), An Englishman's Home/Madmen of Europe (1939).
	From 1940 onwards all Gwenn films – except where indicated – made in the US: The Earl of Chicago (1940), The Doctor Takes a Wife (1940), Mad Men of Europe (1940), Pride and Prejudice (1940), Foreign Correspondent (1940), Cheers for Miss Bishop (1941), Scotland Yard (1941), The Devil and Miss Jones (1941), One Night in Lisbon (1941), Charley's Aunt (1941), A Yank at Eton (1942), The Meanest Man in the World (1943), Lassie Come Home (1943), Forever and a Day (1943), Between Two Worlds (1944), The Keys of the Kingdom (1945), Bewitched (1945), Dangerous Partners (1945), She Went to the Races (1945), Of Human Bondage (1946), Undercurrent (1946), Miracle on 34th Street (1947), Life With Father (1947), Green Dolphin Street (1947), Thunder in the Valley (1947), Apartment for Peggy (1948), Hills of Home (1948), Challenge to Lassie (1949), A Woman of Distinction (1950), Pretty Baby (1950), Mister 880 (1950), Peking Express (1952), Sally and Saint Anne (1952), Bonzo Goes to College (1952), Les Misérables (1952), Something for the Birds (1952), Mister Scoutmaster (1953), The Bigamist (1953), Them (1954), The Student Prince (1954), The Trouble With Harry (1955), It's a Dog's Life (1955), Calabuch/The Rocket from Calabuch (Spain, 1956).
Lyn Harding	The Barton Mystery (1920), A Bachelor Husband (1920), When Knighthood Was In Flower (as Henry VIII, US, 1921), Les Misérables (as Jean Valjean, short in 'Tense Moments with Great Authors' series, 1922), Yolanda (US, 1924), Further Adventures of the Flag Lieutenant (1927), Land of Hope and Glory (1927), The Speckled Band (1931), The Constant Nymph (1933), Wild Boy (1934), The Lash (1934), The Man Who Changed His Name (1934), The Triumph of Sherlock Holmes (1935), Escape Me Never (1935), Spy of Napoleon (as Bismarck, 1936), The Invader/An Old Spanish Custom (1936), Fire Over England (1937), Knight Without Armour (1937), Underneath the

Arches (1937), Please Teacher (1937), Silver Blaze/Murder at the Baskervilles (1937), The Mutiny of the Elsinore (1937), Goodbye Mr Chips (1939), The Missing People (1939), The Prime Minister (1941).

Anthony Hopkins The White Bus (short, 1967), The Lion in Winter (as Prince Richard) (1968), Hamlet (as Claudius) (1969), The Looking Glass War (1970), When Eight Bells Toll (1971), Young Winston (as Lloyd George) (1972), A Doll's House (1973), The Girl from Petrovka (US, 1974), Juggernaut (US, 1974), Audrey Rose (US, 1977), A Bridge Too Far (1977), International Velvet (1978), Magic (1978), The Elephant Man (US, 1980), A Change Of Seasons (US, 1980), The Bounty (as Captain Bligh) (1984), 84 Charing Cross Road (US, 1986), The Good Father (1986), The Dawning (1989), A Chorus of Disapproval (1989), Silence of the Lambs (as Hannibal Lecter) (US, 1991), Freejack (US, 1991), Spotswood (Australia, 1991), Howards End (1991), Dracula: The Untold Story (as Van Helsing) (1991), Chaplin (1992), Remains of the Day (1993), The Trial (1993), Shadowlands (1994), The Innocent (1994), August (actor/director, 1994).

TV: The Three Sisters (BBC, 1969), Danton (title role) (BBC, 1970), The Great Inimitable Mr Dickens (title role) (1970), Uncle Vanya (BBC, 1970), Hearts and Flowers (BBC, 1970), Decision to Burn (YTV, 1971), Poet Game (BBC, 1972), War and Peace (as Pierre) (BBC, 1972), The Edwardians (as Lloyd George) (BBC, 1972), QB VII (Columbia TV, US, 1974), Find Me (BBC, 1974), The Childhood Friend (BBC, 1974), Possessions (Granada, 1974), The Arcata Promise (YTV, 1974), All Creatures Great and Small (BBC, 1974), Dark Victory (NBC, Universal, US, 1976), The Lindbergh Kidnapping Case (NBC, Columbia, 1976), Victory at Entebbe (ABC, US, 1976), Kean (title role) (1978), The Bunker (as Hitler) (CBS/Time-Life, 1980), Mayflower (CBS, 1980), Peter and Paul (MCA, US, 1981), Othello (BBC, 1981), Little Eyolf (BBC, 1982), The Hunchback of Notre Dame (as Quasimodo) (CBS/Columbia, US, 1982), A Married Man (LWT series, for Channel Four, 1983), Strangers and Brothers (BBC, 1984), Arch of Triumph (CBC, HTV, 1985), Mussolini: The Rise and Fall of Il Duce (HBO, RAI/Antenne 2, 1985), Guilty Conscience (CBS, US, 1985), Hollywood Wives (ABC, Warners, 1985), Blunt (BBC, 1985), Across the Lake (BBC, 1988), Heartland (BBC Wales, 1989), One Man's War (1989), The Tenth Man (CBS, US, 1989), Great Expectations (as Magwitch) (HTV, 1990), Selected Exits (BBC Wales, 1993).

Donald Houston A Girl Must Live (1941), The Blue Lagoon (1949), A Run For Your Money (1949), Dance Hall (1950), My Death is a Mockery (1952), Crow Hollow (1952), The Red Beret/Paratrooper (1953), Small Town Story (1953), The Great Game (1953), The Large Rope (1953), Doctor in the House (1954), The Happiness of Three Women (1954), Devil's Point (1954), The Flaw (1955), Doublecross (1956), Find the Lady (1956), The Girl in the Picture (1957), Yangtse Incident/Battle Hell (1957), The Surgeon's Knife (1957), Every Valley (documentary, as narrator) (1957), The Man Upstairs (1958), A Question of Adultery (1958), Room at the Top (1958), Danger Within (1959), Letter for Wales (documentary, as narrator) (1960), The Mark (1961), The 300 Spartans (US, 1962), The Longest Day (US, 1962), Twice Round the Daffodils (1962), The Prince and the Pauper (1962), Maniac (1962), Doctor in Distress (1963), Carry on Jack (1963), 633 Squadron (US/UK, 1964), A Study in Terror/Fog (1965), The Viking Queen (1967), Where Eagles Dare (1968), My Lover, My Son (US/UK, 1970), The Bushbaby (1970), Don't You Cry (1970), Tales That Witness Madness (1973), Sunstruck (1973), Voyage of the Damned (1976), The Sea Wolves (1980).

TV: Under Milk Wood (BBC, 1957), Underground (ABC Armchair Theatre, 1958), The Primitives (ATV, Sunday Mystery Theatre, 1964), Out of the Unknown (BBC, one episode, 1965), The Trial and Error of Colonel Winchip (ATV, 1967), Moonbase 3 (BBC series, 1973).

Glyn Houston The Blue Lamp (1950), Girdle of Gold (1952), The Great Game (1953), The Cruel Sea (1953), River Beat (1954), The Sleeping Tiger (1954), The Happiness of Three Women (1954), Payroll (1960), Flame in the Streets (1961), Emergency (1962), Solo for Sparrow (1962), Panic (1963), One Way Pendulum (1964), The Secret of Blood Island (1965), Invasion (1965), Headline Hunters (1968), The Waiting Room (short, 1977), The Sea Wolves (1980).

TV: Deadline Midnight (series, ATV, 1960/1), The Primitives (ATV Sunday Mystery Theatre, 1964), Murder Reported (BBC Softly, Softly series, 1966), Where the Buffalo Roam (BBC, 1966), Dr Who (BBC, one episode, 1977), Better Days (HTV, 1988), Ballroom (HTV, 1988/9).

Gareth Hughes All USA: And the Children Pay (1918), Eternal Mother/Indiscretion (1919), Broken Hearts (formerly Scar of Shame) (1919), Woman Under Oath (1919)*, Isle of Conquest (1919), Mrs Wiggs of the Cabbage Patch (1919), Every Mother's Son (1919), Ginger (1919), The Red Viper (1919), Eyes of Youth (1919), Woman! Woman (1919), The Chorus Girl's Romance (1920), The Woman in his House (1920), The Lure of Youth (1921), Life's Darn Funny (1921), Sentimental Tommy (1921), The Garments of Truth (1921), The Hunch (1921), Little Eva Ascends (1922), I Can Explain (UK: Stay Home) (1922), Don't Write Letters (1922), Forget-Me-Not (1922), Kick In (1923), The Christian (1923)*, The Enemies of Women (1923), Penrod and Sam (1923), The Spanish Dancer (1923), Shadows of Paris (1924), The Sunset Trail (1924), The Midnight Girl (1925), Men of the Night (1926), The Auctioneer (1927), Eyes of the Totem (1927), The Whirlwind of Youth (1927), Better Days (1927), In the First Degree (1927), Heroes in Blue (1927), Broadway After Midnight (1927), Comrades (1928), The Sky Rider (1928), Top Sergeant Mulligan (1928), Old Age Handicap (1928), Broken Hearted (1929), Silent Sentinel (1929), Mister Antonio (1929), Scareheads (1931).

*The NFA hold The Christian and Woman Under Oath.

Dafydd Hywel The Children of Icarus (1977), Frankenstein Must Be Destroyed (1978), The Mouse and the Woman (1979), O.G. (1981), Coming Up Roses (1986), Milwr Bychan/Boy Soldier (1986), Rebecca's Daughters (1991).

TV: Rachel in Danger (Thames, 1977), Something Upstairs (BBC Wales, 1978), Glas-y-Dorlan (BBC Wales, 1980), The Life and Times of David Lloyd George (BBC Wales, 1981), Where There's a Will (S4C, 1984), The Mimosa Boys (BBC, 1984), Yr Alcoholig Llon/The Happy Alcoholic (S4C, 1985), The Works (S4C, 1985), The Poet (S4C, 1986), Iolo Morgannwg (in 'Cracking Up' series, S4C, 1986), A Penny for Your Dreams (BBC, 1987), Out of Love (BBC, 1988), The Billy King (S4C, 1988), Calvert Jones documentary (HTV, 1989), Stanley and the Women (Central, 1991), The Blackheath Poisonings (Central, 1991).

Mervyn Johns Lady in Anger (1934), In the Soup (1936), Pot Luck (1936), Storm in a Teacup (1937), Song of the Forge/The Village Blacksmith (1937), Almost a Gentleman (1938), Jamaica Inn (1939), Convoy (1940), The Girl in the News (1940), Saloon Bar (1940), The Foreman Went to France/Somewhere in France (1942), Next of Kin (1942), Went the Day Well/48 Hours (1942), The Bells Go Down (1943), My Learned Friend (1943), San Demetrio, London (1943), Halfway House (1944), Twilight Hour (1944), Dead of Night (1945), Pink String and Sealing Wax (1945), They Knew Mr Knight (1945), The Captive Heart (1946), Captain Boycott (1947), Easy Money (1948), Counterblast (1948), Quartet (1948), Helter Skelter (1949), Diamond City (1949), Edward My Son (1949), Tony

Draws a Horse (1950), The Magic Box (1951), Scrooge (1951), Tall Headlines/The Frightened Bride (1952), Valley of Song (1953), The Oracle/The Horse's Mouth (1953), The Master of Ballantrae (1953), Romeo and Juliet (1954), The Blue Peter (1955), 1984 (1956), Moby Dick (1956), The Shield of Faith (1956), The Intimate Stranger/Finger of Guilt (1956), The Counterfeit Plan (1957), Doctor at Large (1957), Danger List (short, 1957), The Vicious Circle/The Circle (1957), The Surgeon's Knife (1957), The Gypsy and the Gentleman (1958), The Devil's Disciple (1959), Once More With Feeling (US, 1960), Never Let Go (1960), No Love for Johnnie (1961), Francis of Assisi (US, 1961), The Rebel (1961), Echo of Barbara (1961), The Day of the Triffids (1962), 80,000 Suspects (1963), 55 Days in Peking (US, 1963), The Old Dark House (1963), The Victors (US/UK, 1963), A Jolly Bad Fellow/They All Died Laughing (1963), The Heroes of Telemark (1965), Who Killed the Cat? (1966), House of Mortal Sin (1976), The Confessional (1977).

TV: The Critical Point (BBC, 1960), The Avengers (ABC series, 1965–6).

Roger Livesey   The Old Curiosity Shop (1920), The Four Feathers (1921), Where The Rainbow Ends (1921), East Lynne on the Western Front (1931), The Veteran of Waterloo (1933), A Cuckoo in the Nest (1933), Blind Justice (1934), Lorna Doone (1935), Midshipman Easy/Men of the Sea (1935), The Price of Wisdom (1935), Rembrandt (1936), The Drum/Drums (1938), Keep Smiling/Smiling Along (1938), Spies of the Air (1939), The Girl in the News (1940), 49th Parallel (1941), The Life and Death of Colonel Blimp (1943), I Know Where I'm Going (1945), A Matter of Life and Death/Stairway to Heaven (1946), Vice Versa (1947), That Dangerous Age/If This Be Sin (1949), Green Grow the Rushes (1951), The Master of Ballantrae (1953), The Intimate Stranger/Finger of Guilt (1956), Es geschah am hellichten Tag/It Happened in Broad Daylight (Germany/Switzerland, 1958), The League of Gentlemen (1960), The Entertainer (1960), No, My Darling Daughter (1961), Of Human Bondage (1964), The Amorous Adventures of Moll Flanders (1965), Oedipus the King (1968), Hamlet (1969), Futtocks End (1979).

TV: The Burning Glass (Associated Rediffusion, Play of the Week, 1960).

Ray Milland   The Plaything (1929), The Informer (1929), The Flying Scotsman (1929), The Lady from the Sea/Goodwin Sands (1929), Way for a Sailor (US, 1930), Passion Flower (US, 1930), The Bachelor Father (US, 1931), Just a Gigolo (US, 1931), Bought (US, 1931), Ambassador Bill (US, 1931), Blonde Crazy (US, 1931), The Man Who Played God (US, 1932), Polly of the Circus (1932), Payment Deferred (1932), Orders is Orders (1933), This is the Life (1933), Bolero (US, 1934), We're Not Dressing (US, 1934), Many Happy Returns (US, 1934), Charlie Chan in London (US, 1934), Menace (US, 1934), One Hour Late (US, 1935), The Gilded Lily (US, 1935), Four Hours to Kill (US, 1935), The Glass Key (US, 1935), Alias Mary Dow (US, 1935), Next Time We Love (US, 1936), The Return of Sophie Lang (US, 1936), The Big Broadcast of 1937 (US, 1936), The Jungle Princess (US, 1936), Three Smart Girls (US, 1936), Bulldog Drummond Escapes (US, 1937), Wings Over Honolulu (US, 1937), Easy Living (1937), Ebb Tide (1937), Wise Girl (1937), Her Jungle Love (1938), Tropic Holiday (1938), Men With Wings (1938), Say It in French (1938), French Without Tears (1938), Hotel Imperial (US, 1939), Beau Geste (US, 1939), Everything Happens at Night (US, 1939), Irene (US, 1940), The Doctor Takes a Wife (US, 1940), Untamed (US, 1940), Arise My Love (US, 1940), I Wanted Wings (US, 1941), Skylark (US, 1941), The Lady Has Plans (US, 1942), Reap the Wild Wind (US, 1942), Are Husbands Necessary? (US, 1942), The Major and the Minor (US, 1942), Star Spangled Rhythm (US, 1942), The Crystal Ball (US, 1942), Forever and a Day (US, 1943), The Uninvited (US, 1944), Lady in the Dark (US, 1944),

Till We Meet Again (US, 1944), Ministry of Fear (US, 1944), The Lost Weekend (US, 1945), Kitty (US, 1946), The Well Groomed Bride (US, 1946), California (US, 1947), Golden Earrings (1947), The Imperfect Lady (US, 1947), The Trouble With Women (US, 1947), The Big Clock (US, 1948), So Evil My Love (UK/US, 1948), Miss Tatlock's Millions (US, 1948), Sealed Verdict (US, 1948), Alias Nick Beal (US, 1949), It Happens Every Spring (US, 1949), A Woman of Distinction (US, 1950), A Life of Her Own (US, 1950), Copper Canyon (US, 1950), Circle of Danger (1951), Night into Morning (US, 1951), Rhubarb (US, 1951), Close to My Heart (US, 1951), Bugles in the Afternoon (US, 1952), Something to Live For (US, 1952), The Thief (US, 1952), Jamaica Run (US, 1953), Let's Do It Again (US, 1953), Dial M for Murder (US, 1954), The Girl in the Red Velvet Swing (US, 1955), A Man Alone (also directed) (US, 1955), Lisbon (also directed) (US, 1957), Three Brave Men (US, 1957), The River's Edge (US, 1957), High Flight (1957), The Safecracker (also directed) (1958), Premature Burial (US, 1962), Panic in the Year Zero! (also directed) (US, 1962), The Man With X-Ray Eyes (US, 1963), The Confession (unreleased) (US, 1965), Hostile Witness (also directed) (1967), Rose rosse per il Führer (Italy, 1968), Company of Killers (US, 1970), Love Story (US, 1970), The Big Game (1972), Frogs (US, 1972), The Thing with Two Heads (US, 1972), Embassy (US, 1972), The House in Nightmare Park/Crazy House (1973), Terror in the Wax Museum (US, 1973), Gold (1974), Escape to Witch Mountain (US, 1975), Aces High (1976), The Last Tycoon (US, 1976), Slavers (Germany, 1977), Oil (Italy, 1977), The Swiss Conspiracy (1977), The Uncanny (UK/Canada, 1977), La Ragazza in Pigiamo Giallo (Italy, 1978), Blackout (Canada/France, 1978), Spree (US/Mexico, 1978), Oliver's Story (US, 1978), Game for Vultures (1979).

TV: Markham (CBS/Universal series, 1959/60), Meet Mr McNutley (CBS, 1953), The Ray Milland Show (drama series, CBS, 1954), Look What's Happened to Rosemary's Baby (Paramount, 1968), Daughter of the Mind (TCF, 1969), River of Gold (1971), Black Noon (Columbia, 1971), The Dead Don't Die (1975), Mayday at 40,000 Feet (Warner Bros. 1976), Testimony of Two Men (MCA/Universal, 1977), Cruise Into Terror (1978), Battlestar Galactica (Thames, one episode only, 1980–1).

Ivor Novello* L'Appel du Sang/Call of the Blood (France, 1920), Miarka la Fille a l'Ours/Miarka the Daughter of the Bear (France, 1920), Carnival (1921), The Bohemian Girl (1922), The White Rose (US, 1923), Bonnie Prince Charlie (1923), The Man Without Desire (1923), The Rat (also co-wrote stage play) (1925), The Lodger/The Case of Jonathan Drew (1926), The Triumph of The Rat (1926), Downhill/When Boys Leave Home (also co-wrote play) (1927), The Vortex (1928), The Constant Nymph (1928), A South Sea Bubble (1928), The Gallant Hussar (1928), The Return of The Rat (1929), Symphony in Two Flats (1930), Once a Lady (US, 1931), The Lodger/The Phantom Fiend (sound remake, 1932), Sleeping Car (1933), I Lived With You (scripted, from his own stage play) (1933), Autumn Crocus (1934).

Writer only: Mata Hari (US, 1931), Tarzan and the Ape Man (1932), But the Flesh is Weak (scripted from his play: The Truth Game) (US, 1932), The Rat (sound remake, co-wrote play source) (1937), Free and Easy (based on Novello's original stage play, The Truth Game; US, 1941), The Dancing Years (stage play only) (1950), King's Rhapsody (musical play source only) (1955).

*Most Novello films are in the NFA, but Miarka and A South Sea Bubble seem to be lost films. The White Rose is viewable in the US at MOMA (New York) and Eastman House (Rochester, NY).

Siân Phillips Becket (1964), Young Cassidy (1965), Laughter in the Dark (1969), Goodbye Mr Chips

(1969), Murphy's War (1970), Under Milk Wood (1971), Dune (1984), The Doctor and the Devils (1985), Ewoks: The Battle for Ensor (US, 1985), Valmont (US/France, 1989), The Age of Innocence (US, 1993).

TV:	Siwan (BBC, 1960), The Other Man (Granada, 1964), Vessel of Wrath (BBC, 1970), Platonov (1971), Shoulder to Shoulder (as Emmeline Pankhurst) (1974), Jennie – Mrs Randolph Churchill (Thames, 1974), How Green Was My Valley (as Beth Morgan) (BBC, 1976), I Claudius (as Livia) (BBC, 1976), Winston Churchill – the Wilderness Years (as Clementine Churchill) (1978), Tinker, Tailor, Soldier, Spy (BBC, 1979), Tales of the Unexpected (one episode, 1979/80), Crime and Punishment (BBC, 1979), Off to Philadelphia in the Morning (BBC, 1978), George Borrow/It is Wild, Mr Borrow (S4C, 1984), The Mabinogi (S4C/Channel Four, 1984), Out of Time (When Reason Sleeps series) (Channel Four, 1987), The Snow Spider (HTV, 1988), Siân (documentary, S4C, 1988), Emlyn's Moon (HTV, 1990), The Black Candle (Tyne Tees, 1991), The Chestnut Soldier (HTV, 1991).

Jonathan Pryce	Voyage of the Damned (1978), The Day Christ Died (1979), Peter and Paul (1979), Breaking Glass (1980), Loophole (1980), The Ploughman's Lunch (1983), Something Wicked This Way Comes (1983), Two Weeks in Winter (1984), Brazil (1985), The Doctor and the Devils (1986), Haunted Honeymoon (1986), Jumpin' Jack Flash (US, 1986), Man of Fire (Italy, 1987), Consuming Passions (US, 1988), Adventures of Baron Munchausen (1988), The Rachel Papers (1989), Glengarry, Glen Ross (US, 1992), Barbarians at the Gate (1992), The Age of Innocence (US, 1992), Deadly Advice (1994).

TV:	Playthings (BBC, 1976), Partisans (ATV, 1978), Timon of Athens (1981), School for Clowns (Thames, 1981), Praying Mantis (1982), Comedians (BBC, 1983), Martin Luther – Heretic (BBC, 1985), Man on Fire (1986), Tickets for the Titanic (1988), The Man From the Pru (BBC, 1989), Uncle Vanya (1989), Selling Hitler (1991), Mr Wroe's Virgins (BBC, 1992), Great Moments in Aviation (BBC Films, 1992), Thicker Than Water (BBC Wales, 1993).

TV series:	Bill Brand (Thames).

Rachel Roberts	Valley of Song (1953), The Limping Man (1953), The Weak and the Wicked (1954), The Crowded Day (1954), The Good Companions (1956), Our Man in Havana (1959), Saturday Night and Sunday Morning (1962), Girl on Approval (1962), This Sporting Life (1963), La Puce à l'Oreille/A Flea in Her Ear (France/US, 1968), The Reckoning (1970), Doctors' Wives (US, 1971), The Wild Rovers (US, 1971), The Belstone Fox (1973), O Lucky Man! (1973), Alpha Beta (1973), Murder on the Orient Express (1974), Great Expectations (1975), Picnic at Hanging Rock (Australia, 1976), Foul Play (US, 1978), When a Stranger Calls (US, 1979), Yanks (1979).

TV:	Nelson (as Emma Hamilton) (ATV, 1966), Out of the Unknown (BBC, one episode, 1966), Destiny of a Spy (NBC/Universal, 1969), Baffled! (ITC, 1971), Graceless Go I (HTV, 1974), The Old Crowd (LWT, 1978).

Sue Roderick	Rebecca's Daughters (made for BBC and cinema release, 1991), Hedd Wyn (cinema release, made for BBC Wales/S4C, 1992).

TV:	A Penny For Your Dreams (BBC, 1987), Llid y Ddaear/The Angry Earth (Channel 4/S4C, 1989), Morphine and Dolly Mixtures (1990), The Committee (HTV Wales, 1991).

Serials include:	Pobl y Cwm (S4C, BBC Wales), Dinas (S4C), Lazarus (own series, HTV), Lifeboat (BBC Wales, 1994).

Queenie Thomas*	Infelice (1915), The Vengeance of Allah (1915), The White Star (1915), Frills (1916), Won by Losing (1916), The Chance of a Lifetime (1916), Ye Wooing of Peggy (1917), A Man the Army Made (1917), Meg o' the Woods (1918), What Would a Gentleman Do? (1918), Rock of Ages (1918), It's Happiness that Counts (1918), A Little Child Shall Lead Them (1919), Trousers (1920), Rainbow Comedies (series of 12 shorts, 1922), Syncopated Picture Plays (series of 6 shorts, 1923), School for Scandal (1923), Straws in the Wind (1924), The Alley of Golden Hearts (1924), Her Redemption (retitled: The Gayest of the Gay) (1924), The Last Witness (1925), The Gold Cure (1925), Safety First (1926), Vestale du Gage (Temple of Shadows) (1927), Temple of Stars (1928), Warned Off (1928).

*No Thomas films were viewable at the NFA in 1994, but the archive holds copies of Paperhanging (in the Rainbow Comedies series), School for Scandal, The Last Witness, The Gold Cure, Safety First and Vestale du Gage. Temple of Stars may be the same film as Vestale du Gage.

Rachel Thomas	The Proud Valley (1940), Undercover/Underground Guerillas (1943), Blue Scar (1949), David (1951), Valley of Song (1953), Catacombs/The Woman Who Wouldn't Die (1964), Sky West and Crooked (1965), Under Milk Wood (1971).
TV:	Poison Pen (BBC, 1956), After the Funeral (1960), Cat's Cradle (1965), Pancakes (BBC, 1967), Bless This House (BBC, 1953), The Straight and the Narrow – Menace series (BBC, 1970), Hedda Gabler (BBC, 1972), Y Stafell Ddirgel/ The Secret Room (BBC, 1972), Bus to Bosworth (BBC Wales, 1976), Off to Philadelphia in the Morning (BBC Wales, 1978), Nye (BBC Wales, 1981), Joanna Southcott programme in Almanac series (S4C, 1985), That Uncertain Feeling (BBC Wales, 1986), Mam (1988).
Naunton Wayne	The First Mrs Fraser (1931), Going Gay (1933), For Love of You (1934), The Lady Vanishes (1938), Gestapo (retitled) Night Train to Munich/Night Train (1940), Crook's Tour (1941), Next of Kin (1942), Millions Like Us (1943), Dead of Night (1945), The Calendar (1947), It's Not Cricket (1948), Quartet (1948), Passport to Pimlico (1948), Obsession (1949), Highly Dangerous (1950), Treasure Hunt (1952), The Titfield Thunderbolt (1953), You Know What Sailors Are (1953), Nothing Barred (1961), Double Bunk (1964).
TV:	The Rose Affair (ABC, 1961).
Emlyn Williams	The Frightened Lady/Criminal at Large (1932), Men of Tomorrow (1932), Sally Bishop (1932), Friday the Thirteenth (also scripted) (1933), My Song for You (1934), Evensong (1934), Road House (1934), The Iron Duke (1935), The Dictator (retitled) The Love Affair of the Dictator/(US) The Loves of a Dictator (retitled) For Love of a Queen (1935), The City of Beautiful Nonsense (1935), Broken Blossoms (also scripted) (1936), I Claudius (unfinished, 1937), Dead Men Tell No Tales (also additional dialogue) (1938), The Citadel (1938), A Night Alone (1938), They Drive By Night (1938), Jamaica Inn (1939), The Stars Look Down (1939), Mr Borland Thinks Again (short, 1940), The Girl in the News (1940), You Will Remember (1940), This England/Our Heritage (narrator only) (1941), Major Barbara (1941), Hatter's Castle (1941), The Last Days of Dolwyn (also directed, scripted) (1949), Three Husbands (US, 1950), The Scarf (1951), The Magic Box (1951), Another Man's Poison (1951), Ivanhoe (US/UK, 1951), The Deep Blue Sea (1955), I Accuse (1958), Beyond This Place/Web of Evidence (1959), The Wreck of the Mary Deare (US, 1959), The L-Shaped Room (1962), Eye of the Devil (1966), David Copperfield (1969), The Walking Stick (1970).
As writer:	Co-scripted The Man Who Knew Too Much (1934), The Citadel (1938), dialogue for Evergreen (1934).

Plays filmed for cinema:	Night Must Fall (1937 and 1964), The Corn is Green (1945 and 1979).
TV roles:	Past Caring (1986).
Rhys Williams	How Green Was My Valley (1941), Underground Agent (1942), This Above All (1942), Mrs Miniver (1942), Remember Pearl Harbour (1942), Cairo (1942), Random Harvest (1942), Gentleman Jim (1943), No Time for Love (1943), The Corn is Green (1945), Blood on the Sun (1945), You Came Along (1945), The Spiral Staircase (1945), The Bells of St Marys (1946), Voice of the Whistler (1946), A Genius in the Family (1946), Mrs Loring's Secret (1947), Cross My Heart (1947), The Farmer's Daughter (1947), The Strange Woman (1947), Moss Rose (1947), If Winter Comes (1948), The Black Arrow/The Black Arrow Strikes (1948), Master of Lassie/His o Hoe (1948), Tokyo Joe (1949), Bad Boy (1949), The Inspector General (1949), Devil's Doorway (1950), Kiss Tomorrow Goodbye (1950), The Law and The Lady (1951), Lightning Strikes Twice (1951), Les Misérables (1952), Plymouth Adventure (1952), Carbine Williams (1952), Meet Me at the Fair (1952), Scandal at Scourie (1953), Mutiny (1953), Bad for Each Other (1954), Johnny Guitar (1954), Julius Caesar (1954), There's No Business Like Showbusiness (1954), Man in the Attic (1954), The Kentuckian (1955), Many Rivers to Cross (1955), Battle Cry (1955), The King's Thief (1955), How to Be Very, Very Popular (1955), The Fastest Gun Alive (1956), The Scarlet Coat (1956), Nightmare (1956), Mohawk (1956), The Boss (1956), Raintree County (1957), The Desperados Are in Town (1957), Merry Andrew (1958), The Restless Breed (1959), Midnight Lace (1960), The Sons of Katie Elder (1965), Our Man Flint (1966), Skulduggery (1969).

Directors

Stephen Bayly	Films: Loving Memory (1971, producer only), The Great Escape, Part II (1974, short, producer only), Dream City and Smile Until I Tell You To Stop (1976-9, National Film School shorts), Notman (1981, short, producer only), Coming Up Roses (1986, made for S4C but released in cinemas), Just Ask for Diamond (1988).
TV:	The International Henry James (1974–6 series, co-produced only), The Author of Beltraffio (1974–6, producer only), Joni Jones (1982, S4C drama series), Aderyn Papur/And Pigs Might Fly (1983, S4C), Dream Factory (1984, episode 6 of series, French/Belgian/Swiss co-production), Joni Jones (film feature version), Letters from Patagonia (1989, BBC–FR3 France, executive producer only), The Diamond Brothers – South by South East (1990–1, co-executive producer only, TVS series).
Endaf Emlyn	Films: Un Nos Ola Leuad/One Full Moon (made for S4C, 1991, dist. Ffilm Cymru in cinemas), Gadael Lenin/Leaving Lenin (S4C, 1993).
TV:	Shampŵ (Shampoo) (video, 1982), Gaucho (S4C, 1984), Bali, a Pattern of Life (1985), Journey Through Java (1985), The Man Who Stole Christmas (S4C, 1985), Y Cloc/The Clock (S4C, 1986), Stormydd Awst (Storms of August) (S4C, 1988).
Karl Francis As director:	Films: Above Us the Earth (1977), The Mouse and the Woman (1980), Giro City (1982), Milwr Bychan/Boy Soldier (1986), Rebecca's Daughters (1991). Boy Soldier was made for S4C, Rebecca's Daughters for BBC Wales (as a German co-production). Both were released in cinemas.
TV:	A Breed of Men (HTV, 1971) (writer only), Justice Out of Reach (BBC Factfinder series,

1971), Timmy and the Experts (BBC2 Inside Story series) (1977), Rough Justice (BBC 40 Minutes Series) (1980), Mister Perks (BBC 40 Minutes series) (1983), Chekhov in Derry (Channel Four) (1983), Yr Alcoholig Llon (the Happy Alcoholic) (S4C, 1984), Ms Rhymney Valley (BBC 2, 1985), Rhyth y Dŵr (Water Marks) (S4C, 1988), Merthyr and the Girl (HTV Wales, 1989), Llid y Ddaear/The Angry Earth (1989), 1996 (BBC Screen One, 1989), Estonia: Country at the Crossroads (S4C, 1989), Estonia: Keeping the Faith (S4C, 1989), Raymond Williams – a Journey of Hope (Channel Four, 1990), Morphine and Dolly Mixtures (BBC, 1990), Mr Chairman (HTV Wales, 1991), The Committee (HTV Wales, 1991), A Night Out (HTV Wales, 1991), 1996 (1991).

TV series/serials:	A Man in his Place (BBC 2 series), Weekend World (LWT, 1972–3), Second House (1973–5), Civvies (BBC, 1992), Judas and the Gimp (HTV, 1993), Lifeboat (BBC Wales, 1994 production credit, also directed one episode).
Acted in :	A Breed of Men (HTV, 1971), Yr Alcoholig Llon/The Happy Alcoholic (S4C, 1984), The Nation's Health (BBC), The Cormorant (BBC, 1992).
William Haggar	Phantom Train Ride at Burry Port† (1902), Phantom Ride Through Swansea (1902)†, The Maniac's Guillotine (1902), Duel scene from The Two Orphans (1902), The Wild Man of Borneo (1902), True as Steel (1902), Weary Willie and Tired Tim – the Gunpowder Plot* (1903), Mirthful Mary – a Case for the Black List (1903), Weary Willie and Tired Tim Turn Barbers (1903), Desperate Poaching Affray (US: The Poachers) (1903), Weary Willie and Tired Tim – a Dead Shot* (1903), The Tramp and the Washerwoman (1903), The Tramp and the Baby's Bottle (1903), A Dash for Liberty, or The Convicts' Escape and Capture (1903), Whitewashing the Policeman (1904), Mirthful Mary in the Dock (1904), The Sign of the Cross (1904), The Bather's Revenge (1904), Brutality Rewarded (1904), The Meddling Policeman (1904), Flynn's Birthday Celebrations (1904), The Biter Bitten (1904), Snowballing (1904), The Rival Painters (1905), The Squire's Daughter (1905), Charles Peace (The Life of) (1905), DT's or The Effect of Drink (1905), Fun at the Waxworks (1905), Bathing Not Allowed (1905), A Boating Incident (1905), Two's Company, Three's None (1905), The Salmon Poachers – a Midnight Mêlée (1905), Mary is Dry (1905), A Message from the Sea (1905), Desperate Footpads (1907), The Red Barn Crime or Maria Marten (1908), The Dumb Man of Manchester (1908), The Maid of Cefn Ydfa (1908).

*These films attributed to Haggar, tentatively, by Denis Gifford, *British Film Catalogue 1895–1985.*
†No contemporary evidence found of this film.
Only A Desperate Poaching Affray and The Life of Charles Peace survive, in entirety, in the NFA.

Jack Howells	Films as director/writer: The Peaceful Years (1947), Scrapbook for 1933 (1950) (both with Peter Baylis), Here's to the Memory (1951), Mine Shaft Sinking (1965), The World Still Sings (1965).
Films as writer only:	Dover, Spring 1947 (1947, uncredited), The Elstree Story (1952), Front Page Story (1953).
TV, as director/writer:	Dylan (TWW/BBC, 1962), Nye! (TWW, 1965), Return to Rhymney (HTV), Penclawdd Wedding (HTV, 1974), The Green, Green Baize (HTV, 1982).
Chris Monger	Narcissus, Story From a Corner, Cold Mountain (shorts, 1973–6), Aesthete's Foot (1976), Enough Cuts for a Murder (1978), Repeater (1980), Voice Over (1981), Waiting for the Light (1989), Just Like a Woman (1991), The Englishman Who Went Up a Hill and Came Down a Mountain (1994).

TV:	The Mabinogi (S4C, 1984, co-directed), The People Show (1984), Crime Pays (S4C, 1986) .
John Ormond	(All BBC Wales, writer-director): A Sort of Welcome to Spring (1958), Borrowed Pasture (1960, 'Take Two' series), Once There Was a Time (1961), Journey into Snowdonia (1962), The Desert and the Dream (1963, 'Take Two' series), From a Town in Tuscany (1963, 'Take Two' series), Return Journey (1964), Operation Salvation (1964, 'Meeting Point' series), Song in a Strange Land (1964), Mormons (1964), Troubled Waters (1965), Under a Bright Heaven ('Take Two' series, 1966), Horizons Hung in Air (1966), Alone in a Boat (1966), Piano With Many Strings (1967), Music in Midsummer – Llangollen International Eisteddfod (1968), The Ancient Kingdoms (1969), Bronze Mask (1969), The Fragile Universe (1969), R. S. Thomas – Priest and Poet (1971), ('The Land Remembers', 1972, series), Travellers (1973), A Day Eleven Years Long ('Visions Out of Wales' series, 1975), Poems in Their Place (series – programmes on A. E. Housman, Edward Thomas, Thomas Gray, W. B. Yeats, Dylan Thomas, Thomas Hardy, John Clare), The Life and Death of Picture Post (1977), The Colliers' Crusade (five programmes, 1979), A Land Against the Light ('Visions Out of Wales' series, 1979), I Sing to You Strangers (1982), Private View (series – programmes on Kyffin Williams, Danny Abse, John Grierson, George Chapman/Diane Roberts, Robert Graves).
Joanna Quinn	(Director – animation films) Superdog (1983, student film, Middlesex Polytechnic), Dancer (1984, student film, Middlesex Polytechnic), Girls' Night Out (1987, Middlesex Polytechnic, S4C/Channel 4), Moo Glue (1987), Tea at Number 10 (1987), Castle Cant/Century City (1987, group film with some animation by Quinn, S4C), Body Beautiful (1990, S4C/Channel 4 but also shown in cinemas), Elles (1992, Trans Europe Film, France, seen in cinemas), Britannia (1994, S4C/Channel 4, cinemas).
TV only:	Jabas (1989, title sequence only, S4C), Goya ('Cracking Up' series, 1989, Channel Four, title sequence only), Now it's Christmas (1989, BBC 1, title sequence only).
Colin Thomas	All TV: The Irish Way (BBC, 1978), Travellers (RTE, 1979), Poverty (RTE, 1979), Prevention of Terrorism Act (RTE, 1979) (all current affairs programmes), And Did Corruptly Receive (HTV, 1980), Crossing Jordan (BBC 1/2 Tales from Wales series – shown as Croesi Jordan on S4C, 1982/3), And Dogs Delight (1982/3) The Dragon Has Two Tongues (HTV series for Channel Four, 1985), Lest Who Forget (BBC Wales documentary, 1985 – Y Llygaid Na All Agor on S4C), Namibia – Tell The World (documentary, C4, 1986), The African from Aberystwyth (BBC Wales drama-documentary – Yr Affricanwr o Aberystwyth on S4C), Iolo – Bard of Liberty ('Cracking Up' series, C4, 1986 – Myfi Iolo Morgannwg on S4C), The Divided Kingdom (HTV, series for C4, 1988), Voice of the People ('Cracking Up' series, C4, 1988 – Llais y Werin on S4C), Goya – the Impossible Revolution ('Cracking Up' series, C4, 1988), Back to Barcelona (BBC Wales documentary, 1988 – Yn ôl i Barcelona for S4C), Gillray – Freeborn Englishman ('Cracking Up' series, C4, 1989), Cyrchfan Cyfiawnder (S4C documentary, 1989), Liberty Literacy (documentary, C4, 1990), Hughesovka and the New Russia (documentary, BBC 2, 1990–1 – Hughesofka a'r Rwsia Newydd for S4C), Video Letters (BBC 2 access programme, 1991), Pushkin – the Bronze Horseman ('Which Side Are You On' series, C4, 1991–2), Saunders Lewis – An Alien Face in the Mirror ('Writing On the Line' series, C4, 1992), Saunders Lewis – Arwr Cenedlaethol (Saunders Lewis – National Hero) (S4C, 1992)
Paul Turner	Films: Trisgel (1981), Hedd Wyn (1992, made for S4C but also shown in cinemas).
TV:	Out of the Pit (1982–3, BBC 1/2), Wil Six (1984, S4C), Chwedlau Serch (1985, Tales

from Wales series, S4C), Tra Bo Dwy/There's Always Two (1986, S4C), Ysbryd y Nos/Spirit of the Night (1987, S4C), Dihirod Dyfed (1986/7, S4C series), Derfydd Aur/Realms of Gold (1990, S4C, feature, co-production), Cwm Hyfryd/Beautiful Valley (1992, S4C, feature, co-production), Smithfield (as producer only, 1990).

Richard Watkins Films: The Great Depression (1976), Mr Sandman (1976), Milford Fishermen (1977), Memoirs of a Pit Orchestra (1981).

TV: Gone for a Soldier (some sequences, BBC, 1978), Le Cirque en Hiver (Telepress/Antenne 2, 1979), Under the Sea and the Waves (S4C/Nos Netherlands, 1981), Matador (S4C, Video Arts USA, 1983), Gwenallt: Ar Waelod y Cof/Deep in the Memory (S4C, 1984), Marseille . . . Marseille (S4C, 1984), Tenor (biography of singer Dennis O'Neill (S4C, 1986), Night Drums (S4C, 1986), Siân, the Life and Work of Siân Phillips (1988), The President/Mac the Bard/Bogo (1986–8, trilogy for S4C), The Funeral (1989, S4C).

Stephen Weeks Flesh (1967), I, Monster (1971), Gawain and the Green Knight (1973), Ghost Story (1974), Sword of the Valiant (1982), The Bengal Lancers (started 1984, unfinished), Owen's War (STV, 1964), Army Camp (STV, 1964), Deserted Station (STV, 1965), Scars (1976), Black Cat at the Castle Gate (pilot, 1982), Kipling Country (1982).

Editors

Chris Lawrence Ms Rhymney Valley (BBC Wales, 1985), Un Nos Ola Leuad/One Full Moon (S4C, 1991) (cinema release), Hedd Wyn, the Armageddon Poet (S4C, 1992) (cinema release).

TV: Bus to Bosworth (BBC Wales, 1975), The Life and Death of Picture Post (BBC Wales, 1977), Grand Slam (BBC Wales, 1978), Nye! (BBC Wales, 1982), Tom Paine – The Most Valuable Englishman Ever (BBC Wales, 1982), The Fasting Girl (BBC Wales, 1984), Return to Cardiff (BBC Wales, documentary featuring poet Dannie Abse) (some cinema screenings), Shadowlands (BBC London/Wales, 1986), Swallows/Gwenoliaid (BBC Wales for S4C, 1986), Colours/Lliwiau (BBC Wales for S4C), A Penny for Your Dreams (BBC Wales, 1987), New World (BBC London/Wales), Llid y Ddaear/The Angry Earth (S4C/Channel 4, 1989), The Committee (HTV Wales, 1991), 1996 (BBC Wales, 1991).

NOTES

INTRODUCTION

1 Dave Berry, 'A valley puts its agony on record', *South Wales Echo,* 1 April 1977.

2 Under the 1927 Cinematograph Films Act, renters had to offer and exhibitors show a minimum percentage of 'British' footage each year. This figure rose to 20 per cent by 1938. (Rachael Low, *Film-making in 1930s Britain,* George Allen & Unwin, 1985).

3 Author's interview with Pen Tennyson's brother Hallam Tennyson, London, 1982.

4 Author's interviews with Ian Saynor (Katharine Hepburn's leading man in the 1979 **The Corn is Green** version), 1982, and with Patricia Hayes, October, 1984.

5 Peter Stead, 'Wales in the movies', in Tony Curtis (ed.), *Wales: The Imagined Nation* (Poetry Wales Press, 1986), pp.161–79.

6 Rachael Low, *The History of The British Film 1918-1929* (George Allen & Unwin, 1971), pp. 123–7,160–2.

7 Mary-Lou Jennings (ed.), *Humphrey Jennings – Film-maker, Painter, Poet* (Riverside Studios – British Film Institute, 1982), pp.16–17. A letter from Jennings, Tom Harrisson (anthropologist) and Charles Madge (journalist) originated the Mass Observation reports 1937 – 'an anthropology for our own people'.

8 Graham Greene, *The Spectator,* 15 March 1940. Cited in *The Pleasure Dome,* Greene's collected film criticism 1935–40 (Oxford University Press,1980).

9 **Boy Soldier,** screened at the 1986 Edinburgh Film Festival, opened at the Cannon Cinema, Tottenham Court Road, London, and London's Metro Cinema in February 1987. **Coming Up Roses** was shown at selected Cannon cinemas in London and around Britain from March.

10 See **The Dragon Has Two Tongues,** HTV and Channel Four (1985), and Gwyn Williams, *When Was* Wales? (Black Raven Press/Penguin Books, 1985).

CHAPTER 1

1 John Barnes, *The Beginnings of the Cinema in England* (David and Charles, 1976) pp.10, 12, 19 and Terry Ramsaye, *A Million And One Nights* (Simon and Schuster, New York, 1926) pp. 52–9, 62–73, 118–28. See also 'Early cinema in Wales', article by Cecil Price in *Dock Leaves* vol.8, no.21, Summer, 1957. The Kinetoscope, phonograph and Kinetophone – all inventions credited to Thomas Alva Edison (1847–1931) – were displayed at the Welsh National Bazaar of the National Society for the Prevention of Cruelty to Children at Cardiff's Park Hall from 28 to 30 April 1896.

2 *WM,* 24 Dec. 1896.

3 The Empire re-opened on 4 or 5 May 1896, after improvements, as the New Empire. Its shows had been held at the Philharmonic Hall during the renovation work.

4 Charlie Chaplin recalls (in his *My Autobiography,* Bodley Head, 1964, pp.83–4) playing a pageboy in a touring stage version of Sherlock Holmes at Tonypandy and Ebbw Vale *c.* 1901–2, and appearing in burlesque comedy with Harry Weldon at Cardiff, on a tour slightly later.

5 *WM* leader, 27 April 1896.

6 Madame Albertine: 'a lady parachutist' (Louisa May Evans, aged fourteen, from Bristol) disappeared in flight and her body was found at the mouth of the Usk (*WM,* 21 and 22 July 1896).

7 John Barnes, *The Beginnings of the Cinema in England,* pp.178–83.

8 Mrs Anne Adaliza Puddicombe, 1836–1908. See Sally Jones, *Allen Raine* (University of Wales Press/Welsh Arts Council, 1979) .

9 *SWE,* 28 Feb. and 19 Nov. 1896.

10 The Cardiff Photographic Society, in addition to inviting Acres, also hosted in 1896 an exhibition of the Vitagraph camera and projector, the work of the French-based Clement and Gilmer company and 'manipulated by M. Eloss'. The society also congratulated itself on 'introducing both X-rays and animated photographs' in its programmes that year (*SWE,* 21 Nov. 1896).

11 *WM,* 11 April 1896. An advert for the Kineopticon also appeared on the *WM* front page, 10 April.

12 *Amateur Photographer,* 6 Nov. 1896.

13 See William Kennedy Dickson, Antonia Dickson, *History of Kinetograph, Kinetoscope and Kinetophonograph* (Ayer Co., Salem, New Hampshire, 1984) (reprint of 1895 original) and John Barnes, *Beginnings,* pp.26–7, 57–61. The Kinetic Camera was patented in 1895 – Acres's separate projection machine from 1896 was the Kineopticon.

14 Llewellyn's were the first photographs to show waves breaking. See Gus McDonald, *Camera,* pp.138–9 (B. T. Batsford, 1979).

15 Acres submitted a 7ft. x 5ft. photograph of surf breaking on a rockbound coast at a Photographic Society Exhibition in London *(Daily Chronicle,* 24 Sept. 1892) and/or a photo or photos of a 'wild sea' *(Morning Post,* 26 Sept. 1892). 'Mr Acres's masterpiece, however, is a series representing breaking waves on the seashore' *(British Journal of Photography/Kinetic Lantern,* undated photostat).

16 *SWE,* 6 May 1896. **Arrest of a Pickpocket** was described in the *Echo* as 'Capture of a Pickpocket'. The idea of some Kinetoscopic screening at the Cardiff Exhibition had been discussed as early as September,1895.

17 John Barnes *(Beginnings)* describes the event.

18 S. W. Allen, *Reminiscences* (Western Mail Ltd., 1918). Mr Allen was chairman of the Cardiff Exhibition's Photographic Committee in 1896.

19 John Barnes, *Beginnings,* pp.178–83.

20 *Globe,* 31 Aug. 1896, cited in John Barnes's book. Also in *Photographic News,* 11 Sept. 1896.

21 *WM,* 26 Aug. 1896.

22 *Amateur Photographer,* 31 July 1896, reported the whole entertainment was a 'brilliant success' and gave 'due praise to Mr Cecil Hepworth, whose electric arc lamp did its work well, to the entire satisfaction of Mr Acres.' Also see Cecil Hepworth, *Came the Dawn* (London, 1951), and Barnes, *Beginnings,* as above.

23 *Era,* 25 July 1896, and *WM,* 26 Aug. 1896.

24 *Bntish Journal of Photography,* 31 July 1896, and *Photographic News,* 7 August.

25 *CEE,* 3 Sept. 1896; *WM,* 1 Sept. The Kineopticon was also booked – with a Röntgen X-Ray display – for the Cardiff Infirmary Bazaar at the city's Drill Hall in November (*WM* advert, 2 Oct.).

26 See Barnes, *Beginnings,* pp.182–3. Acres's films were also shown at the Collins Music Hall, Islington, in December 1896. The Cinematoscope – probably a machine of London-based exhibitor Fred Harvard – also screened films at Cardiff's Grand Theatre in August 1896 *(WM,* 17 Aug.).

27 *WM* advert (12 May) refers to the 'opening night' of the Lumière Cinématographe at the Cardiff Empire. *SWE* (11 May) advertised 'The Lumière Machine – The Original Not a Copy'. Adverts for the show appeared in *SWE* in April. See *SWE,* May 1896. Louis Lumière (b.1864, d.1948) was the driving force of the family company, aided by brother Auguste (b.1862, d.1954).

28 *WM,* 11 May 1896. Letter from S. H. Faulks to Walter Cook (Exhibition secretary), 27 May 1896.

29 *SWE,* July 1896.

30 The Panopticon advertised shows on the Cameramatographe: 'the marvellous scientific invention similar to the Cinematographe'. But such a machine is not listed by Barnes.
    The Cameramatographe featured the first-known Wales screening of the **Butterfly Dance** film, starring dancer and stripteaser 'La' Loie Fuller, which became a *cause célèbre* in its day (but see Terry Ramsaye, *A Million And One Nights,* pp.253–4). It was shown with films of a comic boxing match and a day at Hampstead Heath, and the machine was operated by a well-

known early bioscope man, the ventriloquist, Lt. Walter Cole (*SWE*, 22 and 30 June; *CEE*, 30 June; *WM*, 23 June).

31 The Lumières operated a factory set-up from 1895, and most of the company's films from all over the world were shot by specialized photographers. Acres's film **A Surrey Garden** (1896) was clearly based on the Lumières' **L'Arroseur Arrosé**.

32 The Theatrograph was first exhibited in Wales at the Public Hall, Morriston, early in October, when it was shown by London-based exhibitor William Dower (*Era* advert, 3 Oct. 1896).

33 Advert in *WM*, 19 Oct. 1896, said Paul 'inventor of the Animatographe would personally superintend' his production in Cardiff. See also *WM*, 26 Oct. 1896. Street scenes in Queen Street are also listed in R. W. Paul's company catalogues in the BFI, London. The Paul Theatrograph's run starting on 26 Oct. is described as a 're-engagement' in the Barnes book, citing Paul's own advertisements, but I have found no details of any earlier booking. *WM*, 27 Oct. 1896, reported 'another scene added' showing Queen Street on a Monday morning. 'This picture was of special interest to the audience, many of whom were delighted to find someone they know' (*sic*).

34 *SWE*, 26 Oct. 1896.

35 Proceedings of British Kinematograph Society No.38 (3 Feb. 1936) in BFI Library. A heated debate about the respective claims of Acres and Paul was conducted in the *British Journal of Photography* in 1978 (31 Mar. and 7 June), between John Barnes and Richard Brown.

36 John Barnes, *Beginnings*, pp.26–36.

37 Ibid.; *Amateur Photographer*, 9 Oct. 1896; *Daily Mail*, London, 31 July 1896. The 'original inventor' claim was made in Acres's publicity for his Birtac projector, an invention for home use, 1898. The August 1895 claim is strongly disputed by Barnes.

38 The Swansea date was mentioned in Paul's own publicity material cited in Barnes's Museum of Cinematography, St Ives, in the late eighties. Barnes's book also refers to a poster of Paul's Swansea show then in the Kodak museum, Harrow. Also see *SWE*, 30 Oct. and 18 Nov. 1896, and *WM*, 24 Nov.

39 *SWE*, 22 Dec. 1896.

40 *CEE*, 31 May and 1 June 1897, and 20 Sept. 1897.

41 *Cardiff Evening Post* (13 July) had an account of a jubilee procession screening, almost certainly on Paul's Animatographe – referred to in John Barnes, *The Rise of the Cinema in Great Britain* (Bishopsgate Press, 1983), p.192. Other Wales cinema shows featuring the jubilee procession in 1897 and 1898 were Slades Animated Photographs, the Cinématographe of Signor Polverini, the Animated Photos of Maskelyne and Cooke and the SO (or OS) Cinematographe of Phil and Bernard.

42 *CEE*, 27 Sept. and 8 and 21 July 1897.

43 *CEE*, 20 July 1897, and *SWDP*, 5 July 1897.

44 *SWE*, July 1897.

45 *SWE*, 3 Aug. 1897.

46 *SWDP*, 5 July 1897.

47 John F. Andrews, *The Story of Solomon Andrews and His Family* (Stewart Williams, Barry, 1976).

48 *CEE*, 18 Dec. 1897. For a full account of this fight's history and impact on early cinema read Charles Musser, *The Emergence of Cinema, The American Screen to 1907* in the History of American Cinema series (Charles Scribner's Sons, New York, 1990).

49 Terry Ramsaye, *A Million and One Nights*, p.289.

50 *CEE*, 28 Dec. 1897. The film was also shown at Swansea's Albert Hall in April 1898. See Cecil Price's article in *Dock Leaves*, Summer 1957.

51 *SWE*, 24 June 1907.

52 See Ramsaye (p.288) for a colourful description of Lubin's chicanery.

53 *SWDP*, 6 Jan. 1900.

54 *100 Years of Showmanship, Poole's 1837–1937* (published by Poole's, May 1937).

55 Edison machines were demonstrated by agents, or entrepreneur/showmen in Cardiff, and elsewhere in Wales, in early years, notably the Edison–Thomas Royal Vitascope, 1898, and the Edison–Rogers Eventographe in 1899.

56 *CEE*, 20 Dec. 1897. Edison's machine was also known as the Projecting Kinetoscope – see Musser, *The Emergence of Cinema*, as above.

57 *CEE*, 13 June 1898.

58 Op.cit., 19 July 1898. Other Wales film shows of 1898 and 1899 included Nestlé and Lever Brothers Cinématographe (cricket scenes of Ranjitsinghi and Tom Hayward batting for England) and Jasper Redfern's Animated Photographs (shots of the Sheffield United/Derby County FA Cup Final) and the Anglo-American Bio-Tableaux Show of Walter Gibbons).

59 *SWDP*, 15 Mar. 1898.

60 Author's interviews with Joseph Danter's daughters Josie and Rowena (Ena), at Hirwaun, Mid Glamorgan, February, 1985.

61 When Edison's Kinetoscope and Phonograph were demonstrated together at the NSPCC bazaar in April. See note 1.

62 The *Showman* newspaper, 6 Dec. 1901.

63 *SWE*, April 1906 advert for 9 April performance.

64 An account of William Haggar's experiment can be found in an unpublished 1969 manuscript biography in the British Film Institute by his daughter Lillian (Mrs Lily May Richards), then living in Cardiff.

65 *SWE*, 8 July 1907. Pringle, who ran cinemas in Bristol before the First World War, first screened films at the Park Hall in 1905, including **Turn-out of the Cardiff Fire Brigade** and a soccer match at Swansea.

66 *SWDP*. The film was probably Hepworth's **The Egg-laying Man**. Terms like 'biograph' and even 'cinematographe' were often used as generic terms for film, or projectors. 'Bioscope' was the usual generic term for travelling cinema, and many other early film shows.

67 *Era*, 7 Jan. 1899. Alexandra, Howe and Cushing's Great United Shows tour of Port Talbot, Bridgend, Cowbridge (*Glamorgan Gazette*, 12 Mar. 1897). Le Clair reference in Barnes, *Beginnings*. Also see *Wrexham Advertiser*, 24 Dec. 1898.

68 All references in *SWE*, 1898.

69 The year Stoll moved to London from Cardiff. Article, 'The sin of theatregoing', in *SWDP*, 8 Jan. 1897.

70 *SWDP*, 10 Aug. 1897, reporting meeting at Oxford Street Bible Christian Chapel. Details of the Swansea and Rhyl penny-in-the-slot cases can be found in John Barnes, *Filming the Boer War* (Bishopsgate Press, 1992).

   In 1899, a shopkeeper, Mr E. Clarke of Queen Street, Cardiff, and High Street, Merthyr, had films confiscated by the Cardiff stipendiary magistrate who considered they were in 'very bad taste, very vulgar and coarse'. The films were shown on a penny-in-the-slot machine, the Haydon and Urry Autocosmoscope. See *CEE*, June 1899.

71 *SWDP*, 11 Aug. 1897.

72 *SWDP*, Dec. 1910. Slogan in *SWE*, 8 Feb. 1908.

73 *Stoll Editorial News*, 15 Jan. 1920 (the Stoll company house journal). Also see Rachael Low, Roger Manvell, *The History of the British Film 1896–1906* (Allen and Unwin, 1949).

74 *SWE*, 23 Mar. 1907.

75 John Barnes, *The Rise of the Cinema in Great Britain* (Bishopsgate Press 1983), pp.24–6; *Photography*, 5 Nov. 1896; *Liverpool Daily Post*, 30 Oct. 1896.

76 *Amateur Photographer*, 31 July 1896.

77 Barnes, *Beginnings*, p.73.

1 Some films were in the possession of Mr Eric Foulkes of Rhyl in 1972, others were located at the home of Cheetham's grandson, Stanley, in Chester in the early eighties (interview with Philip Lloyd, Mold, 1985). At least seven films (or sections of them) survive.

2 Philip Lloyd's article in the *Rhyl Journal*, 19 Jan. 1984, based on much original research, is invaluable for facts on Cheetham, as is close study of the *Rhyl Journal* and *Rhyl Record and Advertiser* from 1897 to the First World War. Some Cheetham films had been sent apparently by Mr Foulkes to the National Film Archive in London, before Philip Lloyd met him.

3 Cheetham advertised 'character delineations' in the *E. H. Williams and His Merrie Men Songbook* (undated, in the Clwyd Record Office, Hawarden).

4 Ibid. The publication refers to Cheetham's Gramophone shop in Queen Street and his ownership of the Victorian Printing Press: 'His shop was the first premises to be lit by electricity.'

5 *Rhyl Journal*, Aug. 1896, cited in Philip Lloyd's article, as above, 'Arthur Cheetham, Rhyl's pioneer film-maker'.

6 Advert in issue 19 Jan. 1897. **Stable on Fire** was Herman Casler's film for the American Biograph the same year (see chapter 2) while **Bicyclists in the Park** is probably the **Bicyclists in Hyde Park** film shown on Edison's 'Kinetograph' (Projectorscope) in London in the same month as the Welsh screening (see John Barnes, *The Rise of the Cinema in Great Britain*, p.169).

7 The *Rhyl Record and Advertiser*, 27 March 1897, advertised Mrs Cheetham singing songs with illustrations during 'the return visit of Mr Cheetham's Living Pictures' from 30 March at the Town Hall. The *Rhyl Record and Advertiser* reported (17 April 1897) songs with pictorial illustration by Mr and Mrs Cheetham and 'Living Pictures and Animated Photographs' and (4 June 1898) 'entertainments by A. Cheetham, electrician', etc. – and 'the loudspeaking talking machine the gramophone'. A few years later, Cheetham's son Gus 'the boy pianist' accompanied all pictures and songs at Aberystwyth Market Hall (*Cambrian News*, April 1904).

8 *WM*, 27 Oct. 1896. Coutts's regular Shakespearian recitals were recalled by a reader in a letter to the *SWEP*, 1965.

9 *SWE*, 1896.

10 *RR and A*, 27 Mar. 1897.

11 Screened 13 Jan. 1898. Also see Philip Lloyd's article, as above. The quote on Cheetham's machine is from *RR and A*, 22 Jan. 1898, cited in article by Lloyd Jones in *North Wales Lifestyle*, Autumn 1990 (North Wales Weekly News Group). The children playing on the beach film – now lost – should not be confused with the surviving 55ft. 1899 short of youngsters paddling on the Rhyl beach.

12 The steamroller film may be the same as his 'comic scene' in Queen Street advertised around the same time. Almost all the films referred to were screened in May 1899 (*Rhyl Journal*, 20 May). Some were shot early in 1898.

13 Cheetham may have been at a relevant Trewey/Cinematograph performance. *RR and A*, 4 June 1898.

14 *Rhyl Journal*, 20 May 1899 and J. W. Jones, *Rhyl, the Town and its People* (Rhyl, 1970). Cheetham also took film of trains at Llanfairfechan and Penmaenmawr. Llanrwst film shot in 1898.

15 Also see *RR and A*, 11 July 1898. *RR and A*, 2 Sept. 1899 and the bill included his film of E. H. Williams and his Merrie Men and Mr Cheetham singing 'The Little Hero, by request'. 'Prof. [*sic*] Cheetham's attractive and racy phrenological lecture' had been a 'source of so much attraction on the foreshore during the season'. See John Barnes, *Filming the Boer War* (Bishopsgate Press, London, 1992), p.189 and *Rhyl Journal*, 20 May 1899.

16 See the *Showman*, 21 June 1901. The group were first known as Tom Wood and his Merrie Men and attracted 3,000 people to Rhyl Sands in 1898 (*RR and A*, 4 June). Wood, described

as Rhyl's favourite entertainer, died of pneumonia that year – his 27th (*RR and A*, 3 Sept. 1898). E. H. Williams was described as 'interlocutor, reciter, vocalist, sketch and pantomime artist' in *Rhyl Journal*'s contemporary pen portraits of the group (undated, in author's possession).

17 No documentary record has been found to attribute this film, but it was with other Cheetham work handed to Philip Lloyd by the pioneer's grandson, Mr Stanley Cheetham, and Mr Lloyd has verbal testimony from a former pupil and teacher who claims to have been present when Cheetham filmed at the schools.

18 *Cambrian News*, 16 Mar. 1900. In 1904, Cheetham screened films at Barmouth and Towyn, including footage of the 1903 Gorsedd at Rhyl and a 'ride on an electric car through historic Chester' (1 April 1904).

19 *RR and A*, 30 May 1903. Cody's show was at Rhyl on 27 May and Bangor on 28 May, and he was made a member of the Rhyl lodge of the RAOB and the Order's Grand Lodge of England. The ceremony took place at the town's Lorne Hotel, featured in the film, and the local Samuel Smith lodge was re-christened the Col. Cody lodge.

20 The re-discovered 'Cheetham films' cans included footage of a boy overturning an applecart, but no documentary evidence links this to the film-maker. A 'comic scene' in Queen Street, Rhyl (*c*.1897) may have been an actual or re-staged incident.

21 Philip Lloyd article, *Rhyl Journal*, 1984, and also Lloyd Jones's article in *North Wales Lifestyle*, Autumn 1990. The shots of the Rhyl cinema sign altercation were taken during Cheetham's tenure at the venue between 1906 and 1919.

22 *RR and A*, 14 July 1906, and same paper, 29 Sept. and 1 Dec.

23 Ibid., 26 May and 2 June.

24 Souvenir brochure in National Library, Aberystwyth, stamped with the date 1913. Admission prices ranged from 4*d*. to 2*s*. 'Cinematagraph' is here used as a generic term for the projector – note the spelling is slightly different from the Lumières' invention.

25 The Blackburn match, shot in Sept. 1898, was screened on the Silvograph at Rhyl's Central Hall, as late as 1906. It is possible that a Wrexham–Rhyl soccer match shown there (*RR and A*, 3 Nov. 1906), was shot by Cheetham. He certainly filmed a Rhyl Town v. Amateurs game (*Rhyl Journal*, 20 May 1899). Also see *RR and A*, 24 Feb. 1906, *Rhyl Journal*, 8 Sept. 1898, *Photography* vol.10, no.517 (6 Oct. 1898), John Barnes op.cit. and J. W. Jones op.cit.

26 Royal Jubilee films were shown on the Velograph – a 35mm. projector – at the Royal Pier Pavilion, where the Gladstone funeral procession short was shown the same year (*Cambrian News*, 28 Jan. and 26 Aug. 1898 and 24 Mar. 1899).

27 Known from 1910 as Cheetham's Picture Palace, it became the Palladium in 1923, but burned down in 1934. Aberystwyth's Coliseum, now the Ceredigion Museum, featured films regularly by 1905.

28 These works, which could have been made by Cheetham or his sons, were shown at the Aberystwyth Film Festival, 1989. Cheetham also appears in an extant film of a family wedding in 1913.

29 The *Kinematograph Year Book*, 1920, lists 'Shannon's Cinema' – capacity 400 (prop. D. Shannon). Derek Shannon took over *circa* 1919.

30 In the *Showman*, Dec. 1900 (vol.1, no.4) Codman advertised the sale of a 'living picture' machine.

31 Details of Codman's career can be found in an article by John East in *Silent Picture* No.13, Winter/Spring, 1972, and John East's book *'Neath the Mask* (George Allen and Unwin, 1967).

32 According to John East in his book and the *Silent Picture* article (above). East claims that John G. Brett (1866–99), John Codman's brother-in-law, also 'exhibited the bioscope' at Llandudno in the 1890s (*'Neath the Mask*, p.173).

33 The details of his New Empire shows come from letter-headed correspondence from Codman

(then at the Coliseum Theatre, Aberystwyth) in 1909. A photostat supplied by magic-lanternist Mervyn Heard is in the author's possession. Also see John East's *'Neath The Mask*.

34 *'Neath the Mask*, as above, pp.159–60. I have been unable to find descriptions of these films. All except *A Tour of North Wales* are mentioned in Denis Gifford's *British Film Catalogue 1895–1985* which also lists **Mr Troublesome** – a film not referred to by East. No lengthy synopsis or definite dates are provided (unusually for Gifford), though all the films are listed for the four-year period. Codman's own adverts refer to his films.

35 *'Neath the Mask*, as above, p.160.

36 Ibid. p.181. Neptune Films were established at Borehamwood in 1914. He was at London Films in 1912.

37 Advert issued from Codman's Llandudno base – in *World's Fair*, 25 July 1908.

38 Others were at Pontycymmer, Newtown, Barmouth, Llandudno, Llanidloes, Bangor, Oswestry, Bethesda and Shrewsbury (article in *Silent Picture*, as above). The *Bioscope*, 8 April 1915, listed other ventures at Menai Bridge and Ebbw Vale.

39 *Silent Picture* article. See also *Llanelli County Guardian*, 7 Jan. 1909, and *Bioscope*, 5 Aug. 1909. The same paper reported (on 8 April 1915), a creditors' meeting at Chester which referred to a 'great loss on pantomime ventures' and 'a loss on picturedromes', with Codman citing particular problems at Oswestry.

40 *Bioscope* 25 Nov. 1909 and *Kinematograph Yearbook*, 1921.

41 Ibid. 25 Nov. 1909. M Saronie-Saronie Enterprises later ran 'La Scala' in Prestatyn and the Rhyl Picture House, according to *Kinematograph Yearbook*, 1920. He converted the town hall, Prestatyn, into a cinema by 1913 and it became the Scala cinema the following year (Lloyd Jones article, *North Wales Lifestyle*, as above). Other notable north Wales ventures were run by Nestlé's and Lever – best known for Nestlé's chocolate and milk and Lever's Sunlight soap. They were at Wrexham as early as 1898 with '40 subjects' – including the queen's diamond jubilee procession and the Henley regatta. Currah's Myriorama showed films 'plus the wonderful gramophone or trumpet-speaking machine' at Coedpoeth, Brymbo and Summerhill, the same year. See *Wrexham Advertiser*, 5 March and 7 May 1898.

42 *Carmarthen Journal*, Jan. 1899, and the *Showman*, 6 Mar. 1901. See also chapter 3.

CHAPTER 3

1 Cast members listed in Denis Gifford, *The British Film Catalogue 1895–1985* (David and Charles, 1986) are Walter, Violet, Henry and Lillian Haggar, though Sarah Haggar also appears. In November 1903, Gaumont released another Haggar chase film **A Dash for Liberty** (300ft.), in five scenes, also centred on a convict's escape.

2 All are listed in the *British Film Catalogue* as above and Gaumont catalogues in the BFI. Of thirty-four Haggar films listed in Gifford, nineteen were distributed by Gaumont, six by Urban, five by the Warwick Trading Co., and one (**Maria Marten**) by Walter Tyler. Three are unattributed. The film copy sales figure can be found in Rachael Low and Roger Manvell, *History of the British Film 1896–1906* (George Allen and Unwin, 1949). They claim **Rescued by Rover** sold 395 copies.

3 Low and Manvell, op.cit., describe **The Life of Charles Peace**, for example, as 'one of the most advanced films of the period'.

4 Lillian Haggar's unpublished manuscript (in the BFI) refers to eleven Haggar children – eight survived into adulthood. One daughter of William and Sarah Haggar (née Walton), Helen Elizabeth (Nell) drowned in the River Wye at Chepstow *c.*1890 – a tragedy recreated in the 1987 BBC Wales TV film **A Penny for Your Dreams** (dir. Ken Howard).

5 The first Haggar film shows were in the Castle Theatre Bioscope – according to Lillian's manuscript. Walter dubbed it the Windsor Castle Biograph (in his unpublished autobiographical manuscript, photostat copy in author's possession). The Castle Theatre, continued as a portable stage show run by Will jun., but was badly damaged by a fire in 1907

during a performance of the drama *The Lucky Horseshoe* (*World's Fair*, 28 Dec. 1907). A playbill survives in Chepstow Museum for a Haggar theatre company performance at Chepstow, 1890.

6 Lillian Haggar's unpublished MS. Alfred Wrench of J. Wrench and Son patented a projector – a 'triennial with three lanterns': two for slides (allowing dissolving effects), one for moving pictures. It was used from 1896, and proved popular in the provinces (John Barnes, *The Beginnings of the Cinema in England*, pp.137–41). Lillian Haggar gives the first film show date as 5 April 1898, when she claims 300 people packed into the performances which earned £15. The year varies between 1897 and 1898 in Walter's accounts (his unpublished MSS and his article in *Dock Leaves*, 1953). In an advert in the 1904 Gaumont catalogue, William Haggar sen. testified to using Gaumont's Chronophone projector for seven years. The year 1898 remains the most probable date on the basis of the MS accounts of the coal strike.

7 Lillian Haggar, ibid.

8 Leslie Wood, *The Miracle of the Movies* (Burke Publishing Co., 1957).

9 Lengths of these poaching and police films (excluding the **Mirthful Mary** series) ranged from the 90ft. **The Rival Painters** to the 275ft. **Bathing Not Allowed** (1905 – similar in content to Haggar's 75ft. **The Bather's Revenge** (1904), distributed by the Urban company).

10 125ft., distributed by Urban.

11 Bromhead's speech was to the Kinematograph Renters' Society 1930 (records in BFI Library, London).

12 Sheffield Photo Company Catalogue, 1906. A colour-tinted version of Haggar's film exists in BFI, with purple, yellow and green used for various interiors, red for exteriors.

13 Sheffield Photo Co. catalogue, as above. *Optical Lantern and Cinematograph Journal*, Nov. 1905. Haggar may have been reciprocating when he stole a march on Mottershaw – for the Sheffield Co.'s **The Tramp and the Washerwoman** (1904) could owe something to Haggar's film of the same title released 1903.

14 Lillian Haggar's unpublished MS, as above. She also featured prominently in **Desperate Footpads** (or **The Farmer's Daughter and the Desperate Footpads**), listed in catalogues as 1907, though she claimed it was shot in Haverfordwest in 1909.

15 Sheffield Photo Co. catalogue, as above. In contrast, Mottershaw's **Daring Daylight Burglary** arguably reveals a more sophisticated grasp of composition than surviving Haggar films.

16 **The Poachers** screening in America reference is in Charles Musser, Carol Nelson, *High-Class Moving Pictures: Lyman H. Howe and the Forgotten Era of Travelling Exhibition 1880–1920* (Princeton University Press, 1991) p.136. See also Musser, *Before the Nickelodeon – Edwin S. Porter and the Edison Manufacturing Company* (University of California Press, 1991), pp.253 and 259.

17 **Message from the Sea** is listed at 420ft. in Gaumont Catalogue 1905 but at 745ft. in *Bioscope*, 1908. Also see *Optical Lantern and Cinematograph Journal* vol 2, 1906.

18 Lillian Haggar's MS. Of the Haggar films listed in Gifford, ten – excluding William Haggar jun.'s **The Maid of Cefn Ydfa** (1913–14) – feature characters flung, or knocked, into the river.

19 Lillian Haggar's MS. Low and Manvell, *The History of British Film 1896–1906* and Gaumont Catalogue, Nov. 1905, which also claims **The Salmon Poachers** was 'beautifully tinted'. Film normally cost 1*s.* a foot in Haggar's day, according to Walter's unpublished MS. But Leslie Wood in *The Miracle of the Movies* says 6*d.* a ft. was common in the 1890s and prices were still around 4*d.*–6*d.* a ft. by 1909. Bromhead's speech was made to the KRS, 1930 – see note 11 above.

20 See, among many, R. Low and R. Manvell *History of the British Film 1896–1906*, David Robinson, *World Cinema* (Eyre Methuen, 1973), Michael Chanan, *The Dream that Kicks* (Routledge and Kegan Paul, 1980) and Thomas Elsaesser (ed.), *Early Cinema: Space, Frame and Narrative* (BFI, 1990). Low and Manvell did not have Lillian Haggar's information to

hand at the time of their first edition. Walter claims to have filmed 'with an assistant' from Moss Empires a walking match at Treorchy (his unpublished MS). Lillian said 'Walter was a very fine actor' and the 'best brain in the family . . . in spite of father's knowledge of acting and photography I don't think he would have got as far as he did in the world of moving pictures without Walter's help.'

21 Lillian claimed in the manuscript that she saw the film in 1948. In Cavalcanti's 1948 documentary about cinema history, **Film and Reality**, the Peace extract made by Haggar is attributed to Mottershaw.

22 Lillian, who claimed her father bought his first projector from Exeter in 1897, said that in 1902–3 her father switched from an Urban machine to 'Pathé's No.2 Mechanism'. These details seem to conflict with Haggar's comments (in Gaumont 1904 Catalogue) that he used a Gaumont Chrono from the late 1890s. There were, of course, two Haggar bioscope shows (Walter's and William sen.'s) at one stage touring Wales. Lillian Haggar also claims her father, influenced by R. W. Paul's original ideas, also invented a double-shutter machine – using purple gelatine which Urban was 'delighted to adopt'. Haggar's first machines worked with limelight – oxygen and hydrogen in cylinders ignited on a circle of lime the size of a cotton reel.

23 In the same year, Wadbrooks showed a Wales–Ireland soccer match (see Lillian Haggar's biography and *The Showman*, 30 Aug. 1901).

24 Lillian Haggar, ibid.

25 Ibid.

26 *Showman*, 16 Aug. and 27 Sept. 1901.

27 Haggar shot alleged footage of the Russian–Japanese war but an audience member spotted a local member in the cast. Lillian (in her manuscript) and Jo Haggar – William jun.'s daughter (in an interview with the author at her home in Pembroke, 17 Feb. 1984) gave slightly different versions of this incident and the films. Walter – in his unpublished MS – recalls taking part with brother James *c.*1904–5, in scenes purporting to be of the Russian–Japanese War. The Charles Urban Trading Company's footage of the war was certainly circulating in America in 1905 (see Charles Musser, *High-Class Moving Pictures*, as above).

28 Madge Rastall, Walter's daughter, interviewed by the author at her home, Tutshill nr. Chepstow, 1984. Ada Roberts, Walter's wife, refers to the same film in a taped interview (undated) obtained by Walter's great-grandson, Roy Haggar jun. of Tenby. A **Women of Mumbles Head** film (on a set of slides) was presented by Haggar based on a play by his company.

29 See Lillian and Walter's unpublished reminiscences. Walter refers to William sen. making several very successful Boer War dramas – 'following the example of a Bradford firm making very fine war films'. These were probably Riley's of Bradford – see John Barnes, *The Rise of Cinema in Great Britain* (Bishopsgate Press, 1983) and Barnes's *Pioneers of the British Film* (Bishopsgate Press, 1989). Walter stated that his father shot several Boer War films in the Rhondda Valley, and some Russian–Japanese films in the Rhymney Valley – and he also claimed he played a Japanese character in one such film, made at Quakers' Yard.

30 Author's interview with Griff Harries, then aged eighty, at Aberdare in the mid-1980s. Mr Harries, a former helper and part-time projectionist at Haggar's cinema there, remembered the showman 'filming processions from the roof of the Boot Hotel, Aberdare, and smashing crockery behind the screen as sound effects in disaster films'. Haggar enjoyed 'a hit' showing a Welsh Pageant film at Brynmawr Fair in 1909 (*World's Fair*, 12 Sept. 1909). Lillian also claimed her father filmed skaters in Aberdare Park (her unpublished biography).

31 **Tramp and Baby's Bottle**, listed as a Haggar film in catalogues, was also made by Bamforths in 1899 (ibid.). Haggar sen. paid £70 for a Méliès film **Wonders of the Deep** (alt. titles **Kingdom of the Fairies/Le Royaume des Fées**) (1903), according to Walter, William Haggar certainly

showed the Frenchman's works **Trip to the Moon** and **Bluebeard** at his popular Aberdare shows – in 1902, for example.

32 120ft., 115ft. and 94ft. respectively.

33 Gaumont catalogue (in BFI).

34 Ibid. Mog also featured in Haggar's film **Snowballing** (1904, 115ft.).

35 Ibid. See Low and Manvell, op.cit. pp. 50–89. Other Weary Willie and Tired Tim films have been attributed, tentatively, to Haggar (see Gifford's catalogue no. 00641) but a number of British directors made shorts in the series. **Weary Willie and Tired Tim at the Races** is attributed to Haggar by Lillian in her manuscript. No film of this title appears in Gifford's catalogue.

36 Walter's article in *Dock Leaves* (later the *Anglo-Welsh Review*) vol.3, no.10. Spring 1953.

37 Will jun. employed the town crier with a handbell to wander the streets announcing his programmes (author's interview, 1985, with Haydn Thomas, former conductor and accompanist of Pontardulais Operatic Society which played seasons at Will jun.'s cinema). Mr Thomas also saw Will's cinema burnt down by fire in 1923 and spoke of the cinema 'going up like a matchbox'. He said Will was held back by his friends as he saw all his props perish in the blaze (interview, 1985, and with Claire Pollak for **The Dream that Kicks**, HTV, 1986). Jenny Linden was the stage name of Jane Emily (Jenny) Haggar.

38 One version was shot at Maesteg, and the surviving film around Pontardulais. Walter Haggar claimed a cameraman was brought down from London for one version, possibly the surviving film (dated August 1914, by Gifford). Walter also wrote of the film's huge box-office popularity.

39 Will Fyffe joined William Haggar sen.'s company around 1898, according to Lillian. (Ada Roberts, Walter's wife, claimed he joined as a clog-dancer.) He was certainly a singer and comedian for Will jun.'s company, appearing at Llanelli in 1911. This company regularly played the *Maid of Cefn Ydfa* on stage and Fred Haggar – another son of William sen. – played Lewis Bach in 1911 (*Llanelli Mercury*, 27 April and 4 May). Fyffe's later screen image is epitomized by his hard-drinking misfit in the British feature **Spring Handicap** (1935).

40 After a BBC radio programme appeal – *SWE*, 26 June 1984. **The Maid** was screened at Cardiff's ABC Olympia in 1938 when it was described as 'the only copy in existence'.

41 One 450ft. version of **The Maid** was shot in seven scenes, according to Lillian. The family claim there were at least three pre-1913 versions. One early version *c*.1902/3 was filmed by Will jun.'s company at Maesteg, according to Walter (unpublished MS). Walter Haggar claims his father made a 450 ft. version of **The Maid** in seven scenes *c*.1902/3, and that it took £40 at Treorchy – a huge sum for that time – on its first day's screening (unpublished MS).

42 Lillian Haggar's MS. She claimed the Haggars failed to take a penny at Pontypridd on Easter Monday, 1898. At Whit they charged only 1*d*. to miners on strike at Mountain Ash. The family's fortunes naturally fluctuated with the coalfields – the Haggar family motto became 'follow the coal' and Lillian was known affectionately for years as 'Coalyard Lil'.

43 *World's Fair*, 21 Sept. 1907. Haggar's show was known late in this period as the Royal Electric Bioscope. Violet Haggar led Haggar's dancing girl paraders on the front-of-house stage and lecturers for Haggar shows included her husband Cyril Yorke and Gus Bendall. A copy of the letterhead for W. Haggar and Sons' Royal Electric Bioscope (undated) is in the author's possession, bearing a business address: 'Gordon House, Buckley Road, Kilburn, London'.

44 *Bioscope*, 31 Dec. 1908.

45 The year of the first Haggar Marenghi organ varies with different sources, Walter claiming the instrument was purchased in 1906 (unpublished MS). The original Marenghi frontage had a domed ceiling, gilded figures either side of the entrance and 840 incandescent lamps. 'The crowd stood for hours at this display – nothing like it had been seen before' (Lillian's biography). The steam traction engines also represented great kudos to the south Wales

bioscope shows. The Haggars, at one stage, boasted a Fowler engine named *The Maid of Cefn Ydfa*.

46 Haggar's 'dancing girls and beautiful cinematograph show' were an attraction at Pembroke Fair in 1909 (*World's Fair*, 23 Oct. 1909, citing the *Pembroke Times*). 'The gorgeous Colosseums [*sic*] of Messrs Haggar and Danter are really works of art,' trilled *World's Fair* (21 Aug. 1909). The reporter was also taken with the 'bevy of beauties [paraders] in short skirts gracefully throwing their nether limbs about'. In 1908, Haggar's 'famous Coliseum of Moving Pictures' was at the Maesteg Pleasure and Flannel Fair (*World's Fair*, Oct. 1908). Haggar sometimes held a bioscope show monopoly at fairs (such as Pembroke) after offering more cash than rivals for a spot (see *Pembroke Times* fairs reports, 1910). Sidney White's Orchestraphone is described in *World's Fair*, 2 Jan. 1909. (See also article on White in *SWE*, 24 June 1977).

47 *CEE*, 14 Sept. and 7 Dec.

48 *SWE*, 7 and 14 Sept. 1906 and 23 Feb. 1907.

49 **The Women of Mumbles Head** (screened with recitals) may also possibly have been a Haggar film, also **Wreck of the Amazon on Margam Sands** shown on the American Bioscope at the Newport Empire (ibid., 31 Dec. 1906).

50 *World's Fair*, 4 Jan. 1907.

51 Haggar sen. paid £3,000 for a spacious theatre at Merthyr in 1912, run for a time by his son, Henry. By 1920, Walter ran the cinema at Nayland (before switching to Aberdare), Bert Richards (husband of Lillian Richards née Haggar), ran the Palace cinema, Mountain Ash, and William jun. the Picturedrome, Pontardulais (*Kinematograph Yearbook*, 1920). Walter took over the cinema at Pembroke from William jun.'s widow in the 1930s when another Haggar, Len, began running the Pembroke cinema. Len's son, John, ran the cinema through the 1970s.

52 Richard Dooner, national president of the Cinematograph Exhibitors' Association in 1935, was a member of the Cinema Veterans' Association – showmen who were screening films before 1903. Walter Haggar's unpublished manuscript confirms Richard Dooner had a cine-camera. I have failed to find documentary evidence to confirm whether the Dooners or Danters shot their own films. There is no extant film of work by any 'Welsh' fairground showman apart from Haggar.

53 *Showman*, Sept. 1901.

54 Gwyn Price, Richard Dooner's son-in-law (interviewed April 1990), recalled Dooner's former Cosy cinema at Maesteg as 'no more than a shack'. Dooner later rented the New Theatre there from former boxing champion Jimmy Wilde and also ran cinemas at Abergavenny, Brynmawr, Bridgend, Cwm and Ogmore Vale – according to *Glamorgan Advertiser*, 7 Sept. 1951. Harry Glover, then aged eighty-three, told in a 1990 interview with the author how his father Walter Glover, manager of Dooner's Abergavenny cinema, acted as lecturer for early silents there – 'pointing out characters with a stick'.

55 An article in the showman's paper *Merry Go Round* (1967) claimed Studt's bioscope show was the largest in Wales.

56 Studt's Cinematograph Show at Hereford Fair boasted a fine new organ costing £1,800 (*World's Fair*, 18 May 1907). Pat Collins took delivery at Wrexham in 1907 of a Marenghi organ costing £2,000. John Studt was renowned for charity work and *World's Fair* in 1911 claimed he had given £30,000 to charities in the previous three years.

57 Edward Danter was a victim of the tough new cinema legislation with the coming of cinemas. He was fined at Ystradgynlais for operating his bioscope on the showground without a cinematograph licence (*World's Fair*, 14 Oct. 1911).

58 Author's interviews with the Danter family arranged by Mrs P. Jenkins of Hirwaun. Joseph Danter's travelling picture-show was wrecked by a blizzard, according to surviving family members.

59 Wadbrook's Ghost and Electrical Cinematographe was at Birmingham Onion Fair as early as

1898 – *The Era*, 19 Jan. 1899, cited in John Barnes, *The Rise of the Cinema in Great Britain*, p.177.

60 *The Showman* vol.2, no.15, March 1901.

61 Ibid. 7 Mar. 1902. Wadbrooks also screened local soccer matches, e.g., Aberdare v. Porth (Welsh League 1903).

62 *World's Fair* 16 July 1910 – citing *Western Mail* article. Mrs Crecraft at ninety-four was still working the paybox when the bioscope visited Nayland, Pembrokeshire (ibid. 27 July 1912).

63 Ibid., 13 April 1912. The Glynneath cinema – the Palace – was known affectionately to locals as 'Mam's'.

64 Ibid., 4 Dec. 1909 and 7 Jan. 1911, for details of Manders shows at Nelson (Glamorgan) and Kidwelly. Pat Collins, former Mayor of Walsall, had unparalleled success at Wrexham Fair with his 'Wonderland Cinematographe de Luxe' (*Wrexham Advertiser*, 10 April 1910). Sidney White later moved into permanent cinemas – first at the New Palace, Haverfordwest, in 1913. Other bioscope shows in Wales were Capt. Rowlands's Bioscope and Lion Show (at Aberavon and Brecon fairs, 1901), George Green's cinema de luxe from Scotland (Wrexham Fair 1910), Charles Farrell's show, Nail's Bioscope of Passing Events, Steel Parry's Crown Electric Bioscope, and J. W. Chipperfield's Electrographe, while Hancocks, the West Country family earlier linked with the Dooners, held short-term bioscope licences at Hereford and Newport.

65 *Showman*, 4 April 1901 and 24 Jan. 1902. *Glamorgan Gazette*, 8 May 1915. Lillian Haggar writes of her father's battles in competition with Jack Scarrott, but Walter's reminiscences refer to rivalry with Bill Samuels of Swansea, a former pugilist with a boxing show. In 1907 at Neath Fair, Scarrott was reduced to wooing crowds with prizefighting exhibitions by his friend, the legendary bareknuckle boxer Jem Mace, then seventy-eight.

66 *World's Fair*, 30 May 1908.

67 Lillian's MS. An Aberdare local, J. Emlyn Evans, recalled attending Haggar's temporary Shanty cinema in pre-Kosy cinema days and seeing 'scantily-dressed high-kicking dancing girls' on the stage facing the road. (Interviewed 1984.)

68 Details of Haggar's council and Board of Guardians links appeared in numerous *Aberdare Leader* reports in 1913 and 1914 and his obit notice in *Aberdare Leader*, 7 Feb. 1925. All are cited by Geoffrey Hill in 'William Haggar, pioneer of the cinema in Wales', in *Old Aberdare* vol.VI (Cynon Valley History Society, 1989).

69 Ibid., *Aberdare Leader*, 16 Mar. 1912.

70 Ibid., 26 April 1913. There were isolated skirmishes with authorities in Wales around the same time – Rhyl magistrates decided, for instance, that no children should attend films after 8.30 p.m. (*Bioscope*, June 1915).

71 The five shows at Portfield Fair in 1909 were Wadbrooks, Dooners, Crecrafts, Haggars and Danters. Certainly some bioscopes were still touring Welsh showgrounds in 1914 – Walter Haggar was at Neath with war films and the Haggars also screened war films at Carmarthen and Llandovery fairs (*World's Fair*, various, 1914).

72 The lobby for increased safety standards gained ammunition from such natural disasters as the fire which swept through Arthur Wildman's Franco-British Bioscopical Exhibition with its 'magnificent showfront' at Connah's Quay on 7 Sept. 1909 (*World's Fair*, 11 Sept. 1909). A fire at an unnamed Newport hall projection booth in the same year – believed to have been caused by careless storage of film – led to threats to withdraw the music licence there; and 200 children were evacuated from a Merthyr cinema in 1906 when flames belched from an operating box, knocking the door off its hinges (*Bioscope*, 18 Nov. 1909 and *Optical Lantern and Cinematograph Journal*, 1906).

73 In taped interview with Roy Haggar jun. (undated but, he says, probably from the 1960s).

1 The *Bookman* ranked Raine as one of the four best-selling novelists of her day – alongside Marie Corelli, Hall Caine and Silas Hocking (Sally Jones, *Allen Raine*, University of Wales Press/Welsh Arts Council, 1979). All three filmed Raine novels were first published between 1897 and 1899. Details of the films' casting are in Denis Gifford's *British Film Catalogue 1895–1985* (David and Charles, 1986).

2 'Speaking of silents – the girls of Vitagraph and Biograph', in *Classic Images*, Sept. 1981. Anthony Slide describes Turner as 'the world's first film star' in his *Early American Cinema* (International Film Guide series – Barnes and Co. and A. Zwemmer Ltd., 1970).

3 In **Daisy Doodad's Dial**, a lone viewable Turner film in the BFI archive and made in 1914 in Britain, she reveals her penchant for mugging as she grimaces and changes expression bewilderingly as a 'funny faces' contest entrant in a dream sequence.

4 Edward Wagenknecht, *The Movies in the Age of Innocence* (University of Oklahoma Press, 1962). Also see the chapter on Florence Turner in Anthony Slide's *The Big V – The History of the Vitagraph Company* (new revised edition, 1987), pp.37–43.

5 Letter from Anthony Slide to the author, and *Kinematograph Weekly*, 9 Dec. 1915. The film was deemed sufficiently important for an elaborate musical programme to accompany it at the London trade show. Garforth Mortimer's orchestra accompanied **A Welsh Singer**'s screening at Cardiff's Park Hall Cinema in 1916 (*SWE*, 4 Mar. 1916). By November that year the film had been booked, at various times, into 800 cinemas in Britain (*Bioscope*, 23 Nov. 1916).

6 *Bioscope*, 9 Dec. 1915.

7 *Kinematograph Weekly*, 9 Dec. 1915. *SWE* praised the exterior settings, particularly views of the 'barefooted heroine seen against a background of a silvery lake and distant mountains drawing along a large flock of shaggy mountain sheep' (8 Dec. 1915).

8 *CEE*, 7 and 10 Mar. 1914.

9 Hepworth's biography *Came the Dawn* (Phoenix House, 1951) said the company's artistic strength lay in these three performers, cited in Rachael Low, *The History of British Film 1918–1929* (George Allen and Unwin, 1971).

10 *By Berwen Banks* is the novel title but the film is listed as **By Berwin Banks** in Gifford's *British Film Catalogue* and as **By Berwyn Banks** in Rachael Low, *The History of British Film 1918–1929*. Also see *Cardigan and Tivyside Advertiser*, 17 Sept. 1920.

11 Filmed at Llangranog, Tresaith and New Quay (*Cardigan and Tivyside Advertiser*, 20 Aug. 1920). A boat overturned and both the company's manager, Mr Harold Francis, and Geoffrey Kerr, who played Ifor, had to abandon ship and were 'picked up by Milton Rosmer' or rescued by bystanders (ibid., 3 Sept. 1920). The sail-shed fire was shot in the London studios. In 1920 Ideal, who made **Torn Sails**, also released **Build Thy House**, a drama about a padre who becomes an MP, from a scenario by Welshman Trevor Jones, which won a £200 screenwriting competition (*Bioscope*, 19 Feb. 1920). The film was described as 'a stirring drama about the reconciliation of capital and labour' in the *Bioscope*, May/June, 1920.

12 Sally Jones, op.cit., p.33.

13 *Bioscope*, 28 Oct. 1920.

14 Mrs Margaret Beckingsale of Newcastle Emlyn, Allen Raine's great-niece, has deposited the writer's diaries and other documents – including Mrs Hope's notes on the author's career – in Carmarthen Library. Mrs Beckingsale tells me Mrs Hope was the wife of Mr Charles Hope, the county's former high sheriff. Article by A. G. Prys-Jones (items 62/16 in Beckingsale Collection) and *Allen Raine's Book* (Hutchinson, 1899).

15 Emlyn Williams praised Allen Raine in the first volume of his autobiography, *George* (Penguin Books, 1976).

16 *Allen Raine's Book*, cited by Sally Jones, op.cit.

17 *Bioscope*, 29 July 1920.

18 Ibid.

19 She is best remembered now for her role as the orphan and love object, Norma, in Abel Gance's 1923 feature **La Roue** (**The Wheel**).

20 Gifford film catalogue (as above).

21 Ibid. **The Witch of the Welsh Mountains** was shown at Cardiff's Olympia (*World's Fair*, 10 Aug. 1912) and at Haggars, Llanelli (*Llanelli Mercury*, 12 Sept. 1912).

22 See entries for Nepean (1890–1969) in *The Oxford Companion to the Literature of Wales*, compiled and edited by Meic Stephens (Oxford University Press, 1986) and *Who's Who in Wales* (Adam and Charles Black, 1937).

23 Gifford, as above. Longish films were still rare. In a survey of exhibitors in 1919, Geo. Roberts, of the Grand Cinema, Porth, Rhondda, described an ideal bill as a five-reel 'star' film, a two-reel comedy, two-reel serial, one-reel short drama and a one-reel 'interest' film (*Kinematograph Weekly*, 1 Jan. 1920).

24 Ibid. and Rachael Low, *History of the British Film 1918–1929*, p.353. (George Allen and Unwin, 1971).

25 Ibid. and Rachael Low, *The History of British Film 1914–1918* (George Allen and Unwin, 1948) p.92. One 'Welsh' film mauled by critics was **People of the Rocks**, a comedy directed by Dalton Somers in 1914. When it was re-issued in 1916 one reviewer said it was 'too amateurish to be successful' when first released and the 'same applies even more severely today, despite its fine, scenic setting and crude, fantastic comedy'.

26 Gifford, as above. **Land of My Fathers** was set in Aberystwyth. It is not to be confused with **Land of My Fathers**, a series of eight single-reel Welsh scenes directed in various parts of Wales by Frank Miller and released in 1928. **Love in the Welsh Hills** was reviewed in the *Bioscope*, 10 Jan. 1924.

27 *Bioscope*, 22 Jan. 1914. The film was adapted from a drama by Anne and Bannister Merwin.

28 Edison also released in 1914 a 350ft. film **Wild Wales** (*Bioscope*, 22 and 29 Jan. 1914).

29 In 1918 and 1919, Elvey went to Caernarfon, Cricieth and Neath to film (some visits were for the Lloyd George feature) and to Cardiff on another subject (unknown) – article on director in the *Bioscope*, 1 Jan. 1920. Sarah Street, 'The memoir of Harry Rowson – David Lloyd George: the man who saved the Empire' in *The Historical Journal of Film, Radio and Television* vol.7, no.1, 1987 (Carfax Publishing Co./International Association for Audio-Visual Media in Historical Research and Education). The film is listed as 06657, 'The Life Story of David Lloyd George' in Denis Gifford, *British Film Catalogue 1895–1985* (David and Charles, 1986).

30 Sarah Street, op.cit. Street was on the staff of the Bodleian Library, Oxford.

31 Sarah Street, op.cit. Hepworth's 'Kine Views' were part of a Cabinet feature later abandoned.

32 Denis Gifford, *British Animated Films 1895–1985* (McFarland and Co., 1987).

33 Scott had written a poem about Chepstow Castle – 'The Norman Horse Shoe'.

34 Article on Brenon in *Films in Review*, March 1955. *Bioscope*, 10 and 24 July 1913.

35 *Moving Picture World*, 1913.

36 *Bioscope*, 24 July 1913. 'The story of Ivanhoe' – as told in the film – by Lewis Roach appeared in *Illustrated Films Monthly* (undated photostat in author's possession). There is a viewing print of **Ivanhoe** at the National Film Archive (BFI) and the Chepstow Society also held a copy in the 1980s, obtained after an auction in the local public hall.

37 Bush also found the military operations on screen confusing and claimed the 'movements of the mob gave one the undesirable impression of long and painful drills before the camera' (16 Sept. 1913). Certainly the antics of the extras scurrying to and from the castle are unwittingly comic.

38 Paul Rotha, writing generally of Brenon's career in *The Film Till Now* (1930) thought his 'sense of pictorial values sound' but his cinematic interpretation 'negligible'. This might be contradicted by anyone who has seen the director's splendid and compassionate **Sorrell and Son** (1927) with H. B. Warner.

39 *Films in Review*, March 1955.

40 **Ivanhoe** opened at Cardiff's Olympia cinema with 'specially selected music by the cinema's Grand English Orchestra' (*SWE*, 2 Sept. 1913). See Rachael Low, *History of the British Film 1906–1914*. The film was one of the last important films to be sold on the open market – at 4*d.* a foot, selling 112 copies (ibid).

41 *SWE*, 23 Sept. 1919.

42 *SWE*, 18 Sept. 1919. The company could possibly lay claim to producing the first comedy *set* in Wales by a Welsh company – but Haggar made several comedies shot in Wales with the setting unspecified. In 1913, music-hall personalities the Egbert Brothers appeared in a short comedy **The Dustmens' Holiday**, set in Swansea and made by London-based Will P. Kellino (Gifford, as above). See Tom Gunning, 'The Cinema of Attractions', in *Early Cinema: Space, Frame, Narrative* (BFI publishing, 1990).

43 *SWE*, 19 Mar., 26 April and 26 June 1920.

44 Ibid., 26 June 1920.

45 Ibid., 18 Mar. and 23 April 1920.

46 Walter Gibbons Bio-Tableaux Boer War films were particularly popular, with prime bookings in 1900 at the Cardiff and Newport Empires and at Cardiff's Andrews Hall. Gibbons, a noted early film-maker, was later boss of the Holborn Empire.

47 Shots of Conwy Castle were shown at the Empire, Cardiff (*CEE*, 13 June 1898). This film was shot from the engine of an express train and was a 'phantom train ride' of the type familiar to audiences of the day. The Heron film – **By Boat to Trefriw Wells** – was made in 1913.

48 Another Hepworth short, the 1904 **Waterfalls of Wales**, is in the National Film Archive. The Warwick Trading Company 1900 catalogue (in the BFI) refers to film of the SS *Tudno*, the biggest steamship of the Liverpool and North Wales Company's fleet, photographed leaving Llandudno Pier 'crowded with passengers waving caps and handkerchiefs'. The company also shot another ship, the *St Elvies* 'approaching the pier at full speed', plus a 125ft. film of Conwy Castle and the town including the Holyhead Express passing under Conwy Bridge, and separate panoramic views of Caernarfon, Church Island and the Menai Straits (records in Charles Urban collection, Science Museum, London).

49 *Bioscope*, 5 May 1910 and 2 Jan. 1911. **River Banks of Wales** is mentioned in correspondence between the Gelli Pictorium cinema, Rhondda, and the Charles Urban Company of Wardour Street, London, 9 Aug. 1918 (Pictorium Papers collection, loaned to author by Martin Roberts, then of Canton, Cardiff, 1987).

50 Details of Urban's Kinemacolor success are in the Science Museum, London. See also D. B. Thomas, *The First Colour Motion Pictures* (Science Museum, 1969).

51 The first Welsh disaster to appear on screen was probably **The Loss** [or **Wreck**] **of the** *Amazon* **at Margam Sands** (1908). The 'Clydach pit disaster' was shown on the American Bioscope at Swansea Empire in 1910, when the pictures 'brought home the devastation caused' (*SWDP*, 28 and 29 Mar. 1910).

52 *Llanelli Mercury*, 24 Aug. 1911.

53 Ibid., 14 Sept. 1911. The same month Sir Stafford and Lady Howard attended Haggar's cinema (the former Royalty at Llanelli) for a screening of their daughter's wedding; James Haggar presented the film to them as a 'novel wedding present'. A copy survives and includes shots of members of the Haggar family. See also *Llanelli Mercury*, 30 Nov. 1911.

54 Ibid., 21 Dec. 1911.

55 *Llanelli Mercury*, 16 Oct. 1913.

56 Charles Butt Stanton (1873–1946), leading figure in the Tonypandy riots, advocated in 1911 setting up a Citizens Army, became Merthyr MP in 1915 (succeeding Keir Hardie) then Aberdare Constituency MP in 1918. He is noted also for the 1903 pamphlet 'Why We Agitate'. The Stanton and Wilson films are in the National Film Archive.

57 *Bioscope*, 3 July 1913.

58 *Gaumont Weekly*, 24 July and 28 Aug. 1913 and *Exhibitors' Pocket Book for Welsh and West Country Showmen*, 4 May 1914.

59 *Bioscope*, 31 July 1913. Also *Exhibitors' Pocket Book*, as above (copy in Cardiff Central Library). Pathé even resurrected an old standby – producing **A Storm on the Welsh Coast** (1914) with 'excellent photography which does justice to the restless ever-changing ocean'.

60 *Bioscope*, Sept. 1913. A string of agents handling company products were operating in Wales by mid-decade: Percy Tatem and Co. handled Britain's popular Clarendon Films and Jurys were agents for Keystone's comedies and Edison's Kinetophone sound system (ibid., 6 May 1915).

61 *Bioscope Annual and Trades Directory*, 1910–11.

62 *Kinematograph Yearbooks* 1920 and 1921. A huge attraction in these days were, of course, Chaplin's early one- and two-reelers. In 1916, the Cardiff Castle and Central cinemas held 'exclusive rights' on them in the city (*SWE*, 29 Jan.).

63 The Electric was opened by October 1909 (*Bioscope*, 11 Nov. 1909). The Imperial – originally sometimes described merely as the Picture Palace Theatre – opened 20 Feb. 1911 (*Bioscope*, 23 Feb. 1911). Miss Maud Jeffreys, one of Wales's first female managers, worked at the Electric from *c*.1911, managed Cardiff's Imperial cinema from 1918 to 1927 and was the first manager of the Odeon (opened 1936–7). (Documents from her relative, Joyce Grant, of Leckwith, Cardiff, 1985.) Miss Julia Jones managed the Cardiff Cinema (or Kinema) Queen Street by 1920 (*Kinematograph Weekly*, 29 Jan. 1920). See Cardiff City Watch Committee minutes 25 Sept. 1909; 24 Jan. 1910; 9 Feb. 1910; 7 June 1911.

64 In 1914–15 Swansea had nineteen cinema venues serving a 114,663 population (*Kinematograph Yearbook*, 1915). William Coutts had taken over the Palace at Swansea by 1905, dubbing it in the grand style of the day The People's Art Gallery and Choice Academy of Bioscope Pictures; and he also ran the Star (2,000 seats) and Shaftesbury (800) by 1910 (*Bioscope Annual and Trade Directory* 1910–11). The biggest Swansea cinema venue remained the Empire (2,500 seats).

65 The Central launch (7 Mar.) is reported in *Bioscope* 16 Mar. 1911, and the same paper noted (12 Aug. 1909) that Oswald Stoll intended opening the Andrews Hall as 'a continuous picture entertainment'. (The Olympia opened Boxing Day, 1910.) See also Cardiff Watch Committee minutes, 7 June 1911. The Penylan opened in August 1914 – 'original, hygienic and up to date, every patriot should patronise this British owned and controlled cinema' (letter from former Cardiff City librarian Geoff Dart to author 28 May 1985). Despite the building boom and the optimism, the period was punctuated by strikes; Crecrafts and Dooner's, for example, handed a share of their takings at special performances to miners' distress funds in 1912.

66 Rachael Low, *The History of the British Film 1906–1914*, and *World's Fair*, 29 May 1909. Kinemacolor was the first natural colour process, and could not reproduce accurately all the colours of the spectrum (D. B. Thomas, *The First Colour Motion Pictures*, Science Museum, London, 1969, pp.9–30).

67 Urban material in Science Museum, London. A coloured film of the Oxford–Cambridge boat race was shown at the Cardiff Cinema in 1913 (*World's Fair*, 23 Mar. 1913). William Coutts advertised 'a mammoth show of Kinemacolor' at the Picture House, High Street, Swansea in 1914 (*Bioscope*, 15 Jan. 1914).

68 The Park Hall re-opening in *SWE*, 10 Nov. 1915. Ystrad Mynach claim in *Kinematograph Weekly*, 29 Jan. 1920.

69 *SWDP*, 6 Jan. 1910. Coutts was working for Walterdaw in Cardiff by 1920, and later ran various Cardiff cinemas, including the Imperial (Cardiff Watch Committee minutes, 1930). John Codman was fined for failing to place a barrier around his projection machine at Bangor in 1912 (*World's Fair*, July 1912). See Cardiff City Watch Committee minutes, 29 July 1909.

70 Ibid., 7 Jan. 1910.

71 See articles by Rowland Davies in *SWEP*, 8 Nov. and 22 Dec. 1976. The Carlton was launched 8 Jan. 1914, the Castle, December 1913. The Electric Tivoli, Cwmbrla, opened Feb. 1910 (*SWDP*, 22 Feb. 1910). The Elysium was the first cinema in Swansea to 'go in for' serials (according to *Bioscope*, 11 Nov. 1915).

72 Hale's Tours at Newport, 'Pictures and Illusions', manager S. G. Boulton and seating 60, is mentioned in *Bioscope Annual and Trade Directory* 1910–11. The tours were launched by an American businessman, George C. Hale, of Kansas City, and first shown at the St Louis Exposition, 1903. See Terry Ramsaye, *A Million and One Nights* (Simon and Schuster, 1926) pp.428–9, 431–2.

73 *Bioscope*, 16 Mar. 1911 and 1 Jan. 1914. Llanelli Cinema opened 25 Sept. 1911 (*Llanelli Express and Star*, 21 Sept. 1911). See also *Bioscope*, 24 June 1915, for references to Vint deals as managing director of Famous Copyrights.

74 The Central Cinema Co. owned the hall in 1920 but it was opened in 1909 by Sidney Bacon's London-based company then running a string of cinemas in Britain, including a hall at Barry (*Bioscope Annual and Trades Directory* 1910–11).

75 Stone operated shows at the Hippodrome, Tonypandy; the town's Empire variety venue (prop. W. H. 'Billy' Willis) was equally popular. A copy exists of a special silk 1909 programme there with film on 'the Empiroscope' last on the bill and the inimitable Robb Wilton fourth.

76 *World's Fair*, 29 Mar. 1913.

77 *Bioscope*, 22 April 1915 and *Bioscope Annual and Trades Directory* 1910–11. *Glamorgan Gazette*, 22 Dec. 1900, contains advert for Boer War pictures screenings at Blaengarw, on the Photorotorscope (inventor, W. C. Hughes).

78 Ibid., Sept. 1913, and 5 Feb. 1914.

79 The workmens' hall at Ton Pentre also ranked as an 'ideal picture show venue' (see *Bioscope*, 15 Jan. 1914 and 27 May 1915).

80 Rhyl had six cinemas by 1921 – Kirks (later Saronies) was opened May 1911 according to Rhyl Library. Wrexham had three cinemas by 1911: the Glynn (September 1910), the Majestic (May 1911) and the Empire Picture Palace (the former music-hall), October 1910. In Aberystwyth, the Rink Picture Theatre opened in 1913 on the site of a roller-skating rink dating from the 1880s. Also see article by Neil Cropper in *Buckley* (the magazine of the Buckley Society), 1981.

81 Palace, Haverfordwest, opened 1913 (*World's Fair*, 9 Aug.; *Pembrokeshire Herald*, 13 Aug. and 5 Nov. 1920). The *Western Telegraph*, 31 Oct. 1984, has an account of White's bioscope days at Portfield Fair, Haverfordwest. An impressive monument to White (1860–1938) stands in Cardiff's Cathays cemetery.

82 Father Cunane, from Cardigan, interviewed for **The Dream that Kicks** (HTV 1986) claimed Free Church ministers at a local temperance society meeting called for a boycott of the film.

83 Father Cunane interview for **The Dream that Kicks**, as above, and by the author, Cardigan, 1986. A local writer, Mr H. Vaughan, who attended the opening night, said: 'It would be hard to imagine a more reverent performance – whilst the rapt attention and reverent behaviour of the spectators were also striking . . .' Mr Vaughan said he had entered the cinema with a prejudiced mind – 'in common with a large proportion, perhaps the majority, of the audience' (*Cardigan and Tivyside Advertiser*, 13 Feb. 1914).

84 Cinema Exhibitors' Association, South Wales branch meeting, February 1922. In 1920 they had complained that a YMCA 'picture house' in Swansea was running shows 'in opposition to bona fide kinemas' (*Kinematograph Weekly*, 1 Jan. 1920). In 1922, there was almost a log-jam of major film companies based within a half-mile radius of Cardiff's city centre – including Fox, Gaumont, Pathé Frères, Oswald Stoll's Film Company, Vitagraph and Famous Players Lasky.

85 *Kinematograph Year Book*, 1920.

86   *South Wales Echo*, 14 June 1920, and Rachael Low, *The History of the British Film 1918–1929*, p.98.

CHAPTER 5

1   W. MacQueen Pope, *Ivor – The Story of An Achievement* (Hutchinson, 1952) p.116. Also see James Harding, *Ivor Novello* (W. H. Allen, 1987); Peter Noble, *Ivor Novello, Man of the Theatre* (Falcon Press, 1951); Sandy Wilson, *Ivor* (Michael Joseph, 1975).

2   Rachael Low, *The History of the British Film 1918–1929* (George Allen and Unwin, 1971) p.124.

3   See Low, ibid., pp.157–8. Margaret Dickinson and Sarah Street, *Cinema and State: The Film Industry and the British Government 1927–1984* (BFI, 1985) and George Perry, *The Great British Picture Show* (Granada Publishing, 1975). By 1928, Stoll had sold off many of the company film premises. They also offered for sale rights in 53 books by famous authors – 'presumably the unfilmable residue of their purchases' (Low, ibid., p.162).

4   Low, as above, p.124; *Stoll's Editorial News*, 21 Aug. 1919; *Bioscope*, 3 and 10 Jan. 1924. Stoll, of course, did not feel it necessary to look to real life drama for his films. After all his years in Wales his company produced just one drama set there, **Gwyneth of the Welsh Hills** – and that was a fantasy.

5   Low, ibid., p.127.

6   Of ten productions announced in January 1920, three were from books by Dell (*Bioscope*, 1 Jan. 1920).

7   *Kinematograph Weekly*, 1 Jan. 1920.

8   Reproduced in *Stoll Editorial News*. Another film producer who also made many films based on literary excerpts or variety acts, was H. B. Parkinson. His 1929 silent, **A Broken Romance**, was about a 'Welsh cripple who stars in a film biography and meets the author she loves at the trade show'. It featured William Freshman and Blanche Adele.

9   **The Barton Mystery**, which provided Newport's Lyn Harding with his first leading screen role, was one of the first Stoll Eminent Authors films (*Kinematograph Weekly*, Feb. 1920). In 1921, Stoll joined the British National Film League to encourage the production and exhibition of British-made films.

10   See Jeffrey Richards, *The Age of the Dream Palace: Cinema and Society in Britain 1930–1939* (Routledge and Kegan Paul, 1984), pp.207–24.

11   Elvey (1887–1967) made around 300 features in a career stretching from *c*.1913 to the 1950s.

12   W. MacQueen Pope, *Ivor – The Story of An Achievement*, pp.157–60.

13   See biographies by Noble and MacQueen-Pope. The latter concluded (p.116) that Novello's film career was not of vital importance to his life story. It was 'short and extremely profitable' – 'a means to an end . . . and he achieved that end.'

14   James Harding, *Ivor Novello*, as above. **The White Rose** opened at the Scala, London, in November 1923.

15   By 1927 Barry, the former *Spectator* critic, had apparently relented, describing Novello and Betty Balfour as 'our only two stars' (*Bioscope*, 18 June 1927), cited in Low *History of the British Film 1918–1929*, p.264). Low herself points out that only Balfour, who specialized in Cockney roles, and Novello could compare with the American stars in audience appeal.

16   *New York Times*, 23 May 1923.

17   Gallico thought he resembled both Barthelmess and Ramon Novarro. Most reviewers praised the direction. 'The artist in Griffith, as the master of photoplay photography, smites the eye constantly,' said one. Another writer thought Griffith presented women as 'mystical beings, especially in motherhood'. Perhaps he furnished the screenplay under his pseudonym, Irene Sinclair, to give more credibility to the film's view of a mother's psychology. See Museum of Modern Art Circulating Film Library Catalogue, New York. No copies of **The White Rose** existed in Britain as at July 1994. Eastman House held a 16mm. viewing print and MOMA in New York a 35mm. print. A viewable copy also exists in the Novotny (National) Film Archive in Prague.

18 Letters from Albert Grey, vice-president of D. W. Griffith inc., to A. H. T. Banzhaf (company lawyer) 23 Nov. 1922, 22 Jan. 1924; Novello to Grey, June 1923; contract between Novello and D. W. Griffith inc., Nov. 1922; salary sheets of the company 1922/3; letters from Grey to Novello, 29 June 1923 and 7 Sept. 1923; cable from Grey 19 Sept. 1923 and from Novello to Grey 12 Sept. 1923; Novello letter to Grey 3 Dec. 1923: all in D. W. Griffith papers at Museum of Modern Art, New York. In his letter to Grey, June 1923 Novello says it was an 'entire joy and privilege' to be associated with Griffith. Material in MOMA includes lists of censored scenes and 'testimonials from prominent ministers about the film's moral value'. (D. W. Griffith papers 1897–1954, a guide to the microfilm edition, produced by MOMA, the University of Louisville, Kentucky and Microfilming Corporation of America, North Carolina.) See also James Harding, *Ivor Novello*, p.52. Novello was said to earn between £3,000 and £4,000 a film at the peak of his career (Low *History of the British Film 1918–1929*, p.277).

19 Peter Noble, *Ivor Novello, Man of the Theatre*, p.28

20 James Harding, *Ivor Novello*, p.48.

21 The film, from Robert Hitchens's novel, was made by Mercanton independently and only finally released here in 1927 by Stoll, after a long financial dispute (*History of the British Film 1918–1929*, pp.125 and 161). A British remake, directed by John Clements, was released in 1947.

22 Mercanton was seemingly confident enough in Novello's abilities to use him again – as a gypsy prince in **Miarka, the Daughter of the Bear** (La Fille d'Ours) 1920. No viewing copy of this movie exists in Britain but most of Novello's films can be found at the National Film Archive.

23 Novello *did* achieve another popular success with **Carnival**, directed for the former London company by Harley Knoles, later managing director of the major British film company Alliance. It took £43,000 in its first few weeks.

24 Harding, *Ivor Novello*, p.52. *Bioscope*, 3 Jan. 1924, cites *The Times*'s comments.

25 The producer's autobiography *Michael Balcon Presents – A Lifetime of Films* (Hutchinson, 1969). Balcon describes his personal affection for Tennyson as 'second only to that for my own son' (pp.21 and 66).

26 The play enjoyed a 283-performance run at London's Prince of Wales Theatre in 1924.

27 C. W. Arnold, who designed the *outré* sets for **The Rat**, was also designer on Hitchcock's silent, **The Lodger**. Cutts's feature has a superb opening. The 'Apache', introduced via a close-up of a rat scurrying into a bolt hole, flees down a cobbled alley, seeking refuge. As he lowers himself through a trap door to safety escaping from police, bars bisect his face, seemingly presaging possible eventual come-uppance (shades of the famous scene in **The Lodger** which might well have been inspired by it). James Agate described the stage play **The Rat** as 'a collector's piece'. 'No cliché in the way of phrases has been omitted – no tag of sentiment neglected' (cited in James Harding, *Ivor Novello*, p.59). Balcon, in his autobiography, admitted he 'could not remember even the vaguest detail' of **Return of the Rat** or **Triumph of the Rat**. But they were both 'immensely successful in commercial terms' (Balcon, pp.22–3).

28 Balcon's autobiography, p.35. But Basil Dean in his autobiographical volume, **My Mind's Eye**, recalls the success of the London première of **The Vortex** and its subsequent British run. **The Constant Nymph** was long believed to be lost but noted silent-film historian Kevin Brownlow has turned up a print recently. See *Missing Believed Lost – The Great British Film Search* (BFI, 1992).

29 Adrian Brunel, *Nice Work* (Forbes Robertson, 1949), p.131.

30 Balcon (op.cit., pp.26–7) said the press 'made' **The Lodger**. He claimed that C. M. Woolf, the company's distribution head, did not want to release it after listening to Graham Cutts, 'who was jealous of Hitchcock'. It went on the shelf but 'I showed it to the press and they received it enthusiastically,' Balcon stressed.

31 **South Sea Bubble**, partly filmed in Algeria from a Roland Pertwee novel, was described as a 'failure' by Balcon. Alma Reville had scripting credits on both **The Constant Nymph** and **South Sea Bubble**. In the 1920s, Novello was successful enough to set up his own company,

Novello-Atlas, which released several Adrian Brunel films including a burlesque of Pathé magazine programmes, the **Pathetic Gazette**, and **Lovers in Araby** – plus a popular Henry Edwards feature, **Owd Bob**.

32 *Bioscope*, 23 July 1930. Novello's play about a blind composer was updated by Balcon for the cinema to accommodate the public's new taste for jazz – and Jack Payne and his Orchestra (Harding, p.84).

33 Novello, quoted in Harding, p.87

34 MGM bought the film rights to *Party*, another play Novello completed in Hollywood. Joan Crawford was mooted as star but it was never made (W. McQueen-Pope, *Ivor*, p.97).

35 A Novello suite still exists at London's Twickenham Studios (St Margaret's).

36 Jeffrey Richards, *The Age of the Dream Palace* (Routledge and Kegan Paul, 1984) p.311. *Picturegoer Weekly* thought Novello had 'never appeared to greater advantage' and *Kine Weekly* (22 June 1933) praised the film's 'excellent situations and biting humour'.

37 Peter Noble, *Ivor Novello, Man of the Theatre*, pp.193–4.

38 Noble, op.cit., p.192.

39 Noble, op.cit., pp.290–1.

40 Hughes played a comparatively minor role in Beaudine's **Penrod and Sam** (1923). Woody Van Dyke directed Hughes in **Forget-Me-Not** (1922) when the Welshman and Bessie Love played young lovers; and in **Eyes of the Totem** (1927), when Hughes was the boyfriend who saved his lover from an attack by her father's murderer. Rowland Lee directed the actor in **Whirlwind of Youth** (1927, starring Lois Moran). Hughes worked for a string of smaller companies such as Trinity, Chesterfield and Sterling.

41 Fulton Oursler described him as 'the charm boy to end all charm boys' and 'a petted darling of a precious set'.

42 The actor played the heroine's lover, a bookworm and failed author. The star was Viola Dana and Hughes was then signed to head her support cast on three further films. (*Photoplay*, 28 April 1921). But later the same year it was announced Hughes would make seven films for Metro distribution, directed by George D. Baker – three of these were never made.

43 George D. Baker was the film-maker Hughes worked for most frequently in his Hollywood career.

44 In **The Lure of Youth** (dir. Philip Rosen, 1921), Hughes was the 'other man' who steps between a famous actress and her lover. In **Life's Darn Funny** (dir. Dallas Fitzgerald, 1921), Hughes again co-starred with Viola Dana. He played opposite Lila Lee in **The Midnight Girl** (dir. Wilfred Noye, 1925), shot by D. W. Griffith's famous cameraman G. W. 'Billy' Bitzer.

45 The film cost between $250,000 and $300,000 dollars. Gloria Swanson starred in a 1927 remake **The Love of Sunya**. See *American Film Institute Catalogue of Feature Films 1911–1920*.

46 In her book *Mrs Fiske: Her Views on the Stage*, she praised Hughes's performance in a stage production of *Moloch* in New York in September 1915 (cutting unattributed and dated October 1920 in Gareth Hughes's file at Museum of Modern Art, New York). A brief résumé of the actor's career and early influences appears in *Coleshill School, Llanelli, 1891–1977: End of an Era*, edited by Denver Phillips. Hughes, as a boy, wrote an article for the school's magazine, on visiting the Royalty at Llanelli (later Haggar's cinema) and Llanelli Fair.

47 Co-written by Anita Loos, it included in the cast Keaton's future sister-in-law Norma Talmadge (lead role), Keaton's future wife Natalie Talmadge (in her début film) and Hedda Hopper, later to win wider recognition as a vitriolic screen columnist.

48 W. C. Fields starred in a 1934 remake.

49 From two J. M. Barrie works, *Sentimental Tommy* (published 1895) and *Tommy and Grizel* (1900). Distributed by Paramount. Some sources list – erroneously – among Hughes's credits, **The Little Minister**, also based on Barrie's Thrums adventures, but he does not appear in the 1921 film of that title or the late thirties version with Katharine Hepburn.

50 Hughes spoke of playing a tramp – and researching on the Bowery for a film called **The**

Hunter (*Pictures and Picturegoer*, Oct. 1922). I can find no record of this film.

51 Directed by Jacques Tyrol. Descriptions from *American Film Institute Catalogue of Feature Films 1911–1920*.

52 *Bioscope*, 13 May 1920. This film, directed by Jacques Tyrol, starts with the beguiling, if unlikely, premise that the father of Billy (Hughes) will send him to a brothel before he enters college – 'to learn of life's necessary evils' (*American Film Institute Catalogue*, as above).

53 The issue of women jurors was contentious at the time and only six states permitted them by the film's release date, including California but not New York. A pre-release screening was held for the Brooklyn Womens' Bar Association (AFT catalogue, as above). *Motion Picture World*, 28 June 1919.

54 In **Shadows of Paris**, Negri played a 'queen of the Apaches' and the film explored the same Paris underworld inhabited by Novello in his **Rat** features.

55 **Kick In**, another Famous Players Lasky feature – starring Betty Compson – was shot by Arthur Miller (later to photograph John Ford's **How Green Was My Valley**).

56 It ended, not untypically at the time, with Richard Dix's religious zealot expiring in the heroine's arms. Incomplete copies of **The Christian** are held by the Dutch Film Museum of Overveen, nr. The Hague, and at the Novotny (National) Film Archive in Prague.

57 In the one surviving reel of **Silent Sentinel** (viewable at the Library of Congress, Washington), the canine hero warns Hughes that his girlfriend is in danger by barking over the telephone. The Library of Congress also hold **Better Days**, **Eyes of Youth**, **Mrs Wiggs of the Cabbage Patch** and a few reels of **Enemies of Women**, but none of these is held at the NFA, London. **Broken Hearted** (1929) had some talking sequences. Hughes also appeared in **Mister Antonio** (1929, directors James Flood, Frank Reicher), made in both a sound and silent version, the 1931 67-minute programmer, **Scareheads**, and the 1932 **The Speed Reporter**.

58 Letter to 'M. E. S.' (undated) in Museum of Modern Art (Gareth Hughes collection) in New York. A Patrick Kent article in the *People* (1965) claimed he left full-time theatre work in 1938 but the obits in the *Daily Telegraph* (14 Oct. 1965) and Hollywood Reporter (7 Oct. 1965) say he quit the stage in 1944. Throughout these years Hughes returned periodically to Llanelli.

59 *Pictures and Picturegoer*, Oct. 1922.

60 See Fulton Oursler, *Lights Along the Shore* (Hanover House, New York, 1954) and syndicated newspaper article by Oursler, the 'Star in the desert' for Hearst Publishing Co. Extract in *Reader's Digest*, March, 1952. A few years after forsaking Hollywood, Hughes was working for $94 a month for the WPA Theater Project in America.

61 According to Patrick Kent in the *People*, Nov. 1965, Hughes turned down a 1951 offer from RKO to star in a biopic, the **Desert Padre** (Jan. 1952). Marlon Brando was mooted for the film. Hughes's disaffection for the screen has emerged in recorded interviews.

62 *Silent Picture*, Autumn 1971.

63 Rachael Low, in the *History of British Film 1918–1929*, p.140, describes it as 'a travesty of a Napoleonic spectacular which was a rough version of the old melodrama'.

64 Very few films of the period were longer, but **Royal Divorce** was a minnow compared to A. E. Coleby's **The Prodigal Son**, his 18,454ft. behemoth for Stoll released in separate parts of eight and nine reels (Low, as above, and Denis Gifford, *British Film Catalogue 1895–1985*, David and Charles).

65 Wells appeared in two other Coleby films, **The Great Game** (1918) and **The Silver Lining** (1919). Local fights were constantly screened in cinemas between 1911 and 1913, notably involving Peerless Jim Driscoll and Pontypridd-born Freddie Welsh, but Jack Johnson's World Heavyweight title fights with Tommy Burns and James J. Jeffreys were other popular attractions. Review of **The Pitboy's Romance** in *Bioscope*, 29 Mar. 1917; also see *Bioscope* of 31 May and 7 June 1917.

66 *Stoll Editorial News*, 21 Aug. 1919. Wilde ran the Coliseum at Tylorstown and the New

Cinema, Maesteg. The film is referred to briefly and erroneously titled in Wilde's *Fighting is My Business* (Lonsdale Classics, 1938). For references to **Excuse my Glove** and **The Ball of Fortune** see Gifford's *British Film Catalogue* as above, entries 09917, 08087. Footage of Wilde at the training quarters of one opponent, Pat Moore, is in the National Film Archive (Gaumont Serial No.867).

67 *SWE*, 1 Jan. 1920. When she played in **The Temple of Stars** at the Park Hall cinema, she was described as an ex-pupil of Canton Secondary School, Cardiff (*SWE*, 7 April 1928). See also *Bioscope*, 10 May 1917 and 23 Aug. 1917.

68 Gifford's *British Film Catalogue 1895–1985*. **A Little Child Shall Lead Them** was at the Olympia, Cardiff, in April 1920 (*SWE*, 26 April) and later that year at the city's Gaiety Theatre. When it was shown in France Victor Marcel, the *Bioscope* reviewer, thought its plot construction was 'weak to the point of childishness. Serious situations were greeted with roars of laughter.' If no better films were available British exporters would render the UK film industry 'a real service by abstaining', the writer added (*Bioscope*, 1 July 1917). The 1917 film **Ye Wooing of Peggy** starring Thomas was described as 'somewhat unsophisticated but a dainty little costume (18th century) drama', but Thomas was seen as a 'sweetly pretty heroine, remarkable for her vivacity and expressive acting' (*Bioscope*, 1917).

69 Gifford, ibid. and *SWE*, 1 Jan. 1920.

70 *SWE*, ibid.

71 Thomas also played the lead for Oswald Stoll's company in W. P. Kellino's film, **The Gold Cure** (1925), with Moore Marriott. She had key roles in two films directed by the comedian, Fred Paul: **The Last Witness** and **Safety First** (1925 and 1926). She also played the lead in Paul's **Infelice** (1915) for Samuelson.

72 **The Skin Game** remake, for BIP at Elstree, was scripted by Hitchcock and Alma Reville. Another Gwenn film made at Elstree was a version of Bernard Shaw's **How He Lied to Her Husband** (dir. Cecil Lewis, 1931).

73 Harding played roles in two 1934 Henry Edwards films: **The Lash** and **The Man Who Changed His Name**. See *Bioscope*, 12 Feb. 1920.

CHAPTER 6

1 Rachael Low, *The History of the British Film 1918–1929*, p.17, citing the *Bioscope* 19 Jan. 1922. The Film Society, forerunner of the entire Film Society movement in Britain was co-founded by film-maker Ivor Montague, run by critic Iris Barry and its members included H. G. Wells, George Bernard Shaw, artist Roger Fry, economist John Maynard Keynes, and actress Ellen Terry (Low, as above, p.34).

2 One writer, G. A. Atkinson, noted the 'outcry' for more houses after the war and thought it likely that councils would veto cinema buildings because of the shortage of labour and materials. The number of builders in the trade had slumped from 817,000 in 1911 to 700,000 in 1919 (*Kinematograph Yearbook*, 1920, p.10).

3 *Kinematograph Yearbook,* 1921, p.112.

4 Influential Welsh cinema men, sensing they were on the brink of exciting times, formed themselves into a Cardiff-based trading rental exchange club in 1920 with £10,000 capital. The directors of the exchange, for transacting business and holding trade shows, included Swansea pioneer William Coutts, then of St John's Square, Cardiff, the old showman Richard Dooner and Rowland Williams, of Abertridwr and Pengam, owner of Cardiff's Coliseum cinema, the Palladium at Fleur-de-Lys and Palace, New Tredegar (*Kinematograph Weekly*, 8 Jan. 1920, and *Bioscope*, 15 Jan. 1920).

5 *Bioscope*, Jan. 1920; *Kinematograph Weekly*, 8 Jan. 1920; Annette Kuhn, *Cinema: Censorship and Sexuality 1909–1925* (Routledge, 1988), pp.55–9; and James C. Robertson, *Hidden Cinema* (Routledge, 1989) pp.12–14. A copy of **Damaged Goods** is viewable at the National Film Archive, London. See *Bioscope*, 16 Nov. 1916.

6 *SWE*, March 1928 and 2 July 1928.

7 *Bioscope*, Jan. 1920, but see Deian Hopkin, 'Social reactions to economic change' and Dennis Thomas, 'Economic decline', in Trevor Herbert and Gareth Elwyn Jones (eds.) *Wales Between the Wars* (University of Wales Press/Open University, 1988).

8 Rachael Low, *The History of the British Film 1918–1929*, p.49.

9 Neil Cropper, 'The Palace Picture House, Buckley' in *Buckley*, the magazine of the Buckley Society No.6, Jan. 1981.

10 *CEE*, 24 Dec. 1921; *Bioscope*, 10 Jan. 1924.

11 Balfour, in the mid-1920s, had a British following only equalled by Novello (Low, *History of the British Film 1918–1929*, pp.121 and 301).

12 *SWE*, 14 Jan. and 18 Feb. 1928; *SWDP*, August, 1928; *Bioscope*, 20 May 1920.

13 *SWE*, 20 Oct. 1928; *Bioscope* 24 Oct. 1928. Other cinemas were slightly more unorthodox. Madame Bessie Griffiths sang at a showing of **Sunrise** at the Elysium, Swansea (*SWDP*, 6 Nov. 1928).

14 *Kinematograph Yearbook*, 1928, pp.211–13.

15 *SWE*, 20 Oct. 1928.

16 *Kinematograph Yearbook*, 1928, pp.161–4. The Cinematograph Films Act (1927) fixed minimum percentages of British product to be exhibited in cinemas. Exhibitors' quota was set at 5 per cent and distributors' quota at 7 per cent, initially, both rising to 20 per cent by 1936. The British feared the economic and moral effects of American film industry domination. Prime Minister Stanley Baldwin, who gave the Board of Trade responsibility for film, expressed worries about placing such an enormously powerful instrument of propaganda in the hands of 'foreign countries'. See James Curran and Vincent Porter, (eds.) *British Cinema History* (Weidenfeld and Nicolson, 1983), p.60. See *SWDP*, 28 Sept. 1928.

17 *Kinematograph Yearbook*, 1928, p.199.

18 *Kinematograph Yearbook*, 1928, p.201, and *Bioscope* 26 Dec. 1928.

19 *Bioscope*, 13 June 1928.

20 Pembroke Dock cinema closed in 1929 and was re-opened briefly by the Haggar family in the 1970s. See note 4 *re* Rowland Williams. Rialto cinema was formerly the White Palace.

21 The film made three million dollars profit, according to Clive Hirschorn, *The Warner Bros Story* (Octopus, 1979), p.59, but **The Singing Fool** was the company's most successful film.

22 The Capitol cinema showed **The Jazz Singer** with the first six-reel comedy, **Tillie's Punctured Romance**, starring Chaplin. It also offered 'a prologue to **The Jazz Singer**' and 'incidental vocal effects by the Radom Quartette' (*SWE*, 9 Feb. 1929 and 12 Mar. 1929).

23 *SWE*, 10 June 1929 and 12 Mar. 1929. The Pavilion closed for a while in 1929 and re-opened, after extensive refurbishment, with **Broadway Melody** (*SWE*, 2 Sept. 1929).

24 **The Covered Waggon** was James Cruz's celebrated 1923 silent. The Queen's was billed, for a short time, as The Queen's Talking Picture Theatre.

25 *SWE*, 2 Sept. 1929. Jones also appeared in Hitchcock's **Downhill**.

26 *SWE*, 28 Sept. 1929. The *SWE*, on 12 Oct. 1929, also referred to John Longden as 'a young Welsh actor', but on 24 Nov. 1928 the paper described him as 'a former South Wales miner, born in the West Indies'.

27 *SWE*, 17 April 1929, and 1 June 1929.

28 *SWE*, June 1929, and 2 July 1929.

29 *SWDP*, 5, 9 and 23 Feb. 1929.

30 *SWDP*, 19 Feb. 1929.

31 *SWDP*, 23 and 24 April 1929.

32 *SWDP*, 27 April, 7 May and 8 June 1929.

33 *SWDP*, 6 Sept. 1928 and 14 Dec. 1929.

34 *SWDP*, 21 and 22 May 1929.

35 *SWDP*, 18 and 21 June, 2 and 16 July.

36 *SWDP*, 4 Oct. 1929.

37 *SWDP*, 25 April 1929, 20 July 1929, 25 Aug. 1928, 24 Oct. 1928.

38 *SWE* 22 June 1929. 'His director on the screen version of Tolstoy's **Redemption** claimed: 'He's one of the finest talking picture actors I've heard.' Gilbert's career was popularly supposed to have been destroyed by sound but recent historians and biographers have attributed his screen decline to a row with his former studio head, L. B. Mayer.

39 *SWE*, April 1929. **Showboat** is not to be confused with the 1935 version starring Paul Robeson.

40 The Canton Cinema, Cardiff, switched to sound in December 1929 with **The Rainbow Man**, starring Eddie Dowling and Marion Nixon. The Central, curiously, advertised its British Phototone sound for talking pictures in the *SWE*, 11 Mar. 1929, but announced its first talkies in June 1930 (ibid.). See also *SWE*, 22 Oct. 1929, and 3 and 15 Mar. 1930.

41 Talkies made their début at the Plaza with **The Flying Marine**, starring Ben Lyon, and the sound film *Painted Faces*, starring Joe E. Brown, was screened the same week.

42 *SWE*, 30 Dec. 1929. *Kinematograph Yearbook*, 1929.

43 *SWE*, 24 July 1929. The Albert Hall, Swansea, also installed Western Electric, and announced exactly the same cost for equipment.

44 *SWE*, 13 April 1929.

45 *SWE*, 13 Sept. 1929. Hill was appointed scenario editor for Stoll's around 1920.

46 *SWE*, 6 July 1929.

47 *SWE*, 10 Sept. 1929.

48 *SWE*, 8 Dec. 1928.

49 *SWDP*, 24 July 1929.

50 *SWDP*, 19 Nov. 1929.

51 *SWDP*, 5 Oct. 1929.

52 *SWDP*, Oct. 1928.

53 Article by Rowland Davies – then the Swansea City Council pictorial archivist – in *SWEP*, 22 Dec. 1976.

54 For years the Andrews Hall was rented by Moss Empires after Oswald Stoll used it in 1899 as a short-term replacement for the former Empire, destroyed by fire. John F. Andrews, *Solomon Andrews and his Family* (Stewart Williams, Barry, 1976). The Andrews Hall was rebuilt in 1935, opened as a cinema on 12 Nov. that year, and let from Sept. 1936 to Associated British Cinemas.

55 *Wrexham Leader* articles, 7 Mar. 1958 and 9 Mar. 1962.

56 Jeffrey Richards, *The Age of the Dream Palace, Cinema and Society in Britain 1930–1939*, p.14. The Rowson Report in 1934 estimated there were then 4,305 cinemas in the UK open six days a week. In 1917, there were between 4,000 and 5,000 'cinemas' – but many of these were small public halls screening films once or twice weekly.

CHAPTER 7

1 Author's interview, 1987, with Gordon Holten, (former divisional administrative officer, National Coal Board). Also see Bert Hogenkamp's article 'Miners' cinemas in south Wales in the 1920s and 1930s' in *Llafur* – the journal of the Society for the Study of Welsh Labour History (vol.4, no.2, 1985).

2 Holten interview, ibid.

3 D. J. Davies's history, *The Tredegar Workmen's Hall 1861–1951*, copy in South Wales Miners' Library, Swansea; Hogenkamp, op.cit.

4 TMI Hall committee minutes, 23 Sept. 1933 and 30 Oct. 1933 (in records at South Wales Miners' Library, Swansea).

5 TMI cinema committee minutes, June 1937, 28 Dec. 1933 and 10 May 1935. Minute books in SWML, Swansea.

6 D. J. Davies, *The Tredegar Workmen's Hall 1861–1951*.

7 Ibid.

8 Ibid.

9 Celynen Workmen's Institute 1898–1948 Jubilee programme (in SWML, Swansea).

10 Ferndale minutes, 16 April 1931. Ferndale Workmen's Hall Institute Golden Anniversary publication 1909–59 (in SWML, Swansea) and *Kinematograph Yearbook*, 1921.

11 The workmen at Mardy ran the Picturedrome, which boasted 1,000 seats in 1919 (*Kine Yearbook*). See Bert Hogenkamp, op.cit.

12 Author's interview with Gordon Holten 1987, as above.

13 See *The History of the Oakdale Institute 1912–1946*, foreword by George H. Hoare, copy in SWML.

14 Ibid.

15 Oakdale Institute minutes, 14 Oct. 1930 (SWML).

16 Ibid, 18 Oct. 1930. The reduction in prices for the unemployed 'until such time as work is resumed and the first pay received' caused 'much heated discussion'.

17 *SWE*, 6 and 13 Dec. 1928; *Bioscope*, 28 Nov. 1928. J. R. Payne is listed in the main role and as director in Denis Gifford's *British Film Catalogue 1895–1985*, where the film's release date is given as Nov. 1927. ('Lord's son poses as highwayman to aid sister's elopement'.) A Welsh amateur production of the period was **That Lass of Chandler's** (1929) set in Conwy, centred on a girl's romance with a sailor and directed by W. J. Sargent for North Wales Screen Productions.

18 *SWE*, 29 Dec. 1928 and 13 Dec. 1928.

19 Seating capacities taken from official record books in possession of Gordon Holten. Ferndale Institute bought the Picture House premises at Ferndale in 1941. The workmen's hall at Nantymoel – dating from 1901 – later became the Berwyn Centre. Also see *Kinematograph Yearbook*, 1921.

20 The General Post Office Film Unit, first under John Grierson, then Alberto Cavalcanti, existed from 1933 to 1940, replacing the unit at the Empire Marketing Board. The GPO film directors, including Basil Wright, Harry Watt and Edgar Anstey, helped give Britain an unrivalled reputation in the new 'documentary' field.

21 Bond, 'Making films with a purpose', *Kino News*, Winter 1935. The label 'incorruptible left-winger' comes from Paul Rotha's *Documentary Diary (1928–1939)* (Hill and Wang, New York, 1973).

22 *Kino News*, Winter 1935, as above, cited in Don MacPherson (ed.), *British Cinema – Traditions of Independence* (BFI, 1980).

23 *Plebs*, Aug. 1931. Also Bond article in *Close Up*, the British film magazine, January 1930.

24 Author's interview with Ralph Bond at his London home, Feb. 1985. The fleapit quote can also be found in Bond's essay 'Workers' films: past and future', in *Labour Monthly*, Jan. 1976. In *Deadly Parallels* (Lawrence and Wishart, 1986), p.51, Bert Hogenkamp cites an unsuccessful attempt by the Swansea Independent Labour Party to show **Mother** in 1930, when they were foiled by the town's watch committee according to the *Kinematograph Weekly*, 18 Sept. 1930. But the film was shown in Cwmbach, Nantymoel and Mardy miners' institutes, according to the *Daily Worker*. (See Hogenkamp's essay on miners' cinema in *Llafur* vol.4, no.2, 1985.)

25 See Paul Marris, 'Politics and independent film in the decade of defeat', in *British Cinema – Traditions of Independence*. Bond wrote a long article advising people to set up their own film societies (in *Kino News*, Winter 1935). He told me at his London home in 1985: 'Montagu was a communist. I was a card-carrying member. Kino, an organization distributing Russian and German films, was set up by a number of people . . . not directly by the Communist Party – some were connected with International Class Wars Prisoners Aid (ICWPA) – a world-wide

organization to help people who for one reason or another had been victimized or put in prison for their activities.' Bond said he was not employed by Kino but helped them and also wrote for *Kino News*.

26 Bond interview, London, Feb. 1985.

27 Elvin's comments were made at the 1936 Annual General Meeting of Kino, set up in 1933 as an offspring of the Workers' Theatre Movement. Information also from interview with Bond, London, 1985.

28 Cardiff City Watch Committee minutes, 10 Jan. 1934.

29 Author's interviews with Bond, London 1984 and 1985. See also Paul Rotha's *Documentary Diary*.

30 Author's interview with Ralph Bond, 1984. In an interview given to Claire Pollak in July 1985 for the HTV programme **The Dream that Kicks**, Bond said one of the film's basic objects was to emphasize 'the contributions that ordinary people made to the industrial and social life of the country'.

31 See Trevor Ryan, 'Film and political organisation in Britain 1929–1939' in *British Cinema – Traditions of Independence* (BFI, 1980). See also Bert Hogenkamp, 'Miners' cinema in south Wales in the 1920s and 1930s', *Llafur* vol.4, no.2, 1985; and Hogenkamp's *Deadly Parallels – Film and the Left in Britain 1929–1939*.

32 Strand employees were paid £6 a week on a film by film basis but the director Donald Alexander was adamant he received £3. 10*s.* a week on **Eastern Valley** (author's interview with Alexander, Dundee, 1985).

33 Ibid. Also see Ralph Bond, 'Making **Today We Live**', *World Film News*, vol.2, no.6, Sept. 1937. The South Cerney sequences were directed by John Grierson's sister, Ruby.

34 Author's interview with Bond, 1984, and Bond's article in *World Film News*, as above. See also Bert Hogenkamp's, 'Miners' cinemas in south Wales', op.cit.

35 Bond, 'Making **Today We Live**', op.cit.

36 Alexander's observations are contained in his diary of the time, kindly loaned to me.

37 Ralph Bond interview, 1984.

38 Ibid.

39 Glyn Lewis interviewed by the author in 1984 at Pentre.

40 Interview with Ralph Bond, 1984.

41 Paul Rotha, op.cit, pp.147–9.

42 Author's interview with Les Adlam at his home, in Pentre, 1984.

43 Author's interview with Ralph Bond, 1984. Also see 'Rotha on Rotha', interview by Lynne Fredlund and Paul Marris in *Paul Rotha*: BFI Dossier No.16 (BFI, 1982).

44 See interview by Lynne Fredlund and Paul Marris, as above. Rotha said the film would have gone 50 per cent over budget had he not intervened on the first day.

45 Author's interview with Ralph Bond, 1984.

46 Lynne Fredlund, Paul Marris interview, 'Rotha on Rotha', in BFI Dossier No.16.

47 Ibid. Also, Rotha said in *Documentary Diary* that both **Today We Live** and **Eastern Valley** moved his friend the writer Eric Knight deeply. 'We could hardly believe that such conditions of poverty existed in Britain.'

48 Fredlund and Marris, op.cit.

49 Rotha, *Documentary Diary*, pp.147–9.

50 Bond's comments in interview in 1984, 'I never attempted to film in the pits of South Wales', are interesting in the light of Alexander's observations (made in telephone conversation in 1983 and repeated in the 1984 meeting with him in Dundee). Alexander thought Bond had taken a 'lazy approach' to obtaining the pit footage.

51 Rotha, *Documentary Diary*, p. 149.

52 Paul Marris, 'Politics and the independent film in the decade of defeat', op.cit.

53 Interestingly enough, Alexander studied Russian history at St John's College, Cambridge. 'I made a film about the Rhondda – about which I knew nothing really – but I had developed a social conscience' (telephone conversation, 1983).

54 Author's interview with Donald Alexander, Dundee, 1985. Judy Birdwood became involved with film through the Socialist Film Council, Alexander said. **Housing Problems** (1935), co-directed by Elton and Edgar Anstey, was a key film of the British documentary movement.

55 Loaned to author, 1984.

56 Interview with Alexander, Dundee, 1985. He insisted the shots in this film were better than those he took at the same spots, at Rotha's insistence, for **Today We Live**.

57 Ibid., and see Hogenkamp, *Deadly Parallels*, pp.127 and 134

58 Budget according to Alexander in telephone conversation, 1983. The term 'social experiment' is used in the film, and the commentary describes the Subsistence Society as 'a co-operative of unemployed men'.

59 This was Alexander's recollection in the Dundee interview but S. D. Onions is credited with the photography in standard reference works.

60 Alexander also employed the Trehafod Choir on the sound-track, notably over general farm scenes and opening credits, an early montage of steel and mining shots over images of the unemployed, and later in the haymaking scenes.

61 In *Night and Day Magazine*, 16 Dec. 1937; also included in *The Pleasure Dome*, Greene's collected film criticism 1935–40 (OUP, 1980).

62 Interview with Alexander, 1984, as above and *Documentary News Letter* No.47 (vol.5, no.6) 1944–5 (published by Film Centre, London – a group of documentary film-makers set up by John Grierson, but the head of the magazine's editorial board initially was Arthur Elton.

63 Viewable, though incomplete, in NFA. In a letter to me from Southern Illinois University on 6 June 1985, Professor Marshall said: 'I did a newsreel about the Wrexham disasters . . . and I discovered they were forced to work in a pit that had been labelled dangerous . . . I remember writing about it for the *Daily Worker* of that time and also making some newsreel shots of it, probably then for the Film and Photo League.'

64 Ibid. See also Wal Hannington, *Unemployed Struggles 1919–1936* (first published 1936, reprinted by Lawrence and Wishart, 1977).

65 **March Against Starvation** was a film made by the Left including the Scots film-maker Helen Biggar and the Socialist Film Council in support of the National Protest Against the Unemployment Assistance Board by the National Unemployed Workers Movement.

66 Trevor Ryan, 'Film and political organisation in Britain 1929–1939', op.cit. Hogenkamp (*Deadly Parallels*, p.140) provides details of a Kino tour of Eisenstein's film **Battleship Potemkin** in the south Wales valleys, 1936, and an abortive attempt by a newly formed Cardiff Kino Workers' Film Committee to stage a première in the city.

67 Bert Hogenkamp, 'Miners' cinemas in south Wales in the 1920s and 1930s (Llafur, 1989, op.cit.). The article mentions Kino's outlet at Collett's – the left-wing book shop then in the Castle Arcade, Cardiff. The organization's agency in Wales was set up in 1937. The article also mentions the film **Rhondda**, and the involvement with the south Wales miners.

68 Michael Chanan, *Labour Power in the British Film Industry* (BFI, 1976), quoting Bert Hogenkamp's article 'The use of film by the workers' movement in Great Britain 1929–1939', in *Skrien*, a Dutch magazine, No.51, Aug. 1975. The article was abridged for *Sight and Sound* (BFI, Spring, 1976). See also Hogenkamp's 'Film and the workers' movement in Great Britain 1929–1939' (*Sight and Sound*, Spring 1976); Hogenkamp's *Deadly Parallels*, as above, and his article in *Llafur*, op.cit., and also Trevor Ryan, op.cit., for detailed accounts of film in these years.

69 Tredegar Institute minutes (particularly for 1933–40) and D. J. Davies, 'Tredegar Workmen's Hall 1861–1951', both in SWML, University College, Swansea. **Professor Mamlock** was

shown by the Tredegar Institute (see Hogenkamp, *Deadly Parallels*, p.214).

70 Tredegar Institute minutes, as above. Also see Hogenkamp, *Deadly Parallels*; details of Tredegar's involvement with booking two Spanish films, **They Shall Not Pass** and **Spanish Earth**, can be found in Hogenkamp's essay in *Llafur* vol.4, no.2, 1985.

71 See Hogenkamp's chapter 'Workers' film societies' in *Deadly Parallels*, pp.28–82, which includes fascinating accounts of miners' institute screenings.

72 'The Workers Film Movement slowly petered out. The Soviet Union was a bit behind America in developing the sound film. Our sources of supply dried up' (interview with Bond, 1985). In *Kino News*, Winter 1935, Bond commented on: 'The enthusiasm that has everywhere greeted the showing of the great Russian and other films which are available from Kino', and the 'desire in many districts such as Sheffield . . . Manchester . . . Tonyrefail . . . to show and produce films of real cultural and social value'.

73 See references to Dand in Rachael Low, *Film-making in 1930s Britain: The History of the British Film 1929–1939* (George Allen and Unwin, 1985), pp.107 and 184.

74 See Rachael Low, *Films of Comment and Persuasion of the 1930s* (George Allen and Unwin, 1979).

75 *Sight and Sound* vol.3, no.9, 1934 and *Monthly Film Bulletin* vol.1, no.5, 1934.

76 R. E. Griffith, *Urdd Gobaith Cymru*, vol. 1 (extract translated by the film-maker's son, Owen Edwards, for the present author). A Mr J. M. Howells gave £500 towards making the film. John Ellis Williams recalled that the mainly amateur company spent almost all day rehearsing before recording the sound on disc at Ealing and worked from 8.15 a.m. to 7 p.m.

77 Ibid. and interview with Owen Edwards, Cardiff, 1983.

78 Much interesting material on this has been written by the author and film producer Herbert Marshall, in letter to the present writer, 6 June 1985, and in internal publications at Southern Illinois University, Carbondale, Illinois.

CHAPTER 8

1 Michael Powell, telephone conversation with the author, Sept. 1983.

2 Ibid. Kevin Gough Yates thought **Phantom Light** drew heavily 'on Powell's predilection for the fairy tale' and he thought Wales was presented in the lighthouse-keeper's 'arrival' scene as a 'dream-like wonderland' (Michael Powell monograph, Film Museum, Brussels, 1973). **Edge of The World** was released in 1938.

3 Ibid. The film also starred Binnie Hale, Ian Hunter and Donald Calthrop.

4 Powell, in letter to the author, 1984. 'Gents Only' was in *The Best of Rhys Davies* (David and Charles, 1979 edition). There was a subsequent reference to the project in *Michael Powell: Million Dollar Movie*, the second volume of his autobiography (William Heinemann, 1992) pp. 223–4.

5 Another film, shot in Cardiff, was **High Seas** (working title 'The Silver Rosary'), a romance adventure story completed in 1929, directed by American Dennison Clift and starring Lillian Rich, John Stuart and Randle Ayrton. See *SWE*, 15 and 16 Oct. 1928 - the paper referred only to the working title. The film was made as a silent but sound was added to the film in 1930.

6 **Landslide** was made for Paramount by Pedelty and Victor Greene's company Crusade at the Wembley Studios (Rachael Low, *Film Making in 1930s Britain*, George Allen and Unwin, 1985), pp.189, 303. Pedelty directed and produced. I have been unable to view this film.

7 Telephone conversation with Freddie Young, 1986.

8 James C. Robertson, *The British Board of Film Censors, Film Censorship in Britain 1896–1950* (Croom Helm, 1985), pp.73–4, and Jeffrey Richards, *The Age of the Dream Palace, Cinema and Society in Britain, 1930–1939* (Routledge and Kegan Paul, 1984), pp.230–2, 306–7.

9 Cronin fictionalized his experiences in *Adventures in Two Worlds* (Victor Gollancz, 1952) describing events in 'Tregenny' (Treherbert) in the Rhondda Valley, and Tredegar. *The Citadel* was published by Gollancz in 1937.

10 See Elaine Morgan's article in *Radio Times*, 15–21 Jan. 1983.

11 Rachael Low, op.cit., pp.268–9. The other films were **A Yank at Oxford** (dir. Jack Conway, 1938) and **Goodbye Mr Chips** (dir. Sam Wood, 1939). Michael Balcon was production head but left in 1938, before shooting on **The Citadel**, and Victor Saville assumed his responsibilities.

12 In his autobiography *A Tree is a Tree* (Harcourt Brace, New York, 1952), Vidor talked of Donat arriving with notes, comments, books and sketches and insisting on visiting the locations.

13 Film publicity material stated that trams and other mining equipment were transported from the Welsh collieries. A photostat in the author's possession from the BFI contains reminiscences of railwaymen involved in the shooting of opening scenes at Treherbert. Emlyn Williams confirmed in interview with the author, August 1985, that he never went on location in Wales during the film. Basil Wright's comments are in *Spectator*, 6 Jan. 1939.

14 See J. C. Trewin, *Robert Donat* (Heinemann, 1968). See also Kenneth Barrow, *Mr Chips: The Life of Robert Donat* (Methuen, 1985).

15 King Vidor interviewed by Nancy Dowd in the 1970s and David Shepard in 1980, 1988. See *King Vidor* in the Directors Guild of America oral history series (Directors Guild of America, Scarecrow Press, 1988), p.173.

16 Saville shot some of the film and Pen Tennyson, who had an editing credit on **The Citadel**, also claimed to have directed certain scenes.

17 Margaret Sullavan reference in Raymond Durgnat and Scott Simmon, *King Vidor, American* (University of California Press, 1988), p.211. Saville acquired the rights for £14,000 and later claimed he sold them to MGM for that sum – according to Rachael Low, *Film Making in 1930s Britain*, p. 268.

18 Made by Peter Jefferies and dramatized by Don Shaw for BBC with Ben Cross as Manson.

19 Williams worked primarily on the Welsh scenes and on his own dialogue (Williams's interview with the author and with Claire Pollak for HTV's programme **The Dream that Kicks**, 1986). John Van Druten (1901–57), a former lecturer at University College of Wales, Aberystwyth, is perhaps best known for his adaptations of Christopher Isherwood stories, filmed as **I am a Camera** (director Henry Cornelius, 1955) and later as the inspiration for Bob Fosse's **Cabaret** (1972). But Van Druten wrote several TV plays, notably **The Druid's Circle** for BBC Wales, set on the Welsh borders, with William Devlin, Mary Merrall and Emrys James (screened 3 Dec. 1960).

20 *Film Comment*, July–August 1973.

21 Ibid.

22 See full discussion of Vidor's changes and the film in Durgnat and Simmon, as above, pp.205–11.

23 Ibid.

24 Raymond Durgnat and Scott Simmon, *King Vidor, American*, p.207.

25 Film publicity material (obtained from BFI) and *SWE*, 18 March 1939. See Philip M. Taylor (ed.), *Britain and the cinema in the Second World War* (Macmillan, 1988).

26 *Kinematograph Yearbook* 1939 and Durgnat and Simmon, op.cit., pp.208–9.

27 Op.cit., p.207.

28 Peter Stead, speaking in seminars, Images of Wales season, Cardiff, Chapter Arts Centre, 1986.

29 Peter Stead, *Film and the Working Class* (Routledge, 1989), pp.112–13.

30 Photostat of article (source uncredited) in author's possession.

31 Durgnat and Simmon, op.cit., p.209.

CHAPTER 9

1 Michael Balcon, *Michael Balcon Presents: A Lifetime of Films* (Hutchinson, London, 1969); Geoff Brown and Laurence Kardish *Michael Balcon: The Pursuit of British Cinema* (Museum of

Modern Art, New York, 1984), pp.54–5, Charles Barr, *Ealing Studios* (Cameron and Tayleur, David and Charles, 1977), pp.18–23, and George Perry, *Forever Ealing* (Michael Joseph/Pavilion, 1981), p.49.

2   The Crisp character was modelled on Ford's Irish father, according to Joseph McBride and Michael Wilmington, *John Ford* (Secker and Warburg, 1974), p.8. The book also asserts that the director spoke Gaelic. One regular Ford screenwriter Frank Nugent claimed the film-maker was a great reader of Irish literature (Lindsay Anderson, *About John Ford*, Plexus Publishing, 1981). The **How Green Was My Valley** mining village set was used later by Fox for **The Moon is Down** (1948), a resistance drama set in a snowbound Norwegian village and adapted from a Steinbeck novel by frequent Ford collaborator Nunnally Johnson. The **How Green** cottages and chapel were built in the Ventura Hills, according to Bosley Crowther, *New York Times*, 29 Oct. 1941.

3   Peter Stead, 'Wales in the movies', in Tony Curtis (ed.), *Wales: The Imagined Nation* (Poetry Wales Press, 1986).

4   Ford's **The Long Voyage Home** is based partly on Eugene O'Neill's short play *Bound East for Cardiff*.

5   In the 1960 eight-part BBC TV version (producer Dafydd Gruffydd), Eynon Evans was Gwilym; William Squire, Gruffydd; Rachel Thomas, Beth Morgan; Islwyn Maelor Evans played Huw. (Shot in the Cardiff studios and around Gilfach Goch.) The 1976 version (dir. Ronald Wilson) starred Siân Phillips and Stanley Baker as the Morgans.

6   Parallels between the films are drawn by Andrew Sarris, *The John Ford Movie Mystery* (Secker and Warburg, 1976).

7   Jeffrey Richards, 'Ford's lost world', *Focus on Film* magazine, Spring 1971, and Richards's book *Visions of Yesterday* (Routledge and Kegan Paul, 1973).

8   Andrew Sarris, op.cit., questions whether it is Rhys Williams's voice on the sound-track as credited, and there were two separate commentaries provided for the film, one by the actor and later director Irving Pichel.

9   Richard Llewellyn, *How Green Was My Valley* (Michael Joseph, 1939). Llewellyn's father W. Llewellyn Lloyd – 'a former cinema proprietor' – played Lloyd George in the film **The Guns of Loos**, with Bobby Howes and Madeleine Carroll in 1940 (according to *SWE*, 2 Nov. 1940).

10 Peter Bogdanovich, *John Ford* (Movie Magazine/Studio Vista, 1967).

11 *Time* review, 24 Nov. 1941.

12 See Andrew Sarris, op.cit., pp.103–9.

13 Greg Toland, photographic director on **Citizen Kane**, was originally assigned to the picture, says screenwriter Philip Dunne in his autobiography *Take Two* (McGraw Hill, 1980). But Toland was delayed on the set of Wyler's **The Little Foxes** (*Screen*, Spring 1972, vol.13, no.1 and *New York Times*, 26 May 1941).

14 Dunne had originally been asked to adapt a studio-written script which he found 'long, turgid and ugly' (*Take Two*, McGraw Hill, 1980, p.97). The *SWE*, 21 Nov. 1941, reported – curiously enough, considering the final casting: 'John Ford has insisted that the cast shall be as near as possible 100 per cent Welsh or with Welsh associations. He admits that finding the cast was about the most exacting job he ever had in his life since Welsh players of screen experience are very rare.' The *Echo* observed that at least Rhys Williams was a 'South Glamorgan man', the singers and Tudor Richards, musical director, were also Welsh and Richards had been working as a mechanic in the Fox studios for years. The singers were from a Los Angeles Welsh church.

15 Dunne, *Take Two*, p.98.

16 Ford also won the New York Critics' Best Director award – even though Citizen Kane was voted Best Film.

17 Dai Smith's 1980s BBC TV programme in the **Wales! Wales?** series touching on **How Green Was My Valley** is instructive.

18 Paramount's news magazine programme **Inside Goods** No.2, 1939, made with the co-operation of the south Wales miners, had presented a picture of 'master and man' fighting to save the pits . . . and to reduce unemployment (*SWE*, 20 May 1939). One reason for the change in 'propaganda line' on **Proud Valley** was the 'fine response' by the miners at this time to the call for more production, Balcon claimed in 'Realism or tinsel', a paper to the Workers' Film Association in Brighton, copy in BFI.

19 Paul Robeson jun. in interviews with the author in 1985. *The Times* Robeson obit (24 Jan. 1976) described **Proud Valley** as 'the finest of his British films'.

20 *Welsh Rarebit*, a stepping stone for much Welsh talent, began in 1940 as a programme for British forces in France, and continued on Radio Wales until 1947, returning on the Light Programme in 1956.

21 Author's interview with Pen Tennyson's brother Hallam, 1984, and transcription of interview with Hallam by Claire Pollak for HTV's programme **The Dream that Kicks**, 1986. Pen's suggestion for the title was turned down by 'the management' (*Pen Tennyson*, a limited-edition biography by his father Charles Tennyson, A. S. Atkinson, 1944).

22 Balcon's tribute to Tennyson, *Cine-Technician,* 22 July 1941. The director was a member of the ACT council from 1936 to 1938 (Charles Tennyson, *Pen Tennyson,* as above).

23 *Cine-Technician*, July–August, 1941.

24 Paul Robeson jun. said in 1985 (in an interview with the author) that his father became involved in **Proud Valley** 'because he worked with Herbert Marshall and Alfie Bass in London's Unity Theatre. Herbert Marshall was director of that theatre.'

25 Balcon's account differs. The studio's own publicity material claimed an encounter with a miner on a train journey set him thinking over the possibilities – then Marshall and his wife provided 'the right story'. Marshall talked about the film's origins in an interview with the author at his home, Henfield, Sussex, December 1990.

26 Ironically, Robeson was seen singing 'Joe Hill' in a TV documentary biopic **Sons of Freedom**, screened in Britain, *c.*1986. Marshall claimed Robeson wanted him to direct **Proud Valley** but Balcon would not agree (letter from Marshall to author, 6 June 1985, from Southern Illinois University, Carbondale, Illinois). Marshall headed the Center for Communist and East European studies at Southern Illinois University. His obituary tribute to Robeson can be found in the Center's bulletin, No.17, Spring 1976.

27 Interview with the present author, Henfield, Sussex, Dec. 1990.

28 Dilys Davies featured in the play *Rhondda Roundabout* in London's West End and both Thomas and Davies repeated their film roles in the radio version of **Proud Valley**, which featured Tom Jones as David Goliath and Jack James as Dick Parry. Pen Tennyson's brother Hallam (interviewed at his London home, 1984) told of the film's detailed writing collaborations. Louis Golding had written *Magnolia Street*, a popular novel of the Manchester slum.

29 **Proud Valley** was broadcast in February 1940. Much pertinent material can be found in the Jack Jones collection at the National Library of Wales, Aberystwyth, and in Rowland Lucas, *Voice of a Nation?*, a history of BBC Wales (Gomer Press, 1981).

30 Robeson's pro-Russia pronouncements on the heels of the signing of the German–Russian pact and the Soviet attack on Finland incensed Beaverbrook, who banned all mention of the film or Robeson in his newspapers (George Perry, *Forever Ealing*, pp.49–50). Paul Robeson jun., in 1985, claimed his father donated proceeds of an Albert Hall concert to the south Wales miners as early as 1929 and an Associated Press Agency report in the *SWE* (11 Sept. 1941) claimed Robeson first visited Wales in 1925. He was certainly in Wales in 1935 and 1938.

31 Marshall alleged he was initially 'shunted aside to placate Lord Beaverbrook' (letter to author, 1985). Robeson spoke over the airwaves to south Wales miners' leader Will Paynter.

32 Black dockers from Cardiff were imported to play roles in **Sanders of the River** (dir. Zoltan

Korda). See Jeffrey Richards and Tony Aldgate, *The Best of British: Cinema and Society 1930–70* (Oxford, 1983), p.15. Robeson played a stevedore in **Song of Freedom**.

33 In the film's only oblique early reference to the war, Robeson says he is seeking work and on his way to the 'armament factory at Darran Valley'.

34 Marshall claimed, in his 1985 letter, that the inspiration for these lines lay in lyrics by Bertolt Brecht for Hanns Eisler. An approximation of the lines, he said, was: 'Und nicht in weissen Hosen/Schwartz kommen wir heraus.' (And not in white trousers do we come out [of the pits] but in black').

35 *Sunday Chronicle*, 10 March 1940.

36 Michael Driver in *Reynolds News*, 10 March 1940. *The Monthly Film Bulletin* (No.7, 1940) was more generous, praising the film as 'an outstanding achievement for all concerned'. Crowther's review is in *New York Times*, 17 May 1941.

37 10 March 1940.

38 Graham Greene's review, *Spectator*, 15 March 1940.

39 Dyer concluded that, for the most part, **Proud Valley** was a 'very honourable film'.

40 Paul Robeson jun. in interview with author (1985) said his father accepted that David Goliath was not about to end the film 'triumphant or going into the sunset'; but he said Paul sen. was impressed by **Proud Valley**'s emphasis on the 'common struggle against Fascism'.

41 The only exception to being a tragic victim was in **Jericho** 'where he wrote the ending' (Robeson jun., ibid). Also see Susan Robeson's *The Whole World in his Hands* (Citadel Press, Secaucus, New Jersey, 1981) and Martin Baum Duberman's biography *Paul Robeson* (Ballantine Books/Pan, 1989).

42 Robeson jun. at NFT, 1985.

43 The film featured the London Welsh and Pendyrus male voice choirs.

44 *Spectator*, 15 March 1940; *SWE*, 20 May 1939.

45 The mining sequences were mainly shot in Staffordshire after south Wales private pit-owners denied co-operation. The shots of men scrambling for coal were filmed at the Silverdale Colliery, owned by the Shelton Iron, Steel and Coal Co. of Stoke. The crew were only given permission for the Staffordshire mining sequence once shooting began. I am grateful for information supplied by miners such as Alfred 'Pal' Rowley, a pitman for fifty years who took part in filming at Silverdale, and by Ray Johnson, a lecturer at the North Staffordshire Polytechnic, Stoke-on-Trent, who says the first pit-head long shot was taken at Leycett, nr. Newcastle-under-Lyme. Other pits were used for individual sequences and the main interiors were filmed on a specially built set at Ealing Studios.

46 *The Times* reviewer said Miss Thomas 'gives the screen distinction every time she appears on it' (11 March 1940). A cutting in Rachel Thomas's scrapbook (source unknown) cites Balcon's view that she brought to the screen what Gracie Fields brought to comedy – a warmth of personality and understanding that 'goes straight to the heart of the audience'.

47 See note 4. **Undercover** was to be called 'Chetnik', after the Yugoslav Resistance movement under General Milhailovic – then Tito gained UK government support and the script was amended. Rachel Thomas played the mother of the central Petrovich family.

48 See note 30.

49 Balcon, cited in *The Times* obit, 22 July 1941.

50 Outlook's publicity material for **Blue Scar** described Craigie as 'Britain's only woman film director' – and she certainly seems to have been the only woman director working in fiction that year.

51 William MacQuitty claims Outlook were 'advised a love story was essential if we were to gain the feature distribution hoped for' (William MacQuitty, *A Life to Remember*, Quartet Books, 1991, pp.300–3). Miners at Coednant Colliery were filmed for **Blue Scar** and other shots were taken at Wyndham Colliery, Ogmore Vale, and inside the pitcage at Llanharan Colliery,

according to the film's publicity material. The technical adviser was Dai Davies – a face-worker at Cwmllynfell – with 'partial silicosis' (Outlook press release). The star, Emrys Jones, was born of Welsh parents in Manchester, and brought up there.

52 Williams, a member of the BBC Wales radio repertory company, suffered from silicosis.

53 Just after release the *Evening Standard*, London, gave the budget as £80,000. See William MacQuitty, *A Life to Remember*, as above.

54 Author's interview with William MacQuitty, London, 1983.

55 Author's interview with MacQuitty, 1983.

56 Critic Richard Winnington, who championed **Blue Scar**, stressed 'the almost suicidal courage' involved in 'the act of faith' required to make the film without distribution guarantees (*News Chronicle*, 11 April 1949 – reproduced in Richard Winnington, *Film Criticism and Caricatures 1943–1953*, Elek Books, London, 1975).

57 Outlook said, even at that stage, there was 'no chance of the film being seen in the London area and little hope of a circuit deal' (press release). A separate company publicity release quoted Craigie as 'facing ruin' after the movie's rejection by the Rank circuit's 544 cinemas – unless it was accepted by ABC.

58 Cuts were made after the first preview when 80 per cent of cards returned by audience members contained favourable reactions, but there were only four adverse cards at the Granada, Tooting, where the film was 'wildly applauded' (Outlook press release). The film finally went into 421 cinemas in the ABC chain.

59 Craigie, letter to the author.

60 Craigie told me in 1985 that she deliberately employed a woman, Barry's Grace Williams, to write the music. Elizabeth Lutyens had composed the music for the director's **Born to be a Woman**. Grace Williams also composed the score for Paul Dickson's eloquent short Welsh film **David** (1951).

61 The script was banned by the British Board of Censors through the 1930s but the film was eventually passed uncut in 1941 (James Robertson, *The British Board of Film Censors, Film Censorship in Britain 1896–1950* (Croom Helm, 1985).

62 The *New York Times* reviewer 'TS' claimed the film focused on 'a catastrophe in a *Welsh* town [*sic*]'. He found it a film 'struck off at white heat'. 'It is so stinging in its attack on those who made the disaster inevitable that one wonders how it came to be made at all' (24 July 1941). Graham Greene doubted whether there had even been a better English film (*Spectator*, 26 Jan. 1940) reproduced in *The Pleasure Dome*, his collected criticism, 1935–40 (Oxford University Press, 1972).

63 Group Three was formed in 1951 as an offshoot of the government-backed National Film Finance Corporation.

64 The *SWE* (27 May 1942) reminded readers that 'Howard Spring [was] once an office boy in the reporters' room of this paper.'

Roy Boulting: 'I think MacDonald was a more overtly vain man than Radshaw, much more simplistically vain' (interview with the author, Twickenham Studios, 1984).

65 Boulting told me he thought Rank – and Rank's chief John Davis in particular – did not like it very much and Boulting himself, in retrospect, found the final cut film 'terribly episodic'. He claimed the first cut was 2hrs. 20mins. after losing around 35 mins. The final release print was 116 mins. 'Subjects like strikes, rioting and politics, and human beings involved in politics weren't the kind of material they were used to offering the public' (interview, Twickenham Studios, 1984). The film cost £300,000, a big budget at the time, but it was perhaps hardly surprising Spring did not like the truncated film.

66 Winnington found the scene when Hamer was rejected by the miners offered the film's 'sole moment of compulsion' (*News Chronicle*, 11 Oct. 1947). His unfavourable review still rankled with Boulting nearly forty years later. The film was also meant to be a tilt at the lack of

radicalism in the Attlee government but, released in 1947, it proved a trifle premature.

67 Interview, Twickenham Studios, as above.

68 This film aroused widely varying feelings: see Dai Vaughan, *Portrait of an Invisible Man – a study of Stewart McAllister* (BFI, 1983).

CHAPTER 10

1 *SWE*, 6 July 1940 and 28 May 1941. See also Roy Armes, *A Critical History of the British Cinema* for a detailed study of the impact of war on the national cinema and the documentary movement (Oxford University Press, 1978), pp.145–58.

2 *Bioscope*, 10 May and 16 Aug. 1917. *SWE*, 14 Jan. 1941.

3 *SWE*, 13 Mar. 1941.

4 *Michael Balcon: The Pursuit of British Cinema* (Museum of Modern Art, New York, 1984) pp.53–8. See *SWE*, 18 Jan. 1941.

5 In *Dylan Thomas* (Hodder and Stoughton/Penguin, 1977–8), pp.188–9, Paul Ferris writes briefly of two or three of these films and Thomas's working association with Strand writers such as Julian McLaren-Ross and Ivan Moffatt.

6 The film was compiled partly from the record of the 1934 Reich Party Congress at Nuremberg. It was no.4 in the **Into Battle** series made by Strand for the M.o.I.

7 Paul Ferris, *Dylan Thomas* pp.190–2, as above and Dylan Thomas's essay 'Reminiscences of childhood' (first version) in his collection, *Quite Early One Morning* (J. M. Dent, 1954).

8 Meredith's presence emphasized the propaganda value of such M.o.I. films and the Ministry's consciousness of the need to market them overseas (see Paul Swann, *The British Documentary Film Movement 1926–1946*, Cambridge University Press, 1989).

9 *Monthly Film Bulletin*.

10 *DNL*.

11 *DNL* vol.5, no.8, 1945. The newsletter's same issue printed a substantial extract from the sound-track on its back page.

12 Paul Ferris, op.cit. p.192.

13 Ibid. The British Council prepared versions, without Thomas's contribution – one, **Wales in Peace and War**, was screened in Rhyl and Cardiff in the early 1940s. A version with a Dutch sound-track is also available at the Imperial War Museum and another version known as **Wales** had Hywel Davies as commentator and a prosaic sound-track, minus Thomas's prose-poetry. The British Council was anxious to reflect an anodyne, favourable view of British culture in their films generally. The documentarists, working through the M.o.I., were more anxious to highlight the wider facets of UK life. See *The British Documentary Film Movement, 1926–1946*, as above.

14 The Clair incident is described in Buñuel's *My Last Breath* (Robert Laffont, 1982).

15 The reviewer in *Documentary News Letter*, March 1943, found Thomas's democrats ('ordinary peaceful citizens of the world') in the film's opening section, 'over-passive to the point of becoming puny in moral stature'. The full commentary is in *DNL*, Feb. 1943. The entry in the written material in the Imperial War Museum archive describes it as 'brilliant, especially by comparison with much other British propaganda'.

16 The entry in the IWM archive for **The Battle for Freedom** states: 'In spite of its author there is nothing very distinguished about the documentary.'

17 **A City Reborn** can easily be compared with **New Towns for Old**, **Our Country** and Jill Craigie's film on Plymouth, **The Way We Live** (1946), and as usual the ubiquitous 'town planner' is well to the fore on screen, explaining his schemes in the didactic manner of documentaries of the period.

18 Set in the fictional town of Smokedale, the film is reviewed in *Documentary News Letter* vol.3, no.9 and *Monthly Film Bulletin* vol.9, no.92.

19 Lines in **The Three Weird Sisters** recall Caradoc Evans's work. See his *My People* (Seren Books,

1987). The budget is mentioned in the *Daily Graphic*, 29 Oct. 1948.

20 Dai Jones is reviewed in *DNL* vol.2, no.67 and *Monthly Film Bulletin* vol.8, no.36.

21 *Daily Worker* (30 Nov. 1948) said the story 'still has meaning and moral today' and thought local authorities were 'still inclined to hide their heads in the sand and people who try to take action against social evils are still called mischief makers'.

22 *MFB* vol.15, no.178. The *Kine Weekly* reviewer (23 Sept. 1948) said: 'The genius of the film is its ability to mirror the truth and convert its ugly facts into entertainment.'

23 29 Oct. 1948.

24 30 Oct. 1948.

25 29 Oct. 1948. The *Observer* (31 Oct. 1948) also found it 'rather dreadful'.

26 1 Nov. 1948.

27 The story-line was freely adapted from a 1943 mystery novel *The Case of the Three Weird Sisters* by the American writer Charlotte Armstrong.

28 Telephone conversation with Nova Pillbeam, London, 1983.

29 Paul Ferris, op.cit. p.230.

30 Ferris lists four Thomas/Gainsborough projects – 'Rebecca's Daughters' (about the Rebecca riots), 'The Beach of Falesa', from a Robert Louis Stevenson short story, 'Me and My Bike' (1979) (an original Thomas idea) and a version of Thackeray's *Vanity Fair*. The Rebecca project was finally filmed, with an updated script, by Karl Francis in 1991, and 'Me and My Bike' has also been filmed, by BBC Wales. Thomas's other doomed forties projects proved to be 'Adventures in the Skin Trade', from his own unfinished novel, and 'Twenty Years A-Growing', based on Maurice O'Sullivan's book on the Blasket Islands. Another Thomas film script 'The Doctor and the Devils', based on the relationship between Dr Knox and corpse-stealers Burke and Hare, was filmed in the 1980s by Mel Brooks's Brooksfilms.

31 Dai Vaughan, *Portrait of an Invisible Man* (BFI, 1983) pp.111–14. Balcon thought **Silent Village** the 'best anti-Nazi' propaganda yet projected (letter to Jennings, 22 May 1943, in Jennings material at BFI library).

32 Noel Joseph, 'The Silent Village, the story of Wales and Lidice' (*Cinegram Preview* No.14, foreword by Jan Masaryk, Pilot Press Ltd.). Letter from M.o.I. to Horner, 29 July 1942 (in Jennings collection at BFI). **Coalminer**, made for the M.o.I. and the Ministry of Fuel and Power was directed by Charles de Lautour. Charlie Jones, fifty-six, was returning to the coal face after thirteen years.

33 Letter in Jennings collection at BFI.

34 *Humphrey Jennings, Film-maker, Painter, Poet* (BFI/Riverside Studios, 1982) edited by his daughter Mary-Lou Jennings. She says Humphrey Jennings was introduced to the Welsh miners by left-wing writer and newspaper designer Allen Hutt.

35 **Silent Village** material in BFI Library. Jennings stayed with miner Dave Hopkins and his wife (Mary-Lou Jennings, op.cit.). Lidice was burned to the ground by the Nazis and only 159 residents survived the occupation. A new village with a population of 500 has grown up near the original site.

36 McAllister's work for Jennings is discussed fully in Dai Vaughan, op.cit.

37 The assassination of Heydrich by the Czech underground which preceded the Nazi reprisals at Lidice is dealt with in a fine British fictionalized film **Operation Daybreak** (director, Lewis Gilbert, 1975).

38 The Education Report of 1847, known as the Blue Books, attacked the Welsh language and Welsh Nonconformity.

39 There were much more favourable notices. The *MFB* reviewer 'E.O.' cited its 'passionate sincerity and acute observation' and considered that 'without being pretentious the film has done what is asked of it magnificently' (vol.10, no.114, 30 June 1943).

40 Memo from Ministry of Information in Jennings papers at BFI.

41 Mary-Lou Jennings, op.cit. p.33 (letter to Cicely Jennings, 10 Sept. 1942). The director's respect for Cwmgïedd's pitmen probably led to the presence of 'Goronwy' a Welsh miner, in his **Diary for Timothy** (1946).

42 Mary-Lou Jennings, op.cit. p.33, letter to Cicely Jennings. Mass observation was launched with anthropologist Tom Harrisson from Bolton and poet-journalist Charles Madge.

43 Lindsay Anderson 'Only connect', *Sight and Sound* vol.23, no.4, April/June, 1954, reproduced in Mary-Lou Jennings op.cit., pp.53–9, including postscript added Oct. 1981.

44 Script by Arthur Calder-Marshall, who around 1944, worked for DATA with Chambers, with a team including Donald Alexander, Alexander's wife Budge Cooper, Mary Beales and Wolfgang Suschitzky (*DNL* issues, 1944). Summary in printed material in the IWM archives. See also *SWE* of 9 June 1942 for a description of the film and its screening to the workforce at the ordnance factory.

45 **Dance Hall**, directed by Charles Crichton, is discussed in chapter 13.

CHAPTER 11

1 Film writer/historian Peter Stead has perceptively defined the characteristics of the Williams villain, apropos **The Stars Look Down**. Stead notes the way Williams blends 'charm and a feline opportunism with a thoroughly ambivalent sexual narcissism' ('Wales in the movies', in Tony Curtis (ed.), *Wales: The Imagined Nation*, Poetry Wales Press, 1986).

2 Williams stressed his lack of interest in 'the political side' in discussions about **Last Days of Dolwyn** (author's interview with Williams, 1984 and typescript of interview with Claire Pollak for HTV series **The Dream that Kicks**, 1986).

3 Many of Williams's plays were screened in BBC Wales's first years in the 1950s – including **The Wind of Heaven** (April 1956) made in the Cardiff studios with Rachel Thomas and Helen Shingler, **Light of Heart** with John Longden and Maxine Audley, and **Trespass**, starring John Stratton and Ivor Novello's regular stage foil, Mary Ellis.

4 *Film Weekly*'s poll was in May 1933. Also see *Film Weekly*, 2 June 1933. *Film Pictorial* (13 Aug. 1932) considered the film 'a masterly adaptation' with an 'eerie atmosphere, brilliantly created'.

5 Author's interview with Emlyn Williams, London, 9 Aug. 1985.

6 Saville (b. 1897, d. 1976) also directed **Hindle Wakes** (1931) and **The Good Companions** (1933), among many others.

7 *Sunday Times* reviewer Sydney Carroll (4 July 1937) felt Montgomery's performance was as 'unintelligent as it is unsuccessful' and claimed Rosalind Russell drifted 'vapidly through the film with an entire absence of memorable personality'. But the *SWE* critic (28 Jan. 1939) thought Montgomery gave a 'brilliant study of a cunning criminal'.

8 'Van Druten also wrote a couple of extra scenes, frightfully good' – including kitchen scenes between the girl and the murderer (author's interview with Emlyn Williams, 9 Aug. 1985). Van Druten wrote for BBC Wales a well-remembered fifties TV play, **Druid's Circle**, about a domineering university professor, played initially by Ralph Michael and, in a 1960 production, by William Devlin.

9 Williams interview, Aug. 1985. The 1964 film script was extensively adapted by Clive Exton who aimed to 'reveal the attitude of the society which bred the psychopath' but it caught the backlash from reviewers who objected to seeing Finney in an unsympathetic role after **Tom Jones** (Alexander Walker, *Hollywood, England*, Michael Joseph, 1974), pp.149–50.

10 He made an impact on stage, for example, in 1937 in Tyrone Guthrie's *Richard III* at The Old Vic.

11 To be made for Korda from the Robert Graves novel; the film's problems also ruptured the relationship between Korda and Laughton.

12 **The Epic That Never Was** was televised in 1965.

13 Griffith had seen Williams in *Night Must Fall* on stage (interview with Williams, London, 1986). Williams said it was intentional that the dialogue of **Broken Blossoms** was kept to a minimum (interview, 1986).

14 'Dorothy (Dolly) Haas has a strong accent and the combination of her Austrian Cockney and Emlyn Williams's Welsh Chinaman struck a strange note' (Rachael Low, *Film-making in 1930s Britain*, George Allen and Unwin, 1985, p.177).

15 Favourable notices came from Brooks Atkinson and Walter Winchell, among others. By 1940, Williams was reputedly earning £15,000 from the stage alone ('The story of Emlyn Williams', *Picture Post*, 16 March 1940).

16 Ivor Brown found the Emlyn Williams/Sybil Thorndike production 'deeply moving, broadly amusing and vividly original' (cutting in Williams's scrapbook). In the 1956 BBC TV version Hugh David played Morgan Evans to Robson's Miss Moffat, with Eynon Evans as Mr Jones. Richard Burton also played Morgan Evans on TV and radio after Williams turned down the role to give Burton the opportunity (interview with Williams, London, 1985).

17 Davis later took the lead in *Miss Moffat*, a stage musical adaptation by Emlyn Williams, set in America's Deep South and directed by Joshua Logan. It proved a disaster, closed on the road and never reached Broadway. Charles Higham, *Bette* (New English Library, 1981). James Agee thought Davis's film performance too 'set, official and first-ladyish' (*The Nation*, 14 April 1945).

18 Morgan, born in Hopkinstown, said her work examined the conflicts of people moving from a mining community to Oxford, and her own dilemma. 'Do I stay and keep their outlook in life or do I think this could limit me and go on and identify with the other lot? I never felt it much of a conflict. I always liked the Welsh end more' (interview with the author, Mountain Ash, 1986). **A Matter of Degree** starred Meredith Edwards and Jessie Evans.

19 Williams interview, 9 Aug. 1985. In a letter to Miss Cooke, 23 Mar. 1938, he wrote: 'It would be useless to pretend that the character of Miss Moffat is not based very largely on yourself though, as you'd realize, there has to be a great deal of dramatic licence' (from Williams's scrapbook).

20 *New York Times,* 30 March 1945.

21 The *Monthly Film Bulletin* reviewer (31 March 1946) found the film 'deeply moving' and thought Bette Davis had 'never been better cast'. Also see *New York Times*, 30 March 1945.

22 *The Corn is Green* (Heinemann, 1938) won the New York Critics' Best Foreign Drama award, 1941. The Morgan Evans part in the film at least was originally written for Cardiff-born Richard Waring but he was drafted into the services, according to *The Passionate Life of Bette Davis* (Robson Books, 1990).

23 Darryl Zanuck wanted Hepburn to play the female lead in a planned screen version of Emlyn Williams's stage play *The Light of Heart*. She wanted John Barrymore as co-star, but the project was never realized. It *was* finally filmed as **Life Begins at 8.30** (1942) with Monty Woolley and Ida Lupino.

24 Studio publicity material issued on cinema release and interview with Williams, London, 1984. Dilys Powell thought Edith Evans brought 'a new range and authority to the British cinema' (*Sunday Times*, 24 April 1949). Williams said the Evans role was based on his own mother 'who was a Welsh peasant in a Welsh village and was exactly the sort of humble person I wanted to write for Edith Evans' (transcript of Williams interview for HTV programme **The Dream that Kicks**, 1986).

25 The film was shot at Isleworth Studios, London, and on location near Dolgellau, north Wales (see the *Listener*, 23 June 1949) and premièred at the Plaza, Bangor. There are comparatively few Welsh lines in the film though Edith Evans took special tuition from 'Welsh technical adviser Kenneth Evans' (studio publicity, 1949).

26 See Williams's two volumes of autobiography, *George* (Hamish Hamilton, 1961) and *Emlyn* (The Bodley Head, 1973). Both were issued in Penguin in 1976. Raine's influence is discussed in Don Dale-Jones, *Emlyn Williams* (University of Wales Press/Welsh Arts Council, 1979).

27 *Listener*, 23 June 1949. Williams told Claire Pollak (**The Dream that Kicks**, HTV, 1986): 'I

didn't want it to be an English villain because . . . it would have looked like an attack on England, which I didn't want.' There is surviving Pathé footage of the real life drama of the flooding of Capel Celyn in the Tryweryn Valley to supply water to Liverpool – a *cause célèbre* of the 1960s.

28 'We had an ending where the body [of Rob Davies] is shut up in a house but then we thought better of it. It didn't seem to work. It becomes too melodramatic at the end' (Emlyn Williams interviews with author, London, 1984 and 1985). 'The ending was changed because Emlyn was to fall into the well but he couldn't do it. It was always as if he was acting. We did endless re-takes but he couldn't get it right' (author's interview with associate director Russell Lloyd at St Donat's, South Glamorgan, 1985).

29 Colin McArthur (ed.), *Scotch Reels* (BFI, 1982), p.8. See also Colin McArthur, *The Cinema Image of Scotland* (Tate Gallery Publications, 1986). Williams, on stage at a Welsh screening in 1949, said he would have preferred to make the film entirely in Welsh. Later he said he wanted 'a quite unglamorous film, a simple picture of Wales, as I knew it as a child' (interview for **The Dream that Kicks**, HTV, 1986). He also claimed it was inspired by the success of such films as Rossellini's **Rome: Open City** (1945).

30 'Emlyn didn't know much about the technical side. Whenever I met Richard Burton afterwards he introduced me as his first director . . . Korda considered that Emlyn needed someone who could handle composition and camera movements. I was designing the shots for the film. I can't remember Emlyn being behind the camera, he supervised the acting' (Russell Lloyd interview, St Donats, 1985). Williams confirmed: 'I had expert advice on the camera . . . tracking, dissolving . . . I was really more concerned with myself and the acting' (interview for **The Dream that Kicks**, HTV, 1986).

CHAPTER 12

1 George Perry, *Forever Ealing* (Michael Joseph, 1981) and Charles Barr, *Ealing Studios* (Cameron and Tayleur Books, David and Charles, 1977).

2 The film paid tribute to the work of the Auxiliary Fire Service – including many part-timers – during the blitz. The Johns character, Sam, is caught pilfering by a policeman/part-time fireman but later redeems himself, rescuing his accuser from drowning.

3 Author's interview with Clifford Evans, Welshpool, 1984. Evans told me he coached Hugh Griffith at RADA, where Griffith gained a Gold Medal as the outstanding student of his year.

4 Ibid.

5 Ibid.

6 The charmed newspaper war correspondent and hero of Evelyn Waugh's novel *Scoop*.

7 The British comedy, from Charles Dyer's stage and screen play.

8 Terence Pettigrew, *British Film Character Actors* (David and Charles, 1982) p.96.

9 Edwards doubtless felt more at ease because he had played alongside Houston in many 1940s stage productions for the touring Pilgrim Players, based at Oxford.

10 In an interview with the author, London, 1985.

11 Interview with Meredith Edwards at his home near Mold, 1985.

12 Ealing made their last seven films at Borehamwood and they were produced and distributed by MGM. The part of 'Thomas' in **The Long Arm** was written specially for Edwards by Frend but the actor claimed the Chester line was his own. (Interview, as above.)

13 Ibid.

14 In a cutting (uncredited) in Edwards's scrapbook.

15 In the Watt film Edwards played Gwyl, an experienced trapper employed by Anthony Steel's game-warden hero and he was a pro-Welsh-language clergyman in **Only Two Can Play**.

16 Houston also played the Welsh medic – yet another 'Taffy' (Evans) – in **Doctor in the House** (1954) and significant roles in a string of small British films including **My Death is a Mockery** (1952), **Small Town Story** (1953) and **The Man Upstairs** (1958). He made fewer screen

appearances in the 1960s and 1970s but was Dr Watson to John Neville's Holmes in **A Study in Terror** (1975).

17 Interviewed by the author, Edinburgh Film Festival, 1988.

18 Patti (1843–1919) was born in Spain but had a fashionable retreat at Craig-y-Nos, Breconshire.

19 Interview with Mervyn Johns, London, 1985.

20 Interview with Rachel Thomas, Cardiff, 1985.

21 Individual episodes were directed by Cavalcanti, Charles Crichton, Basil Dearden and Robert Hamer.

22 See Ealing books by Barr and Perry (above), and Philip M. Taylor (ed.), *Britain and the Cinema in the Second World War* (Macmillan Press, 1988).

23 *The Sketch*, 3 June 1942. The *New Statesman* reviewer (23 May 1942) praised Johns's 'faultless performance' and 'drab melancholy'.

24 From a Denis Ogden stage play *The Peaceful Inn*. Ealing writer Diana Morgan insisted that 'nobody used a word of it, only the idea of going back in time' and claimed the rights were bought for a mere £100.

25 T. E. B. Clarke worked on only a small part of **Halfway House** – extending the Françoise Rosay role. 'She wanted a bigger part as she'd arrived from occupied France without money – and "the Frenchwoman" in the film initially had only a line or two' (author's interview with Clarke, Edinburgh Film Festival, 1988).

26 The commander in **Blue Peter** was mentor to the film's star Kieron Moore playing a Korean war hero.

27 Evans appeared in several of Warner's British 'quota' films but not the sole Warner's quota feature with a Welsh subject – **The Midas Touch** (1937) a *ménage à trois* second-feature drama about a Welsh millionaire (Frank Cellier) jealous of his son's romance. Barry K. Barnes and Judy Kelly played the leads.

28 Lewis's most memorable screen role was probably the murderous villain in Seth Holt's superb 1961 Hammer horror thriller **Taste of Fear**. Glyn Houston was best known on TV from the mid-1950s but played prominent cinema roles in B films such as **Payroll** (1960) and the lead in **Solo for Sparrow** (dir. Gordon Flemyng, 1962). At Ealing he had bit parts as a deskbound sergeant in **The Long Arm** and a barrowboy in **The Blue Lamp**.

29 O'Shea also featured in three unremarkable post-war films, the million-dollar flop musical **London Town** (dir. Wesley Ruggles, 1946) with Sid Field, Sonnie Hale and Claude Hulbert and low-budget features directed by John E. Blakeley at his Mancunian Studios in Manchester: **Holidays with Pay** (1948) and **Somewhere in Politics** (1949), both with the Lancashire comedian Frank Randle.

30 Interview with Diana Morgan, London, 1985. Cavalcanti claimed the women turned into 'absolute monsters' (article by Elizabeth Sussex in *Sight and Sound*, Autumn 1975 – cited in Geoff Brown and Lawrence Kardish, *Michael Balcon – The Pursuit of the British Cinema*, (Museum of Modern Art, New York, 1984). Morgan also had a soft spot for a script she wrote for Philip Leacock's feature **Hand in Hand**, a 1960 Associated British release about seven-year-olds finding friendship across racial barriers.

31 Robert Hamer, uncredited, directed most of **Fiddlers Three**, taking over from Watt, according to Morgan. She also claimed Hamer made most of **San Demetrio, London**, after the assigned director Charles Frend fell ill.

32 Charles Barr, (op.cit., p.178) rates it the most vigorous of Ealing's Boreham Wood features and claims its 'intelligence and energy' makes most British films of the 1950s look 'positively geriatric'.

1 **The Old Dark House** was co-written by Sheriff and Benn W. Levy and culled from Priestley's novel *Benighted*.

2 Havelock-Allen, formerly married to **Small Voice** star Valerie Hobson, went on to produce Olivier's screen **Othello** (1965).

3 Scripted by Derek Neame and Julian Orde, the film was made for under £150,000 in just forty-three days.

4 *Observer*, 14 Nov. 1948.

5 Ibid.

6 *News Chronicle*, 16 Nov. 1948.

7 The theme of an American outsider investigating strange events in Britain was again explored in Tourneur's celebrated **Night of the Demon** (1957). Mining sequences for the **Circle of Danger** were shot at the Windsor Colliery, Abertridwr (*Cinema Studio* supplement to *Cinema*, Oct./Nov. 1950).

8 *MFB*, 1951.

9 Interviews in *Film and Filming*. In 1992, J. Lee Thompson was reported to have announced his plans to direct a remake of **Tiger Bay** set in America with a US cast, but later he said he had merely taken out an option on it to prevent anyone else remaking it.

10 **Elenya**'s similarities to **Tiger Bay** were frequently alluded to by critics, and by audiences at screenings of Steve Gough's film in Wales in 1992.

11 Telephoned interview, London, 1985.

12 Ibid.

13 Scott had a two-film Rank contract and claimed they promised he could make a film based on Richard Hilary's *The Last Enemy* if he directed **Bitter Harvest**: 'but they went back on their word later' (interview, Cardiff, August, 1987). The film was shot partly in Cardiff and Senghenydd.

14 Contrary to received opinion, Thomas has played many unsympathetic roles on TV and radio in Wales (Rachel Thomas interview, Cardiff, 1984).

15 The *MFB* reviewer found the film, which included the London Welsh Choral Society, refreshing and pleasing 'with no suggestion of the music-hall conception of the Welsh' (April, 1953). Campbell Dixon, *Daily Telegraph*, thought it evoked the world of Caradoc Evans (6 June 1953).

16 The film's distributors traded on the 'Welshness' of **Valley of Song**. Posters were designed in English and Welsh (title: **Dyffryn y Gan**) and publicity material advised cinema managers to 'dress a number of usherettes in Welsh national costume and let them walk around the town during the peak shopping periods'.

17 Author's interview with Rachel Thomas, Cardiff, 1984.

18 The Cardiff director should not be confused with the screen and stage actor and **Last Days of Dolwyn** director. The drama became one of the first works in Welsh to be shown on Channel Four and boasted fine performances from Charles Williams and Nesta Harris.

19 Reviews can be found in *MFB*, Sept. 1952, and *Kine Weekly*, 24 July 1952.

20 Author's interview with Meredith Edwards, Mold, 1985.

21 Interview with Eynon Evans, Caerphilly, 1984. The film was produced by publisher David Dent for his company Advance.

22 *Spectator*, Nov. 1954; *Financial Times*, 15 Nov. 1954. The *Evening Standard* review (4 Nov. 1954) was generally favourable.

23 Interview with the author, Caerphilly, 1984.

24 It also featured Harry Secombe in a cameo, as a humorous passenger, entertaining fellow passenger Sybil Thorndike.

25 Amis said he wrote only one scene of **Lucky Jim** – Jim's tutorial class: 'the worst scene in the film'. He thought Carmichael 'miscast'. The novel was 'a farcical love story critical of

academics in a mild way' but he thought 'the small serious bits of the novel were forgotten' in the screen treatment (author's interview with Amis, London, 1985).

26 In a radio talk Amis said it was too late to save the Welsh language. 'When the language ceases to be common coin it's dead. It's better to study it as an academic subject – it's artificial to try and sustain it.'

    'Amis has an inbuilt thing against the arty-crafty, against a determination to find a virtue in a minority language' (author's interview with Gilliat at his home nr. Swindon, Summer, 1985).

27 Griffith, interviewed London, 1985. He also appeared to advantage in the Boultings' **Heavens Above!** (1963).

28 Gilliat said he always had trouble with the end: ' . . . the last scene between husband and wife. Bryan [Forbes] re-wrote it – I re-wrote it. In the end it was a hotch-potch of everybody's ideas and it didn't quite come off' (interview, 1985).

29 Interview with Amis, London, 1985. Forbes made headlines in south Wales with his **The Angry Silence** (1960) produced with, and starring, Richard Attenborough and centred on a strikebreaker sent to Coventry. The film was initially 'blacked' by the south Wales miners who called on the public to boycott it, alleging that it was 'anti-union'.

30 'I know Wales fairly well, certainly the atmosphere on certain bodies, from being a director of TWW for ten years. I knew that certain things could be very parochial and very set and I was interested in and liked satire' (Gilliat interview at his Wiltshire home, 1985). Gilliat was chairman of TWW's West Regional council.

31 Cecil Parker's medic 'found seven wives for the Rex Harrison character who thought there were only six' (Gilliat interview as above).

32 Gilliat interview, March, 1985. The success of **Only Two Can Play** contributed, ironically, to the Government's decision to sell off British Lion (Alexander Walker, *Hollywood, England*, Michael Joseph, 1974), p.254.

33 Interview, London, 1985.

34 In a 1980s radio talk on Wales, Amis referred to the decline of Welsh industry and culture and its replacement with an 'international culture – something pretty squalid'. Aspects of this culture were satirized in Amis's novel *The Old Devils* (filmed by BBC TV Wales, 1991).

35 Amis felt aspects of the society he depicted, particularly in **Only Two Can Play**, applied much more generally in Britain than was appreciated. He did not like the attitude that 'in a Welsh novel Welshness must be top of the agenda' (author's interview with Amis, London, 1985).

36 Gilliat suspected there was 'a lobby for Siân Phillips' who had been tested unsuccessfully for the role (interview, summer, 1985).

37 Sellers disliked the film and sold his interest in it, losing out financially, according to Peter Evans (in *Peter Sellers, The Mask Behind the Mask,* Leslie Frewin, 1969, p.136). But Gilliat insists the sale was at the screenwriter's behest after Forbes had seen a rough-cut (Gilliat interview, 1985). But see Geoff Brown, *Launder and Gilliat*, (BFI, 1977) pp.147–8. Gilliat said of Sellers: 'I never thought he was a good actor, technically. He was an absolute impersonator to the point where he could seem to be a good actor' (1985 interview).

38 Interview, ibid.

39 Amis interview, London, 1985.

40 Gilliat interview, London, 1985. 'Someone said Mai would like to do comedy and she agreed to test.' Gilliat, who claimed Amis didn't like the adaptation, admitted the film was difficult to edit 'because certain parts of it didn't work'.

CHAPTER 14

1 Roberts Williams became editor of *Y Cymro* (formed 1931) just after the Second World War and was still at the helm when the Welsh-language edition reached a peak circulation of 28,000-plus in the 1950s (author's interview with John Roberts Williams, Cardiff, 1987).

2 According to Williams, Charles was the first professional photographer to work for a Welsh-

language paper (ibid.). Freddie had been in the Llangybi area, with its small primary school of 30–5 pupils, for three or four years when the film was made.

3 Interview with Williams.

4 Ibid.

5 Glyn Thomas, in the *News Chronicle*, praised the camerawork of Geoff Charles: 'He has caught and reflected the spirit of the mountains, rivers, the fields and glens in a wonderful manner' (29 July 1949).

6 Williams interview, Cardiff, 1987. Robin Griffith, now of Cardiff, then a schoolboy and later a press photographer with *Y Cymro*, recalled touring the film with Tom Morgan and showing it in Llŷn villages, including in the chapel vestries at Edern and Tudweiliog. At Tudweiliog and nearby Dinas, the projectionists used their own generator as there was no electricity supply. Griffith confirmed that the screenings were 'very well attended' (interview, Cardiff, May, 1993).

7 Williams interview, Cardiff, 1987.

8 **David** was made for the Festival's Welsh committee. An extract from the shooting script is in *Sight and Sound* vol.21, no.2, Oct.–Dec. 1951. Dickson, interviewed by the author in 1987 said D. R. Griffiths was chosen on the recommendation of the BBC's Aneurin Talfan Davies who recalled his contribution to a radio series. 'They'd selected D. R. as the voice of Wales – I thought maybe he could become its image and its heart' (Dickson said).

9 Griffiths, formerly at Bettws pit, dug anthracite for thirty-three years (feature by Donald Zec, *Daily Mirror*, 20 March 1951). He joined the Ammanford County School in 1932 and was still there in the year of the film's release. The gas explosion scene was re-staged for the film at the nearby Butcher's Colliery (Zec, ibid.).

10 Dickson scripted a film on the UN charter to be produced by Basil Wright for the Crown Film Unit but it was never made. He was later involved with the 'Britain Can Make It' series produced by Paul Rotha's Film of Fact company. Gavin Lambert (*Sight and Sound*, June 1951) thought D. R. Griffiths re-lived episodes from his life with 'touching dignity and simplicity'. 'These scenes . . . describe ordinary people, [and] infuse life and colour into a background in a way very rare in film in this country. **David** is not only one of the few authentic regional films made here but reasserts the human values that documentary film has lacked for so long.' See also *MFB*, June 1951.

11 Interview with Paul Dickson (National Film School, Beaconsfield, 1987).

12 The film was shot entirely on location. 'World Wide had a marvellous producer, James Carr, who had enormous faith in people. His confidence made you rise to the challenge and he had a marvellous story sense' (interview with Dickson, as above).

13 The film's structure is similar to an episode in the 'Workers and Warfront' series (no. 14), a non-theatrical short made in 1944. In this episode, shot partly in Wales, an injured miner is taken to a casualty unit, then on to rehabilitation.

14 Dickson interview as above. Professionals in **The Undefeated** included Kynaston Reeves, Betty Marsden and Alfie Bass. **Lady in the Lake** was a 1946 version of the Raymond Chandler novel, directed by actor Robert Montgomery, and the action was seen entirely through the eyes of the hero (played by Montgomery) who was only seen through mirrors.

15 Dickson claimed Zinnemann had told him 'The Undefeated** showed the plight of the wounded better than **The Men**' (Dickson interview, 1987).

16 Winnington, in the *News Chronicle*, said the response to **The Undefeated**'s screening at the Edinburgh Festival had confirmed the film's 'wide and instantaneous appeal'. Associated British Pathé had booked the film for distribution through Associated British but seemed reluctant to release it and had given it only 'trial runs' in certain cinemas. **The Undefeated** finally had its London première at the Leicester Square Theatre. Forsyth Hardy (*Films in 1951 Festival of Britain*, published by *Sight and Sound* and BFI, p.60) claimed **The Undefeated** proved there was 'still fire and force in the documentary idea'.

17 Interview with Dickson, as above. See *Films in 1951 Festival of Britain*, a special publication from *Sight and Sound* (BFI, 1951).

18 Dickson's features included the sci-fi movie **Satellite in The Sky** (1956) and **The Depraved** (1957).

19 Leo Genn, who supplied the narrator's voice in **The Undefeated**, starred in Litvak's acclaimed **The Snake Pit** (1948).

CHAPTER 15

1 In the opening scenes Lon Chaney jun.'s character, Lawrence Talbot, is first seen in bed at 'Queen's Hospital, Cardiff', claiming he comes from 'Llanwenny village' nearby. Records show that Talbot died four years previously . . . He then travels to Europe.

2 See Ian Christie, 'Blimp, Churchill and the State' in Ian Christie (ed.), *Powell, Pressburger and Others*, pp.105–20 (BFI, 1978), and Michael Powell, *A Life in Movies* (William Heinemann, 1986), pp.404–6, the film-maker's autobiography.

3 Powell previously chose Livesey for the main naval role in **The Phantom Light** (1935), set partly in Wales, but was over-ruled at Gaumont-British by Michael Balcon who disliked the actor's voice (*A Life in Movies*, as above p.236).

4 Ibid., p.404 and Ian Christie, *Powell, Pressburger and Others*, pp.105–20. Olivier was set to play Candy but the Fleet Air Arm would not release him. Powell's gamble on Livesey for the role was 'probably one of the happiest inspirations I have ever had' (Powell autobiography, as above).

5 See Ian Christie, 'Blimp, Churchill and the state', in *Powell, Pressburger and Others*, pp.105–20.

6 Sam Livesey's films included the 1928 version of Edgar Wallace's **The Forger**, Thomas Bentley's **Young Woodley** (1929) and the controversial – and censored – **Maisie's Marriage** (1923), based on the Marie Stopes sex advice book *Married Love* (Roger also appeared in this film).

7 Michael Powell, *A Life in Movies* (Heinemann, 1986), pp.475–6. Ironically, James Mason was originally invited to play the McNeil role but balked at the privations facing cast and crew during Western Isles filming.

8 *Wide Eyed in Babylon* (Bodley Head, 1974) pp.8 and 15.

9 His 1931 Hollywood films alone included **The Bachelor Father**, with Marion Davies, **Just a Gigolo**, **Bought**, with Constance Bennett, and **Blonde Crazy**.

10 Ronald Colman and Ralph Richardson also played Bulldog Drummond on screen in the 1930s.

11 Typical of Milland's early roles was the amused aristocrat opposite Deanna Durbin in **Three Smart Girls** (1936).

12 Wilder described **The Major and the Minor** as 'the first American film about paedophilia', made well before Stanley Kubrick's **Lolita** (1962) (Maurice Zolotow, **Billy Wilder in Hollywood**, Pavilion Books, 1988, p.107).

13 The 'hocking the typewriter' scene was shot on one Sunday, with Milland 'walking all the time' and a truck following him (Zolotow, op.cit., p.131). A distillery syndicate reputedly tried to buy up all the Paramount prints for five million dollars (op.cit., p.133).

14 **The Safecracker**, like **The Circle of Danger**, was produced by David Rose for Coronado, an independent set-up. It was released through MGM.

15 'I think . . . he did his best work with me. He never was bad in a picture of mine, he was always exceptional. I don't think that can be said of any of the others that I've worked with' (Michel Ciment, *Conversations with Losey*, Methuen, 1985, p.175).

16 **The Cruel Sea** offered Baker his first significant part.

17 Basil Dearden's film, with Baker tackling a gunman in the classroom, was, for 1958, advanced in subject matter, and in its reliance on location filming. Baker's character Truman is partially

transformed from blinkered disciplinarian by his relationship with the troubled teenager Johnny (David McCallum) (John Hill, *Sex, Class and Realism, the British Cinema 1956–1963*, BFI, 1986). **Hell is a City** (dir. Val Guest, 1960) was also set in a working-class milieu – in Manchester.

18 Michel Ciment, op.cit., pp.174–7. The inspector's role had been written for Peter O'Toole, but the film's financiers would not accept him. Losey said he wanted the character to be aggressive in a 'class and sexual way. And I knew that Stanley was both of these.' Losey attributed this to a childhood of extreme poverty and his being Welsh with their 'natural aggressiveness as a nation . . . Particularly the ones from the Rhondda Valley.' See also Peter Stead, *Film and the Working Class* (Routledge, 1989), p.190.

19 Losey decided on certain characteristics when Peter O'Toole arrived for an early interview suffering from a cold.

20 Josef Herman's drawings of Welsh miners were used as an inspiration for the paintings in **Blind Date**. Richard Macdonald, frequent Losey collaborator, aped Herman's style for Van Rooyen's paintings (Michel Ciment, op.cit., p.218). See comments on Herman in chapter 16.

21 Losey's first version was 2hrs. 48mins., but he trimmed it to 2hrs. 30mins. The director claimed the Hakim Brothers took out another 20 minutes, introduced lines into the script and gave Moreau 'a phoney voice'. Baker later said Moreau, Losey and he had all asked for their names to be taken from the credits and publicity after the UK release, Baker claiming the film was now 'nonsense' after cuts (*Daily Mail*, 16 Oct. 1963). Gala distributed a 1hr. 51mins. version in 1966, and a two-hour version was shown by the BFI the same year.

22 Ibid. Losey described **Eve** as 'an intensely personal project'. 'I was not only working out my exile . . . to be dislocated in terms of background and place, to the extent that I was, was to dislocate your personal relationships.'

23 Losey claimed the Hakims removed a final line of dialogue which established she would return, Ciment, op.cit., p.218.

24 Dilys Powell said she 'didn't believe a word of it', but praised Moreau as both 'basilisk' and 'boa constrictor' for 'one of the outstanding performances of the cinema' (*Sunday Times*, 7 June 1963). John Coleman (*New Statesman*, 26 July 1963) referred to some 'wretchedly rhetorical wording, biblical Dylan and splash'.

25 See Alexander Walker's *Hollywood, England* (Michael Joseph, 1974) pp.368–9.

26 A Harry Green drama, with Jessie Evans as Baker's wife. Baker described it as 'full of the reality of life in South Wales' (*SWE*, 26 Oct. 1960). His own father had lost a leg in the mines.

27 According to Baker obits. Anthony Storey in *Stanley Baker, Portrait of an Actor* (W. H. Allen, 1977), claimed the film had made £8 million profit by publication date.

28 *MFB*, Feb. 1964; Alexander Walker, *Evening Standard* 1 Jan. 1964.

29 *Evening Standard,* 1 Jan. 1964.

30 *Variety,* 8 Dec. 1963, referred to a world première in Johannesburg due January 1964. *Daily Express*, 14 Dec. 1963.

31 Baker later formed another company, Oakhurst Enterprises, 'to film pop concerts for cinema release' (*SWE*, 20 May 1970).

32 **Graceless Go I** was directed by Patrick Dromgoole, based on an Anthony Storey novel, and **Fade Out**'s director was John Nelson Burton. **Perfect Friday** was produced by the British-based Dimitri de Grunwald.

33 Richard Burton waived his fee – £50! (author's interview with John Ormond, Cardiff, 1985). 'Much of the film was shot silent, with sound added later. I wanted less equipment between myself and the subject,' ibid. See also Melvyn Bragg, *Rich, The Life of Richard Burton* (Hodder and Stoughton, 1988, Coronet paperback, 1989) for references to Burton and HTV.

34 Burton's tribute in the *Observer* 11 July 1976. Wayne Drew's comments are in National Film Theatre programme notes for **Zulu** in 'Views of the Valleys', a section of the NFT brochure

devoted to a Wales Film Season, 1985. In his notes to **Eve** in the same season, Drew said the designation of 'Welsh star' (also applied to Burton) 'carried with it a clear notion of sexual prowess and cultural credibility . . . derived from its Celtic origins'. See also Michel Ciment, op.cit., p.175.

35 English was Burton's second language.

36 C. A. Lejeune, *Observer*, 11 Jan. 1953.

37 He was moving between the Old Vic and Hollywood until 1956 when he quit the British stage.

38 Dilys Powell thought he had never given 'such a commanding' performance on screen as in **Becket**, from Jean Anouilh's stage play (*Sunday Times*, March 1964).

39 Burton was paid 250,000 dollars for three months' work on **Cleopatra**, which began production in September 1961 and ceased shooting in mid-1962. For **Where Eagles Dare** (1967) he earned a million dollars for 16 weeks' work plus 50,000 dollars 'living expenses' (Paul Ferris, *Portrait of Richard Burton*, Weidenfeld and Nicolson, 1984). The Burtons' first film as a married couple was **The Sandpiper** (1965). For details of **Cleopatra** and its problems see Melvyn Bragg, *Rich*, as above pp.191–215 and 225. The film was first planned in 1958, with Rouben Mamoulian directing.

40 He also played a sinning cleric in **The Sandpiper**.

41 **Brief Encounter** was produced by Loren's husband Carlo Ponti. See Melvyn Bragg's *Rich*, pp.579–81.

42 Burton also appeared in HTV's **This World of Wales** in 1963, broadcast on St David's Day, presenting (with writer Gwyn Thomas) poetry by Dylan Thomas and Gerard Manley Hopkins. He performed commentary duties with Wynford Vaughan-Thomas for HTV, at the 1969 investiture of Prince Charles as the Prince of Wales, and appeared in a two-part networked TV series, co-starring with Liz Taylor, **Divorce His, Divorce Hers**, a portrait of a marriage from the respective points of view of the participants, scripted by John Hopkins and directed by Waris Hussein. See Melvyn Bragg, *Rich*, as above, p.559.

43 Dirk Bogarde turned down the Trotsky role because he did not like the script, which was re-written anyway (Michel Ciment, op.cit., pp.324–5).

44 Nine-hour and five-hour versions of **Wagner**, made mainly for TV, were screened at the National Film Theatre, London, in 1984. A six-hour version has since been shown on British television.

45 *Sight and Sound*, Summer 1971.

46 Ibid.

47 Ibid.

48 Ray Smith, who played Waldo, said: 'It's not a very good film. I told the director I can't dance, I can't sing. The singing teacher gave up in half an hour, no dancing instructor ever showed, so [we] made up some drunken clowning. It wasn't a very happy experience' (interview with the author, Cardiff, 1985).

49 Author's interview with Aubrey Richards, London, 1986.

50 Author's interview with Siân Phillips, Cardiff, 1988.

51 See *No Bells on Sunday*, the journals of Rachel Roberts, edited with a documentary biography by Alexander Walker (Pavilion, 1984). Roberts's early films included J. Lee Thompson's 1956 version of **The Good Companions**, set partly in Wales, with Hugh Griffith also in the cast.

52 Ibid. p.163.

53 *This Sporting Life* was produced by the same team, Julian Wintle/Leslie Parkyn, responsible for the Cardiff-based **Tiger Bay** and also Losey's film **Blind Date**.

CHAPTER 16

1 See Rowland Lucas, *The Voice of a Nation, A Concise Account of the BBC in Wales 1923–73* (Gomer Press, 1981).

2 Luke McKernan, *Topical Budget* (BFI, 1992).

3 Ibid. Three files of Topical Budget material are in the BFI's Cataloguing Dept., London.

4 See *Films on Coal* (Catalogue of NCB titles available, Sept. 1979 – NCB, 1979).

5 In the *WM*, 5 March 1968, Tinniswood described the company as 'an outstanding commercial success, consistently topping £1 million gross profits'. One documentary **Hot Spot**, with writer Gwyn Thomas visiting the French Riviera, won a prize at the Prague Film Festival. See *SWE*, 14 Feb. 1957, for details of the cinema exhibitor's concern.

6 *WM*, 13 June 1967.

7 *SWE*, 15 Feb. 1963.

8 *SWE*, 21 May 1963.

9 *SWE*, 1964.

10 *SWE*, 14 June 1967; *WM*, 22 Sept. 1967; *Sunday Times*, 18 June 1967. Sir Geraint Evans, the Burtons, and Baker's company were all large shareholders.

11 Interviewed, Cardiff, March, 1992.

12 Typical was **Spring on the Farm** (1942), written and directed by Ralph Keene, for the Ministries of Agriculture and Information, which focused on typical farming jobs in the Ross-on-Wye area. **Welsh Magic** (1946) (Paul Barralet Productions) presented 'the scenery of north Wales'. Ralph Keene later made **Angle Bay** (1962), a documentary on Milford Haven, sponsored by BP. **Dragon of Wales** was reviewed in *MFB* vol.10, 1943.

13 In the late forties and fifties, Archie Pipe, a businessman from Pontardawe near Swansea, formed the Octagon company and shot five shorts, including film of American links with Milford Haven (see Wil Aaron, 'Film', in Meic Stephens (ed.), *The Arts in Wales 1950–1975*, Welsh Arts Council, 1979).

14 The Brunner Lloyd films are reviewed in *MFB* issues of 1950 and 1954. The reviewer of **A Letter from Wales** criticized the Welsh boy's accent as 'very English'. **West of the Border**, an Associated Independent Producers (1945) 16-minute film on Wales distributed by Warner Bros., is reviewed in *MFB* vol.12, 1945. Another 1940s documentary set in Wales is **The Road to Yesterday**, with its relentlessly patronizing commentary and views of Welsh beauty spots from narrow-gauge railways to horse fairs, folk crafts and pit ponies. It starts typically with a montage of shop façades bearing the legend 'Jones', and continues with facetious references to Llanfair PG with the usual panning shot over the famous station sign.

15 Author's interview with Jack Howells at Bonvilston, South Glamorgan, 1983.

16 Howells interview, as above. Howells claimed to have written, uncredited, much of the dialogue for DATA's documentary **Dover, Spring 1947** (1947, dir. Mary Beales), which allowed him some tongue-in-cheek humour in a film viewing post-war Kent through the eyes of an American visitor. The film was shown that year at the first Edinburgh Film Festival, then solely a documentary event.

17 Ibid.

18 The 1922 film embraced the death of Michael Collins in Ireland, Shackleton's death and the Thompson–Bywater murder case, but made more use of stills and newspaper cuttings than the 1933 **Scrapbook**.

19 Interview with Jack Howells, Bonvilston, 1985.

20 Howells interview, 1983. A. Milner-Gardner is credited as film editor but there is no doubt that Howells and Baylis shaped the film.

21 Cutting from Jack Howells's personal scrapbook, kindly loaned by the director.

22 Interview with Howells, 1983.

23 Forsyth Hardy thought it was as skilful a piece of compilation as anything from overseas in the 1950 Edinburgh Festival (*Films in the 1951 Festival of Britain*, published by *Sight and Sound* and the BFI, 1951.)

24 Cuttings (undated) from Jack Howells's scrapbook.

25 Ibid.

26 Interview with Howells, 1983.

27 Ibid.

28 Ibid.

29 **Elstree Story** was directed by Gilbert Gunn. The screenplay of **The Dancing Years** (director Harold French) is officially credited to Jack Whittingham and Warwick Ward. An extract from **The Dancing Years** appears in **Elstree Story**.

30 See HTV leaflet published 1991, to accompany a tribute season of Howells films.

31 Howells also made **Mine Shaft Sinking** (1965) for Thyssen (GB), about miners' work at Cynheidre Colliery, Carmarthenshire, and **New Neighbours**, focusing on the problems of building a nuclear power station at Wylfa, Anglesey. They were distributed by the National Coal Board and Central Electricity Generating Board respectively.

32 *Films and Filming*, June 1974.

33 Howells played Pete Seeger's song 'The Bells of Rhymney' over train shots in the Rhymney Valley. It was arranged by Seeger and inspired by Idris Davies's poem.

34 Later Howells failed to obtain Welsh Arts Council funding for another work based on Davies's forthright, astringent verse. Another **Return to Rhymney**, centred on Davies's work but seen through the eyes of women, was directed by Michele Ryan for Cardiff's Teliesyn in the late 1980s.

35 See Michael Foot, *Aneurin Bevan, 1945–1960* (Granada Publishing, 1975).

36 There was a rash of these 'travelogue' films in the 1960s and 1970s in the mould of **Pembrokeshire – My County** (dir. Ronald Stark, 1960) and Walt Disney's 25-minute **People and Places** (dir. Geoffrey Foot), shot partly at the home of Portmeirion creator Clough Williams-Ellis. A film in the Celtic mists and mythology tradition was **The Land of the Proud Dragon**, Shirley Cobham's 1970 film for the British Petroleum Company, which focused on much archaic legend and folklore.

37 The belated advent of TV in Wales was itself deemed good dramatic material. In 1956 Wales TV produced **Without Vision**, a play by Elaine Morgan centring on a family's comments about the box, with Sheila Gill and Eynon Evans in the leads (produced by Peter Lambert, screened 10 July). By 1962 Hywel Davies, the new BBC Wales head of programmes, claimed it was 'generally accepted that outside London, Cardiff is the leading centre of television drama', (Rowland Lucas, op.cit., pp.186–7).

38 Interview with John Ormond, Cardiff, 1983.

39 Ibid.

40 Ibid. In 1977 Ormond directed for BBC a documentary **The Life and Death of Picture Post**. His contribution to the magazine is noted in Tom Hopkinson's book *Of This Our Time* (Hutchinson, 1982).

41 Interview with John Ormond, Cardiff, 1983.

42 Ibid.

43 Ibid.

44 Ibid. Dafydd Gruffydd produced a TV documentary **Strangers in Our Midst** (screened 29 Nov. 1956) which presented the plight and life-style changes of the 'thousands of Poles living in Wales since the war', following the disbanding of the Polish army.

45 Interview with John Ormond, Cardiff, 1983.

46 Ibid.

47 **Borrowed Pasture** was shown at the Edinburgh Festival.

48 Interview with Ormond, Cardiff, August, 1983. Shooting ratio is the proportion of footage shot to footage used.

49 Ibid. According to Ormond, letters of praise were torn up by Myall who 'then dropped them into the bin and said, "I never want to hear another word about that film." ' Jack Mewett was

film department head, with Norman Swallow as his assistant.

50 Author's interview with Harley Jones, Cardiff, 1983. Jones was assistant on **The Desert and the Dream** and sole editor on **From a Town in Tuscany**.

51 Interview with Ormond, Cardiff, 1986.

52 Ibid.

53 Ibid.

54 Ibid.

55 Interview with Ormond, Cardiff, 1984.

56 Ibid. 'As I'd taken so much from this extraordinary, endearing country I thought I'd like to give something back' (Sutherland, quoted in the programme).

57 Interview with Ormond, Cardiff, 1984.

58 Ibid.

59 Ibid. Other documentaries about the poet include **Dylan Thomas – A Personal Memoir** (dir. Bayley Silleck for London Weekend Television in 1972) and a tribute by Kevin Marsland, narrated by Donald Houston.

60 Ormond also made **The Fragile Universe** (1969), a documentary about Welsh poet Alun Lewis, edited by Chris Lawrence.

61 Made for Films of Scotland, where Grierson was a committee member. Grierson asked Henson to direct and Ormond was invited to write the commentary, 'because of his poetry, his films, his sensibility, and his outstanding gift with words'. Grierson and he met quite a lot in Cardiff 'to work on the commentary, and developed quite a rapport' (author's interview with Lawrence Henson, Inverness, April, 1987).

CHAPTER 17

1 Cardiff Film Society booklet, published September 1950, and CFS programme, Dec. 1950. Both in National Library of Wales, Aberystwyth.

2 Transcript of *Now's Your Chance* (Light Programme, 15 Nov. 1949) in BFI library. The programme was recorded at St Illtyd's Hall, Splott, Cardiff.

3 The debate, recorded 8 March 1966, was hosted by journalist and documentary film-maker, John Morgan. Bossak, ousted in the political turmoil of 1968, was also head of one of Poland's seven major state film units.

4 Grierson, then living at Calne, Wiltshire, edited the programmes in the *WM* offices, Cardiff, from around 1959 – STV and the *WM* were both owned by Roy Thomson. 'We assembled four programmes at a time and travelled up to Glasgow to record them' (author's interview in Inverness, 1987, with Lawrence Henson, film editor in Cardiff on the series).

5 Author's interview with Richard Watkins, Cardiff, 1984. The Grierson influence was not direct as Watkins did not arrive at the college until the mid-seventies.

6 Interview with John Wright, Nov, 1983.

7 Ibid.

8 Author's interview with Henry Luttman and Peter Turner (at Newport College of Higher Education, 1984), and interview with John Wright, November, 1983. The canal film was made by Alan Flower and the Newport transporter bridge short won a National Film School place for its student producer, Jim Sullivan. The nine-minute **Resurrection**, made by Harley Jones with Chris Bellinger, was taken for distribution by Contemporary Films who described it as 'a beautifully atmospheric short which brings to life, with some brilliant camerawork, an age that is now almost past' (contemporary catalogue, 1970).

9 Interview with John Wright, Nov. 1983.

10 Early ambitious college films cited by Luttman and Turner as worth special attention include **Variants** by Michael Barnes, **Narcissus** by Alex Kirby and **Firewatch** and **Inside Outside** by Brian Ashby.

11 Interview with Richard Watkins, Cardiff, 1984.

12 Ibid. 'Wildtrack' means recording the sound live and independently, then adding to the film in the studio.

13 Ibid.

14 **Milford Fisherman** was made with a Welsh Arts Council grant of about £2,000 and later bought by the BBC. **Trawling Out of Swansea** information from Francis Worsley's Cardiff-born son, writer, broadcaster and film-maker Roger Worsley (b. 1933), who says the 16mm. film, on acetate, could be dated from the early 1930s, although the can containing the movie was labelled 1926/7. 16mm. stock became available in 1923.

15 Interview with Richard Watkins, Cardiff, 1984.

16 Ibid.

17 A private screening at Milford Haven raised more than £500 for the Fishermens' Benevolent Fund and the Royal National Lifeboat Institution.

18 Interview with Watkins, Cardiff, 1984.

19 Ibid. The film was narrated by Neil Kinnock and included footage from **Green Mountain, Black Mountain**.

20 Ibid. **Memoirs** is Watkins's personal favourite.

21 Ibid.

22 Ibid.

23 Ibid.

24 Ibid.

25 Author's interview with Geoff Thomas, Cardiff, 1984.

26 Ibid. 'To interview a raddled prostitute of 50 years standing on the game and people of that ilk was a brave effort. A lot of people didn't like it – they didn't want to think that these people actually live in Cardiff' (interview with Frances Gallaher, Thomas's wife and business partner, 1984).

27 Interview with Geoff Thomas, as above.

28 Author's interview with Harley Jones, Cardiff, 1983.

29 The film won praise from Wil Aaron in his film article in *The Arts in Wales 1950–1975* (Welsh Arts Council, 1979).

30 Jones's sponsored work in the 1980s included **Wales's Best Blacksmiths**, shot for around £20,000, for the Welsh Tourist Board, and centred on the hotel where George Borrow stayed while writing *Wild Wales*.

31 Author's interview with Henry Luttman, Newport, November 1983. He thought it a 'very bad film' and acknowledged his serious mistake in trying to animate an existing story before preparing a sound-track and music arrangement.

32 Ibid.

33 Ibid.

34 Ibid.

35 Interview with Peter Turner, Newport, 1984.

36 Ibid. Turner acknowledged the influence of Grierson and **This Wonderful World**: 'I watched it avidly and Harley had access to the film and we had the run of the archives and Grierson's Steenbeck. What I learned from him, and from Harley afterwards, is that film is a very wide-ranging open activity – it wasn't just features, documentary or animation.'

37 Ibid.

38 Interview with Chris Monger, Cardiff, 1982.

39 Monger thought in retrospect they were two 'terribly pretentious' films. On the **Cold Mountain** project cash dried up and Monger and his actor Ian McNeice tried to make a virtue of penury and improvise scenes: 'It ends with a shot of my fiancée and myself tired and bored, sitting on a couch, with voice-overs about what the film might have been like' (interview, 1982).

40 Ibid.

41 Ibid.

CHAPTER 18

1 Interview with Euryn Ogwen Williams, S4C programme director, Cardiff, 1983.

2 Monger received £7,719 (with completion grant) for **Repeater**. By the mid-1980s, the council had changed its policy, with emphasis on film and video workshop funding rather than production grants, which were cut by £30,000 to £20,000.

3 Interviews with John Brown of the Scottish Film Council and Professor Ian Locherbie, chairman Scottish Film Production Fund, Edinburgh 1983. Also see Eddie Dick (ed.), *From Limelight to Satellite* (Scottish Film Council and BFI, 1990) and Forsyth Hardy, *Scotland in Film* (Edinburgh University Press, 1990).

4 Wil Aaron's essay in *The Arts in Wales 1950–1975* (Welsh Arts Council, 1979). Aaron in an interview in Caernarfon, June 1984, said that when he was on the WAC film panel: 'We were giving students money which I thought should be coming from the college.'

5 Author's interview with Martyn Howells, then WAC films officer, Cardiff, June 1984.

6 Ibid.

7 Ibid.

8 Ibid. In 1977/8 the WAC film panel gave its first grant to the Welsh Film Board, which had previously received some financial support from other WAC committees.

9 Article by Wil Aaron, in *Barn*, the Welsh-language magazine, October 1976. In the mid-seventies, all the board's 'admin' work was done by the North Wales Arts Association who also distributed the films (ibid.). The NWAA, National Westminster Bank, and Gulbenkian Foundation were among early sponsors.

10 Author's interview with Norman Williams, of the Welsh Film Board, at Bangor Normal College, 1984.

11 Wil Aaron, *Barn*, op.cit. Seven of the twenty had been produced by the board. The Welsh Arts Council officially took over funding the board in 1973; later the grant was given direct by the Welsh Office.

12 Interview with Norman Williams, Welsh Film Board, as above, and 'The Future of Bwrdd Ffilmiau Cymraeg' (discussion paper for Welsh Arts Council, 1980).

13 In an interview with the author, Caernarfon, 1983, Aaron said that at one stage he was virtually the only film-making member of the board. By 1980/1 Richard Lewis and Gareth Wynn Jones were also on the board, which included film-makers turned administrators Euryn Ogwen Williams and Aled Vaughan.

14 Interview with Norman Williams, as above, Bangor, 1984. But Emyr Humphreys (interviewed by the author 1993) said Lewis had been co-operative on various screen projects.

15 Discussion paper for WAC, 1980.

16 In an interview with the author in Caernarfon, June 1984. See also Aaron's article 'Film', in *The Arts in Wales 1950–1975* (WAC, 1979), pp.306–7. The BFI comments were cited in the *WM*, 9 May 1977. A BFI spokesman said, of the board: 'It seems their only aim is to produce material in Welsh and develop the language.'

17 Wil Aaron interview, Caernarfon, 1983.

18 Ibid. Ifas, played by Stewart Jones, was a 'reactionary boor, something like Alf Garnett' (from a Ffilmiau'r Nant treatment of **Gwaed ar y Sêr** submitted to Welsh Film Board). In 1985, Emlyn Williams directed an S4C feature film **Ifas Y Tryc**.

19 Screened on S4C, 9 June 1983.

20 Author's interview with Alan Clayton, Cardiff, 1983. Clayton had previously directed drama series for HTV including **The Enemy Within**, a spy story set at a Welsh Arts Council weekend conference of minority linguistic groups.

21 Ibid.

22 Ibid. There are echoes of the script's ideas in Sul Y Blodau, another eighties work, directed by Richard Lewis (made by BBC for S4C) also written by Michael Povey, a drama-documentary based on the arrest of more than forty suspected Welsh extremists.

23 Aaron interview, June 1984.

24 'The Future of Bwrdd Ffilmiau Cymraeg' (discussion paper for WAC, 1980).

25 See chapter 19. Owen was previously part-time administrator.

CHAPTER 19

1 Author's interview with James Hill, London, 1984. The film was produced by the independent Opix company (Ray Marshall and Terry Ryan), based from the early 1980s in London. Script credit was shared by Hill with Ifor Wyn Williams and Jane Edwards, with Dafydd Huw Williams as script editor. **Owain Glyndŵr** was first screened in English, 1 Nov. 1983.

2 'There were seven or eight scripts worked on by Welsh writers. I don't think they wanted to spend all that money for a seven or eight film series and they asked if we could make a feature-length film' (interview with James Hill as above). 'I knew we had to move, winter was coming and I tailored three of the scripts into a two-hour film.'

3 S4C programmes head Euryn Ogwen Williams later confirmed that lack of finance caused the change of heart but claimed the original plan was for a six-film series (a possible twelve-film series was mooted in the local press in 1982).

4 In back-to-back shooting, often with the same cast, actors play the scenes in English and Welsh.

5 Author's interview with Gwilym Owen, 13 May 1991. Roberts (interviewed 13 June 1991) also claimed Williams requested 'a blockbuster'. **Madam Wen** was based on the story by William David Owen (1874–1925).

6 Gwilym Owen interview as above.

7 Ibid.

8 Twm Sion Catti was first popularized by novelist T. J. Llewelyn Prichard (1790–1862) between 1828 and 1839 and the stories spawned **Hawkmoor**, based on a 1977 novel by Lynn Hughes. See *The Oxford Companion to the Literature of Wales*, compiled and edited by Meic Stephens (Oxford University Press, 1986).

9 A 90-minute version went out later. Owen estimated the final cost at £350,000, but Roberts claimed the final bill was £540,000. 'Euryn and I agreed we would pay for the London-based production team on the whole six-week shoot, though other crew members were brought in later at extra expense. The one thing we didn't have was a film accountant' (Owen, interviewed 13 May 1991). Roberts was an experienced director formerly working with the Wales, West and the North company, forerunners of TWW, before joining the BBC, and going freelance in 1969.

10 Owen, head of BBC Wales news and current affairs by May 1991, stressed that none of his previous Welsh Film Board works had exceeded budget. Roberts claimed Williams specified a £300,000 budget maximum, though an S4C press release later claimed the sum was £335,000 in a 'fixed price contract'. Before production, Roberts originally quoted £350,000 as the cost but revised *his* estimated sum upwards to £445,000 (then £480,000) after detailed discussions with his assistant director. He claimed Owen said it would be OK (interview, June, 1991).

11 He said costs were difficult to assess in advance and preparations could not be made properly because he had no script or treatment a few weeks before shooting began. Roberts claimed he was told they must stick to the original £300,000 budget four weeks into the shoot, too late to trim costs to that extent. Interestingly, he also thought, in retrospect, that Owen had been made a scapegoat.

12 Made by Wynn Jones's company Ty Gwyn from a Dwynwen Berry story and screened in November 1983, it was based loosely on the *Mabinogion*.

13 Clifford Evans narrated the Welsh-language version of the Scan **Hearst** programme, known

originally as 'My Wonderful Place'. Hearst was, of course, the real subject of Orson Welles's 1941 masterpiece **Citizen Kane**.

14 See Marion Davies, *The Times We Had* (Angus and Robertson, 1976).

15 Author's interview with Stephen Bayly, London, 1985.

16 Ibid. Between 1971 and 1977, Bayly also produced **In Loving Memory** for director Tony Scott for the BFI and Michael Medwin's Memorial Enterprises and helped originate a script 'The Duel', eventually directed by Tony's brother, Ridley Scott, as the acclaimed cinema film **The Duellists**.

17 **Gwenoliaid** (dir. Gwyn Hughes Jones) centres on the impact of Cockney children on Rhydderch Jones's home village of Aberllefenni, north Wales, and includes footage shot in the writer's former home. It was shown on S4C on 7 Jan. 1986. Another Rhydderch Jones drama for S4C, **Lliwiau** (Colours) (dir. Gareth Rowlands) also explored childhood memories.

18 'The Evacuees' was first screened 18 Nov. 1982. Bayly and James formed their London-based Red Rooster company in 1983 and the feature film version of **Joni Jones**, surprisingly shorn of 'The Evacuees' episode, was shown on S4C in March 1991.

19 In a 1988 interview with the present author, Euryn Ogwen Williams rated **Aderyn Papur** (screened 23 April 1984) among the four most impressive films from independents screened by the channel. The other three were Francis's **Yr Alcoholig Llon**, **Y Gosb** (The Punishment) directed by Siôn Humphreys from his father Emyr's work, and **Ysglyfaeth** (dir. Gareth Wynn Jones).

20 Author's interview with Stephen Bayly, Cardiff, 1987.

21 'Work isn't the be-all-and-end-all. It really is the quality of life that's important and where you stand in the workplace' (Bayly, ibid.).

22 Ibid.

23 Ibid.

24 Ibid. 'We did each scene, each set-up, first in English, then in Welsh. You can imagine how painful that was – not only for me, but for the actors. Each time we had to make a huge mental adjustment.'

25 Bayly admitted he was forced to use almost 'anybody who could speak a smattering of Welsh – there were people who were not used to acting in Welsh.'

26 'The resources we had in terms of the lighting budget [on **The Works**] were ridiculous for the job in hand' (Bayly, ibid.).

27 Ibid.

28 See *SWE*, 29 Jan. 1987.

29 *Observer*, 18 May 1986.

30 The film won the Pierrot d'Or for the outstanding first feature at Vevey (see *SWE*, 19 Nov. 1986 and 29 Jan. 1987). It was also screened at the 1986 London Film Festival.

31 Author's interview with Euryn Ogwen Williams, Cardiff, 1984.

32 'Slate' was originally planned as a four-hour film, for 1989 cinema release and a TV mini-series to be screened just after the film première (Euryn Ogwen Williams interview, Aug. 1987). Later Ogwen Williams accused Hines of 'trying to recreate **Comrades** [Ken Loach's Tolpuddle Martyrs film] in north Wales. He [Hines] saw it purely in terms of conflict between workers and owners. There was a tendency to see the baddies as English yet there were those in the chapel hierarchy who favoured the English-speaking management, and there was scab labour. It was never as simple as workers v. bosses.' (Interview, 1989.)

33 Begun as a series of twelve 8-minute cartoons, launched by S4C in May 1983. Around twelve animators worked on each of three series, with each film taking twenty weeks to animate, and the first thirty-six programmes cost around £3 million.

34 Author's interview with Wil Aaron, Caernarfon, 1984.

35 Ibid.

36 Ibid.

37 Pawelko's work included **Stud**, a genial and disarming examination of macho leather fetishism. Thomas's resignation was finally triggered by then BBC head Billy Cotton jun. interfering directly to cut out a shot of a gravestone referring to a 'murder' by British troops on Bloody Sunday (author's interview with Thomas, 1991).

38 Both Thomas and Turner shot programmes in the Anglo-Welsh **Tales from Wales** series.

39 Interview with Paul Turner, Cardiff, 1984. The film was shot in just five days.

40 Edwards acted as narrator, playing an elderly version of Wil Jones's friend Wil 'Ginger Beer', and adapted the original Huw K. Evans story.

41 Interview with Paul Turner, Cardiff, 1984. **Wil Six** was screened on S4C on 7 May 1984.

42 It was customary for S4C to pay costs of the independent companies supplying it, including overheads, a 'management fee' (with inbuilt profit margin) and to add a bonus payment (a percentage of the budget) for those who had spent a year working for S4C (interview with Euryn Ogwen Williams, 1989).

43 Interview with Richard Staniforth of Teliesyn, 1983.

44 'You can produce an English-language version at half the normal cost – if you use back-to-back but you should be committed to getting the best possible Welsh version first' (Staniforth, ibid.).

45 Ibid.

46 **Enka** was Teliesyn's first video production.

47 *SWE*, 19 Aug. 1987 and 20 June 1988. Two programmes in the **Cracking Up** series appeared on S4C – devoted to the poet Niclas y Glais (Thomas Evan Nicholas) and the poet-antiquary Iolo Morganwg (Edward Williams).

48 See Bayly's article 'Sianel Pedwar Cymru – the Welsh perspective', *Sight and Sound*, 1983. Also see David Berry, 'TV giants attacked for failing Wales', *SWE*, 1 April 1985.

49 Euryn Ogwen Williams interview, at S4C, Aug. 1987.

50 Ibid.

51 S4C later screened Marc Evans's **Homing (Ymgartrefu)**, a Red Rooster feature centring on a seventy-year-old widow threatened with a future in an old folks' home.

52 **Gaucho** was first shown Boxing Day, 1983. Endaf Emlyn also directed **Y Cloc** (The Clock), screened by S4C at Christmas 1986, twelve months after **Y Dyn Nath Ddwyn y Nadolig**. **Shampŵ**, well shot by Dafydd Hobson, was screened by S4C in November 1982.

53 Author's interview with Siôn Humphreys, nr. Caernarfon, Dec. 1992.

54 The film took three years to make and was begun while Quinn was a student at Middlesex Polytechnic (Quinn interview in *Animator* magazine No.21, Oct./Dec. 1987). 'People don't think animation has a serious intention because it is funny. Making people laugh is a good way of getting the message about feminism across without drumming it in' (Quinn quoted in *Animator* magazine No.20, July/Sept. 1987). See also Linda Pariser's interview with Quinn, in Jayne Pilling (ed.), *Women and Animation* (BFI, 1992), pp.85–7.

CHAPTER 20

1 Roland Denning's article 'Another fine mess' in Chapter's film and video magazine *One Eye*, Aug./Sept. 1984.

2 Author's interview with Chris Monger, chair of Chapter's board of management in the mid-1980s. Quotes are from his interview with Paul Jackson *WM*, 22 Feb. 1982.

3 See Monger's article in *Undercut* magazine, No.6, Winter 1982–3. McNeice, former Royal Shakespeare Company actor, previously played in Monger's short **Aesthete's Foot** (1977).

4 Cinema of Women leaflet circulated at Edinburgh Film Festival that year. The film was also criticized by the Leeds Film Group in a letter to the Welsh Arts Council when LFG refused to pay the hiring fee. Chapter Film Workshop's own spirited defence of the film is in *Undercut* magazine, no.6, 1982–3, citing Steve Jenkins's review in *Monthly Film Bulletin*, July 1982. The South Wales Women's Co-op's comments were in *Undercut*, as above.

5 *SWE*.

6 *Undercut* magazine, as above.

7 Ibid. See Monger's own BFI programme notes comment at the LFF screening.

8 *SWE* review, May 1982. The film was screened at the Edinburgh Festival that year.

9 *SWE*.

10 Review in *SWE*, 6 Dec. 1984.

11 See John Hessey review in *One Eye*, Chapter's own magazine, no.2, Aug./Sept. 1984. **Contortions** was among the films shown in an evening programme at the National Film Theatre devoted to Chapter films. Ken Wlaschin, London Film Festival director and the then NFT programmer, said he was most impressed with the workshop's work and thought it a 'model of what film production outside London should be'.

12 Some exchanges between the bureaucrats and Lowenthal, the kitemaker forced to surrender the boy into care, recalled the menace of Pinter's *Caretaker*.

13 A Welsh film-maker even more preoccupied with form in the eighties was Cerith Wyn Evans (b. Llanelli, 1958), a protégé of the English director Derek Jarman. Evans, who learned his skills at the Royal College of Art, London, used graphics, montage and collage to produce semi-abstract films which won regular subsidy from the Arts Council of Great Britain and the British Film Institute Production Board. Typical was **Degrees of Blindness** (1988), a subjective, impressionistic work seeking to convey the experience of those often falsely regarded as blind.

14 Red Flannel moved to Cardiff in 1994 just before embarking on **All in the Game**, a BBC documentary about women's football (televised 13 May 1994).

15 Bowyer was also a key contributor to the Belfast Film Workshop's stimulating **Under the Health Service** which linked medical problems in the city to the problems of squalid housing and a general planning malaise.

16 Wilks made her shorts at South Glamorgan Institute of Higher Education, Cardiff. **Zombie UB40** was screened on Channel Four, 3 July 1988, when she was co-ordinator of Chapter Film Workshop, before becoming a director of the workshop's self-financing successor, Filmworks.

17 Cardiff Street Television adopted a critical stance from the outset: witness **Welcome to Cardiff** (1974), a 20-minute short attacking the emphasis on building office blocks rather than tackling housing problems; it stressed the ill-fated Centreplan scheme for the city's redevelopment.

18 **Miners' Strike** (1981) was made with the South Wales NUM, the South Wales Miners' Library and the Coalfield Research project at the instigation of the NUM research officer, Kim Howells (later MP for Pontypridd). Other Chapter Film Workshop productions of note included **Whose Law?**, an examination of the legal implications of picketing and a critique of the government's use of the legislative process, and **In The National Interest** (1986), an examination of government attitudes to censorship and freedom of information (made in collaboration with other UK workshops).

19 **The Rumours** tape was winner of top prize in the video section at the 1981 Celtic Festival. **Burning Burning** (1989) used a similar form, revealing the decline of local industries, new developments and the social preoccupations through the comments by locals. More fluid and visually arresting than the **Rumours** films, it never quite captured their spontaneity and gusto. The Video Community Workshop gravitated at one stage to Tudor Street, Riverside, a Cardiff inner-city area where it could be closer to the grassroots (author's interview with Terry Dimmick, Cardiff, Sept. 1992).

20 Chapter Video Workshop final report to Welsh Arts Council, on All-Wales Video project 1982–3, refers to the huge financial contribution made by Channel Four to the workshop. Terry Dimmick and Eileen Smith shot the second **Rumours** programme, with Dimmick doing off-line edit (interview with Terry Dimmick, Cardiff, 1992).

21 Total Welsh Arts Council film funding in 1987–8 was £97,500 and the bulk of that went to

workshops, with only £5,000 for film production (and that was spent on script development) (*SWE*, 7 Aug. 1987). Other cash help for Chapter Community Video came from WAC, the Manpower Services Commission and the Gulbenkian Foundation.

22 The film centred on the family of bus drivers Alan and Ann Thomas. Ann Thomas's life at work and as a pacifist was also the subject of a Frances Bowyer/Claire Pollak documentary, **Something to Hide**.

23 Welsh Women's Aid press release, 3 Mar. 1982, explained the education project and the Chapter Video Workshop's role in training the communications workers.

24 Author's interviews with Susan Twizzy Evans and Liz Forder, Cardiff, 1984 and 1985, and with Evans, Cardiff, 1987.

25 Review in *SWE*, 26 March 1982. 'I'd been looking for years for this sort of subject to film and Shirley was a very strong courageous character' (collective member Ann Lamche quoted in *SWE*, 3 March 1982). Butts was at the time the only woman shop steward on the Amalgamated Union of Engineering Workers' district committee, Llantrisant.

26 Francis was co-author with Dai Smith of *The Fed, A History of the South Wales Miners in the Twentieth Century* (Lawrence and Wishart, 1980) and also founder of the South Wales Miners' Library at University College, Swansea.

27 See Linda Pariser's interview with Candy Guard in Jayne Pilling (ed.) *Women and Animation: A Compendium* (BFI, 1992), p.88.

28 *SWE*, 18 April 1987.

 CHAPTER 21

1 **The Prodigal Tenor** was televised on St David's Day, 1956, **The Bachelor Brothers** 22 Oct. 1960, and **Jubilee Concert** 4 May 1961. Lynn Joshua was the original Tommy Trouble and *Welsh Rarebit* was networked nationally between 1947 and 1952, and again from 1956.

2 Emlyn Williams plays televised in the fifties included **Trespass**, **The Wind of Heaven**, **The Corn is Green** and **The Light of Heart**. A 45-minute extract from the stage play of **Under Milk Wood** was televised from the Edinburgh Film Festival, 20 Aug. 1956, and Llewellyn's **Poison Pen** was performed on BBC 13 Nov. 1956.

3 With William Squire as Captain Cat, Marion Grimaldi as Polly Garter, Meredith Edwards as Revd Eli Jenkins, Aubrey Richards as Mog Edwards. A 1964 TV production, with Donald Houston in the lead, featured Aubrey Richards as Captain Cat.

4 Author's interview with Alexander, Ystradgynlais, Feb. 1994. A Rhydderch Jones four-film tribute season was screened in 1986: **Mr Lollypop, MA** (dir. John Hefin), **Man a Lle (A Plot of Earth**, dir. Gwyn Hughes Jones), **Gwenoliaid** (dir. Gwyn Hughes Jones) and **Broc Mor (Driftwood**, dir. George Owen).

5 Author's interviews with John Hefin, March 1990 and with Alun Owen, London, Dec. 1992. Owen's work is discussed in detail in John Russell Taylor, *Anger and After* (Methuen, 1962). Owen also wrote the screenplay for The Beatles' **Hard Day's Night** (dir. Richard Lester, 1964) and, as an actor, appeared in the Welsh comedy **Valley of Song** (1953). See the interview with Alun Owen by Derek Owen, *Film Dope* no. 49, June 1993, pp.1–7.

6 Interview with Elaine Morgan, Mountain Ash, 1987. Morgan considered Jack Jones's work 'good and gutsy' but found his novel 'impossible' to adapt and thought in retrospect that the last episodes tailed off as Jones's philosophizing took over from the narrative. HTV also made their own drama-doc on Lloyd George – **The Politics of Derision**, with Ian Holm.

7 **The Rescuers** was first televised 6 Dec. 1956, **The Squeeze** in Nov. 1960.

8 Welshman John Geraint directed a much-praised BBC documentary **A Place Like Hungerford** in 1988. Another outsider to make a contribution to Wales in this period was Robert Vas, a documentary director who, with Lindsay Anderson and Tony Richardson, had created important experimental short films in the fifties as one of the British-based Free Cinema. Vas made **The Master Singers** (1965).

9   John Hartley played Nye (1982), with Rachel Thomas as Jenny Lee; Ronald Lacey was Dylan. Lewis also produced **The Fasting Girl** (1984, dir. Robin Rollinson), a rather pedestrian if painstakingly lit and designed version of documented incidents surrounding farmer's daughter Sarah Jacob in the 1860s when she claimed to be pregnant by Christ and to have fasted for a year. The film, despite its shortcomings, won the Best Fiction drama at the Celtic Festival, Brittany, in 1985.

10 The arson was the climax of a long campaign by the Welsh Nationalists against establishing an armaments training programme on Llŷn. A favourable review and discussion of the film by Mario Basini can be found in *WM*, 26 Feb. 1988.

11 Author's interview with William Jones at the Celtic Film Festival, 1986. The film was screened 24 Feb. 1985, on S4C in Welsh and a subtitled version on BBC 2 on 28 Dec. 1985. An **Almanac** (screened 20 Dec. 1982 on S4C) devoted to Lewis Valentine's recollections of 1936, was directed, for Ffilmiau'r Nant, by Robin Evans.

12 Ibid.

13 Ibid.

14 The film provided the first significant role on BBC Wales television for Stanley Baker's son, Glyn.

15 John Hefin, in a 1990s interview, cited among TV work which gave him pleasure **The Loss**, from a Kate Roberts short story, and Rhys Davies's **The Dilemma of Catherine Fuchsias**.

16 **The Shining Pyramid**, a supernatural tale set on the banks of the Usk, starred Anton Rogers and Edward Petherbridge, with music by one of Wales's leading composers, Alun Hoddinott.

17 The cinema feature, set in Ireland, was directed by Cyril Frankel and starred Eileen Herlie, Betty McDowell, Jack MacGowran.

18 Critic and former TV producer Gethin Stoodley Thomas thought Griffith 'an inspired choice' who had 'never given a better performance on television'. 'No other actor in the Welsh canon could have accomplished the wider range of those deceptively plain verses' (*WM*, 24 March 1984). Dai Smith in **Bitter Broken Bread** (in his **Wales! Wales?** series) contrasted Davies's involvement in industrial south Wales with Dylan Thomas's work: 'His [Dylan's] was the voice of the suburbs – the middle class not involved with the struggle which has shaped Swansea.'

19 The **Zola Budd** film, directed by Griffith, was screened on BBC 2 in April 1989. In **Perils of Pendragon**, a 1975 BBC comedy series, Griffith also played the quintessential mean-spirited self-centred Welsh shopkeeper who has become a bogeyman of Welsh folklore since the type surfaced in the Tonypandy riots.

20 Author's interview with Kenneth Griffith, London, 1987. **The Tenby Poisoner**, a BBC Wales documentary on Griffith, dir. John Hefin, 1993.

21 Griffith article in *Stills* magazine, Oxford, vol.1, no.3, Autumn 1981. 'The IBA went secretly to Lew Grade and asked him not to offer the film to them' (author's interview, London, 1983). Griffith, typically, used some money paid out in settlement to buy the home he christened 'Michael Collins's House' in Islington (interviews, 1983 and 1984). His Collins film was screened at the National Film Theatre in 1980. Another portrait – of Baden Powell – was abandoned after technicians refused to shoot in South Africa.

22 Ibid. See Griffith's book *Curious Journey* (Hutchinson, 1982).

23 Ibid. Author's interview with the actor, London, 1987. 'The Thomas Paine work is the film I'm most pleased with as an all-round presentation of a man of enormous importance and significance' (interview, London, 1983).

24 Hefin also revealed a gift for comedy when directing **Grand Slam** (1978), scripted by Gwenlyn Parry and starring Hugh Griffith and Windsor Davies (screened BBC Wales, 17 Mar. 1978). Hefin (interviewed 1987) insisted that he based **Bus to Bosworth** largely on his own father, a teacher.

25 Author's interview with Kenneth Griffith, 19 Feb. 1984.

26 Ibid.

27 Ibid. Griffith wrote on the Relief of Ladysmith in his book *Thank God We Kept the Flag Flying* (Hutchinson, 1974).

28 Author's interview with Griffith, 19 Feb. 1984

29 Ibid.

30 Interview with Griffith, Feb. 1984.

31 Ibid. Griffith has occasionally directed his own films, notably **Sons of the Blood** (produced by David Gerrard and made thanks to cash help from his then business associate, the actor Patrick McGoohan), **Keep Pretoria Clean**, a study of the black refuse collectors in Pretoria and **A Famous Journey**, shot partly in Israel, about the journey of the Magi, in which he played Christ.

32 Griffith had previously played Napoleon in Granada's 1963 **War and Peace** (dir. Silvio Narizzano) and in an episode of **The Prisoner** with Patrick McGoohan. Narizzano said of Griffith's performance: 'He was the best Napoleon. He *was* Napoleon – Kenneth has a Napoleonic complex but he was never any trouble – a true professional.' Narizzano said when he and friends saw Griffith's more personal films, 'all that shouting and bawling', they thought, 'you can't show these. We were wrong, he beat us all down' (interview with Narizzano, London, May 1993). See *TV Times*, 22–8 March 1975. Griffith was later denied a visa to travel to India to make a documentary on Dr Ranji Ambedkar, a contemporary of Gandhi and Nehru and a leader of the Untouchables. Ambedkar helped draw up the Indian Constitution. See also Griffith's *The Discovery of Nehru* (Michael Joseph, 1989).

33 Ibid. 'I thought Israel's case was very urgent. I've derived through my life enormous benefits from the Jewish people – culturally, intellectually, inspirationally. Increasingly, I've wanted to be Israel's advocate' (author's interview with Griffith, London, 1988).

34 As Colin Smith observed, it was a film likely to infuriate everyone from dogmatic Zionists to PLO sympathizers: 'Mr Griffiths enjoys tilting at the prevailing orthodoxy' (*Observer* 31 Aug. 1988).

35 *Nothing But the Truth*, a dossier on the work of the Roger Graef team (BFI publishing/ Institute of Contemporary Arts, 1982).

36 Interview, Claire Pollak, Cardiff, 1982.

37 Screened at the London Film Festival 1981, and included in the LFF touring package the same year.

38 A 'Celtic Countries' series programme on Wales was screened 7 April 1976, written by Harri Pritchard Jones, and Wales and the Welsh had also been examined in **How to be Celtic**, a TV series made in the early eighties in Scotland (Douglas Eadie and Mike Alexander).

39 The 1985 programmes led to a series of study packs, published by HTV, Channel Four and Gwynedd Archives Service. The series aimed to 'turn passive viewers into active participants in the search for our past' (introductory note to study packs).

CHAPTER 22

1 Francis has spoken consciously of the works as a trilogy, in an interview with the author, 1989.

2 The director has lived in both Cardiff and west Wales in the past two decades but the family home – used for key scenes in **Above Us the Earth** – remains in Bedwas.

3 This is most obvious in **Above Us the Earth**.

4 Francis only discussed shooting the planned contest after he had decided to make a film of the Bedwas pit closure and the strike. Interview with Karl Francis, Cardiff, 1987.

5 **The Miners' Tapes**, collected by various video and film workshops, including Cardiff's Chapter Arts Centre, during the strike, are an invaluable record of the dispute.

6 The Dilys Hardacre **Rough Justice** film was made in 1980, and prefigured much of the material in the director's HTV film **The Committee** (1990).

7 See *SWE* review of **The Angry Earth**, 10 Aug. 1989.

8   HTV still has a viewable copy. The Spencer Union was the South Wales Miners' Industrial Union, active between 1926 and 1938 (and 21 branches were formed in January 1927 alone), mostly in the Rhymney Valley. George Spencer became president at the annual meeting in Cardiff in 1936. See Hywel Francis and Dai Smith, *The Fed: A History of the South Wales Miners in the Twentieth Century* (Lawrence and Wishart, 1980).

9   Author's interview with Karl Francis, Cardiff, 1987.

10 *WM*, 24 Feb. 1975. Also author's interview with Francis as above.

11 Author's interview with Karl Francis, Cardiff, 1982.

12 Ibid.

13 Ibid.

14 Ibid.

15 *Daily Mail*, 19 July 1979; *Morning Star* 18 July 1979.

16 Interview with Karl Francis, Cardiff, 1982.

17 Francis has constantly fought for more emphasis on TV in urban South Wales and more scope for English-language film-makers, perhaps via a fifth channel.

18 The name for the *femme fatale* was clearly inspired by Rita Hayworth's performance in Charles Vidor's **Gilda** (1946) (interview with Francis, Cardiff, 1982). **The Mouse and the Woman** was produced by Alvicar and financed by Caerphilly businessman Alf Gooding to the tune of £250,000, according to *SWE*, 23 June 1981, but an Alvicar press release of the time stated the budget was £89,000. The film was screened in the Directors' Fortnight at Cannes in 1980.

19 Dafydd Hywel thought an incestuous relationship with the sister was clearly implied in the screenplay, though Francis has never confirmed this (author's interview with Dafydd Hywel, Cardiff, 1984).

20 Interview with Francis, Cardiff, 1982.

21 Anthony Hopkins was originally pencilled in for the lead role (according to *WM*, 27 April 1977).

22 *SWE* review, 1 April 1983.

23 **Giro City**, screened by Channel Four in the Films on Four slot (1 Feb. 1982), was distributed in the cinema by Cinegate in Britain. In early 1981, Francis submitted a grant application to the Welsh Arts Council for a proposed film 'First Love' which was never made but contained elements of **Timmy and the Experts** and his later films **Giro City** and **Ms Rhymney Valley**.

24 'The media are condemned to look at the world through glass and I don't think the media change anything, yet they are fickle, often irresponsible, elements in the present political set-up' (Francis interviewed by Martyn Auty, *Time Out*, Oct. 1982). See also *WM*, 24 Feb. 1975.

25 Chris Dunkley (*Financial Times*, 8 Dec. 1982) claimed **Giro City** 'benefited enormously from its location work' but among 'minor faults' he considered: 'Bribers and bribed rarely stand in large open spaces accommodatingly counting fivers for anyone who happens along with a telephoto lens.' John Coleman (*New Statesman*, 22 Oct. 1982) was more complimentary: 'Here at last is the kind of British political cinema some of us have been pleading for.'

26 *SWE*, 6 Dec. 1984. Also article in *SWE*, 31 Oct. 1984.

27 Gethyn Stoodley Thomas (*WM*, 9 Nov. 1986) doubted 'if a more moving and clinically realistic portrait of this dire disease has ever before been seen'.

28 'Ordinary people are shown, by their deeds and words, to be extraordinary,' Dai Smith quoted in *Raymond Williams: Film/TV Culture* (BFI, 1989) and cited in Steve Freer, *Karl Francis: A Sense of Direction* (HTV booklet, 1990). **Ms Rhymney Valley** was televised on BBC 2, 10 July 1985.

29 Bill Nind is frequently referred to in Francis's film **A Breed of Men**. His activities in helping edit the pit paper *The Bedwas Rebel* in the 1930s are recalled in Hywel Francis and Dai Smith, *The Fed* (Lawrence and Wishart, 1980).

30 Interview with Karl Francis, Cardiff, 1987.

31 Ibid.

32 Ibid.

33 'The centre of the film, the theme, is the Welshness. Because of the film's Welsh language and Wil's Welsh speaking, it explains a lot of issues about the language in a very real, not an artificial way' (Francis interview, 1986). The Lt.-Col.'s name was an obvious, slightly-barbed reference to Ray Milland's real name Reginald Truscott-Jones.

34 It was not until Francis had re-edited the film, delaying showing the killing to the audience, that he actually 'liked' Wil, who in the re-cut version, beginning with scenes in prison, is more clearly established as victim.

35 Film reviewed in *Daily Express*, *Guardian*, *SWE*, 29 Jan. 1987. Richard Lynch, a University College Aberystwyth student hailing from Bedwas, Francis's home village, received particularly good reviews (*SWE*, 1 Dec. 1986). **Boy Soldier** won three prizes at the Mannheim Festival, West Germany.

36 Interview with Karl Francis, London, November, 1986.

37 *SWE*, 29 Jan. 1987.

38 Interview with Francis, Nov. 1986.

39 **Merthyr and the Girl** was the first commission given by HTV Wales to an independent film-maker under the government requirement for ITV companies to commission part of their programming from independents from 1989 (HTV press release, 1988).

40 Francis faced much flak from letter-writers to the *SWE* for his allegedly unflattering portrait of the community in **Ms Rhymney Valley**. When he won the Celtic Film Festival Best Documentary prize he referred to the hostility of 'a very small minority of small-minded bigots'.

41 Reviewed *SWE*, 10 Aug. 1989.

42 Screened 10 March 1991. Based on the novel of the same name, published by Honno, Welsh Women's Press, 1989.

43 Interview with the author, Inverness, March, 1991.

44 Francis undoubtedly remembered not merely Nottingham's recent role but the history of the Bedwas Colliery dispute between the SWMF and the Spencer Union, led by George Spencer, of the Nottingham Non-Political Union.

45 Interview, Karl Francis, Cardiff, 1990. **1996** was screened 17 Sept. 1989.

46 The project was brought to Francis after an American contact of the German company recommended him (interview, Chris Sievernick, Caerphilly, May, 1991).

■■■■■■■ **CHAPTER 23**

1 'British Independents: Stephen Weeks', article by the present author in *Film*, the magazine of the British Federation of Film Societies, May 1976. Penhow Castle article in *Country Life*, 4 Oct. 1979.

2 *Sir Gawain and the Green Knight* (Penguin Classics, 1959) and J. R. R. Tolkien's translation (George Allen & Unwin, 1975).

3 See *WM*, 6 Nov. 1976, for article by Weeks on the film's production.

4 Sutcliff (d. 1992) was also an admirer of Kipling (interview, *Sunday Times* magazine, 1984).

5 A French film with Italian backing, starring Fabrice Luchini as the Welsh knight and based on an unfinished twelfth-century poem by Chrétien de Troyes. French director Robert Bresson (b. 1907), noted for such films as **Pickpocket**, **Balthazar** and **Four Nights of a Dreamer**, also made a stylized, elliptical version of the Arthurian romance, **Lancelot du Lac** (1974).

6 See Robert Murphy 'Riff raff: British cinema and the underworld' in Charles Barr (ed.), *All Our Yesterdays* (BFI Publishing, 1986).

7 'The First World War has an extraordinary fascination. It was so barbaric, so horrific . . . yet there are people walking around the streets who were in the last of these medieval wars where the countries fought with knives in mud holes' (Weeks interview, Penhow, Gwent, May 1984). Also see article on Weeks *WM*, 6 Nov. 1976.

8 In 1967 Weeks also made **Two at Thursday**, 'a 10-minute experimental romantic drama' scripted by journalist Philip Norman (interview, May 1984).

9 Weeks imported mud from the docks and dead trees from the Port Talbot area to build up the atmosphere at his film setting, Vemelles, a village on the Somme (*WM*, Nov. 1976).

10 David Berry, 'British independents', as above. Weeks stated he was given the director's assignment at three *days'* notice.

11 Ibid. and interview with Weeks, Sept. 1982.

12 Interview with Weeks, Sept. 1982. He thought Subotsky's idea was a 'crackpot scheme'.

13 Ibid.

14 Ibid.

15 *Cinefantastique*, Summer 1973. Raven thought the film 'had a curse on it of the worst sort', and that the screenplay was uncinematic.

16 The director claimed the title was used by Milton Subotsky – who had read his script – for his Amicus film **Asylum** (1972). Weeks's film is referred to as 'Asylum', then a forthcoming project, in 'New blood', an article by David Pirie in *Sight and Sound*, vol.14, no.2, Spring 1971).

   The film was shot in Ootacumund in Tamil Nadu state. Weeks said his interest in India sprang from his fascination with the Roman Empire and 'the idea of lost empires generally . . . I was fascinated by the sort of atmosphere in Rosemary Sutcliff's books such as *The Lantern Bearers*' (interview, May 1984).

17 Significantly, perhaps, **Ghost Story** is Weeks's own particular favourite of all his films (interview, August 1985).

18 It won a top award at the festival in Sitges, Spain, for example. Marjorie Bilbow in *Cinema and TV Film Today*, described the film as 'like a vintage P. G. Wodehouse story as it might have been ghosted by Edgar Allan Poe'. Nigel Andrews praised the film's 'bravura editing, sumptuous Gothic interiors . . .'

19 Interview with Weeks, May 1984.

20 Interview with Weeks, 23 Aug. 1983.

21 Ibid.

22 Ibid. Weeks claimed he sold all his UA rights to Carlo Ponti for 2,000 dollars, then had to pay 150,000 dollars to buy back the film from UA for the remake. In his *Sight and Sound* article, 'New blood' (vol.14, no.2, Spring 1971), David Pirie, who had obviously seen only the test sequence, thought it 'tremendously powerful'.

23 *Film* magazine, May 1976. The director (in a 1982 interview with the author), claimed UA had accepted the Ponti deal, to team up Loren and Peter O'Toole – but did not want to do the Gawain screenplay and made ridiculous demands for changes in the screenplay (from Weeks and co-writer Philip Breen).

24 Interviews with Weeks, Aug. 1983 and Aug. 1985.

25 *Film*, as above, and interview 23 Aug. 1983. Exterior battle scenes were shot near Pembroke and at Merthyr Mawr, Glamorgan; a waterfall scene was filmed at Swallow Falls, Betws-y-coed, and a 90 ft. castle silhouette was also used at a cliff at Pembroke and matched with the Cardiff castle scenes.

26 Weeks claimed UA saw the adventure in 'prosaic terms. They couldn't accept spiritual challenges, they wanted actual fighting' (interview, May 1982).

27 David Pirie 'New blood' *Sight and Sound* (vol.14, no.2, Spring 1971).

28 Weeks said Cannon did not distribute the money properly or spend money on its US publicity, and sold the film for 11.8 million dollars without informing him, and the cable rights in the US for 2.5 million dollars (*SWE*, 5 Jan. 1987).

29 The director (23 Sept. 1983) commented: 'The publicity about his [Connery's] salary was correct. It was the highest "per hour" fee ever negotiated.' Weeks claimed he had been denied

his rightful share of profits and that the film cost only four million dollars to produce despite Cannon's document stating the cost at seven to eight million dollars (*SWE*, Jan. 1987).

30 'I gave the character a chance to win whereas in the original film he (theoretically) had no chance, which was rather depressing' (Weeks interview, Aug. 1985).

31 Ibid.

32 'We needed someone a bit more heavyweight than Peter Hurst, not because we were dissatisfied. We were working with major artists in France and a scene shot in the Great Hall in the Palace of Popes at Avignon was difficult to light and shoot, with 141 set-ups in four days . . . an unbelievable amount of pressure' (interview, Aug. 1985). Young had previously shot **Knights of the Round Table** (1956).

33 Interview with the author, Penhow, Gwent, 23 Sept. 1983.

34 Ibid.

35 Interview, Aug. 1985.

36 'Sipra had this huge ego. He wanted to be the star of the picture . . . He wanted to ride off on a white horse at the end of the film and carry a hawk which pecked out an Englishman's eye' (Weeks interview, May 1984). Weeks told the *SWE*: 'There is no doubt Sipra wanted control of the production. When he suspended production, Sipra announced the script would be re-written by John Goldsmith' (see *SWE*, 19 March and 18 April 1984).

37 Interview with Weeks, August 1985.

38 See *Independent on Sunday* 10 Jan. and 21 Mar. 1993 for a full account of the Bengal Lancers project and Sipra's fall from grace. The first account claimed he borrowed £60 million from Johnson Matthey. The second article is by Chris Blackhurst.

39 *SWE*, 23 July 1985.

40 Interview, Aug. 1985; *SWE*, 5 Jan. 1987.

41 See *Independent on Sunday*, 21 March 1993.

42 The film series was due to be made, in English and Welsh, for Channel Four and S4C. (Article on making the pilot in *SWE*, 16 Aug. 1982.)

CHAPTER 24

1 *SWE*, 2 June 1988. Grieve was earlier an assistant director on Ken Loach's film **Poor Cow** (1967), partly shot in Wales.

2 Prichard (1904–80), born in Bethesda, drew on his own memories of committing his mother to an asylum.

3 Interview, *SWE*, June 1988.

4 **On the Black Hill** was originally budgeted at £1.2 million, but found no backers and was finally made for half the cost (*SWE*, 1 Dec. 1987).

5 Other notable stage roles in the late 1980s included the lead in *King Lear* and Antony in *Antony and Cleopatra* (both for the National Theatre).

6 The **Star Wars** film cost £32 million, compared with **Heart of Fire**'s initial £7 million budget.

7 Menges won the Special Jury prize at Cannes in 1988 with **A World Apart**.

8 **Act of God** showed the fate of twenty (fictitious) people struck by lightning.

9 **Just Ask for Diamond** was released through the Children's Film and TV Foundation. Reviewed *Monthly Film Bulletin*, Dec. 1988.

10 Previously filmed as **The Maltese Falcon** in 1931 (dir. Roy Del Ruth) and 1941 (dir. John Huston) and as **Satan Met a Lady**, 1936 (dir. William Dieterle).

11 The film – working title 'The Englishman Who Went Up a Hill and Came Down a Mountain' – was originally intended as a BBC production, but was finally produced by Ken Loach's company, Parallax, and fully financed by Miramax (US).

12 At the Celtic Film Festival in Rennes, 1985. The Foundation he visualized had broader functions than Ffilm Cymru, which was initially known as the National Film Foundation for Wales but was essentially a film production organization. Back in 1981 Francis said the WAC

should pump £250,000 at least into film production rather than the then current £40,000 a year (*SWE*, 8 June 1981). By 1992 WAC's total contribution *to all aspects of film* had crept up to £250,000, with only a small proportion of that available for production.

13 *Wales on Sunday*, 13 May 1990 and *SWE*, 24 Nov. 1989.

14 By 1992 there were fifteen full-time screens in operation in Cardiff, at six separate venues. These included the new five-screen Capitol-Odeon and two venues, the Monico and the Monroe, run by independent commercial operator Brian Bull of Circle Films.

15 *SWE*, 4 Sept. 1990, 2 April and 27 July 1991. Valley Pictures was formed independently in 1990 and received a Welsh Development Agency grant, and sought to bring new films to smaller halls and new venues. Valley Cinemas was an initiative linking local authorities and seeking to re-open cinemas, or organize conversions of halls to cinemas, with WAC and South East Wales Arts Association support. The new network was created as part of a £4.5 million government-backed Valleys Initiative.

16 Evans's report claimed another £20,000 a year was needed from WAC and the BFI to benefit production, preserve copies of film and perform essential cataloguing work.

17 Author's interview with Ffilm Cymru director John Hefin, May 1990.

18 In **The Vision**, Lee Remick played the chillingly clinical station head prepared to make Bogarde's screen front man a scapegoat and wreck his home life after adverse publicity affected the station. **New World** revolved around a clash of wills between a puritanical governor of the Brethren community (James Fox) and a materialistic opportunist (Bernard Hill). It was shown at the 1986 London Film Festival.

19 Articles on the production are in *SWE*, 17 July and 14 Dec. 1987.

20 Welsh cast members included Paul Rhys – compellingly volatile in Robert Altman's Van Gogh film **Vincent and Theo** (1991) – Dafydd Hywel and Sue Roderick.

21 Interview with Edwards, *SWE*, April 1992. The latter company also produced a lively children's series, **Funnybones** for S4C in 1992. Its animation head Garry Hurst was responsible for the oriental look of **Turandot**.

22 Colin McArthur (ed.), *Scotch Reels* (BFI Publishing, 1982) and Janet McBain, *Pictures Past* (Moorfoot Publishing, 1985).

23 In 1991, HTV's tribute season to Francis included the specially commissioned films **The Committee**, **Mr Chairman** and **A Night Out**.

PICTURE CREDITS

The publishers acknowledge the following for permission to reproduce illustrations or for providing copies:

Dion Alexander: p. 138

Broadcasting, Entertainments, Cinematograph and Theatre Union: p. 131

BBC Wales: pp. 293, 357, 358, 362, 357, 389, 431

The British Film Institute: pp. 6, 12, 26, 27, 46, 49, 51, 53, 56, 67, 68, 70, 72, 73, 78, 92, 94, 98, 99, 101, 104, 105, 109, 134, 136, 151, 155, 162, 165, 167, 170, 172, 175, 192, 194, 208, 211, 216, 220, 222, 225, 230, 233, 238, 247, 255, 256, 258, 263, 267, 271, 275, 379, 382, 386, 403, 407, 415, 421.

Chepstow Museum: p. 124

Cinéclair Films and Steve Benbow (photographer): p. 304

Alan Clayton: p. 366

Paul Dickson: p. 248

Columbia Pictures: p. 424

The Dave Edwards Siriol Animation Studio: p. 330

John East: p. 44

Mary Giles (photographer) and Teliesyn: p. 374

Dane Gould: p. 348

Roy Haggar sen.: pp. 48, 62

HTV: pp. 288, 317, 366

Mervyn Heard: p. 43

Angela Ungoed Hughes: p. 350

Imperial War Museum: p. 187

Philip Lloyd: pp. 36, 37, 38, 39, 40, 41, 42

William MacQuitty: pp. 172, 175, 176

Chris Monger: p. 346

Museum of Modern Art, New York: p. 95

National Library of Wales and the Wales Film and TV Archive: pp. 8, 76, 145, 245

Joanna Quinn: p. 340

The Science Museum: pp. 21, 24, 25

Siriol Productions (Robin Lyons): pp. 434, 435

South Glamorgan County Libraries: pp. vi, 121

S4C: pp. 11, 318, 326, 332, 333, 337, 392, 417, 419, 420

Mick Stubbs: p. 347

Teliesyn: pp. 332, 374

Geoff Thomas: p. 307

Christine Wilks: p. 351

Jacket credits:

Ifan ab Owen Edwards: National Library of Wales

On the Black Hill: BFI

A Welsh Singer: BFI

Gadael Lenin: S4C

Today We Live: BFI